# The Gospels & Acts: Questions & Problems

# The Gospels & Acts: Questions & Problems

Elliott Lesser, Ph.D.

Noble House
Baltimore, Maryland

# THE GOSPELS & ACTS: QUESTIONS & PROBLEMS



Library of Congress
Cataloging in Publication Data
ISBN 1-56167-599-7

Library of Congress Card Catalog Number:
00-104412

Published by

Noble House

8019 Belair Road, Suite 10
Baltimore, Maryland 21236

Manufactured in the United States of America

# TABLE OF CONTENTS

# INTRODUCTION

There are approximately 100 different English language translations of the documents comprising what is known as the Bible. Each differs to some extent, but tends to be accepted by its adherents as the "Word of God" or as divinely inspired. Most biblical scholars believe that the New Testament books were originally written in Greek, although the Gospel of Matthew may have been in Aramaic. The latter, like ancient Hebrew, lacked written vowels, lower case letters, and punctuation. Thus one may understand how translation problems could arise, be exacerbated, and lead to a diversity of translations. The ancient Greek, however, did have written vowels, but, until the 9th century A.D., frequently did not utilize a space between words, thus, resulting in more translation problems. The difficulty in translating ancient Greek may have been best stated by The New English Bible: "Only those who have meditated long upon the Greek original are aware of the richness and subtlety of meaning that may lie within the most apparently simple, or know the despair that attends all efforts to bring it out through the medium of a different language." An excellent example of this problem is seen in JOHN 21:15-18 wherein on three occasions Jesus asked Peter if he loved him, and Peter on three occasions told Jesus that he did love him, The first two times that Jesus used "love," the Greek word so translated was "agape," meaning a general feeling of love or affection, but Peter responding used the Greek, "philos," meaning an intense, passionate love. The third time, Jesus also used "philos." In English, however, both Greek words translate as "love," without a distinction.

Bible study classes when dealing with individual verses do so to relate them to the specific theology of the church or group sponsoring the study. Verses which justify theological belief are emphasized and related to similar supporting verses. Furthermore, the student frequently is inculcated with the concept of biblical inerrancy. Verses which may not fit in with the theology being promulgated or that may cast doubt on the concept of inerrancy tend to be avoided or quickly glossed over. Except in rare instances, questioning the accuracy or veracity of any verse is unthinkable. Similarly, the relationship of the verses to known history is rarely discussed unless both concur. An occasional apparent contradiction may be noted but dismissed with a reasonably rational or more often an irrational explanation. The student, or the average Bible reader, consequently, remains unaware of the thousands of verse discrepancies and the thousands of questions they inspire in the minds of those who do not accept the Bible as inerrant. The similarities between the biblical stories and those of ancient pagan religions, at best, are barely mentioned. Furthermore, few modern Christians know that into the 4th century, the early followers of Jesus observed the biblical sabbath, Saturday, and they celebrated Passover, not Easter. It was the Roman Emperor Constantine who after converting to Christianity commanded Christians to observe Sunday the pagan Roman sabbath; and to observe Easter, the centuries old celebration of pagan deities who died and were resurrected around the time of the vernal equinox, instead of the biblical Passover. He ordered the execution of any Christian who refused. Constantine thus began to merge original Christianity with Roman paganism. Shortly thereafter, the Virgin Birth, a popular pagan concept, and the cross, a pagan sun-god symbol, which replaced the lamb as a Christian symbol, entered into Christianity. The cross had been denounced by early Church leaders because of its association with pagan deities. In fact, some early Christians, the Docetists, did not believe that Jesus was crucified. Others, such as the Ebionites, did not believe that he was the Son of God, but just a human man through whom God performed miracles (see ACTS 2:22 - Jesus was a man of whom God approved and through whom He worked miracles).

Rarely questioned is the generally accepted depiction of Jesus as a relatively tall man with a light complexion and reddish brown hair - a European type figure. It is a picture that does not seem to have come into vogue until after Christianity came to Greece. If Jesus looked this way, it is difficult to imagine the gospel writers not noting it; he would have been so unlike the typical relatively short, swarthy, Middle Easterner with black hair that most certainly the writers would have commented about it. Indeed, Jesus' depiction is how one would expect a Greek sun-god to appear. Along this line, it is of interest to observe that the virgin birth, being the son of a god, death and resurrection, disciples, and miracles, among other things are also associated with many pagan deities. The early Christians in their writings, however, conceived of Jesus as ugly and misshapen as "the suffering servant" described in ISA. 53:2 (with whom they identified him)—"he hath no form nor comeliness, and when we shall see him, there is no beauty that we should desire him."

The Gospels and Acts were selected for this study because they form the heart of Christian theology. All the verses which are discussed individually or in groups are from the Authorized King James Version. Consequently, readers using other Bible translations will observe discrepancies (see above). Some verses have been shortened to avoid redundancy, and pronouns pertaining to the biblical God are capitalized for clarity.

Believers who find items mentioned that they do not understand or about which they may have questions, are urged to discuss them with their particular clergyman or Bible study teacher. They are not intended to change one's belief, but, rather to provide background material to better understand the verses and the stories to which they pertain. Those who are not believers, will find more reasons to justify their skepticism. It is hoped that both believers and skeptics will be encouraged to engage in serious Bible study in conjunction with the study of ancient history and pre-Christian religions. To this end, an extensive, but not all inclusive, bibliography covering a variety Bible related topics and viewpoints is appended. Many of the publications listed were also used as sources for much of the material herein presented.

# *CHAPTER ONE*

## THE GOSPEL ACCORDING TO ST. MATTHEW

1:1 - THE BOOK OF THE GENERATION OF JESUS CHRIST, THE SON OF DAVID, THE SON OF ABRAHAM.

**Language:**
Jesus is the Greek form of the Hebrew Jeshua (Joshua).
Christ is the English form of the Latin, "Christus, " and the Greek, "Khristos," meaning, "one who has been anointed" or "the anointed one." In Hebrew, one who has been anointed is called, "Mashiach" ("Messiah"). The name Jesus Christ, therefore, may be translated as "Joshua the anointed one."

**History:**
The word, Christ, was also used as a title for political and religious figures, Israelite and other kings, as well as for deities. For example, Cyrus, a king of Persia, was called, "Christ," and "Anointed of God." The Israelite kings, after being anointed, like other Near Eastern and Roman kings (Caesars) were also called, "sons of God."

**Pagan parallels:**
The title of "Christ" ("Anointed One") was used for the Roman and Zoroastrian god Mithra and for other pagan deities.

**Contradictions:**
MATT. 22:42-45 - Jesus, upon being called "The Son of David, " said, "If David then call him [Jesus] 'Lord,' how is he [Jesus] his son?"
MARK 12:37 - Jesus: "David calleth him Lord; whence is he [Jesus] then his son?...."
LUKE 20:44 - Jesus: "David calleth him Lord, how is he [Jesus] then his son?"
[Was, or was not Jesus the son (descended from) of David?]
MATT. 1: 18 - ...When his [Jesus' ] mother Mary was espoused to Joseph...she was found with child of the Holy Ghost.
MATT. 1:20-21 - An angel told Joseph, " that which is conceived in her [Mary] is of the Holy Ghost. She shall bring forth a son and thou shalt call his name 'Jesus.'"
MATT. 3:17 - A voice from heaven said, "This is My beloved son."
MATT. 26:63-64 - The high priest said to Jesus, "...tell us whether thou be the Christ, the Son of God. Jesus: "Thou hast said" [a phrase meaning "yes" in Aramaic].
MARK 1:1 The beginning of the gospel of Jesus Christ, the Son of God.
MARK 3:11 Unclean spirits cried, "Thou art the Son of God."
MARK 14:61-62 - .... The high priest asked him, "Art thou the Christ, the Son of the Blessed?" Jesus said, "I am...."
LUKE 1:35 - An angel said to Mary, "That holy thing that shall be born of thee shall be called the Son of God."
LUKE 8:28 - ...he [A man who had devils] cried out..., "What have I to do with thee, Jesus, thou Son of God most high?"
JOHN 1:13 - [Jesus was] born, not of blood, nor of the will of the flesh, nor of the will of man, but of God.

JOHN 1: 14 - The Word was made flesh, and dwelt among us as the only begotten of the Father.
JOHN 1:49 - Nathanael saith, "Rabbi, thou art the Son of God."
JOHN 3:16-18 - God...gave His only begotten Son.... God sent not His Son to condemn the world.... He that believeth on...the only begotten Son of God.
JOHN 6:68-69 - Peter answered, "...thou art that Christ, the Son of the living God."
JOHN 9:35-37 - Jesus...said, "Dost thou believe on the Son of God?" .... Jesus said, "...it is he that talketh with thee."
JOHN 10:36 - Jesus: "Say ye of him, whom the Father...sent into the world, 'Thou blasphemeth,' because I said, 'I am the Son of God?'"
JOHN 20:31 - ...Jesus is the Christ, the Son of God....
GAL. 4:4 - Paul: "...God sent forth His Son, made of a woman."
The astute Bible reader will find additional comparable verses.
[Was Jesus the son of (descended from) David, or was he the Son of God conceived by the Holy Ghost, and the Word made flesh?]

**Perplexing:**
If Jesus was descended from David, why did he deny it? If Jesus was descended from David, how could he also be God's Son? Note that Jews of biblical times traced genealogies patriarchally, and did not maintain matriarchal genealogies, so Jesus could not have been descended from David through his mother Mary. If Jesus was the Son of God, why did MATT. present a human paternal genealogy for him in vv. 1-18?

1:2-16 - A GENEALOGY IS PRESENTED STARTING WITH ABRAHAM AND ENDING WITH JESUS. IT INDICATES 42 GENERATIONS, BUT SINCE JECHONIAS IS CITED TWICE, THERE ACTUALLY ARE ONLY 41 GENERATIONS. THE TIME FRAME COVERS OVER 2000 YEARS.

**History:**
There is no record of any ancient people having maintained unbroken accurate genealogies covering the preceding two millennia.

**Contradiction:**
LUKE 3:23-34 - A cited genealogy from Abraham to Jesus covers 56 generations, only 19 of which are also reported by MATT.
[Were there 41 or 56 generations from Abraham to Jesus? (In an effort to explain the discrepancy between the two, some individuals allege that the LUKE genealogy is that of Mary, whereas that in MATT. pertains to Joseph. Aside from the fact that LUKE 3:23 says that the genealogy is Joseph's, it contains 15 more generations than the one in MATT.).]

**Perplexing:**
How could the Hebrews have kept accurate records through migrations, enslavement, wars, assorted upheavals, and without a written language of their own until the llth century B.C.?
If Jesus was the Son of God, what was the purpose of giving him a paternal human genealogy? Was the genealogy prepared at a time when he was believed to have been the Jewish Messiah, a man descended paternally from David? Was the appelation, "Son of God," originally meant to imply that Jesus was or was to be a king? Was it later erroneously interpreted to mean that he was literally the Son of God?

1:3-6 - THE GENEALOGY CITES: THAMAR (TAMAR), RACHAB (RAHAB), RUTH, AND THE WIFE (BATHSHEBA) OF URIAS. [THESE ARE THE ONLY WOMEN MENTIONED IN THE GENEALOGY, OTHER THAN JESUS' MOTHER MARY.]

**Contradiction:**
The genealogy in LUKE 3:23-38 does not cite any women, not even Mary. [Were, or were not Tamar, Ruth, and Bathsheba related to Jesus?]

**Perplexing:**
Why were the only women appearing in the genealogy prior to Mary, those who had engaged in illicit sexual relations? Tamar acted as a prostitute to have sex with and bear out of wedlock children for her father-in-law Judah. Rahab was a prostitute in Jericho; Ruth had premarital sex with Booz (Boaz) in exchange for six measures of barley (the phrase used in RUTH 3:8, "lay at his feet," is a literal translation of a Hebrew idiom meaning "to have sexual relations"); and Bathsheba committed adultery with David.

1:7 - DAVID'S SON SOLOMON IS CITED AS ONE OF JESUS' ANCESTORS.

**Contradiction:**
LUKE 3:31 - David's son Nathan is cited as one of Jesus' ancestors.
[Was Jesus descended from David through Solomon, or through Nathan?]

**Old Testament:**
2 CHRON. 7:17-18 - The LORD [said to Solomon]: "...then will I establish the throne of thy kingdom, as I have covenanted with David thy father...there shall not fail thee a man to be ruler in Israel."
[This has been interpreted by some as meaning that the Messiah will be descended from David through his son Solomon, not Nathan.]

1:8 - ...JORAM BEGAT OZIAS [UZZIAH].

**Contradiction:**
2 CHRON. 26:1 - Uzziah was made king in the room of his father Amaziah.
[Did Joram beget Uzziah, or was Amaziah the father of Uzziah?]

**History:**
Joram died in 844 B.C., but Uzziah did not begin his reign until 780 B.C., 76 years later. During the interval, Joram's son Ahaziah succeeded him; he was followed by Queen Athaliah, then by his son Joash who was, in turn, followed by his son Amaziah. He, in turn, was succeeded by his son Uzziah. (Note that it was Amaziah, not Joram, who begat Uzziah.)

**Perplexing:**
Why did MATT. state that Uzziah was the son of Joram, when he was actually Amaziah's son? Why did MATT. fail to cite Ahaziah, Athalia, Joash, and Amaziah, in his genealogy?

1:11-12 - JOSIAS BEGAT JECHONIAS...ABOUT THE TIME THEY WERE CARRIED AWAY TO BABYLON. AFTER THEY WERE BROUGHT TO BABYLON, JECHONIAS BEGAT SALATHIEL, AND SALATHIEL BEGAT ZOROBABEL.

**History:**
Josias had been dead for over 20 years at the time of the Babylonian Exile (587 - 538 B.C.). He was the grandfather, not the father of Jechonias.

**Contradictions:**
1 CHRON. 3:15 - The sons of Josiah were Johanan, Johoiakim, Zedekiah, and Shallum.
[Was Jechonias a son of Josias, or were Johanan, Johoiakim, Zedekiah, and Shallum his sons?]
1 CHRON. 3:16; JER. 24:1; 27:20; 28:4; 37:1 - Jechoniah (Jechonias; Corniah) was the son of Jehoiakim.
[Was Jechonias a son of Josias, or of Jehoiakim?]
LUKE 3:27 - Salathiel was the son of Neri.
[Was Salathiel the son of Jechonias, or of Neri?]
1 CHRON. 3:19 - Zerubbabel (Zorobabel) was the son of Pedaiah.
[Was Zorobabel the son of Salathiel, or Pedaiah?]

**Perplexing:**
In JER. 22:24-30, the LORD cursed Jechonias (Corniah) - "Write ye this man childless...no man of his seed shall prosper, sitting upon the throne of David and ruling anymore in Judah." Why then was a man cursed by the LORD cited twice in this genealogy of Jesus? If none of his descendants were to prosper, how could he be one of Jesus' ancestors? Did the LORD's curse fail? Did MATT. not know about the curse?

1:13 - ZOROBABEL BEGAT ABIUD; ABIUD BEGAT ELIAKIM, AND ELIAKIM BEGAT AZOR.

**Contradiction:**
1 CHRON. 3:19-20 - the sons of Zerubbabel were, Meshullam, Hananiah...Hashubah, Ohel, Berechiah, Hasadiah, Jushabhesed....
[Was, or was not Abiud one of Zorobabel's sons?]
LUKE 3:27 - Rhesa was the son of Zorobabel.
[Was, or was not Rhesa a son of Zorobabel?]
2 KINGS 23:34 - Eliakim was the son of Josiah.
[Was Eliakim the son of Abiud, or the son of Josiah?]
2 KINGS 24:6 - Eliakim (Jehoiakim) was succeeded by his son Jehoiachin.
[Was Eliakim succeeded by Azor, or by Jehoiachim?]

**Perplexing:**
Abiud and Azor were not mentioned in the Old Testament. From where then did MATT. obtain these names?

1:16 - JACOB BEGAT JOSEPH THE HUSBAND OF MARY, OF WHOM WAS BORN JESUS, WHO IS CALLED CHRIST.

**Contradiction:**
LUKE 3:23 - Jesus...being (as was supposed) the son of Joseph, which was the son of Heli.
[Was Joseph the son of Jacob, or Heli? (In an effort to avoid this contradiction, some claim that Heli was Joseph's father-in-law. There is no biblical or other support for this assertion. Even if accurate, there would still be a contradiction between "father" and "father-in-law." Individuals who make the above claim also allege that the LUKE genealogy is really that of Mary, not Joseph's. LUKE, however, does not confirm

this; and the ancient Hebrews and the Jews of biblical times did not maintain or recognize a matriarchal genealogy. Furthermore, according to LUKE 1:5, Mary's cousin Elisabeth was a descendant of Aaron; thus Mary also would be descended from Aaron, and, thus, a Levite - of the tribe of Levi. David, however, was of the tribe of Judah (RUTH 4:12-22). Consequently, the LUKE genealogy going back to David and Judah cannot be that of Mary.]
See also under 1:2-16.

**Language:** See under 1:1.

1:17 - All THE GENERATIONS FROM ABRAHAM TO DAVID ARE 14; FROM DAVID UNTIL THE CARRYING AWAY INTO BABYLON ARE 14, AND FROM THE CARRYING AWAY INTO BABYLON UNTO CHRIST ARE 14 GENERATIONS.

**Contradictions:**
MATT. 1:7-11 - There are 13 generations cited between David and the Babylonian Exile: Solomon, Roboam, Abia, Asa, Josaphat, Joram, Ozias, Joatham, Achaz, Ezekias, Manasses, Amon, and Josias. (MATT., in v.11, reported that Jechonias, the son of Josias was born about the time of the Exile, and, in v.12, as living during the Exile. Nonetheless, MATT. included him in both the list of the 14 generations prior to the Exile, and in the 14 generations during the Exile. If he is included in the pre-Exile list, the claim that there were 14 generations from the Exile until Christ would be incorrect, as without Jechonias there would be only 13 generations. Similarly, if he is included in the Exile list, there would be only 13, not 14, generations in the list preceding the Exile.)
[Were there 14, or 13 generations prior to the Babylonian Exile?]
[Were there 14, or 13 generations from the Exile until Christ?]
[Did Jechonias belong in the list from David to Babylon, or in the list from Babylon to Christ?]
1 CHRON. 29:22 - 2 CHRON. 36:6 cited 18 generations starting with Solomon and going to Jehoiakim and the Babylonian Exile.
[Were there 14 or 18 generations between David and the Babylonian Exile?]
[Did, or did not MATT. list all the generations between David and the Babylonian Exile?]

**Perplexing:**
Why did MATT. fail to list all of the generations cited by CHRON.?

1:18 - THE BIRTH OF JESUS CHRIST WAS ON THIS WISE: WHEN HIS MOTHER MARY WAS ESPOUSED TO JOSEPH, BEFORE THEY CAME TOGETHER, SHE WAS FOUND WITH CHILD OF THE HOLY GHOST.

**Contradictions:**
MATT. 1:1 - ...Jesus Christ, the son of David....
LUKE 1:32 - An angel [said to Mary]: "...the Lord God shall give unto him [Jesus] the throne of his father David."
LUKE 3:23-31 presented a human genealogy for Jesus going back to David.
ACTS 2:30 - Peter: "...God had sworn with an oath to him [David], that of the fruit of his loins, according to the flesh, He would raise up Christ to sit on his throne."
ACTS 13:23 - Paul: "Of this man's [David's] seed hath God according to His promise raised unto Israel a Saviour Jesus."
ROM. 1:3-4 - Paul: "Concerning His Son Jesus Christ our Lord, which was made of the seed of David

according to the flesh, and declared to be the Son of God...by the resurrection from the dead."
2 TIM. 2:8 - Paul: "Remember that Jesus Christ of the seed of David was raised from the dead...."
REV. 22:16 - Jesus: "I Jesus am the root and offspring of David...."
[Was Jesus the Son of God, the Holy Ghost, or descended from David?]
JOHN 8:40 - Jesus: "Now ye seek to kill me, a man that hath told you truth which I heard of God."
[Was Jesus the Son of God, or a man who heard the truth from God?]
ACTS 2:22 - Peter: "Jesus of Nazareth, a man approved of God among you by miracles, wonders, and signs, which God did by him in the midst of you...."
[Was Jesus the Son of God, or a man of whom God approved and through whom He performed miracles?]
ACTS 10:38 - Peter: "God anointed Jesus with the Holy Ghost and power, who went about doing good...for God was with him."
[Was Jesus God's Son, or a man anointed by God to do good?]
ACTS 17:31 - Paul: "...He will judge the world...by that man whom he hath ordained...that He hath raised from the dead."
[Was Jesus the Son of God, or a man ordained by God to judge the world?]

**Perplexing:**
Why was the Virgin Birth not mentioned by MARK, JOHN, and Paul?
Why did God select Mary, a married woman (1: 18 - she was esposed to Joseph; in LUKE 1:27-31, also, she was espoused to Joseph before she conceived) to bear Jesus? Why did God engage in adultery with a married woman even if she was still a virgin? And since Mary was not first asked whether she wanted to be impregnated by the Holy Ghost, was God also guilty of rape? Why was no reason given for God's decision to have an espoused woman bear His child. If God knew that He wanted Mary to bear His Son, why did He fail to marry her rather than let her marry Joseph? Why did God not ask Mary first whether she would be agreeable to having the Holy Ghost impregnate her? Why did God not send His Son directly down to earth, rather than engage in fornication, rape, and adultery? Could not MATT.'s accusations against God be viewed as blasphemy by anyone refusing to believe that God would denigrate Himself by engaging in fornication, adultery, and the rape of a human woman for the purpose of propagating Himself?
What form did the Holy Ghost take when it impregnated Mary? In MATT. 3:16; MARK 1:10; LUKE 3:22; and JOHN 1:32, it was said to have descended upon Jesus in the form of a dove. In ACTS 2:3-4, it had the form of "cloven tongues like as of fire" when it sat on the disciples. How did the Holy Ghost impregnate Mary? Does the Holy Ghost have sperm? If so, does It (God) have genes?

**Pagan parallels:**
Many pagan divinities were born out of a union between a god and a virgin human female. Some examples are, Krishna, Dionysus, Heracles (Hercules), and Aeolus. Zeus had sexual relations with numerous women, all of whom bore his children. In one instance, he assumed the form of a swan to impregnated Leda. (Did the Holy Ghost take the form of a dove to impregnate Mary?)
The belief in a Holy Spirit (Ghost) existed in some pre-Christian religions in which it was depicted as a dove.

1:20 - THE ANGEL OF THE LORD APPEARED UNTO HIM IN A DREAM SAYING, "JOSEPH, THOU SON OF DAVID, FEAR NOT TO TAKE UNTO THEE MARY THY WIFE; THAT WHICH IS CONCEIVED IN HER IS OF THE HOLY GHOST."

**Contradictions:** See under 1:18.

**Perplexing:**
Why did the angel specifically identify Joseph as a descendant of David, if he was not Jesus' real father? Why was Joseph selected to be Jesus' stepfather? As the Holy Ghost concept is a New Testament Christian concept, not a Jewish concept, how did Joseph know about what the angel was speaking? What is an angel? When were they created? Why did God need angels?
See also under 1:18.

**Pagan concept:**
In pagan religions, angels were considered to be messengers from a god.

**History:**
Some biblical scholars believe that originally, Jesus was believed to have been the son of Joseph and, thus, legitimately the Jewish Messiah; the Son of God concept having been developed at a later date. Some early Christians, such as the Ebionites also believed that Jesus was a human man who God favored. (See also under 1:18, Contradictions; and under 1:2-16, Perplexing.)

1:21 - THE ANGEL: "SHE SHALL BRING FORTH A SON, AND THOU SHALT CALL HIS NAME JESUS; HE SHALL SAVE HIS PEOPLE FROM THEIR SINS."

**Contradictions:**
LUKE 1:26-35 - The angel Gabriel told Mary, a virgin, espoused to Joseph, of the house of David, "Thou art highly favoured, the Lord is with thee...." ..."Thou hast found favour with God. Thou shalt...bring forth a son, and call his name JESUS. ...the Lord God shall give unto him the throne of his father David, and he shall reign over the house of Jacob forever...."
[Did the angel speak to Joseph, or to Mary?]
[Did the angel say that Jesus will save "his people from their sins," or that he will rule over the house of Jacob forever?]
LUKE 12:49 - Jesus: "I am come to send fire on the earth...."
LUKE 12:51 - Jesus: "Suppose ye that I am come to give peace on earth? Nay, rather division."
[Was Jesus to save people from their sins, or bring fire and division on the earth?]
MARK 4:11-12 - Jesus: "...unto them that are without, these things are done in parables...lest at any time they should be converted, and their sins be forgiven."
[Did Jesus come to save people from their sins, or to prevent them from having their sins forgiven?]
I JOHN 3:8 - John: "The Son of God was manifested, that he might destroy the works of the devil."
[Was Jesus to save people from their sins, or destroy the works of the devil?]

**Perplexing:**
Why did God want His Son to be named "Jesus?" Did Jesus save his people from their sins? Why was it assumed that all people have sins?

**Language:** See under 1:1.

1:22-23 - ALL THIS WAS DONE, THAT IT MIGHT BE FULFILLED WHICH WAS SPOKEN OF THE LORD BY THE PROPHET, "A VIRGIN SHALL BE WITH CHILD, AND SHALL BRING FORTH A SON, AND THEY SHALL CALL HIS NAME EMMANUEL."

**Old Testament:**
ISA. 7:14-16 - Isaiah: "The Lord Himself shall give you [Ahaz, King of Judea (c. 735-715 B.C.)] a sign; a virgin shall conceive, bear a son, and call his name Immanuel. Butter and honey shall he eat, that he may know to refuse the evil, and choose the good. Before the child shall know to refuse the evil, and choose the good, the land that thou abhorrest shall be forsaken of both her kings [the kings of Syria and Israel]." [The sign was to assure Ahaz that he would be victorious in an impending war with Syria and Israel.]
ISA. 8:3 - Isaiah: "I went unto the prophetess, and she conceived, and bore a son. [Isaiah's prophecy, however, failed to materialize; according to 2 CHRON. 28:5 - The LORD delivered Ahaz into the hand of the king of Syria and the king of Israel, who smote him with great slaughter. The prophecy, consequently, did not pertain to the birth of Jesus centuries later. Isaiah, also, did not say that the child would be the Son of God.]

**Language:**
The ISA. 7:14 verse uses the Hebrew word, "almah," meaning "young woman," which was mistakenly translated into Greek as "parthenos," meaning "virgin." Isaiah's prophecy, therefore, did not necessarily refer to a virgin.

**Perplexing:**
Why was a failed prophecy for a Judean king applied to Jesus' birth centuries later? Why was the child to be named Jesus, not Emanuel?

**Pagan parallels:**
Many pre-Christian deities were reputed to have had virgin mothers. Some examples are, Mithra, Krishna, Tammuz, and Horus.

**History:**
The "virgin birth" concept was officially brought into Christian theology by the Council in Ephesus in A.D. 431 at which time Mary was declared to be a virgin and the mother of Jesus through divine intervention. The concept, therefore, may not have been in the original MATT. and LUKE gospels, but inserted at a later date.

1:25 - [JOSEPH] KNEW HER NOT TILL SHE HAD BROUGHT FORTH HER FIRSTBORN SON; HE CALLED HIS NAME JESUS.

**Perplexing:**
If Jesus was Mary's firstborn, how many other children did she have? (Later verses will say that Jesus had brothers and sisters.) Was Joseph their father? (In Catholic theology, Jesus was Mary's only child.)

2:1-2 - WHEN JESUS WAS BORN IN BETHLEHEM OF JUDAEA IN THE DAYS OF HEROD THE KING, THERE CAME WISE MEN FROM THE EAST TO JERUSALEM, SAYING, "WHERE IS HE THAT IS BORN KING OF THE JEWS? WE HAVE SEEN HIS STAR IN THE EAST, AND ARE COME TO WORSHIP HIM."

**Contradictions:**
LUKE 2:1-7 - Jesus was born when Cyrenius was governor of Syria.
[Was Jesus born when Herod was king, or when Cyrenius was governor? (See History, below.)]
LUKE 2:8-15 - An unidentified number of shepherds are told by an angel about Jesus' birth and instructed

to go to Bethlehem to see him.
[Did wise men come looking for the infant Jesus, or were shepherds told to go to him?]

**History:**
King Herod died in 4 B.C., and Cyrenius did not become governor until A. D. 6. (Consequently, if Cyrenius was already governor of Syria, Jesus could not have been born when Herod was king.)

**Perplexing:**
How could Jesus have been born when Herod was king, if he was born when Cyrenius was governor? Who were the wise men? Why were they not identified? How many were there? From where in the east did they come? How did they hear about Jesus? Why did they refer to Jesus as "King of the Jews?" How did they know that the star pertained to Jesus? Why did they follow the star to Jerusalem, instead of to Bethlehem? If the men were Jews, why did they not know that according to Jewish belief the Messiah ("King of the Jews") was to be born in Bethlehem? Why did LUKE not mention the wise men and the star? Why did the star guide unidentified wise men, rather than scholars, historians, political figures, or other people of whom there is some historical record?

**Pagan parallels:**
The birth of the Hindu god Krishna was heralded by a star, as was the birth of the Egyptian god Horus, and other pre-Christian deities. In non-biblical Hebrew mythology, an unusually bright star moved across the sky to signify the birth of Abraham. Zoroaster (some time between 1000-600 B.C.) stated in his holy book the Zend Avesta, that a star would guide his followers (Zoroastrians) to the birthplace of a divine being who would be their lord and everlasting king.

2:3 - WHEN HEROD THE KING HEARD THESE THINGS, HE WAS TROUBLED, AND ALL JERUSALEM WITH HIM.

**Perplexing:**
Did the wise men speak with Herod? Why was Herod troubled? Why was all Jerusalem troubled? How did all Jerusalem learn why the wise men had come? Why had Herod and the people of Jerusalem not seen the star? Why was the star not seen by anyone other than the wise men?

2:4 - WHEN HE HAD GATHERED ALL THE CHIEF PRIESTS AND SCRIBES TOGETHER, HE DEMANDED OF THEM WHERE CHRIST SHOULD BE BORN.

**History:**
There was bitter hostility between the chief priests and Herod. They were not subject to his orders, so he would not have been able to convene them quickly, if at all, at his convenience.

**Perplexing:**
Why did Herod not know that the Messiah was to be born in Bethlehem?

**Pagan parallels:** See under 1:1.

**Language:** See under 1:1.

2:5-6 - THEY SAID, "IN BETHLEHEM OF JUDAEA; IT IS WRITTEN BY THE PROPHET, 'AND THOU BETHLEHEM, IN THE LAND OF JUDA, ART NOT LEAST AMONG THE PRINCES OF JUDA, FOR OUT OF THEE SHALL COME A GOVERNOR, THAT SHALL RULE MY PEOPLE ISRAEL.'"

**Old Testament:**
MIC. 5:1-6 - Micah: "Now gather thyself in troops, O daughter of troops; he ["they," in Hebrew] hath laid siege against us; they shall smite the judge of Israel with a rod upon the cheek. But thou, Bethlehem Ephratah, though thou be little among the thousands of Judah, out of thee shall he come forth unto Me that is to be ruler in Israel.... .... ...thus shall he deliver us from the Assyrians...."

**Contradictions:** See Old Testament, above; the Old Testament verses have been misquoted and taken out of context.
[Did the prophet refer to Bethlehem the city, or to the small clan of Bethlehem Ephratah?]
[Did the prophet refer to "princes of Juda," or to "thousands of Judah?"]

**Perplexing:**
Why did MATT. equate Jesus with a prophecy about someone who was to save Judah from the Assyrians?

2:7 - HEROD, WHEN HE HAD PRIVILY CALLED THE WISE MEN, INQUIRED OF THEM DILIGENTLY WHAT TIME THE STAR APPEARED.

**Perplexing:**
Why did Herod have to ask the wise men when the star appeared? Did not Herod, any of his associates, the priests, or anyone else in Jerusalem see the star? Why was the star seen only by the wise men? See also under 2:1-2.

2:8 - HE SENT THEM TO BETHLEHEM, AND SAID, "GO AND SEARCH DILIGENTLY FOR THE YOUNG CHILD; WHEN YE HAVE FOUND HIM, BRING ME WORD, THAT I MAY COME AND WORSHIP HIM ALSO."

**Contradiction:**
LUKE 2:10-12 - An angel told shepherds that Jesus was born in the city of David (Bethlehem) and could be found there in a manger.
[Did Herod tell the wise men to go to find Jesus in Bethlehem, or did an angel tell shepherds that he would be found there?]

**Perplexing:**
If he wanted to find Jesus, why did he not send his own people to Bethlehem? Why did he need the wise men to try and locate Jesus? Why did he not send members of his staff with them? If the star was meant to guide the wise men to Jesus, why did it lead them to Jerusalem and to Herod, rather than directly to Bethlehem?
Why was no specific data given for determining the date of Jesus' birth?

2:9 - ...THEY DEPARTED, AND THE STAR , WHICH THEY SAW IN THE EAST, WENT BEFORE THEM, TILL IT CAME AND STOOD OVER WHERE THE YOUNG CHILD WAS.

**Contradiction:**
LUKE 2:15-16 - The shepherds found Jesus without being guided by a star and without first meeting with Herod.
[Did a star guide wise men to Jesus, or did shepherds find him without following a star?]

**Geography:**
Bethlehem is south of Jerusalem.

**History:**
A star changing from an easterly to a southerly course and then stopping its celestial movement would have been such a fantastic astronomical phenomenon that it would have been recorded around the world. There is no record, however, outside of MATT., not even in the other gospels, that such an event ever took place.

**Perplexing:**
Why did the star change its course for Bethlehem only after Herod informed the men that Jesus was there? Why were the shepherds able to locate Jesus without the aid of a star? Why is there no record outside of MATT. of the phenomenon of a star changing its course and stopping, or of anyone other than the wise men seeing it?
See also under 2:1-2 and 2:8.

2:11 - WHEN THEY WERE COME INTO THE HOUSE, THEY SAW THE YOUNG CHILD WITH MARY HIS MOTHER. AND FELL DOWN, AND WORSHIPPED HIM; WHEN THEY OPENED THEIR TREASURES, THEY PRESENTED UNTO HIM GIFTS: GOLD, FRANKINCENSE, AND MYRRH.

**Contradictions:**
LUKE 2:12-16 - An angel informed the shepherds that they will find the infant Jesus wrapped in swaddling clothes in a manger; the shepherds went to Bethlehem and found Jesus in a manger. They are not said to have brought gifts.
[Was the infant Jesus first visited by wise men, or by shepherds? (Anyone not reading the Gospel of LUKE would believe that Jesus was born in a house and visited first by wise men. Such a person would not know the story about the shepherds and the manger. In non-biblical Christian mythology, Jesus was said to have been born in a cave.)]
[Was Jesus found in a house, or in a manger? (In an effort to avoid the contradiction, some contend that the house was not in Bethlehem; this, however, is refuted by ensuing verses in which an angel instructed Joseph to flee with Jesus and Mary to Egypt because Herod wanted to kill Jesus; then Herod is reported to have had children in and around Bethlehem killed. If, however, Jesus was not in Bethlehem, there would have been no need for him to flee.)]
[Did he receive gifts from the wise men, or no gifts from shepherds?]

**History:**
Some early Christians, such as Father Tertullian (3rd century), Father Jerome (4th century), and the fourth century Church historian Eusebius contended that Jesus was born in a cave. There was also a second century tradition that Jesus' birthplace was a cave. And during the reign of the Roman Emperor Constantine (4th century), a church was erected at the site of a cave where Jesus was alleged to have been born.

**Pagan parallels:**
Wise men brought gifts of gold, frankincense, and myrrh to the newborn god Krishna. Shepherds brought the first fruit of their flocks and their harvests to the newborn god Mithra.

**Perplexing:**
Why did the wise men need a star to guide them to Jesus' house in Bethlehem, whereas the shepherds could find Jesus' manger in Bethlehem without any guidance? Of what use were the gifts to the infant Jesus? Why did he need gifts? Was the MATT. account based on the Krishna story, and LUKE's on that of Mithra?

2:12 - BEING WARNED OF GOD THAT THEY SHOULD NOT RETURN TO HEROD, THEY DEPARTED INTO THEIR OWN COUNTRY ANOTHER WAY.

**Perplexing:**
How long did the wise men remain with Jesus? To what country did they return? Why did MATT. fail to identify their nationality? What did they do when they returned home? Did they publicize Jesus' birth?

2:13 - WHEN THEY WERE DEPARTED, THE ANGEL OF THE LORD APPEARETH TO JOSEPH IN A DREAM, SAYING, "ARISE; TAKE THE YOUNG CHILD AND HIS MOTHER, AND FLEE INTO EGYPT; BE THERE UNTIL I BRING THEE WORD, FOR HEROD WILL SEEK THE YOUNG CHILD TO DESTROY HIM."

**Perplexing:**
Why did Jesus and family have to flee from Herod? Why could not the angel or God protect them? How could Herod destroy a divine being, the Son of God? How did the family manage to elude Herod who had an army at his disposal and already knew that they were in the small village of Bethlehem?

**Pagan parallel:**
When an infant, the Hindu god Krishna and his family fled at night after his step-father was warned by a heavenly voice that a king planned to kill the infant.

2:14 - WHEN HE AROSE, HE TOOK THE YOUNG CHILD AND HIS MOTHER BY NIGHT, AND DEPARTED INTO EGYPT.

**Contradiction:**
LUKE 2:22 - When the days of her purification...were accomplished, they brought him [Jesus] to Jerusalem, to present him to the Lord.
[After Jesus' birth, did the family flee to Egypt to escape from Herod, or did they go to Jerusalem where Herod resided?]

**Perplexing:**
How was the family able to travel at night? Did they travel only at night? If so, where did they hide during the day, especially on the desert? The distance to Egypt from Bethlehem is about 200 miles. How did they traverse this distance? How long did it take? How were they able to survive on the desert? From where did they obtain money, food, water, and clothes? Where did they rest? Did Joseph and/or Mary speak Egyptian? If so, how and where did they learn it?
If Herod wanted to kill Jesus, why did LUKE say that he was taken to Jerusalem where Herod resided?

**Old Testament:**
GEN. 12:10 - ...Abram went down into Egypt....
GEN. 39:1 - Joseph was brought down to Egypt....
GEN. 46:5-6 - Jacob his sons, their children, their wives, and cattle came into Egypt.
EX. 4:20 - Moses, his wife, and sons returned to the land of Egypt.

2:15 - [THEY WERE] THERE UNTIL THE DEATH OF HEROD, THAT IT MIGHT BE FULFILLED WHICH WAS SPOKEN OF THE LORD BY THE PROPHET, SAYING, "OUT OF EGYPT HAVE I CALLED MY SON."

**Old Testament:**
HOS. 11:1-5 - "When Israel was a child, then I loved him, and called My son out of Egypt. .... He shall not return into the land of Egypt, but the Assyrian shall be his king, because they refused to return."

**Perplexing:**
Why did MATT. equate a statement pertaining to the Exodus of the Israelites from Egypt with Jesus?

2:16 - HEROD WHEN HE SAW THAT HE WAS MOCKED OF THE WISE MEN, WAS EXCEEDING WROTH...AND SLEW ALL THE CHILDREN THAT WERE IN BETHLEHEM, AND IN ALL THE COASTS THEREOF, FROM TWO YEARS OLD AND UNDER....

**History:**
There is no Jewish, Roman, pagan, or other record or evidence that Herod killed children in and around Bethlehem. The alleged incident is not even reported by the other gospels. Had such an action been taken by Herod, it would have precipitated riots and possibly a rebellion by the Jewish population which was not particularly supportive of the pro-Roman Herod. It is also unlikely that the Roman authorities would have permitted Herod to engage in any action that might have provoked an insurrection.

**Perplexing:**
If the event occurred, why did God allow Herod to massacre innocent children because of His Son? What kind of God would allow such a thing to happen? Why did God fail to stop Herod? Why did not any historian, other gospel writer, or anyone else report it? Why were Herod's men unable to locate Jesus before he was taken into Egypt? See also under 2:13.

**Contradictions:**
LUKE 2:10-11 - An angel said unto them [shepherds], "I bring you good tidings of great joy, which shall be to all people. Unto you is born this day in the city of David a Saviour, Christ the Lord."
[Did the birth of Jesus bring joy, or sorrow to the people of Bethlehem?]
[Did the birth of Jesus bring joy, or suffering to the tens of millions of people tortured and killed in Jesus' name over the centuries?]

**Old Testament:**
EX. 1:16 - The king of Egypt ordered the killing of newborn male Hebrew babies.

**Pagan parallel:**
In an effort to kill the infant Krishna, King Kansa ordered the killing of all male children born on the same night as Krishna. (In non-biblical Hebrew mythology, King Nimrod of Babylon is said to have ordered the killing of 70,000 boys, because of a prediction that a recently born boy, Abraham, would dethrone him.)

2:17-18 - THEN WAS FULFILLED THAT WHICH WAS SPOKEN BY JEREMY [JEREMIAH] THE PROPHET, "IN RAMA WAS THERE A GREAT VOICE HEARD, LAMENTATION, AND WEEPING WITH GREAT MOURNING; RACHEL WEEPING FOR HER CHILDREN...BECAUSE THEY ARE NOT."

**Old Testament:**
JER. 31:15-17 - The LORD: "A voice was heard in Ramah, lamentation, and bitter weeping; Rahel weeping for her children...because they were not. Refrain thy voice from weeping, and thine eyes from tears; thy work shall be rewarded; they shall come again from the land of the enemy. There is hope in thine end, that thy children shall come again to their own border." [The verses were a prophecy that the children of Israel would return from exile in Babylon.]

**Perplexing:**
Why did MATT. equate a prophecy about the Israelites returning to their land from Babylon with the alleged killing of children in Bethlehem?

**History:**
Every year in Bethlehem there was a lamentation by women over the death of the god Tammuz (Adonis, the Lord, Adonai).

2:19-23 - WHEN HEROD WAS DEAD, AN ANGEL APPEARETH TO JOSEPH, SAYING, "TAKE THE CHILD AND HIS MOTHER, AND GO TO ISRAEL HE TOOK THE CHILD AND HIS MOTHER INTO ISRAEL...." WHEN HE HEARD THAT ARCHELAUS DID REIGN IN JUDAEA IN THE ROOM OF HIS FATHER HEROD, HE WAS AFRAID TO GO HITHER...BEING WARNED OF GOD IN A DREAM, HE TURNED ASIDE INTO PARTS OF GALILEE. HE CAME AND DWELT IN NAZARETH, THAT IT MIGHT BE FULFILLED WHICH WAS SPOKEN BY THE PROPHETS, "HE SHALL BE CALLED A NAZARENE."

**Contradiction:**
LUKE 2:22-39 - They (Mary and Joseph] brought him to Jerusalem. When they had performed all things according to the law of the Lord, they returned into Galilee, to their own city Nazareth.
[Was Jesus taken to Nazareth from Egypt, or from Jerusalem?]

**Perplexing:**
How long were Jesus, Mary, and Joseph in Egypt? Where in Egypt were they? What did they do in Egypt? How were they able to survive in Egypt? Why could the angel or God not protect them from Archelaus? See also under 2:14.

**Old Testament:**
Neither the cited prophecy nor Nazareth appear in the Old Testament.

**History:**
Prior to his death, Herod made Archelaus, one his sons, governor of Judea and Samaria. This son antagonized the Jews and Samarians to such an extent that after ten years the Romans removed him from office. Meanwhile, Herod's son Antipas was assigned as ruler of Galilee. He remained in power there over 40 years.

3:1-2 - IN THOSE DAYS CAME JOHN THE BAPTIST, PREACHING IN THE WILDERNESS OF JUDAEA, "REPENT YE, FOR THE KINGDOM OF HEAVEN IS AT HAND."

**Perplexing:**
How old was John when he started to preach? From where did he come? Why did he preach in the wilderness, rather than in the cities? Why did he say that the kingdom of heaven was at hand? Why has it not yet arrived? Was John an Essene? (Neither John, nor Jesus were ever reported to have criticized the Essenes.)

**History:**
The Essenes believed in confessing sins and in an imminent end of the world.

3:3 - THIS IS HE THAT WAS SPOKEN OF BY THE PROPHET ESAIAS [ISAIAH], SAYING, "THE VOICE OF ONE CRYING IN THE WILDERNESS, 'PREPARE YE THE WAY OF THE LORD, MAKE HIS PATHS STRAIGHT.'"

**Old Testament:**
ISA. 40:3 - "The voice of him that crieth in the wilderness, 'Prepare ye the way of the LORD, make straight in the desert a highway for our God.'"

**History:**
The ISA. verse was written in the 6th century B.C. during the Babylonian Exile, and is an instruction to the Israelites to prepare a way through the wilderness for their return to Jerusalem.

**Perplexing:**
Why did the gospel writer use an Old Testament verse pertaining to the Babylonian Exile as a reference to Jesus?

3:4 - JOHN HAD HIS RAIMENT OF CAMEL'S HAIR, AND A LEATHERN GIRDLE ABOUT HIS LOINS; HIS MEAT WAS LOCUSTS AND WILD HONEY.

**Old Testament:**
2 KINGS 1:8 - Messengers said [to Ahaziah]: "He was an hairy man, and girt with a girdle of leather about his loins." He said, "It is Elijah the Tishbite."

**Perplexing:**
Why did MATT. equate John with Elijah, when in JOHN 1:21, John said that he was not Elijah? (Why, in MATT. 17:11-13, did Jesus imply that John was Elijah?)

**History:**
The Dead Sea Scrolls said that honey and locusts were acceptable foods to be eaten by Qumran monks (generally believed to have been Essenes). See also under 3:1-2 - Perplexing.

3:5-6 - THEN WENT OUT TO HIM JERUSALEM, ALL JUDAEA, AND THE REGION ROUND ABOUT JORDAN, AND WERE BAPTIZED OF HIM IN JORDAN, CONFESSING THEIR SINS.

**Contradiction:**
LUKE 3:3 - He [John] came into all the country about Jordan preaching the baptism of repentance for the remission of sins.

[Did people come to him, or did he travel around the country preaching?]

**Pagan concept**:
Baptism is an ancient pre-Christian religious rite the origins of which are lost in antiquity. The ritual, believed to wash away sins, moral faults, and lead to spiritual cleanliness, was a part of many pagan religions. In Mithraism, for example, it was also believed to eliminate guilt. Some pagan practices involved just sprinkling, whereas others required full immersion.

**History:**
The Essenes practiced immersion in water as a religious ritual for spiritual cleanliness, rather than for the remission of sins. It was an essential daily act for them. Judaism at that time required converts to be totally immersed for the purpose of purifying the body after the soul had been cleansed by righteous conduct. Confession of sins and baptism were not a part of traditional Judaism.
According to Josephus, John commanded the Jews to exercise virtue, righteousness towards each other and piety towards God, See also under 3:1-2.

**Old Testament:**
The Old Testament does not cite a requirement for baptism. In ISA. 36:24-25, however, God said, "I will take you from among the heathen...bring you into your own land. Then will I sprinkle clean water upon you, and ye shall be clean...."
[This was to be a one-time act on the part of God. There was no command to the Israelites to engage in such a practice.]

**Perplexing:**
Why did John resort to baptism, an ancient non-Jewish, pagan ritual?
How did the entire region learn about John? Why did they all go to him? How did they find him in the wilderness? Why did they believe him? If the people who came to him were Jewish, why did they participate in a pagan baptism rite and the non-Jewish practice of confessing sins?

**History:** See under 3:1-2.

3:7 - WHEN HE SAW MANY OF THE PHARISEES AND SADDUCEES COME TO HIS BAPTISM, HE SAID, "O GENERATION OF VIPERS, WHO HATH WARNED YOU TO FLEE FROM THE WRATH TO COME?"

**History:**
The Pharisees were held in high repute, even by the Romans, because of their dedication to upholding religious ideals, supporting leniency and mercy in the application of laws, supporting the rights of the poor against oppression by the rich, supporting one's right to disagree on religious matters, and opposing the Roman occupation. The historical record of the Pharisees is much different from the way in which it is portrayed in the gospels. Unlike the Pharisees, the Sadducees cooperated with the Romans, comprised much of the priesthood, and accepted only the written Law (the Torah) as divinely inspired. They did not believe in angels, demons, that there was scriptural authority for the concept of resurrection, an afterlife, an immortal soul, or that God was concerned about the activities of people. At the time the gospels were being compiled, the Sadducees had lost their influence; consequently, the Pharisees had become the dominant Jewish sect and were in competition with the adherents of Jesus for converts.

**Perplexing:**
Why did Pharisees and Sadducees come to John to be baptized and confess sins, things that were not part of their religious beliefs? Why was John hostile towards both the Pharisees and Sadducees? Why did John imply that the "wrath" would come upon the Pharisees and Sadducees to whom he was speaking?

3:11 - JOHN: "I BAPTIZE YOU WITH WATER UNTO REPENTANCE, BUT HE THAT COMETH AFTER ME...WHOSE SHOES I AM NOT WORTHY TO BEAR, SHALL BAPTIZE YOU WITH THE HOLY GHOST AND WITH FIRE."

**Contradictions:**
MARK 1:7-8 - John: "There cometh one...the lachet of whose shoes I am not worthy to unloose. I have baptized you with water, but he shall baptize you with the Holy Ghost."
LUKE 3:16 - John: "...one...cometh, the lachet of whose shoes I am not worthy to unloose; he shall baptize you with the Holy Ghost and fire."
JOHN 1:27 - John: "He it is, who coming after me whose shoe's latchet I am not worthy to unloose."
[Did John say that he is not worthy to bear Jesus' shoes, or that he is not worthy to unloose the lachet of Jesus' shoes?]
[Was Jesus to baptize with the Holy Ghost and fire, or just with the Holy Ghost?]
JOHN 4:2 - Jesus himself baptized not....
[Did Jesus baptize, or did he not baptize?]
ACTS 19:1-3 - Paul found disciples of John, who had been baptized by him, say, "We have not so much heard whether there be any Holy Ghost."
[Did, or did not John mention the Holy Ghost to his disciples?]

**Pagan concept:**
The Babylonians referred to the sun at the time of the summer solstice, as the "baptism of fire."

3:13 - THEN COMETH JESUS FROM GALILEE TO JORDAN UNTO JOHN, TO BE BAPTIZED.

**Contradictions:**
LUKE 3:20-21 - ...he (Herod the tetrarch) shut up John in prison. it came to pass, that Jesus also being baptized....
[Was, or was not, Jesus baptized by John?]
[Was John imprisoned before, or after Jesus came to him to be baptized?]

**Perplexing:**
Why did Jesus have to undergo baptism, something that was originally a pagan purification rite? If he was the Son of God, would he not be pure and free from sin? If those who were baptized confessed their sins, what sins did Jesus confess? Why did the gospel writers present him as a repentant sinner?
Was MATT. saying that Jesus really was a human - the son of Joseph descended from David? Were Jesus' baptism verses written before the Jesus as Son of God concept came unto being?

**History:**
Early Christians, the Ebionites, believed that Jesus was a human man favored by God and used by Him to perform miracles (see ACTS 2:22 - Jesus of Nazareth, a man approved of God among you by miracles....).
Some biblical scholars also contend that Jesus became God's adopted Son after his baptism.
See also under 1:20.

3:15 - JESUS SAID, "...IT BECOMETH US TO FULFILL ALL RIGHTEOUSNESS."

**Perplexing:**
What was meant by righteousness?

3:16 - JESUS WHEN HE WAS BAPTIZED, WENT UP OUT OF THE WATER; THE HEAVENS WERE OPENED UNTO HIM, AND HE SAW THE SPIRIT OF GOD DESCENDING LIKE A DOVE, AND LIGHTING UPON HIM.

**Pagan parallels:**
The dove was a symbol of a holy spirit in a number of pagan religions. The goddesses Juno, Astarte, Cybele, Isis, and others were at times represented with a dove upon or associated with them.
Zeus in the form of a swan descended upon the woman Leda.
See also under 1:18.

**Perplexing:**
In ACTS 2:3-4, the Holy Ghost (the Spirit) descended upon the disciples as tongues of fire, and the disciples spoke in tongues. Why did the Spirit descend on Jesus in the form of a dove, rather than tongues of fire? Did Jesus speak in tongues after the Spirit descended on him? Did anyone besides Jesus and John (JOHN 1:32) see the dove? Why did it descend upon Jesus? Why did It wait until after he was baptized to descend onto him? Why did It not descend on him when he was born? How were the heavens opened? How far and how fast did the dove have to fly to reach Jesus? How old was Jesus when he was baptized? LUKE 3:23 implied that he was about 30 years of age. If so, why did he wait until he was an adult to be baptized? If John knew who Jesus was, why in MATT. 11:2-3, did he instruct two of his disciples to ask Jesus, "Art thou he that should come, or do we look for another?"

**History:**
Some Gnostics considered the Spirit, to be feminine and the "Mother of all Things"; and when in the shape of a dove, as "the Word of the Mother from above." Some early Christians even viewed the Holy Spirit to be the mother of Jesus. (In Hebrew, the word for spirit, "ruach," is feminine.]

3:17 - A VOICE FROM HEAVEN, SAYING, "THIS IS MY BELOVED SON, IN WHOM I AM WELL PLEASED."

**Contradictions:** See under 1:18.

**Old Testament:**
PS 2:7 - "...the LORD hath said unto me, 'Thou art My Son; this day have I begotten thee.'" [The words were spoken by a recently crowned king.]

**History:**
In the ancient Middle East and Rome it was customary for kings to consider themselves to be the adopted sons of God. The coronation day was viewed as the day on which they were begotten by God. Some manuscripts, such as the Codex Bezae, dating to between the 4th to the 6th centuries translate the verse, "Thou art My Son; today I have begotten thee." Some Bibles, such as The New Jerusalem Bible, translate God's words as, "You are My Son; today I have fathered you." The Codex Bezae consisting of the four gospels and ACTS has, "Thou art My Son; today I have begotten thee." Thus, these Bibles and the Codex

imply that at least some early Christians considered Jesus to be God's adopted Son, not His procreated Son.
[In HEB. 1:5, Paul, referring to Jesus, said, "For unto which of the angels said He at any time, 'Thou art My Son; this day have I begotten thee, and I will be to him a Father, and he shall be to Me a Son?'"]
See also under 1:1.

**Perplexing:**
What had Jesus done to cause God to say that He is well pleased with him? Why did God wait until this time to say that He is pleased with Jesus? Why did MATT. fail to report anything that Jesus did up until now? Was MATT. saying that Jesus was God's adopted Son? If Jesus and God are one, as claimed in JOHN 10:30, was God saying that he is pleased with Himself?
Did the gospel writer view Jesus as God's adopted Son?

**Pagan parallel:**
A voice resembling thunder - that of Mother Universe - speaking about Buddha, said, "This is my beloved son."

4:1-2 - THEN WAS JESUS LED UP OF THE SPIRIT INTO THE WILDERNESS TO BE TEMPTED OF THE DEVIL. WHEN HE HAD FASTED 40 DAYS AND NIGHTS, HE WAS AFTERWARD AN HUNGERED.

**Contradictions:**
MARK 1:12-13 - Immediately the spirit driveth him into the wilderness. He was in the wilderness 40 days, tempted of Satan...the angels ministered unto him.
LUKE 4:1-2 - Jesus...was led by the Spirit into the wilderness, being 40 days tempted of the devil. he did eat nothing; when they were ended he afterward hungered.
[Did the Spirit lead, or drive Jesus into the wilderness?]
[Was Jesus in the wilderness 40 days before the devil came to him (in 4:3), or was he tempted for 40 days?]
[Did Jesus fast for 40 days before meeting the devil, not fast 40 days while with Satan, or fast 40 days while with the devil?]
[Did angels minister to Jesus during the 40 days, or after the 40 days (in 4:11)?]
JOHN 1:28-43 - Jesus went from Bethabara beyond Jordan where John was baptizing to Galilee after encountering two of John's disciples and Simon.
[After being baptized by John, did Jesus go to the wilderness and meet the devil, or did he go to Galilee?]
LUKE 3:20-22; 4:1 - John was imprisoned before Jesus was tempted by the devil.
[Was John imprisoned (MATT. 4:12) after, or before the devil tempted Jesus?]

**Old Testament:**
EX. 24:18 - Moses was in the mount 40 days and 40 nights.
EX. 34:28-29 - Moses did not eat or drink for 40 days and nights when he was on mount Sinai with the LORD.
1 KINGS 19:8 - Elijah spent 40 days and nights on mount Horeb the mount of God.
(The number "40," appears numerous times in the Old Testament and may have had mystical meaning for the ancient Hebrews that carried over into the New Testament where it appears several times.)
Some examples, other than the above are:
GEN. 7:12 - The rain was on the earth 40 days and 40 nights.
GEN. 50:3 - Forty days were fulfilled for him (Jacob) the days of those which are embalmed....

1 SAM. 4:18 - .... He [Eli] had judged Israel 40 years.
1 KINGS 2: 11 - The days that David reigned over Israel were 40 years....
1 KINGS 11:42 - The time that Solomon reigned...over Israel was 40 years....
2 CHRON 24:1 - Joash...reigned 40 years in Jerusalem....

**Perplexing:**
Why did Jesus have to be taken to the wilderness to be tempted by the devil? Why would the devil want to tempt Jesus the Son of God? Why would the devil think that he could succeed in tempting Jesus? What did Jesus do in the wilderness for 40 days while waiting for the devil? Why did he go without food for 40 days? Why could Jesus not control his hunger? Why could he not perform a miracle to create food for himself? Did the number "40" have a special significance for the Bible writers?

**Pagan concept:**
The wilderness was believed to be the abode of evil spirits.

4:3 - WHEN THE TEMPTER CAME TO HIM, HE SAID, "IF THOU BE THE SON OF GOD, COMMAND THAT THESE STONES BE MADE BREAD."

**Contradiction:**
LUKE 4:3 - The devil said, "If thou be the Son of God, command this stone be made bread."
[Did the devil ask Jesus to turn numerous stones, or just one stone, into bread?]

**Perplexing:**
From where did the devil come? Was he created by God? If so, why and when? If he was evil, why did the Bible writers fail to cite any evil that he perpetrated? Why did MATT. fail to provide some introductory material about the devil? Was the devil concept, which is not a Jewish concept, so well known that it required no explanation? If one was not familiar with Christian theology, one would not know that the devil is supposed to be evil.
Why was the devil the first being, other than God, in MATT. to refer to Jesus as the "Son of God?"
Why was the conversation between Jesus and the devil not reported by MARK and JOHN?

**Pagan parallels:**
Belief in one or more deities (or forces) of evil is found in many pre-Christian religions such as Zoroastrianism, Buddhism, and the ancient Etruscan faith. The evil deity, or main evil deity, usually existed as a rival of a good god or person. In sun-god religions, the evil being represented the personification of the sun's enemy - the dark cloud that could obscure the sun (the good god).
The Etruscan devil Charun (c.500 B.C.) ruled a realm of darkness and was depicted with flaming eyes, wings, and cloven hoofs (very similar in appearance to the usual depiction of the Christian Satan).
In Zoroastrianism, the evil god Ahriman (Angra Mainyu), known as the prince of darkness, had an army of demons, was a tempter, corrupter, and the enemy of the good god Ahura Mazda (Ohrmazd). He tried unsuccessfully with grandiose promises to dissuade Zoroaster (usually dated to between 1000 - 600 B.C.), who was about 30 years old at the time, from worshiping the good god.
Buddha (6th century B.C.) was tempted by Mara the evil one.

**Dead Sea Scrolls:**
In the Dead Sea Scrolls, those who are "righteous" are called, "sons of God."

4:4 - JESUS: “IT IS WRITTEN, ‘MAN SHALL NOT LIVE BY BREAD ALONE, BUT BY EVERY WORD THAT PROCEEDETH OUT OF THE MOUTH OF GOD.’”

**Old Testament:**
DEUT. 8:3 - Moses: “...man doth not live by bread only, but by every word that proceedeth out of the mouth of the LORD doth man live.”

4:5-6 - THE DEVIL TAKETH HIM INTO THE HOLY CITY, SETTETH HIM ON A PINNACLE OF THE TEMPLE, AND SAITH, “IF THOU BE THE SON OF GOD, CAST THYSELF DOWN, FOR IT IS WRITTEN, ‘HE SHALL GIVE HIS ANGELS CHARGE OF THEE; IN THEIR HANDS THEY SHALL BEAR THEE UP. LEST AT ANY TIME THOU DASH THY FOOT AGAINST A STONE.’”

**Contradiction:**
LUKE 4:5 - The devil, taking him up into a high mountain, shewed him all the kingdoms of the world in a moment of time.
[Did the devil take Jesus from the wilderness to a pinnacle of the temple in Jerusalem, or did he take him to an unidentified mountain?]

**Old Testament:**
PS. 91:2-13 - “I will say of the LORD, He is my refuge.... .... There shall no evil befall thee, neither shall any plague come nigh thy dwelling. He shall give His angels charge over thee, lest thou dash thy foot against a stone. Thou shalt tread upon the lion and the adder; the young lion and the dragon shalt thou trample under feet.”
[The verses referred to those who trust in God; they did not pertain to Jesus or even to jumping from a height.]

**Perplexing:**
Why did the devil believe that Jesus, the Son of God, would require the assistance of angels? How could Jesus be hurt? Why did Jesus fail to point out that the devil had misused the Old Testament verses?

4:7 - JESUS SAID, “IT IS WRITTEN, ‘THOU SHALT NOT TEMPT THE LORD THY GOD.’”

**Old Testament:**
DEUT. 6:16 - Moses: “Ye shall not tempt the LORD your God, as ye tempted Him in Massah.”
[The verse pertained to EX. 17:2-7 in which Moses accused the Israelites of tempting the LORD when they doubted that the LORD was with them in the wilderness.]

**Perplexing:**
Why did Jesus take the verse out of its context?

4:8 - THE DEVIL TAKETH HIM UP INTO AN EXCEEDINGLY HIGH MOUNTAIN, AND SHEWETH HIM ALL THE KINGDOMS OF THE WORLD, AND THE GLORY OF THEM.

**Contradiction:**
LUKE 4:9 - The devil brought him to Jerusalem, and set him on a pinnacle of the temple....
[Did the devil take Jesus from a temple pinnacle to a mountain, or from a mountain to a pinnacle of the temple?]

See also under 4:5-6.

**Perplexing:**
Onto what mountain did the devil take Jesus? Where was this mountain? As the world is spherical, it would not be possible to see the opposite side of the planet from a mountain peak no matter how high it might be. Consequently, the devil would not have been able to show Jesus the Indian kingdoms of the Western Hemisphere, such as the Olmec, Maya, Chavin, Mocha, Inca, and others. There also is no mountain on the earth high enough to enable one to see from its summit more than a few of the kingdoms (or nations), and then not in their entirety. If, however, the earth was relatively small and flat, it might have been possible to see all of the kingdoms. Did MATT. and LUKE believe that the earth was flat? Did Jesus believe that the world was flat? Why did Jesus fail to inform people that the world was round, not flat? Were MATT., LUKE. and Jesus ignorant of the size and shape of the earth, and the existence of kingdoms on the other side of the planet? If so, why?
As God's Son, why would Jesus need or want the glory of human kingdoms when he already had the glory of the entire universe and heaven? Did the devil have the power to give the glory of the kingdoms? If so, how and why did he get it?

4:9 - THE DEVIL: "ALL THESE THINGS WILL I GIVE THEE, IF THOU WILT FALL DOWN AND WORSHIP ME."

**Perplexing:**
How could the devil offer to Jesus anything which Jesus, as God's Son, did not already own?

4:10 - JESUS: "GET THEE HENCE SATAN; IT IS WRITTEN, 'THOU SHALT WORSHIP THE LORD THY GOD, AND HIM ONLY SHALT THOU SERVE.'"

**Old Testament:**
EX. 20:3 - "Thou shalt have no other gods before Me."
EX. 20:5 - "Thou shalt not bow down thyself to them [other gods], nor serve them...."
EX. 34:14 - "Thou shalt worship no other god...."
DEUT. 6:13 - "Thou shalt fear the LORD thy God and serve Him...."
DEUT. 10:20 - "Thou shalt fear the LORD thy God; Him shalt thou serve...."

**Perplexing:**
Why did Jesus wait until now to tell Satan to leave?

**Pagan parallel:**
Buddha told the Evil One who was trying to tempt him, "Get thee away from me."

**Language:**
The word, "satan," is derived from the Hebrew word meaning, "adversary," not "devil." (See MATT. 16:23 and MARK 8:32-33 - Jesus, after being rebuked by Peter, said, "Get thee behind me, Satan." By so doing, Jesus was calling Peter an adversary, not the devil.)

4:11 - THEN THE DEVIL LEAVETH HIM, AND ANGELS CAME AND MINISTERED UNTO HIM.

**Contradictions:**
MARK 1:13 - He was in the wilderness 40 days tempted of Satan and...the angels ministered unto him.
[Did angels minister to Jesus after the devil departed, or during the 40 days that he was in the wilderness?]
LUKE 4:13 - When the devil ended the temptation, he departed...[after the incident at the pinnacle].
[Did the devil leave Jesus from the mountain, or from the pinnacle?]

**Perplexing:**
Why did Jesus need angels to minister to him? Why did the Son of God require any ministering? Why did LUKE not state that angels ministered to Jesus? Why did JOHN not report the devil's efforts to tempt Jesus? If one read only JOHN, one would not know about the temptations.

4:12 - WHEN JESUS HAD HEARD THAT JOHN WAS CAST INTO PRISON, HE DEPARTED INTO GALILEE.

**Contradictions:**
LUKE 3:20-21 - ...He [Herod] shut up John in prison. Now when all the people were baptized, it came to pass, Jesus also being baptized...the heaven was opened [before being tempted by the devil].
[Was John imprisoned after, or before the devil tried to tempt Jesus?]
JOHN 1:32-43; 3:24 - John bear record, saying, "I saw the Spirit descending from heaven like a dove, and it abode upon him [Jesus]. ".... Jesus then met Andrew and Peter. The day following Jesus would go forth into Galilee.... John was not yet cast into prison.
[Did Jesus go to Galilee after, or before John was imprisoned?]
[Did Jesus go to Galilee before, or after meeting Andrew and Peter?]
See also under 4:1-2.

**Perplexing:**
How did Jesus learn about John's imprisonment? Why did Jesus go to Galilee when he heard the news about John? Why did he not come to John's aid and perform a miracle to free him?

4:13 - LEAVING NAZARETH, HE CAME AND DWELT IN CAPERNAUM, WHICH IS UPON THE SEA COAST, IN THE BORDERS OF ZABULON AND NEPHTHALIM.

**Contradictions:**
MARK 1:16-21 - Jesus went from the sea of Galilee to Capernaum with Peter, Andrew, James, and John.
[Did Jesus go to Capernaum from Nazareth, or from the Sea of Galilee?]
[Did Jesus go to Capernaum alone, before he acquired any disciples, or did he go with four disciples?]
JOHN 2:1-12 - Jesus went to Capernaum from Cana in Galilee with his disciples, mother, and brethren.
[Did Jesus go to Capernaum from Nazareth, or Cana?]
[Did Jesus go to Capernaum alone, or with his disciples, mother, and brethren?]

**Perplexing:**
Why did Jesus choose to dwell in Capernaum, rather than in Nazareth? Why was he referred to as Jesus of Nazareth, rather than Jesus of Capernaum?

4:14-16 - THAT IT MIGHT BE FULFILLED, WHICH WAS SPOKEN BY ESAIAS [ISAIAH] THE PROPHET, "THE LAND OF ZABULON, AND THE LAND OF NEPHTHALIM, BY WAY OF THE SEA, BEYOND JORDAN, GALILEE OF THE GENTILES; THE PEOPLE WHICH SAT IN DARKNESS SAW GREAT LIGHT; AND TO THEM WHICH SAT IN THE REGION AND SHADOW OF DEATH LIGHT IS SPRUNG UP."

**Old Testament:**
ISA. 8:22 - 9:2 - Isaiah: "They [Israelites] shall look unto the earth, and behold trouble and darkness...they shall be driven to darkness. Nevertheless the dimness shall not be such as was in her [Israel's] vexation, when at the first he [a king] lightly afflicted the land of Zebulun and the land of Naphtali, and afterward [God] did more grievously afflict her by the way of the sea, beyond Jordan, in Galilee of the nations. The people that walked in darkness have seen a great light; they that dwell in the land of the shadow of death; upon them hath the light shined."
[In some Bibles, ISA. 8 ends with "nations," because it relates to the conquest of Israel by the Assyrians; the next verse beginning with "The people," starts ISA. 9 and refers to the coronation of a new Israelite king. The verses, consequently, are not a prophecy pertaining to Jesus.]

**Perplexing:**
Why did MATT. take verses relating to Israel and apply them to Jesus?

4:17 - FROM THAT TIME JESUS BEGAN TO PREACH, "REPENT, FOR THE KINGDOM OF HEAVEN IS AT HAND."

**Contradiction:**
JOHN 3:3-24 - Jesus was preaching before John was cast into prison.
[Did Jesus begin preaching after, or prior to John's imprisonment?]

**Perplexing:**
Why did Jesus say to his listeners that the kingdom of heaven was about ready to arrive during their lifetime? Why, about two millennia later, has it still not come? Did Jesus deliberately lie to his listeners?

**History:**
The Pharisees used the phrase, "kingdom of God," to mean either the reign of God, or His future reign over the world during the Messianic age.
Note: The terms "kingdom of heaven" and "kingdom of God" are used inter-changeably in the New Testament.

**Old Testament:**
EZEK. 30:3 - "The day is near; the day of the LORD is near...."
JOEL 1:15 - "Alas for the day! The day of the LORD is at hand...."
JOEL 3:14 - "...the day of the LORD is near...."
OBAD. 15 - "The day of the LORD is near...."
ZEP. 1:7 - "...the day of the LORD is at hand...."
ZEP. 1:14 - "The great day of the LORD is near, it is near and hasteth greatly...."

4:18-20 - JESUS, WALKING BY THE SEA OF GALILEE, SAW TWO BRETHREN, SIMON CALLED PETER, AND ANDREW HIS BROTHER, CASTING A NET INTO THE SEA; THEY WERE FISHERS. HE SAITH, "FOLLOW ME; I WILL MAKE YOU FISHERS OF MEN." THEY LEFT THEIR NETS AND FOLLOWED HIM.

**Contradictions:**

LUKE 5:1-11 - ...Jesus stood by the lake of Gennesaret (Sea of Galilee], and saw two ships; the fishermen were out of them while washing their nets. He entered one of the ships, Simon's, prayed him that he would thrust out a little from the land. He taught the people out of the ship. When he left speaking, he said unto Simon, "Launch out into the deep, and let down your nets for a drought ...." ...they inclosed a great multitude of fish, and their net brake. .... They [their partners] came and filled both ships.... .... He [Simon Peter] was astonished, and all that were with him...so was also James, and John, the sons of Zebedee, which were partners with Simon. Jesus said unto Simon, "...henceforth thou shalt catch men." When they brought their ships to land, they forsook all, and followed him.

[Were Simon and Andrew casting a net into the sea, or was Simon, without Andrew, washing nets?]

[Did Jesus speak only with the men who were to become his followers, or did he also speak to the people on the shore?]

[Did Jesus go to the Sea of Galilee where he saw Simon and Andrew fishing, or, did he go to the Sea of Galilee, board Simon's ship, teach people on the shore, and help Simon, James, and John catch fish?]

[Did Jesus call Simon and Andrew, or Simon, James, and John to follow him?]

JOHN 1:35-42- ...John stood, and two of his disciples; and looking upon Jesus as he walked, saith, "Behold the Lamb of God!" The two disciples...followed Jesus. .... One of the two was Andrew, Simon Peter's brother. He findeth Simon, and saith, "We have found the Messias,".... He brought him to Jesus.

[Did Jesus meet Simon and Andrew at the Sea of Galilee, or while at Bethabara [JOHN 1:28] encounter two of John's disciples, one of whom was Andrew, who later introduced him to Simon.]

[Did Jesus call Simon and Andrew to follow him, or did Andrew follow him without being called?]

**Perplexing:**

Why did Jesus select these fishermen to be his first disciples? Why did they desert their livelihood to follow a stranger? Why did LUKE fail to report Andrew's presence? LUKE did not mention Andrew as a disciple until 6:14. Why did Jesus fail to ask the men whether or not they had a family including children dependent upon them?

**Language:**

"Peter" is derived from the Greek, "petros," and the Latin "petrus," which mean "rock."

4:21-22 - GOING ON FROM THENCE, HE SAW TWO OTHER BRETHREN, JAMES THE SON OF ZEBEDEE, AND JOHN HIS BROTHER, IN A SHIP WITH ZEBEDEE THEIR FATHER, MENDING THEIR NETS; HE CALLED THEM. THEY IMMEDIATELY LEFT THE SHIP AND THEIR FATHER, AND FOLLOWED HIM.

**Contradictions:**

LUKE 5:7-11 - James and John, Simon's partners, were on a ship fishing. When they brought the ship to land, they forsook all, and followed Jesus.

[Did Jesus call James and John to follow him when he saw them mending nets on a ship, or after they finished fishing and brought their ship to land?]

[Did James and John follow Jesus after Simon and Andrew followed him, or did they follow him at the

same time as Simon, without Andrew?]
JOHN 1:43 - The day following Jesus would go forth into Galilee, findeth Philip, and saith, "Follow me."
[Were Simon, Andrew, James, and John, or Andrew, Simon, and Philip Jesus' first disciples?]
See also under 4:18-20.

**Perplexing:**
Why did Jesus not tell Zebedee to follow him?

4:23 - JESUS WENT ABOUT ALL GALILEE, TEACHING IN THEIR SYNAGOGUES, PREACHING THE GOSPEL OF THE KINGDOM, AND HEALING ALL MANNER OF SICKNESS, AND DISEASE.

**Contradictions:**
LUKE 4:33-35 - Jesus drove an unclean spirit out of a man, before he acquired any followers.
LUKE 4:38-39 - Jesus healed Simon's mother-in-law of a fever, before Simon and others became his followers.
[Did Jesus begin performing miracles before or after he acquired disciples?]
JOHN 2:6-11 - Jesus converted water into wine. This beginning of miracles did Jesus in Cana in Galilee.
[Did Jesus' first miracles involve healing the sick and infirm, or was his first miracle the conversion of water into wine?]

**Perplexing:**
How was Jesus able to walk into and preach in synagogues, especially when he was not preaching Jewish theology? How was he able to obtain authorization from the presiding priest to do so?

**Pagan parallels:**
Many pagan deities healed the sick and infirm including the deaf and blind. Some examples are, Krishna, Tammuz, Serapis, and Asclepius (Aesculapius) who also was a resurrected "son of god."

**History:**
During and prior to Jesus' time, the causes of illness and various infirmities were not known. Consequently, they were attributed to spirits and/or demons (devils), or as punishments from God. The latter belief still persists among some religious individuals. People were not knowledgeable about disease-causing microorganisms, toxic substances, chemical imbalances in the body, genetic disorders, and other factors capable of producing physical and mental problems.

4:24-25 - HIS FAME WENT THROUGHOUT ALL SYRIA; THEY BROUGHT SICK PEOPLE WITH DIVERS DISEASES AND TORMENTS, THOSE POSSESSED WITH DEVILS, AND...LUNATICK, AND...THE PALSY; HE HEALED THEM. THERE FOLLOWED HIM GREAT MULTITUDES OF PEOPLE FROM GALILEE, DECOPOLIS, JERUSALEM, JUDAEA, AND BEYOND JORDAN.

**History:**
Despite being famous throughout the region, traveling around, teaching, preaching, being seen and followed by great multitudes, and healing all manner of ailments, there is no non-biblical record of Jesus or any of his accomplishments.
Decopolis was the name given to a league of ten cities established by the Romans extending from Damascus

to what is now Amman.

**Perplexing:**

Why did Jesus fail to explain the nature and causes of diseases, how to prevent them, and how to develop treatments for them? Did his failure to have done so make him responsible for all of the plagues and various diseases that have inflicted untold suffering and death on humanity over the centuries? Why did Jesus not perform a miracle to eliminate diseases?

Who or what were the "devils?" When and why were they created? Why did they posses people? How did they enter people? Where did they go and what did they do when they were cast out of a person? If God created them and knew what they would do, should He not be held responsible for their actions and the problems they cause? Is it possible that they are not real, but were invented to explain illnesses, ailments, and misfortunes, the causes of which were not known? Why did Jesus not eradicate them?

Why did Jesus' miraculous achievements fail to encourage political figures, government officials, physicians, important military people, and merchants to meet with him and try to utilize his services and/or make a notation about him in their records? Why did the soldiers and merchants from Rome, Greece, and elsewhere fail to mention or write about him when they returned home? Why did not any of the people healed by Jesus fail to record their miraculous cures? Why did Jesus, himself, fail to leave any written documents citing and explaining his teachings unambiguously so that people would know exactly what he wanted them to do?

**Pagan concept:**

Devils/demons/evil spirits were beings or deities found in some ancient pre-Christian religions including those of Sumer, Babylonia, Iran, Greece, and India. They also appeared in non-biblical Hebrew mythology as spiritual creatures who received permission from God to tempt people and to punish them for their sins. Thus, they functioned under the auspices of God, not, as in Christianity, under the control of Satan.

5:1-2 - SEEING THE MULTITUDES, HE WENT UP A MOUNTAIN; WHEN HE WAS SET, HIS DISCIPLES [ONLY FOUR HAVE BEEN REPORTED] CAME UNTO HIM. HE OPENED HIS MOUTH, AND TAUGHT THEM.

**Contradictions:**

LUKE 6:12-19 - ...he went into a mountain, to pray.... ...he called unto him his disciples; of them he chose twelve.... He came down with them, and stood in the plain...and a great multitude...came to hear him and be healed of their diseases.... ...[he] healed them all [before speaking to them].

[Did Jesus go onto a mountain to speak to the multitude, or did he come down from a mountain to address them?]

[Did his four disciples come to him on the mountain, or did he call an unspecified number of disciples to him and select 12 of them?]

[Did Jesus go onto a mountain and teach, or did come down from a mountain after praying, heal multitudes, and then teach?]

5:3 - JESUS: "BLESSED ARE THE POOR IN SPIRIT FOR THEIRS IS THE KINGDOM OF HEAVEN."

**Contradictions:**

MATT. 5:10 - Jesus: "Blessed are they which are persecuted for righteousness' sake, for theirs is the kingdom of heaven."

[Must one be poor in spirit, or persecuted for righteousness' sake to enter the kingdom of heaven?]

MATT. 5:20 - Jesus: "Except your righteousness shall exceed the righteousness of the scribes and Pharisees, ye shall in no case enter into the kingdom of heaven."
[Must one be poor in spirit, or more righteous than the scribes and Pharisees to enter the kingdom of heaven?]
MATT. 7:21 - Jesus: "Not everyone that saith unto me, 'Lord, Lord,' shall enter into the kingdom of heaven, but he that doeth the will of my Father which is in heaven."
[Must one be poor in spirit, or do the will of Jesus' Father to enter the kingdom of heaven?]
MATT. 18:3 - Jesus: "Except ye be converted, and become as little children, ye shall not enter into the kingdom of heaven."
[Must one be poor in spirit, or become as little children to enter the kingdom of Heaven?]
LUKE 6:20 - Jesus: "Blessed be ye poor, for yours is the kingdom of God."
[Must one be poor in spirit, or just poor to enter the kingdom of heaven (God)?]
JOHN 3:3 - Jesus: "Except a man be born again, he cannot see the kingdom of God."
[Must one be poor in spirit, or born again to enter the kingdom of heaven (God)?]
JOHN 3:5 - Jesus: "Except a man be born of water and the Spirit, he cannot enter into the kingdom of God."
[Must one be poor in spirit, or born of the water and Spirit to enter the kingdom of heaven (God)?]
See also under 19:17-19 (for obtaining eternal life).
Note: See under 4:17.

5:5 - JESUS: "BLESSED ARE THE MEEK FOR THEY SHALL INHERIT THE EARTH."

**Old Testament:**
PS. 37:11 - "The meek shall inherit the earth...."

**Perplexing:**
Why would the meek want to inherit the earth? Why would anyone want to inherit the earth? Why will the meek inherit the earth rather than being admitted to heaven?

5:8 - JESUS: "BLESSED ARE THE PURE IN HEART, FOR THEY SHALL SEE GOD."

**Contradictions:**
COL. 1:15 - Paul: "...the invisible God...."
1 TIM. - 1:17 - Paul: "The King eternal, immortal, invisible, the only wise God...."
2 TIM. - 6:16 - "[God] whom no man has seen, nor can see...."
[Can God be seen, or is He invisible?]

5:9 - JESUS: "BLESSED ARE THE PEACEMAKERS FOR THEY SHALL BE CALLED CHILDREN OF GOD."

**Contradiction:**
GAL. 3:26 - Paul: "Ye are all the children of God by faith in Christ Jesus."
[Are the children of God those who have faith in Jesus, or the peacemakers?]

5:10 - JESUS: "BLESSED ARE THEY WHICH ARE PERSECUTED FOR RIGHTEOUSNESS' SAKE FOR THEIRS IS THE KINGDOM OF HEAVEN."

**Contradictions:**
ROM. 3:10 - Paul: "There is none righteous, no, not one."
[Are some people righteous, or is no one righteous?]
See also under 5:3.

**Perplexing:**
Are righteous people who are persecuted by Jesus' followers also eligible to reach the kingdom of heaven? See also under 3:15.

5:11-12 - JESUS: "BLESSED ARE YE, WHEN MEN SHALL REVILE YOU, PERSECUTE YOU, AND SAY...EVIL AGAINST YOU FALSELY, FOR MY SAKE. GREAT IS YOUR REWARD IN HEAVEN...."

**Perplexing:**
Do those persecuted by Jesus' followers also receive a reward in heaven? What kind of reward can one receive in heaven? Why is being in heaven not a sufficient reward?

**Pagan parallel:**
Orpheus (between the 13th and 6th centuries B.C.) asserted that there was a place in the sky for the "pure" where they had eternal life.

5:14 - JESUS: "YE [THE DISCIPLES] ARE THE LIGHT OF THE WORLD."

**Contradiction:**
JOHN 8:12 - Jesus: "I am the light of the world...."
[Were the disciples, or Jesus the light of the world?]

**Perplexing:**
Why did Jesus say that his disciples were the light of the world? What did they do or say that provided light to the world?

5:16 - JESUS: "LET YOUR LIGHT SO SHINE BEFORE MEN, THAT THEY MAY SEE YOUR GOOD WORKS, AND GLORIFY YOUR FATHER IN HEAVEN."

**Contradiction:**
MATT. 6:1 - Jesus: "Take heed that ye do not your alms before men, to be seen of them, otherwise ye have no reward of your Father in heaven."
MATT. 6:3-4 - Jesus: "When thou doest alms, let not thy left hand know what thy right hand doeth, that thine alms may be in secret; thy Father which seeth in secret shall reward thee openly."
[Should good works be performed openly for all to see, or should they be done secretly?]

5:17-18 - JESUS: "THINK NOT THAT I AM COME TO DESTROY THE LAW...BUT TO FULFILL. TILL HEAVEN AND EARTH PASS, ONE JOT OR ONE TITTLE SHALL IN NO WISE PASS FROM THE LAW, TILL ALL BE FULFILLED."

**Contradictions:**

ACTS 15:24-19 - Apostles: "We have heard that certain which went out from us troubled you with the words..., 'Ye must be circumcised, and keep the law, to whom we gave no such commandment.... It seemed good to the Holy Ghost, and to us, to lay upon you no greater burden than these: abstain from meats offered to idols, from blood, from things strangled, and from fornication...."

[Could not one tittle the law not be changed, or could the apostles change the law?]

ROM. 7:6 - Paul: "Now we are delivered from the law, that being dead wherein we were held; we should serve in newness of spirit, not in the oldness of the letter."

[Will the law not change, or is it dead?]

GAL. 3:13 - Paul: "Christ hath redeemed us from the curse of the law...."

[Did Jesus come to uphold the law, or to deliver and redeem people from it?]

See also below under 5:31-32.

5:19 - JESUS: "WHOSOEVER SHALL BREAK ONE OF THESE LEAST COMMANDMENTS, AND SHALL TEACH MEN TO DO SO, HE SHALL BE CALLED THE LEAST IN THE KINGDOM OF HEAVEN...."

**Perplexing:**

Is Jesus saying that people who break commandments will still be admitted into the kingdom of heaven?

5:20 - JESUS: "EXCEPT YOUR RIGHTEOUSNESS SHALL EXCEED THE RIGHTEOUSNESS OF THE SCRIBES AND PHARISEES, YE SHALL IN NO CASE ENTER THE KINGDOM OF HEAVEN."

**Contradictions:**

MATT. 12:34 - Jesus [to the Pharisees]: "0 generation of vipers, how can ye, being evil, speak good things...?"

MATT. 23:33 - Jesus [to the scribes and Pharisees]: "Ye serpents; ye generation of vipers, how can ye escape the damnation of hell?"

[Did Jesus say that the scribes and Pharisees were righteous, or did he say that the they were evil and vipers?]

MATT. 15:3 - Jesus [to the scribes and Pharisees]: "Why do ye also transgress the commandment of God by your tradition?"

[Did Jesus say that the scribes and Pharisees were righteous, or that they transgressed the commandment of God?]

MATT. 16:6-12 - Jesus said [to his disciples], "...beware of the leaven of the Pharisees and Sadducees." .... Then understood they how he bade them not beware of the leaven of bread, but of the doctrine of the Pharisees and Sadducees.

[Did Jesus tell his disciples that the Pharisees were righteous, or to beware of their doctrine?]

MATT. 15:7 - Jesus [to the scribes and Pharisees]: "Ye hypocrites...."

MATT. 23:13, 14, 15, 23, 25, 27, 29 - Jesus: "Woe unto you, scribes and Pharisees, hypocrites!"

[Did Jesus say that the scribes and Pharisees were righteous, or that they were hypocrites?]

MATT. 23:28 - Jesus [to the scribes and Pharisees]: "Ye outwardly appear righteous, but within ye are full of hypocrisy and iniquity."

[Did Jesus say that the scribes and Pharisees were righteous, or that they were full of hypocrisy and iniquity?]

LUKE 20:46-47 - Jesus; "Beware of the scribes the same shall receive greater damnation."

[Did Jesus say that the scribes were righteous, or that they would be damned?]

See also under 5:10.

**Perplexing:**
In 5:19, Jesus said that people who break commandments are in the kingdom of heaven. Was he now saying that the righteousness of such people exceeds the righteousness of the scribes and Pharisees?

5:22 - JESUS: "...WHOSOEVER SHALL SAY, 'THOU FOOL,' SHALL BE IN DANGER OF HELL FIRE."

**Perplexing:**
In MATT. 23:17 and 19, Jesus called the scribes and Pharisees, "Ye fools...."
In LUKE 11:40, Jesus called the Pharisees, "Ye fools...."
In LUKE 24:25, Jesus said to two disciples, "O fools...."
Is Jesus, by calling people fools, in danger of hell fire, or is he exempt from following his own teachings?

**Language:**
The word translated as "hell fire," is "Gehanna." This was the name of a site, also known as the "Valley of Hinnom," where the bodies of executed criminals were burned.

5:27-28 - JESUS: "YE HAVE HEARD... 'THOU SHALT NOT COMMIT ADULTERY'; I SAY THAT WHOSOEVER LOOKETH ON A WOMAN TO LUST AFTER HER HATH COMMITTED ADULTERY WITH HER IN HIS HEART."

**Old Testament:**
EX. 20:14 - God: "Thou shalt not commit adultery."

**Perplexing:**
Based on Jesus' statement, is there any heterosexual man who has not committed adultery in his heart? Is adultery in one's heart a violation of the commandment against adultery? By referring only to men, was Jesus saying that a woman may lust after a man without committing adultery in her heart? Was adultery so common prior to and during Jesus' time that a special commandment had to be given to prohibit it?

**Judaism:**
The Talmud says, "Whoever regards even the little finger of a woman has already violated matrimony in his heart."

5:29-30 - JESUS: "IF THY RIGHT EYE OFFEND THEE, PLUCK IT OUT...IT IS PROFITABLE FOR THEE THAT ONE OF THY MEMBERS SHOULD PERISH, AND NOT THAT THY WHOLE BODY SHOULD BE CAST INTO HELL. IF THY RIGHT HAND OFFEND THEE, CUT IT OFF...NOT THAT THY WHOLE BODY SHOULD BE CAST INTO HELL."

**Perplexing:**
Hands, feet, and eyes do not function independently. They are controlled by the brain, which, therefore, is the offending body part. Why, then, did Jesus accuse a limb or eye of being responsible for its actions? The brain, however, cannot be easily removed, so it may be a bit more difficult to avoid hell than Jesus implied. Was Jesus saying that the physical body with its imperfections including missing parts is what enters heaven? Does this mean that prostheses are available in heaven? Does a person with an artificial limb or other prosthesis enter heaven with it? If so, would this include false teeth? And those early Christians who castrated themselves - do they receive new gonads in heaven or must they spend eternity without them? Jesus did not say that a person who mutilated himself would be made whole in heaven.

**Pagan concept:**
Many pre-Christian religions (such as those of Egypt, Persia, India, Assyria, Babylonia, and Etruria) had the concept of a place of punishment for the wicked.

5:31-32 - JESUS: "IT HATH BEEN SAID, 'WHOSOEVER SHALL PUT AWAY HIS WIFE, LET HIM GIVE HER A WRITING OF DIVORCEMENT.' I SAY THAT WHOSOEVER SHALL PUT AWAY HIS WIFE, SAVING FOR THE CAUSE OF FORNICATION, CAUSETH HER TO COMMIT ADULTERY; WHOSOEVER SHALL MARRY HER THAT IS DIVORCED COMMITTETH ADULTERY."

**Old Testament:**
DEUT. 24:1-2 - When a man hath taken a wife, and it come to pass that she find no favour in his eyes, because he hath found some uncleanness in her, let him write her a bill of divorcement.... When she is departed, she may go and be another man's wife.

**Contradictions:**
DEUT. 24:1-2, above.
[Can a man divorce his wife only for fornication, or if she finds no favour in his eyes?]
[Does she commit adultery if she remarries, as Jesus said, or is it acceptable for her to marry again, as God said?]
MATT. 5:17-18 - Jesus: "Think not that I have come to destroy the law...I am not come to destroy, but to fulfil. Till heaven and earth pass, one jot or one tittle shall in no wise pass from the law."
[Did Jesus come to uphold the law, or to change it regarding divorce?]
[Can the law not be changed one tittle, or can it be changed regarding divorce?]

**Perplexing:**
Why did Jesus contradict the Old Testament by saying that fornication was the only justification for divorce? Was Jesus saying that God changed His mind about divorce? Why would a woman who is divorced because of fornication be guilty of adultery if she married again? Why was Jesus so cruel that he wanted people to remain married despite how unhappy, unpleasant, violent, or loveless the marriage might be, or even if one spouse abused the other? How much misery and suffering including violence and murder have resulted from people being forced to comply with Jesus' statements? Why did Jesus view fornication as being worse than physical and mental abuse? Why did he fail to condemn violence in marriage? Why did he fail to condemn polygamy? Why did he fail to condemn child abuse? Why did Jesus fail to say that a woman should be able to divorce her husband on grounds of fornication?

**History:**
During the first century, Jewish men, not Jewish women could initiate a divorce.
The Essenes and a branch of the Pharisees known as Shammaites, founded in the first century B.C. by Shannai, opposed divorce except in the case of a wife's infidelity.

5:34-35 - JESUS: "SWEAR NOT AT ALL, NEITHER BY HEAVEN, FOR IT IS GOD'S THRONE, NOR BY THE EARTH, FOR IT IS THE FOOTSTOOL; NEITHER BY JERUSALEM, FOR IT IS THE CITY OF THE GREAT KING."

**Old Testament:**
LEV. 19:12 The LORD: "Ye shall not swear by My name falsely...."
ISA. 66:1 The LORD: "The heaven is My throne, and the earth is My footstool...."

**Contradictions:**
DEUT. 6:13 - Moses: "Thou shalt fear the LORD thy God, serve Him, and swear by His name."
[Should one not swear, or is it permissible to swear?]
DEUT. 7:12-13 - Moses: "He sware unto thy fathers...He sware unto thy fathers...."
JER. 22:5 - "I swear by Myself, saith the LORD...."
[Should one not swear, or is it permissible for the LORD to swear?]

**Perplexing:**
In GEN. 21:23-24, Abimelech and Phichol spake unto Abraham, "Swear by God that thou wilt not deal falsely with me...." Abraham said, "I will swear."
In GEN. 24:9, Abraham's servant sware to him.
In GEN. 25:33, Esau swore to Jacob.
In GEN. 31:53, Jacob sware by the fear of his father Isaac.
In GEN. 47:31, Joseph swore to Jacob.
In 2 SAM. 19:7 - Joab: "...I swear by the LORD...."
Why was it acceptable for Abraham, Jacob, Esau, and Joab to swear?
In JER. 22:5 (see above under Contradictions) and in HEB. 6:13, God swore by Himself.
In REV. 10:6, [an angel] sware by Him that liveth forever and ever....
Are God and angels exempt from Jesus' prohibition against swearing?

**History:**
The Essene sect prohibited oaths except to join the group.

5:38 - JESUS: "YE HAVE HEARD THAT IT HATH BEEN SAID, 'AN EYE FOR AN EYE, AND A TOOTH FOR A TOOTH.'"

**Old Testament:**
EX. 21:23-24 - The LORD: "...thou shalt give life for life, eye for eye, tooth for tooth...."
LEV. 24:19-20 - The LORD: "...as he hath done, so shall it be done to him; breach for breach, eye for eye, tooth for tooth; as he hath caused a blemish in a man, so shall it be done to him."
DEUT. 19:21 - The LORD: "...life shall go for life, eye for eye, tooth for tooth...."

**Pagan parallel:**
Laws engraved on a stone tablet, known as the Code of Hammurabi, given to the Babylonian King Hammurabi (18th century B.C.) on a mountain by the god Shamash, said, "If a man shall put out the eye of another, then let his own eye be put out. If a man shall knockout the tooth of another who is higher in rank, then let his own tooth be knocked out."

**Judaism:**
The above verses were not taken literally. The Pharisees, in particular, interpreted the verses as meaning that any injury caused to a person should be compensated monetarily based on the seriousness of the injury.

5:39-40 - JESUS: "RESIST NOT EVIL, BUT WHOSOEVER SHALL SMITE THEE ON THY RIGHT CHEEK, TURN TO HIM THE OTHER; IF ANY MAN WILL SUE THEE AT THE LAW, AND TAKE AWAY THY COAT, LET HIM HAVE THY CLOAK ALSO."

**Old Testament:**
ISA. 50:6 - Isaiah: "I gave my back to the smiters, and my cheeks to them that plucked off the hair...."

**Judaism:**
A Jewish proverb is, "If any demand thy ass, give him the saddle also."

**Perplexing:**
How long would people or nations survive if they did not resist evil? Why do the vast majority, if not all, of those who believe in Jesus fail to follow these teachings of Jesus in MATT. 5:39-40?

5:43 - JESUS: "YE HAVE HEARD THAT IT HATH BEEN SAID, 'THOU SHALT LOVE THY NEIGHBOUR, AND HATE THINE ENEMY.'"

**Perplexing:**
From where did Jesus obtain this saying? It is not in the Old Testament.

5:44 - JESUS: "LOVE YOUR ENEMIES, BLESS THEM THAT CURSE YOU; DO GOOD TO THEM THAT HATE YOU; PRAY FOR THEM WHICH DESPITEFULLY USE YOU, AND PERSECUTE YOU."

**Old Testament:**
EX. 23:4-5 - The LORD: "If thou meet thine enemy's ox or ass going astray, thou shalt bring it back to him."
EX. 23:9 - The LORD: "Thou shalt not oppress a stranger...."
LEV. 19:18 - The LORD: "...thou shalt love thy neighbour as thyself."
PROV. 24:17 - "Rejoice not when thine enemy falleth, and let not thine heart be glad when he stumbleth."
PROV. 25:21 - "If thine enemy be hungry, give him bread to eat; if he be thirsty, give him water to drink."

**Judaism:**
The Talmud says, "Thou shalt not hate, not even internally." "Love him that punishes thee." "It is better to be wronged by others than to wrong." "Be rather among the persecuted than the persecutors."

**Perplexing:**
Why do all or almost all of the believers in Jesus fail to obey these MATT. 5:44 teachings by Jesus?
In MATT. 12:32, Jesus: "...whosoever speaketh against the Holy Ghost, it shall not be forgiven him, either in this world, neither in the world to come."
In MATT. 23:13-33, Jesus in a tirade against Pharisees and scribes called them hypocrites, fools, serpents, and vipers.
In MARK 16:16, Jesus said, "...he that believeth not shall be damned."
Are Jesus and the Holy Ghost exempt from adhering to Jesus' teaching about loving one's enemies? Why did Jesus fail to practice what he preached?

5:48 - JESUS: "BE YE THEREFORE PERFECT, AS YOUR FATHER WHICH IS IN HEAVEN IS PERFECT."

**Perplexing:**
How is it possible for anyone to be as perfect as God?

6:1 - JESUS: "TAKE HEED THAT YE DO NOT YOUR ALMS BEFORE MEN, TO BE SEEN OF THEM, OTHERWISE YE HAVE NO REWARD OF YOUR FATHER WHICH IS IN HEAVEN."

**Contradiction:**
MATT. 5:16 - Jesus: "Let your light so shine before men, that they may see your good works, and glorify your Father in heaven."
[Should one do good works secretly, or openly for all to see?]
See also under 5:16.

**Perplexing:**
Why should one do good works in expectation of a reward, rather than just for the sake of doing good? What is the reward that God will give?

**Pagan concept:**
Buddha: "True offering springs spontaneously from one's heart with no thought of return."

**Judaism:**
The concept of doing good in secret is also found in the Talmud.

6:3-4 - JESUS: "WHEN THOU DOEST ALMS, LET NOT THY LEFT HAND KNOW WHAT THY RIGHT HAND DOETH, THAT THINE ALMS MAY BE IN SECRET; THY FATHER WHICH SEETH IN SECRET SHALL REWARD THEE OPENLY."

**Contradiction:** See under 6:1.

**Perplexing:** See under 6:1.

**Judaism:** See also under 6:1.

6:5-6 - JESUS: "WHEN THOU PRAYEST, THOU SHALT NOT BE AS THE HYPOCRITES; THEY LOVE TO PRAY STANDING IN THE SYNAGOGUES AND...STREETS, THAT THEY MAY BE SEEN OF MEN.... WHEN THOU PRAYEST, ENTER INTO THY CLOSET, AND WHEN THOU HAST SHUT THY DOOR, PRAY TO THY FATHER IN SECRET; THY FATHER WHICH SEETH IN SECRET SHALL REWARD THEE OPENLY."

**Perplexing:**

Why do Christians disobey Jesus' command and pray openly in groups (meetings, churches, political gatherings, etc.)? Why do many Christians try to impose public prayers on people in schools, at athletic events, etc.? According to Jesus, people should not even know that one is praying. Why then do Christians pray like the hypocrites who Jesus criticized?

6:8 - JESUS: "...YOUR FATHER KNOWEST WHAT THINGS YE HAVE NEED OF, BEFORE YE ASK HIM."

**Perplexing:**
If God knows what one needs before praying for it, why pray? Why does God not give what is needed without requiring one to pray for it? Why would a good and merciful God want a person to beg Him for anything, especially, since He knows beforehand whether or not He will answer the person's prayer? He also knows whether what is needed will be provided even if one does not pray. Did Jesus, therefore, mean that it is pointless to pray for anything?

6:13 - JESUS: "[FATHER] LEAD US NOT INTO TEMPTATION...FOR THINE IS THE KINGDOM, THE POWER, AND THE GLORY FOREVER."

**Contradictions:**
JAM. 1:13 - James: "...neither tempteth He any man."
[Can God lead people into temptation (so that people have to pray that He does not so lead them), or does he not tempt anyone?]
ISA. 43:10 - the LORD: "...before Me there was no God formed, neither shall there be after Me."
[Is God's kingdom, power, and glory forever, or will He be gone at some point in the future with no god coming after Him?]

**Perplexing:**
Why would God lead anyone into temptation?

6:17 - JESUS: "WHEN THOU FASTEST, ANOINT THY HEAD, AND WASH THY FACE...."

**Pagan concept:**
The custom of fasting which originated in antiquity was an ancient pagan religious ritual. Abstinence from food may have been aimed at purifying the body to make it more receptive to being taken over by a divine spirit. The rite eventually became a means of self-mortification for sins that had been committed, as in Judaism's Day of Atonement.

**Judaism:**
It was and still is a Jewish custom to fast on the Day of Atonement ("Yom Kippur").

**Old Testament:**
In LEV. 23:27, the LORD: "On the tenth day of this seventh month there shall be a day of atonement; it shall be an holy convocation, and ye shall afflict your souls...." ["Afflict" is interpreted to mean "fasting." Presumably, this is the fasting to which Jesus referred.]

6:19 - JESUS: "LAY NOT UP FOR YOURSELVES TREASURES UPON EARTH, WHERE MOTH AND RUST DOTH CORRUPT, AND WHERE THIEVES BREAK THROUGH AND STEAL."

**Perplexing:**
Why is this command by Jesus ignored or rejected by many (most?) Christians, especially the clergy? Why do many Christian leaders and other self-proclaimed Christians amass fortunes here on earth contrary to Jesus' teaching? Why did God or Jesus fail to eliminate thievery?

**Old Testament:**
ECCL. 5:13-14 - "There is a sore evil which I have seen namely, riches kept for the owners, thereof to their hurt.Those riches perish by evil travail...."

6:20 - JESUS: "LAY UP FOR YOURSELVES TREASURES IN HEAVEN...."

**Perplexing:**
What did Jesus mean by, "treasures?" What kind of treasures can one lay up in heaven? Of what use are treasures in heaven?

6:23 - JESUS: "IF THINE EYE BE EVIL, THY WHOLE BODY SHALL BE FULL OF DARKNESS...."

**Perplexing:**
What did Jesus mean by an eye that is evil? How can an eye be evil? Did Jesus believe in the "evil eye" concept?

**Pagan concept:**
The belief in an evil eye — an eye that could cause misfortune for those upon whom it looked — originated in antiquity. It was in existence during Jesus' time and still exists among superstitious people including Christians in different parts of the world.

6:24 - JESUS: "...YE CANNOT SERVE GOD AND MAMMON."

**Perplexing:**
If Jesus is correct, why are many Christian clergy and other self-proclaimed Christians (modern disciples) obsessed with obtaining wealth — worshiping mammon?
See also under 6:19.

**Language:**
"Mammon" is an Aramaic word meaning "wealth."

6:25 - JESUS: "TAKE NO THOUGHT FOR YOUR LIFE, WHAT YE SHALL EAT, DRINK, NOR FOR YOUR BODY, WHAT YE SHALL PUT ON...."

**Contradiction:**
1 TIM. 5:8 - Paul: "If any provide not for his own, and specially for those of his own house, he hath denied the faith, and is worse than an infidel."
[Should one not be concerned about one's life, food, drink, clothes, etc., or should one be concerned and provide things that are needed?]

**Perplexing:**
How can a person survive without thinking about the necessities of life and doing what may be necessary to obtain them — food, water, clothes, medications, etc.? How could one's family survive? What would happen in the world, if everyone adhered to this command by Jesus? Would not mass starvation, disease, unemployment, and universal misery result? Are these reasons why Christians do not obey Jesus' command?

6:26 - JESUS: "BEHOLD THE FOWLS OF THE AIR; THEY SOW NOT, NEITHER DO THEY REAP...YET YOUR HEAVENLY FATHER FEEDETH THEM. ARE YE NOT MUCH BETTER THAN THEY?"

**Perplexing:**
Birds of prey feed on smaller birds as well as other animals. Did Jesus, therefore, mean that God provides small birds and animals for hawks, eagles, etc. to eat? Did he mean that God created insects to be food for many other birds? Jesus referred to "fowls of the air"; was he unaware of flightless birds such as ostriches and penguins? Jesus did not point out that birds do not require clothes or money. If people are much better than birds, why does God, who benevolently provides food for birds, allow people to suffer and die from starvation and malnutrition?

6:28 - JESUS: "WHY TAKE THOUGHT FOR RAIMENT?"

**Perplexing:**
Did Jesus mean that people should not care if they lack clothes and, consequently, have to go around naked?

6:31 - JESUS: "THEREFORE TAKE NO THOUGHT, SAYING, 'WHAT SHALL WE EAT? WHAT SHALL WE DRINK? WHEREWITHAL SHALL WE BE CLOTHED?'"

**Contradiction:** See under 6:25.

**Perplexing:** See under 6:25.

6:33 - JESUS: "SEEK YE FIRST THE KINGDOM OF GOD, AND HIS RIGHTEOUSNESS, AND ALL THESE THINGS SHALL BE ADDED UNTO YOU."

**Perplexing:**
Why does one need food, drink, and clothing in the kingdom of God?
See also under 4:17.

6:34 - JESUS: "TAKE NO THOUGHT FOR THE MORROW, FOR THE MORROW SHALL TAKE THOUGHT FOR THE THINGS OF ITSELF. SUFFICIENT UNTO THE DAY IS THE EVIL THEREOF."

**Contradiction:** See under 6:25.

**Perplexing:**
If one need not be concerned about tomorrow, why save money? Why buy and store food for ensuing days? Why bother to grow and prepare food? Why be concerned about education, employment, shelter, healthy living, and taking care of one's family? See also under 6:25.

7:1-2 - JESUS: "JUDGE NOT, THAT YE BE NOT JUDGED; WITH WHAT JUDGMENT YE JUDGE, YE SHALL BE JUDGED; WITH WHAT MEASURE YE METE, IT SHALL BE MEASURED TO YOU."

**Contradiction:**
JOHN 7:24 - Jesus: "Judge not according to the appearance, but judge righteous judgment."
[Should one not judge, or should one judge righteous judgment?]

**Perplexing:**
How could courts function without someone judging? How could legal problems be resolved without judgments?

**Judaism:**
The Talmud says, "Judge everyone as favorably as possible," and "Judge not thy neighbor until thou hast stood in his place."

7:7-8 - JESUS: "ASK, AND IT SHALL BE GIVEN YOU; SEEK, AND YE SHALL FIND; KNOCK, AND IT SHALL BE OPENED UNTO YOU. EVERYONE THAT ASKETH RECEIVETH; HE THAT SEEKETH FINDETH; TO HIM THAT KNOCKETH IT SHALL BE OPENED."

**Perplexing:**
Jesus implied that whatever one may want can be ottained by asking for it. In reality, however, how many people, if any, receive everything, or anything, they request? Why do those who ask for such things as peace, health, prosperity for humanity, and the conversion of unbelievers fail to receive them? Did Jesus lie?

7:11 - JESUS: "IF YE BEING EVIL...GIVE GOOD GIFTS UNTO YOUR CHILDREN, HOW MUCH MORE SHALL YOUR FATHER IN HEAVEN GIVE GOOD THINGS TO THEM THAT ASK HIM?"

**Perplexing:** See under 7:7-8.

7:12 - JESUS: "ALL THINGS WHATSOEVER YE WOULD THAT MEN SHOULD DO TO YOU, DO YE SO TO THEM; THIS IS THE LAW AND THE PROPHETS."

**Perplexing:**
Why during about two millennia have relatively few Christians opted to follow this command by Jesus? If they had obeyed his command, humanity would have been spared such heinous atrocities as the Crusades, Inquisition, Holocaust, witch burnings, slavery, religious wars, religious persecution, etc.

**Pagan parallel:**
Confucius (c. 551-478 B.C.) said that you should not do to others as you would not wish done to yourself.

**Judaism:**
Rabbi Hillel (lst century B.C.) and other Jewish teachers preached as Confucius did. Jesus, by having stated that it "is the law," acknowledged that he was teaching a Jewish concept.

**Old Testament:** See under 5:44.

7:15 - JESUS: "BEWARE OF FALSE PROPHETS, WHICH COME TO YOU IN SHEEP'S CLOTHING, BUT INWARDLY ARE RAVENING WOLVES."

**Perplexing:**
Is Jesus' warning applicable to the numerous clergy who incessantly solicit money, preach intolerance, hate, and violence, establish cults and claim to preach in his name or claim to be him, and those who do not accept the commandments in the old testament?

7:21 - JESUS: "NOT EVERYONE THAT SAITH UNTO ME, 'LORD, LORD,' SHALL ENTER INTO THE KINGDOM OF HEAVEN, BUT HE THAT DOETH THE WILL OF MY FATHER WHICH IS IN HEAVEN."

**Contradictions:** See under 5:3.

7:23 - JESUS: "THEN WILL I PROFESS UNTO THEM...DEPART FROM ME, YE THAT WORK INIQUITY."

**Old Testament:**
PS. 6:8 - "Depart from me, all ye workers of iniquity...."

**Perplexing:**
What did Jesus mean by "iniquity?"

7:28 - WHEN JESUS HAD ENDED THESE SAYINGS, THE PEOPLE WERE ASTONISHED AT HIS DOCTRINE.

**Perplexing:**
If all or most of the people listening to Jesus were Jewish, why were they astonished at hearing him reiterate concepts that came from the Old Testament and Jewish doctrine?

8:1-3 - WHEN HE WAS COME DOWN FROM THE MOUNTAIN, GREAT MULTITUDES FOLLOWED HIM. THERE CAME A LEPER AND WORSHIPPED HIM, SAYING, "IF THOU WILT, THOU CANST MAKE ME CLEAN." JESUS TOUCHED HIM, SAYING, "I WILL; BE THOU CLEAN." IMMEDIATELY HIS LEPROSY WAS CLEANSED.

**Contradictions:**
LUKE 7:1-3 - When he had ended all his sayings in the audience of the people, he entered into Capernaum. A centurion's servant...was sick, and ready to die. When he heard of Jesus, he sent unto him the elders of the Jews, beseeching that he would come and heal his servant.
[After giving his sermon, did Jesus encounter and heal a leper, or did he go to Capernaum where he was asked to heal a centurion's servant?]
LUKE 5:12-13 - The incident with the leper took place before Jesus began his sermon in LUKE 6:17.
[Did Jesus heal the leper after, or before his sermon?]
MARK 1:30-44 - After healing Simon's Mother-in-law, Jesus healed many that were sick, prayed in a solitary place, and preached in synagogues throughout Galilee, before encountering and healing the leper.
[Did Jesus heal the leper after giving his sermon, or after healing Simon's mother-in-law and other people,

and preaching and traveling throughout Galilee?]
See also under 4:23.

**History:**
Lepers were ostracized and forced to reside in remote areas away from towns and cities.

**Perplexing:**
How could a man full of leprosy be among a multitude of people, if lepers were prohibited from coming into populated areas? Why did Jesus fail to heal all lepers and eliminate leprosy from the earth? Why did he fail to educate people about the cause of and give a cure for leprosy and other diseases?

**Old Testament:**
2 KINGS 5:7-14 - Elisha healed a leper.

**Pagan parallel:** See under 4:23.

**Language:**
The Greek word, "lepra," meaning "scaly condition," was translated as "leprosy," and anyone so afflicted was identified as a "leper." In the Old Testament, the Hebrew word was, "tzara'at," which was used to designate a number of different skin conditions such ast eczema, psoriasis, impetigo, or leprosy. Consequently, the words, "leper" and "leprosy," in English language versions of the Bible may not be accurate.

8:4 - JESUS SAITH UNTO HIM, "TELL NO MAN; GO THY WAY; SHEW THYSELF TO THE PRIEST, AND OFFER THE GIFT THAT MOSES COMMANDED...."

**Perplexing:**
Why did Jesus instruct the man not to tell anyone that he had been healed? Did not any of the great multitudes around Jesus witness the cure? Would not the miracle have been a topic of conversation? Would not his relatives, friends, acquaintances, and others who knew the man observe that he had been cured? Would they not ask him how it happened? Did Jesus want the man to lie to them about how he was cured?
See also under 8:1-3.

**Old Testament:**
LEV. 14:2-32 described "the law of the leper" including the offerings that were to be made.

8:5-6 - WHEN JESUS WAS ENTERED INTO CAPERNAUM, THERE CAME UNTO HIM A CENTURION, SAYING, "LORD, MY SERVANT LIETH AT HOME SICK OF THE PALSY...."

**Contradiction:**
LUKE 7:1-3 - The centurion who had the sick servant sent elders of the Jews to ask Jesus to heal his servant.
[Did the centurion ask Jesus to heal his servant, or did he send elders to do so?]

8:8 - THE CENTURION: "LORD, I AM NOT WORTHY THAT THOU SHOULDEST COME UNDER MY ROOF...."

**Contradiction:**
LUKE 7:6 - ...the centurion sent friends to him saying, "Lord, trouble not thyself; I am not worthy that thou shouldest enter under my roof."
[Did the centurion speak to Jesus, or did he send friends to speak to him?]

8:10 - JESUS...MARVELLED...AND SAID, "I HAVE NOT FOUND SO GREAT FAITH, IN ISRAEL."

**Perplexing:**
JOHN 18:4 said that Jesus knew all things that should come upon him. Why then did Jesus marvel? Why did he not know what the centurion would say?

8:11 - JESUS: "MANY SHALL COME FROM THE EAST AND WEST, AND SIT DOWN WITH ABRAHAM, ISAAC, AND JACOB, IN THE KINGDOM OF HEAVEN."

**Perplexing:**
Do people sit around in heaven? Is there enough room for a large number of people to sit with Abraham, Isaac, and Jacob? How are people able to recognize these Patriarchs? Besides sitting, what else is there to do in heaven? On what do they sit? Are there chairs in heaven? of what material are they made? What are they like? Who makes them?

8:12 - JESUS: "THE CHILDREN OF THE KINGDOM SHALL BE CAST INTO OUTER DARKNESS."

**Contradiction:**
MATT. 13:38 - Jesus: "...the good seed are the children of the kingdom."
[Are the children of the kingdom to be cast into outer darkness, or are they "the good seed?"]

**Perplexing:**
Who are the children of the kingdom? Why are they to be cast into outer darkness, if they are "the good seed?" What is the outer darkness? In EX. 34:6-7, the LORD proclaimed that He is merciful, abundant in goodness, and forgives iniquity, transgressions, and sin. Why would merciful, forgiving God cast anyone into outer darkness, rather than forgiving or reforming them?

**Pagan parallels:**
In Hinduism, evil doers are hurled into an abyss of darkness. In Etruscan belief (c. 500 B.C.) , the evil deity Charun ruled over a realm of darkness. In Zoroastrianism, the evil deity Ahriman resided in a place called "Endless Darkness" where souls of the wicked are sent.

8:14-15 - WHEN JESUS WAS COME INTO PETER'S HOUSE, HE SAW HIS WIFE'S MOTHER SICK OF A FEVER. HE TOUCHED HER HAND, AND THE FEVER LEFT HER....

**Contradictions:**
MARK 1:29-31 ...they [Jesus and disciples] entered the house of Simon and Andrew, with James and John. Simon's wife's mother lay sick of a fever.... He took her by the hand, lifted her up, and the fever left her....
[The incident occurred after Jesus healed a man of an unclean spirit in MARK 1:23-26.]
LUKE 4:38-39 - He [Jesus]...entered Simon's house. Simon's wife's mother was taken with a great fever.... He...rebuked the fever, and it left her.... [The incident occurred before Peter became a disciple of

Jesus in LUKE 5:11, and before the centurion's servant was healed in LUKE 7:2-10.]
[Did Jesus cure the fever by touching the woman's hand, or by rebuking it?]
[Did Jesus cure Peter's mother-in-law's fever after, or before Peter became a disciple?]
[Did Jesus heal the centurion's servant, after or before curing Simon's mother-in-law?]
LUKE 7:11 - [After healing the centurion's servant]...Jesus went into a city called Nain....
[After healing the centurion's servant, did Jesus go to Simon's house, or to a city called Nain?]

**Perplexing:**
Why did Jesus not point out that a fever is a symptom of an infection, not a disease itself? What caused the fever? Was the cause of the fever also eliminated?

8:16-17 - ...THEY BROUGHT UNTO HIM MANY THAT WERE POSSESSED WITH DEVILS; HE CAST OUT THE SPIRITS WITH HIS WORD, AND HEALED ALL THAT WERE SICK, THAT IT MIGHT BE FULFILLED WHICH WAS SPOKEN BY ESAIAS THE PROPHET: "HIMSELF TOOK OUR INFIRMITIES, AND BEAR OUR SICKNESS."

**Contradictions:**
MARK 1:32-34 - ...they brought unto him all that were diseased, and them possessed with devils. .... He healed many...and cast out many devils....
LUKE 4:40-41 - ...all they that had any sick with diverse diseases brought them to him; he laid his hands on every one of them, and healed them. Devils also came out of many....
[Did Jesus heal all, or just many that were sick?]
[Did Jesus heal by means of his word, or by laying on his hands?]

**Old Testament:**
ISA. 53:4 - Isaiah: "He has borne our griefs and carried our sorrows, yet we did esteem him stricken, smitten of God, and afflicted."
[The verse taken out of context by MATT. is part of a series of verses pertaining to the Israelite people.]

**Perplexing:**
Why did MATT. apply a verse related to the Israelites to Jesus? Where did the devils and spirits go when they were cast out? What did they look like? Why did no one write about or otherwise record these healing miracles by Jesus?
See also under 4:24-25.

**History:** See under 4:23.

**Pagan parallels:** See under 4:23.

8:18 - WHEN JESUS SAW GREAT MULTITUDES ABOUT HIM, HE GAVE COMMANDMENT TO DEPART UNTO THE OTHER SIDE (TO THE LAND OF THE GERGESENES IN 8:28).

**Contradictions:**
MARK 1:35 - [After curing Peter's mother-in-law's fever and many sick people] Jesus rising a great while before day, went out, departed into a solitary place, and prayed.
LUKE 4:42 - [After curing Peter's mother-in-law's fever and healing the sick but before obtaining disciples] Jesus, when it was day, departed and went into a desert place....

[Did Jesus give a command, presumably to his disciples, to depart for "the other side," or did he rise before day to go to a solitary place and pray?]
[Did Jesus go to the other side (to the Gergesenes), or to a solitary, desert place?]
[Did Jesus depart after, or before obtaining disciples?]

**Perplexing:**
How was Jesus able to move around, if there were great multitudes about him?

8:20 - JESUS: "...THE SON OF MAN HATH NOT WHERE TO LAY HIS HEAD."

**Language:**
In Aramaic, the term, "son of man," meant simply, "man" or "human being." As there were no upper case letters in ancient Aramaic or Hebrew, the use of capitals was at the option of the translators. Therefore, some use "Son," whereas others use "son." The term as used in DAN. has also been interpreted by some scholars as an allegorical reference to the Jewish state.

**History:**
"Son of man" was a title used by Judean kings.

**Old Testament:**
NUM. 23:19 - Balaam: "God is not a man, that He should lie, neither the son of man, that He should repent...."
JOB 25:6 - Bildad: "How much less man, that is a worm? And the son of man, which is a worm?"
PS. 146:3 - "Put not your trust in princes, nor in the son of man, in whom there is no help."
EZEK. 2:1 and numerous other verses- The LORD referred to Ezekiel as, "Son of man."
DAN. 7:13 - Daniel: "I saw in the night visions, one like the Son of man came with the clouds of heaven, and came to the Ancient of days...."
DAN. 8:17 - Daniel: "He said [to me], "O son of man, at the time of the end shall be the vision."
There are numerous additional Old Testament verses mentioning "Son (son) of man."

**Perplexing:**
Why did Jesus refer to himself as the "Son of man?" Did he mean that he was only a man, or that he was a king?

8:21-22 - ANOTHER OF HIS DISCIPLES SAID, "LORD, SUFFER ME FIRST TO GO AND BURY MY FATHER." JESUS SAID, "FOLLOW ME; LET THE DEAD BURY THEIR DEAD." [THIS INCIDENT OCCURRED BEFORE JESUS SENT HIS DISCIPLES FORTH TO PREACH IN 10:5, AND BEFORE THEY WALKED THROUGH A CORNFIELD IN 12:1.]

**Contradictions:**
LUKE 9:59-60 - He said unto another, "Follow me," but he said, "Lord, suffer me first to go and bury my father." Jesus said, "Let the dead bury their dead; go thou and preach the kingdom of God." [The incident is reported to have occurred after Jesus and the disciples walked through a cornfield in LUKE 6:1, and after he sent the disciples forth to preach (LUKE 9:2.)]
[Did Jesus say that the dead should bury their dead before, or after walking through a cornfield?]
[Did Jesus say that the dead should bury their dead before, or after sending the disciples out to preach?]

8:23 - WHEN HE WAS ENTERED INTO A SHIP, HIS DISCIPLES FOLLOWED HIM.

**Contradictions:**
MARK1:35-39 - ...he departed into a solitary place.... Simon and they that were with him followed. .... He said, "Let us go into the next towns, that I may preach there...." He preached in their synagogues throughout Galilee, and cast out devils.
[Did Jesus board a ship with his disciples shortly after healing Simon's mother-in-law, or did he go to a solitary place and then to preach in synagogues in Galilee?]
LUKE 4:44 - Jesus preached in the synagogues of Galilee [prior to finding his first disciples in LUKE 5:10-11].
[Shortly after curing Peter's mother-in-law of a fever, did Jesus board a ship with his disciples, or did he go to preach in the synagogues of Galilee before obtaining any disciples?]

8:24-25 - THERE AROSE A GREAT TEMPEST IN THE SEA, THAT THE SHIP WAS COVERED WITH WAVES, BUT HE WAS ASLEEP. HIS DISCIPLES AWOKE HIM, SAYING, "LORD, SAVE US; WE PERISH."

**Contradiction:**
MARK 4:37-38 - The above incident is reported to have occurred after Jesus recited a series of parables, walked through a cornfield, ordained twelve disciples, discoursed with Pharisees, healed the sick, and refused to meet with his mother and brethren.
LUKE 8:23-24 - The reported incident is comparable to that in MARK but with more of Jesus' adventures and discourses mentioned.
[Was Jesus on the ship shortly after he cured a fever, or at a much later time?]

**Perplexing:**
Why did the Son of God require sleep? How was Jesus able to remain asleep on a relatively small boat that was being tossed around by the wind and being f illed with water? Why did he not know that a storm would arise to endanger the passengers? Why did he fail to prevent the storm?

**Old Testament:**
JON. 1:3-6 - Jonah boarded a ship; there was a mighty tempest in the sea, so that the ship was like to be broken. Jonah was fast asleep. The shipmaster came to him and told him to arise and call upon his God so that they would not perish.

8:26 - JESUS: "WHY ARE YE SO FEARFUL...?" HE AROSE AND REBUKED THE WINDS AND THE SEA, AND THERE WAS A GREAT CALM.

**Contradictions:** See under 8:24-25.

**Old Testament:**
PS. 89:9 - "Thou [LORD God] rulest the raging of the sea; when the waves thereof arise, Thou stillest them."
PS. 107:29 - "He [the LORD] maketh the storm calm, so that the waves thereof are still."

8:27 - THE MEN MARVELLED, SAYING, "WHAT MANNER OF MAN IS THIS, THAT EVEN THE WINDS AND THE SEA OBEY HIM?"

**Perplexing:**
After the numerous healing miracles that Jesus performed and which were witnessed by multitudes, why did the men wonder about what kind of man he is?

8:28 - WHEN HE WAS COME TO THE OTHER SIDE INTO THE COUNTRY OF THE GERGESENES, THERE MET HIM TWO POSSESSED WITH DEVILS, COMING OUT OF THE TOMBS....

**Contradictions:**
MARK 5:1 and LUKE 8:26 - They came into the country of the Gadarenes.
[Did they arrive at the country of the Gergesenes, or the Gadarenes?]
MARK 5:2 - When he was out of the ship, immediately there met him out of the tombs a man with an unclean spirit.
[Was Jesus met by two possessed with devils, or a man with an unclean spirit?]
LUKE 8:27 - When he went forth to land, there met him out of the city a man, which had devils long time, and ware no clothes, neither abode in any house but in the tombs.
[Was Jesus met by two possessed with devils, or a man who had devils?]

**Perplexing:** See under 4:24-25.

8:29 - THEY CRIED OUT, "WHAT HAVE WE TO DO WITH THEE, JESUS, THOU SON OF GOD? ART THOU COME HITHER TO TORMENT US BEFORE THE TIME?"

**Contradictions:**
MARK 5:7 - [The man] cried with a loud voice, "What have I to do with thee, Jesus, thou Son of the most high God? I adjure thee by God, that thou torment me not."
LUKE 8:28 - When he [the man] saw Jesus, he cried out, and fell down before him, and with a loud voice said, "What have I to do with thee Jesus, thou Son of God most high? I beseech thee, torment me not."
[Did two spirits speak to Jesus and ask whether he came to torment them, or did one ask that he not torment him?]
1 JOHN 4:2 - John: "Hereby know ye the spirit of God; every spirit that confesseth that Jesus Christ is come in the flesh is of God."
[Were the spirits devils, or were they of God because they acknowledged Jesus to be God's Son?]

**Perplexing:**
Why were devils and Satan (in 4:3, 6) the first beings on earth, in MATT., to refer to Jesus as the "Son of God?"
See also under 4:3.

**History:**
Some early Christians such as the Ebionites did not believe that Jesus was the Son of God. They saw him as a man who found favor with God and who was used by God to perform miracles. (See ACTS 2:22 - Jesus was "a man approved of God among you by miracles...which God did by him....")

8:30-32 - THERE WAS...A HERD OF SWINE FEEDING. THE DEVILS BESOUGHT HIM, "IF THOU CAST US OUT, SUFFER US TO GO INTO THE HERD OF SWINE." HE SAID, "GO."...THEY WENT INTO THE HERD OF SWINE; THE WHOLE HERD RAN VIOLENTLY DOWN A STEEP PLACE INTO THE SEA, AND PERISHED.

**Perplexing:**
Why did Jesus comply with the devils' request? Why did Jesus allow them to destroy a herd of innocent animals and, hence, the livelihood of those who were dependent upon the swine? Why was Jesus so cruel? Why could Jesus not dispose of the devils without killing the animals? Why could the devils not go into the swine without being ordered to do so by Jesus? What happened to the devils when the swine died?

8:33-34 - THEY THAT KEPT THEM FLED, INTO THE CITY, AND TOLD EVERYTHING, AND WHAT WAS BEFALLEN TO THE POSSESSED OF THE DEVILS. THE WHOLE CITY CAME TO MEET JESUS, AND BESOUGHT THAT HE WOULD DEPART OUT OF THEIR COASTS.

**Perplexing:**
How long did it take the swineherds to travel around the city telling people what had occurred? How long did it take the whole city to reach Jesus? How many people were there? Why did Jesus fail (1) to perform a miracle giving the owners a new supply of animals or recompense them for their loss; (2) to perform a miracle to bring the swine back to life; (3) to apologize to the people for destroying their animals; (4) to preach to the people or tell them about his Father? Did he fail to preach to them because they were not Jewish? Can the people be faulted for asking Jesus to leave?

9:1-2 - JESUS ENTERED A SHIP AND CAME INTO HIS OWN CITY. THEY BROUGHT TO HIM A MAN SICK OF THE PALSY, ON A BED; JESUS SEEING THEIR FAITH SAID UNTO THE SICK OF PALSY, "SON, BE OF GOOD CHEER; THY SINS BE FORGIVEN THEE."

**Contradiction:**
MARK 5:21-23 - When Jesus passed over by ship unto the other side, much people gathered unto him.... There cometh one of the rulers of the synagogue...saying, "My little daughter lieth at the point of death; I pray thee, come and lay thy hands on her, that she may be healed, and shall live."
LUKE 8:40-42 - similar to MARK.
[When Jesus arrived, was he met by people who brought a man sick with palsy, or by a ruler of the synagogue asking him to heal his sick daughter?]

**Perplexing:**
Why was it necessary for Jesus to forgive the man's sins? Why did he forgive the man's sins? Why did he fail to explain the nature and cause of palsy? Why did he fail to provide people with a cure for palsy? Why did he not eradicate palsy from the world?

9:3 - CERTAIN OF THE SCRIBES SAID WITHIN THEMSELVES, "THIS MAN BLASPHEMETH."

**Perplexing:**
Why did the scribes believe that Jesus had committed blasphemy, when, according to Jewish law, blasphemy is the denigration of God, which Jesus did not do?

9:4 - JESUS KNOWING THEIR THOUGHTS....

**Contradiction:**
MATT. 9:28 - ...Jesus saith unto them [two blind men], "Believe ye that I am able to do this?"
MARK 5:30 - Jesus...said, "Who touched my clothes?]
MATT. 20:21 - He said unto her [the mother of Zebedee's children], "What wilt thou?"

MARK 9:16 - He asked the scribes, “What question ye with them?”
MARK 10:36 - He said unto them [James and John], “What would ye that I should do for you?”
LUKE 18:41 - Jesus: “What wilt thou that I should do unto thee [a blind man]?”
JOHN 1:38 - Jesus saith anto them [Andrew and an unidentified person], “What seek ye?”
JOHN 5:6 - ...he saith unto him [an infirm man], “Wilt thou be made whole?”
[There are several additional verses in which Jesus asked people what they thought or wanted?]
[Could Jesus read thoughts, or did he have to ask people what they thought or wanted?]

9:7-8 - HE [THE MAN WHO HAD PALSY] AROSE, AND DEPARTED TO HIS HOUSE. WHEN THE MULTITUDES SAW IT, THEY MARVELLED, AND GLORIFIED GOD....

**Perplexing:**

If multitudes witnessed the healing miracle, why did not any of them make a written report of it or tell someone who would document the event?

9:9 - JESUS...SAW A MAN, NAMED MATTHEW, SITTING AT THE RECEIPT OF CUSTOM, AND SAITH, “FOLLOW ME.” HE AROSE AND FOLLOWED HIM.

**Contradictions:**

MARK 2:14 - he saw Levi the son of Alphaeus sitting at the receipt of custom, and said, “Follow me.” He arose and followed him.
LUKE 5:27-28 - ...he saw a publican, named Levi, sitting at the receipt of custom; he said, “Follow me.” He left all, and followed him.
[Did Jesus see and tell Matthew, or Levi, to follow him?]
[Did the incident occur after, or before the incident with the swine (in MARK 5:12-13; and LUKE 8:32-34)?]

**Perplexing:**

Why did MATT. say that Jesus saw Matthew, whereas MARK and LUKE say that he saw Levi? (Some theologians contend that Matthew and Levi are the same. The gospels, however, do not make this claim.) How could a publican, an employee of the Roman government, involved in the collection of taxes simply walk away from a relatively secure government job and salary without notifying his supervisor and follow a stranger? Was he not risking arrest, possible imprisonment, and even execution for deserting his assignment? Why did JOHN fail to mention either Matthew or Levi as one of Jesus’ disciples?

9:11 - ...THE PHARISEES SAID UNTO HIS DISCIPLES, “WHY EATETH YOUR MASTER WITH PUBLICANS AND SINNERS?”

**Contradictions:**

MARK 2:16 - The scribes and Pharisees...said unto his disciples, “How is it that he eateth with publicans and sinners?”
[Did Pharisees, or scribes and Pharisees speak to the disciples?]
LUKE 5:30 - Scribes and Pharisees murmured against his disciples, saying, “Why do ye eat and drink with publicans and sinners?”
[[Did the Pharisees ask the disciples why Jesus ate with publicans and sinners, or did Pharisees and scribes ask the disciples why they ate with publicans and sinners?]
[Did the event take place after, or before the incident with the swine?]

**Perplexing:**
Why were Pharisees at a meal with Jesus, his disciples, publicans, and sinners? If not, how did they know with whom he was eating, and how were they able to speak with his disciples?
Was the meal in Jesus' house? If so, why did Jesus permit Pharisees to eat with him?

9:13 - JESUS: "GO AND LEARN WHAT MEANETH, 'I WILL HAVE MERCY, AND NOT SACRIFICE'; I AM NOT COME TO CALL THE RIGHTEOUS, BUT SINNERS TO REPENTANCE."

**Contradictions:**
ROM. 3:10 - Paul: "There is none righteous, no, not one."
[Are there any who are righteous, or is no one righteous?]
MATT. 10:35 - Jesus: "I am come to set a man at variance against his father; the daughter against her mother, and the daughter in law against her mother in law."
[Did Jesus come to call sinners to repentance, or to cause family dissension?]
MATT, 20:28 - Jesus: "The Son of man came...to give his life a ransom for many."
[Did Jesus come to call sinners to repentance, or to give his life as a ransom for many?]
MARK 1:38 - Jesus; "Let us go into the next towns, that I may preach there also, for therefore came I forth."
[Did Jesus come to call sinners to repentance, or to preach?]
MATT. 13:11 - He said unto them [his disciples], "It is given unto you to know the mysteries of the kingdom of heaven, but to them it is not given."
MARK 4:11-12 - He said unto them [his disciples], "Unto you it is given to know the mystery of the kingdom of God; unto them that are without, all these things are done in parables...lest at any time they should be converted, and their sins should be forgiven."
[Did Jesus want to bring sinners to repentance, or did he speak in parables so they would not have their sins forgiven?]
LUKE 12:49 - Jesus: "I am come to send fire on the earth...."
[Did Jesus come to call sinners to repentance, or did he come to send fire onto the earth?]
LUKE 12:51 - Jesus: "Suppose ye that I have come to give peace on earth? Nay, but rather division."
[Did Jesus come to call sinners to repentance, or to division?]
MATT. 18:11 - Jesus: "The Son of man is come to save that which was lost."
LUKE 19:10 Jesus: "The Son of man is come to seek and save that which was lost."
[Did Jesus come to call sinners to repentance, or to save that which was lost?]
JOHN 12:47 - Jesus: " I came to save the world."
[Did Jesus come to call sinners to repentance, or to save the world?]
1 JOHN 3:8 - John: "For this purpose the Son of God was manifested, that he might destroy the works of the devil."
[Did Jesus come to call sinners to repentance, or to destroy the works of the devil?]
The astute reader will find additional contradictory verses about why Jesus came.

**Old Testament:**
HOS. 6:6 - Hosea [citing the LORD]: "I desired mercy, not sacrifice, and the knowledge of God more than burnt offerings."

9:15 - JESUS SAID, "CAN THE CHILDREN OF THE BRIDECHAMBER MOURN, AS LONG AS THE BRIDEGROOM IS WITH THEM?"

**Contradiction:**

MARK 2:19 - Jesus said, "Can the children of the bridechamber fast, while the bridegroom is with them?"
LUKE 5:34 - He said, "Can ye make the children of the bridechamber fast, while the bridegroom is with them?"
[Did Jesus speak about the children of the bridechamber mourning, or fasting?]

9:18 - ...THERE CAME A CERTAIN RULER, AND WORSHIPPED HIM, SAYING, "MY DAUGHTER IS EVEN NOW DEAD, BUT COME; LAY THY HAND UPON HER, AND SHE SHALL LIVE."

**Contradictions:**

MARK 5:22-23 - [When Jesus returned from the country of the Gadarenes] There cometh one of the rulers of the synagogue, Jairus by name; when he saw him, he fell at his feet, and besought him greatly, saying, "My little daughter lieth at the point of death; I pray thee, come and lay hands on her, that she may be healed and live."
LUKE 8:41-42 - [When Jesus returned from the country of the Gadarenes] There came a man named Jairus, a ruler of the synagogue; he fell down at Jesus' feet, and besought him that he would come into his house; he had one daughter, about twelve years of age, and she lay dying....
[Was the ruler's daughter dead, or was she dying?]
[Did the ruler ask Jesus to bring his daughter back to life, or to heal her?]
[Did the ruler come to Jesus after Jesus acquired Matthew as a disciple and after eating with publicans and sinners (9:9-17), or when Jesus arrived from the country of the Gadarenes after casting devils into swine?]
See also under 9:1-2.
MARK 5:35 - There came from the ruler of the synagogue's house certain which said, "Thy daughter is dead...."
LUKE 8:49 - There cometh one from the ruler of the synagogue's house, saying, "Thy daughter is dead...."
[Did the ruler say that his daughter was dead, or did one or more people from the ruler's house say that she was dead?]

9:19 - JESUS AROSE, AND FOLLOWED HIM; SO DID HIS DISCIPLES.

**Contradiction:**

MARK 5:37 - He suffered no man to follow him, save Peter, James, and John the brother of James.
[Did all of Jesus' disciples follow him, or did he permit only Peter, James, and John to follow him?]

9:20-22 - A WOMAN WITH AN ISSUE OF BLOOD TWELVE YEARS, CAME BEHIND HIM, AND TOUCHED THE HEM OF HIS GARMENT"; SHE SAID WITHIN HERSELF, "IF I MAY BUT TOUCH HIS GARMENT, I SHALL BE WHOLE." JESUS TURNED, AND WHEN HE SAW HER, SAID, "...THY FAITH HAS MADE THEE WHOLE." THE WOMAN WAS MADE WHOLE FROM THAT HOUR.

**History:**

The Essene sect believed in faith healing.

9:25 - WHEN THE PEOPLE WERE PUT FORTH, HE WENT IN, TOOK HER BY THE HAND, AND THE MAID AROSE.

**Contradictions:**

MARK 5:40 - ...he taketh the father and mother of the damsel, and them that were with him, and entereth in where the damsel was lying.

[Did Jesus go to the girl alone, or with her parents and his disciples?]

MARK 5:41-42 - He took the damsel by the hand, and said, “Talitha cumi,” which is, “I say unto thee, arise.” Straightway, the damsel arose....

LUKE 8:54-55 - He put them all out, took her by the handt and called, “Maid, arise.” ...she arose straightway....

[Did the girl return to life after Jesus took her hand, or after he took her hand and told her to arise?]

ACTS 26:23 - Paul: “Christ should suffer, and then be the first that should rise from the dead....”

REV. 1:5 - Jesus Christ...the first begotten of the dead....

[Was the girl brought back from the dead before Jesus was resurrected, or was he the first to be resurrected (in 28:5-6)?]

**Old Testament:**

1 KINGS 17:20-23 - Elijah resurrected a dead boy.

2 KINGS 4:32-35 - Elisha resurrected a dead boy.

**Pagan parallels:**

The Hindu god Krishna went to the home of a dead girl and asked those present, “Why do you weep? Do you not see that she is sleeping?” He then told her to arise, and she did. Asclepius (Aesculapius) also resurrected the dead. The Egyptian god Horus resurrected the dead Osiris.

9:26 - THE FAME THEREOF WENT ABROAD INTO ALL THAT LAND.

**Perplexing:**

If the account of this resurrection was publicized throughout the land, why is there no record of it outside of the Bible? Why did not multitudes of people, especially government, military, and other influential people come to Jesus and ask him to resurrect their loved ones?

As brain damage begins to occur shortly after death, what was the girl’s mental condition?

9:27 - WHEN JESUS DEPARTED, TWO BLIND MEN FOLLOWED HIM, SAYING, “THOU SON OF DAVID, HAVE MERCY ON US.”

**Perplexing:**

How were the blind men able to recognize and follow Jesus? Why did they refer to him as the “Son of David?” Did people at that time consider him to be a human descended from David through Joseph, rather than the Son of God? (Since Jews only recognized a patriarchal genealogy, a genealogy through Mary would not have been accepted.)

9:28-30 - WHEN HE WAS COME INTO THE HOUSE, THE BLIND MEN CAME TO HIM, AND JESUS SAITH, “BELIEVE YE THAT I AM ABLE TO DO THIS?” THEY SAID, “YES, LORD.” THEN TOUCHED HE THEIR EYES, SAYING, “ACCORDING TO YOUR FAITH BE IT UNTO YOU.” THEIR EYES WERE OPENED; JESUS CHARGED THEM, “SEE THAT NO MAN KNOW IT.”

**Contradiction:**

9:4 - Jesus knowing their thoughts....

12:25 - Jesus knew their thoughts....
MARK 2:8 - ...Jesus perceived in his spirit what they had reasoned within themselves....
LUKE 5:22 - When Jesus perceived their thoughts....
LUKE 6:8 - He knew their thoughts....
LUKE 9:47 - Jesus perceiving the thought of their heart....
LUKE 11:17 - He knowing their thoughts....
[Did Jesus know people's thoughts, or did he have to ask them if they believed?]

**Perplexing:**
Why were the blind men in this incident able to obtain sight through faith and by Jesus touching their eyes, when (1) in MATT. 20:34, Jesus healed two blind men by just touching their eyes; (2) in MARK 8:23-25, Jesus spit upon the eyes of a blind man and touched his eyes twice; (3) in MARK 10:51-52, faith alone healed a blind man; (4) in JOHN 9:6-7, Jesus healed a blind man by first spitting on the ground and making clay which he put on the man's eyes and then ordering him to wash in the pool of Siloam?
How could the blind men keep secret the fact that they could now see?
If Jesus knew people's thoughts, why did he have to ask the blind men if they believed?
See also under 4:24-25.

**Pagan parallels:** See under 4:23.

9:31 - THEY, WHEN THEY WERE DEPARTED, SPREAD ABROAD HIS FAME IN ALL THAT COUNTRY.

**Perplexing:**
Why did Jesus fail to know that they would spread "his fame in all that country?" Why is there no secular record of Jesus healing any blind people? Why did Jesus fail to heal all blind people?

9:32-33 - ...THEY BROUGHT TO HIM A DUMB MAN, POSSESSED WITH A DEVIL. WHEN THE DEVIL WAS CAST OUT, THE DUMB SPAKE, AND THE MULTITUDES MARVELLED....

**Perplexing:**
Why was this miracle, witnessed by multitudes, not recorded in the secular literature of the time? Where did the devil go when it was cast out? Why was it in the man? Was demonic possession used to explain infirmities which the people at that time could not otherwise explain?
See also under 4:24-25.

**History:** See under 4:24-25.

9:35 - JESUS WENT ABOUT ALL THE CITIES AND VILLAGES, TEACHING IN THEIR SYNAGOGUES, PREACHING THE GOSPEL OF THE KINGDOM, AND HEALING EVERY SICKNESS, AND DISEASE AMONG THE PEOPLE.

**Perplexing:**
How did Jesus travel? From where did he obtain funds for food, lodging, and clothes? How much time did he spend traveling? How was he able to obtain permission to teach in the synagogues, since he was not teaching traditional Judaic beliefs? If he traveled throughout "all the cities and villages" and healed every "sickness, and disease among the people," why is there no documentation of his achievements? Certainly,

curing incurable ailments and diseases would have come to the attention of historians, government officials, and others who would have made notations of his accomplishments? Why did the merchants and military personnel, especially from Rome, visiting the area not report what he had done when they returned to their homeland? Why did the Roman officials not summon him to Rome or come to meet him to have their ailments cured? Why did Jesus fail to teach the people how to treat and prevent diseases? Why did Jesus fail to eliminate disease from the planet, and, thereby, convince the world beyond any doubt of his divinity? If Jesus had the power to eradicate diseases, but failed to do so, is he not then responsible for all the pain, suffering, misery, and deaths caused by diseases? Was it not an act of cruelty for Jesus not to have saved all of humanity from the ravages of diseases?
See also under 4:23 and 4:24-25.

**History:** See under 4:24-25.

9:36 - WHEN HE SAW THE MULTITUDES, HE WAS MOVED WITH COMPASSION, BECAUSE THEY FAINTED, AND WERE SCATTERED ABROAD, AS SHEEP HAVING NO SHEPHERD.

**Old Testament:**
1 KINGS 22:17 - He [Micaiah] said, "I saw all Israel scattered upon the hills, as sheep that have not a shepherd...."

10:1 - WHEN HE HAD CALLED UNTO HIM HIS 12 DISCIPLES, HE GAVE THEM POWER AGAINST UNCLEAN SPIRITS, TO CAST THEM OUT, AND TO HEAL ALL MANNER OF SICKNESS, AND DISEASE. [THIS OCCURRED BEFORE JESUS AND THE DISCIPLES WENT THROUGH A CORNFIELD IN 12:1-8.]

**Contradictions:**
MATT. 17:14-21 - A man brought his sick son to Jesus and said, "I brought him to thy disciples, and they could not cure him." After ridding the boy of a devil, Jesus said to his disciple, "This kind goeth not out but by prayer and fasting."
[Did Jesus give his disciples power "to heal all manner of sickness, and disease," or did he give them power to heal only those sicknesses and diseases that did not require "prayer and fasting?"]
MARK 3:14-15 - [Before Jesus resurrected the daughter of the ruler of a synagogue] He ordained twelve, that they should be with him, and that he might send them to preach, have power to heal sickness, and cast out devils.
[Did Jesus give his twelve disciples power to heal sicknesses after, or before having resurrected the daughter of a synagogue's ruler?]
LUKE 6:13-16 - Jesus called and selected the twelve disciples after having gone through the cornfield in 6:1-5.
[Did Jesus call his disciples before, or after going through the cornfield?]

**History:**
There is no secular record of the twelve disciples.

**Perplexing:**
Why did Jesus select twelve disciples? When did he acquire all twelve of them? Why did Jesus fail to inform the disciples that some cases would require fasting and prayer? Why is there no historical record of the disciples?

**Old Testament:**

GEN. 49:1-28 - Jacob had 12 sons, from whom arose twelve Israelite tribes.
GEN. 22:20-24 - Abraham's brother Nahor had twelve children.
NUM. 1:44 - the princes of Israel being twelve men....
DEUT. 1:23 - Moses: " I took twelve men of you...."
JOSH. 3:12 - Joshua: "Therefore take you twelve men out of the tribes of Israel...."
JOSH. 4:4 - Joshua called the twelve men....
1 KINGS 4:7 - Solomon had twelve officers over all Israel
(There are numerous other Old Testament verses citing twelve people or things.)

**Dead Sea Scrolls:**

The Teacher of Righteousness had twelve priests.

**Pagan parallels:**

Pagan deities such as Mithra, Tammuz, and others traveled with followers or disciples. Buddha and Confucius also had disciples. Ancient Zodiacs had twelve signs. In Hinduism, Aditi the mother of gods had twelve sons (Aditya). The Greek Olympian pantheon also had twelve gods.

10:2-4 - THE NAMES OF THE 12 APOSTLES ARE: SIMON, CALLED PETER, ANDREW HIS BROTHER JAMES THE SON OF ZEBEDEE, JOHN HIS BROTHER, PHILIP, BARTHOLOMEW, THOMAS, MATTHEW THE PUBLICAN, JAMES THE SON OF ALPHAEUS, LEBBAEUS THADDAEUS, SIMON THE CANAANITE, AND JUDAS ISCARIOT....

**Contradictions:**

LUKE 6:16 and ACTS 1:13 listed Judas the brother of James as a disciple in place of Lebbaeus Thaddaeus.
JOHN 14:22 - Judas, not Iscariot, was reported as one of the disciples.
[Was Lebbaeus Thaddaeus, or Judas (not Iscariot) one of the twelve?]
JOHN 21:2 - Nathanael was cited as one of the disciples.
[JOHN did not mention Bartholomew, Matthew, James the son of Alphaeus, Labbaeus Thaddaeus, or Simon the Canaanite.]
[Was, or was not Nathanael one of the twelve?]
MARK 2:14 and LUKE 5:27-28 identified Levi as a follower of Jesus.
[Was Lebbaeus Thaddaeus, or Levi a disciple?]

**Perplexing:**

Why did the gospels fail to agree on the names of Jesus' disciples? Why were the twelve not clearly identified to avoid confusion? Why was James specifically reported to be the son of Alphaeus, when MARK 2:14 stated that Levi was the son of Alphaeus? MARK did not say that James and Levi are brothers.

**Language:**

"Canaanite" is derived from the Greek, "Kamanaios" and the Aramaic, "Kannai." It means "one who is zealous" - "a Zealot." In LUKE 6:15 and ACTS 1:13, Simon is identified as "Zelotes" - "a Zealot."
"Apostle" is derived from the Greek, "apostellein," meaning "send forth" as an envoy, messenger, or missionary.

**History:**
The Zealots were Jewish religious fanatics who engaged in acts of terrorism against both Romans and other Jews. They were responsible for initiating the rebellion that eventually led to the destruction of Jerusalem and the temple by the Romans.

10:5-6 - THESE 12 JESUS SENT FORTH, AND COMMANDED THEM, "GO NOT INTO THE WAY OF THE GENTILES, AND INTO ANY CITY OF THE SAMARITANS ENTER YE NOT; GO RATHER TO THE LOST SHEEP OF THE HOUSE OF ISRAEL."

**Contradictions:**
MATT. 24:14 - Jesus: "This gospel of the kingdom shall be preached... unto all nations...."
MATT. 28:19 - Jesus: "Go ye therefore, and teach all nations...."
MARK 13:10 - Jesus: "The gospel must first be published among all nations."
MARK 16:15 - Jesus: "Go ye into all the world, and preach the gospel...."
ACTS 1:8 - Jesus: "...ye shall be witnesses unto me both in Jerusalem. and in all Judaea, Samaria, and unto the uttermost part of the earth."
ACTS 13:47 - Paul and Barnabas: "So hath the Lord commanded us, saying, 'I have set thee to be a light of the Gentiles, that thou shouldest be for salvation unto the ends of the earth.'"
[Did Jesus instruct his disciples not to go to the Gentiles or into Samaria, but only to the lost sheep of Israel, or did he tell them to go to the Gentiles, Samaria, and all nations?]
MARK 6:7 - Jesus sent the disciples forth after having gone through the cornfield in 2:23.
[Did Jesus send his disciples forth before, or after having gone through a cornfield?]

**History:**
Samaritan beliefs were similar to those of the Jews. They differed primarily by believing that their temple on Mount Garizim, not the temple in Jerusalem, was the legitimate place for worship. This led to extreme hostility between the two groups. It may also be the reason why Jesus, a Jew, prohibited the disciples from going into Samaritan areas.

10:7-8 - JESUS: "AS YE GO, PREACH, 'THE KINGDOM OF HEAVEN IS AT HAND.' HEAL THE SICK, CLEANSE THE LEPERS, RAISE THE DEAD, CAST OUT DEVILS; FREELY YE HAVE RECEIVED, FREELY GIVE."

**Contradictions:**
MARK 6: 7 - He...began to send them forth by two and two, and gave them power over unclean spirits.
[Did Jesus instruct the disciples to heal the sick, to cast out devils, and to preach that the kingdom of heaven (God) is imminent, or did he just give them power over unclean spirits?]
LUKE 9:1-2 - He...gave them power and authority over all devils, and to cure diseases. He sent them to preach the kingdom of God, and to heal the sick.
[Did Jesus give, or not give the disciples power to raise the dead?]
See also under 10:1.

**Perplexing:**
Why do not modern clergy follow Jesus' command to preach and work freely? Why do many (almost all?) always solicit money for their services? If the kingdom of heaven was at hand, why has it not yet arrived? Did Jesus erroneously believe that his kingdom was about to materialize? If not, why did he tell the disciples to lie about it being near? Why did God need people, especially uneducated individuals to preach for Him?

Why could God Himself not speak to people and thereby convince everyone of His existence? Why did Jesus fail to pray for everyone's conversion?

10:9 - JESUS: "PROVIDE NEITHER GOLD, SILVER, NOR BRASS IN YOUR PURSES."

**History:**
Members of the Essene sect did not carry money with them when they traveled. The Essene communities in which they stopped provided lodging and sustenance for them.

**Perplexing:**
From where could the disciples have obtained gold, silver, and brass ("copper," in some Bibles), since they had deserted their occupations, and were not reported to be engaged in any gainful employment?

10:10 - JESUS: "NOR SCRIP FOR YOUR JOURNEY, NEITHER TWO COATS, NEITHER SHOES, NOR STAVES...."

**Contradictions:**
MARK 6:8-9 - [Jesus] commanded that they should take nothing for their journey, save a staff [a stave] only; no scrip, no bread, no money in their purse, but be shod with sandals, and not put on two coats.
[Did Jesus tell the disciples not to take staves, or did he say to take a staff?]
[Did Jesus tell the disciples not to take shoes, or did he say to wear sandals?]
LUKE 9:3 - Jesus: "Take nothing for your journey, neither staves, nor scrip, neither bread, neither money, neither have two coats apiece."
[Did Jesus allow, or not allow bread to be taken?]

10:14-15 - JESUS: "WHOSOEVER SHALL NOT RECEIVE YOU, NOR HEAR YOUR WORDS.... IT SHALL BE MORE TOLERABLE FOR SODOM AND GOMORRHA IN THE DAY OF JUDGMENT, THAN FOR THAT CITY."

**Judaism:**
According to Jewish tradition, Sodom and Gomorrha were destroyed because their inhabitants were inhospitable to and mistreated visitors. (This conflicts with the usual Christian belief that their populace engaged in homosexual activities.)

**Pagan parallel:**
According to Zoroastrianism, there will be a day of judgment. Such a concept also occurs in many other pre-Christian religions.

10:16 - JESUS: "I SEND YOU FORTH AS SHEEP IN THE MIDST OF WOLVES; BE YE THEREFORE WISE AS SERPENTS AND HARMLESS AS DOVES."

**History:**
During the ensuing two millennia, it was the followers of Jesus who acted worse than vicious wolves. They perpetrated some of the most heinous atrocities imaginable against humanity including: the Crusades, the Inquisition, the Holocaust, the slaughter of American Indians, innumerable religious wars and crimes in the name of Jesus, as well as promulgating religious hate, intolerance, murders, and persecution.

**Perplexing:**
Why did Jesus say that serpents are wise? Why have many (most?) Christians rejected Jesus' command to be as harmless as doves? Why have they instead opted to be like wolves?

10:17 - JESUS: "BEWARE OF MEN; THEY WILL DELIVER YOU UP TO THE COUNCILS, AND SCOURGE YOU IN THEIR SYNAGOGUES."

**Contradiction:**
MATT. 11:1 - 12:1 - The disciples departed and then returned to Jesus without any report of them having been delivered up to councils or scourged.
[Were the disciples persecuted, or did they return to Jesus without having faced any untoward situations?]

**History:**
Followers of Jesus were not delivered to councils and scourged in synagogues. The persecution of Christians which occurred briefly was by Romans.

**Perplexing:**
Why did Jesus' prophecy fail to materialize? Why did Jesus fail to prophesy persecution by the Romans? Why could Jesus not protect his disciples from any persecution that might be directed against them? Why did he fail to prophesy that over the centuries his followers would do the persecuting?

10:21 - JESUS: "BROTHER SHALL DELIVER UP THE BROTHER TO DEATH, THE FATHER THE CHILD; THE CHILDREN SHALL RISE UP AGAINST THEIR PARENTS, AND CAUSE THEM TO BE PUT TO DEATH."

**History:**
There is no record of such widespread intra-family conflict having taken place during the time the disciples were supposed to have been traveling and preaching.

**Perplexing:**
Why did this prophecy by Jesus fail?

10:23 - JESUS: "WHEN THEY PERSECUTE YOU IN THIS CITY, FLEE INTO ANOTHER; YE SHALL NOT HAVE GONE OVER THE CITIES OF ISRAEL, TILL THE SON OF MAN BE COME."

**Contradictions:**
MATT. 12:1 - The disciples returned to Jesus without any report of them having faced persecution. Jesus was still around; he had not yet left (died) or returned (been resurrected).
[Were the disciples persecuted, or not persecuted?]
[Did Jesus say, or not say that he would return before the disciples had traveled over the cities of Israel?]
MATT. 24:14 - Jesus: "This gospel of the kingdom shall be preached in all the world for a witness unto all nations; then shall the end come."
[Did Jesus say that he would return before the disciples had gone over the cities of Israel, or after the gospel had been preached to all nations?]
See also under 10:5-6 and 10:17.

**Perplexing:**
Why did Jesus say that the disciples would be persecuted? Why did he say that he would return before they had gone over the cities of Israel? Why now, about two millennia later, after Jesus' disciples (followers) have traversed not only Israel but the entire planet, has Jesus still failed to return?
See also under 10:17.

10:25 - JESUS: ".... IF THEY HAVE CALLED THE MASTER OF THE HOUSE BEELZEBUB...."

**Pagan concept:**
Beelzebub, also known as Baalzebub, Baal-Zebul, and Baal Zephon was the name of a Middle Eastern deity believed to have the power to heal the sick and to prevent insect plagues. Since in Phoenician, "zebub" meant "a fly," he was also known as the "fly god" and "Lord of the Flies." He was the chief god of the Philistine city of Ekron (see 2 KINGS 1:2, 3, 6, 16). Christians later denigrated and equated him with a demon or the devil. Philistines and Canaanites also worshiped him as a god of prophecy and fertility. (Later in 12:24, Jesus will be accused of being able to heal people because of an association with Beelzebub - not surprising, as Beelzebub was a god of healing.)

**Old Testament:**
2 KINGS 1:2-3 - Ahaziah...was sick, and sent messengers, and said, "Go, inquire of Baalzebub the god of Ekron whether I shall recover of this disease." An angel: "...and say unto them, 'Is it not because there is not a God in Israel, that ye go to inquire of Baalzebub the god of Ekron whether I shall recover of this disease?'"

**Language:**
"Beelzebub" is derived from the Ugaritic, "Baalzebul," meaning, "Lord of the Temple."

10:28 - JESUS: "...FEAR HIM WHICH IS ABLE TO DESTROY BOTH SOUL AND BODY IN HELL."

**Contradiction:**
EX. 34:6 - The LORD proclaimed, "The LORD God, merciful, gracious, long suffering, and abundant in goodness...."
DEUT. 4:31 - Moses: "The LORD thy God is a merciful God...."
NEH. 9:17 - Nehemiah: "...Thou art a God ready to pardon, gracious and merciful, slow to anger, and of great kindness...."
PS. 37:26 - "He is ever merciful...."
JER. 3:12 - Jeremiah: "...'I am merciful,' saith the LORD; 'I will not keep anger forever.'"
LUKE 6:36 - Jesus: "Be merciful, as your Father is merciful."
(Many other verses proclaim God to be merciful.)
[Does God destroy souls and bodies in hell, and want to be feared, or is He merciful, forgiving, and kind?]

**Perplexing:**
Why would a merciful God want people to fear Him? What pleasure does He derive from people who are afraid of Him? Why would almighty God, creator of the universe, care whether on not piddling, short-lived people on an obscure planet in an obscure solar system on the fringe of an obscure galaxy feared Him? Why would He even care about what people said, did, or believed? Would a merciful, good, and kind God kill people? Would He condemn them to an eternity in hell? Why did He create people that He would cast

into hell? How could God, merciful, good, and kind create something as terrible as hell? Is killing and creating a hell rather what one would expect from an evil deity - a devil? Was Jesus just trying to frighten people into following him?
What is a soul? When was it created? Why was it created?

10:34 - JESUS: "THINK NOT THAT I AM COME TO SEND PEACE ON EARTH; I CAME NOT TO SEND PEACE, BUT A SWORD."

**Contradictions:**
LUKE 2:11 - An angel: "Unto you this day in the city of David a Saviour, which is Christ the Lord."
ACTS 10:36 - Peter: "The word which God sent unto the children of Israel, preaching peace by Jesus Christ...."
1 JOHN 4:14 - John: "...the Father sent the Son to be the Saviour of the world."
[Did Jesus come not to bring peace, or was he a Savior who preached peace?]
See also under 9:13.

**Perplexing:**
Why did Jesus say, in MATT. 26:52, "Put up thy sword into his place, for all they that take the sword shall perish with the sword," if he came to bring a sword, not peace to the earth?

10:35-36 - JESUS: "I AM COME TO SET A MAN AT VARIANCE AGAINST HIS FATHER, THE DAUGHTER AGAINST HER MOTHER, AND THE DAUGHTER-IN-LAW AGAINST THE MOTHER- IN-LAW."

**Old Testament:**
MIC. 7:6 - Micah: "The son dishonoureth the father; the daughter riseth up against her mother, the daughter in law against her mother in law; a man's enemies are the men of his own house."
[In MIC., the verses pertain to an existing situation; they are not, as Jesus used them, something that he will cause to occur.]

**Contradictions:**
EX. 20:12 - GOD: "Honour thy father and mother...."
MATT. 19:19 - Jesus: "Honour thy father and mother...."
[Did Jesus come to cause trouble between children and their parents, or did he want them to honor their parents?]
See also under 9:13 and 20:28.

**Perplexing:**
In DEUT. 27:16 - Moses: "Cursed be he that setteth light by his father or mother." Did Jesus, therefore, mean that he came so that people would be cursed?

10:37 - JESUS: "HE THAT LOVETH FATHER OR MOTHER MORE THAN ME IS NOT WORTHY OF ME; HE THAT LOVETH SON OR DAUGHTER MORE THAN ME IS NOT WORTHY OF ME."

**Perplexing:**
Why did Jesus, a divinity, care whether or not mere ignorant, short-lived mortals loved him? Why did he

want people to love him more than their parents and children?

10:38 - JESUS: "HE THAT TAKETH NOT HIS CROSS, AND FOLLOWETH AFTER ME, IS NOT WORTHY OF ME."

**History:**

The concept of a cross as one's burden did not come into existence until after Jesus' crucifixion. Why, therefore, did Jesus use the expression at this time? How would his listeners have known what he meant? Was the reference to the cross an anachronism?

Prior to becoming a Christian symbol, the cross was a pagan symbol for sun gods and adorned pagan temples; it also served as a phallic symbol. Consequently, early Christians into the fifth century condemned it and opposed its use as a Christian symbol.

10:41 - JESUS: "...HE THAT RECEIVETH A RIGHTEOUS MAN IN THE NAME OF A RIGHTEOUS MAN, SHALL RECEIVE A RIGHTEOUS MAN'S REWARD."

**Contradiction:**

ROM. 3:10 - Paul: "There is none righteous, no, not one."

[Are there righteous men, or is no one righteous?]

**Perplexing:**

What is a righteous man? What is a righteous man's reward?

11:2-3 - WHEN JOHN HAD HEARD IN PRISON THE WORKS OF CHRIST, HE SENT TWO OF HIS DISCIPLES, AND SAID UNTO HIM, "ART THOU HE THAT SHOULD COME, OR DO WE LOOK FOR ANOTHER."

**Contradiction:**

MATT. 3:13-17 - John did not believe that Jesus should be baptized; the Spirit of God in the form of a dove descended onto Jesus, and a voice from heaven said that Jesus "is My beloved Son, in whom I am well pleased?"

MARK 1:9-11 is comparable to MATT. 3:13-17.

LUKE 1:41 - "When Elisabeth heard the salutation of Mary, the babe [John] leaped in her womb, and Elisabeth was filled with the Holy Ghost."

JOHN 1:29 - John saw Jesus and said, "Behold the Lamb of God, which taketh away the sin of the world."

JOHN 1:34 - John: "I saw, and bare record that this is the Son of God."

[Did John not know, or did he know who Jesus was?]

**Perplexing:**

How was the imprisoned John able to hear about Jesus' works? How was he able to contact his disciples? If John as a fetus recognized the embryonic Jesus (LUKE 1:44), and later identified him as the son of God (JOHN 1:34), why did he now wonder whether Jesus was "he that should come?" Did John also forget that he and Jesus were cousins (LUKE 1:36-44)?

11:5 - JESUS: "THE BLIND RECEIVE THEIR SIGHT; THE LAME WALK; THE LEPERS ARE CLEANSED; THE DEAF HEAR; THE DEAD ARE RAISED UP, AND THE POOR HAVE THE GOSPEL PREACHED TO THEM."

**Contradiction:**
ACTS 26:23 - Paul: "Christ should suffer, and be the first that should rise from the dead...."
REV, 1:5 - Jesus Christ, who is the first begotten of the dead...."
[Did Jesus resurrect the dead, or was he the first to be resurrected?]

**Perplexing:** See under 9:35.

**Old Testament:**
ISA. 26:19 - Isaiah: "[When the LORD cometh] Thy dead men shall live, together with my dead body shall they arise...."
ISA. 35:4-6 - Isaiah: "...God will come with vengeance.... Then the eyes of the blind shall be opened, and the ears of the deaf shall be unstopped. Then shall the lame man leap as a hart, and the tongue of the dumb sing...."
ISA. 61:1 - Isaiah: "...the LORD hath anointed me to preach good tidings unto the meek...."
[The Septuagint and some other Bibles say, "the poor," instead of, "the meek."]

11:10 - JESUS: "THIS IS HE [JOHN], OF WHOM IT IS WRITTEN, 'I SEND MY MESSENGER BEFORE THY FACE, WHICH SHALL PREPARE THY WAY BEFORE THEE.'"

**Old Testament:**
MAL. 3:1 - "I will send My messenger, and he shall prepare the way before Me...the messenger of the covenant, whom ye delight in, shall come," saith the LORD of hosts."

**Perplexing:**
In JER. 23:24, the LORD said, ".... Do not I fill heaven and earth?"
[If God fills heaven and earth, and therefore, is everywhere, why does He need a messenger?]
See also under 3:3.

**History:**
The MAL. verse was written around 460 B.C. when the Israelites were under Persian domination, and ritual observances were lax. The implication was that the LORD would suddenly appear, preceded by his messenger, an angel. (Note how the verse has been changed from "prepare the way before Me," to "prepare thy way before thee.")

11:12 - JESUS: "FROM THE DAYS OF JOHN THE BAPTIST UNTIL NOW THE KINGDOM OF HEAVEN SUFFERETH VIOLENCE, AND THE VIOLENT TAKE IT BY FORCE."

**Perplexing:**
Why does God allow the kingdom of heaven to suffer violence and to be taken by the violent? Is God powerless to prevent the violence? Why does God fail to eliminate violence and the violent?

11:13-14 - JESUS: "ALL THE PROPHETS AND THE LAW PROPHESIED UNTIL JOHN. IF YE WILL RECEIVE IT, THIS IS ELIAS [ELIJAH] WHICH WAS TO COME."

**Old Testament:**
MAL. 4:5 - The LORD: "I will send you Elijah the prophet before the coming of the great and dreadful day of the LORD."

**Judaism:**
In Jewish belief, Elijah is expected to return to the earth immediately prior to the Day of the LORD.

**Contradiction:**
JOHN 1:21 - They [Jews] asked him [John], "Art thou Elias?" He saith, "I am not." [They:] "Art thou that prophet?" He answered, "No."
[Was, or was not John the prophet Elijah?]

**Perplexing:**
Why did Jesus say that John was Elijah? Why did John deny being Elijah? If John was Elijah, why did the Day of the LORD fail to come? Was the writer of the Gospel of John unaware that in MATT. Jesus had equated John with Elijah?

11:19 - JESUS: "THE SON OF MAN CAME EATING AND DRINKING, AND THEY SAY, 'BEHOLD, A MAN GLUTTONOUS, AND A WINEBIBBER....' BUT WISDOM IS JUSTIFIED OF HER CHILDREN."

**Perplexing:**
Jesus acknowledged that he drank wine. By so doing, he was complying with God's commandment in DEUT. 14:26, one of the more than 600 commandments given by God, that "Thou shalt bestow that money for whatsoever thy soul lusteth after...for wine, for strong drink, or whatsoever thy soul desireth...and thou shalt rejoice...." Why, then, do some Christians endeavor to impose prohibition or sanctions on drinking alcoholic beverages?

**Old Testament:**
DEUT. 14:26 - see above.
PROV. 1:20-33 - "Wisdom crieth without... "How long...will ye...fools hate knowledge? .... I have stretched out my hand, and no man regarded; ye have set at nought all my counsel.... .... Whoso hearkeneth unto me shall dwell safely, and shall be quiet from fear of evil."

11:20-23 - THEN BEGAN HE TO UPRAID THE CITIES WHEREIN MOST OF HIS MIGHTY WORKS WERE DONE, BECAUSE THEY REPENTED NOT; "WOE UNTO THEE, CHORZIN! WOE UNTO THEE, BETHSAIDA! .... IT SHALL BE MORE TOLERABLE FOR TYRE AND SIDON AT THE DAY OF JUDGMENT THAN FOR YOU. THOU, CAPERNAUM, WHICH ART EXALTED UNTO HEAVEN, SHALT BE BROUGHT DOWN TO HELL...."

**Contradiction:**
5:44 - Jesus: "Love your enemies; bless them that curse you; do good to them that hate you; pray for them which despitefully use, and persecute you."
6:14-15 - Jesus: "If ye forgive men their trespasses, you heavenly Father will forgive you; if ye forgive not, neither will your heavenly Father forgive your trespasses."
LUKE 6:27 - Jesus: "Love your enemies; do good to them which hate you."
[Did Jesus believe in upbraiding and cursing those he deemed to be his enemies, or did he believe in loving and forgiving them?]

**Perplexing:**
Did Jesus mean that all the people in the cities he cited did not repent? Did these people who did not repent

include all those that he healed or resurrected? If so, why did they not repent? Why did Jesus not order them to repent? Why did he fail to know that they would not repent? Why did he not perform a miracle to make them repent? Why did he not pray for them to repent? Is it possible that they had done nothing for which to repent?
If Jesus believed in loving and blessing enemies, why did he denounce the cities?
Was Jesus exempt from following his own teachings?

**Old Testament:**
ISA. 14:12-15 - Isaiah: "...O Lucifer, son of the morning! .... Thou hast said, 'I will ascend into heaven.... .... Thou shalt be brought down to hell, to the sides of the pit."
EZEK. 26:3-14 - Saith the Lord God, "I am against thee, O Tyrus [Tyre].... .... I will make thee like the top of a rock thou shalt be built no more...."
EZEK 26:21 - "...thou [Tyre] shalt be no more though thou be sought for, shalt thou never be found," saith the Lord God.
EZEK. 27:36 - The LORD: "thou [Tyre] never shalt be any more."
EZEK. 28:19 - The LORD: "never shalt thou [Tyre] be any more."
[Despite the LORD's prophecies that Tyre would be destroyed and not rebuilt, it was still in existence in Jesus' time.]

12:1 - JESUS WENT ON THE SABBATH DAY THROUGH THE CORN; HIS DISCIPLES WERE HUNGERED, AND BEGAN TO PLUCK THE EARS OF CORN, AND EAT. [THE INCIDENT OCCURRED AFTER JESUS GAVE HIS TWELVE DISCIPLES POWER TO HEAL SICKNESS AND SENT THEM FORTH TO PREACH IN 10:1-8.]

**Contradictions:**
MARK 2:23 - He [Jesus] went through cornfields on the sabbath day; his disciples began. ...to pluck the ears of corn. [The incident took place before Jesus sent the twelve disciples forth to preach and gave them power to heal sickness in MARK 3:14-15.]
[Did the disciples eat the ears of corn or did they just pluck them?]
LUKE 6:1 - ...he [Jesus] went through the cornfields; his disciples plucked the ears of corn, and did eat. [The incident occurred before Jesus gave his disciples power to cure diseases and sent them to preach in LUKE 9:1-2.]
[Did Jesus and his disciples go through the cornfields after, or before he had given them power to heal sickness and had sent them out to preach?]
MATT. 10:23 - [Jesus told his disciples] "... ye shall not have gone over the cities of Israel, till the Son of man be come."
[Did, or did not the disciples go over the cities of Israel?]
See also under 10:23.
MARK 6:30-31 - The apostles gathered unto Jesus, and told him what they had done, and taught. He said, "Come ye apart into a desert place...."
LUKE 9:10 - The apostles when they returned, told him all that they had done. He took them into a desert place...."
[When the apostles returned, did they go through a cornfield, or to a desert place?]

**Perplexing:**
How long were the disciples away? When did they return from their travels? How did they know where to find Jesus? Why were they so hungry that they ate raw grain? Why did not Jesus perform a miracle to provide food for them?

**History:**
Corn, a Western Hemisphere crop, was not present in the Middle east during biblical times. The word, "corn," used here, is correctly translated as "grain," in many other Bibles.

12:2 - WHEN THE PHARISEES SAW IT, THEY SAID UNTO HIM, "THY DISCIPLES DO WHAT IS NOT LAWFUL TO DO ON THE SABBATH DAY."

**Perplexing:**
Why were the Pharisees in the cornfield? What were they doing there? Why did they say that it is unlawful to hand pick grain on the Sabbath, when Jewish law permits it if one is hungry?

**Old Testament:**
DEUT. 23:25 - Moses: "When thou comest into the standing corn of thy neighbour, thou mayest pluck the ears with thine hand...."

12:3-4 - HE SAID, "HAVE YE NOT READ WHAT DAVID DID, WHEN HE WAS HUNGERED, AND THEY THAT WERE WITH HIM; HE ENTERED INTO THE HOUSE OF GOD, AND DID EAT THE SHEWBREAD, WHICH WAS NOT LAWFUL FOR HIM TO EAT, NEITHER FOR THEM WHICH WERE WITH HIM, BUT ONLY FOR THE PRIESTS?"

**Contradiction:**
I SAM. 21:1-6 - David came to Ahimelech the priest and asked for five loaves of bread for him and his servants. The priest said that only hallowed bread was available, but he would allow them to have it if the men had been kept from women. David said that women had been kept away from them for three days. The priest gave David the hallowed bread.
[Did David take the bread unlawfully as stated by Jesus, or was it given to him lawfully by the priest?]

**Judaism:**
Jewish law permitted a hungry army to eat even if the food was "unclean."

**Perplexing:**
Why did Jesus fail to cite the David incident correctly? Why did the Pharisees fail to correct him?

12:7 - JESUS: "IF YE HAD KNOWN WHAT THIS MEANETH, 'I WILL HAVE MERCY, NOT SACRIFICE,' YE WOULD NOT HAVE CONDEMNED THE GUILTLESS."

**Old Testament:** See under 9:13.

12:9-10 - WHEN HE DEPARTED THENCE, HE WENT INTO THEIR SYNAGOGUE; THERE WAS A MAN WHICH HAD HIS HAND WITHERED. THEY ASKED HIM, "IS IT LAWFUL TO HEAL ON THE SABBATH DAYS?"

**Contradiction:**
MARK 3:1-2 - He entered into the synagogue; there was a man which had a withered hand. They watched, whether he would heal him on the sabbath day....
[Was Jesus asked whether it was lawful to heal on the sabbath, or was he watched to see if he would heal the man?]

**History:**
The Pharisees did not oppose healing on the Sabbath. Their writings stated that healing activities were permitted on the Sabbath. They said that saving life took precedence over the law of the Sabbath. Pharisee law books used the same arguments that Jesus will use later to justify healing on the Sabbath.

**Perplexing:**
Why did Jesus fail to remind the Pharisees that their own teachings allowed healing to take place on the Sabbath? Why did the Pharisees fail to know that they did not object to healing on the Sabbath? Was the gospel writer ignorant of Pharisee beliefs, or was he trying to incite hostility towards them?

12:13 - SAITH HE TO THE MAN, "STRETCH FORTH THINE HAND." HE STRETCHED IT FORTH, AND IT WAS RESTORED WHOLE, LIKE THE OTHER.

**Old Testament:**
1 KINGS 13:6 - The king said unto the man of God, "Intreat the LORD thy God, and pray that my hand may be restored. The man of God besought the LORD, and the king's hand...became as it was before.

**Perplexing:**
Why did Jesus not ask the man if he had faith?

12:14 - THEN THE PHARISEES HELD A COUNCIL, HOW THEY MIGHT DESTROY HIM.

**Contradictions:**
MARK 3:6 - The Pharisees took counsel with the Herodians, how they might destroy him.
[Did the Pharisees counsel with themselves, or with the Herodians?]
LUKE 13:31 - ...there came Pharisees, saying unto him, "Get thee out, and depart hence, for Herod will kill thee."
[Did Pharisees want to destroy Jesus, or protect him?]

**Perplexing:**
Why did the Pharisees want to kill someone for doing what they taught was legitimate? Why did they not want to befriend someone who could perform such miracles as healing a withered hand and other ailments? Why were they not in awe of such a person? Why did they not want Jesus to heal their relatives and friends? If they became ill or infirm, would they not be glad to have Jesus help them? If the Pharisees wanted to kill Jesus, why in LUKE 13:31, did they urge him to flee because Herod wanted to kill him?

12:15-16 - WHEN JESUS KNEW IT, HE WITHDREW FROM THENCE; GREAT MULTITUDES FOLLOWED HIM, AND HE HEALED THEM ALL, AND CHARGED THEM THAT THEY SHOULD NOT MAKE HIM KNOWN.

**Contradiction:**
LUKE 6:12 - [After the withered hand incident] He went into a mountain to pray....
[Did Jesus heal multitudes, or did he go onto a mountain to pray?]

**History:**
There is no secular record of these great multitudes having been healed by Jesus?

**Perplexing:**
Why did Jesus flee? Why could his Father not protect him from the Pharisees? Why is there no historical documentation of these great multitudes having been healed by Jesus?

12:17-21 - JESUS: "THAT IT MIGHT BE FULFILLED WHICH WAS SPOKEN BY ESAIAS THE PROPHET, 'BEHOLD MY SERVANT, WHOM I HAVE CHOSEN; MY BELOVED, IN WHOM MY SOUL IS WELL PLEASED; I WILL PUT MY SPIRIT UPON HIM, AND HE SHALL SHEW JUDGMENT TO THE GENTILES. HE SHALL NOT STRIVE, NOR CRY; NEITHER SHALL ANY MAN HEAR HIS VOICE IN THE STREETS. A BRUISED REED SHALL HE NOT BREAK, AND SMOKING FLAX SHALL HE NOT QUENCH, TILL HE SEND FORTH JUDGMENT INTO VICTORY. IN HIS NAME SHALL THE GENTILES TRUST.'"

**Old Testament:**
ISA. 42:1-4 - The LORD: "My servant, whom I uphold, Mine elect, in whom My soul delighteth, I have put My spirit upon him; he shall bring forth judgment to the Gentiles. He shall not cry, nor lift up, nor cause his voice to be heard in the street. A bruised reed shall he not break; the smoking flax shall he not quench; he shall bring forth judgment unto truth. He shall not fail nor be discouraged, till he have set judgment in the earth; the isles shall wait for his law."

**Perplexing:**
Why did Jesus modify the ISA. verses and apply them to himself, when they were God's comments about Israel?
How did Jesus' words relate to the Pharisees' desire to kill him or to his healing the multitudes?

12:22 - THEN WAS BROUGHT UNTO HIM ONE POSSESSED WITH A DEVIL, BLIND AND DUMB; HE HEALED HIM...THE BLIND AND DUMB BOTH SPAKE AND SAW.

**History:** See under 4:24-25.

**Perplexing:**
Why is there no secular record of this amazing miracle? Who was the man? Why did neither he nor his relatives, friends, or others report the event? Why had the devil entered the man? How did it enter? Why did it make the man blind and dumb? Of what use could a blind and dumb man be to a devil?
See also under 4:24-25 and 9:32-33.

12:23 - ALL THE PEOPLE WERE AMAZED, AND SAID, "IS THIS NOT THE SON OF DAVID?"

**Perplexing:**
Why did the people not refer to Jesus as the son of Joseph? By referring to him as the "son of David," did they mean that they believed him to be descended from David, or that his father's name was David?
See also under 9:27.

12:24 - THE PHARISEES: "THIS FELLOW DOTH NOT CAST OUT DEVILS BUT BY BEELZEBUB THE PRINCE OF THE DEVILS."

**Pagan concept:** See under 4:24-25 and 10:25.

**Old Testament:** See under 10:25.

**Perplexing:** See under 4:24-25.

12:25 - JESUS KNEW THEIR THOUGHTS

**Contradictions:** See under 9:4.

12:30 - JESUS: "HE THAT IS NOT WITH ME IS AGAINST ME...."

**Perplexing:**
Why did Jesus assert that anyone not with him was against him? Why was he unable to accept the fact that such people would not necessarily be against him? Did he want to incite his followers to hate and possibly attack those who did not accept him?

12:31-32 - JESUS: "ALL MANNER OF SIN AND BLASPHEMY SHALL BE FORGIVEN UNTO MEN, BUT BLASPHEMY AGAINST THE HOLY GHOST SHALL NOT BE FORGIVEN. WHOSOEVER SPEAKETH A WORD AGAINST THE SON OF MAN, SHALL BE FORGIVEN, BUT WHOSOEVER SPEAKETH AGAINST THE HOLY GHOST, SHALL NOT BE FORGIVEN, NEITHER IN THIS WORLD, NEITHER THE WORLD TO COME."

**Perplexing:**
Why would the Holy Ghost, part of the Trinity with God and Jesus, care about blasphemy? Why is blasphemy against the Holy Ghost so serious that it cannot be forgiven? It cannot be harmed by blasphemy. Why cannot blasphemy be ignored or laughed at? Why cannot a merciful God forgive blasphemy against the Holy Ghost? How can blasphemy against one part of the Trinity not be blasphemy against the other parts? How can one commit blasphemy against only one part of the Trinity? Why would almighty God and/or the Holy Ghost care about what puny, short-lived human beings say?
Is not the Bible with its depravity, pornography, and accusations that God perpetrated heinous atrocities the worst possible blasphemy? Why did God create people who would commit blasphemy?
In 5:44, Jesus said, "Love your enemies; bless them that curse you; do good for them that hate you." In LUKE 6:27, Jesus also said, "Love your enemies; do good to them which hate you." Why does not the Holy Ghost abide by these teachings of Jesus? How can the parts of the Trinity disagree about anything? Why would God, who is reported to be merciful and/or abundant in goodness and kindness, in such verses as, EX. 34:6, NUM. 14:18, PS. 103:8. 117:2, and JOEL 2:15, condemn anyone to eternal damnation?
See also under 5:44 - Old Testament and Judaism.

**Pagan concept:**
Orphism, which originated between the 13th and 6th centuries B.C., introduced the concept of sin into Greek thought. The Orphics also believed in eternal life in a heaven in the sky.

12:34 - JESUS: "O GENERATION OF VIPERS, HOW CAN YE [PHARISEES], BEING EVIL, SPEAK GOOD THINGS?...."

**Contradiction:**
5:20 - Jesus: "Except your righteousness shall exceed the righteousness of the scribes and Pharisees, ye shall in no case enter the kingdom of heaven."
[Did Jesus say that the Pharisees were vipers and evil, or did he say that they were righteous?]

12:36 - JESUS: "EVERY IDLE WORD THAT MEN SHALL SPEAK, THEY SHALL GIVE ACCOUNT IN THE DAY OF JUDGMENT."

**Pagan parallel:** See under 10:14-15.

12:37 - JESUS: "BY THY WORDS THOU SHALT BE JUSTIFIED, AND BY THY WORDS THOU SHALT BE CONDEMNED."

**Contradictions:**
MATT. 16:27 - Jesus: "The Son of man shall reward every man according to his works."
ROM. 2:5-6 - Paul: "God, who will render to every man according to his deeds."
JAM. 2:24 - James: "Ye see then how by works a man is justified, not by faith only."
REV. 22:12 - "I come quickly, and my reward is with me, to give every man according as his work shall be."
[Is a person justified by words, or by works?]
ROM. 3:28 - Paul: "We conclude that a man is justified by faith without the deeds of the law."
GAL. 2:16 - Paul: "...we have believed in Jesus Christ, that we might be justified by the faith of Christ, not by the works of the law...."
[Are people justified by their words, or by faith?]
EPH. 2:8 - Paul: "By grace ye are saved through faith, and not of yourselves; it is the gift of God."
[Is a person justified by words, or by grace through faith?]
MARK 16:16 - Jesus: "...he that believeth not shall be damned."
[Is one condemned by one's words, or is one damned because of unbelief?]
There are many additional contradictory verses about how to be saved, justified, or condemned.

12:38-39 - CERTAIN SCRIBES AND PHARISEES ANSWERED, "MASTER, WE WOULD LIKE TO SEE A SIGN FROM THEE." HE SAID, "AN EVIL AND ADULTEROUS GENERATION SEEKETH A SIGN; THERE SHALL NO SIGN BE GIVEN TO IT, BUT THE SIGN OF THE PROPHET JONAS."

**Contradictions:**
MATT. 24:3-7 - ...the disciples came, saying, ".... What shall be the sign of thy coming, and the end of the world?" Jesus: ".... Many shall come in my name, saying, 'I am Christ....Ye shall hear of wars.... ...there shall be famines, pestilences, and earthquakes...."
[Did Jesus say that the only sign would be that of Jonah, or did he mention several signs?]
MARK 8:11-12 - The Pharisees came...seeking of him a sign.... He saith, "There shall no sign be given unto this generation."
[Did Jesus say that there would be the sign of Jonah, or no sign?]

**History:**
The Pharisees did not believe in signs.

**Perplexing:**
If the Pharisees did not believe in signs, why did they ask Jesus for a sign? Why did Jesus fail to remind them that they did not believe in signs?

12:40 - JESUS: "JONAS WAS THREE DAYS AND THREE NIGHTS IN THE WHALE'S BELLY, SO SHALL THE SON OF MAN BE THREE DAYS AND THREE NIGHTS IN THE HEART OF THE EARTH."

**Contradictions:**

JON. 1:17 - Jonah was in the belly of the fish three days and three nights.
[Was Jonah in the belly of a whale, or a fish?]
MATT. 16:21 - ...began Jesus to shew unto his disciples, how he must...be killed, and be raised the third day.
MATT. 17:23 - Jesus: "They shall kill him [Jesus], and the third day he shall be raised."
MATT. 20:19 - Jesus: "...the Gentiles...crucify him, and the third day he shall rise."
MARK 9:31 - Jesus: "...after he is killed, he shall rise the third day."
MARK 10:34 - Jesus: "They...shall kill him, and the third day he shall rise."
LUKE 9:22 - Jesus: "The Son of man must...be slain, and be raised the third day."
LUKE 18:33 - Jesus: "They shall...put him to death, and the third day he shall rise."
LUKE 24:7 - Two men (angels?): "The Son of man must be...crucified, and the third day rise."
LUKE 24:46 - Jesus: " it behooved Christ to rise from the dead the third day."
1 COR. 15:4 - Paul: "He [Jesus] was buried, and rose the third day...."
[Did Jesus say that he would spend three days and three nights in the heart of the earth, or that he would rise the third day?]
MARK 8:31 - "He began to teach them, that the Son of man must...be killed, and after three days rise."
[Did Jesus say that he would spend three days and nights in the heart of the earth, or that he would rise some time after three days?]
MATT. 27:60; MARK 15:46; and LUKE 23:53 - Joseph placed Jesus' body in a sepulchre near the surface of the earth.
JOHN 19:41-42 - Joseph and Nicodemus placed Jesus' body in a sepulchre near the surface of the earth.
[Was Jesus to be three days and nights in the heart of the earth, or in a sepulchre near the surface of the earth?]

**Perplexing:**

Why did Jesus say that he would spend three days and nights in the heart of the earth, when he would spend only about one and a half days (Friday evening until before dawn on Sunday) in a near surface sepulchre according to MATT. 27:57 - 28:6; MARK 15:42 - 16:6; LUKE 23:54 - 24:6; and JOHN 19:42 - 20:8? Why did he fail to spend three full days and nights in the heart of the earth?

**Old Testament:**

EX. 10:22 - ...there was a thick darkness in all Egypt for three days.
EX. 19:16-17 - On the third day in the morning Moses brought forth the people...to meet with God....
2 KINGS 20:5 - The LORD: "Tell Hezekiah on the third day thou shalt go up unto the house of the LORD...."
EST. 5:1- On the third day, Esther put on her royal apparel....
HOS. 6:2 - Hosea: "After two days will He revive us; in the third day he will raise us up...."

**Pagan parallels:**

Tammuz spent three days and nights in the earth before being resurrected. Baal was resurrected after being entombed for three days and nights.

12:41 - JESUS: "THE MEN OF NINEVAH SHALL RISE IN JUDGMENT WITH THIS GENERATION AND CONDEMN IT...."

**History:**
The origins of Ninevah are not known, but it was already in existence in the 6th millennium B.C. The city was located by the Tigris River and served as the capital of Assyria.

12:42 - JESUS: "THE QUEEN OF THE SOUTH SHALL RISE UP IN THE JUDGMENT WITH THIS GENERATION, AND CONDEMN IT; SHE CAME FROM THE UTTERMOST PARTS OF THE EARTH TO HEAR THE WISDOM OF SOLOMON...."

**Perplexing:**
Who was the "queen of the south?" Did Jesus' reference to her visit to Solomon mean that she was the Queen of Sheba (I KINGS 10:1)?

**History:**
The Ptolemaic kings of Egypt were called, "Kings of the South." It is not known whether the Queen of Sheba was Egyptian, Ethiopian, or Arabian.

12:43-45 - JESUS: "WHEN THE UNCLEAN SPIRIT IS GONE OUT OF A MAN, HE WALKETH THROUGH DRY PLACES, SEEKING REST, AND FINDETH NONE. HE SAITH, "I WILL RETURN UNTO MY HOUSE FROM WHENCE I CAME OUT.... THEN HE TAKETH SEVEN OTHER SPIRITS...AND THEY ENTER IN AND DWELL THERE.... ...."

**Perplexing:**
Where does an unclean spirit reside when it is not in a person? Is an unclean spirit visible? REV. 16:13 said that three unclean spirits were like frogs. Do all unclean spirits look like frogs? Why does an unclean spirit need rest?
See also under 4:24-25.

**History:** See under 4:24-25.

**Pagan parallel:**
There are numerous Babylonian references about seven demons living together.

12:46-50 - WHILE HE TALKED TO THE PEOPLE, HIS MOTHER AND BRETHREN STOOD WITHOUT, DESIRING TO SPEAK WITH HIM. ONE SAID, "THY MOTHER AND BRETHREN STAND WITHOUT DESIRING TO SPEAK WITH THEE." HE SAID, "WHO IS MY MOTHER AND MY BRETHREN?" .... "WHOSOEVER SHALL DO THE WILL OF MY FATHER IN HEAVEN, IS MY BROTHER, SISTER, AND MOTHER." [THIS INCIDENT OCCURRED LONG AFTER JESUS CAST DEVILS INTO SWINE IN 8:32.]

**Contradiction:**
MARK 3:31-35 - The incident is reported to have occurred before Jesus cast devils into swine in 5:13.
LUKE 8:19-21 - The incident is reported to have occurred before Jesus cast devils into a herd of swine in LUKE 8:33.
[Did Jesus refuse to speak with his mother and brethren after, or before casting devils into a herd of swine?]

**Perplexing:**

Why did Jesus refuse to speak with his mother and brethren? Why did Jesus disobey the commandment to honor one's father and mother? Did Jesus' comment mean that his mother and brethren were not doing the will of his Father?

13:1-9 - ...JESUS SAT BY THE SEASIDE. GREAT MULTITUDES WERE GATHERED UNTO HIM, SO HE WENT INTO A SHIP...THE MULTITUDE STOOD ON THE SHORE. HE SPAKE UNTO THEM IN PARABLES, SAYING, "A SOWER WENT FORTH TO SOW...." [THE INCIDENT OCCURRED AFTER JESUS CAST DEVILS INTO A HERD OF SWINE.]

**Contradictions:**

MARK 4:2-8 - He taught them many things by parables..."There went out a sower to sow.... ...."
[The incident occurred before Jesus cast devils into a herd of swine.]
LUKE 8:4-8 - When much people...were come to him...he spake by a parable; "A sower went out to sow.... ...."
[The incident occurred before Jesus cast devils into a herd of swine in LUKE 8:33.]
[Did, or did not Jesus go onto a ship to recite the parable?]
[Did the incident occur after, or before Jesus cast devils into a herd of swine?]

**History:**

Teaching by parables was an ancient Jewish technique that was used by the Pharisees.

**Pagan parallel:**

Buddha taught by means of parables.

13:10-13 - THE DISCIPLES: "WHY SPEAKEST THOU UNTO THEM IN PARABLES?" HE SAID, "BECAUSE IT IS GIVEN UNTO YOU TO KNOW THE MYSTERIES OF THE KINGDOM OF HEAVEN, BUT TO THEM IT IS NOT GIVEN. .... THEREFORE SPEAK I TO THEM IN PARABLES, BECAUSE THEY SEEING SEE NOT, AND HEARING HEAR NOT, NEITHER DO THEY UNDERSTAND."

**Contradictions:**

MATT. 9:13 - Jesus: "...I am not come to call the righteous, but sinners to repentance."
MARK 2:17 and LUKE 5:32 - Jesus: "...I came not to call the righteous, but sinners to repentance."
[Did Jesus want to restrict knowledge about the kingdom of heaven, or did he want to call sinners to repentance?]
JOHN 3:17 - God sent not His Son into the world to condemn the world, but that the world through him might be saved.
[Did Jesus want to prevent people from understanding his teachings, and, hence, from being saved, or did he come to save the world?]
See also under 9:13.

**Perplexing:**

Why did Jesus want to restrict knowledge about "the mysteries of the kingdom of heaven" to his disciples? Why did he want his teachings to be secret? How could people kept in ignorance of the kingdom of heaven be saved? If Jesus did not want people to know about what he was speaking, what was the point of him coming into the world? How did Jesus decide when, where, and to whom to speak in parables?
Does God have a moral right to punish people, if His Son was responsible for keeping them from knowing what He wanted?

**Pagan parallels:**
In some pagan religions, which became known as "mystery religions," the doctrines and mysteries of the faith were revealed only to initiates. Thus, outsiders were kept in ignorance about their rites, doctrines, etc.

13:14-15 - JESUS: "IN THEM IS FULFILLED THE PROPHECY OF ESAIAS, 'BY HEARING YE SHALL HEAR, AND SHALL NOT UNDERSTAND; SEEING YE SHALL SEE, AND NOT PERCEIVE. THIS PEOPLE'S HEART IS WAXED GROSS; THEIR EARS ARE DULL OF HEARING; THEIR EYES HAVE CLOSED, LEST AT ANY TIME THEY SHOULD SEE, HEAR, UNDERSTAND...BE CONVERTED, AND I SHOULD HEAL THEM.'"

**Old Testament:**
ISA. 6:9-11 - He [the LORD] said [to Isaiah], "Go, and tell this people, 'Hear ye, but understand not; see but perceive not.' Make the heart of this people fat, their ears heavy, and shut their eyes, lest they see, hear, understand...convert, and be healed." Said I, "Lord, how long?" He answered, "Until the cities be wasted without inhabitant...."

**Perplexing:**
Why did Jesus take the verses out of context? Why did Jesus not want the people to understand, be converted, and healed?

13:17 - JESUS: "MANY PROPHETS AND RIGHTEOUS MEN HAVE DESIRED TO SEE THOSE THINGS WHICH YE SEE, AND HAVE NOT SEEN THEM...."

**Contradictions:** See under 10:41.

13:22 - JESUS: "...THE DECEITFULNESS OF RICHES CHOKE THE WORD [OF THE KINGDOM]. AND HE [THE WORD] BECOMETH UNFRUITFUL."

**Perplexing:**
If riches "choke the word" and make it unfruitful, why do most followers of Jesus, especially the clergy, seek and try to acquire as many riches as possible?"

13:31-32 - .... JESUS: "THE KINGDOM OF HEAVEN IS LIKE A GRAIN OF MUSTARD SEED... WHICH IS THE LEAST OF ALL SEEDS...."

**Perplexing:**
Why did Jesus say that the mustard seed was the smallest of all seeds? Was he ignorant about the seeds of many fungi, some cacti, and other plants that are smaller than those of mustard?

13:35 - JESUS: "...WHICH WAS SPOKEN BY THE PROPHET, 'I WILL OPEN MY MOUTH IN PARABLES; I WILL UTTER THINGS WHICH HAVE BEEN KEPT SECRET FROM THE FOUNDATION OF THE WORLD.'"

**Old Testament:**
PS. 78:2-3 - "I will open my mouth in a parable; I will utter dark sayings of old, which we have heard and known, and our fathers have told us."

**Perplexing:**
Why did Jesus attribute the PS. verses to a prophet?

**History:** See under 13:1-9.

**Pagan parallel:** See under 13:1-9.

13:38-39 - JESUS: "...THE GOOD SEED ARE THE CHILDREN OF THE KINGDOM; THE TARES ARE THE CHILDREN OF THE WICKED ONE; THE ENEMY THAT SOWED THEM IS THE DEVIL...."

**Contradiction:**
MATT. 8:12 - Jesus: "The children of the kingdom shall be cast into outer darkness; there shall be weeping and gnashing of teeth."
[Are the children of the kingdom the good seed, or are they to be cast into outer darkness?]

**Perplexing:**
Why could Jesus not reform the children of the wicked one? Why did God allow the wicked one to exist? Since God created the wicked one, is He not morally responsible for the devil's wickedness? Is He, then, not also wicked?
If the devil is the wicked one, what wickedness has he perpetrated? Jesus has not accused him of violating any of the Old Testament commandments or any of those given by Jesus. If the devil is the wicked one, why does the Bible accuse God of being responsible for, among other things, (1) a deluge that killed millions of people including unborn embryos en utero (GEN. 6 - 8); (2) killing all the firstborn Egyptian children and cattle after having hardened the pharaoh's heart (EX. 12:29; 11:10)); (3) sending a plague that killed 14,700 Israelites (NUM. 16:44-49); (4) ordering the decapitation of people and the displaying of their heads in daylight (Num. 25:4); (5) killing people with a great slaughter (JOSH. 10:10); (6) killing 50,070 men for looking in the ark of the LORD (1 SAM. 6:19); (7) ordering the killing of all Amalekite men, women, infants, and animals (1 SAM. 15:3); (8) killing Uzzah for touching the ark of the LORD to steady it (2 SAM. 6:6-7); (9) killing Bathsheba's and David's baby because of their adultery (2 SAM. 12:14-19); (10) creating evil (ISA. 45:7); (11) ordering the killing of all the old, the young, the girls, women, and babies in Jerusalem (EZEK. 9:5-6); (11) committing adultery and possibly rape with Mary (MATT. 1:18 and LUKE 1:35); (12) and many more comparable atrocities. See also EX. 32:27, NUM. 11:1, 11:33, 21:6, DEUT. 7:16, 1 SAM. 6:19, JER. 11:22, 25:29, EZEK. 5:17, and many other comparable verses. See also under 4:3 and 8:12.

**Pagan parallels:** See under 4:3.

13:40 - JESUS: "AS THE TARES ARE GATHERED AND BURNED IN THE FIRE, SO SHALL IT BE IN THE END OF THIS WORLD."

**Perplexing:**
Why are the tares, the children of the wicked one, to be burned in the fire? What have they done that is wicked? What did Jesus consider wickedness to be? Whatever they may have done, was it not what God created them to do?
By burning the tares, instead of reforming them, is Jesus not violating his command in MATT. 7:12 - "All things whatsoever ye would that men should do to you, do ye so to them; this is the law and the prophets?"

**Old Testament:**
PS. 106:18 - "A flame was kindled in their company; the flame burned up the wicked."

13:41-42 - JESUS: "THE SON OF MAN SHALL SEND FORTH HIS ANGELS; THEY SHALL GATHER OUT OF HIS KINGDOM ALL THINGS THAT OFFEND, AND THEM WHICH DO INIQUITY, AND SHALL CAST THEM INTO A FURNACE OF FIRE; THERE SHALL BE WAILING AND GNASHING OF TEETH."

**Perplexing:**
Why are some people consigned to burn in a furnace, whereas others are cast into outer darkness (8:12)?
Why are angels needed to cast people into a furnace? Why cannot Jesus or his Father do it?
Is God morally justified in casting people into a furnace for doing what He knew they would do and what He allowed them to do? Is a God who cannot or will not prevent iniquity, a good god?
See also under 13:40.

**Old Testament:**
GEN. 15:17 - ...when the sun went down, and it was dark, a smoking furnace...passed between those pieces.
PS. 9:17 - "The wicked shall be turned into hell, and all nations that forget God."
PS. 145:20 - "The LORD preserveth all that love Him, but all the wicked will He destroy."
See also under 13:40.

**Pagan concept:**
The belief in fiery punishment is found in many pre-Christian religions. For one example, in Egyptian belief, the deity Afu-Ra cast his enemies and the wicked into a fiery hell.

**Dead Sea Scrolls:**
"Cursed are thou for all thy wicked guilty works. .... Cursed are thou, beyond the hope of mercy. ...mayest thou be damned in the gloom of the fire eternal." (In "The Manual of Discipline.")

13:43 - JESUS: "THEN SHALL THE RIGHTEOUS SHINE FORTH AS THE SUN IN THE KINGDOM OF THEIR FATHER...."

**Contradiction:** See under 10:41.

**Perplexing:** See under 10:41.

13:49-50 - JESUS: "AT THE END OF THE WORLD, THE ANGELS SHALL COME, AND SEVER THE WICKED FROM AMONG THE JUST, AND CAST THEM INTO THE FURNACE OF FIRE...."

**Perplexing:** See under 13:38-39.

**Pagan concept**: See under 13:41-42.

**Old Testament:** See under 13:40 and 13:41-42.

**Dead Sea Scrolls:** See under 13:41-42.

13:54 - WHEN HE WAS COME INTO HIS OWN COUNTRY, HE TAUGHT IN THEIR SYNAGOGUES....

**Perplexing:**
What was Jesus' own country? Was it all of Galilee, just Nazareth, or just Capernaum?
See also under 4:23.

13:55 - PEOPLE: "IS NOT THIS THE CARPENTER'S SON? ...."

**Contradiction:**
MARK 6:3 - People: "Is this not the carpenter...."
[Did people say that Jesus was the carpenter's son, or that he was the carpenter?]

13:56 - PEOPLE: "HIS SISTERS, ARE THEY NOT ALL WITH US?"

**Perplexing:**
How many sisters did Jesus have? Why were they not cited by name?

13:58 - HE DID NOT MANY MIGHTY WORKS THERE BECAUSE OF THEIR UNBELIEF.

**Contradiction:**
MARK 6:5-6 - He could there do no mighty work, save that he laid his hands upon a few sick folk, and healed them. He marvelled because of their unbelief.
[Did Jesus opt not to do any mighty work because of the people's unbelief, or was he unable to do mighty work because of their unbelief?]

**Perplexing:**
Why did Jesus not work miracles because of the people's unbelief? Would not performing miracles for those who lacked belief have been an excellent way to elicit belief? Was belief a prerequisite for the performance of miracles by Jesus? Was Jesus just being spiteful, because the people did not believe?

14:1 - AT THAT TIME HEROD THE TETRARCH HEARD OF THE FAME OF JESUS.

**Perplexing:**
Why did Herod not hear about Jesus before now, considering that multitudes had already witnessed his miracles?

**History:**
After the death of King Herod, the Romans eliminated the "kingdom," and divided it into four parts, each one governed by one of King Herod's sons who was titled, a "tetrarch." The tetrarch mentioned by MATT. is Antipas.

14:2 - HEROD SAID UNTO HIS SERVANTS, "THIS IS JOHN THE BAPTIST; HE IS RISEN FROM THE DEAD, AND THEREFORE MIGHTY WORKS DO SHEW FORTH THEMSELVES IN HIM."

**Contradiction:**
LUKE 9:7 - Herod the tetrarch heard of all that was done by him [Jesus]; he was perplexed, because it was

said of some, that John was risen from the dead.
[Did Herod, or did some unidentified individuals say that John had risen from the dead?]

**Perplexing:**
Jesus had been traveling throughout the region performing miracles witnessed by multitudes prior to and during the time that John was imprisoned. How then could Herod not have heard about Jesus' accomplishments? How could he possibly believe that Jesus was a resurrected John the Baptist?
See also under 14:1.

14:3-4 - HEROD HAD LAID HOLD ON JOHN...AND PUT HIM IN PRISON FOR HERODIAS' SAKE, HIS BROTHER PHILIP'S WIFE. JOHN SAID, "IT IS NOT LAWFUL FOR THEE TO HAVE HER."

**History:**
Herodias was the daughter of Aristobulus, one of Herod Antipas' brothers; she married another brother - Philip, but divorced him to marry Antipas. Although each of the brothers had a different mother, Antipas was her uncle (actually half-uncle) and, consequently, his relationship with her was viewed by some to be incestuous even though sexual relations between an uncle and niece were not specifically prohibited by LEVITICUS. (LEV. 18:12, however, did prohibit such relations between an aunt and nephew.)
According to Josephus, John was imprisoned by Herod Antipas out of fear that John was causing political trouble that could lead to a rebellion against him. It was also contrary to Essene doctrine for a person to have more than one spouse in a lifetime; some historians believe that John was an Essene.
See also under 3:1-2.

**Perplexing:** See under 3:1-2.

**Old Testament:**
LEV. 18:16 - The LORD: "Thou shalt not uncover the nakedness of thy brother's wife...."

14:5 - WHEN HE WOULD HAVE PUT HIM TO DEATH, HE FEARED THE MULTITUDE, BECAUSE THEY COUNTED HIM AS A PROPHET.

**History:**
According to Josephus, John was killed immediately after his imprisonment.

14:6-8 - WHEN HEROD'S BIRTHDAY WAS KEPT, THE DAUGHTER OF HERODIAS DANCED AND PLEASED HEROD. HE PROMISED WITH AN OATH TO GIVE HER WHATSOEVER SHE WOULD ASK. SHE, BEING BEFORE INSTRUCTED OF HER MOTHER, SAID, "GIVE ME JOHN BAPTIST'S HEAD IN A CHARGER."

**Contradiction:**
MARK 6:22-24 - When the daughter of Herodias danced and pleased Herod...the king said, "Ask of me whatsoever thou wilt, and I will give it thee...." She said unto her mother, "What shall I ask?" She said, "The head of John the Baptist."
[Did Herodias instruct her daughter beforehand to ask for John's head, or did she tell her after she finished dancing?]

**Perplexing:**
How did Herodias know beforehand that her daughter would be asked to dance, that it would please Herod, and that he would promise to give her whatever she might ask for?

**History:**
Herodias' daughter was named Salome and was the child from her previous marriage to Herod Antipas' brother Philip.

14:9 - THE KING WAS SORRY, NEVERTHELESS...HE COMMANDED IT BE GIVEN TO HER.

**Contradiction:**
MATT. 14:5 - When he would have put him to death, he feared the multitude....
[Was Herod sorry to have John killed, or did he want to have him killed?]

**History:**
This Herod was a tetrarch, not a king.
See also under 14:1.

14:10-12 - HE SENT, AND BEHEADED JOHN IN THE PRISON. HIS HEAD WAS BROUGHT...AND GIVEN TO THE DAMSEL; SHE BROUGHT IT TO HER MOTHER. HIS DISCIPLES CAME, TOOK THE BODY, BURIED IT, AND WENT AND TOLD JESUS.

**Perplexing:**
How did John's disciples find out that John had been killed? How were they able to obtain his body? What did Herodias do with John's head? Did the disciples obtain and bury the head with the body? Why did they tell Jesus? Why did Jesus not come to John's assistance by performing a miracle to free him? Why did he not resurrect John? Why did Jesus fail to denounce Herod for killing his cousin (see LUKE 1:36)?
If John the Baptist was Elijah, as Jesus implied in 11:13-14 and in 17:12-13, how could he be killed? According to MAL 4:5, Elijah was to come prior to the day of the LORD. Did John's death mean that the day of the LORD would not come? Was Jesus wrong in equating John with Elijah? (See JOHN 1:21 - John denied being Elijah.)

14:13 - WHEN JESUS HEARD OF IT, HE DEPARTED BY SHIP INTO A DESERT PLACE APART; WHEN THE PEOPLE HEARD THEREOF, THEY FOLLOWED HIM ON FOOT OUT OF THE CITIES.

**Contradiction:**
JOHN 6:1-3 - Jesus went over the sea of Galilee.... A great multitude followed him.... Jesus went up into a mountain, and sat with his disciples.
[Did Jesus go to a desert place, or to a mountain?]

**Perplexing:**
Why did Jesus leave after learning about John's death? Would not resurrecting a decapitated body have been a sufficient miracle to induce belief even in Herod?
How did the people know where to go? How far did they have to travel? How long did it take over 5000 people (see 14:21) on foot to reach Jesus' location? Why did the Romans allow this mass movement of people to take place, especially since such a large number would have clogged the roads and footpaths?

14:14 - JESUS SAW A GREAT MULTITUDE, WAS MOVED WITH COMPASSION TOWARD THEM, AND HEALED THEIR SICK.

**Perplexing:**
How were the sick able to travel to Jesus? How many were there? How long did it take Jesus to heal them all?

14:15-17 - WHEN IT WAS EVENING, HIS DISCIPLES CAME, SAYING, "THIS IS A DESERT PLACE...SEND THE MULTITUDE AWAY, THAT THEY MAY GO INTO THE VILLAGES, AND BUY VICTUALS." JESUS SAID, "THEY NEED NOT DEPART; GIVE THEM TO EAT." THEY SAY, "WE HAVE BUT FIVE LOAVES, AND TWO FISHES."

**Contradictions:**
JOHN 6:5-9 - Jesus...saith unto Philip, "Whence shall we buy bread, that these may eat? .... Philip answered, "Two hundred pennyworth of bread is not sufficient for them...." Andrew...saith, "There is a lad here, which hath five barley loaves, and two small fishes, but what are they among so many?"
[Did Jesus tell the disciples to give the multitude food, or did he ask Philip where bread could be purchased?]
[Did the disciples say that they had five loaves and two fish, or did Andrew say that a lad had five loaves and two fish?]

**Perplexing:**
Why did Jesus not know how much food was available? How long had the people been with Jesus? Did they have nothing to eat during this time? Did not some of them get hungry? Why did they stay? What was Jesus doing? The writer does not say that he was teaching or healing.

**Judaism:**
In Jewish tradition, fish were associated with the Messiah.

**Pagan parallels:**
Many pagan deities such as Ea, Apollo, Vishnu, and Aphrodite were associated with fish.

14:19 - HE COMMANDED THE MULTITUDE TO SIT ON THE GRASS, TOOK THE FIVE LOAVES, AND TWO FISHES, AND LOOKING UP TO HEAVEN, BLESSED, BRAKE, AND GAVE THE LOAVES TO HIS DISCIPLES, AND THE DISCIPLES TO THE MULTITUDE.

**Contradictions:**
MATT. 14:13 - Jesus...departed...into a desert place...the people followed....
MATT. 14:15 - his disciples came saying, "This is a desert place...."
MARK 6:32 - They departed into a desert place....
LUKE 9:10 - ...He took them...into a desert place....
[Were Jesus and the people in a place with enough grass for over 5000 people to sit, or were they in a desert place?]
MARK 6:39 - He commanded them [his disciples] to make all sit down....
LUKE 9:14 - .... He said to his disciples, "Make them sit down...."
[Did Jesus command the multitude to sit down, or did he order his disciples to make them sit down?]

**Perplexing:**
Why was it necessary for the multitude to be told to sit? How large a grassy area would have been needed to seat over 5000 people (14:21)? Why were the people not already sitting? Were they not tired (exhausted) from traveling by foot to reach Jesus? What if any sanitary facilities were available for the people to use to avoid polluting the area? As Jews traditionally washed their hands before eating, where could thousands of people go to wash? How could thousands of people hear Jesus? Did the disciples also distribute the fish? Were the fish eaten raw, dried, or were they cooked? What did the people have to drink? Was fresh water available? Where? Did they not get thirsty on the desert or after eating dry bread and fish? How long did it take the disciples to distribute the food to the multitude? Did each disciple carry a basket in which the bread and fish reproduced? If there were 5000 men plus an unspecified number of women and children, it may be estimated that there were at least 6000 people. Each disciple, therefore. would have had to feed about 500 individuals. If it took only 20 seconds to feed and move from one person to another, it would have taken about two hours and 45 minutes for all the people to be fed. What did those waiting to be fed do? What did Jesus do?

**Old Testament:**
1 KINGS 17:11-16 - Elijah used a handful of meal and some oil to feed an unspecified number of people for many days.
2 KINGS 4:42-44 - Elisha fed 100 men with 20 loaves of barley and some corn.

14:20 - THEY DID ALL EAT, AND WERE FILLED; THEY TOOK UP OF THE FRAGMENTS THAT REMAINED 12 BASKETS FULL.

**Perplexing:**
Why were there fragments left over? Why did Jesus not know how much food would be needed so that there would be no leftovers? How long did it take the disciples to collect the leftovers? How large were the baskets? From where were they obtained? What happened to the fish bones and skin, and bread crumbs? Were they also collected, or were they just left as litter? How long did it take the more than 5000 people to finish eating?

14:21 - THEY THAT HAD EATEN WERE ABOUT 5000 MEN, BESIDE WOMEN AND CHILDREN.

**Contradiction:**
MARK 6:44 - They that did eat were about 5000 men.
LUKE 9:14 - They were about 5000 men.
JOHN 6:10 - .... The men sat down, in number about 5000.
[Were there about 5000 men and an unspecified number of women and children, or were there just about 5000 men?]

**Perplexing:**
Why was there no secular record made of this miraculous event, especially when such a large number of people were involved? Who counted the number of people?

14:22-23 - JESUS CONSTRAINED HIS DISCIPLES TO GET INTO A SHIP, AND GO BEFORE HIM UNTO THE OTHER SIDE, WHILE HE SENT THE MULTITUDES AWAY. WHEN HE HAD SENT THE MULTITUDES AWAY, HE WENT INTO A MOUNTAIN APART TO PRAY; WHEN THE EVENING WAS COME, HE WAS THERE ALONE.

**Contradictions:**
MATT. 14:15 - When it was evening, his disciples came to him....
MARK 6:35 - When the day was now far spent, his disciples came unto him....
[Was it evening after, or before the multitudes had eaten and departed?
LUKE 9:18 - [After the fragments had been put into 12 baskets] As he was alone praying, his disciples were with him; he asked them, "Whom say the people that I am?" [The disciples were not told to board a ship.]
[Did Jesus send his disciples away by ship and then go onto a mountain to pray alone, or did his disciples remain with him while he went onto a mountain to pray?]
JOHN 6:14-17 - [After the fragments had been put into 12 baskets] Those men, when they had seen the miracle, said, "This is that prophet that should come into the world." When Jesus perceived that they would come and take him by force to make him a king, he departed onto a mountain alone. When even was come, his disciples...entered a ship, and went over the sea toward Capernaum.
[Did Jesus send the multitudes away, or did they remain saying that he was a prophet and want to take him by force to make him a king?]
[Did Jesus go onto a mountain to pray alone, or did he flee to a mountain to escape from the multitude?]

**Perplexing:**
How were the thousands of people able to travel and find their way home in the dark? Why did Jesus send the disciples ahead of him? Did ships sail at night? Why did Jesus pray? As the Son of God, he knew what was to occur and why. He also said in MATT. 6:8, "...your Father knoweth what things ye have need of before ye ask Him." Why then bother praying? In JOHN 10:30, he said, "I and my Father are one," and in MATT. 28:19 he identified himself as part of the Trinity. Therefore, If the JOHN and MATT. verses are accepted, Jesus was praying to himself. If God knows beforehand what you want, as He should, why does He want people to pray (beg) for something that He already knows He will or will not give?

14:25 - IN THE FOURTH WATCH OF THE NIGHT JESUS WENT UNTO THEM, WALKING ON THE SEA.

**Old Testament:**
GEN. 1:2 - ...the Spirit of God moved upon the face of the waters.
JOB 9:8 - Which [God] alone...treadeth upon the waves of the sea.

**Perplexing:**
Why did Jesus walk on the water rather than take another ship? Were no other ships available? Why was this the only time that Jesus is said to have walked on water? Why could Jesus not fly to the ship or materialize on it? Why did LUKE not consider Jesus' feat of walking on water important enough to include in his gospel?

**Contradiction:**
JOHN 9:4 - Jesus: "I must work the works of Him who sent me, while it is day; the night cometh when no man can work."
[Could, or could not Jesus perform miracles at night?]

**Pagan parallel:**
A disciple of Buddha walked across the water of a river.

14:26 - WHEN THE DISCIPLES SAW HIM WALKING ON THE SEA, THEY WERE TROUBLED, SAYING, "IT IS A SPIRIT"; THEY CRIED OUT IN FEAR.

**Perplexing:**
How were the disciples able to see Jesus walking on the sea at night with the ship being tossed by the waves and wind (14:24)?

14:27-28 - JESUS SPAKE, "BE OF GOOD CHEER; IT IS I; BE NOT AFRAID. "PETER SAID, "LORD, IF IT BE THOU, BID ME COME UNTO THEE ON THE WATER."

**Perplexing:**
With a strong wind and heavy sea tossing the ship, how were Jesus and Peter able to hear each other and converse? See also under 14:26.

14:29-31 - HE SAID, "COME." WHEN PETER WAS COME DOWN OUT OF THE SHIP, HE WALKED ON THE WATER, TO GO TO JESUS. WHEN HE SAW THE WIND BOISTEROUS, HE WAS AFRAID; BEGINNING TO SINK, HE CRIED, "LORD, SAVE ME." JESUS...CAUGHT HIM, AND SAID, "O THOU OF LITTLE FAITH, WHEREFORE DIDST THOU DOUBT?"

**Perplexing:**
How was Peter able to step off a ship being tossed by heavy seas and strong wind? Why did the other gospels not report the amazing occurrence of Peter walking on the water?

**Pagan parallel:**
One of Buddha's disciples was walking across a river when he saw the waves, became frightened, and began to sink. He regained his faith in Buddha and was able to finish walking on the water until he reached the opposite shore.

**History:**
Buddhist missionaries traveled through the Middle East as early as the second century B.C. bringing with them the Buddhist religion and stories. (Some historians believe that the Jewish Essene sect evolved from Buddhism.)

14:32 - WHEN THEY WERE COME INTO THE SHIP....

**Perplexing:**
Were not both Jesus and Peter soaking wet from being on the water with waves being tossed around them? Did they change clothes? Did they have extra clothing with them? Did they continue to wear the wet clothes? How were they able to get dry?

14:33 - THEN THEY THAT WERE ON THE SHIP CAME...SAYING, "...THOU ART THE SON OF GOD."

**Perplexing:**
Why is this the first time that people, rather than the devil or unclean spirits, called Jesus the "Son of God?" See also under 4:3.

14:34 - ...THEY CAME INTO THE LAND OF GENNESARET.

**Contradiction:**
LUKE 9:18-29 - [After the feeding miracle] Jesus spoke to the disciples and then took Peter, John, and James to a mountain where his countenance was altered.
[After the feeding miracle, did Jesus and the disciples go by ship to Gennesaret, or did they remain on land and go to a mountain where Jesus' countenance was altered?]
JOHN 6:16-24 - The disciples entered into a ship; Jesus walked on the water to join them, and they arrived in Capernaum.
[Did Jesus and the disciples go to Gennesaret (a town on the northwest part of the Sea of Galilee south of Capernaum), or to Capernaum?]

14:35-36 - WHEN THE MEN OF THAT PLACE HAD KNOWLEDGE OF HIM, THEY WENT INTO ALL THE COUNTRY, BROUGHT UNTO HIM ALL THAT WERE DISEASED, AND BESOUGHT HIM THAT THEY MIGHT TOUCH THE HEM OF HIS GARMENT; AS MANY AS TOUCHED WERE MADE PERFECTLY WHOLE.

**Contradictions:**
MARK 6:56 - Withersoever he entered villages, cities, or country, they laid the sick in the streets...as many as touched him were made whole.
[Did the men go around the country and bring the sick to Jesus, or did Jesus travel around the country to where the sick were?]
JOHN 6:22-40 - The people who participated in the feeding miracle took ships and went to Capernaum to seek Jesus. He entered into a discourse with them. No healing was said to have occurred.
[Did Jesus heal people in Gennesaret, or did he converse in Capernaum with people for whom he had recently performed the feeding miracle?]

**Perplexing:**
Why is there no historical record of Jesus having healed diseased people in Gennesaret? Why was merely touching the hem of Jesus' garment sufficient to heal people?

15:1-2 - THEN CAME TO JESUS SCRIBES AND PHARISEES, OF JERUSALEM, SAYING, "WHY DO THY DISCIPLES TRANSGRESS THE TRADITION OF THE ELDERS? THEY WASH NOT THEIR HANDS WHEN THEY EAT BREAD."

**History:**
Although hand washing before eating was customary for Jews, and obligatory for priests, it did not become mandatory for all Jews until A.D. 70. Guests in Jewish homes were also expected to wash their hands. The Essenes, however, used to bathe the entire body, not just the hands, before eating. Hand washing prior to eating or handling food is now recognized as a means of preventing many enteric diseases.

**Perplexing:**
Why did Jewish disciples fail to comply with Jewish custom?

15:3-6 - HE SAID, "WHY DO YE TRANSGRESS THE COMMANDMENT OF GOD...? ...HONOUR THY FATHER AND MOTHER.... YE SAY, 'WHOSOEVER SHALL SAY TO HIS FATHER OR MOTHER, "IT IS A GIFT, BY WHATSOEVER THOU MIGHTEST BE PROFITED BY ME";

AND HONOUR NOT HIS FATHER OR MOTHER, SHALL BE FREE.' THUS HAVE YE MADE THE COMMANDMENT OF NONE EFFECT...."

**Perplexing:**
Why did Jesus cite the commandment to honor one's father and mother to the scribes and Pharisees? Why did they not respond?

**Old Testament:**
EX. 20:12 - "Honour thy father and thy mother."
[This is one of the Ten Commandments in EX. 20; it does not, however, appear as one of the Ten Commandments in EX. 34:14-28.]

**Language:**
The Hebrew word used for "gift" is "corban," meaning, "a gift dedicated to God."

15:7-9 - JESUS: "YE HYPOCRITES, WELL DID ESAIAS [ISAIAH] PROPHESY OF YOU: 'THIS PEOPLE DRAWETH NIGH UNTO ME WITH THEIR MOUTH, AND HONOURETH ME WITH THEIR LIPS, BUT THEIR HEART IS FAR FROM ME. IN VAIN THEY WORSHIP ME, TEACHING FOR DOCTRINES THE COMMANDMENTS OF MEN.'"

**Old Testament:**
ISA. 29:13-14 - Isaiah: "The Lord said, 'Forasmuch as this people draw near Me with their mouth, and with their lips honour Me, but have removed their heart far from Me, and their fear toward Me is taught by the precept of men, I will proceed to do a marvellous work and a wonder; the wisdom of their wise men shall perish, and the understanding of their prudent men shall be hid.'"
[The verses are part of a series in which God spoke about the people of Jerusalem.]

**Contradiction:**
MATT. 5:20 - Jesus: "Except your righteousness shall exceed that of the scribes and Pharisees, ye shall in no case enter into the kingdom of heaven."
[Were the scribes and Pharisees hypocrites, or were they righteous?]

**Perplexing:**
Why did Jesus distort ISA.'s verses, take them out of context, and apply them to the scribes and Pharisees? Why did the Pharisees fail to correct him?

15:11 - JESUS: "NOT THAT WHICH GOETH INTO THE MOUTH DEFILETH A MAN, BUT THAT WHICH COMETH OUT OF THE MOUTH; THIS DEFILETH A MAN."

**Contradiction:**
LEV. 11:42-43 - The LORD: "Whatever goeth upon the belly, goeth upon all four, or hath more feet among all creeping things...ye shall not eat; they are an abomination. Ye shall not make yourselves abominable with any creeping thing...that ye should be defiled."
LEV. 11:44 - The LORD: "...neither shall ye defile yourselves with any manner of creeping thing...."
LEV. 22:8 - The LORD: "That which dieth of itself, or is torn with beasts, he shall not eat to defile himself
[Is there nothing that can be eaten (go into one's mouth) that will defile a person, or are there certain things which, if ingested, can defile a person?]

**Perplexing:**
Why did Jesus fail to know that many enteric diseases are spread by unclean hands and food contaminated with pathogenic bacteria, viruses, and parasites? Why did Jesus not so inform his disciples? Why was Jesus as ignorant of the causes of diseases as the people who wrote about him? Since people at that time ate with their fingers, clean hands were essential for the prevention of such diseases as typhoid, hepatitis, amebiasis, cholera, salmonellosis, shigellosis, and numerous other bacterial, parasitic, and viral infections. Can these verses implying that God is ignorant of how certain diseases are transmitted be construed as blasphemy?
Was Jesus repudiating the LORD's commandments in LEV.? Was he unaware that the LORD had identified certain food that would defile a person? Why did Jesus not view the ingestion of contaminated material or filth as defilement? Why did he fail to enlighten people about the causes and prevention of enteric diseases and also food poisoning such as botulism? Because of Jesus' failure to do so, millions of people have suffered and died. Can Jesus, consequently, be held responsible for the misery that these diseases have wrought on humanity?
See also under 4:24-25.

**History:** See under 15:1-2.

15:14 - JESUS: "...THEY [SCRIBES AND PHARISEES] BE BLIND LEADERS OF THE BLIND. AND IF THE BLIND LEAD THE BLIND, BOTH SHALL FALL INTO THE DITCH."

**Contradiction:** See under 15:7-9.

15:20 - JESUS: "...TO EAT WITH UNWASHEN HANDS DEFILETH NOT A MAN."

**Perplexing:** See under 15:11.

15:21 - JESUS DEPARTED INTO THE COASTS OF TYRE AND SIDON.

**Perplexing:**
How did Jesus travel to Tyre which was about 35 miles northeast of Capernaum?

**Old Testament:** See under 11:20-23.

15:22-24 - A WOMAN OF CANAAN CAME...SAYING, "HAVE MERCY ON ME, 0 LORD, SON OF DAVID: MY DAUGHTER IS GRIEVOUSLY VEXED WITH A DEVIL." HE ANSWERED NOT A WORD. HIS DISCIPLES CAME, SAYING, "SEND HER AWAY...." HE SAID, "I AM NOT SENT BUT UNTO THE LOST SHEEP OF THE HOUSE OF ISRAEL."

**Contradictions:** See under 10:5-6.

**Perplexing:**
Why did the woman refer to Jesus as "Son of David?" Why did Jesus not have the courtesy to answer the woman? Why did he not want to help her? Was it because she was not Jewish? Why did Jesus say at this time that he had been sent only to "the lost sheep of the house of Israel?" Why did he imply that he was only interested in bringing back to Judaism those Jews ("the lost sheep") who had drifted away from its religious practices? Why was Jesus not interested in assisting or converting non-Jews to him? Why did a devil want to vex the woman's daughter? See also under 4:23, 4:24-25, and 9:27.

**History:**
The woman mentioned the prevailing belief, which Jesus did not correct, that ailments were caused by devils (demons/evil spirits).
See also under 4:23.

15:26-27 - HE SAID, "IT IS NOT MEET TO TAKE THE CHILDREN'S BREAD, AND CAST IT TO DOGS." SHE SAID, "LORD, THE DOGS EAT OF THE CRUMBS WHICH FALL FROM THEIR MASTER'S TABLE."

**Perplexing:**
Why did Jesus refer to non-Jews or non-Israelites as "dogs?" Was he demonstrating religious and/or ethnic bigotry? ("Children" referred to the Jews; "bread" referred to his teachings, and "dogs" referred to non-Jews.) Why did he exhibit this intolerance toward those who were not of his faith? Why was he anti-Gentile?

15:28 - JESUS SAID, "WOMAN, GREAT IS THY FAITH; BE IT UNTO THEE AS THOU WILT." HER DAUGHTER WAS MADE WHOLE THAT VERY HOUR."

**Contradiction:**
MARK 7:28-29 - She said, "The dogs under the table eat of the children's crumbs." He said, "For this saying go thy way; the devil is gone out of thy daughter."
[Did Jesus say that because of the woman's faith he healed her daughter, or because of her saying that the dogs under the table eat the children's crumbs?]

15:29-30 - JESUS DEPARTED, CAME NIGH UNTO THE SEA OF GALILEE, WENT UP A MOUNTAIN, AND SAT DOWN. GREAT MULTITUDES CAME UNTO HIM, WITH THOSE THAT WERE LAME, BLIND, DUMB, MAIMED, AND MANY OTHERS, AND CAST THEM AT JESUS' FEET; HE HEALED THEM.

**Contradiction:**
MARK 7:31-32 - Departing from Tyre and Sidon, he came unto the sea of Galilee.... They bring unto him one that was deaf, and had a speech impediment....
[Did people bring the sick and infirm to Jesus, or only one deaf person with a speech impediment?]

**Perplexing:**
How much time did Jesus spend in Tyre and Sidon? Were his disciples with him?
How did the multitudes know where to find Jesus? How were the lame, blind, maimed, and other infirm people able to travel to and up a mountain to Jesus? How many individuals with infirmities were there? How did Jesus heal all the sick and infirm? Were they required to have faith, or did he just touch them?
See also under 14:14.

15:31 - THE MULTITUDE WONDERED, WHEN THEY SAW THE DUMB SPEAK, THE MAIMED TO BE WHOLE, THE LAME WALK, AND THE BLIND SEE; THEY GLORIFIED THE GOD OF ISRAEL.

**Contradiction:**
MARK 7:37 - [They] were beyond measure astonished, saying, "...he maketh the deaf to hear, and the dumb to speak."

[Did the multitude wonder and glorify God after Jesus healed the sick and infirm, or were they astonished that Jesus healed a deaf man?]

**Perplexing:**
Why was there no secular report of these healing miracles? Why was the God of Israel glorified, rather than God without qualification? Did the people believe that the God of Israel was a specific god, and that other people or nations had different gods? Were these people expressing a belief in polytheism? Did they believe that Jesus' God was only the God of Israel, not the God of others? (The term, "God of Israel," appears but one other time in the New Testament; in LUKE 1:68 - Zacharias said, "Blessed be the Lord God of Israel.")

**Old Testament:**
EX. 34:23 - God referred to Himself as, "the God of Israel" [not "the God of all people" or "of the universe."]

15:32 - JESUS CALLED HIS DISCIPLES AND SAID, "I HAVE COMPASSION ON THE MULTITUDE, BECAUSE THEY CONTINUE WITH ME NOW THREE DAYS, AND HAVE NOTHING TO EAT; I WILL NOT SEND THEM AWAY FASTING, LEST THEY FAINT IN THE WAY."

**Perplexing:**
Why did it take three days for Jesus to have compassion on the multitude, especially as children were there (15:38)? Why did mothers allow their children to go three days without eating? Why did they not leave to obtain food in nearby villages? Were they not near such villages? How could they have remained with Jesus for three days without anything to eat and, presumably, with nothing to drink? Did Jesus and the disciples also go without food for three days? What did the multitude, Jesus, and the disciples do for the three days? What sanitary facilities were available for the multitude to avoid polluting the area? Where did the people sleep?

15:33-35 - HIS DISCIPLES SAY, "WHENCE SHOULD WE HAVE SO MUCH BREAD IN THE WILDERNESS, AS TO FILL SO GREAT A MULTITUDE?" JESUS SAITH, "HOW MANY LOAVES HAVE YE?" THEY SAID, "SEVEN AND A FEW LITTLE FISHES." JESUS COMMANDED THE MULTITUDE TO SIT DOWN ON THE GROUND.

**Perplexing:**
Why did the disciples wonder about being able to feed the multitude when they had recently witnessed Jesus' miracle of feeding over 5000 people with five loaves and two fish (MATT. 14:15-21)? Were the disciples absent-minded? Why did Jesus fail to remind the disciples of his previous feeding miracle and rebuke them for their lack of faith until later in 16:8-9? Why did Jesus allow the multitude to go three days without food? What did they do during the three days? Did Jesus and the disciples also go without food? If so, why did the disciples not complain about being hungry? Why was it necessary for Jesus to order the people to sit down? Why would people who have not eaten in three days have to be told to sit down?
See also under 14:19 and 15:32.

15:36-38 - HE TOOK THE SEVEN LOAVES AND THE FISHES, GAVE THANKS, BRAKE THEM, GAVE TO HIS DISCIPLES, AND THE DISCIPLES TO THE MULTITUDE. THEY DID ALL EAT, AND WERE FILLED; THEY TOOK UP OF THE BROKEN MEAT THAT WAS LEFT SEVEN BASKETS FULL. THEY THAT DID EAT WERE 4000 MEN, BESIDE WOMEN AND CHILDREN.

**Contradiction:**
MARK 8:9 - They that had eaten were about 4000....
[Were there 4000 men plus women and children, or were there just about 4000 people?]

**Perplexing:**
How long did it take the disciples to feed 4000 men plus, one may estimate, about 1000 women and children? If it took each disciple about 20 seconds to distribute the food and move from person to person, the event would have taken nearly 2½ hours. Why is there no historical evidence for this occurrence? Was this story a variant of the account in MATT. 14:15-21? Why was this feeding miracle not reported by LUKE and JOHN?
See also under 14:19, 20, and 21.

15:39 - HE SENT AWAY THE MULTITUDE, TOOK SHIP, AND CAME INTO THE COASTS OF MAGDALA.

**Contradiction:**
MARK 8:10 - He entered into a ship with his disciples and came to the parts of Dalmanutha.
[Did Jesus go to Magdala, or to Dalmanutha?]

16:1 - THE PHARISEES WITH THE SADDUCEES CAME, AND TEMPTING DESIRED THAT HE WOULD SHOW THEM A SIGN FROM HEAVEN.

**Contradiction:**
MARK 8:11 - The Pharisees began to question with him, seeking of him a sign from heaven, tempting him.
[Did the Pharisees and Sadducees, or only the Pharisees try to tempt Jesus for a sign?]

**History:** See under 12:38-39.

**Perplexing:** See under 12:38-39.

16:3 - JESUS: ".... O YE HYPOCRITES...CAN YE NOT DISCERN THE SIGNS OF THE TIMES?"

**Contradiction:** See under 15:7-9.

16:4 - JESUS: "A WICKED AND ADULTEROUS GENERATION SEEKETH AFTER A SIGN; THERE SHALL NO SIGN BE GIVEN UNTO IT, BUT THE SIGN OF THE PROPHET JONAS."

**Contradictions:** See under 12:38-39.

16:6-12 - JESUS: "TAKE HEED AND BEWARE OF THE LEAVEN OF THE PHARISEES AND SADDUCEES." THEY [THE DISCIPLES] REASONED, "IT IS BECAUSE WE HAVE TAKEN NO BREAD." .... JESUS: "HOW IS IT YE DO NOT UNDERSTAND...YE SHOULD BEWARE OF THE LEAVEN OF THE PHARISEES AND SADDUCEES?" THEN UNDERSTOOD THEY THAT HE BADE THEM NOT BEWARE OF THE LEAVEN OF BREAD, BUT OF THE DOCTRINE OF THE PHARISEES AND SADDUCEES.

**Contradictions:**

MATT. 23:2-3 - Jesus: "The scribes and Pharisees sit in Moses' seat; all therefore whatsoever they bid you observe, that observe and do, but do not after their works, for they say, and do not."

[Did Jesus tell the disciples to beware of the doctrine of the Pharisees, or to do what they teach?]

MARK 8:15 - Jesus: "Take heed; beware of the leaven of the Pharisees, and the leaven of Herod."

[Did Jesus warn his disciples to beware of the doctrine of the Pharisees and Sadducees, or that of the Pharisees and Herod?]

LUKE 12:1 - Jesus: "Beware ye of the leaven of the Pharisees, which is hypocrisy."

[Did Jesus say that the leaven of the Pharisees was their doctrine, or their hypocrisy?]

See also under 15:7-9.

16:13 - WHEN JESUS CAME INTO THE COASTS OF CAESAREA PHILIPPI, HE ASKED HIS DISCIPLES, "WHOM DO MEN SAY THAT I THE SON OF MAN AM?"

**Contradictions:**

MARK 8:22 - He cometh to Bethsaida....

[Did Jesus go to Caesarea Philippi, 25 - 30 miles north of the Sea of Galilee, or to Bethsaida, on the shore of the Sea of Galilee?]

LUKE 9:18 - [After feeding about 5000 men in Bethsaida] Jesus asked them (his disciples], "Whom say the people that I am?"

[Did Jesus ask his disciples in Caesarea Philippi who people say he is, or after feeding about 5000 men in Bethsaida?]

16:14 - THEY: "SOME SAY THAT THOU ART JOHN THE BAPTIST, SOME, ELIAS; OTHERS, JEREMIAS, OR ONE OF THE PROPHETS."

**Perplexing:**

Why did some people believe that Jesus was John the Baptist? Was Jesus unknown before John was killed, although both traveled and preached at the same time? Why did some equate Jesus with Elijah and Jeremiah?

16:16 - SIMON PETER: "THOU ART THE CHRIST, THE SON OF THE LIVING GOD."

**Perplexing:**

Why did Peter say that Jesus was "the Son of the living God?" The concept of God or a god having a son is not found in Judaism. It was, however, an ancient pagan belief that gods could have children borne for them by human women. This is the first time that any identified person has said that Jesus is the Son of God. In 14:33, unidentified people on a ship had referred to him as such. Why was Peter the only disciple to so identify Jesus?

16:20 - THEN CHARGED HE HIS DISCIPLES THAT THEY SHOULD TELL NO MAN THAT HE WAS JESUS THE CHRIST.

**Perplexing:**

Why did Jesus want his disciples to keep his identity as Christ secret, especially after performing miracles for multitudes? He had already been called "the prophet that should come," in JOHN 6:14-17, by the people involved in his first feeding miracle; and in MATT. 14:33, people on a ship said, "Thou art the Son of God."

By referring to himself as "Christ," was Jesus saying that he was the Messiah or a king? (See under 1:1 - Language, History, and Pagan parallels.)

**Old Testament:**
ISA. 8:16 - "Bind up My testimony; seal the law among My disciples."

16:21 - ...BEGAN JESUS TO SHEW UNTO HIS DISCIPLES, THAT HE MUST GO UNTO JERUSALEM, SUFFER MANY THINGS OF THE ELDERS, CHIEF PRIESTS, AND SCRIBES, BE KILLED, AND BE RAISED THE THIRD DAY.

**Contradictions:**
MATT. 12:40 - Jesus: "...so shall the Son of man be three days and three nights in the heart of the earth."
[Did Jesus say that he would be raised the third day, or spend three days and three nights in the earth?]
MARK 8:31 - He began to teach them that the Son of man must...be killed, and after three days rise.
[Did Jesus say that he would rise on the third day, or after three days?]
JOHN 20:9 - They [the disciples] knew not...that he must rise again from the dead.
[Were the disciples told that Jesus would rise from the dead, or did they not know?]
See also under 12:40.

**Old Testament:** See under 12:40.

**Perplexing:** See under 12:40.

16:23 - HE SAID UNTO PETER, "GET THEE BEHIND ME, SATAN; THOU ART AN OFFENSE UNTO ME, FOR THOU SAVOUREST NOT THE THINGS THAT BE OF GOD, BUT THOSE THAT BE OF MEN."

**Perplexing:**
In MATT. 16:18-19, Jesus: "Thou art Peter, and upon this rock I will build my church," and "I will give unto thee the keys of the kingdom of heaven...." If Peter was the rock on which Jesus would build his church, and if Jesus is to give him the keys to the kingdom of heaven, how could Jesus now refer to him as "Satan" and as "an offense?" Did Jesus not know, that Peter would be an offense to him and that he would call him, "Satan?"

**Judaism:**
In Jewish theology, "Satan" ("satan") was the name for an adversary, one who opposed or obstructed. It was also the designation for the "prosecutor" who pointed out Israel's sins to a heavenly court. The word did not refer to the devil, a being that was not part of traditional Jewish belief.

16:24 - SAID JESUS, "IF ANY MAN COME AFTER ME, LET HIM DENY HIMSELF, TAKE UP HIS CROSS, AND FOLLOW ME."

**Perplexing:**
Was Jesus' comment about the cross an anachronism? The cross had not yet become a symbol of a burden that one bears. At this time, the cross was still a pagan symbol for sun-gods, adorned pagan temples, and was also a phallic symbol. Did the disciples understand about what Jesus was speaking?

**History:** See under 10:38.

16:26 - JESUS: "...WHAT SHALL A MAN GIVE IN EXCHANGE FOR HIS SOUL?"

**Perplexing:** See under 10:28.

16:27 - JESUS: "THE SON OF MAN SHALL COME IN THE GLORY OF HIS FATHER WITH HIS ANGELS; THEN HE SHALL REWARD EVERY MAN ACCORDING TO HIS WORKS."

**Contradictions:**
MATT. 12:37 - Jesus: "By thy words thou shalt be justified, and by thy words thou shalt be condemned."
[Are people to be rewarded according to their works,or by their words?]
ROM. 3:20 - Paul: "By the deeds of the law there shall no flesh be justified...."
[Are people to be rewarded, or not, based upon their deeds (works)?]
ROM. 3:28 - Paul: "...a man is justified by faith without the deeds of the law."
GAL. 2:16 - Paul: "A man is not justified by the works of the law, but by the faith of Jesus Christ...by the works of the law shall no flesh be justified."
[Are people rewarded according to their works, or by their faith?]
EPH. 2:8-9 - Paul: "By grace ye are saved through faith, and that not of yourselves; it is the gift of God, not of works...."
[Are people to be rewarded according to their works, or by a gift of God?]
See also under 12:37.

16:28 - JESUS: "THERE BE SOME STANDING HERE, WHICH SHALL NOT TASTE OF DEATH, TILL THEY SEE THE SON OF MAN COMING IN HIS KINGDOM."

**Perplexing:**
Why did Jesus fail to return? What has delayed him? Why did Jesus say that some of his disciples would not be dead before he returned? Why did Jesus mislead them by implying that the end of the world was near? In MATT. 26:64 and MARK 14:62, Jesus also told the high priest, "Ye shall see the Son of man sitting on the right hand of power, and coming in the clouds of heaven." In this verse, Jesus clearly indicated that he expected the high priest to be alive when he returned. In MATT. 10:23, he stated that he would return before the disciples had gone over the cities of Israel. The disciples and the high priest are long dead, and about two millennia later, Jesus' prophecy to return has failed to come to pass. Some individuals contend that Jesus' transfiguration (in 9:29) fulfilled the prophecy, but he made the prophecy to the high priest after the transfiguration; and in LUKE 10:9, also after the transfiguration, he said "...the kingdom of God is come nigh unto you," again implying that it was about to arrive. Many additional verses also specify that Jesus expected to return during the lifetime of the people to whom he was speaking.

**Old Testament:**
EZEK. 30:3 - The LORD: "The day is near, the day of the LORD is near...."
JOEL 1:15 - The LORD: "...the day of the LORD is at hand...."
OBAD. 1:15 - The LORD: "The day of the LORD is near...."
ZEPH. 1:7 - The LORD: "...the day of the LORD is at hand...."
ZEPH. 1:14 - The LORD: "The great day of the LORD is near, and hasteth greatly...."

17:1 - AFTER SIX DAYS JESUS TAKETH PETER, JAMES, AND JOHN HIS BROTHER, UP INTO AN HIGH MOUNTAIN.

**Contradiction:**
LUKE 9:28 - About eight days after these sayings [about Jesus' return], he took Peter, John, and James into a mountain to pray.
[Did Jesus and three disciples go onto the mountain after six days, or after about eight days?]

**Perplexing:**
To what mountain did they go? Where was the mountain? Why did Jesus take only Peter, James, and John with him? Where were the other disciples?

17:2 - [JESUS] WAS TRANSFIGURED BEFORE THEM; HIS FACE DID SHINE AS THE SUN, AND HIS RAIMENT WAS WHITE AS THE LIGHT.

**Old Testament:**
EX. 34:29-30, 35 - When Moses came down from mount Sinai the skin of his face shone.... When Aaron and all the children of Israel saw Moses, the skin of his face shone....

**Pagan parallel:**
When Buddha went onto Mount Pandava in Sri Lanka, his body became bright and shone like the sun and moon.

**Perplexing:**
Why did the Gospel of JOHN not consider the transfiguration important enough to report?

17:3-4 - THERE APPEARED UNTO THEM MOSES AND ELIAS TALKING WITH HIM. PETER SAID, "LORD, IT IS GOOD FOR US TO BE HERE; IF THOU WILT, LET US MAKE HERE THREE TABERNACLES, ONE FOR THEE, ONE FOR MOSES, AND ONE FOR ELIAS."

**Perplexing:**
How was Peter able to recognize Moses and Elijah? Were there pictures of them that he had seen? Did they appear as they did in old age or when they were younger? What were they wearing, or were they naked? If clothed, by whom were the clothes made, and of what material? Why did Jesus fail to respond to Peter's request to make tabernacles? In 11:14 and later in 17:12-13, Jesus identified John the Baptist as Elijah. Was the Elijah with him here also John the Baptist?
See also under 14:10-12 and below under 17:11-13.

17:5 - ...A BRIGHT CLOUD OVERSHADOWED THEM, AND A VOICE OUT OF THE CLOUD SAID, "THIS IS MY BELOVED SON, IN WHOM I AM WELL PLEASED; HEAR YE HIM."

**Old Testament:**
The concept of God being in a cloud is found in several Old Testament verses. For examples:
EX. 13:21 - The LORD went before them by day in a pillar of a cloud....
EX. 16:10 - ...the glory of God appeared in the cloud.
EX. 19:9 - The LORD said unto Moses, "I come unto thee in a thick cloud...."

**Contradiction:**
JOHN 5:37 - Jesus: ".... Ye have neither heard His voice at any time, nor seen his shape."
[Was, or was not the voice of God heard?]
See also under 1:18.

**Perplexing:**
If God could speak out of a cloud to three disciples, why can He not speak to everyone?
See also under 3:17.

**Pagan parallel:** See under 3:17.

**History:** See under 1:20.

17:6 - WHEN THE DISCIPLES HEARD IT, THEY FELL ON THEIR FACE, AND WERE AFRAID.

**Contradiction:** See under 17:5.

**Perplexing:** See under 17:5.

17:9 - ...JESUS CHARGED THEM, "TELL THE VISION TO NO MAN UNTIL THE SON OF MAN BE RISEN AGAIN FROM THE DEAD."

**Contradiction:**
JOHN 20:9 - They knew not that he must rise again from the dead.
[Did Jesus tell the disciples that he would rise from the dead, or did they not know that he would be resurrected?]
See also under 16:21.

17:11-13 - JESUS SAID, "ELIAS SHALL FIRST COME, AND RESTORE ALL THINGS. I SAY, ELIAS IS COME ALREADY, AND THEY KNEW HIM NOT, BUT HAVE DONE UNTO HIM WHATSOEVER THEY LISTED. LIKEWISE SHALL ALSO THE SON OF MAN SUFFER OF THEM." THE DISCIPLES UNDERSTOOD THAT HE SPOKE OF JOHN THE BAPTIST.

**Contradiction:** See under 11:13-14.

**Perplexing:**
Why did Jesus say that Elijah would "restore all things?" What did he mean by "restore all things?" If John the Baptist was Elijah, why did he deny it, and why did he not "restore all things"? Why did the "great and dreadful day of the Lord" not come (MAL. 4:5)? Why, now, about two millennia later, has the day of the Lord still not arrived?Why did Jesus believe that the day of the Lord was imminent? Why did jesus imply that John the Baptist was Elijah? Why did Jesus impy that Jews killed John, and that they will cause him to suffer, when John was killed by Herod for personal reasons?
See also under 11:13-14, 14:10-12, and 17:3-4.

**Old Testament:** See under 11:13-14.

17:15 - A MAN: "LORD, HAVE MERCY ON MY SON; HE IS LUNATICK, AND SORE VEXED; OFTTIMES HE FALLETH INTO THE FIRE, AND OFT INTO THE WATER."

**Contradictions:**
MARK 9:18 - [After the transfiguration] A man: "I have brought my son, which hath a dumb spirit; wheresoever he taketh him, he teareth him, and he foameth, gnashes his teeth, and pineth away...."
[Was the man's son a lunatick who fell into fire and into water, or possessed by a dumb spirit?]
LUKE 9:38-39 - [After the transfiguration] A man cried out, "Look upon my son.... A spirit taketh him, and he suddenly crieth out; it teareth him that he foameth, and bruising him hardly departeth from him."
[Was the boy a lunatic who fell into fire and into water, or was he harmed by a spirit?]
MARK 9:21-22 - Jesus: "How long is it since this came unto him?" He said, "Of a child. Ofttimes it hath cast him into the fire, and into the waters to destroy him...."
[Did the man say that his son had fallen into fire and into water before, or after Jesus spoke to him?]

**Perplexing:** See under 4:24-25.

**History:** See under 4:23.

17:16 - THE MAN: "I BROUGHT HIM TO THY DISCIPLES, AND THEY COULD NOT CURE HIM."

**Contradiction:**
MATT. 10:1 - ...he gave them [his disciples] power against unclean spirits, to cast them out, and to heal all manner of sickness and disease. [Jesus did not mention any exceptions or attach any conditions to the power he gave to the disciples.]
[Did, or did not Jesus give his disciples unconditional power against unclean spirits and to heal all diseases?]

**Perplexing:**
Why did Jesus fail to inform the disciples that they would not be able to heal certain ailments? Did he not know that they might find such ailments? Did Jesus fail to transfer all of his healing power to the disciples?

17:17 - JESUS: "O FAITHLESS AND PERVERSE GENERATION, HOW LONG SHALL I BE WITH YOU...."

**Perplexing:**
How could the disciples lack faith, after witnessing Jesus' miracles involving healing, feeding, and the meeting with Elijah and Moses?

17:18 - JESUS REBUKED THE DEVIL, AND HE DEPARTED OUT OF HIM; THE CHILD WAS CURED FROM THAT VERY HOUR.

**Contradiction:**
MARK 9:21-27 - Jesus conversed with the boy's father and said, "If thou canst believe, all things are possible to him that believeth." The father said, "Lord, I believe; help thou mine unbelief." Jesus...rebuked the foul spirit, saying, "Thou dumb and deaf spirit come out of him, and enter no more into him. "The spirit cried, rent him sore, came out of him, and he was as one dead.... Jesus...lifted him up, and he arose.
[Did Jesus just rebuke the devil to make it leave the boy, or did he speak first with the boy's father, ask him about having faith, and then rebuke the spirit?]

**Perplexing:**
How did the devil/spirit enter the boy? Why did it enter him? What benefit did the devil/spirit derive by vexing the boy? Where did it go when it left the boy? Why did Jesus not heal all sick children?

17:19-21 - THE DISCIPLES SAID, "WHY COULD NOT WE CAST HIM OUT?" JESUS SAID, "BECAUSE OF YOUR UNBELIEF; IF YE HAVE FAITH AS A GRAIN OF MUSTARD SEED, YE SHALL SAY UNTO THIS MOUNTAIN, 'REMOVE HENCE TO YONDER PLACE,' AND IT SHALL REMOVE; AND NOTHING SHALL BE IMPOSSIBLE UNTO YOU. HOWBEIT THIS KIND GOETH NOT OUT BUT BY PRAYER AND FASTING."

**Perplexing:**
If this particular devil could be cast out only through prayer and fasting, why did Jesus accuse the disciples of lacking faith? Why was Jesus able to cast the devil out just by rebuking it, rather than resorting to prayer and fasting? Why did Jesus not warn his disciples that there would be some devils against which the power he gave them (MATT. 10:1) would be ineffective?
If faith as small as a mustard seed can move a mountain, why has no one been able to move a mountain by faith? Does no one have even the faith of a mustard seed?
See also under 17:17.

17:22-23 - WHILE THEY ABODE IN GALILEE, JESUS SAID, "THE SON OF MAN SHALL BE BETRAYED INTO THE HANDS OF MEN; THEY SHALL KILL HIM, AND THE THIRD DAY HE SHALL BE RAISED AGAIN." THEY [THE DISCIPLES] WERE EXCEEDINGLY SORRY.

**Contradictions:** See under 16:21.

**Old Testament:** See under 12:40.

**Perplexing:** See under 12:40.

17:24-25 - WHEN THEY WERE COME TO CAPERNAUM, THEY THAT RECEIVED TRIBUTE MONEY CAME TO PETER, AND SAID, "DOTH NOT YOUR MASTER PAY TRIBUTE?" HE SAITH, "YES."

**Perplexing:**
Why did Jesus pay tribute money (taxes), whereas modern clergy do not?

17:27 - JESUS: "LEST WE SHOULD OFFEND THEM [TAX COLLECTORS], GO THOU [PETER] TO THE SEA; CAST AN HOOK, AND TAKE UP THE FISH THAT FIRST COMETH UP; WHEN THOU HATH OPENED HIS MOUTH, THOU SHALT FIND A PIECE OF MONEY; TAKE AND GIVE UNTO THEM FOR ME AND THEE."

**Perplexing:**
Why did Jesus make Peter go fishing to obtain a coin (for paying tax)? Why did he not give Peter the coin, or perform a miracle to manifest the money? If Jesus did not oppose paying tax, why do not modern clergy pay tax? Why was Jesus fearful of offending the tax collectors?

18:1 - CAME THE DISCIPLES UNTO JESUS, SAYING, "WHO IS THE GREATEST IN THE KINGDOM OF HEAVEN?"

**Contradictions:**
MARK 9:33-34 -...Jesus: "What was it ye [the disciples] disputed among yourselves by the way?" They held their peace for by the way they had disputed among themselves who should be the greatest.
[Did the disciples ask Jesus who is the greatest in heaven, or did Jesus ask them what they disputed?]
LUKE 9:46-47 - There arose a reasoning among them, which of them should be the greatest. Jesus perceiving the thought....
[Did the disciples want to know who is the greatest in heaven, or which of them should be the greatest?]
[Did the disciples ask Jesus who is the greatest in heaven, or did he perceive their thought?]

18:3 - JESUS: "EXCEPT YE BE CONVERTED, AND BECOME AS LITTLE CHILDREN, YE SHALL NOT ENTER INTO THE KINGDOM OF HEAVEN."

**Contradictions:** See under 5:3.

18:8-9 - JESUS: "IF THY HAND OR FOOT OFFEND THEE, CUT THEM OFF AND CAST THEM FROM THEE; IT IS BETTER TO ENTER INTO LIFE HALT OR MAIMED, THAN HAVING TWO HANDS OR FEET TO BE CAST INTO EVERLASTING FIRE. IF THINE EYE OFFEND THEE PLUCK IT OUT, AND CAST IT FROM THEE; IT IS BETTER TO ENTER INTO LIFE WITH ONE EYE, RATHER THAN TWO EYES TO BE CAST INTO HELL FIRE."

**Perplexing:** See under 5:29-30 and 6:23.

**Pagan concept:** See under 5:29-30 and 6:23.

**Language:** See under 5:22.

18:10 - JESUS: "...DESPISE NOT ONE OF THESE LITTLE ONES, FOR IN HEAVEN THEIR ANGELS DO ALWAYS BEHOLD THE FACE OF MY FATHER IN HEAVEN."

**Perplexing:**
How many angels are there? Is there nothing else for angels to do in heaven but always behold the face of the Father? Is God so pompous and conceited that He wants angels to spend their time looking at His f ace? See also under 1:20.

18:11 - JESUS: "THE SON OF MAN IS COME TO SAVE THAT WHICH WAS LOST."

**Contradictions:** See under 9:13.

18:16 - JESUS: "...IN THE MOUTH OF TWO OR THREE WITNESSES EVERY WORD MAY BE ESTABLISHED."

**Old Testament:**
DEUT. 19:15 - Moses: at the mouth of two witnesses, or three witnesses, shall the matter be established."

18:17 - JESUS: "IF HE SHALL NEGLECT TO HEAR THEM, TELL IT UNTO THE CHURCH; IF HE NEGLECT TO HEAR THE CHURCH, LET HIM BE UNTO THEE AS A HEATHEN AND A PUBLICAN."

**Perplexing:**

Is the use of the word "church" an anachronism? As of yet, Jesus only had his twelve disciples; no church had been established.

18:18 - JESUS: "WHATSOEVER YE SHALL BIND ON EARTH SHALL BE BOUND IN HEAVEN, AND WHATSOEVER YE SHALL LOOSE ON EARTH SHALL BE LOOSED IN HEAVEN."

**Perplexing:**

In MATT. 16:19, Jesus [said to Peter] "I will give unto thee the keys of the kingdom of heaven; whatsoever thou shalt bind on earth shall be bound in heaven; whatsoever thou shalt loose on earth shall be loosed in heaven." Why did he now extend this authority to all the disciples?

18:21-22 - PETER SAID, "LORD, HOW OFT SHALL MY BROTHER SIN AGAINST ME, AND I FORGIVE HIM? TILL SEVEN TIMES?" JESUS SAITH, "I SAY NOT, UNTIL SEVEN TIMES, BUT UNTIL SEVENTY TIMES SEVEN."

**Old Testament:**

GEN. 4:24 - Lamech: "If Cain shall be avenged sevenfold, truly Lamech seventy and sevenfold."

18:34 - JESUS: "HIS LORD WAS WROTH, AND DELIVERED HIM [A SERVANT WHO OWED MONEY AND WHO DID NOT FORGIVE ANOTHER SERVANT'S DEBT] TO THE TORMENTORS, TILL HE SHOULD PAY ALL THAT WAS DUE UNTO HIM [HIS LORD]."

**Perplexing:**

Why did Jesus support the imprisonment and torture of debtors? How could one obtain money to pay a debt if imprisoned?

19:1-2 - JESUS...DEPARTED FROM GALILEE, AND CAME INTO THE COASTS OF JUDAEA BEYOND JORDAN; GREAT MULTITUDES FOLLOWED HIM AND HE HEALED THEM THERE.

**Perplexing:**

Why is there no historical record of this mass healing?

19:3-4 - THE PHARISEES CAME, SAYING, "IS IT LAWFUL FOR A MAN TO PUT AWAY HIS WIFE FOR EVERY CAUSE?" HE SAID, "HAVE YE NOT READ, THAT HE WHICH MADE THEM AT THE BEGINNING MADE THEM MALE AND FEMALE."

**Old Testament:**

GEN. 1: 27 - God created man in His own image; in the image of God created He him; male and female created He them.

**Contradiction:**
GEN. 2:7-22 - The LORD God formed man out of the dust of the ground.... .... LORD God...took one of his [the man's] ribs and...made He a woman...[Between the time that man was created and then woman, God planted a garden and created animals. Only when man could not find a help meet from among the animals did God create the woman.]
[Did God create man male and female at the same time (after the animals had been created, in GEN. 1:20-25), or did He first create a man, then animals, and last a woman?]

**Perplexing:**
Did Jesus not believe the creation story in GEN. 2?

19:5 - HE SAID, "FOR THIS CAUSE SHALL A MAN LEAVE FATHER AND MOTHER, AND SHALL CLEAVE TO HIS WIFE, AND THEY TWAIN SHALL BE ONE FLESH."

**Old Testament:**
GEN. 2:24 - Therefore shall a man leave his father and mother, and shall cleave unto his wife, and they shall be one flesh.

19:6 - JESUS: "THEY ARE NO MORE TWAIN, BUT ONE FLESH. WHAT THEREFORE GOD HATH JOINED TOGETHER, LET NOT MAN PUT ASUNDER."

**Perplexing:**
Why did Jesus want people to remain married even if they were unhappy, if one spouse was physically or mentally abusive, if the marriage was loveless, or if it was a forced marriage against the will of one or both spouses? Why did Jesus lack compassion and understanding in the matter of marriage?
See also under 5:31-32.

**History:** See under 5:31-32.

19:7-8 - THEY [PHARISEES] SAY, "WHY DID MOSES THEN COMMAND TO GIVE A WRITING OF DIVORCEMENT, AND TO PUT HER AWAY?" HE SAITH, "MOSES BECAUSE OF THE HARDNESS OF YOUR HEARTS SUFFERED YOU TO PUT AWAY YOUR WIVES, BUT FROM THE BEGINNING IT WAS NOT SO."

**Old Testament:**
DEUT. 6:1 - Moses: "These are the commandments, statutes, and judgments, which the LORD your God commanded to teach you...."
See also under 5:31-32.

**Contradiction:**
See Old Testament - DEUT. 6:1, above.
[Did Moses give the commandment because of the hardness of the Pharisees' hearts, or did God order Moses to give the commandment to the people?]

**Perplexing:**
Why did Jesus repudiate God's law about divorce? Was Jesus saying that God changed His mind about divorce? Why did Jesus say that Moses authorized divorce because of the Pharisees' hardness of heart, when the Pharisees were not in existence during Moses' time (even Judaism had not yet come into existence)?

19:9 - JESUS: "WHOSOEVER SHALL PUT AWAY HIS WIFE, EXCEPT FOR FORNICATION, AND SHALL MARRY ANOTHER, COMMITTETH ADULTERY, AND WHOSO MARRIETH HER WHICH IS PUT AWAY DOTH COMMIT ADULTERY."

**Contradictions:** See under 5:31-32.

**Perplexing:** See under 5:31-32.

19:12 - JESUS: "THERE ARE SOME EUNUCHS, WHICH WERE SO BORN FROM THEIR MOTHER'S WOMB; THERE ARE SOME EUNUCHS WHICH WERE MADE EUNUCHS OF MEN; AND THERE BE EUNUCHS, WHICH HAVE MADE THEMSELVES EUNUCHS FOR THE KINGDOM OF HEAVEN'S SAKE...."

**Perplexing:**
Why did Jesus fail to explain why God would want anyone to make himself a eunuch for His kingdom's sake? Why do all or almost all modern Christians ignore this method of reaching heaven?

**History:**
Some early Christians took the above verse seriously, and castrated themselves. One prominent example was Bishop Origin (A.D. 185 - 253).

**Pagan concept:**
Priests and some followers of the goddess Cybele (a virgin known as the "Mother of God," whose lover died and was resurrected, and whose adherents said that they were "born again" and " washed in the blood of the lamb") castrated themselves. This religion which dates back to about the 13th century B.C., existed in Greece and Rome during biblical times. (Worshipers of Cybele also considered a black stone to be sacred, as do modern Muslims with their stone in Mecca.)

**Old Testament:**
ISA. 56:4-5 - "Saith the LORD, 'Unto the eunuchs that keep My Sabbath, choose the things that please Me, and take hold of My covenant, unto them will I give in Mine house and within My walls a place and name better than of sons and daughters; I will give them an everlasting name....'"

19:16 - ONE SAID, "GOOD MASTER, WHAT GOOD THING SHALL I DO, THAT I MAY HAVE ETERNAL LIFE?"

**Perplexing:**
Why would anyone want eternal life, even in heaven? What could one do for eternity?

**Pagan concept:**
Some pre-Christian religions such as Mithraism, Orphism, Zoroastrianism, and that of ancient Egypt had the concept of eternal life in a heaven or in a future existence.
Similarities between Orphism and Christianity are noted under JOHN 6:63.

19:17-19 - HE [JESUS] SAID, “WHY CALLEST THOU ME GOOD? THERE IS NONE GOOD BUT ONE, THAT IS GOD; BUT IF THOU WILT ENTER INTO LIFE, KEEP THE COMMANDMENTS.” HE SAITH, “WHICH?” JESUS SAID, “THOU SHALT DO NO MURDER; THOU SHALT NOT COMMIT ADULTERY; THOU SHALT NOT STEAL; THOU SHALT NOT BEAR FALSE WITNESS; HONOUR THY FATHER AND MOTHER; AND, THOU SHALT LOVE THY NEIGHBOR AS THYSELF.”

**Contradictions** (for God being good):
ISA. 31:2 - Isaiah: “Yet He is wise, and will bring evil....”
ISA. 45:7 - The LORD: “I...create evil....”
JER. 4:6 - The LORD: “ I will bring evil....”
JER. 6:19 - The LORD: “Hear O earth, I will bring evil upon this people....”
JER. 11:11 - “Saith the LORD, ‘I will bring evil upon them... and though they shall cry unto Me, I will not hearken unto them.”
JER. 11:23 - The LORD: “I will bring evil upon the men of Anathoth....”
JER. 19:3 - Saith the LORD, “I will bring evil upon the place....”
JER. 25:29 - “‘I begin to bring evil on the city...,’ saith the LORD.”
JER. 36:31 - The LORD: “...I will bring upon them...all the evil that I have pronounced against them....”
JER. 42:10 - The LORD: “...I will repent of the evil that I have done unto you.”
JFR. 44:2 - “Saith the LORD, ‘Ye have seen all the evil that I have brought upon Jerusalem, and the other cities of Judah....’”
JER. 45:5 - “‘...I will bring evil upon all flesh,’ saith the LORD....”
JER. 49:37 - “‘I will bring evil upon them, even My fierce anger,’ saith the LORD....”
For similar verses see JER. 18:11, 19:15, 23:12, 32:42, 35:17, and 42:17.
JUDG. 9:23 - God sent an evil spirit between Abimelech and the men of Shechem....
1 SAM. 6:14 - Saul’s servants said, “An evil spirit from God troubleth thee.”
2 SAM. 12:11 - Saith the LORD, “I will raise up evil against thee [David] out of thine own house....”
1 KINGS 14:10 - The LORD: “I will bring evil upon the house of Jeroboam....”
JOB 42:11 - ...they comforted him over the evil that the LORD had brought upon him....
PS. 78:49 - “He cast upon them the fierceness of His anger...by sending evil angels among them.”
For similar verses see 1 KINGS 9:9, LAM. 3:38, and DAN, 9:12.
See also under 13:38-39 - Perplexing for a list of some of the atrocities perpetrated by God; see also below under Perplexing (for God being good).
[Is God good, or evil?]

**Perplexing** (for God being good):
Why is Jesus, the Son of God, not good? In JOHN 10:30, Jesus said, “I and my Father are one.” By saying this, Jesus equated himself with God, and, therefore, if God is good, must not Jesus also be good? If Jesus is not good, how can he be one with God or be God’s Son? If he is not good, can God really be good? If God is good, why did He create hell? Why does He permit evil to exist? Why does He bring evil into the world? Why does He not prevent suffering, diseases, infirmities, poverty, crime, wars, and other evils? Could a deity of evil, the devil, have created more misfortunes, misery, disasters, etc. than are attributed to God?
See also under 13:38-39.

**Contradictions** (for obtaining eternal life):
MATT. 5:20 - Jesus: "Except your righteousness shall exceed the righteousness of the scribes and Pharisees, ye shall in no case enter into the kingdom of heaven."
[Must one observe certain commandments, or be more righteous than the scribes and Pharisees to obtain eternal life?]
MATT. 19:29 - Jesus: "Everyone that hath forsaken houses, brethren, father, mother, wife, children, or lands, for my sake shall inherit...everlasting life."
MARK 10:29-30 and LUKE 18:29-30 - similar to MATT. 19:29.
[Must one obey the cited commandments, or forsake one's relatives and property to obtain eternal life?]
[Must one honor one's father and mother, or forsake them?]
MARK 10:19 - Jesus: "Do not commit adultery; do not kill; do not steal; do not bear false witness; defraud not; honour thy father and mother."
[Must one love one's neighbor, or defraud not to obtain eternal life?]
LUKE 18:20 - Jesus: "...do not commit adultery, do not kill, do not steal, do not bear false witness, honour thy father and mother."
[Must one obey the six cited commandments including loving one's neighbor, or five commandments without loving one's neighbor?]
[Is only murder, or all killing prohibited?]
MARK 16:16 - Jesus: "He that believeth and is baptized shall be saved, but he that believeth not shall be damned."
[Must one obey the cited commandments, or believe and be baptized?]
LUKE 10:25-28 - A lawyer stood up, saying, "What shall I do to inherit eternal life?" He [Jesus] said, "What is written in the law?" He said, "Thou shalt love the Lord thy God with all thy heart, soul, strength, and mind, and love thy neighbour as thyself." He said, "Thou hast answered right; this do, and thou shalt live."
[Must one obey the cited commandments, or just love God and one's neighbor?]
LUKE 19:8-9 - Zacchaeus said, "Lord, half of my goods I give to the poor; if I have taken anything from any man by false accusations, I restore him fourfold." Jesus said, "This day is salvation come to this house...."
[Must one obey the cited commandments, or give half of one's goods to the poor?]
JOHN 5:24 - Jesus: "He that heareth my word, and believeth on Him that sent me, hath everlasting life...."
[Must one obey the cited commandments, or listen to Jesus and believe in God?]
JOHN 6:40 - Jesus: "...everyone which seeth the Son, and believeth on him, may have everlasting life, and I will raise him up at the last day."
[Must one obey certain commandments, or see and believe in Jesus?]
JOHN 6:44 - Jesus: "No man can come to me, except the Father ...draw him; I will raise him up at the last day."
ACTS 13:48 - ...as many as were ordained to eternal life believed.
EPH. 2:8 - Paul: "By grace ye are saved through faith, and that not of yourselves; it is a gift of God."
[Must one obey the cited commandments, or be selected (ordained, gifted) by God to obtain eternal life?]
JOHN 3:36 - John: "He that believeth on the Son hath everlasting life, and he that believeth not the Son shall not see life...."
JOHN 6:47 - Jesus: "He that believeth on me hath everlasting life."
JOHN 11:26 - Jesus: "Whosoever liveth and believeth in me shall never die."
JOHN 20:31 - ...believe that Jesus is the Christ, the Son of God, and believing ye might have life through his name.

ACTS 16:31 - Paul and Silas: "Believe on the Lord Jesus Christ, and thou shalt be saved, and thy house."
[Must one obey the cited commandments, or believe in Jesus to obtain eternal life?]
JOHN 5:28-29 - Jesus - "...all that are in the graves...shall come forth; they that have done good, unto the resurrection of life...."
[Must certain commandments be obeyed, or must one have done good to obtain eternal life?]
JOHN 6:54 - Jesus: "Whosoever eateth my flesh, and drinketh my blood, hath eternal life...."
[Must one obey the cited commandments, or eat Jesus' flesh and drink his blood?]
JOHN 8:51 - Jesus: "If a man keep my sayings, he shall never see death."
[Must one obey the cited commandments, or keep Jesus' sayings?]
JOHN 12:25 - Jesus: "...he that hateth his life in this world shall keep it unto life eternal."
[Must one obey the cited commandments, or hate one's life?]
ACTS 2:21 - Peter: "Whosoever shall call on the name of the Lord shall be saved."
[Must one obey the cited commandments, or call on the name of the LORD to be saved?]
[Must one obey certain commandments, or call on the name of the LORD?]
ACTS 5:11 - Peter; "We believe that through the grace of the Lord Jesus Christ we shall be saved...."
[Must one obey the cited commandments, or be saved through the grace of Jesus Christ?]
There are many additional verses similar to the above.
See also under 5:3.
JOB 14:12 - Job: "Man lieth down, and riseth not, till the heavens be no more; they shall not awake, nor be raised out of their sleep."
ECCL. 9:5 - "...the dead know nothing, neither have they anymore reward...."
[Is there, or is there not a reward of eternal life?]

**Perplexing** (for obtaining eternal life):
What must one do to obtain eternal life? Must one comply with all of the requirements stated by Jesus, Peter, Paul, and John, or any one of them? Why did MARK 10:19 and LUKE 18:20 cite slightly differing commandments? If one is preordained to have eternal life through the grace of God or Jesus, what difference does it make what one does? If God already decided beforehand who will be saved and received eternal life, what was the point of Jesus coming into the world?
Why were only six commandments cited? Why did Jesus not cite the commandments to keep the Sabbath day holy (EX. 20:8-11), or those prohibiting incest (LEV. 18:6-16)? In MATT. 25:46, Jesus said, "These [the unrighteous] shall go into everlasting punishment, but the righteous into life eternal." Is not everlasting punishment also eternal life?
See also under 19:16.

**Old Testament:**
The first five cited commandments are found in EX. 20:12-16. The commandment to love thy neighbor as thyself is from LEV. 19:18.

**Pagan parallels:**
Buddha: "A child should honor his parents and do for them all that he is supposed to do. He should serve them, help them at their labor, cherish the family lineage, protect the family property, and hold memorial services after they have passed away."
A set of laws, known as the "Code of Hammurabi," engraved on stone tablets and given to the Babylonian King Hammurabi (c. 1728-1686 B.C.) on a mountain by the god Shamash, contained penalties for bearing false witness, stealing, adultery, and killing, among others.

**Judaism:**
According to some Jewish scholars, the commandment against stealing is a prohibition against stealing a person - kidnapping.

19:21 - JESUS SAID, "IF THOU WILT BE PERFECT, GO AND SELL THAT THOU HAST, AND GIVE TO THE POOR, AND THOU SHALT HAVE TREASURE IN HEAVEN; COME FOLLOW ME."

**Perplexing:**
Why do few, if any, modern professed followers of Jesus, especially the self-proclaimed men of God, sell their belongings (or even half of their belongings as in LUKE 19:8-9) and give the proceeds to the poor? In ACTS 2:45, the disciples sold their possessions and goods, and parted them to all men as every man had need. If the proceeds are given to the poor, would the poor still be poor? Would those who disposed of their belongings then be poor and, therefore, eligible to receive funds from others?
What kind of treasure is there in heaven? Of what use is treasure in heaven? Why would admittance into heaven not be enough of a reward without the need for treasure?

19:23-24 - JESUS SAID, "A RICH MAN SHALL HARDLY ENTER INTO THE KINGDOM OF HEAVEN. IT IS EASIER FOR A CAMEL TO GO THROUGH THE EYE OF A NEEDLE, THAN FOR A RICH MAN TO ENTER THE KINGDOM OF GOD."

**History:**
The early Christian congregations were composed primarily of the poor who were hostile to the rich. The phrase "eye of a needle" referred to a sewing needle; it was derived from an old Jewish saying, "Are you from Pombeditha (in Babylonia), where they can drive an elephant through the eye of a needle?" The question was asked of someone who appeared to believe in the impossible. As Christianity began to have a wider appeal and to attract richer people, the "eye of the needle" was said to refer to a narrow gate in Jerusalem through which a fully laden camel could not pass until some of the load was removed. This was further interpreted to mean that a rich person would have to donate some of his wealth to the Church and/or the poor.

**Perplexing:**
If it is so difficult for a rich person to enter into the kingdom of God, why do many (most?) Christians, especially the clergy strive to acquire as much wealth as possible? Why are they obsessed with amassing fortunes in this life? Do they not believe Jesus? Do they even believe in Jesus and the kingdom of God?

**Pagan concept:**
Plato (5th century B.C.) said, "It is impossible for an exceptionally good man to be exceptionally rich."

19:26 - ...JESUS: "WITH GOD ALL THINGS ARE POSSIBLE."

**Old Testament:**
GEN. 18:14 - The LORD: "Is anything too hard for the LORD?"

**Contradictions:**
GEN. 2:18-20 - LORD God: "...I will make an help meet for him [Adam]." Out of the ground the LORD God formed every beast of the field, and every fowl of the air, and brought them to Adam.... ...but for

Adam there was not found an help meet.
[Are all things possible with God, or was it not possible for Him to create a help meet out of the ground for Adam?]
GEN. 3:16-19 - Unto the woman He said, "...in sorrow thou shalt bring forth children...and thy husband, shall rule over thee." Unto Adam He said, "...cursed is the ground...in sorrow shalt thou eat of it all the days of thy life...in the sweat of thy face shalt thou eat bread...."
[Are all things possible with God, or was it not possible for Him to foresee the development of modern medicine and anesthesia which have eliminated much of the pain of childbirth; or agricultural techniques and machinery which made farming easier and more productive; or the development of the tremendous number of non-agricultural occupations which eliminated the need for most people to engage in farming?]
[Are all things possible with God, or was it impossible for Him to foresee the development of social and occupational freedom for women which eliminated the need for many (most?) women to be dependent upon and subservient to their husbands?]
GEN. 6:5-6 - God saw that the wickedness of man was great in the earth, and that every imagination of the thoughts of his heart was only evil continually. It repented the LORD that He had made man on the earth; it grieved Him at His heart.
GEN. 6:12 - God looked upon the earth, and, behold, it was corrupt....
[Are all things possible with God, or was it not possible for Him to create an earth that was not corrupt?]
GEN. 8-21 - The LORD: "...the imagination of man's heart is evil from his youth...."
[Are all things possible with God, or was it impossible for Him to create people who were not wicked and who did not have evil thoughts and evil imagination?]
EX. 13:17 - ...God led them [the Israelites] not through the land of the Philistines...for God said, "Lest peradventure the people repent when they see war, and they return to Egypt."
[Are all things possible with God, or was it not possible for Him to prevent war between the Israelites and the Philistines, and prevent the Israelites from returning to Egypt?]
JUDG. 1:19 - ...the LORD was with Judah...but [Judah] could not drive out the inhabitants of the valley, because they had chariots of iron.
[Are all things possible with God, or was He powerless to help Judah against people who had iron chariots?]
MATT. 2:12-13 - Being warned of God...that they should not return to Herod.... ...the angel of the Lord appeareth to Joseph...saying, "Take the young child and his mother, and flee into Egypt...for Herod will seek the young child to destroy him."
[Are all things possible with God, or was it not possible for Him to protect His Son against Herod?]
REV. 12:7 - There was war in heaven....
[Are all things possible with God, or was He unable to prevent war in heaven?]

**Perplexing:**
If all things are possible with God, why did He fail to create a perfect world without suffering, disease, poverty, crime, war, and other evils? If He is incapable of preventing war in heaven, how can He be expected to prevent wars on the earth? Is this why praying for peace has been futile?

19:27 - PETER SAID, "WE HAVE FORSAKEN ALL, AND FOLLOWED THEE; WHAT SHALL WE HAVE THEREFORE?"

**Perplexing:**
Why did Peter ask what he and the others would receive for following Jesus? Peter's words may be translated as, "What is in it for me?" Why was being given the keys of the kingdom of heaven (16:19) not sufficient for Peter? Why was being Jesus' disciples, witnessing his miracles, being rewarded with admission into heaven, being rewarded with treasure there, and being made judges (see 19:28, below) not adequate compensation for them? What more could they want? Did they also want material wealth in this life?

19:28 - JESUS SAID, "...YE ALSO SHALL SIT UPON TWELVE THRONES, JUDGING THE TWELVE TRIBES OF ISRAEL."

**Contradictions:**
LUKE 22:29-30 - [At the Passover meal] Jesus: "I appoint unto you [the disciples] a kingdom...and sit on thrones judging the twelve tribes of Israel."
[Did Jesus promise the disciples that they would judge the tribes of Israel before, or at the Passover meal?]
PS. 7:11 - "God judgeth the righteous...."
PS. 9:8 - "He [the LORD] shall judge the world in righteousness; He shall minister judgment to the people in uprightness."
PS. 96:13 - "...He [the LORD] cometh to judge the earth; He shall judge the world with righteousness."
PS. 98:9 - "He [the LORD] cometh to judge the earth; with righteousness shall He judge the world...."
ECCL. 12:14 - "God shall bring every work into judgment, with every secret thing, whether it be good, or evil."
EZEK. 7:8 - "'Now will I [the Lord]...judge thee according to thy ways....'"
EZEK. 7:27 - "...according to their deserts will I judge them, and they shall know that I am the LORD.'"
EZEK. 18:30 - "'I will judge you, O house of Israel, every man according to his ways,' saith the Lord God...."
ROM. 2:5-6 - Paul: "...the day...of the righteous judgment of God, who will render unto every man according to his deeds."
HEB. 12:23 - Paul: "...God the Judge of all...."
HEB. 13:4 - Paul: "...God will judge."
[Will the disciples do judging, or will God do the judging?]
JOHN 5:22 - Jesus: "The Father judgeth no man, but hath committed all judgment unto the Son."
JOHN 5:26-27 - Jesus: "As the Father...hath given him [the Son] authority to execute judgment...."
JOHN 5:30 - Jesus: "...I judge...."
ACTS 10:42 - Peter: "...it is he [Jesus] which was ordained of God to be the judge of the quick and the dead."
[Will the disciples, or Jesus do the judging?]
1 COR. 6:2 - Paul: "Do ye not know that the saints shall judge the world?"
[Will the disciples, or saints do the judging?]

**History:**
Over the ensuing centuries through intermarriage and the loss of tribal records, the twelve tribes of Israel have lost their identities and ceased to exist.

**Perplexing:**
Why did Jesus fail to know that the twelve tribes of Israel would cease to exist? Why did he believe that the tribes would still be in existence at the end of the world? Did he believe that the world would end while the tribes were in existence? If so, why? Why did Jesus promise his twelve disciples including Judas Iscariot

that they would sit on thrones judging the Israelite tribes? Was Jesus unaware that Judas would betray him? In MATT. 26:24 and MARK 14:21, Jesus said, "Woe unto that man by whom the Son of man is betrayed!" Why then did Jesus say that Judas would be rewarded with a throne? Why did Jesus imply that only the tribes of Israel, not other people, would be judged? Did he not know that he was to be the Savior for all people, not just the Israelites (Jews)?
Who will do the judging - the disciples, God, Jesus, or saints? (In JOHN 8:15 and 12:47, Jesus said that he does not judge.)

19:29 - JESUS: "EVERYONE THAT HATH FORSAKEN HOUSES, OR BRETHREN, OR SISTERS, OR FATHER, OR MOTHER, OR WIFE, OR CHILDREN, OR LANDS, FOR MY NAME'S SAKE, SHALL RECEIVE AN HUNDREDFOLD, AND SHALL INHERIT EVERLASTING LIFE.

**Contradictions:**
1 TIM. 5:8 - Paul: "If any provide not for his own, and specially for those of his own house, he hath denied the faith, and is worse than an infidel."
[Should one desert one's family for Jesus, or should one provide for one's family?]
See also under 19:17-19 (for obtaining eternal life).

**Perplexing:**
Why did Jesus not explain why it is necessary to forsake (desert) one's property and family members, thus, perhaps destroying their lives for an unspecified "hundredfold" and everlasting life? How would those family members dependent upon Jesus' followers support themselves? Why did Jesus advocate the renunciation of familial responsibilities, but oppose divorce? What will be increased a hundredfold? Of what use would such be in heaven? What is so desirable about everlasting life that would make one want it?
Why did Jesus not instruct his followers to love and take care of their families?

20:1-15 - JESUS RECITED A PARABLE IN WHICH A HOUSEHOLDER AGREED TO PAY SOME MEN A PENNY FOR WORKING A FULL DAY IN HIS VINEYARD; BUT HE PAID OTHERS A PENNY FOR WORKING ONLY AN HOUR IN THE EVENING. THE HOUSEHOLDER THEN REJECTED THE CLAIM BY THE FIRST GROUP THAT HE WAS UNFAIR BY PAYING AS MUCH TO THOSE WHO WORKED ONLY AN HOUR AS HE PAID TO THEM. JESUS SUPPORTED THE HOUSEHOLDER, CONTENDING THAT HE COULD DO WHAT HE WANTED WITH HIS MONEY. THE HOUSEHOLDER SAID, "IS THINE EYE EVIL, BECAUSE I AM GOOD?"

**Perplexing:**
Why should anyone agree to work a full day for such a householder, when he could wait until the evening and get paid just as much for an hour's work? If, instead of working the full day, suppose the men only worked for one hour and then took the rest of the day off, would Jesus still want them paid for the full day? If not, what is the difference between working for one hour in the morning and being idle the rest of the day, and being idle all day except for the last hour?

**Pagan concept:** See under 6:23, for "evil eye."

20:18-19 - JESUS: "WE GO TO JERUSALEM; THE SON OF MAN SHALL BE BETRAYED UNTO THE CHIEF PRIESTS AND SCRIBES; THEY SHALL CONDEMN HIM TO DEATH, AND DELIVER HIM TO THE GENTILES...TO CRUCIFY HIM; THE THIRD DAY HE SHALL RISE AGAIN."

**Contradictions:** See under 16:21.

**Perplexing:**
Why did Jesus at this time say that he will be crucified by the Gentiles? Why have many Christians over the centuries ignored this verse and accused and persecuted the Jews for allegedly crucifying Jesus? See also under 12:40.

**Old Testament:** See under 12:40.

20:20-21 - THEN CAME TO HIM THE MOTHER OF ZEBEDEE'S CHILDREN WITH HER SONS, WORSHIPPING HIM, AND DESIRING A CERTAIN THING OF HIM. HE SAID, "WHAT WILT THOU?" SHE SAITH, "GRANT THAT THESE MY TWO SONS MAY SIT, THE ONE ON THY RIGHT HAND, AND THE OTHER ON THE LEFT, IN THY KINGDOM."

**Contradictions:**
MATT. 9:4, 12:25; LUKE 5:22, 6:8, 9:47, and 11:17 - Jesus knew people's thoughts.
[Did Jesus know what people were thinking, or did he have to ask what was wanted?]
MARK 10:35-37 - James and John, the sons of Zebedee, came to Jesus saying, "We would that thou shouldest do for us whatsoever we shall desire." Jesus: "What would ye that I should do for you?" They: "Grant unto us that we may sit, one on thy right hand, and the other on thy left hand, in thy glory."
[Did the mother of Zebedee's children speak to Jesus, or did her sons speak to him without her?]

**Perplexing:**
If Jesus could read minds, why did he have to ask the mother of James and John what she wanted?

20:28 - JESUS: "THE SON OF MAN CAME NOT TO BE MINISTERED UNTO, BUT TO MINISTER, AND TO GIVE HIS LIFE A RANSOM FOR MANY."

**Contradictions:**
MATT. 9:13 - Jesus: " I am not come to call the righteous, but sinners to repentance."
[Did Jesus come to minister and give his life as a ransom, or to call sinners to repentance?]
See also under 9:13.

**Old Testament:**
ISA. 53:11 - The LORD: "...by his knowledge shall My righteous servant justify many...."

20:29 - AS THEY DEPARTED FROM JERICHO, A GREAT MULTITUDE FOLLOWED HIM.

**Contradiction:**
LUKE 18:35 - As he was come nigh unto Jericho....
[Was Jesus departing from, or entering Jericho?]

**Old Testament:**
JOSH. 6:26 - [After the destruction of Jericho] Joshua adjured them, saying, "Cursed be the man before the LORD, that riseth up and buildeth this Jericho...."

**Perplexing:**
Why did Jesus go to a city, the rebuilding of which had been cursed? Did the person or persons who rebuilt Jericho suffer from Joshua's curse?

20:30-31 - TWO BLIND MEN SITTING BY THE WAY, WHEN THEY HEARD THAT JESUS PASSED BY, CRIED OUT, "HAVE MERCY ON US, 0 LORD, THOU SON OF DAVID." THE MULTITUDE REBUKED THEM...BUT THEY CRIED THE MORE, "HAVE MERCY ON US, O LORD, THOU SON OF DAVID."

**Contradiction:**
MARK 10:46-48 - ...blind Bartimaeus, the son of Timaeus, sat by the highway side begging. When he heard that it was Jesus of Nazareth, he began to cry out, "Jesus, thou Son of David, have mercy on me." Many charged him that he should hold his peace, but he cried the more, "Thou Son of David, have mercy on me."
LUKE 18:35-39 - ...a blind man sat by the way begging; hearing the multitude pass, he asked what it meant. They told him, that Jesus of Nazareth passeth by. He cried: "Jesus, thou son of David, have mercy on me." They which went before rebuked him...but he cried the more, "Thou Son of David, have mercy on me."
[Were there two blind men, or just one?]

**Perplexing:** See under 9:27.

20:32 - JESUS CALLED THEM, AND SAID, "WHAT WILL YE THAT I SHALL DO UNTO YOU?"

**Contradiction:**
MATT. 9:4, 12:25; MARK 2:8; LUKE 5:22, 6:8, 9:47, and 11:17 - Jesus knew people's thoughts.
[Did not, or did Jesus know people's thoughts?]
See also under 20:20-21.

**Perplexing:**
If Jesus was capable of discerning people's thoughts, why did he have to ask the blind men what they wanted? Why did Jesus fail to know their thoughts? Why could Jesus not logically have assumed that they would want to to see?

20:33-34 - THEY SAY: "LORD, THAT OUR EYES MAY BE OPENED." JESUS HAD COMPASSION ON THEM, TOUCHED THEIR EYES, AND IMMEDIATELY THEIR EYES RECEIVED SIGHT, AND THEY FOLLOWED HIM.

**Contradictions:**
MARK 10:51-52 - The blind man: "Lord, that I might receive my sight." Jesus said unto him, "Go thy way; thy faith hath made thee whole"; immediately he received his sight, and followed Jesus....
LUKE 18:41-43 - ...He said, "Lord, that I may receive my sight." Jesus said unto him, "Receive thy sight; thy faith has saved thee." Immediately he received his sight, and followed him....

[Were there two blind men who told Jesus that they wanted to see, or was there just one blind man who spoke to Jesus?]
[Did Jesus touch the eyes of the two blind men enabling them both to see, or did faith enable one blind man to see?]

**History:**
There are no secular records of Jesus healing any blind persons.

**Perplexing:**
Why did Jesus not heal them before they asked? Why did Jesus fail to heal all blind people? In MARK 8:23-25, Jesus had to spit on and touch a blind man's eyes to make him see. In JOHN 9:6-7, Jesus spit on the ground, made clay with the saliva, anointed the eyes of a blind man, and sent him to the pool of Siloam to wash; after having washed, the man could see. Why did Jesus use different methods to heal these blind men? Why are there no accounts outside the Bible of such amazing miracles as healing the blind?
See also under 9:28-30.

21:1-2 - WHEN THEY...WERE COME TO BETHPHAGE, UNTO THE MOUNT OF OLIVES, THEN SENT JESUS TWO DISCIPLES, SAYING, "GO INTO THE VILLAGE OVER AGAINST YOU, AND STRAIGHTWAY YE SHALL FIND AN ASS TIED, AND A COLT WITH HER; LOOSE THEM, AND BRING THEM UNTO ME."

**Contradictions:**
MARK 11:2 and LUKE 19:30 - Jesus told two disciples to go into a village where upon entering they would find a colt tied, upon which no man has sat; they were to loose it and bring it to him.
[Did Jesus send disciples to find and bring to him an ass and a colt, or just a colt?]
JOHN 12:14 - Jesus...found a young ass.... He did not send disciples to find an ass and/or a colt.]
[Did Jesus send disciples to find an ass and colt, or did Jesus, himself, find an ass?]

**Perplexing:**
If Jesus had to send disciples for an ass (and/or a colt), it may be assumed that he and the disciples did not have any with them. If so, how did they travel? Did they walk everywhere, other than when they were on a ship?

21:3 - JESUS: "IF ANY MAN SAY OUGHT UNTO YOU, YE SHALL SAY, 'THE LORD HATH NEED OF THEM....'"

**Perplexing:**
Why did Jesus not know with certainty whether any one would question the disciples?"

21:4-5 - THIS WAS DONE, THAT IT MIGHT BE FULFILLED WHICH WAS SPOKEN BY THE PROPHET, "TELL YE THE DAUGHTER OF SION [ZION], 'BEHOLD, THY KING COMETH UNTO THEE, MEEK, AND SITTING UPON AN ASS, AND A COLT THE FOAL OF AN ASS.'"

**Old Testament:**
ZECH. 9:9 - Zechariah: "...O daughter of Zion; O daughter of Jerusalem, behold, thy king cometh unto thee...lowly, and riding upon an ass, and upon a colt the foal of an ass." [This, however, is a mistranslation of the Hebrew which reads, "O daughter, thy king cometh unto thee; he is triumphant, and victorious,

lowly, and riding upon an ass, even upon a colt the foal of an ass.] (The version in Hebrew identifies only one animal: an ass' colt. MARK and LUKE did not cite the ZECH. verse, but correctly translated it to mean one animal; see Contradictions under 21:1-2; JOHN 12:15 cited part of the verse correctly by reporting only one animal, "an ass's colt.")

**Pagan parallel:**
In Greek mythology, the god Dionysus rode on two asses.

**Perplexing:**
Did MATT. misinterpret the Hebrew in ZECH., or did MATT. deliberately mix Greek mythology with ZECH?

21:6-7 - THE DISCIPLES...BROUGHT THE ASS, AND COLT, PUT ON THEM THEIR CLOTHES, AND SET HIM THEREON.

**Contradictions:**
MARK 11:7 - They brought the colt to Jesus, cast their garments on him, and he sat upon him."
LUKE 19:35 - They brought him to Jesus, cast their garments upon the colt, and set Jesus thereon.
[Did Jesus sit on an ass and a colt, or only on a colt?]
[Did the disciples put their clothes on an ass and colt, or only on a colt?]
JOHN 12:14 - Jesus, when he had found a young ass, sat thereon....
[Did the disciples bring an ass and colt to Jesus, or did he find an ass? ]
[Did the disciples set Jesus on an ass and colt, or did he, by himself, sit on an ass?]

**Perplexing:**
How could Jesus sit on the ass and colt at the same time, especially when the colt was probably smaller than the ass?

**Old Testament:**
1 KINGS 1:38-39 - Zadok...Nathan...Beniah...the Cherethites, and Pelethites caused Solomon to ride upon king David's mule, and brought him to Gihon. .... They blew the trumpet, and all the people said, "God save King Solomon."

21:8-9 - A VERY GREAT MULTITUDE SPREAD THEIR GARMENTS IN THE WAY.... AND...CRIED, "HOSANNA TO THE SON OF DAVID; BLESSED IS HE THAT COMETH IN THE NAME OF THE LORD; HOSANNA IN THE HIGHEST."

**Contradictions:**
MARK 11:8-10 - Many spread their garments in the way.... And...cried, "Hosanna; Blessed is he that cometh in the name of the Lord; Blessed be the kingdom of our father David, that cometh in the name of the Lord; Hosanna in the highest."
[Did the multitude say, "Hosanna to the Son of David," or "Hosanna; Blessed is he that cometh in the name of the Lord?"]
LUKE 19:36-38 - ...they spread their clothes in the way.... ...the whole multitude of disciples began to rejoice and praise God for all the mighty works that they had seen, saying, "Blessed be the King that cometh in the name of the Lord; peace in heaven, and glory in the highest."
[Did a great multitude cry, "Hosanna to the Son of David...Hosanna in the highest," or did the disciples praise God and say, " glory in the highest?"]

**Language:**
"Hosanna," used in the verses as a greeting, is a Hebrew word meaning, "save now."

**Old Testament:**
2 KINGS 9:13 - Then they hasted, and took every man his garment, and put it under him [Jehu] on the top of the stairs, and blew with trumpets, saying, "Jehu is king."
PS. 118:26 - "Blessed is he that cometh in the name of the LORD...."
See also under 21:6-7.

**Perplexing:**
Why did the multitude call Jesus, "Son of David?" Why was the Hebrew, "Hosanna," misused?
See also under 9:27.

21:10-11 - WHEN HE WAS COME INTO JERUSALEM, ALL THE CITY WAS MOVED, SAYING, "WHO IS THIS?" THE MULTITUDE SAID, "THIS IS JESUS, THE PROPHET OF NAZARETH OF GALILEE."

**Perplexing:**
Why did the people have to ask who Jesus was, considering that multitudes had seen and heard him and witnessed his miracles, and that his fame had spread throughout the land? Why was he identified as "the prophet of Nazareth," rather than as "the prophet of Capernaum," or the "Son of David" or the "Son of God, " or even as what Jesus called himself, "the Son of man?" Why was Jesus associated with Nazareth, his childhood home, when he was born in Bethlehem and resided in Capernaum?

21:12-13 - JESUS WENT INTO THE TEMPLE OF GOD, CAST OUT ALL THAT SOLD AND BOUGHT IN THE TEMPLE, OVERTHREW THE TABLES OF THE MONEYCHANGERS, AND THE SEATS OF THEM THAT SOLD DOVES, AND SAID, "IT IS WRITTEN, 'MY HOUSE SHALL BE CALLED THE HOUSE OF PRAYER,' BUT YE HAVE MADE IT A DEN OF THIEVES."

**History:**
At this time in Jerusalem, Roman, Greek, Persian, Syrian, Arabian, and Tyrian coins were in circulation. The temple tax which had to be paid by all adult Jewish males, other than priests, however, had to be paid with Tyrian coins. The moneychangers, therefore, served to exchange the foreign currencies for the required Tyrian money; for this, they charged a 4% fee. The birds and other animals were used for religious sacrifices and offerings in the temple.

**Contradictions:**
MARK 11:11-17 - Jesus entered...the temple; when he had looked around, the eventide was come; he went to Bethany with the twelve. On the morrow [after having cursed a fig tree].... ...Jesus went into the temple, and began to cast out them that bought and sold, overthrew the tables of the moneychangers, and the seats of them that sold doves.... He taught, "Is it not written, 'My house shall be called of all nations the house of prayer?' But ye have made it a den of thieves."
[Did Jesus cast out the moneychangers and others when he first entered the temple, or did he just look around?]
[Did Jesus cast out the moneychangers and others the first day that he entered the temple, or did he wait and do it the next day?]
JOHN 2:12-16 - Jesus went from Capernaum, where he was with his mother, brethren, and disciples, to

Jerusalem when Passover was at hand, and found in the temple those that sold oxen, sheep, and doves, and changers of money. When he had made a scourge of small cords, he drove them all out of the temple, and the sheep and oxen, and poured out the changers' money, and overthrew the tables, and said unto them that sold doves, "Take these things hence; make not my Father's house an house of merchandise."
[Did Jesus go to the temple after leaving Jericho with a multitude of people, or after leaving Capernaum with his disciples, brethren, and mother?]
[Was it not, or was it Passover?]
[Did the event take place towards the end of his ministry, or at the beginning (shortly after acquiring disciples in JOHN 1 and after converting water into wine in JOHN 2:7-11)?]
[Did Jesus say (quoting Scripture) that the temple was a house of prayer, but the merchants had turned it into a den of thieves, or did he say that it should not be turned into a house of merchandise?]

**Old Testament:**
ISA. 56:4-7 - Isaiah: "Saith the LORD unto the eunuchs that keep My sabbaths.... ...them will I bring to My holy mountain, and make them joyful in My house of prayer; their burnt offerings and sacrifices shall be accepted...for Mine house shall be called an house of prayer for all people."
JER. 7:9-11 - "'Will ye steal, murder, commit adultery, swear falsely burn incense unto Baal, and walk after other gods...and come...in this house.... Is this house, which is called by My name, become a den of robbers in your eyes? I have seen it,' saith the LORD."
ZECH. 14:21 (In the Masoretic Text) - Zechariah: "Every pot in Jerusalem and Judah shall be holy unto the LORD...and in that day there shall be no trafficker in the house of the LORD of hosts."

**Perplexing:**
Why did Jesus not first ask the merchants to leave? Why did he not ask the priests to remove them? Why did Jesus resort to violence? Why could he not control his temper? Why did he not perform a miracle that would have removed the merchants without the need for a violent temper tantrum? Why did he not ask his "Father" to remove them? Why did God tolerate them? Why did the merchants not retaliate and attack Jesus? Why did Jesus fail to comply with his order in 5:39 - "Resist not evil...?" Why did Jesus combine the ISA. and JER. verses and take them out of context to apply to the merchants?

21:14 - THE BLIND AND THE LAME CAME TO HIM IN THE TEMPLE, AND HE HEALED THEM.

**Perplexing:**
Why did the priests and others permit Jesus to remain in the temple after his violent outburst? How many people were healed? Why is there no historical record of this miraculous healing of the blind and lame in the temple? Why also do the other gospels fail to record these miracles in the temple?

21:15 - WHEN THE CHIEF PRIESTS AND SCRIBES SAW THE WONDERFUL THINGS THAT HE DID, AND THE CHILDREN IN THE TEMPLE, SAYING, "HOSANNA TO THE SON OF DAVID," THEY WERE SORE DISPLEASED.

**Perplexing:**
Why were the chief priests and scribes displeased? Why were they not in awe of someone with the power to heal the blind and lame? Why did they not want to befriend such a person and have him perform wonderful things for them? Why did the children now call Jesus, "the Son of David," rather than "the prophet of Nazareth" as he was called in 21:11?
See also under 9:27.

**Language:** See under 21:8-9.

21:16 - THE CHIEF PRIESTS AND SCRIBES: "HEAREST THOU WHAT THESE SAY?" JESUS SAITH, "HAVE YE NEVER READ, 'OUT OF THE MOUTH OF BABES AND SUCKLINGS THOU HAST PERFECTED PRAISE?'"

**Old Testament:**
PS. 8:2 - "Out of the mouth of babes and sucklings hast Thou ordained strength because of Thine enemies, that Thou mightest still the enemy and the avenger."

**Perplexing:**
Why did Jesus misquote and misuse the verse? Why did the priests and scribes fail to correct him?

21:17-19 - HE LEFT, WENT INTO BETHANY, AND LODGED THERE. IN THE MORNING AS HE RETURNED INTO THE CITY, HE HUNGERED. WHEN HE SAW A FIG TREE, HE CAME TO IT, FOUND NOTHING THEREON, BUT LEAVES, AND SAID, "LET NO FRUIT GROW ON THEE HENCEFORWARD FOREVER." THE TREE WITHERED AWAY.

**Contradictions:**
MARK 11:12-15 - On the morrow, when they were come from Bethany [after having visited the temple the previous day], he was hungry; seeing a fig tree...he came...he found nothing but leaves, for the time of figs was not yet. Jesus said, "No man eat fruit of thee hereafter forever." His disciples heard it. ...Jesus went to the temple and began to cast out them that sold and bought....
[Did Jesus curse the fig tree after, or before he threw the merchants out of the temple?]
JOHN 18:4 - Jesus, knowing all things that should come upon him, went forth....
[Did Jesus know, or not know that the tree would lack fruit?]

**Perplexing:**
Where in Bethany or with whom did Jesus and the disciples lodge? Did they have to pay for the lodging? Why did they not eat where they lodged? Why could Jesus not control his hunger? Why did Jesus fail to know that the tree would not have any figs on it? Why did Jesus destroy the tree rather than perform a miracle to put fruit on it or otherwise provide food for himself? (He was able to provide food for himself, his disciples, and thousands of people in MATT. 15 and 16.) Why was Jesus unable to control his temper and avoid cursing a tree? Why did Jesus engage in this act of cruelty that deprived other people of the opportunity to obtain fruit from the tree? Was this the action that one would expect from a Son of God, a Messiah, or a compassionate and merciful person? Why did he not bless the tree to bear fruit all year?

**Old Testament:**
JER. 8:13 - '"...'saith the LORD, 'There shall be no grapes on the vine, nor figs on the fig tree; the leaf shall fade, and the things that I have given them shall pass away from them.'"
HAB. 3:17 - Habakkuk: "The fig tree shall not blossom, neither shall fruit be on the vines...."

21:21 - JESUS SAID, "IF YE HAVE FAITH, AND DOUBT NOT, YE SHALL NOT ONLY DO THIS WHICH IS DONE TO THE FIG TREE, BUT ALSO IF YE SHALL SAY UNTO THIS MOUNTAIN, 'BE THOU REMOVED, AND BE THOU CAST INTO THE SEA,' IT SHALL BE DONE."

**Perplexing:**
In the approximately two millennia that have elapsed since Jesus was said to have uttered the above, why has no one been able to move a mountain, or a hill, or a pebble, or even a grain of sand by means of faith? Does no one have faith? Did Jesus lie? If faith is so powerful, why did Jesus fail to use it to grow figs on the fig tree, to remove the merchants from the temple, and cause everyone to accept his divinity? Why has faith failed to prevent crime, war, poverty, disease, or any natural disaster?

21:22 - JESUS: "ALL THINGS, WHATSOEVER YE SHALL ASK IN PRAYER, BELIEVING, YE SHALL RECEIVE."

**Perplexing:**
Why do not believers receive what they ask for in prayer? Do people really not believe that they will receive whatever is asked for? If prayer combined with faith is supposed to be so effective, why did Jesus fail to pray for acceptance by everyone? If what Jesus said is true, why do his followers not pray for the mass conversion to Christianity of everyone in the world? Why are prayers for peace, health, and for the elimination of crime, poverty, etc. not answered? Did Jesus lie? What would happen if two people believing, prayed for opposite things?

**Pagan concept:**
Some pagan religions, such as Wicca (witchcraft), also claim that if one wishes (prays) hard enough for something, it will be obtained.

21:23 - WHEN HE WAS COME INTO THE TEMPLE, THE CHIEF PRIESTS AND ELDERS OF THE PEOPLE CAME UNTO HIM AS HE WAS TEACHING, AND SAID, "BY WHAT AUTHORITY DOEST THOU THESE THINGS, AND WHO GAVE THEE THIS AUTHORITY?"

**Contradiction:**
MARK 11:27-28 - ...as he was walking in the temple, there come to him the chief priests, scribes, and elders, and say, "By what authority doest thou these things, and who gave thee this authority?"
[Was Jesus teaching, or walking in the temple when he was questioned by the chief priests and others?]

**Perplexing:**
How was Jesus able to teach in the temple without authorization from the chief priests? How could Jesus have obtained such authorization after his violent actions in the temple (21:12) and after having viciously denounced the Pharisees as "vipers" (12:34)? Why did the priests fail to order Jesus out of the temple or have him forcibly removed?

21:25-27 - JESUS: "THE BAPTISM OF JOHN, WHENCE WAS IT, FROM HEAVEN, OR OF MEN?" .... .... THEY ANSWERED, "WE CANNOT TELL."

**Perplexing:**
Jews did not practice baptism. Why, therefore, did Jesus ask them the question? Why did they not answer that it did not matter, since baptism was not a Jewish rite?
See also under 3:5-6.

**History:** See under 3:5-6.

**Pagan concept:** See under 3:5-6.

**Old Testament:** See under 3:5-6.

21:31 - .... JESUS SAITH [TO THE CHIEF PRIESTS AND ELDERS], "THE PUBLICANS AND HARLOTS GO INTO THE KINGDOM OF GOD BEFORE YOU."

**Perplexing:**
Why did the priests fail to inform Jesus that the concept of a "kingdom of God" is not a Jewish concept? Why did they fail to ask him to explain what he meant by the "kingdom of God?" Jesus did not condemn harlots. Why then do Christians tend to persecute them?

21:33-36 - JESUS: "HEAR ANOTHER PARABLE. THERE WAS A HOUSEHOLDER, WHICH PLANTED A VINEYARD, HEDGED IT ROUND ABOUT, DIGGED A WINEPRESS, BUILT A TOWER, AND LET IT OUT TO HUSBANDMEN, AND WENT TO A FAR COUNTRY; WHEN THE TIME OF FRUIT DREW NEAR, HE SENT HIS SERVANTS, THAT THEY MIGHT RECEIVE THE FRUITS; THE HUSBANDMEN BEAT ONE, KILLED ANOTHER, AND STONED A THIRD. OTHER SERVANTS WERE SENT, BUT THEY WERE TREATED LIKE THE FIRST ONES.

**Contradictions:**
MARK 12:1-5 - On three separate occasions one servant was sent; the husbandmen beat the first two and killed the third. The owner then sent more servants some of whom were beaten, others killed.
LUKE 20:10-12 - On three separate occasions, one servant was sent. Each was beaten by the husbandmen.
[Did Jesus say in the parable that the owner initially sent three servants to the husbandmen, or that on three separate occasions only one was sent?]
[Did Jesus say that one of the first three servants was killed, or that the three were just beaten?]
[Did Jesus say that several servants were sent after the first three, or that only three were sent?]

**Old Testament:**
ISA. 5:1-2 - .... My wellbeloved hath a vineyard...he fenced it...built a tower in the midst, and made a winepress therein....

21:37-39 - JESUS: "LAST OF ALL HE [THE OWNER] SENT UNTO THEM HIS SON.... WHEN THE HUSBANDMEN SAW THE SON, THEY SAID...'LET US KILL HIM....' THEY CAUGHT HIM, CAST HIM OUT OF THE VINEYARD, AND SLEW HIM.

**Contradiction:**
MARK 12:6-8 - "Having one son...He sent him.... The husbandmen .... They took him, killed him, and cast him out of the vineyard."
[Did Jesus say that the son was cast out of the vineyard and then killed, or that he was killed before being cast out?]

21:42 - JESUS SAITH, "DID YE NEVER READ THE SCRIPTURES, 'THE STONE WHICH THE BUILDERS REJECTED, IS BECOME THE HEAD OF THE CORNER; THIS IS THE LORD'S DOING, AND IT IS MARVELLOUS IN OUR EYES.'"

**Old Testament:**
PS. 118:22-23 - "The stone which the builders refused is become the head stone of the corner. This is the LORD's doing; it is marvelous in our eyes."

21:43 - JESUS: "THE KINGDOM OF GOD SHALL BE TAKEN FROM YOU, AND GIVEN TO A NATION BRINGING FORTH THE FRUITS THEREOF."

**Perplexing:** See under 21:31.

22:15-16 - THE PHARISEES, TOOK COUNSEL HOW THEY MIGHT ENTANGLE HIM IN HIS TALK. THEY SENT UNTO HIM THEIR DISCIPLES WITH HERODIANS....

**History:**
The Pharisees were anti-Roman; the Herodians were pro-Roman. It is highly unlikely, if not impossible, that the Herodians would have taken orders from or worked with the Pharisees, and highly unlikely, if not impossible, that the Pharisees would have been involved with the Herodians for any purpose. The two groups were bitter enemies, and at this time the Pharisees were advocating revolution against the Romans; the extremist Pharisees became a group of fanatics known as Zealots who perpetrated acts of violence against and murdered both Romans and Jews. They also began the failed rebellion that eventually led to the destruction of the Jerusalem temple by the Romans.

**Perplexing:**
Why did the gospel writer imply that the Pharisees and Herodians cooperated with each other?

22:17-21 - [THEY:] "...IS IT LAWFUL TO GIVE TRIBUTE UNTO CAESAR?" JESUS SAID, ".... SHEW ME THE TRIBUTE MONEY." THEY BROUGHT HIM A PENNY. HE SAITH, "WHOSE IS THIS IMAGE AND SUPERSCRIPTION?" THEY SAY, "CAESAR'S." SAITH HE, "RENDER UNTO CAESAR THE THINGS WHICH ARE CAESAR'S, AND UNTO GOD THE THINGS THAT ARE GOD'S."

**Perplexing:**
If Jesus did not object to paying tax, why do modern Christian clergy oppose doing so?
See also under 17:27.

**History:**
Copper coins of Judea did not bear any human likeness. Only the name of the emperor and innocuous symbols appeared on them. Roman denarii, however, depicted the figure of the emperor.

22:23-28 - CAME TO HIM THE SADDUCEES, WHICH SAY THAT THERE IS NO RESURRECTION, SAYING, "MOSES SAID, 'IF A MAN DIE, HAVING NO CHILDREN, HIS BROTHER SHALL MARRY HIS WIFE, AND RAISE UP SEED UNTO HIS BROTHER.'" THEY THEN POSED THE QUESTION THAT IF THERE WERE SEVEN BROTHERS, AND AFTER EACH DIED CHILDLESS, THE WOMAN MARRIED ONE OF THE REMAINING BROTHERS UNTIL SHE DIED, "IN THE RESURRECTION WHOSE WIFE SHALL SHE BE OF THE SEVEN?"

**Old Testament:**
DEUT. 25:5-6 - Moses: "If brethren dwell together, and one of them die, and have no child, the wife of the dead shall not marry without unto a stranger; her husband's brother shall go in unto her, and take her to wife, and perform the duty of an husband's brother unto her. It shall be, that the firstborn which she beareth shall succeed in the name of his brother, which is dead...."

**Perplexing:**
If the Sadducees did not believe in a resurrection, why did they ask Jesus a question pertaining to the resurrection?

22:30 - JESUS SAID, "IN THE RESURRECTION THEY NEITHER MARRY, NOR ARE GIVEN IN MARRIAGE, BUT ARE AS THE ANGELS OF GOD IN HEAVEN."

**Contradiction:**
GEN. 6:2-4 - The sons of God [generally accepted to mean angels] saw the daughters of men...and took wives of all which they chose...the sons of God came in unto the daughters of men, and they bare children to them....
[Do not, or do angels marry?]

**Perplexing:**
If angels do not marry as Jesus said, do they engage in sex without getting married? If Jesus meant that angels do not engage in sexual activity, why, according to biblical stories, do they resemble men, have male genitalia, and produce sperm (they were able to have sex with and impregnate human females in GEN. 6:2, 4)? Why are no angels said to look like women? If there are no female angels, are the male angels homosexual, or do they have sex with human females who are admitted into heaven? Do people have sexual relations in heaven without getting married? Why were angels not created as non-sexual creatures?

22:31-32 - JESUS: "...HAVE YE NOT READ THAT WHICH WAS SPOKEN BY GOD, 'I AM THE GOD OF ABRAHAM, ISAAC, AND JACOB?' GOD IS NOT THE GOD OF THE DEAD, BUT OF THE LIVING."

**Old Testament:**
EX. 3:4-6 - ... God called unto him [Moses] out of the midst of the [burning] bush. .... He said, "I am the God of thy father, of Abraham, of Isaac, and Jacob." ....

**History:**
The burning bush out of which God is reported to have spoken is a natural phenomenon. It is a shrub known botanically as Dictamnus albus. The plant has oil sacs that secrete a volatile oil in hot weather which ignites in direct sunlight; it burns away so rapidly, however, that the bush does not catch fire, but creates the illusion of a burning bush.

**Contradiction:**
LUKE 20:37 - Jesus: "...Moses shewed at the bush, when he calleth the Lord the God of Abraham, Isaac, and Jacob."
[Did Jesus say that God called Himself the God of Abraham, Isaac, and Jacob, or did he say that Moses called God the God of Abraham, Isaac, and Jacob?]

**Pagan parallels:**
Many ancient peoples believed that deities and spirits resided in bushes and trees. A number of pagan gods were also associated with mountains; for examples: Zeus, Baal, Indra, and Parvati.

22:35-38 - ONE OF THEM [PHARISEES], A LAWYER, ASKED, "MASTER, WHICH IS THE GREAT COMMANDMENT OF THE LAW?" JESUS SAID, "THOU SHALT LOVE THE LORD THY GOD WITH ALL THY HEART, ALL THY SOUL, AND WITH ALL THY MIND. THIS IS THE FIRST AND GREAT COMMANDMENT."

**Contradictions:**
EX. 20:2-3 and DEUT. 5:6-7 - [The first commandment is] "I am the LORD God, which have brought thee out of the land of Egypt, out of the house of bondage. Thou shalt have no other gods before me."
EX. 34:14 - [The first commandment is] "Thou shalt worship no other god, for the LORD, whose name is Jealous, is a jealous God."
[Is the first commandment to love God, or to have (worship) no other gods?]
MARK 12:28 - One of the scribes came, and...asked, "Which is the first commandment of all?"
[Did a Pharisee, or a scribe ask Jesus which is the first commandment?]

**Old Testament:**
DEUT. 6:5 - Moses: "Thou shalt love the LORD thy God with all thine heart, all thine soul, and with all thy might."

**Perplexing:**
If loving God is the great commandment, why is it not one of the ten commandments of EX. 20 or EX. 34? Why does an almighty deity of a universe of unimaginable proportions care about whether or not piddling, little, short-lived, humans love Him? Is God so vain, lonely, and insecure that He needs to be loved? Does God not receive enough love from His angels and other celestial creations? Is the belief that God wants human love an example of human pomposity—that humans consider themselves to be so important that even God needs their affection?

**History:**
The Pharisees considered this commandment to be so important that they believed it should be recited twice a day.

22:39 - JESUS: "THE SECOND IS LIKE UNTO IT, THOU SHALT LOVE THY NEIGHBOR AS THYSELF."

**Old Testament:**
LEV. 19:18 - The LORD said, "...thou shalt love thy neighbour as thyself."

**Perplexing:**
Why is this commandment, identified by Jesus as the second, not listed as one of the ten commandments in EX. 20 or 34?

**History:**
According to Hillel (c. 60 B.C. - c. A.D. 9), the doctrine of Judaism may be summed up as, "What thou dost not like do not to thy neighbor."

**Contradictions:**
EX. 20:4-5 and DEUT. 5:8-9 - [The second commandment is: ] “Thou shalt not make any graven image, or likeness of anything in heaven above, the earth beneath, or the water under the earth; thou shalt not bow down to, nor serve them....”
[Is the second commandment to love one’s neighbor, or not to make and serve any graven images?]
EX. 34:17 - [The second commandment is:] “Thou shalt make no molten gods.”
[Is the second commandment to love one’s neighbor, or make no molten gods?]

**Pagan parallels:**
Buddhism says that a Buddhist should love all people. Confucius (6th century B.C.) said, “Love your neighbor as yourself. Do to another what you would he should do unto you; do not unto another what you would not be done unto you.”

22:41-45 - WHILE THE PHARISEES WERE GATHERED TOGETHER, JESUS ASKED THEM, “WHAT THINK YE OF CHRIST? WHOSE SON IS HE?” THEY SAY, “THE SON OF DAVID.” HE SAITH, “HOW THEN DOTH DAVID IN SPIRIT CALL HIM LORD, SAYING, ‘THE LORD SAID UNTO MY LORD, “SIT ON MY RIGHT HAND, TILL I MAKE THINE ENEMIES THY FOOTSTOOL?” IF DAVID CALL HIM LORD, HOW IS HE HIS SON?’”

**Contradictions:** See under 1:18.

**Old Testament:**
PS. 110:1 - “The LORD said unto my Lord [“my lord,” in the Masoretic text; the term was used in addressing a king], ‘Sit thou at My right hand, until I make thine enemies thy footstool.’” [Jesus has taken the verse, which referred to God addressing a king, possibly David, out of context and applied it to himself.]

**Judaism:**
According to Jewish belief, the Messiah (Christ) is to be a king descended paternally from David.

**Perplexing:**
By denying that he was descended from David, was Jesus also denying that he was the Jewish Messiah - the Christ? If he was descended paternally from God, he could not be paternally descended from David. If, however, he claimed paternal descent from David, he could not be God’s Son.

IN MATT. 9:27, 15:22, 20:30-31, 21:9, 21:15; MARK 10:47-48; and LUKE 18:38-39, Jesus was addressed as “son of David,” and never denied it. Why? Why did he deny it now?

22:46 - NO MAN WAS ABLE TO ANSWER HIM A WORD....

**Perplexing:**
Why did the Pharisees fail to correct Jesus’ misinterpretation of the PS. verse?

23:1-3 - SPAKE JESUS TO THE MULTITUDE AND TO HIS DISCIPLES, “THE SCRIBES AND PHARISEES SIT IN MOSES’ SEAT; THEREFORE WHATSOEVER THEY BID YOU OBSERVE; THAT OBSERVE AND DO; BUT DO NOT AFTER THEIR WORKS, FOR THEY SAY, AND DO NOT.”

**Contradiction:**
MATT. 16:11-12 - Jesus: "...ye should beware of the leaven of the Pharisees and Sadducees?" Then understood they that he bid them...beware...of the doctrine of the Pharisees and Sadducees.
[Were the disciples to observe and do what they were bid by the Pharisees, or were they to beware of their doctrine?]

23:5 - JESUS: "ALL THEIR WORKS THEY DO TO BE SEEN OF MEN; THEY MAKE BROAD THEIR PHYLACTERIES, AND ENLARGE THE BORDERS OF THEIR GARMENTS."

**Old Testament:**
EX. 13:16 - The LORD: "It shall be for a token upon thine hand, and for frontlets between thine eyes...."
DEUT. 6:8 - Moses: "Thou shalt bind them for a sign upon thine hand, and they shall be as frontlets between thine eyes."
DEUT. 11:18 - Moses: "Therefore shall ye lay up these words in your heart, your soul, and bind them for a sign upon your hand, that they may be as frontlets between your eyes."
[These frontlets, or phylacteries, are small leather pouches containing parchment on which are written parts of EX. and DEUT. They are attached to the upper left arm and the forehead by thin straps; some fundamentalist Jews still wear them.]
NUM. 15:38 - The LORD: "Speak unto the children of Israel, and bid them make fringes in the borders of their garments...that they put upon the fringes a ribband of blue."

23:9 - JESUS: "CALL NO MAN YOUR FATHER UPON THE EARTH, FOR ONE IS YOUR FATHER, WHICH IS IN HEAVEN."

**Perplexing:**
If one should not call anyone "father" on earth, what should one call a male parent? Why are the clergy of certain Christian religions called "Father?" Why is the above command by Jesus ignored?

23:13 - JESUS: "WOE UNTO YOU, SCRIBES AND PHARISEES, HYPOCRITES! YE SHUT UP THE KINGDOM OF HEAVEN AGAINST MEN; YE NEITHER GO IN YOURSELVES, NEITHER SUFFER THEM THAT ARE ENTERING TO GO IN."

**Contradiction:** See under 15:7-9.

**Perplexing:**
Can one be a hypocrite and be righteous (5:20)? Why did the Pharisees fail to respond to Jesus' accusations? Why did they fail to ask Jesus what he meant by "the kingdom of heaven?"
See also under 15:7-9.

**History:** See under 3:7.

23:14 - JESUS: "WOE UNTO YOU, SCRIBES AND PHARISEES, HYPOCRITES! YE DEVOUR WIDOWS' HOUSES, AND FOR A PRETENCE MAKE LONG PRAYERS; THEREFORE YE SHALL RECEIVE THE GREATER DAMNATION."

**Contradiction:** See under 15:7-9.

**Perplexing:**
How can the Pharisees who Jesus said are righteous (5:20) receive damnation? Do the righteous "devour widows' houses?"

**History:** See under 3:7.

23:15 - JESUS: "WOE UNTO YOU, SCRIBES AND PHARISEES, HYPOCRITES! YE COMPASS SEA AND LAND TO MAKE ONE PROSELYTE, AND WHEN HE IS MADE, YE MAKE HIM TWOFOLD MORE THE CHILD OF HELL THAN YOURSELVES."

**Contradiction:** See under 15:7-9.

**Perplexing:**
How can the righteous (Pharisees) be children of hell? Since hell, as used by Jesus, is not a Jewish concept, why did the Pharisees fail to answer him?

**History:** See under 3:7.

23:17 - JESUS: "YE FOOLS AND BLIND...."

**Perplexing:**
In MATT. 5:22, Jesus said, " ...whosoever shall say, 'Thou fool,' shall be in danger of hell fire." Why did Jesus use a term that he had denounced? By calling the scribes and Pharisees, "fools," did Jesus place himself in danger of "hell fire?" Was Jesus exempt from following his own teachings? How could the scribes and Pharisees be fools, if they were righteous (5: 20)?

23:18 - JESUS: "WHOSOEVER SHALL SWEAR BY THE ALTAR, IT IS NOTHING...."

**Contradiction:**
MATT. 5:34 - Jesus: "Swear not at all...."
[ Is it acceptable to swear by the altar, or should one swear not at all?]

23:19 - JESUS: "YE FOOLS AND BLIND...."

**Perplexing:** See under 23:17.

23:23 - JESUS: "WOE UNTO YOU, SCRIBES AND PHARISEES, HYPOCRITES! YE PAY TITHE OF MINT...AND HAVE OMITTED THE WEIGHTIER MATTER OF THE LAW, JUDGMENT, MERCY, AND FAITH...."

**Contradiction:** See under 15:7-9.

**Perplexing:** See under 23:13.

**History:** See under 3:7.

23:25 - JESUS: "WOE UNTO YOU, SCRIBES AND PHARISEES, HYPOCRITES! YE MAKE CLEAN THE OUTSIDE OF THE CUP AND PLATTER, BUT WITHIN THEY ARE FULL OF EXTORTION AND EXCESS."

**Contradiction:** See under 15:7-9.

**Perplexing:**
How could the Pharisees be righteous (5:20) and be full of extortion.
See also under 23:13.

**History:** See under 3:7.

23:27 - JESUS: "WOE UNTO YOU, SCRIBES AND PHARISEES, HYPOCRITES! YE ARE LIKE WHITED SEPULCHRES, WHICH APPEAR BEAUTIFUL OUTWARD, BUT ARE WITHIN FULL OF DEAD MEN'S BONES, AND UNCLEANNESS."

**Contradiction:** See under 15:7-9.

**Perplexing:** See under 23:13.

**History:**
It was a Jewish custom to whitewash the exterior of tombs to warn passers-by of the uncleanness within. This was done, because a Jew who touched a tomb was considered to be ceremonially unclean and would be barred from the temple area, and have to undergo ritual purification.
See also under 3:7.

23:28 - JESUS: "YE ALSO OUTWARDLY APPEAR RIGHTEOUS UNTO MEN, BUT WITHIN YE ARE FULL OF HYPOCRISY AND INIQUITY."

**Contradiction:** See under 15:7-9.

**Perplexing:**
How could the Pharisees be righteous (5:20) and also be full of iniquity?
See also under 23:13.

**History:** See under 3:7.

23:29 - JESUS: "WOE UNTO YOU, SCRIBES AND PHARISEES, HYPOCRITES! YE BUILD THE TOMBS OF THE PROPHETS, AND GARNISH THE SEPULCHRES OF THE RIGHTEOUS."

**Contradictions:** See under 10:41 and 15:7-9.

**Perplexing:** See under 23:13.

**History:** See under 3:7.

23:30-31 - JESUS: "[PHARISEES AND SCRIBES] SAY, 'IF WE HAD BEEN IN THE DAYS OF OUR FATHERS, WE WOULD NOT HAVE BEEN PARTAKERS WITH THEM IN THE BLOOD OF THE PROPHETS.' YE BE WITNESSES UNTO YOURSELVES, THAT YE ARE THE CHILDREN OF THEM WHICH KILLED THE PROPHETS."

**Old Testament:**
There is no account of prophets being killed by the Hebrews/Jews or any ancestors of the Pharisees.

**Perplexing:**
Why did Jesus say that prophets were killed? Why did he not identify these prophets? Why did the Pharisees fail to point out that their fathers did not kill any prophets?

23:33 - JESUS: "YE SERPENTS, YE GENERATION OF VIPERS, HOW CAN YE ESCAPE THE DAMNATION OF HELL?"

**Contradictions:**
MATT. 5:44 - Jesus: "Love your enemies; bless them that curse you; do good to them that hate you, and pray for them which despitefully use you, and persecute you."
[Did Jesus believe that you should call your enemies names, or love and bless them?]
See also under 15:7-9.

**Perplexing:** See under 23:14.

23:34 - JESUS: " I SEND UNTO YOU PROPHETS, AND WISE MEN, AND SCRIBES; SOME OF THEM YE SHALL KILL AND CRUCIFY; SOME SHALL YE SCOURGE IN YOUR SYNAGOGUES, AND PERSECUTE FROM CITY TO CITY."

**History:**
There is no record of Jesus having sent any prophets, wise men, or scribes who were killed or persecuted by the Jews or anyone else.

**Perplexing:**
What prophets, wise men, and scribes did Jesus send? When and where were they killed, crucified, scourged, or persecuted? As crucifixion was a Roman, not a Jewish means of execution, why did Jesus erroneously say that the Pharisees would crucify some of the people he will send? Why would Jesus have been unable to protect the people he is to send?
Why did Jesus' prophecy fail?

23:35 - JESUS: "UPON YOU MAY COME ALL THE RIGHTEOUS BLOOD SHED UPON THE EARTH, FROM THE BLOOD OF RIGHTEOUS ABEL UNTO THE BLOOD OF ZACHARIAS SON OF BARACHIAS, WHOM YE SLEW BETWEEN THE TEMPLE AND THE ALTAR."

**Contradictions:**
GEN. 4:2-8 - Abel was a keeper of sheep and was killed by his brother Cain.
[Was Abel killed by the ancestors of the Pharisees, or by his brother?]
[Was Abel a prophet, or a keeper of sheep?]
ZECH. 1:1, 7 and the rest of the Old Testament - "Zechariah, the son of Berechiah," was not killed.

[Was Zacharias [Zechariah] the son of Berechiah killed, or was he not killed?]
See also under 10:41.

**History:**
Zacharias the son of Baruch was killed in the temple by Zealots in A. D. 68.
Zacharias the prophet and son of Berechiah was not killed.

**Perplexing:**
In 2 CHRON. 24:20-22, Zechariah the son of Jehoiada the priest was stoned to death at the commandment of Joash the king in the court of the house of the LORD. Why did Jesus confuse Zechariah the priest's son, who was not a prophet, with Zechariah the prophet? Since Zacharias the son of Baruch was killed after the time of Jesus, could MATT. have confused him with Zechariah the son of Berechiah? Why did the Pharisees, who were well versed in the Old Testament, fail to correct Jesus?

23:37 - JESUS: "O JERUSALEM, THOU THAT KILLEST THE PROPHETS...."

**History:**
There is no record of biblical prophets having been killed in Jerusalem.

**Perplexing:** See under 23:30-31.

23:39 - JESUS: "YE SHALL NOT SEE ME HENCEFORTH, TILL YE SHALL SAY, 'BLESSED IS HE THAT COMETH IN THE NAME OF THE LORD.'"

**Old Testament:** See under 21:8-9.

**Perplexing:**
Did Jesus forget that in 21:9, the multitude had already said, "Blessed is he that cometh in the name of the lord?"

24:1-2 - JESUS DEPARTED FROM THE TEMPLE; HIS DISCIPLES SHOWED HIM THE BUILDINGS OF THE TEMPLE. JESUS SAID, "...THERE SHALL NOT BE LEFT HERE ONE STONE UPON ANOTHER, THAT SHALL NOT BE THROWN DOWN."

**History:**
The temple had been built originally in the 6th century B.C. Then in 19 B.C., King Herod began to restore and enlarge it. The rebuilding, however, was not completed until A.D. 62, about 82 years later. It was destroyed by the Romans in A.D. 70. Historians and biblical scholars generally believe that MATT. was written some time after A.D. 70, so his report of Jesus' prophecy was very likely inserted by the gospel writer after the fact. Consequently, the prophecy may not be attributable to Jesus.

24:3-7 - ...THE DISCIPLES CAME SAYING, "WHEN SHALL THESE THINGS BE? WHAT SHALL BE THE SIGN OF THY COMING, AND THE END OF THE WORLD?" JESUS SAID, "TAKE HEED THAT NO MAN DECEIVE YOU. MANY SHALL COME IN MY NAME, SAYING, 'I AM CHRIST,' AND SHALL DECEIVE MANY. YE SHALL HEAR OF WARS AND RUMOURS OF WARS.... NATION SHALL RISE AGAINST NATION, AND KINGDOM AGAINST KINGDOM; THERE SHALL BE FAMINES, PESTILENCES, AND EARTHQUAKES, IN DIVERS PLACES."

**Contradictions:**

MATT. 12:39-40 - Jesus: "An evil and adulterous generation seeketh after a sign. There shall be no sign given to it, but the sign of the prophet Jonas; as Jonas was three days and three nights in the whale's belly, so shall the Son of man be three days and three nights in the heart of the earth."
MATT. 16:4 - Jesus: "...there shall no sign be given, but the sign of the prophet Jonas."
LUKE 11:29 - ...Jesus he [Jesus] began to say, "...there shall no sign be given, but the sign of Jonas the prophet."
[Did Jesus cite numerous signs that would foretell his return, or only the sign of Jonah?]
MARK 8:12 - He [Jesus]...saith, "Why doth this generation seek after a sign? There shall no sign be given unto this generation."
[Did Jesus say that there would be numerous signs foretelling his return, or that there would be no sign?]
LUKE 17:20 - ...Jesus: "The kingdom of God cometh not with observation."
[Did Jesus say that there would be numerous signs, or that the kingdom would not come with observation?]
See also under 12:38-39.

**Perplexing:**

Why in MATT. 10:23, did Jesus say to the disciples, "...ye shall not have gone over the cities of Israel, till the Son of man be come?" Why did Jesus fail to condemn war and teach people how to prevent it? Why did Jesus not eliminate famines, pestilences, and earthquakes? Was there any period in human history when the disasters forecast by Jesus did not occur? Why did Jesus not know that governments other than kingdoms would come into existence? Why did he fail to instruct people about democracy, freedom, and human rights? Why did Jesus fail to inform his disciples that they would not live to see the end of the world and his return?
Why can neither Jesus, nor his Father prevent false Christs from coming and deceiving people?
Why did Jesus speak as though his return would be imminent? The things he predicted have occurred repeatedly over the ensuing nearly two millennia, except in recent times when few kingdoms remain to engage in war with each other. Why has he failed to return?

**Pagan parallel:**

In Zoroastrianism, the end of the world is to be preceded by wars, pestilence, famine, and other calamities.

24:9 - JESUS: "THEN SHALL THEY DELIVER YOU UP TO BE AFFLICTED, SHALL KILL YOU, AND YE SHALL BE HATED OF ALL NATIONS FOR MY NAME'S SAKE."

**Perplexing:**

Why would Jesus not be able to protect his disciples from affliction, hate, and being killed? Why did he fail to inform his disciples that his future followers would become experts at the religious persecution, torture, and murder of others throughout the centuries to come?
See also under 10:23.

**History:**

Over the centuries, Jesus' followers have hated, persecuted, tortured, and killed countless tens of millions of innocent non-Christians in Jesus' name, although there are no biblical verses in which Jesus ordered them to do so. There is no historical evidence that Jesus' twelve disciples were hated, beaten, and killed, although for a brief time the Romans persecuted some early Christians. Historically, it was the Christians, who, as they increased in number, became the mass murderers of Jews, pagans, and even of each other.

24:11 - JESUS: "MANY FALSE PROPHETS SHALL RISE, AND SHALL DECEIVE MANY."

**Perplexing:**
Did Jesus prophesy the coming existence of modern evangelists and religious leaders all claiming to preach Jesus' teachings while soliciting money with which to enrich themselves?
Why can neither Jesus, nor his Father prevent people from being deceived by false prophets?

24:14 - JESUS: "THIS GOSPEL OF THE KINGDOM SHALL BE PREACHED IN ALL THE WORLD FOR A WITNESS UNTO ALL NATIONS; THEN SHALL THE END COME."

**Contradictions:**
MATT. 10:5-6 - ...Jesus: "Go not into the way of the Gentiles, and into any city of the Samaritans enter ye not; go rather to the lost sheep of the house of Israel."
MATT. 10:23 - Jesus: "Ye shall not have gone over the cities of Israel, till the Son of man be come."
MATT. 15:24 - Jesus: "I am not sent but unto the lost sheep of the house of Israel."
[Did Jesus tell the disciples to preach in all the world, or just to the lost sheep of Israel?]
[Will the end come after the gospel is preached to all nations, or was it to come before the disciples traveled over all of the cities of Israel?]
See also under 10:23.

**Perplexing:**
Why does almighty God need piddling human beings to travel around preaching His gospel? Why can He not do it Himself? If He did, there would be no question about his existence. If, however, God has decided beforehand whether or not a person is to be saved (JOHN 6:44 - Jesus: "No man can come to me, except the Father which hath sent me draw him...."), why must the gospel be preached at all?
In COL. 1:23, Paul said, "...the gospel, which ye have heard, and which was preached to every creature which is under heaven...."
Therefore, if the gospel has already been preached to all creatures, why has Jesus still failed to return? Why do missionaries continue to travel around the planet preaching?
See under 10:23.

24:15-16 - JESUS: "WHEN YE THEREFORE SHALL SEE THE ABOMINATION OF DESOLATION, SPOKEN OF BY DANIEL THE PROPHET, STAND IN THE HOLY PLACE ... LET THEM WHICH BE IN JUDAEA FLEE INTO THE MOUNTAINS."

**Old Testament:**
DAN. 11:31 - "Arms shall stand on his part, and shall pollute the sanctuary of strength, shall take away the daily sacrifice, and they shall place the abomination that maketh desolate."
DAN. 12:11 - "From the time that the daily sacrifice shall be taken away, and the abomination that maketh desolate be set up, there shall be 1290 days."

**History:**
The "abomination of desolation" was a name given to an altar dedicated to Zeus that Antiochus Epiphanes had placed on top of the altar of burnt offerings in the temple, in 168 B.C. Antiochus, who wanted to Hellenize the population of Jerusalem, prohibited Jewish worship and ceremonies including observance of the biblical Sabbath and circumcision. He ordered worship of and sacrifices made to Greek gods.

**Perplexing:**
Why did Jesus refer to something that occurred about two centuries earlier as something that is to happen in the future? Could MATT. have inserted the reference to the "abomination" for a Greek or other non-Jewish community that did not know to what it referred and that it was no longer in existence?
Why did Jesus say that only those in Judaea should flee? Will not people elsewhere be affected? Why will they not have to flee? Also, what good would it do to flee to the mountains?
According to MAL. 4:5, the LORD said, "I will send Elijah the prophet before the coming of the great and dreadful day of the LORD." Why, then, has the "day" not yet arrived, since in MATT. 11:14 and 17:12, Jesus said that Elijah had come?
See also under 17:11-13.

24:20 - JESUS: "PRAY THAT YOUR FLIGHT BE NOT IN WINTER, NEITHER ON THE SABBATH DAY."

**Perplexing:**
Why did Jesus tell his disciples to pray that his return would not be in the winter or on a Sabbath day? Why did he mislead them by implying that they would still be alive when he returned? Why did Jesus fail to know that most future Christians would discard the Lord's Sabbath day (Saturday) which he observed, and replace it with the Roman pagan Sabbath day (Sunday) in the fourth century?

24:21 - JESUS: "THEN SHALL BE GREAT TRIBULATION, SUCH AS WAS NOT SINCE THE BEGINNING OF THE WORLD TO THIS TIME, NO, NOR EVER SHALL BE."

**Old Testament:**
DAN. 12:1 - "...there shall be a time of trouble, such as never was since there was a nation... and at that time thy people shall be delivered, everyone found written in the book."

**Perplexing:**
Why would a good, merciful god create a great tribulation? Would such an action be more appropriate for a deity of evil?

24:22 - JESUS: "EXCEPT THOSE DAYS BE SHORTENED, THERE SHOULD NO FLESH BE SAVED; FOR THE ELECT'S SAKE THOSE DAYS SHALL BE SHORTENED."

**Perplexing:**
Why did God create people to destroy them? If God already selected those that He is going to save (His elect), why was it necessary for Jesus to come? Why believe in or obey Jesus or any of the commandments? What criteria did God use for choosing His elect?

24:24 - JESUS: "THERE SHALL ARISE FALSE CHRISTS, AND FALSE PROPHETS...IF IT WERE POSSIBLE, THEY SHALL DECEIVE THE VERY ELECT."

**Perplexing:** See under 24:11.

24:29 - JESUS: "IMMEDIATELY AFTER THE TRIBULATION OF THOSE DAYS SHALL THE SUN BE DARKENED; THE MOON SHALL NOT GIVE HER LIGHT; THE STARS SHALL FALL FROM HEAVEN, AND THE POWERS OF THE HEAVENS SHALL BE SHAKEN."

**Perplexing:**
If the sun was darkened, temperature on earth would plummet to well below 0° F in a relatively short time, and sink towards absolute zero. Consequently, no human life and probably no other life could survive. Why was Jesus unaware of this? Meanwhile, without sunlight, the moon would be darkened, because its light is reflected sunlight; the moon itself does not produce light; consequently, it cannot shine if the sun is darkened. Why did Jesus not know this? Why did Jesus say that the stars would fall from heaven? Stars, like all celestial bodies, are already falling (traveling) through space. Why was Jesus ignorant of this? To where did Jesus believe the stars would fall? If he believed that they would fall onto the earth, he was ignorant of the tremendous size of most stars and the huge number (googols) of them. If so, he was also ignorant of the intense heat that they generate—heat that would incinerate the planet if even one star came within several million miles of the earth. Why was Jesus also ignorant of the gravitational effect that an approaching star would have on the earth—disrupting its orbit and rotation? Why was Jesus as ignorant of astronomy as were his contemporaries and the people who wrote about him?

**Old Testament:**
ISA. 13:9-10 - The LORD: "The day of the LORD cometh, cruel with wrath and fierce anger.... The stars of heaven and the constellations thereof shall not give their light; the sun shall be darkened in his going forth, and the moon shall not cause her light to shine."
ISA. 13:13 - The LORD: "I will shake the heavens, and the earth shall remove out of her place...."

24:30-31 - JESUS: "THERE SHALL APPEAR THE SIGN OF THE SON OF MAN IN HEAVEN; THEN SHALL ALL THE TRIBES OF THE EARTH MOURN; THEY SHALL SEE THE SON OF MAN COMING IN THE CLOUDS OF HEAVEN WITH POWER AND GREAT GLORY. HE SHALL SEND HIS ANGELS WITH A GREAT SOUND OF A TRUMPET; THEY SHALL GATHER TOGETHER HIS ELECT FROM THE FOUR WINDS, FROM ONE END OF HEAVEN TO THE OTHER."

**Perplexing:**
Why has Jesus failed to return after approximately two millennia, and after telling his disciples in MATT. 10:23 that he would return before they finished going over the cities of Israel? Even if Jesus returned, who would be alive to see him and the angels in the terrible cold and darkness resulting from the sun being darkened, and after approaching stars had incinerated the earth? Who would be alive to hear the trumpet? Why did Jesus continually give the impression that his return would take place during the lifetime of his disciples? Why was he not honest with them and say that even in two millennia, after they were long dead, he would not return? Are there trumpets in heaven? If so, why? Of what are they made? Who makes them? Does anyone besides God and Jesus play them? Who writes the music for them? Are God and Jesus musicians? Are other musical instruments also played in heaven? If so, by whom?
See also under 24:20 and 24:29.

**Old Testament:**
DAN. 7:13-14 - Daniel: "I saw in the night visions, one like the Son of man came with the clouds of heaven, and came to the Ancient of days.... There was given him dominion, glory, and a kingdom...."
ZECH. 9:14 - Zechariah: "The LORD shall be seen...and the Lord GOD shall blow the trumpet...."

**Language:** See under 8:20.

**History:** See under 8:20.

24:33-34 - JESUS: "WHEN YE SHALL SEE ALL THESE THINGS, KNOW THAT IT IS NEAR, EVEN AT THE DOORS. THIS GENERATION SHALL NOT PASS TILL ALL THESE THINGS BE FULFILLED."

**Contradictions:** See under 24:3-7.

**Perplexing:**
Why did Jesus tell his disciples that they and their generation would see the things that he prophesied? He said that the events he mentioned were "even at the doors." Why did his prophecy fail? Why did he lie to the disciples? If Jesus had not meant that the existing generation would see his prophecy fulfilled, why did he make such a definitive statement? Why did he not qualify his prophecy by saying that it pertained to events to occur thousands of years into the future?
See also under 3:2, 10:23, 16:28, and 24:30-31.

**Old Testament:** See under 16:28.

24:35 - JESUS: "HEAVEN AND EARTH SHALL PASS AWAY, BUT MY WORDS SHALL NOT PASS AWAY."

**Old Testament:**
ISA. 65:17 - God: "I create new heavens and a new earth; the former shall not be remembered, nor come into mind."

**Contradiction:**
ECCL. 1:4 - "One generation passeth away, and another generation cometh, but the earth abideth forever." [Will the earth pass away, or will it endure forever?]

**Pagan parallel:**
Buddha: "Though heavens were to fall to earth, and the great world swallowed up and pass away...the words of Buddha are true."

24:36 - JESUS: "OF THAT DAY AND HOUR KNOWETH NO MAN; NO, NOT THE ANGELS OF HEAVEN, BUT MY FATHER ONLY."

**Perplexing:**
If Jesus is the Son of God, part of the Trinity with God, and one with God (JOHN 10:30), how could he not know when the end would come? If he did not know, why did he speak with such certainty that it would occur during the life of his disciples and that of the high priest (26:64 - Jesus saith unto him (the high priest), "Hereafter shall ye see the Son of man sitting on the right hand of power, and coming in the clouds of heaven.")? In 11:14 and 17:12, Jesus said that Elijah who was to precede the end of the world had come.

**Judaism:** See under 11:13-14.

24:42 - JESUS: "WATCH THEREFORE, FOR YE KNOW NOT WHAT HOUR YOUR LORD DOTH COME."

**Perplexing:** See under 24:36.

24:44 - JESUS: "BE READY, FOR IN SUCH AN HOUR AS YE THINK NOT THE SON OF MAN COMETH."

**Perplexing:**
Why did Jesus again speak to his disciples as though they would be alive to see him return? Why did he fail to even hint that he would not return for millennia?
See also under 24:36.

25:13 - JESUS: "WATCH THEREFORE, FOR YE KNOW NEITHER THE DAY NOR THE HOUR WHEREIN THE SON OF MAN COMETH."

**Perplexing:** See under 24:36 and 24:44.

25:14-30 - JESUS RECITED A PARABLE IN WHICH A MAN HAVING TO TRAVEL TO A DISTANT COUNTRY ENTRUSTED VARIOUS SUMS OF MONEY WITH THREE SERVANTS. TWO OF THEM ENGAGED IN SPECULATION OR USURY AND DOUBLED THE AMOUNT OF MONEY THAT HAD BEEN LEFT WITH THEM. THE THIRD SERVANT WAS HONEST, KEPT THE MONEY SAFE, AND RETURNED IT TO THE MAN WHEN HE RETURNED. THE FIRST TWO SERVANTS WERE REWARDED, BUT THE THIRD WAS CALLED "WICKED" AND WAS PUNISHED BY BEING CAST "INTO OUTER DARKNESS."

**Perplexing:**
Why did Jesus believe that an honest servant who did not engage in speculation or usury was wicked and deserved to be cast into outer darkness? Why did Jesus approve of speculation or usury? Why did he not commend the servant for his honesty? Why did he not denounce the man for his greed?
See also under 8:12 and 13:41-42.

**Pagan concept:** See under 8:12.

25:31-33 - JESUS: "WHEN THE SON OF MAN SHALL COME IN HIS GLORY, AND ALL THE HOLY ANGELS WITH HIM...BEFORE HIM SHALL BE GATHERED ALL NATIONS; AND HE SHALL SEPARATE THEM, AS A SHEPHERD DIVIDETH HIS SHEEP FROM THE GOATS"; HE SHALL SET THE SHEEP ON HIS RIGHT HAND, BUT THE GOATS ON THE LEFT."

**Old Testament:**
EZEK. 34:17 - The LORD GOD: "As for you, My flock, I judge between cattle and cattle, between the rams and the he goats."

**Pagan parallel:**
In Zoroastrianism, at the time the dead are resurrected, the righteous will be separated from the wicked.

**Perplexing:**
There are gradations of good and evil, and these may vary from society to society. How then can a clear-cut distinction be made between them? Can anyone be totally good or totally bad?

25:37 - JESUS: "THEN SHALL THE RIGHTEOUS ANSWER HIM...."

**Contradiction:** See under 10:41.

25:41 - JESUS: "THEN SHALL HE SAY UNTO THEM ON THE LEFT HAND, 'DEPART FROM ME, YE CURSED, INTO EVERLASTING FIRE, PREPARED FOR THE DEVIL AND HIS ANGELS.'"

**Contradictions:**
EX. 34:6 - The LORD...proclaimed, "The LORD God, merciful and gracious, long suffering, and abundant in goodness and truth."
NUM. 14:18 - Moses: "The LORD is long suffering, and of great mercy, forgiving iniquity and transgression...."
PS. 86:15 - "Thou, O Lord, art a God full of compassion, gracious, long suffering, and plenteous in mercy and truth."
[Does God curse and send people into everlasting fire, or is He compassionate, long suffering, merciful, and forgiving?]
MATT. 5:44 - Jesus: "Love your enemies; bless them that curse you; do good to them that hate you; pray for them which despitefully use you, and persecute you."
[Should one's enemies be loved and blessed, or should they be cursed and cast into everlasting fire?]

**Perplexing:**
Since evil cannot exist without the connivance of God, and since God, being omniscient, knew who and what would be evil but did nothing to prevent it, is He morally justified in punishing anyone? Is He also not responsible for the evil perpetrated by His creations? He could have prevented it, if He wanted to do so. Even Satan could not exist without God's permission. Is punishment in everlasting fire what one would expect from a merciful God? Why would God consign individuals to an eternity of everlasting fire for what they did during a very brief, infinitesimal, time on earth? Was Jesus attempting to induce belief in him and his Father by inciting fear in people?
See also under 13:40 and 13:41-42.

**Old Testament:** See under 13:40 and 13:41-42.

**Pagan concept:** See under 13:41-42.

25:46 - JESUS: "THESE SHALL GO AWAY INTO EVERLASTING PUNISHMENT, BUT THE RIGHTEOUS INTO LIFE ETERNAL."

**Contradictions:**
ECCL. 9:5 - "The living know that they shall die, but the dead know not anything, neither have they anymore a reward...."
[Is there, or is there not, a reward after death?]
See also under 10:41 and 19:17-19 (for obtaining eternal life).

**Perplexing:**
Would an endless life be so monotonous as to be worse than death? Is not everlasting punishment, also eternal life? Is not everlasting punishment an evil that one would expect to be inflicted by a fiendish deity—a devil—not by a merciful God? What shape will people have in eternal life? Will they look as they

did when they died? Will they be composed of flesh and blood? Will they wear clothes or be naked? Why did Jesus resort to threats and fear, rather than reason and logic to convert people to his teachings? Can a belief predicated on fear be sincere?
See also under 5:29-30, 10:41, 19:16, and 25:41.

**Pagan concept:** See under 13:41-42 and 19:16.

26:2 - JESUS: "AFTER TWO DAYS IS THE FEAST OF PASSOVER, AND THE SON OF MAN IS BETRAYED TO BE CRUCIFIED."

**History:**
The Jewish holiday known as Passover is a combination of two ancient pagan festivals that were in existence long before the time the Exodus is supposed to have taken place. One was a thanksgiving rite in which an agricultural animal was sacrificed; the other celebrated the beginning of the grain harvest at which time unleavened bread was eaten. (The two holidays are noted in MARK 14 :1 - (1) the feast of Passover and (2) the feast of unleavened bread.)
Passover was observed by the early followers of Jesus into the fourth century. It was then that the Roman Emperor Constantine commanded them to cease observing the biblical Passover that Jesus observed and, instead, to observe the ancient pre-Christian Easter celebration of the resurrection of pagan gods who after being killed rose from the dead around the vernal equinox. Constantine also ordered the execution of any Christian who continued to observe Passover. Furthermore, it was this emperor who ordered the execution of any Christian who observed the biblical Sabbath, Saturday, rather than the Roman pagan Sunday Sabbath. Now, about 1700 years later, the vast majority of Christians are still obedient to Constantine, and reject the biblical God's commandments to observe the Saturday Sabbath (EX. 12:14-27, 13:6-7, 34:18, NUM. 9:2-4, DEUT. 16:1, and other verses). Thus, after converting to Christianity, Constantine merged the religion of Jesus and Paul with Roman paganism to create modern Christianity with all of its sects.
By saying that he was to be crucified, a Roman method of execution, Jesus said that he would be killed by the Romans.

26:3-4 - ASSEMBLED TOGETHER THE CHIEF PRIESTS, SCRIBES, AND ELDERS OF THE PEOPLE, UNTO THE PALACE OF THE HIGH PRIEST, CALLED CAIAPHAS, AND CONSULTED THAT THEY MIGHT TAKE JESUS BY SUBTILITY, AND KILL HIM.

**Perplexing:**
What did Jesus do to incite the priests, scribes, and elders to want to kill him? He has not been said to have violated any Jewish laws. Why also would they want to kill someone who could heal the sick and infirm and raise the dead? Why were they not in awe and fear of Jesus? Why did they not want to cultivate his friendship so as to benefit from his miraculous abilities?
See also under 12:14.

26:6-7 - WHEN JESUS WAS IN BETHANY [TWO DAYS BEFORE PASSOVER (26:2)], IN THE HOUSE OF SIMON THE LEPER...A WOMAN HAVING AN ALABASTER BOX OF VERY PRECIOUS OINTMENT, POURED IT ON HIS HEAD, AS HE SAT AT MEAT.

**Contradictions:**
LUKE 7:36-38 - [Long before Jesus went to Jerusalem (LUKE 19:41-45)] One of the Pharisees, named Simon (7:40), desired that he would eat with him. He went into the Pharisee's house, and sat down to meat. A woman, a sinner, brought an alabaster box of ointment, stood at his feet behind him weeping, and began

to wash his feet with tears, wiped them with her hair, kissed his feet, and anointed them with the ointment.
[Did the incident take place in Bethany after Jesus had been in Jerusalem and the temple, or before Jesus went to Jerusalem?]
[Was he in the house of a Simon the leper, or Simon the Pharisee?]
[Did a woman anoint Jesus' head, or his feet?]
JOHN 12:1-3 - Jesus six days before Passover came to Bethany, where Lazarus was...whom he raised from the dead. There they made him a supper; Martha served.... Then took Mary a pound of ointment of spikenard, very costly, anointed the feet of Jesus, and wiped his feet with her hair....
[Did the incident occur two days, or six days before Passover?]
[Was Jesus in the house of Simon the leper, or the house of Martha, Mary, and Lazarus?]
[Did the incident occur after Jesus made his first and only trip to Jerusalem, or before Jesus made his third trip to Jerusalem?]
[Was Jesus' head anointed by an unidentified woman, or were his feet anointed by Mary?]
[Were not, or were Jesus' feet washed with tears, kissed, and wiped with hair?]

**Perplexing:**
Why did the woman pour the ointment on Jesus? Was this Simon the leper the same person as the Pharisee cited in LUKE? If so, why did a Pharisee invite Jesus into his home? Why did Jesus accept the invitation? Did Jesus heal Simon? Did Simon really have leprosy? If he did have the disease, why was he not forced to reside outside the city as other lepers were compelled to do? Why was Jesus not anointed before now, as his title, Christ, means "anointed" or "the anointed one?" (See under 1:1 - Language.) Why was Jesus anointed by a woman who was identified as a sinner in LUKE 7:37? If she was a sinner, why did Simon allow her to come into his house?

**Pagan concept:**
The Hindu god Krishna was anointed by a woman pouring oils and perfumes onto his head.

26:8-9 - HIS DISCIPLES HAD INDIGNATION, SAYING, "TO WHAT PURPOSE IS THIS WASTE? THIS OINTMENT MIGHT HAVE BEEN SOLD FOR MUCH, AND GIVEN TO THE POOR."

**Contradictions:**
LUKE 7:39 - When the Pharisee saw it, he spake within himself, "This man, if he were a prophet, would have known who and what manner of woman this is that toucheth him, she is a sinner." [The disciples were not said to be present.]
[Did the disciples speak to Jesus about the ointment, or did the Pharisee speak to himself about the woman?]
JOHN 12:4-5 - Then saith Judas Iscariot, Simon's son, which should betray him, "Why was not this ointment sold for 300 pence, and given to the poor?"
[Did the disciples, or Judas Iscariot question Jesus about the ointment?]

26:11 - JESUS: "YE HAVE THE POOR ALWAYS WITH YOU, BUT ME YE HAVE NOT ALWAYS."

**Contradictions:**
MATT. 19:21 - Jesus: "If thou wilt be perfect, go and sell that thou hast, and give to the poor, and thou shalt have treasure in heaven; come and follow me."
[Should people ignore the poor, because they will always be present, or should they give the proceeds from the sale of their belongings to the poor?]
MATT. 28:20 - Jesus: "...I am with you alway [sic]...."

[Did Jesus say that he will not, or will always be with the disciples?]

**Perplexing:**
Why did Jesus not eliminate poverty?

26:13 - JESUS: "WHERESOEVER THIS GOSPEL SHALL BE PREACHED IN THE WHOLE WORLD, THERE SHALL ALSO THIS, THAT THIS WOMAN HATH DONE, BE TOLD FOR A MEMORIAL OF HER."

**Contradictions:**
MATT. 10:5-6 -...Jesus commanded, "Go not into the way of the Gentiles, and into any city of the Samaritans enter not. Go rather to the lost sheep of the house of Israel."
[Did Jesus say that the gospel shall be preached to the whole world, or just to the lost sheep of the house of Israel?]
MATT. 10:23 - Jesus: "Ye shall not have gone over the cities of Israel till the Son of man be come."
[Did Jesus say that this gospel shall be preached in the whole world, or just in some of the cities of Israel?]

**Perplexing:**
If what the woman did was so important, why was her name not given? Why is her action virtually never mentioned by Christians? Why was she not canonized? Why has she been consigned to obscurity, whereas Pilate's wife, Claudia Procula, was canonized by the Greek Orthodox and Coptic churches for merely having a dream about Jesus (MATT. 27:19)? Why has Jesus prophecy about her failed to materialize?

26:14-16 - ONE OF THE TWELVE, JUDAS ISCARIOT, WENT UNTO THE CHIEF PRIESTS, AND SAID, "WHAT WILL YE GIVE ME, AND I WILL DELIVER HIM UNTO YOU?" THEY COVENANTED WITH HIM FOR 30 PIECES OF SILVER. FROM THAT TIME HE SOUGHT OPPORTUNITY TO BETRAY HIM.

**Perplexing:**
Why was Judas the one to betray Jesus? Why did the chief priests agree to pay him for betraying Jesus? They have had no difficulty meeting and speaking with Jesus. Obviously, they knew where he could be located, so there was no need for them to pay Judas or anyone else for this information. Paul, in his Epistles which were written before the gospels, did not mention a betrayal by Judas. Why? Why was a betrayal necessary? If Jesus was to die and be resurrected, why did he not voluntarily turn himself over to the priests? Why could he not have been resurrected after dying a natural death?
If the crucifixion and resurrection were preordained, why was it necessary for Judas to betray Jesus?
See also under 26:3-4.

**Old Testament:**
ZECH. 11:12-13 - Zechariah: "If ye think good, give me my price; if not, forbear. So they weighed for my price 30 pieces of silver. The LORD said unto me, 'Cast it unto the potter, a goodly price that I was prised at of them.' I took the 30 pieces of silver and cast them to the potter [treasury] in the house of the LORD."

26:17-18 - THE FIRST DAY OF THE FEAST OF UNLEAVENED BREAD THE DISCIPLES CAME TO JESUS, SAYING, "WHERE WILT THOU THAT WE PREPARE TO EAT THE PASSOVER?" HE SAID, "GO INTO THE CITY TO SUCH A MAN, AND SAY, 'MY MASTER SAITH, MY TIME IS AT HAND; I WILL KEEP THE PASSOVER AT THY HOUSE WITH MY DISCIPLES.'"

**Contradictions:**

MARK 14:12-14 - The first day of unleavened bread...his disciples said, "Where wilt we go and prepare the Passover?" He sendeth forth two of his disciples, and saith, "Go into the city, and there shall meet you a man bearing a pitcher of water; follow him. Wheresoever he shall go in, say to the goodman of the house, 'The Master saith, where is the guestchamber, where I shall eat the Passover with my disciples?'"

LUKE 22:7-11 - Came the day of unleavened bread.... He sent Peter and John, saying, "Go and prepare the Passover.... They said, "Where wilt thou that we prepare?" He said, "When ye are entered into the city, there shall a man meet you, bearing a pitcher of water; follow him into the house where he entereth, and say unto the goodman of the house, 'The Master saith, where is the guestchamber, where I shall eat the Passover with my disciples?'"

[Did Jesus instruct the disciples to go directly to a specific man and say that he will keep the Passover at his house, or did he tell the disciples to meet and follow a man bearing a pitcher of water to a house and ask about a guestchamber?]

[Did Jesus send all the disciples into the city, or did he send only two of them?]

JOHN 19:1-14 - Jesus was questioned by Pilate at the time of the preparation of the Passover.

[Was Jesus with his disciples preparing to eat the Passover meal, or was he being interrogated by Pilate?]

LUKE 8:1 - [After being anointed by a woman] He went throughout every city and village, preaching....

[After being anointed, did Jesus prepare for Passover, or did he go around preaching?]

JOHN 12:12-50 - [After being anointed by Mary] Jesus went to Jerusalem where people greeted him saying, "Hosanna; Blessed is the King of Israel...." He then engaged in a discourse with his disciples and others.

[After being anointed, did Jesus prepare for Passover or did he go to Jerusalem where he was greeted and where he spoke to the people and his disciples?]

**Perplexing:**

Why was the homeowner not identified?

**History:** See under 26:2.

26:19-21 - THE DISCIPLES...MADE READY THE PASSOVER. WHEN THE EVEN WAS COME, HE SAT DOWN WITH THE TWELVE DISCIPLES. AS THEY DID EAT, HE SAID, "ONE OF YOU SHALL BETRAY ME."

**Contradictions:**

JOHN 13:1-21 - Before the feast of the Passover...Supper being ended...Jesus said "One of you shall betray me."

[Did Jesus say at the Passover meal, that he would be betrayed, or did he say it at the supper prior to Passover?]

[Did Jesus say while eating, or after eating that he would be betrayed?]

[Was Jesus' last supper a Passover meal, or was it a meal the day before Passover?]

JOHN 19:1:31 - Pilate scourged and conversed with Jesus and had him crucified just prior to the eve of Passover.

[Was Jesus with his disciples at the Passover meal, or was he with Pilate and crucified prior to the Passover meal?]

**Perplexing:**

Why was a betrayal needed? Why could Jesus not have been seized by the Romans or the chief priests

without first being betrayed?
See also under 26:14-16.

**Pagan parallel:**
Mithra, primarily a Persian and Roman resurrected savior god, had a last supper with twelve disciples, at least 400 years before the time of Jesus.

26:22 - THEY WERE EXCEEDING SORROWFUL, AND BEGAN EVERY ONE OF THEM TO SAY, "LORD, IS IT I?"

**Contradictions:**
LUKE 22:23 - They began to inquire among themselves, which of them should do this thing.
[Did each of the disciples ask Jesus if he was the one to betray him, or did they ask among themselves who it would be?]
JOHN 13:22-25 - The disciples looked one on another, doubting of whom he spake. There was leaning on Jesus' bosom one of his disciples, whom Jesus loved. Peter beckoned to him, that he should ask Jesus of whom he spake. He lying on Jesus' breast saith, "Lord, who is it?"
[Did each of the disciples ask Jesus if he would betray Jesus, or did Peter ask another disciple to ask Jesus?]

26:23 - HE [JESUS] SAID, "HE THAT DIPPETH HIS HAND WITH ME IN THE DISH, THE SAME SHALL BETRAY ME."

**Contradictions:**
LUKE 22:21 - [Before the disciples inquired in LUKE 22:31 about who will betray Jesus] Jesus said, "The hand of him that betrayeth me is with me on the table."
[Did Jesus say that his betrayer would dip his hand with him in a dish, or that the betrayer's hand is on the table?]
[Did Jesus indicate who would betray him after, or before the disciples asked about it?]
JOHN 13:26 - Jesus answered, "He it is, to whom I shall give a sop, when I have dipped it."
[Did Jesus say that his betrayer would be the one to dip his hand with him in a dish, or the one to whom he will give a sop?]

26:24 - JESUS: "...WOE UNTO THAT MAN BY WHOM THE SON OF MAN IS BETRAYED! IT HAD BEEN GOOD FOR THAT MAN IF HE HAD NOT BEEN BORN."

**Contradiction:**
MATT. 19:28 - Jesus said, "...ye [the disciples including Judas Iscariot] shall sit upon twelve thrones, judging the twelve tribes of Israel."
LUKE 22:29-30 - Jesus: "I appoint unto you a kingdom...that ye may eat and drink at my table in my kingdom, and sit on thrones judging the twelve tribes of Israel."
[Did Jesus say, "woe" unto his betrayer and that it would have been good for him not to have been born, or did he promise him a throne from which to judge the Israelite tribes?]

**Perplexing:**
Why did Jesus speak so vehemently against the man who was to betray him—a man for whom Jesus promised a throne from which to judge the Israelite tribes? Jesus knew that he was to be betrayed and

selected Judas to do it. Why was Judas selected? Was not Judas doing the will of God by betraying Jesus? If he had not betrayed Jesus, there would have been no arrest, trial, crucifixion, resurrection, or Christianity. Rather than condemning Judas, should not Jesus have thanked him? Should not Judas be honored and praised for making it possible for Jesus to fulfill his mission? By denouncing Judas, was Jesus saying that he did not want to be killed and resurrected in accordance with his Father's plan?
See also under 19:28 and 26:14-16.

26:25-28 - JUDAS SAID, "MASTER IS IT I?" HE SAID, "THOU HAST SAID." AS THEY WERE EATING, JESUS TOOK BREAD, BLESSED IT, BRAKE IT, GAVE IT TO THE DISCIPLES, AND SAID, "TAKE, EAT; THIS IS MY BODY." HE TOOK THE CUP, GAVE THANKS, AND GAVE IT TO THEM, SAYING, "DRINK ALL OF IT; THIS IS MY BLOOD OF THE NEW TESTAMENT, WHICH IS SHED FOR MANY FOR THE REMISSION OF SINS."

**Contradictions:**
MARK 14:22-24 - Jesus took bread.... He took the cup...and they all drank. He said, "This is my blood of the new testament, which is shed for many."
[Did Jesus say that his blood is shed for the remission of sins, or for many?]
LUKE 22:17-21 - He took the cup... and said, "Take this, and divide it among yourselves...." He took bread.... [Jesus:] "...this cup is the new testament in my blood, which is shed for you. The hand of him that betrayeth me is with me on the table."
[Did Jesus give the disciples the bread, or the cup first?]
[Did Jesus say that his blood is shed for the remission of sins, or for the disciples?]
[Did Jesus give his disciples bread and wine after, or before saying that he will be betrayed?]

**Judaism:**
At a Passover meal the wine is taken before the bread.

**Pagan concept:**
The concept of bread and wine representing the body and blood of a god is found in some pre-Christian religions such as those involved in the worship of Mithra, Osiris, Dionysus, and Tammuz.

**Pagan parallels:**
Those persons being initiated into Mithraism partook of a Eucharistic sacrament of bread and wine. In the worship of Osiris, bread, in the form of buns or wafers, inscribed with a cross, was eaten.

**History:**
The belief that bread and wine can represent the body of a deity existed at least as far back as 3000 B.C. In the Dead Sea Scrolls, members of the Qumran community, generally believed to have been Essenes, referred to themselves as "a community of the New Testament of the Covenant."

**Perplexing:**
Why did Jesus resort to an ancient pagan belief and ritual? Why did Jesus, by taking the bread before the wine, fail to adhere to Jewish ritual? Why did Jesus and the disciples permit Judas to partake of the Eucharist? Why, after Jesus said that he would be betrayed, and after identifying Judas as the one who will betray him, did things proceed as if there had been no mention of a betrayal? Why did the disciples not question Jesus further about the matter, not ask Judas why he would do it, or condemn him for it? Is it possible that the verses about the betrayal were carelessly added to the gospels by a redactor at a later date?

**Old Testament:**
GEN. 14:18 - Melchizedek king of Salem brought forth bread and wine....
DEUT. 14:26 - Moses: "Thou shalt bestow that money for whatever thy soul lusteth after...for wine, or strong drink...and thou shalt rejoice...." [Contrary to claims by some Christian groups, God approved of drinking alcoholic beverages.]
PROV. 9:5 - Wisdom: "Come eat of my bread, and drink of the wine which I have mingled."
ECCL. 9:7 - "Go thy way, eat thy bread with joy, and drink thy wine with a merry heart...."
ISA. 22:13 - Isaiah: "...eating flesh, and drinking wine, let us eat and drink, for tomorrow we shall die."
JER. 31:31 - "Saith the LORD, 'I will make a new covenant with the house of Israel, and the house of Judah.'"

26:29 - JESUS: "I WILL NOT DRINK HENCEFORTH OF THIS FRUIT OF THE VINE, UNTIL THAT DAY WHEN I DRINK IT NEW WITH YOU IN MY FATHER'S KINGDOM."

**Perplexing:**
If there is wine in heaven, what varieties are there? If so, are there wineries and vineyard workers? If so, are the vineyard workers angels, people, or other heavenly beings? Do people and/or angels get drunk? Are there alcoholics in heaven? Do God and the Holy Ghost also drink? Are there any prohibitionists in heaven? As the act of drinking implies the existence of physical bodies, do the inhabitants of heaven including God have to urinate? (In GEN. 18:1-8, God and angels ate and drank.) If so, what type of sanitary and plumbing facilities are available?
If Jesus drank, and if wine is available in heaven, why are some Christians prohibitionists?

26:30 - WHEN THEY HAD SUNG AN HYMN, THEY WENT OUT INTO THE MOUNT OF OLIVES.

**Contradiction:**
JOHN 18:1 - [After the supper] Jesus...went with his disciples over the brook Cedron, where was a garden into which he entered....
[Did Jesus and the disciples go to the Mount of Olives, or cross the brook Cedron and enter a garden?]

**Old Testament:**
EX. 12:22 - The LORD: "...none of you shall go out the door of his house until morning," [Jews, consequently, did not leave their home after the Passover meal.]

**Perplexing:**
Why did Jesus and his disciples, Jews, violate the LORD's command and go outside after the Passover meal? Was the gospel writer unaware of the EX. verse and the Jewish custom? Did Judas go with them?

26:31 - SAITH JESUS, "...IT IS WRITTEN, 'I WILL SMITE THE SHEPHERD, AND THE SHEEP OF THE FLOCK SHALL BE SCATTERED ABROAD.'"

**Old Testament:**
ZECH. 13:7 - "...saith the LORD of hosts, 'Smite the shepherd, and the sheep shall be scattered, and I will turn Mine hand upon the little ones.'"

**Pagan parallel:**
At least 500 years before Jesus, Zoroaster referred to himself as a "shepherd" and to his followers as "sheep."

26:32 - JESUS: "AFTER I AM RISEN AGAIN, I WILL GO BEFORE YOU INTO GALILEE."

**Contradictions:**
LUKE 24:49 - Jesus: "...tarry ye in Jerusalem, until ye be endued with power from on high."
ACTS 1:4 - [Jesus]...commanded that they should not depart from Jerusalem, but wait for the promise of the Father....
[Did Jesus instruct his disciples to meet him in Galilee, or tell them to remain in Jerusalem?]
JOHN 20:9 - As yet they [the disciples] knew not the scripture, that he must rise again from the dead.
[Did Jesus inform the disciples that he would rise and precede them into Galilee, or did they not know that he would rise?]

**Perplexing:**
If Jesus told the disciples that he would go before them into Galilee, why in MARK 16:14, LUKE 24:36, and JOHN 20:19 did he come to them in Jerusalem?

26:34 - JESUS SAID UNTO HIM [PETER], "THIS NIGHT BEFORE THE COCK CROW, THOU SHALT DENY ME THRICE."

**Contradictions:**
MARK 14:30 - Jesus saith, "...in this night, before the cock crow twice, thou shalt deny me thrice."
[Did Jesus say that Peter would deny him before the cock crowed once, or twice?]
LUKE 22:34-39 - [Before they went out to the mount of olives] Jesus: "The cock shall not crow this day, before thou shalt thrice deny that thou knowest me."
[Did Jesus say that Peter will deny him thrice after, or before they went to the mount of Olives?]

**History:**
At the time the incident is reported to have taken place (first century A.D.), there was a prohibition against keeping cocks in Jerusalem.

26:35 - PETER SAID, "THOUGH I SHOULD DIE WITH THEE, YET WILL I NOT DENY THEE." LIKEWISE ALSO SAID ALL THE DISCIPLES.

**Perplexing:**
Judas Iscariot has not been said to have left the group; therefore, the term, "all the disciples" implied, that Judas was still with them and made the same pledge. Since Judas was identified openly by Jesus in v.25 as the one to betray him, why did not the disciples and Jesus denounce him for his hypocrisy? Why did not the other disciples try to prevent the betrayal?
See also under 26:25-28.

26:36 - COMETH JESUS WITH THEM TO GETHSEMANE, AND SAITH, "SIT HERE, WHILE I GO AND PRAY YONDER."

**Contradiction:**
JOHN 18:1 - Jesus went forth with his disciples over the brook Cedron, where was a garden, into which he entered, and his disciples.
[Did Jesus and his disciples go to Gethsemane where he went to pray, or did they cross a brook and go into a garden?]

**Perplexing:** See under 14:22-23 (for praying).

26:37-39 - HE TOOK PETER AND THE TWO SONS OF ZEBEDEE, AND BEGAN TO BE SORROWFUL AND HEAVY. SAITH HE, "MY SOUL IS EXCEEDING SORROWFUL, EVEN UNTO DEATH...." HE WENT A LITTLE FURTHER, FELL ON HIS FACE, AND PRAYED, "MY FATHER, IF IT BE POSSIBLE, LET THIS CUP PASS FROM ME; NEVERTHELESS NOT AS I WILL, BUT AS THOU WILT."

**Contradictions:**
LUKE 22:39-42 - He went to the mount of Olives; his disciples followed him. He said, "Pray that ye enter not into temptation." He was withdrawn from them...kneeled down, and prayed, saying, "Father, if Thou be willing, remove this cup from me, nevertheless not my will, but Thine be done."
[Did Jesus take only Peter, James, and John with him, or did all of the disciples follow him?]
[Did Jesus pray in Gethsemane, or at the mount of Olives?]
[Did Jesus say that he was sorrowful to three disciples, or did he tell all of the disciples to pray to avoid temptation?]

**Perplexing:**
Why did Jesus say that he was sorrowful unto death? Why did he even think about asking his Father that "this cup" pass from him? He knew that he would not actually die, but be resurrected and be with his Father. As a divine being, he had nothing about which to worry or fear—he could not suffer or die. Why was he not happy that his mission was nearing completion and that he would be returning to his Father in heaven? Why did he pray as if he was a fearful human? What is the point of praying for or against something that is inevitable?
Instead of praying, why did Jesus not perform a miracle to cause everyone to believe in him and his Father? By failing to do so, does he not bear responsibility for all the religious hate, intolerance, persecution, violence, torture, and wars inflicted on humanity in his name by his followers over the ensuing centuries? Consequently, are not his hands as well as his Father's drenched with the blood of the countless tens of millions of people who suffered and were killed in their names? Could the devil have done worse?
See also under MATT. 14:22-23 and MATT. 19:26 (about praying).

26:40 - HE COMETH UNTO THE DISCIPLES, FINDETH THEM ASLEEP, AND SAITH UNTO PETER, "WHAT, COULD YE NOT WATCH WITH ME ONE HOUR?"

**Perplexing:**
Under the circumstances, knowing that Jesus was to be betrayed and killed and resurrected, how could the disciples fall asleep? Why were they not too excited or anxious to sleep? Why did Jesus fail to know that Peter would not watch with him and that the disciples would sleep (in JOHN 18:4 - Jesus knew all things that would come upon him)?

26:41 - JESUS: "WATCH AND PRAY, THAT YE ENTER NOT INTO TEMPTATION...."

**Contradictions:**
LUKE 22:39-42 - He went to the mount of Olives; his disciples followed him. When he was at the place, he said, "Pray that ye enter not into temptation." He was withdrawn from them...kneeled down, and prayed, saying, "Father if Thou be willing...."
[Did Jesus tell his disciples to pray not to enter into temptation, after, or before he prayed to his father?]
JAM. 1:2 - James: "My brethren, count it all joy when ye fall into divers temptations."

[Should one watch and pray not to enter temptation, or should one count it all joy to enter temptations?]

**Perplexing:**
Were the disciples now awake? When did they wake?
Why would the disciples have to pray to avoid temptation? Why would their faith not protect them from temptation? Why would God not protect them from temptation?

26:42 - HE WENT AWAY THE SECOND TIME, AND PRAYED, "O MY FATHER, IF THIS CUP MAY NOT PASS AWAY FROM ME, EXCEPT I DRINK IT, THY WILL BE DONE."

**Contradiction:**
LUKE 22:41-47 - Jesus only prayed once before Judas and a multitude arrived.
[Did Jesus pray more than once, or only once?]

**Perplexing:** See under 14:22-23 (about praying) and 26:37-39.

26:43 - HE CAME AND FOUND THEM ASLEEP AGAIN, FOR THEIR EYES WERE HEAVY.

**Contradiction:**
LUKE 22:41-47 - Jesus found the disciples asleep only once.
[Did Jesus find the disciples asleep more than once, or only once?]

**Perplexing:** See under 26:40.

26:44 - HE LEFT THEM, WENT AWAY AGAIN, AND PRAYED THE THIRD TIME, SAYING THE SAME WORDS.

**Contradiction:** See under 26:42.

**Perplexing:**
Why did Jesus pray three times?
See also under 14:22-23 (about praying) and 26:37-39.

26:45-46 - THEN COMETH HE TO HIS DISCIPLES, AND SAITH, "SLEEP, AND TAKE YOUR REST; THE HOUR IS AT HAND; THE SON OF MAN IS BETRAYED INTO THE HANDS OF SINNERS. RISE, LET US BE GOING; HE IS AT HAND THAT DOTH BETRAY ME."

**Perplexing:**
If Jesus had to die and be resurrected, why did he not just turn himself in to the authorities voluntarily? Why could he not have died from a disease such as smallpox or pneumonia and then be resurrected? Why was the manner of his death more important than the resurrection?
See also under 26:14-16.

26:47 - WHILE HE YET SPAKE, JUDAS CAME, WITH A GREAT MULTITUDE WITH SWORDS AND STAVES, FROM THE CHIEF PRIESTS AND ELDERS OF THE PEOPLE.

**Contradictions:**
LUKE 22:52 - Jesus said to the chief priests, captains of the temple, and the elders, which were come to him....
[Was the multitude sent by the chief priests and elders, or did they come with the multitude?]
JOHN 18:3 - Judas received a band of men and officers from the chief priests and Pharisees....
[Did the multitude come from the chief priests and elders, or was a band of men and officers sent by the chief priests and Pharisees?]

**Perplexing:**
When did Judas leave Jesus and the other disciples? Why was his absence not noted? How could Judas come with a great multitude on Passover night? (See under 26:30 - Jews did not leave their homes on Passover night.) Therefore, how could a great multitude of people be obtained unless they were not Jewish? If they were not Jewish, why did they take orders from the chief priests and elders? (In MATT. 26:55, however, Jesus identified the people as being Jewish by saying, "I sat daily with you teaching in the temple....") If it was Passover night, the chief priests and elders would also have been at home with their families and would not have been able to arrange for an armed multitude to go after Jesus. See 26:30 above - Jesus and the disciples including Judas would not have left the house where they had eaten the Passover meal. What reason was given to the multitude for seizing Jesus, a man who could work miracles? Why was an armed multitude needed to seize Jesus? Did the people think that Jesus and his disciples were armed? Were they armed? Were all of Jesus' disciples now with him? When did they arrive? (According to 26:37, Jesus only took three disciples with him.)

**Old Testament:** See under 26:30.

26:48-49 - HE THAT BETRAYED HIM GAVE THEM A SIGN, SAYING, "WHOMSOEVER I SHALL KISS, THAT SAME IS HE, HOLD HIM FAST." FORTHWITH HE CAME TO JESUS, AND SAID, "HAIL MASTER," AND KISSED HIM.

**Contradictions:**
MATT. 26:55 - Jesus said to the multitudes, "...I sat daily with you teaching in the temple, and ye laid no hold on me."
[Did the multitudes need a sign to recognize Jesus, or did they recognize him from seeing and hearing him daily in the temple?]
LUKE 22:47-48 - ...Judas...drew near unto Jesus to kiss him. Jesus said, "Judas, betrayeth the Son of man with a kiss?"
[Did Judas greet Jesus and kiss him, or did he approach Jesus to kiss him, but was questioned by Jesus before he could kiss him?]
JOHN 18:4 - Jesus...said unto them [the band], "Whom seek ye?"
[Did Judas greet and kiss Jesus, or did Jesus question the band without Judas speaking to or trying to kiss him?]

**Perplexing:**
If Jesus had been seen by multitudes throughout the region and in the temple, why did the people need Judas to point him out? Why were the people not afraid of seizing a man who could perform healing miracles and raise the dead? Why did they not want to befriend such a person?
See also under 26:47.

26:50 - JESUS: "FRIEND, WHEREFORE ART THOU COME?" THEN THEY LAID HANDS ON JESUS, AND TOOK HIM.

**Contradictions:**

MATT. 26:25 - Jesus identified Judas as the one who would betray him.
JOHN 13:11 - Jesus knew who should betray him....
JOHN 18:4 - Jesus knowing all things that should come upon him....
[Did Jesus know, or not know that Judas had betrayed him?]
[Did Jesus have to ask Judas why he had come, or did he know all the things that were to happen to him?]
LUKE 22:48 - Jesus: "Betrayest thou the Son of man with a kiss?"
[Did Jesus ask Judas why he had come, or did he say that Judas had come to betray him?]
JOHN 18:3-4 - Judas did not kiss Jesus, and Jesus did not speak to Judas; Jesus asked the people, "Whom seek ye?"
JOHN 18:5-12 - They answered, "Jesus of Nazareth." Jesus said, "I am he.".... ...they fell to the ground. Asked he again, "Whom seek ye?" They said, "Jesus of Nazareth." Jesus: "...I am he...." .... Then the band, captain, and officers of the Jews took Jesus and bound him.
[Did Jesus speak to Judas, or to the multitude?]
[Was Jesus seized after being kissed by Judas, or after identifying himself twice to the band?]
See also under 20:20-21 (Jesus knew people's thoughts).

**Perplexing:**

Why was Jesus surprised that Judas came to him and the other disciples? Why did he call Judas, "Friend?" If Jesus knew people's thoughts, why did he have to ask Judas why he came? If Jesus knew that his mission was to die and be resurrected, why did he wait to be betrayed and arrested? Why did he not just turn himself over to the priests or the Romans?
See also under 26:14-16.

26:51 - ONE OF THEM WHICH WERE WITH JESUS DREW HIS SWORD AND STRUCK A SERVANT OF THE HIGH PRIEST'S AND SMOTE OFF HIS EAR.

**Contradiction:**

LUKE 22:50-54 - One of them smote the servant of the high priest, and cut off his right ear. .... Then took they him [Jesus], and led him....
JOHN 18:10-12 - Simon Peter having a sword, smote the high priest's servant, and cut off his right ear.... .... Then the band, captain, and officers of the Jews took Jesus and bound him.
[Was Jesus seized after, or before the servant was attacked?]

**Perplexing:**

In MATT. 5:39, Jesus said, "Resist not evil, but whosoever shall smite thee on thy right cheek, turn to him the other." In 5:44, he said, "Love your enemies...pray for them which despitefully use, and persecute you." Then in 10:16, he said, "...be ye...harmless as doves." Why then was at least one disciple carrying a sword? Why did he attack someone with his sword? Why did Jesus permit any of his disciples to carry a weapon? Why did they not rely on God for protection? Did all of them including Jesus lack faith that they would be protected by God? Why was the high priest's servant attacked? Why was the disciple who struck the servant not attacked or seized by those with the servant? Rather than resort to violence, why did the disciples fail to pray? Jesus had told them, in 21:22, "Whatsoever ye shall ask in prayer, believing, ye shall receive."
See also under 26:47.

**Language:**
The Greek word, "otarion," translated as "ear," means "ear-lobe."

**Old Testament:**
AMOS 3:12 - Saith the LORD, "As the shepherd taketh out of the mouth of the lion two legs, or a piece of an ear...."

26:52 - JESUS SAID, "PUT UP AGAIN THY SWORD INTO HIS PLACE, FOR ALL THEY THAT TAKE THE SWORD SHALL PERISH WITH THE SWORD."

**Contradiction:**
MATT. 10:34 - Jesus: "Think not that I am come to send peace on earth; I came not to send peace, but a sword."
LUKE 22:36 - Jesus: "...he that hath no sword, let him sell his garment, and buy one."
LUKE 22:38 - "They said, "Lord, here are two swords." He said, "It is enough."
[Did Jesus object to, or support the use of swords?]

26:53-54 - JESUS: "THINKEST THOU THAT I CANNOT NOW PRAY TO MY FATHER, AND HE SHALL PRESENTLY SEND ME MORE THAN TWELVE LEGIONS OF ANGELS? BUT HOW THEN SHALL THE SCRIPTURE BE FULFILLED, THAT THUS IT MUST BE?"

**Contradiction:**
JOHN 18:11 - Jesus said, "Put up thy sword into the sheath; the cup which my Father hath given me, shall I not drink it?"
[Did Jesus say that he can pray for angels, or that he will drink what his Father has given to him?]

**Perplexing:**
Why would Jesus have to pray for legions of angels? Why would his Father not send them without requiring Jesus to pray for them? Why would Jesus need angels? What would these angels do? Why would Jesus be unable to perform a miracle to extricate himself from this or any other situation? Why did Jesus fail to perform a miracle that would have caused everyone to recognize who he is, thereby, eliminating the need for his crucifixion and resurrection, and all the persecution, torture, murder, wars, assorted crimes, and suffering that have been perpetrated by and against his followers over the centuries? One miracle performed at this time would have saved humanity from centuries of untold misery in his name.
See also under 26:37-39.

26:55 - SAID JESUS TO THE MULTITUDES, ".... I SAT DAILY WITH YOU TEACHING IN THE TEMPLE, AND YE LAID NO HOLD ON ME."

**Contradictions:**
MATT. 26:48 - Judas had to identify Jesus for the people by kissing him.
JOHN 18:4-8 - Jesus asked the people twice, "Whom seek ye?" They said, "Jesus of Nazareth," twice. Jesus twice told them that he was that person.
[Did, or did not the people recognize Jesus?]
See also under 26:48-49.

**Perplexing:**
Why did Jesus speak as though he did not know that these people came to seize him?
See also under 26:48-49.

26:56 - ...ALL THE DISCIPLES FORSOOK HIM AND FLED.

**Contradiction:**
JOHN 18:8 - Jesus answered, "I have told you that I am he; if therefore ye seek me, let these go their way." [Did the disciples flee, or did Jesus request that they be released?]

**Perplexing:**
Why did the disciples desert Jesus? Did they not have faith in him and his Father? Did they not believe that he could perform a miracle to protect them?

26:57 - THEY LED HIM AWAY TO CAIAPHAS THE HIGH PRIEST, WHERE THE SCRIBES AND ELDERS WERE ASSEMBLED.

**Contradictions:**
LUKE 3:2 - Annas and Caiaphas being the high priests....
[Was Caiaphas the high priest, or were Annas and Caiaphas the high priests?]
JOHN 18:13 - [They] led him away to Annas first; he was the father-in-law to Caiaphas, the high priest that year.
[Was Jesus taken directly to Caiaphas, or was he taken first to Annas?]

**Perplexing:**
It was Passover night, a time when Jews did not leave their homes. Therefore, how could the high priest, scribes, elders, and other Jews be outside seizing Jesus and taking him to the high priest? How could the high priest, scribes, and elders be away from their homes and families in violation of Jewish law?
See also under 26:30.

**History:**
A high priest named Joseph Caiaphas served in that capacity from A.D. 18-36.

26:58 - PETER FOLLOWED HIM AFAR OFF TO THE HIGH PRIEST'S PALACE, WENT IN, AND SAT WITH THE SERVANTS TO SEE THE END.

**Contradictions:**
LUKE 22:54-55 - They took him, and brought him to the high priest's house. Peter followed afar off. When they had kindled a fire in the midst of the hall, and were set down together, Peter sat down among them.
[Did Peter sit with the servants, or with the people who brought Jesus to the house?]
JOHN 18:15-18 - Peter followed Jesus, and so did another disciple, known unto the high priest, and went in with Jesus into the palace of the high priest. Peter stood at the door without. That other disciple...spake unto her that kept the door and then brought in Peter. .... The servants and officers stood there, who had made a fire...Peter stood with them....
[Did Peter follow Jesus from a distance, or did he and another disciple follow Jesus and enter the high priest's palace with Jesus?]
[Was Peter able to enter the palace by himself, or did another disciple have to speak to the doorkeeper before he could be admitted?]
[Did Peter sit with the servants, or did he stand with the servants and officers?]

**Perplexing:**
How was Peter able to walk into the high priest's palace? Could anyone walk into the palace and mingle with the servants? Why did the servants let him sit with them?

26:59-60 - THE CHIEF PRIESTS, ELDERS, AND THE COUNCIL, SOUGHT FALSE WITNESS AGAINST JESUS, TO PUT HIM TO DEATH, BUT FOUND NONE, THOUGH MANY FALSE WITNESSES CAME, FOUND THEY NONE. AT LAST CAME TWO FALSE WITNESSES.

**Contradiction:**
LUKE 22:66 - As soon as it was day, the elders of the people, the chief priests, and scribes came together and led Jesus into their council.
[Was Jesus brought before the religious officials on Passover night, or the next morning?]

**Perplexing:**
How could any witnesses, false or otherwise, be found at night, especially on Passover night when Jews did not leave their homes? How could the chief priests, elders, and Council have a meeting on Passover night? How were witnesses sought?
See also under 26:30.

**History:**
The Council (the Sanhedrin) did not meet during Passover.
At this time in history, Jews did not employ the death penalty, so Jesus could not have been sentenced to death by Jews. (See JOHN 18:31 - .... The Jews said, "It is not lawful for us to put any man to death.")

26:63 - .... THE HIGH PRIEST SAID. "I ADJURE THEE BY THE LIVING GOD, THAT THOU TELL US WHETHER THOU BE THE CHRIST, THE SON OF GOD."

**Contradictions:**
LUKE 22:66-67 - As soon as it was day, the elders, chief priests, and scribes came...saying, "Art thou the Christ?...."
[Was Jesus asked if he was the Christ, the Son of God by the high priest, or was he asked only if he was the Christ by elders, chief priests, and scribes?]
[Was Jesus questioned on Passover night, or the next morning?]
JOHN 18:19 - The high priest asked Jesus of his disciples, and his doctrine.
[Did the high priest ask Jesus if he was the Christ, the Son of God, or did he ask him about his disciples and doctrine?]

**Judaism:**
According to Jewish belief, the Christ—the Messiah—was to be paternally descended from David.
The concept of a Son of God is not part of traditional Jewish belief. (The Koran, the Muslim holy book, falsely accuses Jews of believing that Ezra is the son of God.)

**Perplexing:**
Since it is not part of Jewish belief, why did the high priest ask Jesus if he was the Son of God? Why did he equate being the Christ (the Messiah) with being the Son of God?

**Language:** See under 1:1.

26:64 - JESUS SAITH, "THOU HAST SAID, NEVERTHELESS I SAY UNTO YOU, HEREAFTER SHALL YE SEE THE SON OF MAN SITTING ON THE RIGHT HAND OF POWER, AND COMING IN THE CLOUDS OF HEAVEN."

**Language:**
"Thou hast said," is the literal translation of an Aramaic phrase meaning, "yes."

**Contradiction:**
LUKE 22:67-69 - Jesus: "If I tell you, ye will not believe.... Hereafter shall the Son of man sit on the right hand of the power of God."
[Did Jesus tell the high priest that he would see him on the right hand of power coming in the clouds, or that he will sit on the right hand of the power of God?]

**Perplexing:**
Why did Jesus say that the high priest will see him sitting on the right hand of God and coming in the clouds of heaven? Why did Jesus' prophecy fail? The high priest has been dead for about two millennia, and Jesus still has not come in the clouds of heaven. The high priest and the others were aware of Jesus' miracles including bringing the dead back to life, so why did they not want to utilize his abilities to possibly help them? Why did they not ask him to perform healing miracles for them and their families?
See also under 24:30-31.

26:65 - THE HIGH PRIEST..., "HE HATH SPOKEN BLASPHEMY.... YE HAVE HEARD HIS BLASPHEMY."

**Perplexing:**
Why did the high priest accuse Jesus of blasphemy? According to Jewish law, only denigrating God is considered blasphemy. Jews did not consider claiming to be the Messiah (as many had done at that time and on into the second century) or a Son of God to be blasphemous.

26:66 - "WHAT THINK YE?" THEY ANSWERED, "HE IS GUILTY OF DEATH."

**History:**
Trials were not held during the Passover week. Accused persons were also not required nor permitted to testify against themselves.
See also under 26:59-60.

**Perplexing:**
How could Jesus have been put on trial if trials were not held during Passover? If Jesus had not been accused of a capital crime, how could they say that he was guilty of death?
See also under 26:59-60.

26:67-68 - THEN DID THEY SPIT IN HIS FACE, AND BUFFETED HIM; OTHERS SMOTE HIM WITH THE PALMS OF THEIR HANDS, SAYING, "PROPHESY, THOU CHRIST, WHO IS HE THAT SMOTE THEE?"

**Contradictions:**
LUKE 22:63-64 - The men that held Jesus mocked, smote, struck him, and told him to prophesy who

struck him before he was asked in LUKE 22:67, "Art thou the Christ?"
[Was Jesus struck, etc., after, or before being asked if he was the Christ?"]
JOHN 18:22 - ...one of the officers which stood by struck Jesus with the palm of his hand, saying, "Answerest the high priest so?"
[Was Jesus struck by several men, or by one officer?]
[Was he struck and told to prophesy who struck him, or was he hit for the way in which he answered the high priest?]

**Perplexing:**

How could people fearlessly molest someone who had the power to heal the sick and infirm and raise the dead? Why were they not afraid of such a person? Why did they not want to befriend such a person and have him perform healing miracles for them? Since Jews were at home on Passover night and they did not hold trials during Passover week, and since Jesus was not really guilty of blasphemy, how could the described events have occurred?

26:69 - PETER SAT WITHOUT IN THE PALACE; A DAMSEL CAME, SAYING, "THOU ALSO WAST WITH JESUS OF GALILEE."

**Contradictions:**

MARK 14:66-67 - As Peter was beneath in the palace, there cometh one of the maids of the high priest; when she saw Peter warming himself, she said, "Thou also wast with Jesus of Nazareth."
[Did a woman refer to Jesus as, "Jesus of Galilee," or "Jesus of Nazareth?"]
LUKE 22:56 - [Prior to Jesus being interrogated] A maid beheld him [Peter] as he sat by the fire, looked upon him, and said, "This man was also with him."
[Did a woman speak directly to Peter and say that he was with Jesus, or did she say to others that he was with Jesus?]
JOHN 18:17 - [Prior to Jesus being interrogated] Saith the damsel that kept the door unto Peter, "Art not thou also one of this man's disciples?" ....
[Did the woman associate Peter with Jesus after, or before Jesus had been questioned?]
[Was Peter asked about having been with Jesus after he had entered and sat down in the palace, or when he was at the door entering the palace?]
JOHN 18:18 - The servants and officers stood there, who had made a fire...and Peter stood with them....
[Was Peter sitting, or standing?]

**Perplexing:**

How did the damsel know that Peter had been with Jesus? Was Peter questioned by a damsel, a maid, or a doorkeeper? Why did no one ask Peter why he was in the palace? Why was Peter not arrested for cutting off the ear of a servant of the high priest (JOHN 18:26 identified Peter as the culprit)?

26:70-72 - HE DENIED BEFORE THEM ALL, SAYING, "I KNOW NOT WHAT THOU SAYEST." WHEN HE WAS GONE OUT INTO THE PORCH, ANOTHER MAID SAW HIM, AND SAID UNTO THEM THAT WERE THERE, "THIS FELLOW WAS ALSO WITH JESUS OF NAZARETH." AGAIN HE DENIED WITH AN OATH, "I DO NOT KNOW THE MAN."

**Contradictions:**

MARK 14:68-70 - He denied, saying, "I know not, neither understand what thou sayest." He went out into the porch, and the cock crew. A maid saw him again, and began to say to them that stood by, "This is one

of them." He denied it again.
[Did, or did not a cock crow?]
LUKE 22:57-58 - [Prior to Jesus being questioned] He denied him, saying, "Woman, I know him not." After a little while another saw him. and said, "Thou art also of them." Peter said, "Man, I am not." [Was Peter questioned for the second time after, or before Jesus was questioned?]
[Did a maid tell people around Peter that he was with Jesus, or did a man accuse him of having been with Jesus?]
JOHN 18:25 - Simon Peter stood and warmed himself. They said, "Art not thou also one of his disciples?" He denied it, and said, "I am not."
[Was Peter questioned the second time by a maid, or by a group of people?]
[Was Peter on the porch, or warming himself around a fire in the hall?]

**Perplexing:**
If Jesus and his disciples had been seen by multitudes, how could Peter deny having been with Jesus and expect people to believe him?

26:73-74 - AFTER A WHILE CAME UNTO HIM THEY THAT STOOD BY, AND SAID, "SURELY THOU ART ONE OF THEM, FOR THY SPEECH BETRAYETH THEE." THEN BEGAN HE TO CURSE AND SWEAR, SAYING, "I KNOW NOT THE MAN." IMMEDIATELY THE COCK CREW.

**Contradictions:**
MARK 14:70-72 - He denied it again...they that stood by said, "Surely thou art one of them, for thou art a Galilean; thy speech agreeth thereto. He began to curse and swear, saying, "I know not this man of whom ye speak." The second time the cock crew.
[After Peter denied knowing Jesus for the third time, did the cock crow for the first time, or the second time?]
LUKE 22:59-60 - [Prior to Jesus being questioned] About one hour after another affirmed, "Of a truth this fellow was with him, for he is a Galilean." Peter said, "Man, I know not what thou sayest." Immediately, while he spake, the cock crew."
[Was Peter addressed by people standing near, or did one person say to others that Peter was a Galilean?]
JOHN 18:26-27 - one of the servants of the high priest, being his kinsman whose ear Peter cut off, saith, "Did not I see thee in the garden with him?" Peter denied again; immediately the cock crew.
[Did a group of people say that Peter had been with Jesus, or did a servant ask Peter if he had been with Jesus?]
[Did Peter curse and swear, or did he just deny having been with Jesus?]
LUKE 22:66-67 - [After the cock crowed]...the elders, chief priests, and scribes came...saying [to Jesus], "Art thou the Christ?...."
[Did the cock crow after Jesus was asked if he was the Christ (26:63), or before he was asked?]

**Perplexing:**
Why did a disciple of Jesus curse and swear? Why did Peter violate Jesus' command in MATT. 5:34 - "Swear not at all...."
Since cocks were not in Jerusalem at this time (see under 26:34 - History), how could one be heard? Also, as cocks crow at dawn, how could one be heard crowing at night? Morning did not arrive until 27:1.

**History:** See under 26:34.

26:75 - PETER REMEMBERED THE WORD OF JESUS, "BEFORE THE COCK CROW, THOU SHALT DENY ME THRICE."

**Contradiction:**

MARK 14:72 - Peter called to mind the word that Jesus said, "Before the cock crow twice, thou shalt deny me thrice."

[Did Peter say that Jesus said he would deny him thrice before the cock crowed, or before the cock crowed twice?]

27:1-2 - WHEN THE MORNING WAS COME, ALL THE CHIEF PRIESTS AND ELDERS OF THE PEOPLE TOOK COUNSEL AGAINST JESUS TO PUT HIM TO DEATH. WHEN THEY HAD BOUND HIM, THEY...DELIVERED HIM TO PONTIUS PILATE THE GOVERNOR.

**Contradictions:**

LUKE 22:66-67 - As soon as it was day, the elders of the people, chief priests, and scribes came together, and led him into their council, saying, "Art thou the Christ?"

[Was Jesus questioned before it was morning (in 26:63 - 27:1), or after it was day?]

[Was Jesus taken to Pilate in the morning after having been questioned during the night, or was he taken to the chief priests and scribes in the morning without having been questioned during the night?]

JOHN 18:28 - They led Jesus from Caiaphas unto the hall of judgment; it was early; they went not into the judgment hall, lest they be defiled, but that they might eat the Passover.

[Was Jesus brought to Pilate on Passover day after Jesus and the disciples ate the Passover meal, or on the day before Passover?]

See also under 26:59-60.

**History:**

Jews, especially the clergy, did not hold meetings, trials, or engage in non-religious activities during Passover. The priests would have spent the day in the temple or synagogues. Other Jews would have been engaged in religious activities or at home.

The Council (Sanhedrin) had the authority to punish violators of Jewish law.

Therefore, if Jesus was deemed guilty of having broken Jewish laws, he would not have been brought to Pilate. The governor was concerned only with Roman law. In JOHN 18:31, Pilate said, "Take him, and judge him according to your law." .... In LUKE 23:2-3, the Jews said that Jesus claimed to be a king, and Jesus acknowledged this when Pilate asked him if he was a king. Consequently, Jesus admitted being guilty of treason — claiming to be a king without permission from Rome — and, thus, subject to punishment (execution) under Roman law.

**Perplexing:**

Why did the priests believe that they could put to death someone who had the ability to resurrect the dead and perform other miracles? How could the priests and others have convened a meeting during Passover? Did the people get any sleep during the night? If so, where? Did they stay up all night? Did all of them remain in the palace? How many people were there? Where did they eat?

**Old Testament:**

PS. 2:2 - "The kings of the earth...and the rulers take counsel together, against the LORD, and against His anointed."

27:3-6 - THEN JUDAS...REPENTED, AND BROUGHT THE THIRTY PIECES OF SILVER TO THE CHIEF PRIESTS AND ELDERS, SAYING, "I HAVE SINNED; I HAVE BETRAYED INNOCENT BLOOD." THEY SAID, "WHAT IS THAT TO US? HE CAST DOWN THE PIECES OF SILVER IN THE TEMPLE, DEPARTED, AND HANGED HIMSELF. THE PRIESTS TOOK THE SILVER PIECES....

**Contradictions:**
ACTS 1:18 - Peter: "This man [Judas] purchased a field with the reward of iniquity, and falling headlong, he burst asunder, and all his bowels gushed out."
[Did Judas repent and cast the silver in the temple, or did he use the silver to buy a field?]
[Did Judas hang himself, or did he die in a fall?]

**Perplexing:**
Why did the other gospels and Epistles not mention Judas ' death? How could Judas have sinned, when he did what was preordained by God?

**Old Testament:**
2 SAM. 17:23 - Ahithophel hanged himself after betraying David.

27:7-10 - THEY [THE PRIESTS] BOUGHT WITH THEM THE POTTER'S FIELD TO BURY STRANGERS IN. WHEREFORE THAT FIELD WAS CALLED THE FIELD OF BLOOD.... THEN WAS FULFILLED THAT WHICH WAS SPOKEN BY JEREMY [JEREMIAH] THE PROPHET, "THEY TOOK THE THIRTY PIECES OF SILVER, THE PRICE OF HIM THAT WAS VALUED, WHOM THEY OF THE CHILDREN OF ISRAEL DID VALUE, AND GAVE THEM FOR THE POTTER'S FIELD, AS THE LORD APPOINTED ME."

**Contradiction:**
ACTS 1:18 - Peter: "This man [Judas] purchased a field with the reward of iniquity...."
[Did the priest, or Judas purchase the field?]

**Old Testament:**
ZECH. 11:12-13 - Zechariah: I said, "If ye think good, give me my price; if not, forbear. So they weighed for my price thirty pieces of silver. The LORD said unto me, 'Cast it unto the potter'; a goodly price that I was prised at of them. I took the thirty pieces of silver, and cast them to the potter in the house of the LORD. [Potter referred to the temple "treasury," and is so translated in some Bibles. It did not refer to a field or to the work of a potter.] (The prophecy attributed by MATT. to Jeremiah does not appear in the Old Testament. Apparently, MATT. distorted the words of Zechariah and erroneously attributed them to Jeremiah.)

**Perplexing:**
Why did MATT, misquote the Zechariah verses as a prophecy and attribute them to a prophecy by Jeremiah? Did MATT. confuse the temple potter (the temple treasury) with a potter's field?

27:11 - JESUS STOOD BEFORE THE GOVERNOR [PONTIUS PILATE]; THE GOVERNOR ASKED HIM, "ART THOU THE KING OF THE JEWS?" JESUS SAID, "THOU SAYEST."

**Language:** See under 26:64.

**Contradiction:**
JOHN 18:33-34 - Pilate...said, "Art thou the King of the Jews?" Jesus answered, "Sayest thou this thing of thyself, or did others tell it thee of me?"
[Did Jesus say that he was King of the Jews, or did he ask Pilate if someone told him that he was King of the Jews?]

**History:**
Pontius Pilate was governor (procurator) from A.D. 26-36. He was vehemently and violently anti-Jewish, and was responsible for massacring hundreds if not thousands of Jews. He did not have a reputation of meeting with, listening to, or complying with the desires of Jews. His violence and hostility towards the Jews was eventually too much even for Rome to tolerate and he was removed from office and recalled. Under Roman law, anyone claiming to be a king in Roman occupied territory without the consent of Rome, was subject to execution. If Jesus had been accused of claiming to be a king, in violation of Roman law, Pilate would have had a reason for interrogating him. There is no evidence, however, that Pilate ever questioned Jesus, or that Jesus ever appeared before him. The existing court records of Pontius Pilate do not contain any account of Jesus having been arrested, tried, and executed.

**Perplexing:**
Why did the anti-Jewish Pilate bother meeting with a group of Jews? Why did he condescend to speak with a Jew who had been accused of violating a Jewish law? Why did Pilate not ask Jesus about the miracles attributed to him? Why was Pilate not in awe of someone who could perform miracles of healing and resurrecting the dead? Why did Pilate not want to utilize Jesus' abilities for himself or his family and friends? Why did Pilate ask Jesus if he was a king, unless such an assertion had been made (in LUKE 23:2, Jesus was accused of saying that he is a king)?

27:13 - SAID PILATE UNTO HIM, "HEAREST THOU NOT HOW MANY THINGS THEY WITNESS AGAINST THEE?"

**Perplexing:**
To whom did the "they" refer? Was it to the priests or a group of unspecified people? What things were witnessed against Jesus? Why did not the multitudes who were healed of illnesses, blindness, deafness, being lame, and those he resurrected from the dead, as well as the thousands who participated in the feeding miracles, those who saw his other miracles, and those who believed Jesus to be the Messiah come to his defense?

27:15 - AT THAT FEAST THE GOVERNOR WAS WONT TO RELEASE UNTO THE PEOPLE A PRISONER, WHOM THEY WOULD.

**Contradiction:**
LUKE 23:17 - Of necessity he [the governor] must release one [a prisoner] unto them at the feast.
[Was it the custom to release a prisoner, or was it a necessity?]

**History:**
Neither the Jews nor the Romans had a custom of releasing a prisoner at Passover. The Romans did not give the Jews the privilege of having the governor release a prisoner during Passover. No prisoner had to be or was released at the demand of Jews during Passover. The Romans did not have a custom of releasing a prisoner on the occasion of a local religious festival. And neither the Jews, nor other peoples in the region had such a custom.

27:16 - THEY HAD THEN A NOTABLE PRISONER, CALLED BARABBAS.

**Contradictions:**

MARK 15:7 - There was one named Barabbas, which lay bound with them that had made insurrection with him, who had committed murder in the insurrection.
LUKE 23:18-19 - ...Barabbas, (who for a certain sedition made in the city and for murder was cast into prison).
[Was Barabbas a notable prisoner, or a murderer involved in insurrection and/or sedition?]
JOHN 18:40 - ...Barabbas was a robber.
[Was Barabbas a notable prisoner, or was he a robber?]

**Language:**

In Aramaic, "Barabbas," meant, "Son of the Father." (Some Bibles, such as the New English Bible, use the name, "Jesus Barabbas.")

27:17 - ...PILATE SAID, "WHOM WILL YE THAT I RELEASE UNTO YOU? BARABBAS OR JESUS WHICH IS CALLED CHRIST?"

**Contradiction:**

MARK 15:9 - Pilate answered, "Will ye that I release unto you the King of the Jews?"
JOHN 18:39 - Pilate: " Will ye therefore that I should release unto you the King of the Jews?"
[Did Pilate ask whether he should release "Jesus which is called Christ," or "the King of the Jews?]

**History:**

There is no record of the vehemently anti-Jewish Pilate asking Jews what he should do about any prisoners. The acknowledgment by Jesus that he was a king (27:11), a violation of Roman law, would also have precluded the Jews from having any voice in the matter.
If Barabbas was guilty of insurrection and sedition as claimed in MARK 15:7 and LUKE 23:18-19, Pilate would not have had the authority to release him, or even to ask Jews whether or not he should be released. Similarly, he did not have the authority to release anyone who claimed to be a king. Had he released either individual without first obtaining permission from Rome, he would have been subject to arrest and possible execution.
See also under 27:11.

**Perplexing:**

Why would the historical, vehemently anti-Jewish Pilate, who had looted the temple and who had been responsible for the massacre of hundreds, possibly thousands, of Jews, condescend to meet with Jews, and ask them for instructions about releasing a prisoner?
See also under 27:11.

27:19 - WHEN HE WAS SET DOWN ON THE JUDGMENT SEAT, HIS WIFE SENT UNTO HIM, SAYING, "HAVE THOU NOTHING TO DO WITH THAT JUST MAN; I HAVE SUFFERED MANY THINGS THIS DAY IN A DREAM BECAUSE OF HIM."

**History:**

The name of Pilate's wife was Procula (Procla) . Because of the above verse, she was canonized by the Greek Orthodox Church and the Coptic Church. October 27 is known as St. Procula's (Procla's) Day.

**Perplexing:**
How could she suffer in a dream? What did she suffer?

27:20 - THE CHIEF PRIESTS AND ELDERS PERSUADED THE MULTITUDE THAT THEY SHOULD ASK BARABBAS, AND DESTROY JESUS.

**Perplexing:**
How were the priests able to gather together a multitude on a holy day when they and the people were expected to be in the temple or synagogues, and when no trials or other non-religious activities were permitted? How many people were in the multitude? How many could fit into the judgment hall?
Why were the priests not in the temple and synagogues? How were the priests able to persuade the multitude to be hostile to Jesus? In MATT. 26:3-5, they were fearful that arresting Jesus and having him killed on Passover would create "an uproar among the people." Why was there no "uproar" now? Where were all the people who were healed by Jesus or who had seen his miracles? Where were those that he raised from the dead (MATT. 9:18-26; 11:5)? Why did they all now turn against him? Why were the people not in awe of one who could heal the sick, the blind, the lame, lepers, and others, and who could bring the dead back to life? Why did the people and Pilate not want Jesus to be around to perform miracles for them?

27:21 - THE GOVERNOR SAID, "WHETHER OF THE TWAIN WILL YE THAT I RELEASE UNTO YOU?" THEY SAID, "BARABBAS."

**History:**
There is no record of Pilate asking Jews about what prisoner he should release. He also did not have the authority to release anyone suspected of sedition, or of claiming to be a king, without orders to do so from Rome.
See also under 27:11 and 27:15.

**Perplexing:** See under 27:20.

27:22 - PILATE SAITH, "WHAT SHALL I DO THEN WITH JESUS WHICH IS CALLED CHRIST?" THEY ALL SAY, "LET HIM BE CRUCIFIED."

**Contradiction:**
MARK 15:12-13 - Pilate: "What will ye then that I shall do unto him whom ye call the King of the Jews?" They cried out, "Crucify him."
[Did Pilate refer to Jesus as "Christ" or as "King of the Jews?"]

**History:**
If Pilate released a prisoner (Barabbas) guilty of insurrection, he would have been subject to execution by Rome. If he released someone (Jesus) who claimed, without Roman approval, to be a king, he also would have been subject to execution by Rome. Pilate, consequently, could not have released either Barabbas or Jesus.
There is no record of a multitude of Jews and their priests forsaking their religious obligations in the temple and synagogues to meet with Pilate and to demand the crucifixion or death of anyone on Passover.
See also under 27:11 and 27:15.

**Perplexing:**
Why did the anti-Jewish Pilate ask Jews what to do with a prisoner, especially, when Roman law prohibited him from releasing either Barabbas or Jesus? Why did the Jews say that Jesus should be killed by crucifixion,

a Roman method of execution? Why did Jesus not perform a miracle in front of Pilate and the multitude to demonstrate his divinity and, thus, not only avoid being crucified but convert everyone to his teachings, and prevent almost two millennia of religious persecution, torture, violence, wars, inquisitions, holocausts, and other atrocities causing untold suffering and death for countless tens of millions of innocent people? Consequently, should not Jesus and his Father be held responsible for all the evils inflicted on humanity because of Jesus' failure to conclusively prove his divine nature?
See also under 26:37-39 and 26:53-54.

27:24 - WHEN PILATE SAW THAT HE COULD PREVAIL NOTHING, BUT THAT RATHER A TUMULT WAS MADE, HE TOOK WATER, WASHED HIS HANDS BEFORE THE MULTITUDE, SAYING, "I AM INNOCENT OF THE BLOOD OF THIS JUST PERSON; SEE YE TO IT."

**Contradiction:**

MATT. 27:37 - Over Jesus' head (on the cross) was written his accusation, "THIS IS JESUS THE KING OF THE JEWS."
[Did Pilate say that Jesus was a "just person," or did he place a sign on the cross stating that Jesus was a king, therefore, a criminal according to Roman law?]

**History:**

Pilate, as the Roman governor, had Roman troops at his disposal, so he had no need to be concerned about a tumult by a small number of Jews in his facility. He previously did not hesitate to use the troops to loot the temple and to massacre hundreds, if not thousands, of Jews. He could easily have dispersed or slaughtered a relatively small number of them. Pilate, because of his alleged statement that Jesus was a just person, was canonized by the Coptic and Abyssinian Churches—this—despite having ordered Jesus' crucifixion. (Would they have canonized him if he had freed Jesus?)
See also under 27:11.

**Old Testament:**

DEUT. 21:6-9 - Moses: "All the elders that are next unto the slain man, shall wash their hands over the heifer that is beheaded in the valley; they shall say, 'Our hands have not shed this blood, neither have our eyes seen it.' .... So shalt thou put away the guilt of innocent blood from among you...."
PS. 26:5-6 - "I have hated the congregation of evil doers, and will not sit with the wicked. I will wash mine hands in innocency...."

**Perplexing:**

Why did the viciously anti-Jewish Pilate resort to an ancient Jewish ritual to proclaim his innocence? Would he even have known about this ritual derived from the Old Testament? If Jesus was not guilty of a crime against Rome, Pilate could easily have released him and quickly quelled any tumult. Why did he not do so?

27:25 - ALL THE PEOPLE SAID: "HIS BLOOD BE ON US, AND ON OUR CHILDREN."

**History:**

The above statement attributed to a group of Jews has been used as a basis for centuries of persecution and killing of Jews by Christians. It succeeded in transferring the guilt of Jesus' death from the Romans, who killed him for the capital offense of being a king in violation of Roman law, to the Jews.

**Perplexing:**
Why are not those responsible for Jesus' death, and his subsequent resurrection, praised for doing God's will and for creating the events that brought Christianity into existence?

27:26 - THEN RELEASED HE BARABBAS UNTO THEM, AND WHEN HE HAD SCOURGED JESUS, HE DELIVERED HIM TO BE CRUCIFIED.

**Contradictions:**
LUKE 23:7-25 - Pilate sent Jesus to Herod before delivering him to be crucified, and before releasing Barabbas. Scourging was not reported.
[Did Pilate send Jesus to be crucified directly after scourging him, or did he send him to Herod before having him crucified?]
[Did Pilate send Jesus to be crucified after, or before releasing Barabbas?]
[Did Pilate not send, or send Jesus to Herod?]

**Perplexing:**
If Pilate believed that Jesus was not guilty of any crime, why did he scourge him and have him crucified? As governor he had the authority to release anyone that he deemed to be innocent. Why was Pilate not afraid to order the execution of one who had the power to raise the dead and heal the sick and inf irm? Was he not fearful that Jesus might perform a miracle to harm or create problems for him? How could he have released Barabbas who was guilty of insurrection against Rome? Why was Pilate not arrested and imprisoned and/or executed for releasing Barabbas?
See also under 27:11.

**History:** See under 27:15 and 27:17.

**Pagan parallel:**
Around 2000 B.C., the god Baal was arrested put on trial, found innocent, but sentenced to death.

27:28 - THEY [SOLDIERS] STRIPPED HIM, AND PUT ON HIM A SCARLET ROBE.

**Contradictions:**
MARK 15:17 - They clothed him with purple....
[Did the soldiers put a scarlet robe on Jesus, or did they clothe him in purple?]
LUKE 23:11 - Herod with his men of war...arrayed him in a gorgeous robe, and sent him to Pilate.
[Did Pilate's soldiers put a scarlet robe on Jesus, or did Herod's soldiers put a gorgeous robe on him?]
JOHN 19:2 - [Before the priests told Pilate to crucify Jesus in JOHN 19:16] Pilate scourged him. The soldiers...put on him a purple robe.
[Was Jesus arrayed in the robe after, or before the priests requested that he be crucified?]
See also under 27:26.

**History:**
It was a custom among some primitive people to dress a victim, usually a criminal, as a king and then kill him as a sacrifice to bring the people good fortune.

27:29 - WHEN THEY HAD PLATTED A CROWN OF THORNS, THEY PUT IT ON HIS HEAD....

**Contradiction:**
JOHN 19:2-6 - The soldiers platted a crown of thorns, and put it on his head.... .... When the chief priests and officers saw him, they cried out, "Crucify him."
[Was the crown of thorns put on Jesus' head after Pilate delivered him to be crucified, or before the priests requested that he be crucified?]

27:30 - THEY...TOOK THE REED, AND SMOTE HIM ON THE HEAD.

**Contradictions:**
JOHN 19:3-16 - ...they smote him with their hands. .... Then delivered he him unto them to be crucified.
[Did the soldiers hit Jesus with a reed, or with their hands?]
[Did the soldiers strike Jesus after, or before he was sent to be crucified?]

**Pagan parallel:**
The god Baal was abused by people after being sentenced to be killed.
See also under 27:26.

27:31 - AFTER THEY [SOLDIERS] HAD MOCKED HIM, THEY TOOK THE ROBE OFF...AND LED HIM AWAY TO CRUCIFY HIM.

**Contradiction:**
LUKE 23:25-26 - ...he [Pilate] delivered Jesus to their [the priests'] will. As they led him away....
JOHN 19:16 - Then delivered he [Pilate] him unto them [Jews] to be crucified. They took Jesus, and led him away.
[Was Jesus led away by Pilate's soldiers to be crucified. or by Jews?]

27:32 - AS THEY CAME OUT, THEY FOUND A MAN OF CYRENE, SIMON BY NAME; HIM THEY COMPELLED TO BEAR HIS CROSS.

**Contradiction:**
JOHN 19:17 - He bearing his cross went forth....
[Did Simon carry Jesus' cross, or did Jesus carry the cross?]

**History:**
The cross was an ancient pagan symbol for sun-gods; it adorned pagan temples, and was also used as a phallic symbol.
Until the Council of Nicea (4th century) made the cross a Christian symbol, the lamb had been used to symbolize Christianity. Prior to that time Christians had condemned the cross as pagan.

27:33 - THEY WERE COME TO A PLACE CALLED GOLGOTHA, THAT IS TO SAY, A PLACE OF A SKULL.

**Language:**
"Golgotha," was the Aramaic word for "skull." In LUKE 23:33, the name was given in Latin, "Calvary."
The capitation tax collected by the Roman authorities was also called "golgotha."

27:34 - THEY GAVE HIM VINEGAR TO DRINK MINGLED WITH GALL; WHEN HE HAD TASTED THEREOF, HE WOULD NOT DRINK.

**Contradiction:**
MARK 15:23 - They gave him to drink wine mingled with myrrh, but he received it not.
[Did Jesus taste but not drink vinegar with gall, or did he refuse to taste wine with myrrh?]

**Old Testament:**
PS. 69:21 - "They gave me gall for my meat; in my thirst they gave me vinegar to drink."

27:35 - THEY CRUCIFIED HIM, AND PARTED HIS GARMENTS, CASTING LOTS THAT IT MIGHT BE FULFILLED WHICH WAS SPOKEN BY THE PROPHET, "THEY PARTED MY GARMENTS AMONG THEM, AND UPON MY VESTURE DID THEY CAST LOTS."

**Contradictions:**
ACTS 5:30 - Peter: "The God of our fathers raised up Jesus, whom ye slew and hanged on a tree."
ACTS 10:39 - Peter: "...whom they slew and hanged on a tree."
ACTS 13:29 - Paul: "...they took him down from the tree...."
[Was Jesus crucified (hung on a cross while still alive), or was he killed in an unspecified manner and his body then hung on a tree?]
GAL. 3:13 - Paul: "Christ hath redeemed us from the curse of the law, being made a curse for us... 'Cursed is everyone that hangeth on a tree.'"
[Was Jesus crucified, or hanged on a tree?]
PS. 22:18 - "They part my garments among them, and cast lots upon my vesture."
[Was the statement about the garment and lots spoken by a prophet, or was it taken from PSALMS?]

**Old Testament:** See PS. 22:18 above.

**History:**
There is no documentation of the crucifixion of Jesus. There is, however, evidence that Jesus Ben Pandira (believed to have founded the Essene sect) was killed and his body then hung on a tree just prior to Passover sometime between 106 - 79 B.C. (Could the biblical Jesus have been modeled after or confused with this earlier Jesus? Interestingly, the biblical Jesus is never reported to have spoken adversely about the Essenes, although he frequently denounced the other two major Jewish sects, the Pharisees and Sadducees.) The second century Church leader, Father Irenaeus, wrote that Jesus was not crucified, but died of natural causes at about the age of 50. Some early Christians such as the Docetists did not believe that Jesus was crucified and resurrected.
Jews did not participate in executions (or at this time utilize capital punishment - see under 26:59-60) or in any work related activities during Passover.

**Perplexing:**
Why did MATT. refer to the words in a Psalm as words spoken by a prophet? Why did the multitudes who benefited from Jesus' miracles not come forward to help him? Why did he not perform a miracle freeing himself and convincing everyone that he is the Son of God? Why is there no set date (such as there is for Christmas) for the crucifixion? Why is there no historical record of something as important to Christianity as the crucifixion and resurrection?
See also under 27:20 and 27:22.

**Language:**
The Greek word translated as "cross," was "stauros," which means "stake" or "pole." Consequently, one Bible, The New World Translation of the Holy Scriptures, writes that Jesus was impaled, not crucified.

27:37-38 - SET UP OVER HIS HEAD WAS HIS ACCUSATION WRITTEN, THIS IS JESUS THE KING OF THE JEWS. THEN WERE THERE TWO THIEVES CRUCIFIED WITH HIM....

**Contradictions:**
MARK 15:26 - The superscription of his accusation, THE KING OF THE JEWS.
LUKE 23:38 - A superscription was written over him in Greek, Latin, and Hebrew, THIS IS THE KING OF THE JEWS.
JOHN 19:19 - Pilate wrote a title,, and put it on the cross. The writing was, JESUS OF NAZARETH THE KING OF THE JEWS.
[Did the superscription in MATT., or MARK, or LUKE, or JOHN appear on the cross?]

**Perplexing:**
Why did the gospels disagree about what sign was on the cross? By saying that the accusation against Jesus was that of being the King of the Jews, Pilate was saying that Jesus was executed by the Romans for setting himself up as king without authorization from Rome; that is, he was guilty of treason against Rome. He was not executed for calling himself the "Son of God" or for any violation of Jewish law.

**History:** See under 27:35.

**Pagan parallel:**
Two criminals were also tried with the god Baal.
See also under 27:26.

27:39 - THEY THAT PASSED BY REVILED HIM, WAGGING THEIR HEADS.

**Perplexing:**
Why have all the multitudes helped by Jesus turned against him now?

**Old Testament:**
PS. 22:7-8 - "All that see me laugh me to scorn; they shoot out the lip; they shake the head, saying, 'He trusted on the LORD that He would deliver him; let Him deliver him, seeing He delighted in him.'"

**Pagan parallel:**
The god Baal was reviled by a mob of people.
See also under 27:26.

27:41-42 - THE CHIEF PRIESTS, SCRIBES, AND ELDERS, SAID, "...IF HE BE THE KING OF ISRAEL, LET HIM COME DOWN NOW FROM THE CROSS, AND WE WILL BELIEVE HIM."

**Contradictions:**
MARK 15:32 - The chief priests: "Let Christ the King of Israel descend now from the cross, that we may see and believe."
[Did the chief priests say if Jesus "be the king of Israel, " or did they refer to Jesus as "Christ the King of Israel?"]

LUKE 23:37 - Soldiers: "If thou be the king of the Jews, save thyself."
[Did the chief priests say that they would believe if Jesus came down from the cross, or did the soldiers tell Jesus to save himself?]
JOHN 19:21 - Said the chief priests to Pilate, "Write not, The King of the Jews, but that he said, 'I am King of the Jews.'"
[Did the priests say, "If he [Jesus] be The King of Israel," or did they ask Pilate not to write that Jesus was "The King of the Jews?"]
[Did the priests and others speak to each other about Jesus, or did they speak to Pilate?]

**Perplexing:**
Why did Jesus not miraculously come down from the cross, and, thereby, persuade everyone to believe him?
See also under 27:22.

27:43 - [THE CHIEF PRIESTS, SCRIBES, AND ELDERS:] "HE TRUSTED IN GOD; LET HIM DELIVER HIM NOW...HE SAID, 'I AM THE SON OF GOD.'"

**Old Testament:** See under 27:39.

27:44 - THE THIEVES WHICH WERE CRUCIFIED WITH HIM, CAST THE SAME IN HIS TEETH.

**Contradiction:**
LUKE 23:42-43 - He [one of the malefactors] said, "Lord, remember me when thou comest into thy kingdom." Jesus said, "Today shalt thou be with me in paradise."
[Did the two criminals mock and revile Jesus, or did one of them speak with him and obtain a promise that he would go to paradise that day?]

27:45 - NOW FROM THE SIXTH HOUR THERE WAS DARKNESS OVER ALL THE LAND UNTO THE NINTH HOUR.

**History:**
There is no historical record of three hours of darkness having occurred at any time during which the crucifixion could have taken place. Note that it is not possible to ascertain the date for the event, if it actually happened, other than that it was when Pilate was governor: A.D. 26 - 36. Jews did not hold trials or conduct executions on Passover; they observed the holiday in the temple and synagogues. The Romans, however, did not observe Jewish customs, so they could have held trials and executions whenever it suited them.
See also under 27:35.

**Perplexing:**
Why did JOHN not report something as amazing as the darkness? Why is there no specific date for the crucifixion? Why did no historian, political or military figure, or anyone else ever report the crucifixion or the remarkable phenomenon of three hours of darkness? If there was darkness, how could anyone see what was occurring?

**Pagan parallel:**
Darkness occurred when sun-gods died. It symbolized the setting of the sun which later is resurrected (or

born again) at dawn. Darkness was also reported at the death of several pre-Christian deities, such as: Aesclepius, Hercules, Krishna, and Quirinius.

27:46 - ABOUT THE NINTH HOUR JESUS CRIED WITH A LOUD VOICE, "ELI, ELI, LAMA SABACHTHANI?" THAT IS, "MY GOD, MY GOD, WHY HAST THOU FORSAKEN ME?"

**Contradictions:**
MARK 15:34 - At the ninth hour, Jesus cried with a loud voice, "Eloi, Eloi, lama sabachthani?" which is "My God, my God, why hast thou forsaken me?"
[Did Jesus say, "Eli, Eli," (Hebrew transliterated into Greek) or "Eloi, Eloi" (Aramaic)?]
LUKE 23:46 - When Jesus had cried with a loud voice, he said, "Father, into Thy hands I commend my spirit"....
[Did Jesus say, "My God, why hast Thou forsaken me," or that he commends his spirit to his Father?]
JOHN 19:30 - Jesus...said, "It is finished"....
[Did Jesus ask why God had forsaken him, or say, "It is finished?"]

**Old Testament:**
PS. 22:1 - "My God, my God, why hast thou forsaken me?...."

**Perplexing:**
Why did MARK. assert that Jesus used "Eloi," the Aramaic word for "God," whereas MATT. used "Eli," based on the Hebrew of the PS. verse?
Why did Jesus accuse God of forsaking him, when in MATT. 16:21; 17:23, and a number of other gospel verses he said that he would be killed and then be resurrected? In JOHN 18:4, Jesus was said to know everything that was to happen to him. Why then did MATT. and MARK state that Jesus spoke like a human who was being executed and who would not be resurrected, rather than like a divinity—the Son of God? If Jesus had to die and then rise from the dead, why did God not want him to die from natural causes instead of being killed by crucifixion?

**History:** See under 27:35.

27:50 - JESUS, WHEN HE HAD CRIED AGAIN WITH A LOUD VOICE, YIELDED UP THE GHOST.

**Contradictions:**
LUKE 23:46 - When Jesus had cried out again with a loud voice, he said, "Father into Thy hands I commend my spirit"; having said thus he gave up the ghost.
[Did Jesus cry out and yield up the ghost, or after crying out say, "Father, into Thy hands I commend my spirit," then give up the ghost?]
JOHN 19:30 - ...he said, "It is finished"; he bowed his head and gave up the ghost.
[Did Jesus just cry out in a loud voice, or did he say, "It is finished," before giving up the ghost?]

27:51-53 - THE VEIL OF THE TEMPLE WAS RENT IN TWAIN FROM TOP TO BOTTOM; THE EARTH DID QUAKE, AND ROCKS RENT; GRAVES WERE OPENED, AND MANY BODIES OF THE SAINTS AROSE, CAME OUT OF THE GRAVES AFTER HIS RESURRECTTON, WENT INTO THE HOLY CITY, AND APPEARED UNTO MANY.

**History:**
There is no record of the above fantastic events, including the assertion that resurrected corpses crawled out of graves and went meandering around Jerusalem.

**Perplexing:**
Why did no Roman, Greek, Jewish, other individuals, or the other gospel writers record the earthquake, the opening of graves, and the parade of risen corpses? Why did the earthquake fail to knock down the cross and cause the people to flee? What was the appearance of the resurrected saints? How many were there? Who were they? How long had they been dead? Where did they go? What did they do? Who saw them? What eventually happened to them? Did they return to their graves, or are they still roaming around? If they did return, who reburied them? If this mass resurrection occurred, would it not have been an even greater event than Jesus' resurrection?

27:54 - WHEN THE CENTURION, AND THEY THAT WERE WITH HIM WATCHING JESUS, SAW THE EARTHQUAKE, AND THOSE THINGS THAT WERE DONE, THEY FEARED GREATLY, SAYING, "TRULY THIS WAS THE SON OF GOD."

**Contradictions:**
MARK 15:39 - When the centurion...saw that he so cried out, and gave up the ghost, he said, "Truly this man was the Son of God."
[Did the centurion and those with him say that Jesus was the Son of God, or did only the centurion say it?]
LUKE 23:47 - When the centurion saw what was done, he glorified God, saying, "Certainly this was a righteous man."
[Did the centurion and those with him say that Jesus was the Son of God, or did the centurion say that Jesus was a righteous man?]
[Did the centurion and people with him witness an earthquake, or did they just see Jesus die?]

**Perplexing:**
Why did no one record the earthquake or the damage it caused?
Did people have nothing else to do but stand around for three hours watching Jesus die? How were they able to see anything during the three hours of darkness (27:45)?
See also under 27:51-53.

**History:** See under 8:29.

27:55-56 - MANY WOMEN WERE THERE BEHOLDING AFAR OFF, WHICH FOLLOWED JESUS FROM GALILEE, MINISTERING UNTO HIM, AMONG WHICH WAS MARY MAGDALENE, MARY THE MOTHER OF JAMES AND JOSES, AND THE MOTHER OF ZEBEDEE'S CHILDREN.

**Contradictions:**
JOHN 19:25-27 - There stood by the cross of Jesus his mother, his mother's sister, Mary the wife of Cleophas, and Mary Magdalene. Jesus saw his mother and the disciple he loved, and saith unto his mother, "Woman, behold thy son!" Saith he to the disciple, "Behold thy mother!" That disciple took her unto his own home.
[Were the women far off, or were they by the cross?]
[Were there several women, or just the three women (four according to some Bibles) cited by JOHN?]

[Was, or was not a disciple present by the cross?]
[Did, or did not Jesus speak to his mother and a disciple?]

**Perplexing:**
If someone as important as Jesus' mother was present, as claimed by JOHN, why did not MATT., MARK, and LUKE mention her? In MATT. 13:55, James and Joses are identified as two of Jesus' brethren, with Mary (Jesus' mother) their mother. If it was Passover, why were the women not home, in the temple, or in a synagogue?
How many women were there from Galilee? Where in Jerusalem did these women stay?

**Pagan concept:**
Sun-gods die in the evening, and women are always present. The women represent the stars that appear in the eastern sky (afar off) as the sun dies (sets) in the west. The gods are then resurrected (born again) at dawn.

27:57-58 - WHEN THE EVEN WAS COME, THERE CAME A RICH MAN OF ARIMATHAEA, NAMED JOSEPH, WHO ALSO WAS JESUS' DISCIPLE; HE WENT TO PILATE, AND BEGGED THE BODY OF JESUS. PILATE COMMANDED THE BODY TO BE DELIVERED.

**Contradictions:**
MARK 15:43-45 - Joseph of Arimathaea...went boldly unto Pilate, and craved the body of Jesus. Pilate...calling the centurion, asked whether he had been any while dead; when he knew it of the centurion, he gave the body to Joseph.
[Did Joseph beg Pilate for Jesus' body, or did he boldly crave the body from Pilate?]
JOHN 19:38 - Joseph...besought Pilate that he might take away the body of Jesus; Pilate gave him leave. He came and took the body.
LUKE 23:50-53 - ....He [Joseph] took it [Jesus' body] down....
[Did Pilate give Jesus' body to Joseph, or did Joseph take it down from the cross?]
ACTS 13:29 - Paul: "...they [that dwell in Jerusalem and their rulers] took him [Jesus] down from the tree and laid him in a sepulchre?]
[Did Pilate have Jesus' body delivered to Joseph, or did people from Jerusalem take Jesus' body down from a tree?]

**Perplexing:**
Was the historical anti-Jewish Pilate readily available to meet with any Jew who wanted to speak with him? Did he have the time and willingness to meet with a Jew wanting to take Jesus' body, and give him the body? Would a Jew be out of his home, temple, or synagogue on Passover, a major religious holiday? How could a rich man be a disciple of Jesus? See also under 19:23-24 and 26:30.

**Old Testament:** See under 26:30.

**History:** See under 19:23-24 and 27:11.

27:59-60 - WHEN JOSEPH HAD TAKEN THE BODY, HE WRAPPED IT IN A CLEAN LINEN CLOTH, AND LAID IT IN HIS OWN NEW TOMB, WHICH HE HAD HEWN OUT OF ROCK; HE ROLLED A GREAT STONE TO THE DOOR OF THE SEPULCHRE, AND DEPARTED.

**Contradictions:**

JOHN 19:39-42 - There came Nicodemus...and brought a mixture of myrrh and aloes, about an 100 pound weight. Then took they the body of Jesus, and wound it in linen clothes with the spices.... In the place where he was crucified there was...a new sepulchre.... There laid they Jesus because of the Jews' preparation day, for the sepulchre was nigh at hand.

[Did Joseph alone place Jesus' body in a sepulchre, or did he and Nicodemus do it?]

[Did Joseph wrap Jesus' body in linen, or did he and Nicodemus wrap it in linen?]

ACTS 13:29 - Paul: "...they [that dwell at Jerusalem, and their rulers]...took him down from the tree and put him in a sepulchre."

[Was Jesus' body taken down from a cross, or from a tree? (Some Christians contend that "tree" means "cross.")]

[Did Joseph alone place Jesus' body in the tomb, or did those who dwelt in Jerusalem and their rulers do it?]

**Perplexing:**

In MATT. 12:40, Jesus said, "...so shall the Son of man be three days and three nights in the heart of the earth." Why was Jesus placed into a sepulchre near the surface of the earth, rather than into the heart of the earth as he prophesied?

Where was the sepulchre? Why was its location not specified? How was Joseph able to roll a great stone to the door of the sepulchre? How far did he have to move it?

Why did not Paul mention Joseph of Arimathaea?

**Pagan parallel:**

The god Baal, after being killed, was entombed and a stone used to seal the tomb.

See also under 27:26.

27:61 - THERE WAS MARY MAGDALENE, AND THE OTHER MARY, SITTING OVER AGAINST THE SEPULCHRE.

**Contradictions:**

MARK 15:47 - Mary Magdalene and Mary the mother of Joses beheld where Jesus was laid.

[Was the other Mary, or Mary the mother of Joses with Mary Magdalene? (assuming that the other Mary was not also the Mary who was the mother of Joses).]

LUKE 23:55 - The women which came with him from Galilee, followed after and beheld the sepulchre, and how his body was laid.

[Were there two women, or several women at Jesus' interment?]

**Perplexing:**

Why were Mary Magdalene and the other Mary sitting opposite the sepulchre? How did the women know that Jesus would be removed from the cross, and that Joseph would be able to obtain his body? How did they know where he would be interred? Who was "the other Mary?"

27:62-66 - THE NEXT DAY, THAT FOLLOWED THE DAY OF PREPARATION, THE CHIEF PRIESTS AND PHARISEES CAME UNTO PILATE, SAYING, COMMAND THAT THE SEPULCHRE BE MADE SURE...." PILATE SAID, "YE HAVE A WATCH...."

**Perplexing:**

Why did the other gospels not report that the sepulchre was watched? Why did the anti-Jewish Pilate seem

to have little else to do but meet with, listen to, and comply with the wishes of Jews? Why did the Pilate described in MATT. bear little resemblance to the historical Pilate?
See also under 27:11.

28:1 - IN THE END OF THE SABBATH, AS IT BEGAN TO DAWN TOWARD THE FIRST DAY OF THE WEEK, CAME MARY MAGDALENE AND THE OTHER MARY TO SEE THE SEPULCHRE.

**Contradictions:**
MARK 16:1-2 - When the sabbath was past, Mary Magdalene, Mary the mother of James, and Salome, brought sweet spices, that they might anoint him. Very early in the morning the first day of the week, they came unto the sepulchre at the rising of the sun.
[Did Mary Magdalene and the other Mary come to see the sepulchre, or did Mary Magdalene, the mother of James, and Salome come to anoint Jesus?]
LUKE 24:1 - The first day of the week, very early in the morning, they [women from Galilee] came unto the sepulchre, bringing spices which they had prepared, and certain others with them.
[Did Mary Magdalene and the other Mary come to see the sepulchre, or did several women from Galilee bring spices to the sepulchre?]
JOHN 20:1 - The first day of the week cometh Mary Magdalene early, when it was yet dark unto the sepulchre and seeth the stone taken away from the sepulchre.
[Was it beginning to dawn when Mary Magdalene and the other Mary came to the sepulchre, or was it yet dark when Mary Magdalene came alone to the sepulchre?]
[Did Mary Magdalene and the other Mary come to see the sepulchre, or did only Mary Magdalene come?]

**Perplexing:**
If it was now Sunday, the Sabbath would have been Saturday the regular biblical Sabbath. The crucifixion, however, was reported by MATT. to have taken place on Friday which was said to have been Passover. The Jewish calendar, however, is arranged so that Passover, never falls on a Friday. Did MATT. (as well as MARK and LUKE) confuse the days, or was he or someone who rewrote his account ignorant of Passover and the Jewish calendar? (JOHN, however, had Passover fall on a Saturday.)
Why did the women come to see the sepulchre at dawn?

28:2-4 - THERE WAS A GREAT EARTHQUAKE, FOR THE ANGEL OF THE LORD DESCENDED FROM HEAVEN, AND CAME AND ROLLED BACK THE STONE FROM THE DOOR, AND SAT UPON IT. HIS COUNTENANCE WAS LIKE LIGHTNING, AND HIS RAIMENT WHITE AS SNOW. FOR FEAR OF HIM THE KEEPERS DID SHAKE, AND BECAME AS DEAD MEN.

**Contradictions:**
MARK 16:4-5 - When they looked, they saw that the stone was rolled away; it was very great. Entering the sepulchre they saw a young man sitting, clothed in a long white garment....
[Did the women see an angel sitting on the stone outside the sepulchre, or did they enter the sepulchre where they saw a young man in a white garment?]
[Did the women see, or not see an angel role the stone away?]
LUKE 24:2-4 - They found the stone rolled away. They entered, and found not the body of the Lord Jesus. ...two men stood by them in shining garments.
[Did the women see an angel sitting on the stone outside the sepulchre, or did they enter the sepulchre and see two men in shining garments standing there?]

[Did, or did not the women enter the sepulchre?]
[Was there, or was there not a great earthquake?]
JOHN 20:1-12 - Mary Magdalene early, when it was yet dark...seeth the stone taken away from the sepulchre. She runneth to Peter, and the disciple Jesus loved.... .... Peter and that other disciple came to the sepulchre. He [the other disciple] looking in saw the linen clothes.... Peter went into the sepulchre and saw the linen clothes. .... Then the disciples went away unto their own home. Mary stood by the sepulchre weeping...and looked into the sepulchre, and seeth two angels in white sitting where the body of Jesus had lain.
[Did Mary Magdalene and another woman see an angel roll the stone away, or did Mary Magdalene alone see (in the dark) that the stone had been rolled away?]
[Did, or did not Mary Magdalene speak to the disciples and then make a second visit to the tomb, and see two angels?]
[Did, or did not Peter and another disciple come to the sepulchre?]
[Were, or were not keepers present at the sepulchre?]

**Perplexing:**
Why is there no historical record of this "great earthquake?" Why was it not reported by the other gospels? Why were none of the women or the guards hurt in the great earthquake? Why was the sepulchre not damaged in the great earthquake? What damage did the quake cause anywhere? Why did an angel have to roll the stone away? Why could the resurrected Jesus not do it?
See also under 27:51-53 (there is no record of the previous earthquake).

**Pagan parallel:**
The stone which sealed the entrance of the tomb of the god Baal was found rolled away.
See also under 27:26.

**Old Testament:**
DAN. 7:9 - Daniel: "...the Ancient of days did sit, whose garment was white as snow...."
DAN. 10:6 - Daniel: "...his [a certain man clothed in linen] face as the appearance of lightning...."

28:5-7 - THE ANGEL SAID, "FEAR NOT; I KNOW YE SEEK JESUS.... HE IS RISEN...COME SEE THE PLACE WHERE THE LORD LAY. GO QUICKLY, AND TELL HIS DISCIPLES THAT HE IS RISEN FROM THE DEAD, AND GOETH BEFORE YOU INTO GALILEE; THERE SHALL YE SEE HIM...."

**Contradictions:**
MARK 16:6-7 - He saith unto them, "...ye seek Jesus of Nazareth...he is risen; he is not here; behold the place where they laid him. ...tell his disciples and Peter that he goeth into Galilee, where shall ye see him as he said unto you."
[Did the angel say, "Jesus," or did the young man say, "Jesus of Nazareth?"]
[Did the angel say, "see the place where the Lord lay," or did the young man say, "behold the place where they laid him?"]
LUKE 24:5-6 - ...they said unto them [the women]. "Why seek ye the living among the dead? He...is risen; remember how he spake unto you when he was in Galilee, 'The Son of man must be delivered into the hands of sinful men, be crucified, and the third day rise again.'"
[Did the angel tell the women to convey the news of Jesus' resurrection to his disciples, or did two men not so instruct the women?]
[Did an angel instruct the women to tell the disciples to meet Jesus in Galilee, or did two men not so tell the women?]

JOHN 20:11-14 - Mary [on her second visit to the sepulchre] weeping...looked into the sepulchre, and seeth two angels in white sitting. They say, "Woman, why weepest thou?" She saith, "They have taken away my Lord, and I know not where they have laid him."
[Did an angel tell Mary Magdalene and the other Mary that Jesus had risen from the dead, or did two angels not so inform Mary Magdalene?]
[Was, or was not Mary Magdalene told to inform the disciples to meet Jesus in Galilee?]
[Did, or did not Mary Magdalene weep?]
MATT. 12:40 - [Jesus:] "As Jonas was three days and three nights in the whale's belly, so shall the Son of man be three days and three nights in the heart of the earth."
[Did Jesus spend at most one and a half days and two nights in the earth (he was interred on Friday evening, and resurrected before dawn on Sunday), or three days and nights in the earth?]
MARK 8:31 - "He began to teach them that the Son of man must be killed, and after three days rise."
[Did Jesus rise after about one and a half days, or after three days?]

**Perplexing:**
Why did Jesus fail to spend three nights in the heart of the earth as he had prophesied? Why was Jesus resurrected in secret? Why were not the women, disciples, or anyone else permitted to watch his resurrection? Why did Jesus not remain at the tomb to greet the women when they arrived? How early in the morning did Jesus have to rise to avoid being seen by the women?
Why did the resurrected Jesus fail to appear before Pilate, the high priest, and all people to prove that he had risen from the dead? Why did the angel not inform the disciples that Jesus had risen?
See also under 12:40.

**History:**
There is no date for or historical documentation of the resurrection.
See also under 27:35.

**Pagan parallels:**
The belief in deities that died or were killed and buried, but were resurrected, usually three days thereafter, around then time of the vernal equinox, is a relatively common theme in pagan religions. Some of these resurrected gods were Baal, Mithra, Krishna, Tammuz, Horus, and Attis. Baal even left behind an empty tomb and showed himself resurrected to his followers. His death and resurrection were for the purpose of obtaining eternal life for humanity.
See also under 27:26.

**Old Testament:**
DAN. 10:12 - Daniel: "Said he unto me, 'Fear not....'"

28:8 - THEY DEPARTED QUICKLY FROM THE SEPULCHRE WITH FEAR AND GREAT JOY, AND DID RUN TO BRING HIS DISCIPLES' WORD.

**Contradictions:**
MARK 16:8 - They went out quickly, and fled from the sepulchre; they trembled and were amazed; neither said they anything to any man, for they were afraid.
[Did two women depart with fear and great joy, or were three women trembling, amazed, and afraid?]
[Did two women depart to bring word to the disciples, or were three women too afraid to say anything to anyone?]

JOHN 20:2 - She [Mary Magdalene, alone] runneth to Simon Peter, and to the disciple, whom Jesus loved.... [Did Mary Magdalene and the other Mary run to bring word to the disciples, or did Mary Magdalene alone run to Peter and another disciple?]

28:9-10 - AS THEY WENT TO TELL HIS DISCIPLES, JESUS MET THEM, SAYING, "ALL HAIL." THEY HELD HIM BY THE FEET AND WORSHIPPED HIM. SAID JESUS, "BE NOT AFRAID; GO TELL MY BRETHREN THAT THEY GO INTO GALILEE, AND THERE SHALL THEY SEE ME."

**Contradictions:**

MARK 16:9 - When Jesus was risen early the first day, he appeared first to Mary Magdalene [but is not reported to have conversed with her]....

[Did Jesus encounter Mary Magdalene and the other Mary, or only Mary Magdalene?]

LUKE 24:8-9 - They...returned from the sepulchre, and told all these things to the eleven, and to the rest. [The women did not meet Jesus.]

[Did Jesus meet Mary Magdalene and the other Mary, or did he not meet any women?]

JOHN 20:14-17 - She [Mary Magdalene] saw Jesus standing, and knew not that it was Jesus. Jesus saith, "Woman, why weepest thou?" She, supposing him to be the gardener, saith, "Sir...tell me where thou hast laid him...?" Jesus saith, "Mary"; she saith, "Rabboni...." Jesus saith, "Touch me not, for I am not yet ascended to my Father, but go to my brethren, and say, 'I ascend unto my Father, to my God, and your God.'"

[Did Mary Magdalene and the other Mary recognize Jesus, or did Mary Magdalene after her second trip to the sepulchre alone suppose Jesus to be a gardener, before she recognized him?]

[Did Mary Magdalene and the other Mary hold Jesus' feet and worship him, or did Jesus tell Mary Magdalene not to touch him because he had not yet ascended?]

[Did Jesus tell Mary Magdalene and the other Mary to instruct his disciples to meet him in Galilee, or did he tell Mary Magdalene to inform them that he was ascending to his Father?]

LUKE 24:13-30 - The resurrected Jesus appeared first to two disciples, one of whom was named Cleopas, while they were walking between Emmaus and Jerusalem.

[Did the resurrected Jesus meet first with Mary Magdalene and the other Mary, or with two disciples?]

1 COR. 15:4-5 - Paul: "...he rose the third day...and was seen of Cephas, then of the twelve."

[Did the resurrected Jesus meet Mary Magdalene and the other Mary, or Cephas?]

LUKE 24:49 - Jesus: "...tarry in the city of Jerusalem, until ye be endued with power from on high."

ACTS 1:4 - ...[Jesus] commanded that they should not depart from Jerusalem, but wait for the promise of the Father....

[Did Jesus say that his disciples should go to Galilee, or that they should remain in Jerusalem?]

**Perplexing:**

Why did Jesus tell the women to instruct the disciples to come to Galilee? Why could neither he nor the angel do so? Why did he repeat the instructions given to the women by the angel, when the women were already on their way to the disciples?

**History:**

There is no historical record of the resurrected Jesus having been seen by anyone.

**Pagan parallel:**

The god Baal appeared resurrected and said that he had secured life in the hereafter for all.

See also under 27:26.

28:11-15 - ...SOME OF THE WATCH...SHEWED UNTO THE CHIEF PRIESTS ALL THE THINGS THAT WERE DONE. ...THE ELDERS...GAVE LARGE MONEY UNTO THE SOLDIERS, SAYING, "SAY, 'HIS DISCIPLES CAME BY NIGHT, AND STOLE HIM AWAY WHILE WE SLEPT.' IF THIS COME TO THE GOVERNOR'S EARS, WE WILL PERSUADE HIM AND SECURE YOU." ...THEY DID AS THEY WERE TAUGHT, AND THE SAYING IS COMMONLY REPORTED AMONG THE JEWS UNTIL THIS DAY.

**Perplexing:**

Why did Roman soldiers (see under 27:62-66) report to Jewish priests, instead of to the Roman Authorities? Why were the above verses not reported by the other gospels? If there was a "great earthquake," as reported by MATT. 28:2, how could anyone believe that the guards slept through it? If they were asleep, how could they say that the disciples (or anyone else) stole Jesus' body? Why would they agree, even for money, to say that they were asleep while on guard duty when doing so would get them punished and possibly executed? Would they not also have known that the priests and elders would have little or no influence with Pilate (the historical Pilate)? By seeing and hearing from the angel about what happened, and seeing the empty sepulchre, would the soldiers not have been converted to and become followers of Jesus? What is meant by, "until this day?" Would a Jew have written that the saying is "commonly reported among the Jews?" Could the above verses which interrupt the flow of the narrative from v.10 to the following v.16, have been inserted some time after the original gospel had been compiled?

28:16-17 - THE ELEVEN DISCIPLES WENT INTO GALILEE, INTO A MOUNTAIN WHERE JESUS HAD APPOINTED THEM. WHEN THEY SAW HIM, THEY WORSHIPPED HIM, BUT SOME DOUBTED.

**Contradictions:**

MARK 16:10-11 - She [Mary Magdalene] told them that she had been with him as they mourned and wept. They when they had heard that he was alive, and had been seen of her, believed not.

JOHN 20:18 - Mary Magdalene told the disciples that she had seen the Lord, and that he had spoken these things unto her.

[Did the disciples go to Galilee and meet Jesus, or did they remain in Jerusalem where Mary Magdalene told them that Jesus was alive?]

LUKE 24:9-12 - [The women] returned from the sepulchre, and told all these things unto the eleven, and to the rest. It was Mary Magdalene, Joanna, Mary the mother of James, and other women with them, which told these things unto the apostles. Their words seemed to them as idle tales, and they believed them not. Then Peter, ran unto the sepulchre, stooping down, he beheld the linen clothes, and departed, wondering at that which was come to pass.

[Did the disciples go to Galilee and meet Jesus, or did they remain in Jerusalem where several women told them that Jesus had risen?]

[Did the disciples go to Galilee and worship Jesus, whereas some doubted, or did they refuse to believe that Jesus was alive?]

[Did no disciples, or did Peter visit the empty sepulchre?]

JOHN 20:2-10 - She [Mary Magdalene] cometh to Peter and the disciple Jesus loved, and saith, "They have taken away the Lord out of the sepulchre, and we know not where they have laid him." Peter and the other disciple came to the sepulchre. The other disciple saw the linen clothes. Simon Peter went into the sepulchre, and seeth the linen clothes. .... Then the disciples went unto their own home.

[Did no disciples, or did Peter and another disciple visit the empty sepulchre?]

[Did the disciples go to Galilee, or to their own home?]

MARK 16:12-14 - After [meeting Mary Magdalene (16:10)] he appeared in another form unto two of them [disciples] as they walked in the country. They told it to the residue; neither believed they them. Afterward he appeared unto the eleven...and upbraided them with their unbelief and hardness of heart
[Did Jesus appear to the disciples in Galilee where he was worshiped, or did he appear first to two disciples, then to the rest in Jerusalem where he upbraided them for their unbelief?]
LUKE 24:13-36 - Jesus appeared to two disciples as they walked between Emmaus and Jerusalem, then to all of them in Jerusalem.
[Did all the eleven disciples go to Galilee where they met Jesus, or did two meet him while walking outside of Jerusalem before he met all of them in Jerusalem?]
[Did Jesus meet initially with all eleven disciples, or first with two of them, then with the rest?]
JOHN 20:19-29 - The same day at evening, the first day of the week, when the doors were shut where the disciples were assembled (in Jerusalem)...came Jesus and stood in the midst, and saith, "Peace be unto you." Jesus spoke with them, but Thomas, one of the twelve, was not with them. The other disciples said to him, "We have seen the Lord." He doubted that Jesus really appeared. Eight days again his disciples were within, Thomas with them; then came Jesus...and Thomas believed.
[Did Jesus meet the eleven once in Galilee, or the eleven first in Jerusalem, without Thomas, then twelve (the eleven plus Thomas) in Jerusalem?]
[Was, or was not Thomas with the disciples when they first met Jesus?]
JOHN 21:1-22 - Jesus appeared for a third time to seven disciples while they were fishing; he later ate and conversed with them.
[Did Jesus meet with the disciple once, or three times?]
1 COR. 15:4-7 - Paul: "He was buried, and rose the third day...was seen by Cephas (Peter?), then of the twelve; after that he was seen of above 500 brethren at once time.... After that, he was seen of James, then of all the apostles."
[Was Jesus seen only by the eleven in Galilee, or by Cephas, the twelve (presumably this included Judas Iscariot, who Paul did not know had died), more than 500 others, and James?]
See also under 28:9-10 and 28:16.

**History:** See also under 28:9-10.

**Perplexing:**
Which disciples doubted? Why did they doubt? Why was there gospel confusion about whether Jesus met the disciples in Galilee or in Jerusalem? How many times did Jesus meet with the disciples? Why was there confusion about whether or not he met all eleven at the same time? Why did JOHN and Paul refer to the existence of 12 disciples? Were they unaware that Judas was reportedly deceased? Why did the resurrected Jesus continue to fail to make himself known to the world? Why did MATT. and the other gospels not confirm Paul's allegation that more than 500 people saw the risen Jesus? Why did an account of the crucifixion and resurrection not appear in the records of historians, historical figures, or government and political personages of the period?

28:18-20 - "ALL POWER IS GIVEN ME IN HEAVEN AND EARTH. GO THEREFORE, AND TEACH ALL NATIONS, BAPTIZING THEM IN THE NAME OF THE FATHER, THE SON, AND THE HOLY GHOST, TEACHING THEM TO OBSERVE ALL THINGS WHATSOEVER I HAVE COMMANDED YOU; I AM WITH YOU ALWAY [SIC], EVEN UNTO THE END OF THE WORLD."

**Contradictions:**

MATT. 10:5-7 - These twelve Jesus sent forth, saying, "Go not into the way of the Gentiles, and into any city of the Samaritans enter ye not; but go rather to the lost sheep of the house of Israel. As ye go, preach, 'The kingdom of heaven is at hand.'"

MATT. 10:23 - Jesus: "...ye shall not have gone over the cities of Israel, till the Son of man be come."

[Did Jesus instruct his disciples to teach all nations, or just to go to the lost sheep of the house of Israel?]

[Did Jesus order his disciples to teach what he commanded and to baptize, or to preach that the kingdom of heaven is at hand?]

[Did Jesus say that he is with the disciples always, or that he would return before they went over the cities of Israel?]

MARK 16:15-20 - He said, "Go ye into all the world, and preach the gospel to every creature. He that believeth and is baptized shall be saved; be that believeth not shall be damned; these signs shall follow them that believe; in my name shall they cast out devils, speak with new tongues, take up serpents, and if they drink any deadly thing, it shall not hurt them; they shall lay hands on the sick, and they shall recover." After the Lord had spoken, he was received up into heaven, and sat on the right hand of God. They went forth, and preached everywhere, the Lord working with them and confirming the word with signs.

[Did Jesus tell his disciples to teach all nations and to baptize in the name of the Father, Son, and Holy Ghost, or to preach the gospel, that those who believe and are baptized are saved, whereas others are damned; that they would not be harmed by deadly things, and could heal the sick?]

[Did Jesus say that he is with the disciples always, or did he ascend into heaven from Jerusalem?]

MARK 14:7 - Jesus: "...me ye have not always."

[Did Jesus say that he would always be with the disciples, or that he would not always be with them?]

LUKE 24:47-53 - Jesus: "Repentance and remission of sins should be preached in his [Christ's] name among all nations beginning at Jerusalem . .... I send the promise of my Father upon you, but tarry ye in the city of Jerusalem, until ye be endued with power from on high." He led them to Bethany.... ...he was carried up into heaven. They...returned to Jerusalem with great joy, and were continually in the temple, praising and blessing God.

[Did Jesus order the disciples to teach all things that he had commanded, and to baptize, or to preach repentance and the remission of sins?]

[Did Jesus instruct the disciples to go and teach all nations and baptize, or to remain in Jerusalem until they receive the promise of his Father?]

[Did Jesus say that he is with the disciples always, or did he ascend to heaven from Bethany?]

JOHN 21:1-25 - Jesus appeared (for the third time after his resurrection) to seven disciples as they fished in the Sea of Tiberias (Galilee), helped them catch fish, and spoke with them. He said to Peter, "If I will that he tarry till I come, what is that to thee?" [These were the last words spoken by Jesus based on JOHN.]

[Did the resurrected Jesus appear once, or on three different occasions to the disciples?]

[Were Jesus' final words to his eleven disciples, or only to Peter?]

ACTS 1:2-12 - ...the apostles...to whom he shewed himself alive after his passion by many infallible proofs, being seen of them, 40 days, and speaking of the things pertaining to the kingdom of God, and commanded that they should not depart from Jerusalem, but wait for the promise of the Father.... He said, "...Ye shall receive power, after that the Holy Ghost is come upon you, and ye shall be witnesses unto me both in Jerusalem, all Judaea, Samaria, and unto the uttermost part of the earth." When he had spoken...he was taken up, and a cloud received him.... Then returned they unto Jerusalem from the mount called Olivet....

[Did the resurrected Jesus remain on earth for an unspecified length of time, or did he ascend to heaven from Mount Olivet after 40 days?]

[Did Jesus tell the disciples to teach and baptize, or to wait in Jerusalem until the Holy Ghost comes upon them?]

ACTS 2:38 - Peter: "Repent and be baptized in the name of Jesus Christ for the remission of sins...."
[Is one to be baptized in the name of the Father, the Son, and the Holy Ghost, or only in the name of Jesus Christ?]
See also under MATT. 10:5-6 and 28:9-10.

**Perplexing:**

Why did the gospels disagree about whether Jesus said that the disciples should meet him in Galilee, or whether they should remain in Jerusalem? How long was the resurrected Jesus on the earth?
Did the disciples start preaching, go to the temple, or go fishing? Why did MATT. and JOHN not report the Ascension? Why did JOHN not cite any final instructions from Jesus to all the disciples? Why did Jesus say that he would be with the disciples until the end of the world, when he must have known that they would be dead long before the end of the world, which has yet to occur? Although Jesus instructed his disciples to teach, baptize, and observe his commands (including loving one's neighbors and one's enemies), many of his followers engaged in and still engage in policies of hate, intolerance, torture, and violence against those who do not share their beliefs, and even against those who interpret those beliefs differently. What is there in the teachings of or the belief in Jesus that incites many believers to perpetrate atrocities? Why do many, possibly most, Christians ignore MATT. 10:16, in which Jesus said, "I send you forth as sheep in the midst of wolves; be ye therefore wise as serpents, and harmless as doves?" Why is there no definitive date for the crucifixion and resurrection? Why did Jesus fail to put his teachings into writing? Did he not know that confusion, disagreements, and even violence would result because of different interpretations of what he is reported to have said? Why did much of Jesus life resemble that of a number of pagan gods? Why in a period as well documented as that of Augustus and Tiberius was there no record of Jesus and his reported miraculous works found outside of the Bible? The brief, occasionally cited, notations to Jesus found in the works of Josephus are recognized by historians to have been inserted into Josephus' writings at a later date, probably in the 4th century.

**Pagan parallels:**

The concept of a Trinity was basic to a number of ancient pre-Christian religions. For examples: Hinduism has Brahma (the creative principle), Vishnu (the protecting/preserving principle), and Siva (the destructive/reconstructing principle) as parts of one deity; the ancient Egyptians had Osiris (the father who judged the dead) , Isis (the mother), and Horus (the son) ; the Sumerians had Anu (the keeper of the bread and water of eternal life, and the father of gods), Enlil, and Ea. Similarly, the belief in a god that is both father and son is an ancient pagan concept. Two such examples occur in Hinduism—the god Agni and the god Visvakarman are each both father and son. And, in Sumerian and Babylonian beliefs, there is found the idea of a god being both lover and son of a virgin, much like the biblical God loving (impregnating) Mary who then bares Him as His son. The Sumerian version has Dumuzi as the lover and son of the virgin Inanna; in the Babylonian version it is Tammuz who is the lover and son of Ishtar. Bethlehem was also a holy city for Tammuz.

# CHAPTER TWO

## THE GOSPEL ACCORDING TO ST. MARK

1:1 - THE BEGINNING OF THE GOSPEL OF JESUS CHRIST, THE SON OF GOD.

**Contradictions:** See under MATT. 1:18.

**History:** See under MATT. 3:17 and 8:29.

**Language:** See under MATT. 1:1.

**Pagan parallels:** See under MATT. 1:1.

**Dead Sea Scrolls:** See under MATT. 4:3.

1:2 - IT IS WRITTEN IN THE PROPHETS, "I SEND MY MESSENGER BEFORE THY FACE, WHICH SHALL PREPARE THY WAY BEFORE THEE."

**Old Testament:** See under MATT. 11:10.

**History:** See under MATT. 11:10.

**Perplexing:** See under MATT. 11:10.

1:3 - THE VOICE OF ONE CRYING IN THE WILDERNESS, "PREPARE YE THE WAY OF THE LORD; MAKE HIS PATHS STRAIGHT."

**Old Testament:** See under MATT. 3:3.

**History:** See under MATT. 3:3.

**Perplexing:** See under MATT. 3:3.

1:4-5 - JOHN DID BAPTIZE IN THE WILDERNESS, AND PREACH THE BAPTISM OF REPENTANCE FOR THE REMISSION OF SINS. THERE WENT UNTO HIM ALL JUDAEA, AND THEY OF JERUSALEM, AND WERE ALL BAPTIZED OF HIM IN THE RIVER OF JORDAN, CONFESSING THEIR SINS.

**Pagan concept:** See under MATT. 3:5-6.

**History:** See under MATT. 3:5-6.

**Old Testament:** See under MATT. 3:5-6.

**Perplexing:** See under MATT. 3:5-6.

1:6 - JOHN WAS CLOTHED WITH CAMEL'S HAIR, WITH A GIRDLE OF SKIN ABOUT HIS LOINS, AND HE DID EAT LOCUSTS AND WILD HONEY.

**Old Testament:** See under MATT. 3:4.

**History:** See under MATT. 3:4.

1:7 - JOHN: "THERE COMETH ONE MIGHTIER THAN I AFTER ME, THE LACHET OF WHOSE SHOES I AM NOT WORTHY TO UNLOOSE."

**Contradiction:**
MATT. 3:11 - John: "...he that cometh after me is mightier than I, whose shoes I am not worthy to bear...."
[Did John say that he is not worthy to unloose the lachet of Jesus' shoes, or that he is not worthy to bear them?]

1:8 - JOHN: "I HAVE BAPTIZED YOU WITH WATER, BUT HE SHALL BAPTIZE YOU WITH THE HOLY GHOST."

**Contradictions:**
MATT. 3:11 - John: "I baptize you with water unto repentance, but... he shall baptize you with the Holy Ghost, and fire."
LUKE 3:16 - John answered, "I baptize you with water, but... he shall baptize you with the Holy Ghost and fire."
[Did John say that Jesus will baptize with the Holy Ghost, or with the Holy Ghost and fire?]
See also under MATT. 3:11.

1:9 - JESUS CAME FROM NAZARETH OF GALILEE, AND WAS BAPTIZED OF JOHN IN JORDAN.

**Contradictions:** See under MATT. 3:13.

**Perplexing:**
Why did MARK introduce Jesus as an adult? Why did MARK not report a miraculous virgin birth for Jesus as did MATT. and LUKE?
See also under MATT. 3:13.

**History:** See under MATT. 3:13.

1:10 - COMING UP OUT OF THE WATER, HE SAW THE HEAVENS OPENED, AND THE SPIRIT LIKE A DOVE DESCENDING UPON HIM.

**Perplexing:** See under MATT. 3:16.

**Pagan parallels:** See under MATT. 3:16.

**History:** See under MATT. 3:16.

1:11 - THERE CAME A VOICE FROM HEAVEN, SAYING, "THOU ART MY BELOVED SON, IN WHOM I AM WELL PLEASED."

**Contradiction:** See under MATT. 1:18.

**Perplexing:** See under MATT. 3:17.

**Old Testament:** See under MATT. 3:17.

**History:** See under MATT. 3:17.

**Pagan parallel:** See under MATT. 3:17.

1:12 - IMMEDIATELY THE SPIRIT DRIVETH HIM INTO THE WILDERNESS.

**Contradictions:**
MATT. 4:1 - Then was Jesus led up of the Spirit into the wilderness....
LUKE 4:1 - Jesus being full of the Holy Ghost returned from Jordan, and was led by the Spirit into the wilderness.
[Did the Spirit drive, or lead Jesus into the wilderness?]
[Did the Spirit drive Jesus into the wilderness immediately after his baptism, or did it wait until after he returned from Jordan?]

1:13-14 - HE WAS IN THE WILDERNESS FORTY DAYS, TEMPTED OF SATAN; AND WAS WITH THE WILD BEASTS; THE ANGELS MINISTERED TO HIM. AFTER THAT JOHN WAS PUT IN PRISON, JESUS CAME INTO GALILEE, PREACHING THE GOSPEL OF THE KINGDOM OF GOD.

**Contradictions:**
MATT. 4:2-3 - When he had fasted forty days and nights, he was hungered. ...the tempter came to him....
[Was Jesus tempted by Satan for forty days in the wildernesst or was he tempted after having fasted for forty days in the wilderness?]
LIKE 4:2 - Being forty days tempted of the devil, he did eat nothing....
[Did Jesus not fast, or fast when he was with the devil?]
[Was Jesus ministered to by angels for forty days, or did he fast for forty days?]
MATT. 4:11 - Then the devil leaveth him, and angels ministered unto him.
[Did the angels minister to Jesus while in the wilderness with Satan, or after the devil departed?]
LUKE 3:20-22; 4:1 - ...he [Herod the tetrarch] shut up John in prison. When all the people were baptized, it came to pass, that Jesus also being baptized...the Holy Ghost descended.... Jesus...was led by the Spirit into the wilderness.
[Did Jesus go into the wilderness before, or after John was imprisoned?]
JOHN 1:32-43; 3:24 - JOHN: "I saw the Spirit descending from heaven like a dove, and it abode upon him [Jesus]." .... The day following Jesus would go into Galilee.... John was not yet cast into prison.
[Did Jesus go to Galilee after the Spirit descended upon him and after John was imprisoned, or before John was imprisoned?]

**Old Testament:** See under MATT. 4:1-2.

**Pagan concepts:** See under MATT. 4:1-2.

**Perplexing:** See under MATT. 4:1-2.

**Language:** See under MATT. 4:10.

1:15 - JESUS: "THE TIME IS FULFILLED, AND THE KINGDOM OF GOD IS AT HAND; REPENT YE, AND BELIEVE THE GOSPEL."

**Perplexing:** See under MATT. 4:17.

**Contradiction:** See under MATT. 4:17.

**Old Testament:** See under MATT. 4:17.

**History:** See under MATT. 4:17.

1:16-18 - AS HE WALKED BY THE SEA OF GALILEE, HE SAW SIMON AND ANDREW HIS BROTHER CASTING A NET INTO THE SEA; THEY WERE FISHERS. JESUS SAID, "COME AFTER ME; I WILL MAKE YOU BECOME FISHERS OF MEN." STRAIGHTWAY THEY FORSOOK THEIR NETS, AND FOLLOWED HIM.

**Contradictions:** See under MATT. 4:18-20.

**Perplexing:** See under MATT. 4:18-20.

1:19-20 - WHEN HE HAD GONE A LITTLE FURTHER, HE SAW JAMES THE SON OF ZEBEDEE, AND JOHN HIS BROTHER IN THE SHIP MENDING THEIR NETS. HE CALLED THEM; THEY LEFT...AND WENT AFTER HIM.

**Contradictions:** See under MATT. 4:21-22.

**Perplexing:** See under MATT. 4:18-20 and 4:21-22.

1:21 - THEY WENT INTO CAPERNAUM, AND STRAIGHTWAY ON THE SABBATH DAY HE ENTERED THE SYNAGOGUE AND TAUGHT.

**Contradictions:**
MATT. 4:23 - Jesus went about all Galilee teaching in their synagogues, preaching the gospel of the kingdom, and healing all manner of sickness and disease.
[Did Jesus go directly to a synagogue in Capernaum on the Sabbath and teach, or did he travel around Galilee preaching and healing?]
LUKE 4:13-15 - When the devil...departed from him.... Jesus returned into Galilee.... He taught in their synagogues, being glorified of all [before acquiring his first disciples in LUKE 5:11.]

[Did Jesus teach in a synagogue in Capernaum after obtaining disciples, or did he preach in synagogues around Galilee before obtaining disciples?]
JOHN 1:43 - ...Jesus would go into Galilee, findeth Philip, and saith, "Follow me."
[Did Jesus teach in a synagogue in Capernaum before acquiring Philip as a disciple, or did he go to Galilee and find Philip before preaching in any synagogue?]

**Perplexing:** See under MATT. 4:23.

1:23-24 - THERE WAS IN THEIR SYNAGOGUE A MAN WITH AN UNCLEAN SPIRIT; HE CRIED OUT, "LET US ALONE; WHAT HAVE WE TO DO WITH THEE, JESUS OF NAZARETH? .... ...THOU ART THE HOLY ONE OF GOD."

**Contradictions:**
LUKE 4:33-34 - The incident was reported to have occurred before Jesus acquired his first disciples in LUKE 5:11.
[Did Jesus meet the man with the unclean spirit after, or before he obtained disciples?]
JOHN 2:6-11 - Jesus converted water into wine. This beginning of miracles did Jesus in Cana of Galilee....
[Was Jesus' first miracle driving an unclean spirit out of a man, or converting water into wine?]
[Was Jesus' first miracle in Capernaum or in Cana?]
1 JOHN 4:2 - "Hereby know ye the Spirit of God: Every spirit that confesseth that Jesus Christ is come in the flesh is of God."
[Was the spirit unclean, or was it really clean, because it acknowledged Jesus to be "The Holy One of God."]
See also under MATT. 8:29.

**History:** See under MATT. 4:23.

**Pagan concept:** See under MATT. 4:24-25.

1:25-26 - JESUS REBUKED HIM, "...COME OUT OF HIM." WHEN THE UNCLEAN SPIRIT HAD TORN HIM.... HE CAME OUT OF HIM.

**Contradiction:**
LUKE 4:35 - Jesus rebuked him.... ...he came out of him, and hurt him not.
[Did the unclean spirit leave after having "torn" the man, or did it leave without hurting him?]

**Pagan parallels:** See under MATT. 4:23.

**Perplexing:** See under MATT. 4:24-25.

1:28 - IMMEDIATELY HIS FAME SPREAD THROUGHOUT THE REGION ROUND ABOUT GALILEE.

**History:** See under MATT. 4:24-25.

**Perplexing:** See under MATT. 4:24-25.

1:29-31 - WHEN THEY WERE COME OUT OF THE SYNAGOGUE, THEY ENTERED THE HOUSE OF SIMON AND ANDREW.... SIMON'S WIFE'S MOTHER LAY SICK OF A FEVER.... HE TOOK HER BY THE HAND, LIFTED HER UP, AND THE FEVER LEFT HER....

**Contradictions:**

MATT. 8:14-15 - [After Jesus gave his Sermon on the Mount in MATT. 5-7 and healed a centurion's servant in MATT. 8:5-13] When Jesus was come into Peter's house, he saw his wife's mother sick of a fever. He touched her hand, and the fever left her....

[Did Jesus enter Peter's house after leaving a synagogue, or after delivering his Sermon and healing a centurion's servant?]

[Did Jesus heal Peter's mother-in-law by taking her hand and lifting her up, or just by touching her hand?]

LUKE 4:38-39 - [Before Jesus acquired his first disciples in LUKE 5:5-11] He arose out of the synagogue and entered Simon's house. Simon's wife's mother was taken with a great fever.... He...rebuked the fever, and it left her....

[Did Jesus enter Simon's house and heal his mother-in-law after, or before Simon, Andrew, James, and John became his disciples?]

[Did Jesus heal Simon's mother-in-law by taking her hand and lifting her up, or by rebuking the fever?]

See also under MATT. 8:14-15.

**Perplexing:** See under MATT. 8:14-15.

1:34 - HE HEALED MANY THAT WERE SICK OF DIVERS DISEASES, AND CAST OUT MANY DEVILS; AND SUFFERED THE DEVILS NOT TO SPEAK....

**Contradictions:**

MATT. 8:16 - ...he cast out the spirits with his word, and healed all that were sick.

LUKE 4:40-41 - ...he laid his hands on every one of them [the sick]. and healed them. Devils came out of many, saying, "Thou art Christ, the Son of God." He rebuking them suffered them not to speak....

[Did Jesus heal many, or did he heal all who were sick?]

[Did Jesus rebuke the devils before they had a chance to say anything, or did they have a chance to say that he is Christ before being silenced?]

**Perplexing:** See under MATT. 4:24-25.

**Pagan concept:** See under MATT. 4:24-25.

1:35 - IN THE MORNING...BEFORE DAY, HE DEPARTED INTO A SOLITARY PLACE, AND THERE PRAYED.

**Contradictions:**

MATT. 8:18-23 - [After healing all that were sick in the evening (8:16)]...he gave commandment to depart unto the other side. .... When he was entered into a ship his disciples followed him.

[Did Jesus depart in the morning, or in the evening?]

[Did Jesus go into a solitary place to pray, or did he and his disciples board a ship?]

LUKE 4:42 - [After healing everyone who was sick] When it was day, he went into a desert place...people came unto him....

[Did Jesus go to a solitary place to pray, or did he go to a desert place to where people followed him?]

**Perplexing:** See under MATT. 14:22-23.

1:36-39 - SIMON AND THEY THAT WERE WITH HIM FOLLOWED. .... HE SAID, "LET US GO INTO THE NEXT TOWNS, THAT I MAY PREACH THERE, FOR THEREFORE CAME I FORTH." HE PREACHED IN THEIR SYNAGOGUES THROUGHOUT ALL GALILEE, AND CAST OUT DEVILS.

**Contradictions:**
MATT. 8:28 - He was come into the country of the Gergesenes....
[Did Jesus preach in synagogues throughout Galilee, or did he go to the country of the Gergesenes?]
LUKE 4:43-44 - [Before acquiring any disciples] He said unto them [the people who followed him], "I must preach the kingdom of God in other cities, for therefore am I sent." He preached in the synagogues of Galilee.
[Did Jesus tell his disciples that he wanted to preach in the next towns, or did he tell the people who followed him that he must preach elsewhere?]
[Did Jesus go to preach after, or before acquiring disciples?]

**Perplexing:**
How was Jesus able to obtain approval to preach from the presiding priests of the synagogues throughout Galilee? How did he and the disciples travel? Where did they stay at night? From where did they obtain funds for their food, lodging, etc.?
See also under MATT. 4:23.

1:40-42 - THERE CAME A LEPER TO HIM...SAYING, "IF THOU WILT, THOU CANST MAKE ME CLEAN." JESUS...TOUCHED HIM AND SAITH, "BE THOU CLEAN." ...THE LEPROSY DEPARTED FROM HIM, AND HE WAS CLEANSED.

**Contradictions:**
MATT. 8:2-3 - [After Jesus completed his sermon on the Mount and came down the mountain, and before healing Simon's mother-in-law] There came a leper...saying, "If thou wilt, thou canst make me clean." Jesus...touched him, saying, "Be thou clean." His leprosy was cleansed.
[Did Jesus heal the leper after, or before healing Simon's mother-in-law?]
LUKE 5:12-13 - [Just after acquiring Peter, James, and John as disciples in 5:10-11]...a man full of leprosy...saying, "Lord, if thou wilt, thou canst make me clean." He touched him, saying, "Be thou clean." The leprosy departed from him.
[Did Jesus heal the leper after having preached and traveled around Galilee with four disciples, or after he recently obtained three disciples?]

**Language:** See under MATT. 8:1-3.

**History:** See under MATT. 8:1-3.

**Perplexing:** See under MATT. 8:1-3.

1:44-45 - [JESUS] SAITH, "SEE THOU SAY NOTHING TO ANY MAN; GO THY WAY...." BUT HE BEGAN TO PUBLISH IT MUCH, AND TO BLAZE ABROAD THE MATTER....

**Perplexing:**
According to MATT. 9:4; 12:25; LUKE 5:22; 6:8; 9:47; and 11:17, Jesus knew people's thoughts. And according to JOHN 18:4, he knew all things that were to come upon him. Why then did Jesus fail to know that the man would not obey him, but go around telling people about his miraculous cure? How could Jesus expect the man not to speak about what happened? Anyone who had seen or known the man would have observed that he was now cured and probably would have questioned him about his sudden recovery.

**Old Testament:** See under MATT. 8:1-3.

2:1-4 - HE ENTERED CAPERNAUM...HE WAS IN THE HOUSE. MANY WERE GATHERED TOGETHER INSOMUCH THAT THERE WAS NO ROOM TO RECEIVE THEM.... THEY COME, BRINGING ONE SICK WITH PALSY, BORNE BY FOUR. WHEN THEY COULD NOT COME NIGH HIM, THEY UNCOVERED THE ROOF...WHEN THEY HAD BROKEN IT, THEY LET DOWN THE BED WHEREIN THE SICK OF THE PALSY LAY.

**Perplexing:**
How large was the house? To whom did the house belong? If the house was so full that people could not even enter through the doorway, how could there be room for five additional people, one on a bed, coming into the house through the roof? How were the four able to raise the bed to the roof, break the roof, and then lower the bed into the house? Was not the owner of the house upset about the roof being broken? Who paid for and repaired the roof?

2:5 - WHEN JESUS SAW THEIR FAITH, HE SAID UNTO THE SICK OF PALSY, "SON, THY SINS BE FORGIVEN THEE."

**Perplexing:** See under MATT. 9:1-2.

2:6-7 - THERE WERE SCRIBES THERE, REASONING IN THEIR HEARTS, "WHY DOTH THIS MAN SPEAK BLASPHEMIES? WHO CAN FORGIVE SINS BUT GOD?"

**Contradiction:**
LUKE 5:21 - [After Jesus forgave the man's sins] Scribes and Pharisees began to reason, saying, "Who is this which speaketh blasphemies? Who can forgive sins, but God alone?"
[Did scribes reason in their hearts, or did scribes and Pharisees speak?]

**Perplexing:**
Why did the scribes believe that Jesus had spoken blasphemies? According to Jewish law blasphemy is denigrating God, which Jesus did not do.
See also under MATT. 26:65.

2:8 - WHEN JESUS PERCEIVED THAT THEY SO REASONED WITHIN THEMSELVES, HE SAID, "WHY REASON THESE THINGS IN YOUR HEART?"

**Contradictions:** See under MATT. 9:4.

2:11-12 - "I SAY UNTO THEE, ARISE, TAKE THY BED, AND GO THY WAY INTO THINE HOUSE." HE AROSE, TOOK UP THE BED, AND WENT FORTH....

**Perplexing:**
If the house was so packed with people, how was the healed man able to get up, carry the bed, and leave? Did he depart through the broken roof? Did the four who brought him leave with him?

2:14 - ...HE SAW LEVI THE SON OF ALPHAEUS SITTING AT THE RECEIPT OF CUSTOM, AND SAID, "FOLLOW ME." HE AROSE AND FOLLOWED HIM.

**Contradictions:**
MATT. 9:9 - Jesus...saw Matthew, sitting at the receipt of custom, and said, "Follow me." He arose and followed him.
[After healing the palsy victim, did Jesus see and ask Levi, or Matthew to follow him? (Some Christians contend that Levi is another name for Matthew, but there is no biblical substantiation for this claim.)]
MATT. 10:3; MARK 3:18; LUKE 6:15; and ACTS 1:13 - James was the son of Alphaeus.
[Was Levi, or James the son of Alphaeus? (Matthew is never identified as a son of Alphaeus.)]
MATT. 10:2-5; MARK 3:16-19; LUKE 6:13-16; and the verses in JOHN where disciples are named, Levi is not cited as one of Jesus' disciples.
[Was, or was not Levi a disciple of Jesus?]
See also under MATT. 9:9.

**Perplexing:** See under MATT. 9:9.

2:15 - AS JESUS SAT AT MEAT IN HIS HOUSE, MANY PUBLICANS AND SINNERS SAT WITH JESUS AND HIS DISCIPLES....

**Contradiction:**
LUKE 5:29 - Levi made him a great feast in his own house; there was a great company of publicans and others that sat down with them.
[Was the meal in Jesus' house, or Levi's house?]

**Perplexing:**
Where was Jesus' house? Was it in Capernaum (see 2:1)? Did Jesus live alone in his house? Did any of the disciples reside with him? Did Mary and Joseph also live there? How did he obtain the house? How many people were present? How did Jesus obtain the money to pay for the house and the food? What did they eat? Who prepared the meals?

2:16 - WHEN SCRIBES AND PHARISEES SAW HIM EAT WITH PUBLICANS AND SINNERS, THEY SAID UNTO HIS DISCIPLES, "HOW IS IT THAT HE EATETH AND DRINKETH WITH PUBLICANS AND SINNERS."

**Contradiction:**
MATT. 9:11 - When the Pharisees saw it, "They said, "Why eateth your Master with publicans and sinners?"
[Did the scribes and Pharisees speak to Jesus' disciples, or did just the Pharisees speak to them?]

See also under MATT. 9:11.

**Perplexing:** See under MATT. 9:11.

2:17 - WHEN JESUS HEARD IT, HE SAITH, "...I CAME NOT TO CALL THE RIGHTEOUS, BUT SINNERS TO REPENTANCE."

**Contradictions:** See under MATT. 9:13.

2:18 - THE DISCIPLES OF JOHN AND OF THE PHARISEES USED TO FAST....

**Pagan concept:** See under MATT. 6:17.

**Judaism:** See under MATT. 6:17.

2:23-26 - HE WENT THROUGH CORN [GRAIN] FIELDS ON THE SABBATH DAY; HIS DISCIPLES BEGAN TO PLUCK THE EARS OF CORN. THE PHARISEES SAID UNTO HIM, "WHY DO THEY ON THE SABBATH DAY THAT WHICH IS NOT LAWFUL?" HE SAID, "HAVE YE NEVER READ WHAT DAVID DID, WHEN HE HAD NEED, AND HUNGERED, AND THEY THAT WERE WITH HIM? HOW HE WENT INTO THE HOUSE OF GOD IN THE DAYS OF ABIATHAR THE HIGH PRIEST, AND DID EAT THE SHEWBREAD, WHICH IS NOT LAWFUL TO EAT BUT FOR THE PRIESTS, AND GAVE ALSO TO THEM WHICH WERE WITH HIM?"

**Contradiction:**
MATT. 12:1-4 - Jesus went through the corn with his disciples after they returned to him after he had given them power over unclean spirits and to heal all manner of sickness in 10:1.
[Did Jesus and the disciples go through the cornfields after having eaten and spoken with scribes and Pharisees (2:16-22), or after the disciples received power from Jesus? (It is not until MARK 3:14-15 that Jesus gives the disciples power to heal sickness and to cast out devils.)]
See also under MATT. 12:1 and 12:3-4.

**Old Testament:** See under MATT. 12:2.

**Perplexing:**
How were the disciples able to eat raw grain? According to 1 SAM. 21:1-6, the priest to whom David came was Ahimelech. Why did Jesus identify the priest incorrectly as Abiathar?
See also under MATT. 12:1, 12:2, and 12:3-4.

**Judaism:** See under MATT. 12:3-4.

**History:** See under MATT. 12:1.

3:1-2 - HE ENTERED AGAIN THE SYNAGOGUE, AND THERE WAS A MAN WITH A WITHERED HAND. THEY [PHARISEES] WATCHED HIM, WHETHER HE WOULD HEAL HIM ON THE SABBATH DAY, THAT THEY MIGHT ACCUSE HIM.

**Contradiction:**
MATT. 12:10 - There was a man who had his hand withered. They asked him [Jesus], "Is it lawful to heal on the sabbath days?" that they might accuse him.
[Did the Pharisees watch Jesus to see if he would heal the man, or did they ask him if healing was lawful on Sabbaths?]

**History:** See under MATT. 12:9-10.

**Perplexing:** See under MATT. 12:9-10.

3:4 - HE SAITH TO THEM, "IS IT LAWFUL TO DO GOOD ON THE SABBATH DAYS, OR TO DO EVIL? TO SAVE LIFE, OR TO KILL?" THEY HELD THEIR PEACE.

**History:** See under MATT. 12:9-10.

**Perplexing:**
Why did the Pharisees fail to inform Jesus that their teaching allowed healing to take place on Sabbath days?
See also under MATT. 12:9-10.

3:5 - ...HE SAITH UNTO THE MAN, "STRETCH FORTH THINE HAND." HE STRETCHED IT OUT, AND HIS HAND WAS RESTORED WHOLE AS THE OTHER.

**Old Testament:** See under MATT. 12:13.

**Perplexing:** See under MATT. 12:13.

3:6 - THE PHARISEES TOOK COUNSEL WITH THE HERODIANS, HOW THEY MIGHT DESTROY HIM.

**Contradictions:**
MATT. 12:14 - The Pharisees held a council, how they might destroy him.
[Did the Pharisees counsel with the Herodians, or did they hold their own council?]
LUKE 6:11 - They [scribes and Pharisees] were filled with madness, and communed one with another what they might do to Jesus.
[Did the Pharisees counsel with the Herodians, or did the Pharisees and scribes commune with each other?]
See also under MATT. 12:14.

**Perplexing:**
What had Jesus done to antagonize the Herodians to want to kill him?
See also under MATT. 12:14.

**History:** See under MATT. 22:16.

3:7-8 - JESUS WITHDREW HIMSELF WITH HIS DISCIPLES TO THE SEA; A GREAT MULTITUDE FROM GALILEE FOLLOWED HIM, FROM JUDAEA, JERUSALEM, IDUMAEA, FROM BEYOND JORDAN, AND THEY ABOUT TYRE AND SIDON...WHEN THEY HEARD WHAT GREAT THINGS HE DID.

**Contradiction:**
LUKE 6:12 - In those days, he went out into a mountain to pray, and continued all night in prayer to God.
[Did Jesus go to the sea with his disciples, or did he go onto a mountain to pray?]

**Perplexing:**
How did the multitudes know where to find Jesus? How did they travel? How long did it take all of them to reach him?
See also under MATT. 12:15-16.

3:9 - HE SPAKE TO HIS DISCIPLES, THAT A SMALL SHIP SHOULD WAIT ON HIM BECAUSE OF THE MULTITUDE, LEST THEY SHOULD THRONG HIM.

**Perplexing:**
Why did Jesus need a ship? Why did he not stand or walk on the water?
MATT. 14:25 and MARK 6:48 said that Jesus could walk on water. Why did Jesus not perform a miracle to prevent the people from thronging him?

3:11 - UNCLEAN SPIRITS, WHEN THEY SAW HIM, FELL DOWN BEFORE HIM, SAYING, "THOU ART THE SON OF GOD."

**Contradiction:**
1 JOHN 4:2 - John: "Hereby know ye the spirit of God; every spirit that confesseth that Jesus Christ is come in the flesh is of God."
[Were these spirits unclean, or were they of God because they acknowledged Jesus as the Son of God?]
See also under MATT. 8:29.

**Perplexing:**
What was the appearance of these spirits? Did anyone besides Jesus see them?
See also under 1:23-24; MATT. 8:29 and 12:43-45.

**History:** See under MATT. 8:29.

3:14-19 - HE ORDAINED TWELVE...THAT HE MIGHT SEND THEM FORTH TO PREACH, TO HAVE POWER TO HEAL SICKNESSES, AND CAST OUT DEVILS; SIMON HE SURNAMED PETER, JAMES THE SON OF ZEBEDEE, JOHN THE BROTHER OF JAMES; HE SURNAMED THEM BOANERGES, WHICH IS, "THE SONS OF THUNDER"; ANDREW, PHILIP, BARTHOLOMEW, MATTHEW, THOMAS, JAMES THE SON OF ALPHAEUS, THADDAEUS, SIMON THE CANAANITE, AND JUDAS ISCARIOT...AND THEY WENT INTO AN HOUSE. [THIS OCCURRED AFTER THE INCIDENT IN THE CORNFIELD (2:23-28) AND THE HEALING OF A MAN'S WITHERED HAND (3:1-6).]

**Contradictions:**
MATT. 4:18 - Jesus...saw...Simon called Peter....
LUKE 5:8 and JOHN 1:40 - Simon was identified as Simon Peter before becoming a disciple.
[Did Jesus give the surname Peter to Simon, or was he known as Simon Peter before becoming one of Jesus' disciples?]
MATT. 10:1-4 - Jesus selected his twelve disciples before walking through the cornfields in 12:1, and

before healing a man's withered hand in 12:13.
[Did Jesus select the twelve disciples after, or before walking through the cornfields, and healing a man's withered hand?]
MATT. 10:5-6 - [After having selected his twelve disciples] These twelve Jesus sent forth, and commanded, "Go not into the way of the Gentiles, and into any city of the Samaritans enter ye not, but go to the lost sheep of the house of Israel."
[After having selected his disciples, did Jesus enter a house with them, or did he send them forth to the lost sheep of the house of Israel?]
LUKE 6:17 - [After Jesus selected his disciples (6:13-16)] He came down with them and stood in the plain....
[After having selected his disciples, did Jesus go with them into a house, or onto a plain?]
MATT. 10: 1-8 - He...gave them power over unclean spirits, to cast them out, to heal all manner of sickness and disease.... "As ye go, preach, 'The kingdom of heaven is at hand.' Heal the sick; cleanse the lepers; raise the dead, cast out devils; freely ye have received; freely give."
[Did, or did not, Jesus give the disciples power to raise the dead?]
[Did, or did not, Jesus tell the disciples to preach that the kingdom of heaven is at hand?]
See also under MATT. 10:2-4 and 10:7-8.

**Perplexing:** See under MATT. 10:1 and 10:2-4.

**Language:**
Boanerges may be derived from the Aramaic, "benai regesh," meaning "sons of anger," or from the Sumerian, "pu-angur-ges," meaning "upholder of a heavenly canopy."
Some Bibles translate "Canaanite" as "Cananaean" or as "Zelote," meaning "one who is zealous."
See also under MATT. 10:2-4.

**History:** See under MATT. 10:1 and 10:2-4.

**Pagan parallels:** See under MATT. 10:1.

**Old Testament:** See under MATT. 10:1.

3:20-21 - THE MULTITUDE COMETH TOGETHER AGAIN.... WHEN HIS FRIENDS HEARD OF IT, THEY WENT TO LAY HOLD ON HIM; THEY SAID, "HE IS BESIDE HIMSELF."

**Perplexing:**
Who were these friends of Jesus? The verse implied that they were not disciples. Some Bibles use, "relatives," instead of "friends." Why at this time did his friends, or relatives, believe that he was "beside himself?" Were they unaware of his ability to perform miracles? Aside from his disciples, with whom did he associate? Why were these friends, or relatives, not identified and mentioned more frequently? Why did Jesus and/or Mary fail to inform these friends, or relatives, about his divine nature?

3:22 - THE SCRIBES FROM JERUSALEM: "HE HATH BEELZEBUB, AND BY THE PRINCE OF THE DEVILS CASTETH OUT DEVILS." [THIS IS REPORTED TO HAVE OCCURRED PRIOR TO JESUS SENDING FORTH HIS DISCIPLES IN 6:7.]

**Contradictions:**
MATT. 12:24 - The Pharisees: "This fellow doth not cast out devils, but by Beelzebub the prince of devils." [This is reported to have occurred long after Jesus sent forth his disciples in 10:5, and immediately after he healed a blind and dumb man in 12:22.]
[Did scribes, or Pharisees say that Jesus cast out devils by Beelzebub?"]
[Did the incident occur just after Jesus' friends said that he is beside himself, or after he healed a blind and dumb man?]
LUKE 11:15 - Some of them [people] said, "He casteth out devils through Beelzebub the chief of the devils." [This occurred long after Jesus sent forth his disciples in 9:2, and immediately after he healed a dumb person in 11:14.]
[Did scribes, or unidentified people accuse Jesus of casting out devils by Beelzebub?]
[Did the incident take place before, or after Jesus sent forth his disciples?]

**Pagan concept:** See under MATT. 10:25.

**Language:** See under MATT. 10:25.

**Old Testament:** See under MATT. 10:25.

3:28-29 - JESUS: "ALL SINS SHALL BE FORGIVEN... AND BLASPHEMIES, WHEREWITH SOEVER THEY SHALL BLASPHEME; BUT HE THAT SHALL BLASPHEME AGAINST THE HOLY GHOST HATH NEVER FORGIVENESS, BUT IS IN DANGER OF ETERNAL DAMNATION."

**Perplexing:** See under MATT. 12:31-32.

3:31-35 - CAME HIS BRETHREN AND HIS MOTHER...CALLING HIM. THE MULTITUDE...SAID, "THY MOTHER AND BRETHREN SEEK FOR THEE." HE ANSWERED, "WHO IS MY MOTHER, OR BRETHREN! WHOSOEVER SHALL DO THE WILL OF GOD, IS MY BROTHER, SISTER, AND MOTHER." [THIS PRECEDED THE INCIDENT IN WHICH JESUS CAST DEVILS INTO A HERD OF SWINE (5:13).]

**Contradictions:**
MATT. 12:46-50 - The incident is reported to have occurred after Jesus cast devils into a herd of swine (8:32).
[Did Jesus refuse to heed his mother and brethren before, or after casting devils into a herd of swine?]
LUKE 8:19-21 - The incident is reported to have occurred before Jesus was accused of casting out devils by Beelzebub (11:15).
[Did Jesus refuse to heed his mother and brethren after, or before being accused of casting out devils by Beelzebub?]

4:1 - HE BEGAN AGAIN TO TEACH BY THE SEASIDE; THERE WAS GATHERED A GREAT MULTITUDE, SO HE ENTERED A SHIP...AND THE MULTITUDE WAS ON LAND.

**Contradiction:**
LUKE 8:22 - ...he went into a ship with his disciples, and said, "Let us go over unto the other side of the lake."
[Did Jesus enter a ship and teach a multitude on the land, or did he enter a ship with his disciples and sail to the other side of the lake? ]

**Perplexing:**
Why did Jesus go onto a ship, rather than walk on the water as he did in MATT. 14:25, JOHN 6:19-20, and later in MARK 6:48-50?

4:2-8 - JESUS TAUGHT BY PARABLES, "THERE WENT OUT A SOWER TO SOW.... .... [THE INCIDENT IS REPORTED PRIOR TO JESUS SENDING DEVILS INTO A HERD OF SWINE IN 5:13.]

**Contradiction:**
MATT. 13:3-8 - He spake unto them in parables, "A sower went forth to sow.... .... [The incident is reported after Jesus had cast devils into a herd of swine in 8:32.]
[Did Jesus teach by parables from a ship before, or after sending devils into a herd of swine?]

**History:** See under MATT. 13:1-9.

**Pagan parallel:** See under MATT. 13:1-9.

4:11-12 - HE SAID UNTO THEM [HIS DISCIPLES], "UNTO YOU IT IS GIVEN TO KNOW THE MYSTERY OF THE KINGDOM OF GOD; BUT UNTO THEM THAT ARE WITHOUT, ALL THESE THINGS ARE DONE IN PARABLES, THAT SEEING THEY MAY SEE, AND NOT PERCEIVE, HEARING THEY MAY HEAR, AND NOT UNDERSTAND, LEST AT ANY TIME THEY SHOULD BE CONVERTED, AND THEIR SINS SHOULD BE FORGIVEN THEM."

**Contradictions:**
MATT. 9:13 - Jesus: "...I am not come to call the righteous, but sinners to repentance."
MARK 2:17 and LUKE 5:31-32 - Jesus saith unto them, "...I came not to call the righteous, but sinners to repentance."
[Did Jesus want to prevent sinners from being converted and having their sins forgiven, or did he come to call sinners to repentance?]
JOHN 3:17 - God sent not his Son into the world to condemn the world, but that the world through him might be saved.
[Was Jesus sent into the world to prevent people from being converted and having their sins forgiven, or to save the world?]
ACTS 26:18 - Jesus [to Paul]: "Open their eyes...that they may receive forgiveness of sins...."
[Did Jesus want to prevent people from having their sins forgiven, or did he want them to receive forgiveness for their sins?]
See also under MATT. 9:13 and 13:10-13.

**Perplexing:**
Why did Jesus say that he did not want people to be converted and have their sins forgiven? Was not Jesus supposed to save as many people as possible? MARK 4:1-2 stated that Jesus taught a great multitude by parables. How could the multitude have learned anything, if the parables were unintelligible to them, and prevented them from understanding his teachings?
See also under MATT. 13:10-13.

**Pagan parallel:** See under MATT. 13:10-13.

4:15 - JESUS: "THESE ARE THEY BY THE WAYSIDE, WHERE THE WORD IS SOWN; BUT WHEN THEY HAVE HEARD, SATAN COMETH IMMEDIATELY, AND TAKETH AWAY THE WORD THAT WAS SOWN IN THEIR HEARTS."

**Perplexing:**
Why cannot Jesus and/or God prevent Satan from taking "the word" out of people's hearts? Why does Satan select only certain people from whom to take "the word?"

4:19 - JESUS: "...THE DECEITFULNESS OF RICHES, AND THE LUSTS OF OTHER THINGS ENTERING IN, CHOKE THE WORD, AND IT BECOMETH UNFRUITFUL."

**Perplexing:** See under MATT. 13:22.

4:31 - JESUS: "IT [THE KINGDOM OF GOD] IS LIKE A MUSTARD SEED, WHICH WHEN SOWN IN THE EARTH, IS LESS THAN ALL THE SEEDS THAT BE IN THE EARTH."

**Perplexing:** See under MATT. 13:31.

4:36-39 - WHEN THEY HAD SENT AWAY THE MULTITUDE, THEY TOOK HIM IN THE SHIP. .... THERE AROSE A GREAT STORM OF WIND; WAVES BEAT INTO THE SHIP, SO THAT IT WAS FULL. HE WAS ASLEEP ON A PILLOW; THEY AWAKE HIM.... HE AROSE, REBUKED THE WIND, AND SAID UNTO THE SEA, "PEACE, BE STILL." THE WIND CEASED, AND THERE WAS A GREAT CALM.

**Contradictions:**
MATT. 8:18-26 - The incident is reported to have occurred shortly after Jesus healed Peter's mother-in-law and other people (8:15-16), but before Jesus' twelve disciples were identified (10:1-4).
[Did Jesus calm the wind and sea long after healing Peter's mother-in-law (MARK 1:31), or shortly thereafter?]
[Did the incident take place after Jesus' twelve disciples were identified (3:14-19), or before they were identified?]
See also under MATT. 8:24-25.

**Perplexing:**
How was Jesus able to remain asleep on what must have been a soaking wet pillow, with waves bringing water into the ship?
See also under MATT. 8:24-25.

**Old Testament:** See under MATT. 8:24-25 and 8:26.

4:41 - THEY FEARED, AND SAID, ONE TO ANOTHER, "WHAT MANNER OF MAN IS THIS, THAT EVEN THE WIND AND THE SEA OBEY HIM?"

**Perplexing:** See under MATT. 8:27.

5:1 - THEY CAME UNTO THE OTHER SIDE OF THE SEA, INTO THE COUNTRY OF THE GADARENES.

**Contradiction:**
MATT. 8:28 - He was come to the other side into the country of the Gergesenes....
[Did Jesus arrive in the country of the Gadarenes, or the Gergesenes?]

**History:**
Gadara was a city located approximately five miles southeast of the Sea of Galilee. Some historians equate the Gergesenes with the city of Gerasa situated about 35 miles southeast of the Sea of Galilee.

5:2 - WHEN HE WAS COME OUT OF THE SHIP, IMMEDIATELY THERE MET HIM OUT OF THE TOMBS A MAN WITH AN UNCLEAN SPIRIT.

**Contradiction:**
MATT. 8:28 - ...there met him two possessed with devils, coming out of the tombs....
[Was Jesus met by a man with an unclean spirit, or by two persons possessed by devils?]

**Perplexing:** See under MATT. 4:24-25 and 12:43-45.

**Pagan concept:** See under MATT. 4:24-25.

5:6-7 - WHEN HE SAW JESUS AFAR OFF, HE RAN AND WORSHIPPED HIM, AND SAID, "WHAT HAVE I TO DO WITH THEE, JESUS, THOU SON OF THE MOST HIGH GOD? I ADJURE THEE BY GOD, THAT THOU TORMENT ME NOT."

**Contradictions:**
MATT. 8:29 - They cried out, "What have we to do with thee, Jesus, thou Son of God? Art thou come to torment us before the time?"
[Did the spirit ask Jesus not to torment it, or did two of them ask Jesus if he had come to torment them?]
[Did the spirit refer to Jesus as "Son of the most high God," or as "Son of God"?]
See also under MATT. 8:29.

**Perplexing:**
Why would or how could an unclean spirit worship Jesus? By saying, "most high God," was the spirit saying that there are other gods which are not as "high" as Jesus' God? If the spirit was unclean, why did it adjure by God that Jesus not torment it?

**History:** See under MATT. 8:29.

5:8-9 - HE SAID, "COME OUT OF THE MAN, THOU UNCLEAN SPIRIT. WHAT IS THY NAME?" HE ANSWERED, "LEGION, FOR WE ARE MANY."

**Perplexing:**
Why did the spirit not come out of the man when Jesus commanded it?
Why did Jesus then have to ask for the spirit's name? Why did Jesus not know the spirit's name?

**Pagan concept:**
Ancient people tended to believe that illnesses could be attributed to evil spirits or demons, but if their names were known they could be banished from an afflicted person.

5:10 - HE BESOUGHT HIM THAT HE WOULD NOT SEND THEM AWAY OUT OF THE COUNTRY.

**Contradiction:**
LUKE 8:31 - They besought him that he would not command them to go out into the deep.
[Did the spirits ask Jesus not to send them out of the country, or not to send them into the deep?]

**Perplexing:**
Why did the spirits not want to leave the country?
See also under MATT. 4:24-25.

5:11-13 - THERE WAS NIGH UNTO THE MOUNTAINS A GREAT HERD OF SWINE FEEDING. ALL THE DEVILS BESOUGHT HIM, "SEND US INTO THE SWINE." JESUS GAVE THEM LEAVE, AND THE UNCLEAN SPIRITS ENTERED THE SWINE, AND THE HERD RAN DOWN A STEEP PLACE INTO THE SEA (THEY WERE ABOUT 2000), AND WERE CHOKED IN THE SEA.

**Perplexing:** See under MATT. 8:30-32.

5:14-17 - THEY THAT FED THE SWINE FLED, TOLD IT IN THE CITY, AND THE COUNTRY. THEY WENT TO SEE WHAT WAS DONE. THEY COME TO JESUS, AND SEE HIM THAT WAS POSSESSED WITH THE DEVIL...IN HIS RIGHT MIND.... THEY THAT SAW IT TOLD HOW IT BEFELL TO HIM THAT WAS POSSESSED BY THE DEVIL AND CONCERNING THE SWINE. THEY BEGAN TO PRAY HIM TO DEPART OUT OF THEIR COASTS.

**Perplexing:** See under MATT. 8:33-34.

5:20 - .... HE [THE MAN OUT OF WHOM JESUS CAST THE DEVILS] BEGAN TO PUBLISH IN DECAPOLIS HOW GREAT THINGS JESUS HAD DONE FOR HIM, AND ALL MEN DID MARVEL.

**Contradiction:**
LUKE 8:39 - .... He went and published throughout the whole city how great things Jesus had done unto him.
[Did the man publicize what Jesus had done for him in Decapolis (a league of ten cities), or in one city?]

**History:** See under MATT. 4:24-25.

5:21-22 - WHEN JESUS PASSED OVER BY SHIP UNTO THE OTHER SIDE, MUCH PEOPLE GATHERED UNTO HIM; HE WAS NIGH UNTO THE SEA. THERE COMETH ONE OF THE RULERS OF THE SYNAGOGUE, JARIUS BY NAME....

**Contradiction:**
MATT. 9:1-18 - He entered into a ship...and came into his own city. They brought to him a man sick of palsy, lying on a bed; Jesus...said, "...thy sins be forgiven thee." .... ..."Arise ...." He arose, and departed to his house. .... Jesus saw a man, named Matthew, sitting at the receipt of custom, and saith, "Follow me." He followed him. Jesus sat at meat, publicans and sinners sat with him and his disciples. Pharisees saw it .... .... While he spake, there came a certain ruler....

[Did the ruler come to Jesus immediately after Jesus arrived, or after Jesus had cured a man's palsy, acquired Matthew as a disciple, and ate with publicans and sinners?]

**Language:**
"Jairus," in Aramaic, means "he will awaken."

5:23 - HE BESOUGHT HIM GREATLY, SAYING, "MY LITTLE DAUGHTER LIETH AT THE POINT OF DEATH; I PRAY THEE, COME AND LAY THY HANDS ON HER, THAT SHE MAY BE HEALED, AND SHALL LIVE."

**Contradiction:**
MATT. 9:18 - ...there came a certain ruler...saying, "My daughter is even now dead, but come, lay thy hand upon her, and she shall live."
[Did the ruler ask Jesus to heal his seriously ill daughter, or to bring her back to life?]

**Pagan concept:**
The origins of the practice of attempting to heal the sick by means of laying on of hands are lost in antiquity.

**Pagan parallel:**
The Babylonians believed that a priest could exorcise evil spirits from a sick person by touching the person.

5:25-34 - A WOMAN WHICH HAD AN ISSUE OF BLOOD TWELVE YEARS...TOUCHED HIS GARMENT. SHE SAID, "IF I MAY TOUCH BUT HIS CLOTHES, I SHALL BE WHOLE." STRAIGHTWAY...SHE WAS HEALED. JESUS...TURNED AND SAID, "WHO TOUCHED MY CLOTHES?" .... THE WOMAN...TOLD HIM. HE SAID, "THY FAITH HATH MADE THEE WHOLE; GO IN PEACE...."

**Contradictions:**
MATT. 9:20-22 - A woman, diseased with an issue of blood twelve years...touched the hem of his garment; she said, "If I may but touch his garment, I shall be whole." Jesus turned, and when he saw her, said, "Daughter, be of good comfort; thy faith hath made thee whole." The woman was made whole from that hour.
[Was the woman healed by touching Jesus' clothes before he saw her, or by her faith after he saw her?]
[Did, or did not Jesus have to ask who touched his clothes?]
MATT. 9:4; 12:25; MARK 2:8; LUKE 5:22; 6:8; 9:47; and 11:17 - Jesus knew people's thoughts.
[Did not, or did Jesus know the woman's thoughts and that she had touched him?]

**Perplexing:**
Why did Jesus inquire about who touched his clothes? He knew all the things that would happen to him, according to JOHN 18:4.

**History:** See under MATT. 9:20-22.

5:35 - ...THERE CAME FROM THE RULER OF THE SYNAGOGUE'S HOUSE CERTAIN WHICH SAID, "THY DAUGHTER IS DEAD, WHY TROUBLEST THOU THE MASTER ANY FURTHER?"

**Contradiction:**
MATT. 9:18 - There came a certain ruler, saying, "My daughter is even now dead, but come lay thy hand upon her, and she shall live."
[Did someone from the ruler's house say that his daughter was dead, or did the ruler tell Jesus that she was dead?]

5:37 - HE SUFFERED NO MAN TO FOLLOW HIM, SAVE PETER, JAMES, AND JOHN THE BROTHER OF JAMES.

**Contradiction:**
MATT. 9:19 - Jesus arose, and followed him, and so did his disciples.
[Did only three disciples go with Jesus, or did they all go?]

**Perplexing:**
Why did Jesus select only Peter, James, and John to accompany him?

5:39-42 - WHEN HE WAS COME IN, HE SAITH, ".... THE DAMSEL IS NOT DEAD, BUT SLEEPETH." THEY LAUGHED...HE TAKETH THE FATHER AND MOTHER OF THE DAMSEL, AND THEM THAT WERE WITH HIM, AND ENTERETH IN WHERE THE DAMSEL WAS LYING. HE TOOK THE DAMSEL BY THE HAND, AND SAID, "TALITHA CUMI," WHICH IS, "DAMSEL, I SAY UNTO THEE, ARISE." SHE AROSE AND WALKED.... ....

**Contradictions:**
MATT. 9:18 - 12:1-4 - The incidents with the ruler, the woman with an issue of blood, and the resurrection of the girl took place prior to Jesus, his disciples, and the Pharisees going through a cornfield (12:1-8).
[Did Jesus encounter the ruler, the woman, and the girl, long after passing through a cornfield (MARK 2:23-28), or long before doing so?]
MATT. 9:23-25 - The incident occurred before Jesus' twelve disciples were identified and sent forth to preach (10:1-5).
[Did Jesus resurrect the girl after his disciples were identified and sent forth to preach (MARK 3:14-19), or before the twelve were identified and sent forth?]
MATT. 9:25 - When the people were put forth, he went in, took her by the hand, and the maid arose.
[Did Jesus go to the girl with her father, mother, and three disciples, or did he go alone?]
[Did Jesus take the girl by the hand and tell her to arise, or did he just take her by the hand?]
See also under MATT. 9:25.

**Old Testament:** See under MATT. 9:25.

**Pagan concept:** See under MATT. 9:25.

**Perplexing:**
Why did MARK interject Aramaic words at this point?

5:43 - HE CHARGED THEM THAT NO MAN SHOULD KNOW IT....

**Perplexing:**
How could the girl's resurrection be kept secret, as her relatives, friends, and others knew that she had been

dead?
See also under MATT. 9:26.

6:1-3 - HE WENT FROM THERE INTO HIS OWN COUNTRY, AND HIS DISCIPLES FOLLOW HIM. WHEN THE SABBATH DAY WAS COME, HE BEGAN TO TEACH IN THE SYNAGOGUES; MANY HEARING HIM WERE ASTONISHED, SAYING, ".... IS NOT THIS THE CARPENTER, THE SON OF MARY, THE BROTHER OF JAMES, JOSES, JUDA, AND SIMON? ARE NOT HIS SISTERS HERE WITH US?" THEY WERE OFFENDED AT HIM.

**Contradictions:**
MATT. 9:27 - [After having resurrected the girl] When Jesus departed thence, two blind men followed him, saying, "Thou Son of David, have mercy on us."
[After having resurrected the girl, did Jesus return to his own country, begin to teach in synagogues, and be identified as a carpenter, the son of Mary, with brothers and sisters, or was he followed by two blind men?]
MATT. 13:54-57 - When he had come into his own country, he taught in their synagogue, that they were astonished, and said, "Is this not the carpenter's son? Is not his mother called Mary? .... ...." They were offended in him. ....
[Did people say that Jesus is a carpenter, or a carpenter's son?]
[Did the event occur shortly after Jesus resurrected a girl, or long afterward?]

**Perplexing:**
If Jesus was a carpenter, why is he never reported to have done any carpentry? When and where did Jesus learn carpentry? Why was he said to be Mary's son, not Joseph's son? Why did MARK never mention Joseph? Was MARK saying that Mary was a widow, or possibly unmarried? (The Koran also does not mention Joseph, but has Mary as the unmarried sister of Aaron and Moses.) How could Jesus walk into a synagogue and start teaching without first obtaining permission from the presiding priest? Why was Jesus' family offended? How could they be offended by a family member who was the Son of God? (See MARK 1:1; MATT. 1:18; LUKE 1:32, 35; and other verses.)

6:5 - HE COULD THERE DO NO MIGHTY WORK, SAVE THAT HE LAID HIS HANDS UPON A FEW SICK FOLK AND HEALED THEM.

**Contradiction:**
MATT. 13:58 - He did not many mighty works because of their unbelief.
[Was Jesus unable to do any mighty work there, or did he choose not to do any because of the people's unbelief?]

**Perplexing:**
Why did Jesus have to lay his hands on people at this time to heal them? Why was he unable to do any mighty work? Why could he heal only a f ew sick people? Was Jesus' ability to perform miracles dependent upon people's beliefs? Would not performing miracles for unbelievers have been an effective means of persuading them to believe in him?

6:7-9 - HE CALLED THE TWELVE, BEGAN TO SEND THEM FORTH BY TWO AND TWO, GAVE THEM POWER OVER UNCLEAN SPIRITS, AND COMMANDED THAT THEY TAKE NOTHING FOR THEIR JOURNEY, SAVE A STAFF ONLY, NO SCRIP, NO BREAD, NO MONEY, BUT BE SHOD WITH SANDALS, AND NOT PUT ON TWO COATS.

**Contradictions:**
MATT. 10:10 and LUKE 9:3 - Jesus told the disciples not to take any staves.
[Did Jesus tell the disciples to take a staff, or not to take any staves?]
MATT. 10:10 - Jesus told them not to take shoes.
[Did Jesus instruct the disciples to wear sandals (shoes), or not to take shoes?]
MATT. 10:5 - Jesus sent the disciples forth before they walked through the corn in 12:1.
[Were the disciples sent forth a long time after having gone through the cornfields (MARK 2:23), or before going through cornfields?]
See also under MATT. 10:7-8 and 10:10.

**History:** See under MATT. 10:9.

6:12-13 - THEY WENT OUT, AND PREACHED THAT MEN SHOULD REPENT. THEY CAST OUT MANY DEVILS, ANOINTED WITH OIL MANY THAT WERE SICK, AND HEALED THEM.

**History:**
There is no secular record of the disciples having traveled around preaching and healing anyone.

**Perplexing:**
Why did the disciples have to anoint people with oil to heal them? Why is there no secular record of the disciples traveling around and/or healing anyone?

**Pagan parallel:**
The practice of anointing the sick with oil, resins, sap from trees and plants, or mucous from mushrooms to heal them was an ancient custom. It was predicated on the belief that these substances were the healing unctions of gods.

6:14 - KING HEROD HEARD OF HIM (FOR HIS NAME WAS SPREAD ABROAD) AND SAID, "JOHN THE BAPTIST WAS RISEN FROM THE DEAD, AND MIGHTY WORKS DO SHOW FORTH IN HIM."

**Contradictions:**
MATT. 2:19 - King Herod died when Jesus was an infant in Egypt.
[Did King Herod speak about John the Baptist, or was he dead? (Christian clergy claim that MARK was referring to Herod the Tetrarch.)]
MATT. 14:2 - [After Jesus did not do many mighty works (MATT. 13:58) and long after he sent forth the disciples (MATT. 10:5)] Herod the tetrarch heard of the fame of Jesus, and said, "This is John the Baptist; he is risen from the dead, and mighty works shew forth in him."
[Did Herod equate John with Jesus shortly after Jesus' disciples went forth (MARK 6:12) preaching and healing, or shortly after Jesus failed to do many mighty works and long after the disciples were sent forth?].
LUKE 9:7 - Herod the tetrarch heard of all that was done by him, and was perplexed, because it was said of some, that John was risen from the dead.
[Did Herod, or some people say that John had risen from the dead?]
LUKE 9:9 - Herod said, "John have I beheaded, but who is this, of whom I hear such things?" He desired to see him.
[Did Herod equate Jesus with John, or did he wonder who Jesus was and desire to see him?]

**History:**
King Herod died in 4 B.C.E. The reference to him at this point, therefore, may be an error, unless MARK was referring to Herod Antipas the tetrarch as "king."

**Perplexing:**
As Jesus was reported to have performed miracles witnessed by multitudes, and as his reputation was said to have been spread throughout the region, why had not Herod heard of him prior to John's execution? In LUKE 23:8, Herod said that he heard many things about Jesus and hoped to see him perform a miracle. How then could he have confused him with John the Baptist?

6:16 - WHEN HEROD HEARD THEREOF, HE SAID, "IT IS JOHN WHOM I BEHEADED; HE IS RISEN FROM THE DEAD."

**Contradiction:**
LUKE 9:9 - Herod: "John have I beheaded, but who is this, of whom I hear such things?" He desired to see him.
[Did Herod say that John has risen from the dead, or did he ask who Jesus is?]

6:17-18 - HEROD HAD...LAID HOLD UPON JOHN, AND BOUND HIM IN PRISON FOR HERODIAS SAKE, HIS BROTHER PHILIP'S WIFE, FOR HE HAD MARRIED HER. JOHN HAD SAID, "IT IS NOT LAWFUL FOR THEE TO HAVE THY BROTHER'S WIFE."

**History:** See under MATT. 14:3-4.

6:22-23 - WHEN THE DAUGHTER OF THE SAID HERODIAS CAME IN, DANCED, AND PLEASED HEROD AND THEM THAT SAT WITH HIM, THE KING SAID UNTO THE DAMSEL, "ASK OF ME WHATSOEVER THOU WILT, AND I WILL GIVE IT THEE." HE SWARE, "WHATSOEVER THOU SHALT ASK OF ME, I WILL GIVE IT THEE, UNTO HALF OF MY KINGDOM."

**Contradiction:** See under 6:14.

**Old Testament:**
EST. 5:3 - Said the king unto her, "What wilt thou, queen Esther? What is thy request? It shall be even given thee to the half of the kingdom."
EST 5:6 - The king said unto Esther at the banquet of wine, "What is thy petition? It shall be granted thee; what is thy request? Even to the half of the kingdom it shall be performed."

6:24 - SHE WENT AND SAID UNTO HER MOTHER, "WHAT SHALL I ASK?" SHE SAID, "THE HEAD OF JOHN THE BAPTIST."

**Contradiction:**
MATT. 14:8 - She, being before instructed of her mother, said, "Give me here John Baptist's head in a charger."
[Did Herodias instruct her daughter to ask for John's head after, or before she danced?]

**Perplexing:**
If MARK meant Herod the tetrarch, why did he continue to refer to him as a king and the relatively small region over which he ruled as a kingdom?

**History:** See under 6:14 and under MATT. 14:6-8.

6:25-27 - SHE CAME WITH HASTE UNTO THE KING, SAYING, "I WILL THAT THOU GIVE ME...THE HEAD OF JOHN THE BAPTIST." THE KING WAS SORRY.... THE KING SENT AN EXECUTIONER, AND COMMANDED HIS HEAD TO BE BROUGHT; HE WENT AND BEHEADED HIM IN PRISON.

**Contradictions:** See under 6:14 and under MATT. 14:9.

6:29 - WHEN HIS DISCIPLES HEARD IT, THEY CAME, TOOK HIS CORPSE, AND LAID IT IN A TOMB.

**Perplexing:**
How did John's disciples learn about his execution? How were they able to obtain the corpse? Did they also obtain the head? How? Where was the tomb? Why did Jesus not perform a miracle to save John (his cousin according to LUKE 1:36-44) or resurrect him? Why did Jesus fail to condemn Herod for killing John?

6:30 - THE APOSTLES GATHERED UNTO JESUS, AND TOLD HIM ALL THINGS, BOTH WHAT THEY HAD DONE, AND TAUGHT.

**Contradiction:**
MATT. 10:23 - Jesus: "When they persecute you in this city, flee into another; ye shall not have gone over the cities of Israel, till the Son of man be come."
[Did, or did not, the disciples go over all the cities of Israel before the resurrected Jesus returned?]

**Perplexing:**
Where did the disciples go? Were they persecuted? If so, where, when, and by whom? Did they have to flee from city to city? How were they all able to return at the same time? How did they know where to find Jesus? Why is there no reference to the persecution of the apostles either in the gospels or in secular histories? Why was Jesus not killed and resurrected before the apostles returned?
See also under MATT. 12:1.

6:31 - HE SAID, "COME APART INTO A DESERT PLACE, AND REST A WHILE"; FOR THERE WERE MANY COMING AND GOING, AND THEY HAD NO LEISURE SO MUCH AS TO EAT.

**Contradiction:**
MATT. 14:13 - When Jesus heard of it [John's death], he departed by ship into a desert place....
[Did Jesus depart because he and the disciples had no time for themselves even to eat, or because he heard about John's death?]

**Perplexing:**
Why did Jesus fail to perform a miracle to prevent people from taking up all of his and the disciples' time? Why did he not perform a miracle to allow them time to eat?

6:32-33 - THEY DEPARTED INTO A DESERT PLACE BY SHIP PRIVATELY. PEOPLE SAW THEM DEPARTING; MANY KNEW HIM, AND RAN AFOOT THITHER OUT OF ALL CITIES, OUTWENT THEM, AND CAME TOGETHER UNTO HIM.

**Contradictions:**
MATT. 14:13 - ...Jesus departed by ship into a desert place apart; when the people heard, they followed him on foot out of the cities.
[Did people see Jesus depart, or did they hear that he had departed?]
JOHN 6:1-4 - Jesus went over the sea of Galilee.... A great multitude followed.... Jesus went up into a mountain and there sat with his disciples. The passover, a feast of the Jews, was nigh.
[Did Jesus and his disciples go to a desert place, or did they go into a mountain and sit?]

**Perplexing:**
How many cities did "all cities" mean? Did it refer only to a few cities in a small area? How could people in all the cities have seen Jesus depart? How did they know where he was going? How were they all able to reach the destination before he did? If Jesus was in Capernaum, as the gospels implied, and he went to Bethsaida (LUKE 9:10), the distance would have been about five miles; and MARK 6:44 said that about 5000 men came to him. How many hours would it have taken all these men from "all cities" to traverse the five miles on foot? Would they not have clogged the roads making rapid movement difficult? The trip would also have entailed crossing the Jordan River. Were there enough boats to ferry the 5000 across? How long would it have taken? Was there a bridge? Did they all swim? Could they really have arrived at Jesus' destination before his ship? Would the Roman authorities have permitted such a mass movement of people? Why did Jesus not know that people would follow him?
See also under MATT. 14:13.

6:34 - JESUS...SAW MUCH PEOPLE AND WAS MOVED WITH COMPASSION TOWARD THEM, BECAUSE THEY WERE AS SHEEP NOT HAVING A SHEPHERD; HE BEGAN TO TEACH THEM MANY THINGS.

**Contradictions:**
MATT. 14:14 - Jesus saw a great multitude, was moved with compassion toward them, and healed their sick.
[Did Jesus teach the people many things, or did he heal their sick?]
LUKE 9:11 - ...he received them [the people], spake unto them of the kingdom of God, and healed them that had need of healing.
[Did Jesus teach the people many things, or speak about the kingdom of God and heal the sick?]

**Perplexing:**
According to MARK 6:44, there were about 5000 men. How were all 5000 able to hear Jesus speak? Over how large an area were the men spread?

6:35-38 - THE DAY WAS NOW FAR SPENT; HIS DISCIPLES SAID, "THIS IS A DESERT PLACE...SEND THEM AWAY, THAT THEY MAY GO...INTO THE VILLAGES, AND BUY BREAD, FOR THEY HAVE NOTHING TO EAT." HE SAID, "GIVE YE THEM TO EAT." THEY SAY, "SHALL WE BUY 200 PENNYWORTH OF BREAD...?" HE SAITH, "HOW MANY LOAVES HAVE YE?" ...THEY SAY, "FIVE AND TWO FISHES."

**Contradictions:** See under MATT. 14:15-17.

**Perplexing:** See under MATT. 14:15-17.

**Pagan parallel:** See under MATT. 14:15-17.

**Judaism:** See under MATT. 14:15-17.

6:39 - HE COMMANDED THEM TO MAKE ALL SIT DOWN BY COMPANIES UPON THE GREEN GRASS.

**Contradictions:** See under MATT. 14:19.

**Perplexing:** See under MATT. 14:19.

6:40 - THEY SAT DOWN IN RANKS BY 100s, AND BY 50s.

**Contradiction:**
LUKE 9:14 - .... He said to his disciples, "Make them sit down by 50s in a company."
[Did the people sit down in ranks by 100s and 50s, or were they ordered to sit down by 50s?]

6:41-44 - WHEN HE HAD TAKEN THE FIVE LOAVES AND TWO FISHES...AND BRAKE THE LOAVES, AND GAVE THEM TO HIS DISCIPLES TO SET BEFORE THEM; THE TWO FISH DIVIDED HE AMONG THEM ALL. THEY DID ALL EAT, AND WERE FILLED. THEY TOOK UP 12 BASKETS OF THE FRAGMENTS, AND OF THE FISHES. THEY THAT DID EAT WERE ABOUT 5000 MEN.

**Contradictions:**
MATT. 14:21 - They that had eaten were about 5000 men, beside women and children.
[Were there about 5000 men, or were there about 5000 men plus an unspecified number of women and children?]
LUKE 9:16 - He took the five loaves and two fishes...and gave to the disciples to set before the multitude.
JOHN 6:11 - Jesus took the loaves and...distributed to the disciples, and the disciples to them that were set down; likewise of the fishes....
[Did the disciples distribute only the loaves, and Jesus distribute the fish, or did the disciples distribute both the loaves and the fish?]

**History:** See under MATT. 14:21.

**Perplexing:** See under MATT. 14:19, 14:20, and 14:21.

**Old Testament:** See under MATT. 14:19.

6:45-47 - HE CONSTRAINED HIS DISCIPLES TO GET INTO THE SHIP TO GO TO THE OTHER SIDE BEFORE UNTO BETHSAIDA, WHILE HE SENT AWAY THE PEOPLE. WHEN HE HAD SENT THEM AWAY, HE DEPARTED INTO A MOUNTAIN TO PRAY. WHEN EVEN WAS COME, THE SHIP WAS IN THE MIDST OF THE SEA, AND HE ALONE ON THE LAND.

**Contradictions:** See under MATT. 14:22-23.

**Perplexing:** See under MATT. 14:22-23.

6:48-50 - HE SAW THEM TOILING IN ROWING, FOR THE WIND WAS CONTRARY UNTO THEM; ABOUT THE FOURTH WATCH OF THE NIGHT HE COMETH UNTO THEM, WALKING UPON THE SEA, AND WOULD HAVE PASSED BY THEM. WHEN THEY SAW HIM WALKING UPON THE SEA, THEY...CRIED OUT; THEY ALL SAW HIM....

**Contradiction:** See under MATT. 14:25.

**Perplexing:**
How could the disciples, busy rowing against a strong wind and rough sea, at night, see Jesus? Why would Jesus have passed by the ship if the disciples had not cried out to him? Could not Jesus see the ship in the dark?
See also under MATT. 14:25 and 26.

**Old Testament:** See under MATT. 14:25.

**Pagan parallel:** See under MATT. 14:25.

6:52 - THEY CONSIDERED NOT THE MIRACLE OF THE LOAVES, FOR THEIR HEART WAS HARDENED.

**Perplexing:**
Why was their heart hardened?

6:53 - WHEN THEY HAD PASSED OVER, THEY CAME INTO THE LAND OF GENNESARET....

**Contradictions:** See under MATT. 14:34.

**Perplexing:**
In 6:45, Jesus sent the disciples to Bethsaida. Why then did they go to Gennesaret?

6:54-56 - WHEN THEY WERE COME OUT OF THE SHIP, STRAIGHTWAY THEY KNEW HIM...AND BEGAN TO CARRY IN BEDS THOSE THAT WERE SICK, WHERE THEY HEARD HE WAS. WHITHERSOEVER HE ENTERED, VILLAGES, CITIES, OR COUNTRY, THEY LAID THE SICK IN THE STREETS...AND AS MANY AS TOUCHED HIM WERE MADE WHOLE.

**Contradiction:**
MATT. 14: 35 - When the men of that place had knowledge of him, they sent out into all that country round about, and brought unto him all that were diseased....
[Did Jesus travel around the region healing the sick, or were the sick brought to him?]
See also under MATT. 14:35-36.

**Perplexing:** See under MATT. 14:35-36.

7:1-4 - CAME UNTO HIM THE PHARISEES, AND CERTAIN SCRIBES FROM JERUSALEM. WHEN THEY SAW SOME OF HIS DISCIPLES EAT BREAD...WITH UNWASHEN HANDS, THEY FOUND FAULT. ...ALL THE JEWS, EXCEPT THEY WASH THEIR HANDS OFT, EAT NOT, HOLDING THE TRADITION OF THE ELDERS. WHEN THEY COME FROM THE MARKET, EXCEPT THEY WASH, THEY EAT NOT. ....

**History:** See under MATT. 15:1-2.

**Perplexing:** See under MATT. 15:1-2.

7:6-7 - HE ANSWERED, "ESAIAS [ISAIAH] PROPHESIED OF YOU HYPOCRITES, AS IT IS WRITTEN, 'THIS PEOPLE HONOURETH ME WITH THEIR LIPS, BUT THEIR HEART IS FAR FROM ME. HOWBEIT IN VAIN DO THEY WORSHIP ME, TEACHING FOR DOCTRINES THE COMMANDMENTS OF MEN.'"

**Old Testament:** See under MATT. 15:7-9.

**Contradiction:** See under MATT. 15:7-9.

**Perplexing:** See under MATT. 15:7-9.

7:8-9 - JESUS: "LAYING ASIDE THE COMMANDMENT OF GOD, YE HOLD THE TRADITION OF MEN, AS THE WASHING OF POTS.... FULL WELL YE REJECT THE COMMANDMENT OF GOD, THAT YE MAY KEEP YOUR OWN TRADITION."

**Contradiction:**
MATT. 5:20 - Jesus: "Except your righteousness shall exceed the righteousness of the scribes and Pharisees, ye shall in no case enter the kingdom of heaven."
[Did Jesus accuse the Pharisees of putting aside and rejecting God's commandments, or did he say that they were righteous?]

7:10 - JESUS: "MOSES SAID, 'HONOUR THY FATHER AND MOTHER;' AND 'WHOSO CURSETH FATHER OR MOTHER, LET HIM DIE THE DEATH.'"

**Old Testament:**
EX. 21:17 - God: "He that curseth his father or mother, shall surely be put to death."
LEV. 20:9 - The LORD: "Everyone that curseth his father or mother shall be surely put to death...."
See also under MATT. 15:3-6.

**Perplexing:**
Why was there no commandment prohibiting parents from abusing and killing their children?
See also under MATT. 15:3-6.

7:11 - JESUS: "IF A MAN SHALL SAY TO HIS FATHER, 'IT IS CORBAN,' THAT IS TO SAY, 'A GIFT'...."

**Language:** See under MATT. 15:3-6.

7:15 - JESUS: "THERE IS NOTHING FROM WITHOUT A MAN, THAT ENTERING INTO HIM CAN DEFILE HIM; BUT THE THINGS WHICH COME OUT OF HIM, THOSE ARE THEY THAT DEFILE THE MAN."

**Contradictions:** See under MATT. 15:11.

**Perplexing:** See under MATT. 15:11.

7:18-19 - HE SAITH, ".... DO YE NOT PERCEIVE, THAT WHATSOEVER THING FROM WITHOUT ENTERETH INTO THE MAN, IT CANNOT DEFILE HIM; IT ENTERETH NOT INTO HIS HEART, BUT INTO THE BELLY, AND GOETH OUT THE DRAUGHT, PURGING ALL MEATS?"

**Contradictions:** See above under MATT. 15:11.

**Perplexing:** See above under MATT. 15:11.

7:21-22 - JESUS: "...OUT OF THE HEART OF MEN, PROCEED EVIL THOUGHTS... AN EVIL EYE...."

**Pagan concept:** See under MATT. 6:23.

**History:**
Long before the onset of Christianity many ancient people believed in the concept of an "evil eye." Even in modern times, some individuals still retain the belief.

**Perplexing:**
Did Jesus believe in the "evil eye?"
See also under MATT. 6:23.

7:24 - FROM THENCE, HE WENT INTO THE BORDERS OF TYRE AND SIDON, ENTERED INTO AN HOUSE, AND WOULD HAVE NO MAN KNOW IT, BUT HE COULD NOT BE HID.

**Perplexing:**
Into whose house did he enter? Why was the house owner not identified? Why did Jesus fail to know that people would find him? Why did he not perform a miracle to keep his whereabouts secret?
See also under MATT. 15:21.

**Old Testament:** See under MATT. 11:20-23.

7:25-28 - A WOMAN, WHOSE YOUNG DAUGHTER HAD AN UNCLEAN SPIRIT, CAME AND FELL AT HIS FEET; THE WOMAN WAS A GREEK, A SYROPHENICIAN; SHE BESOUGHT HIM THAT HE, WOULD CAST THE DEVIL OUT OF HER DAUGHTER. JESUS SAID, "LET THE CHILDREN FIRST BE FILLED, FOR IT IS NOT MEET TO TAKE THE CHILDREN'S BREAD AND TO CAST IT UNTO THE DOGS." SHE SAID, "YES, LORD, YET THE DOGS UNDER THE TABLE EAT OF THE CHILDREN'S CRUMBS."

**Contradictions:**
MATT. 15:22-27 - A woman of Canaan came, saying, "Have mercy on me, O Lord, thou Son of David, my daughter is vexed with a devil." He answered her not a word. His disciples came, saying, "Send her away." He said, "I am not sent but unto the lost sheep of the house of Israel." Came she and worshipped him, saying, "Lord help me." He said, "It is not meet to take the children's bread, and to cast it to the dogs." She said, "Lord, yet the dogs eat of the crumbs which fall from their masters' table."
[Did Jesus respond to the woman when she approached him, or did he refuse to speak with her until after his disciples requested that he send her away?]
[Did the woman ask Jesus once, or twice for help?]

**Perplexing:** See under MATT. 15:22-24 and 26.

**History:** See under MATT. 15:22-24.

7:29 - HE SAID, "FOR THIS SAYING GO THY WAY; THE DEVIL IS GONE OUT OF THY DAUGHTER."

**Contradiction:**
MATT. 15:28 - Jesus said, "Great is thy faith; be it unto thee even as thou wilt." Her daughter was made whole from that very hour.
[Did Jesus heal the daughter because of the woman's saying, or because of her faith?]

7:31 - DEPARTING FROM THE COASTS OF TYRE AND SIDON, HE CAME UNTO THE SEA OF GALILEE, THROUGH THE MIDST OF THE COASTS OF DECAPOLIS.

**Contradiction:**
MATT. 15:29 - Jesus departed from thence, came nigh unto the sea of Galilee, and went up into a mountain, and sat down there.
[Did Jesus travel to the Sea of Galilee through Decapolis, or did he go onto a mountain near the Sea of Galilee?]

**Perplexing:**
Traveling from Tyre and Sidon which are northwest of the Sea of Galilee, Jesus would have reached the Sea of Galilee before reaching Decapolis which is southeast of the Sea of Galilee. Tyre, which is about 40 miles from the Sea of Galilee, is closer to it than Sidon. Decapolis, at its closest point by the Sea of Galilee, is an additional ten miles further away from Tyre. Why did Jesus travel the extra distance (to and through the midst of Decapolis then to the Sea)? How did he travel? How long did the trip take? Was MARK ignorant of the geography of Palestine?

**History:** See under MATT. 4:24-25 for Decapolis.

7:32-35 - THEY BRING UNTO HIM ONE THAT WAS DEAF, AND HAD AN IMPEDIMENT IN HIS SPEECH; THEY BESEECH HIM TO PUT HIS HAND UPON HIM. HE TOOK HIM ASIDE, PUT HIS FINGERS INTO HIS EARS, SPIT, AND TOUCHED HIS TONGUE; ...HE SAITH, "EPHPHATHA," THAT IS, "BE OPENED." HIS EARS WERE OPENED...AND HE SPAKE PLAIN.

**Contradiction:**
MATT. 15:30 - Great multitudes came to him [on a mountain near the Sea of Galilee (15:29)]...those that were lame, blind, dumb, maimed, and many others...he healed them.
[Did Jesus heal one deaf man with a speech impediment, or multitudes with a variety of infirmities while on a mountain?]

**History:**
Many ancient people believed that saliva possessed the body's life energy and had healing properties including the ability to heal blindness. It was cited in Egyptian and cuneiform writings as a substance that should be used to heal people.

**Language:**
"Ephphatha," is Aramaic.

**Perplexing:**
Why did Jesus have to put his fingers in the man's ears, spit, and touch his tongue to heal this particular man? Why did Jesus not use faith or words, as he had done on past occasions to heal other people? Did Jesus also believe that saliva had healing properties? Why did MARK use Aramaic at this time?

7:36 - HE CHARGED THEM THAT THEY SHOULD TELL NO MAN, BUT THE MORE HE CHARGED THEM, SO MUCH THE MORE THEY PUBLISHED IT.

**Perplexing:**
If Jesus knew all that was to occur, why did he bother to ask the people not to tell anyone about his miracles? If he did not want news of the healing to be advertised, why did he fail to perform a miracle to keep it confidential?

8:1-4 - THE MULTITUDE BEING VERY GREAT, AND HAVING NOTHING TO EAT, JESUS CALLED HIS DISCIPLES, AND SAITH, "I HAVE COMPASSION ON THE MULTITUDE, BECAUSE THEY HAVE NOW BEEN WITH ME THREE DAYS, AND HAVE NOTHING TO EAT; IF I SEND THEM AWAY FASTING, THEY WILL FAINT BY THE WAY, FOR DIVERS CAME FROM AFAR." HIS DISCIPLES ANSWERED, "FROM WHENCE CAN A MAN SATISFY THESE MEN WITH BREAD HERE IN THE WILDERNESS?"

**Perplexing:** See under MATT. 15:32 and 15:33-35.

8:5-6 - HE ASKED, "HOW MANY LOAVES HAVE YE?" THEY SAID, "SEVEN." HE COMMANDED THE PEOPLE TO SIT DOWN ON THE GROUND....

**Perplexing:**
After going three days without food, why were the people not tired enough to sit down without being told to do so? What sanitary facilities were available for the people (4000, according to 8:9)?
See also under MATT. 14:15-17, 15:32, and 33-35.

8:7-9 - THEY HAD A FEW SMALL FISHES.... SO THEY DID EAT, AND WERE FILLED; THEY TOOK UP OF THE BROKEN MEAT THAT WAS LEFT SEVEN BASKETS. THEY THAT HAD EATEN WERE ABOUT 4000; HE SENT THEM AWAY.

**Contradiction:**
MATT. 15:38 - They that did eat were 4000 men, beside women and children.
[Were there about 4000 people, or 4000 men plus an unspecified number of women and children?]

**Perplexing:** See under MATT. 15:36-38.

**Old Testament:** See under MATT. 14:19.

8:10 - STRAIGHTWAY HE ENTERED A SHIP WITH HIS DISCIPLES, AND CAME INTO THE PARTS OF DALMANUTHA.

**Contradiction:**
MATT. 15:39 - He sent away the multitude, took ship, and came into the coasts of Magdala.
[Did Jesus go to Dalmanutha, or to Magdala?]

8:11-12 - PHARISEES CAME AND BEGAN TO QUESTION HIM, SEEKING OF HIM A SIGN FROM HEAVEN, TEMPTING HIM. HE SAITH, "WHY DOTH THIS GENERATION SEEK AFTER A SIGN? THERE SHALL NO SIGN BE GIVEN UNTO THIS GENERATION?"

**Contradictions:**
MATT. 16:1-4 - Pharisees with Sadducees desired...that he would shew them a sign from heaven. He answered, ".... .... ...there shall be no sign given, but the sign of the prophet Jonas."
[Did only Pharisees, or Pharisees with Sadducees question Jesus?]
[Did Jesus say that no sign would be given, or that the sign of Jonah would be given?]
See also under MATT. 12:38-39.

**History:** See under MATT. 12:38-39.

**Perplexing:** See under MATT. 12:38-39.

8:15 - HE CHARGED THEM [THE DISCIPLES], "BEWARE OF THE LEAVEN OF THE PHARISEES, AND OF THE LEAVEN OF HEROD."

**Contradiction:**
MATT. 16:6 - Jesus said, "...beware of the leaven of the Pharisees and of the Sadducees."
[Did Jesus warn the disciples about the leaven of the Pharisees and Herod, or the leaven of the Pharisees and Sadducees?]
See also under MATT. 16:6-12.

**Perplexing:**
If according to LUKE 12:1, the leaven of the Pharisees is hypocrisy, what did Jesus mean by "the leaven of Herod?"

8:18 - JESUS: "HAVING EYES, SEE YE NOT? HAVING EARS, HEAR YE NOT...."

**Old Testament:**
JER. 5:21 - The LORD: "...O foolish people...which have eyes, and see not; which have ears and hear not."

8:22 - HE COMETH TO BETHSAIDA, AND THEY BRING A BLIND MAN UNTO HIM, AND BESOUGHT HIM TO TOUCH HIM.

**Contradictions:**
MATT. 16:13 - Jesus came into the coasts of Caesarea Philippi....
[No blind man was said to have been brought to him.]
[Did Jesus go to Bethsaida, by the Sea of Galilee, or to Caesarea Philippi, about 25 miles north of Bethsaida and of the Sea of Galilee?]

8:23-25 - HE TOOK THE BLIND MAN BY THE HAND, AND LED HIM OUT OF THE TOWN; WHEN HE HAD SPIT ON HIS EYES, AND PUT HIS HANDS UPON HIM, ASKED IF HE SAW OUGHT. HE SAID, "I SEE MEN AS TREES, WALKING." HE PUT HIS HANDS AGAIN UPON HIS EYES...HE SAW EVERY MAN CLEARLY.

**Perplexing:**
Why was Jesus unable to heal the man the f irst time he touched him? Why did Jesus have to spit on the man's eyes? Why did he not spit on the eyes of all the blind people he healed? Why was the man not healed by faith? In JOHN 9:6-7, Jesus spit on the ground and made clay which he put on the eyes of a blind man and told to him wash in a pool. Why did Jesus not do the same to the man in this MARK incident?

**History:**
Tacitus reported that Vespassian (A.D. 9-79) applied saliva to the eyes of a blind man who was then able to see; this healing was said to have been witnessed by a multitude. [If one believes that Jesus healed a blind man by using saliva, should one not also believe that Vespassian used saliva to heal a blind man?] See also under 7:32-35.

8:26 - HE SENT HIM AWAY, SAYING, "NEITHER GO INTO THE TOWN, NOR TELL IT TO ANY IN TOWN."

**Perplexing:**
How could the man keep secret that he could now see? The people who brought him to Jesus (8:22) and everyone who knew that he had been blind would now know that he had his sight. Did Jesus want the man to lie? How could the man stay away from the town indefinitely?

8:27 - JESUS WENT OUT, AND HIS DISCIPLES, INTO THE TOWNS OF CAESAREA PHILIPPI; HE ASKED THEM, "WHOM DO MEN SAY THAT I AM?"

**Contradictions:** See under MATT. 16:13.

8:28 - THEY ANSWERED, "JOHN THE BAPTIST, BUT SOME SAY, ELIAS, AND OTHERS, ONE OF THE PROPHETS."

**Perplexing:** See under MATT. 16:14.

8:29 - HE SAITH, "BUT WHOM SAY YE THAT I AM?" PETER ANSWERETH, "THOU ART THE CHRIST?"

**Perplexing:** See under MATT. 16:16.

**Language:** See under MATT. 1:1.

**History:** See under MATT. 1:1.

**Pagan parallel:** See under MATT. 1:1.

8:31 - HE BEGAN TO TEACH THEM THAT THE SON OF MAN MUST...BE KILLED, AND AFTER THREE DAYS RISE AGAIN.

**Contradictions:**
MATT. 16:21 - Jesus began to shew unto his disciples that he must be killed, and raised the third day.
MATT. 17:22-23 - Jesus said, "The Son of man...they shall kill him, and the third day he shall be raised."
MARK 9:31 - He taught, "The Son of man...they shall kill him, and...he shall rise the third day."
MARK 10:33-34 - Jesus: "...the Son of man...[they] shall kill him, and the third day he shall rise."
LUKE 9:22 - Jesus: "The Son of man must...be slain, and be raised the third day."
LUKE 18:33 - Jesus: "They shall...put him [Jesus] to death, and the third day he shall rise."
LUKE 24:7 - Two men (angels?): "The Son of man must...be crucified, and the third day rise."
LUKE 24:46 - [Jesus] said, "...it behoved Christ to rise from the dead the third day."
1 COR. 15:4 - Paul: "...he rose again the third day...."
[Did Jesus say that he would rise after three days, or on the third day?]
See also under MATT. 12:40 and 16:21.

**Perplexing:**
Jesus said that he would rise from the dead after three days, but did so in less than two days. He was entombed on a Friday evening and resurrected about dawn or earlier the following Sunday — a period of approximately one and one half days (MATT. 27:57, 28:6; MARK 15:34, 16:6; LUKE 23:54, 24:6; JOHN 19:42, 20:14).

**Old Testament:** See under MATT. 12:40.

**Pagan parallels:** See under MATT. 12:40.

8:33 - ...HE REBUKED PETER, SAYING, "GET THEE BEHIND ME SATAN...."

**Perplexing:** See under MATT. 16:23.

**Judaism:** See under MATT. 16:23.

8:34 - ...HE SAID, "WHOSOEVER WILL COME AFTER ME, LET HIM DENY HIMSELF, TAKE UP HIS CROSS, AND FOLLOW ME."

**Perplexing:** See under MATT. 16:24.

**History:** See under MATT. 16:24.

8:37 - JESUS: "WHAT SHALL A MAN GIVE IN EXCHANGE FOR HIS SOUL?"

**Perplexing:** See under MATT. 16:26.

8:38 - JESUS: "WHOSOEVER SHALL BE ASHAMED OF ME AND MY WORDS IN THIS ADULTEROUS AND SINFUL GENERATION, OF HIM SHALL THE SON OF MAN BE ASHAMED, WHEN HE COMETH IN THE GLORY OF HIS FATHER WITH THE HOLY ANGELS."

**Perplexing:**
Jesus said that he would return to "this adulterous and sinful generation" (his contemporary generation) with his Father's "holy angels." Why did he not return as promised? Did Jesus deliberately lie to his disciples? See also under MATT. 16:28.

**Old Testament:** See under MATT. 16:28.

9:1 - HE SAID, "THERE BE SOME OF THEM THAT STAND HERE, WHICH SHALL NOT TASTE OF DEATH, TILL THEY HAVE SEEN THE KINGDOM OF GOD COME WITH POWER."

**Perplexing:** See under MATT. 16:28.

**Old Testament:** See under MATT. 16:28.

9:2-3 - AFTER SIX DAYS JESUS TAKETH PETER, JAMES, AND JOHN INTO A HIGH MOUNTAIN AND HE WAS TRANSFIGURED BEFORE THEM. HIS RAIMENT BECAME SHINING, EXCEEDING WHITE AS SNOW, AS NO FULLER ON EARTH CAN WHITE THEM.

**Contradiction:** See under MATT. 17:1.

**Perplexing:** See under MATT. 17:1 and 17:2.

**Old Testament:** See under MATT. 17:2.

**Pagan parallel:** See under MATT. 17:2.

9:4-5 - THERE APPEARED UNTO THEM ELIAS [ELIJAH] WITH MOSES; THEY WERE TALKING WITH JESUS. PETER SAID TO JESUS, "...LET US MAKE THREE TABERNACLES, ONE FOR THEE, ONE FOR MOSES, AND ONE FOR ELIAS."

**Perplexing:** See under MATT. 17:3-4.

9:7 - THERE WAS A CLOUD THAT OVERSHADOWED THEM, AND A VOICE CAME OUT OF THE CLOUD, SAYING, "THIS IS MY BELOVED SON, HEAR HIM."

**Contradictions:** See under MATT. 1:18 and 17:5.

**Old Testament:** See under MATT. 17:5.

**Perplexing:** See under MATT. 3:17 and 17:5.

**History:** See under MATT. 1:20.

9:9-10 - AS THEY CAME DOWN THE MOUNTAIN, HE CHARGED THEM THAT THEY SHOULD TELL NO MAN WHAT THEY HAD SEEN, TILL THE SON OF MAN WERE RISEN FROM THE DEAD. THEY KEPT THAT SAYING WITH THEMSELVES, QUESTIONING ONE WITH THE ANOTHER WHAT THE RISING FROM THE DEAD SHOULD MEAN.

**Contradiction:** See under MATT. 17:9.

**Perplexing:**
As recently as MARK 8:31, Jesus taught the disciples that he was to be killed, and after three days rise from the dead. Why did the disciples now not understand about what Jesus was speaking?

9:11 - THEY ASKED HIM, "WHY SAY THE SCRIBES THAT ELIAS (ELIJAH) MUST COME FIRST?"

**Old Testament:** See under MATT. 11:13-14.

**Judaism:** See under MATT. 11:13-14.

9:12-13 - HE ANSWERED, "ELIAS COMETH FIRST, AND RESTORETH ALL THINGS"; AND HOW IT IS WRITTEN OF THE SON OF MAN, THAT HE MUST SUFFER MANY THINGS, AND BE SET AT NOUGHT. "BUT, ELIAS IS INDEED COME, AND THEY HAVE DONE UNTO HIM WHATEVER THEY LISTED, AS IT IS WRITTEN OF HIM."

**Perplexing:** See under MATT. 17:11-13.

**Old Testament:** See under MATT. 11:13-14.

**Judaism:** See under MATT. 11:13-14.

9:16- HE ASKED THE SCRIBES: "WHAT QUESTION YE WITH THEM [HIS DISCIPLES]?"

**Contradictions:** See under MATT. 9:28-30.

**Perplexing:**
Why did not the scribes respond to Jesus?

9:17 - ONE OF THE MULTITUDE SAID, "I HAVE BROUGHT UNTO THEE MY SON, WHICH HATH A DUMB SPIRIT."

**Contradictions:**
MATT. 17:14-15 - ...there came a man...saying, "Lord, have mercy on my son, for he is a lunatick...."
[Did the man say that his son has a "dumb spirit, " or that he is a "lunatick?"]
See also under MATT. 17:15.

9:18 - THE MAN: "...I SPAKE TO THY DISCIPLES THAT THEY SHOULD CAST HIM OUT, AND THEY COULD NOT."

**Contradiction:** See under MATT. 17:16.

**Perplexing:** See under MATT. 17:16.

9:19: HE ANSWERETH, "O FAITHLESS GENERATION, HOW LONG SHALL I BE WITH YOU?...."

**Perplexing:** See under MATT. 17:17.

9:21 - HE ASKED HIS FATHER, "HOW LONG IS IT SINCE THIS CAME UNTO HIM?" HE SAID, "OF A CHILD."

**Perplexing:**
Why did it matter to Jesus how long the spirit had been in the boy? Why did Jesus not ask anyone else, how long a spirit had been present?

9:22 - "OFTTIMES IT HATH CAST HIM INTO THE FIRE, AND INTO WATERS...."

**Contradiction:**
MATT. 17:15 - The man: "Lord, have mercy on my son for he is a lunatick, and sore vexed; ofttimes he falleth into the fire, and oft into water."
[After having conversed with Jesus, did the man say that his son falls into fire and into water, or did he say it when he first came to Jesus?]

9:23-26 - JESUS SAID, "IF THOU CANST BELIEVE, ALL THINGS ARE POSSIBLE TO HIM THAT BELIEVETH." THE FATHER OF THE CHILD SAID, "LORD, I BELIEVE...." ...JESUS REBUKED THE FOUL SPIRIT, "THOU DUMB AND DEAF SPIRIT, I CHARGE THEE, COME OUT OF HIM, AND ENTER NO MORE INTO HIM." THE SPIRIT...CAME OUT OF HIM....

**Contradictions:**
MATT. 17:18 - Jesus rebuked the devil; he departed, and the child was cured....
LUKE 9:42 - .... Jesus rebuked the unclean spirit, and healed the child....
[Did Jesus engage the boy's father in conversation about belief before rebuking the spirit, or dig he rebuke the devil/spirit without first conversing with the boy's father?]
MARK 9:28-29 - When he was come into the house, the disciples asked, "Why could we not cast him out?" He said, "This kind can come forth by nothing, but prayer and fasting."
[Was the spirit cast out because of the father's belief and Jesus' command to the spirit, or by prayer and fasting?]
See also under MATT. 17:18.

**Perplexing:** See under MATT. 17:18.

9:28-29 - ...HIS DISCIPLES ASKED HIM, "WHY COULD WE NOT CAST HIM OUT?" HE SAID, "THIS KIND CAN COME FORTH ONLY BY NOTHING, BUT PRAYER AND FASTING."

**Contradictions:** See under 9:23-26.

**Perplexing:** See under MATT. 17:19-21.

9:30 - THEY DEPARTED THENCE, AND PASSED THROUGH GALILEE, AND HE WOULD NOT THAT ANY MAN KNOW IT.

**Perplexing:**
Why did Christ, the Messiah, want to travel in secret? Why did he not want to demonstrate publicly to everyone who he was so as to elicit belief and acceptance?

9:31 - HE TAUGHT HIS DISCIPLES, AND SAID, "THE SON OF MAN...THEY SHALL KILL HIM; AFTER HE IS KILLED, HE SHALL RISE THE THIRD DAY."

**Contradictions:** See under MATT. 16:21.

**Old Testament:** See under MATT. 12:40.

**Pagan parallels:** See under MATT. 12:40.

9:32 - THEY UNDERSTOOD NOT THAT SAYING....

**Contradiction:**
10: 35-37 - James and John came unto him.... .... They said, "Grant us that we may sit, one on thy right hand, and the other on thy left, in thy glory."
[Did the disciples not understand Jesus, or did at least two of them understand and want to be with him in his glory?]

**Perplexing:**
How could the disciples not understand what Jesus was saying? He had told them what was to occur on several occasions. Why did Jesus not know that the disciples did not understand him? Why did he fail to

make clear to them what he meant? If they did not understand, why did they not ask him to explain his statement?

9:33-34 - HE CAME TO CAPERNAUM; IN THE HOUSE HE ASKED THEM, "WHAT WAS IT THAT YE DISPUTED AMONG YOURSELVES BY THE WAY?" THEY HELD THEIR PEACE, FOR THEY HAD DISPUTED AMONG THEMSELVES, WHO SHOULD BE THE GREATEST.

**Contradiction:**
LUKE 9:46-47 - There arose a reasoning among them, which of them should be greatest. Jesus perceiving the thought of their heart....
[Did the disciples refuse to say about what they disputed, or did Jesus perceive their thoughts?]
See also under 9:16 and MATT. 18:1.

**Perplexing:**
In whose house were they? Was it Jesus' house? Is it the same house, cited in 2:2-4, the roof of which was broken? If so, was the roof repaired?

9:38 - JOHN ANSWERED, "MASTER, WE SAW ONE CASTING OUT DEVILS IN THY NAME, AND HE FOLLOWETH NOT US...."

**Perplexing:**
How could someone who did not receive power from Jesus cast out devils? Does one merely have to use Jesus' name to cast them out? If such is the case, why was it necessary for Jesus to give the disciples power to do so? Why could they not have done it on their own just by using Jesus' name? (In ACTS 3:6-8 - Peter healed a lame man by using Jesus' name; in ACTS 4:30 - Peter and John said that signs and wonders may be done in the name of Jesus; in ACTS 19:13-16, however, people failed to cast out evil spirits by using Jesus' name.)

9:41 - JESUS: "WHOSOEVER SHALL GIVE YOU A CUP OF WATER TO DRINK IN MY NAME, BECAUSE YE BELONG TO CHRIST, HE SHALL NOT LOSE HIS REWARD."

**Contradictions:**
MARK 16:16 - "He that believeth and is baptized shall be saved, but he that believeth not shall be damned."
[Can one be saved by giving a drink of water in Jesus' name, or must one believe and be baptized, and, conceivably, refuse to give the drink?]
See also under MATT. 19:17-19 (for obtaining eternal life).

9:43-47 - JESUS: "IF THY HAND OFFEND THEE, CUT IT OFF; IT IS BETTER TO ENTER INTO LIFE MAIMED, THAN HAVING TWO HANDS TO GO INTO HELL... WHERE THE WORM DIETH NOT, AND THE FIRE IS NOT QUENCHED. IF THY FOOT OFFEND THEE, CUT IT OFF; IT IS BETTER TO ENTER HALT INTO LIFE, THAN HAVING TWO FEET TO BE CAST INTO HELL.... IF THINE EYE OFFEND THEE, PLUCK IT OUT; IT IS BETTER TO ENTER THE KINGDOM OF GOD WITH ONE EYE, THAN HAVING TWO EYES TO BE CAST INTO HELL FIRE."

**Old Testament:**
ISA. 66:24 - The LORD: "They shall go forth,and look upon the carcases of the men that have transgressed against Me; their worm shall not die, neither shall their fire be quenched; they shall be an abhorring unto all flesh."

**Perplexing:**
Why did Jesus take the ISA. verse out of context?
See also under MATT. 5:29-30.

**Pagan parallel:**
In the religion of ancient Egypt, the wicked are cast into a lake of fire, and enemies of the sun god are tossed into pits filled with fire.
See also under MATT. 5:29-30.

9:49 - JESUS: "...EVERY SACRIFICE SHALL BE SALTED WITH SALT."

**Old Testament:**
LEV. 2:13 - The LORD: "Every oblation of thy meat offering shalt thou season with salt...with all thine meat offerings thou shalt offer salt."

9:50 - JESUS: "SALT IS GOOD...."

**Perplexing:**
Why did Jesus fail to point out that salt can cause or exacerbate medical problems for some people?

10:2-5 - PHARISEES ASKED HIM, "IS IT LAWFUL FOR A MAN TO PUT AWAY HIS WIFE?" HE SAID, "WHAT DID MOSES COMMAND YOU?" THEY SAID, "MOSES SUFFERED TO WRITE A BILL OF DIVORCEMENT, AND TO PUT HER AWAY." JESUS SAID, "FOR THE HARDNESS OF YOUR HEART HE WROTE THIS PRECEPT."

**Contradiction:** See under MATT. 19:7-8.

**History:** See under MATT. 5:31-32.

**Old Testament:** See under MATT. 5:31-32.

**Perplexing:** See under MATT. 5:31-32.

10:6 - JESUS: "FROM THE BEGINNING OF THE CREATION GOD MADE THEM MALE AND FEMALE."

**Old Testament:** See under MATT. 19:3-4.

**Contradiction:** See under MATT. 19:3-4.

10:7-9 - JESUS: "FOR THIS CAUSE SHALL A MAN LEAVE HIS FATHER AND MOTHER, AND CLEAVE TO HIS WIFE; ...THEY ARE NO MORE TWAIN, BUT ONE FLESH. WHAT GOD HATH JOINED TOGETHER, LET NOT MAN PUT ASUNDER."

**Old Testament:** See under MATT. 19:5.

**Perplexing:** See under MATT. 19:5.

**History:** See under MATT. 5:31-32.

10:11 - HE SAITH, "WHOSOEVER SHALL PUT AWAY HIS WIFE, AND MARRY ANOTHER, COMMITTETH ADULTERY AGAINST HER."

**Contradiction:** See under MATT. 5:31-32.

**Perplexing:** See under MATT. 5:31-32.

10:12 - JESUS: "IF A WOMAN SHALL PUT AWAY HER HUSBAND, AND BE MARRIED TO ANOTHER, SHE COMMITTETH ADULTERY."

**Contradiction:**
DEUT. 24:2 - The LORD: "When she is departed out of his house, she may go and be another man's wife." [Does a divorced woman who remarries commit adultery, or is she legitimately married?]

**History:**
Jewish women did not have the right to initiate a divorce during the first century A.D. (The Old Testament did not say that a woman can initiate a divorce.) Roman women, however, under certain circumstances could start divorce proceedings.
See also under MATT. 5:31-32.

**Perplexing:**
Why did Jesus say that a divorced woman is guilty of adultery upon marrying again, whereas God voiced no objection to such a remarriage? Why did Jesus not know that a Jewish woman could not divorce her husband? Did Jesus confuse Roman and Jewish laws?
See also under MATT. 5:31-32.

10:17-18 - ...THERE CAME ONE, AND ASKED, "GOOD MASTER, WHAT SHALL I DO THAT I MAY INHERIT ETERNAL LIFE?" JESUS SAID, "WHY CALLEST ME GOOD? THERE IS NONE GOOD BUT ONE, THAT IS, GOD."

**Contradictions:** See under MATT. 19:17-19 (for God being good).

**Perplexing:** See under MATT. 19:16 and 17-19 (for God being good).

**Pagan concept**: See under MATT. 19:16.

10:19 - JESUS: "THOU KNOWEST THE COMMANDMENTS. DO NOT COMMIT ADULTERY; DO NOT KILL; DO NOT STEAL; DO NOT BEAR FALSE WITNESS; DEFRAUD NOT; HONOUR THY FATHER AND MOTHER."

**Old Testament:**
LEV. 19:13 - The LORD: "Thou shalt not defraud thy neighbour...."
See also under MATT. 19:17-19.

**Contradictions:**
MATT. 19:18-19 - ...Jesus: "Thou shalt do no murder" [instead of "Do not kill"]; thou shalt not commit adultery; thou shalt not steal; thou shalt not bear false witness; honour thy father and mother; thou shalt love thy neighbour as thyself."
[Did Jesus say not to kill, or not to murder?"]
[Did Jesus say that one should not defraud, or that one should love one's neighbour to obtain eternal life?]
LUKE 18:20 - Jesus: ".... Do not commit adultery; do not kill; do not steal; do not bear false witness; honour thy father and mother."
[Did, or did not Jesus say that one should not defraud to obtain eternal life?]
See also under MATT. 19:17-19 (for obtaining eternal life).

**Perplexing:** See under MATT. 19:17-19 (for obtaining eternal life).

**Pagan parallels:** See under MATT. 19:17-19.

**Judaism:**
According to Jewish scholars, the commandment stated as "Do not kill," is more correctly translated as "Thou shalt do no murder," as cited in MATT. 19:18.
See also under MATT. 19:17-19.

10:21 - JESUS LOVED HIM, AND SAID, "...SELL WHATSOEVER THOU HAST, GIVE TO THE POOR, AND THOU SHALT HAVE TREASURE IN HEAVEN; COME, TAKE UP THE CROSS, AND FOLLOW ME."

**Perplexing:**
Who was this man that Jesus loved? Why did Jesus love him? Why was no information given about him? Why is this the only time in MARK, MATT., and LUKE, that Jesus is reported to have loved anyone. (An ancient manuscript of MARK has been reported to contain an account, censored out of the Bible in the fourth century, of this man and Jesus having a homosexual relationship. The reference to "love" is the only remaining vestige of that account.)
See also under MATT. 10:38 and 19:21.

**History:** See under MATT. 10:38.

10:23-25 - JESUS SAITH, "HOW HARDLY SHALL THEY THAT HAVE RICHES ENTER INTO THE KINGDOM OF GOD! .... "IT IS EASIER FOR A CAMEL TO GO THROUGH THE EYE OF A NEEDLE, THAN FOR A RICH MAN TO ENTER INTO THE KINGDOM OF GOD."

**Perplexing:** See under MATT. 19:23-24.

**History:** See under MATT. 19:23-24.

**Pagan concept:** See under MATT. 19:23-24.

10:27 - JESUS SAITH, "...WITH GOD ALL THINGS ARE POSSIBLE."

**Contradictions:** See under MATT. 19:26.

**Perplexing:** See under MATT. 19:26.

10:29-30 - JESUS SAID, "THERE IS NO MAN THAT HATH LEFT HOUSE, OR BRETHREN, OR SISTERS, OR FATHER, OR MOTHER, OR WIFE, OR CHILDREN, OR LANDS, FOR MY SAKE, AND THE GOSPEL'S, BUT SHALL RECEIVE AN HUNDREDFOLD NOW IN THIS TIME...AND IN THE WORLD TO COME ETERNAL LIFE."

**Contradictions:** See under MATT. 19:29.

**Perplexing:** See under MATT. 19:29.

10:33-34 - JESUS: "...THE SON OF MAN SHALL BE DELIVERED TO THE CHIEF PRIESTS, AND THE SCRIBES...THEY SHALL DELIVER HIM TO THE GENTILES, AND THEY...SHALL KILL HIM, AND THE THIRD DAY HE SHALL RISE AGAIN."

**Contradictions:** See under MATT. 16:21

**Old Testament:** See under MATT. 12:40.

10:35-36 - JAMES AND JOHN, THE SONS OF ZEBEDEE, COME UNTO HIM, SAYING, "MASTER, WE WOULD THAT THOU SHOULDEST DO, WHATSOEVER WE SHALL DESIRE." HE SAID, "WHAT WOULD YE THAT I SHOULD DO FOR YOU?"

**Contradictions:**
MATT. 20:20-21 - Came to him the mother of Zebedee's children with her sons...desiring a certain thing of him. He said, "What wilt thou?" ....
[Did John and James come to Jesus and speak to him, or did their mother speak to Jesus?]
See also under MATT. 20:20-21.

**Perplexing:**
Why did Jesus ask James and John what they wanted, when he could read people's minds (see under MATT. 20:20-21 - Contradictions)?

10:37 - THEY SAID, "GRANT UNTO US THAT WE MAY SIT, ONE ON THY RIGHT HAND, AND THE OTHER ON THY LEFT HAND, IN THY GLORY."

**Contradictions:**
MATT. 20:21 - ...She saith, "Grant that these my two sons may sit, one on thy right hand, the other on the left, in thy kingdom."
[Did James and John request that one of them sit on Jesus' right and the other on Jesus' left, or did their mother make the request?]
MARK 9:31-32 - Jesus said that he would be killed, but would rise the third day. They understood not that saying.
[Did, at least, James and John understand that Jesus would die, be resurrected, and go to his kingdom, or did they not understand?]

10:45 - JESUS: "THE SON OF MAN CAME NOT TO BE MINISTERED UNTO, BUT TO MINISTER, AND TO GIVE HIS LIFE A RANSOM FOR MANY."

**Contradictions:** See under MATT. 9:13 and 10:34..

**Perplexing:** See under MATT. 9:13.

10:46-47 - ...AS HE WENT OUT OF JERICHO WITH HIS DISCIPLES AND A GREAT NUMBER OF PEOPLE, BLIND BARTIMAEUS, THE SON OF TIMAEUS, SAT BY THE HIGHWAY SIDE BEGGING. WHEN HE HEARD THAT IT WAS JESUS OF NAZARETH, HE BEGAN TO CRY OUT, "JESUS, THOU SON OF DAVID, HAVE MERCY ON ME."

**Contradictions:**
MATT. 20:29-30 - As they departed from Jericho.... Two blind men sitting by the wayside...cried out, "Have mercy on us, O Lord, thou Son of David."
[Upon leaving Jericho, did Jesus encounter one blind man, or two blind men?]
LUKE 18:35-38 - As he was come nigh unto Jericho, a blind man sat by the wayside begging.... He cried, "Jesus thou Son of David, have mercy on me."
[Did Jesus encounter a blind man upon leaving Jericho, or upon nearing Jericho?]

**Perplexing:**
Why did the blind man refer to Jesus as the Son of David? MARK had not mentioned either David or Joseph, nor given a genealogy for Jesus. Furthermore, neither Jesus nor his disciples had referred to him as the son of David.
See also under MATT. 9:27.

**Old Testament:** See under MATT. 20:29.

10:51 - JESUS SAID, "WHAT WILT THOU THAT I SHOULD DO UNTO THEE?" THE BLIND MAN SAID, "LORD, THAT I MIGHT RECEIVE MY SIGHT."

**Contradictions:** See under MATT. 20:20-21.

**Perplexing:** See under MATT. 20:32.

10:52 - JESUS SAID, "GO THY WAY; THY FAITH HATH MADE THEE WHOLE." IMMEDIATELY HE RECEIVED HIS SIGHT....

**Contradictions:**
MATT. 20:34 - Jesus had compassion on them, touched their eyes, and immediately their eyes received sight....
[Did one blind man gain sight because of his faith, or did two blind men receive sight after Jesus touched their eyes?]
See also under MATT. 20:33-34.

**History:** See under MATT. 20:33-34.

**Perplexing:** See under MATT. 20:33-34.

11:1-2 - WHEN THEY CAME NIGH TO JERUSALEM, UNTO BETHPHAGE AND BETHANY, AT THE MOUNT OF OLIVES, HE SENDETH FORTH TWO DISCIPLES, AND SAITH, "GO INTO THE VILLAGE...AND AS SOON AS YE BE ENTERED, YE SHALL FIND A COLT TIED, WHEREON NEVER MAN SAT; LOOSE HIM AND BRING HIM."

**Contradictions:**
MATT. 21:1-2 - When they...were come to Bethphage, unto the mount of Olives, sent Jesus two disciples, saying, "Go into the village and straightway ye shall find an ass tied, and a colt with her; loose them, and bring them unto me."
[Did Jesus tell the disciples that they would find a colt, or that they would find an ass and a colt?]
See also under MATT. 21:1-2.

**Perplexing:** See under MATT. 21:1-2.

11:3 - JESUS: "IF ANY MAN SAY, 'WHY DO YE THIS?' SAY, 'THE LORD HATH NEED OF HIM'...."

**Perplexing:** See under MATT. 21:3.

11:4 - THEY...FOUND THE COLT...AND THEY LOOSE HIM.

**Contradictions:**
MATT. 21:6-7 - The disciples...brought the ass and the colt....
[Did the disciples find only a colt, or did they find an ass and a colt?]
JOHN 12:14 - Jesus found a young ass....
[Did the disciples find a colt, or did Jesus find a young ass?]

11:5 - CERTAIN OF THEM THAT STOOD THERE SAID, "WHAT DO YE, LOOSING THE COLT?"

**Contradiction:**
LUKE 19:33 - ...the owners said, "Why loose ye the colt?"
[Did certain people, or the owners ask the disciples why they were loosing the colt?]

11:7 - THEY BROUGHT THE COLT TO JESUS, CAST THEIR GARMENTS ON HIM, AND HE SAT UPON HIM.

**Contradictions:**
MATT. 21:7 - [They] brought the ass, and colt, put on them their clothes, and they set him thereon.
[Did the disciples put their clothes on a colt, or on an ass and a colt?]
[Did Jesus sit on the colt, or on the ass and colt?]
See also under MATT. 21:6-7.

**Perplexing:**
Would it not be difficult to climb onto and ride a colt that had never been ridden before? Did all the disciples, or only the two who found the colt place their garments on it?

**Old Testament:** See under MATT. 21:6-7

11:8-10 - MANY SPREAD THEIR GARMENTS IN THE WAY; OTHERS CUT DOWN BRANCHES...AND STRAWED THEM IN THE WAY. THEY...CRIED, "HOSANNA; BLESSED IS HE THAT COMETH IN THE NAME OF THE LORD; BLESSED BE THE KINGDOM OF OUR FATHER DAVID, THAT COMETH IN THE NAME OF THE LORD; HOSANNA IN THE HIGHEST."

**Contradictions:**
MATT. 21:8-9 - A very great multitude spread their garments in the way.... The multitudes cried, "Hosanna to the Son of David.... Hosanna in the highest."
[Did the multitude say, "Blessed be the kingdom of our father David," or "Hosanna to the Son of David?]
LUKE 19:37-38 - ...the whole multitude of the disciples began to rejoice and praise God...saying, "Blessed be the king that cometh in the name of the Lord, peace in heaven, and glory in the highest."
[Did people greet Jesus and shout, "Hosanna...," or did the disciples praise God and say, "glory in the highest?]
See also under MATT. 21:8-9.

**Language:** See under MATT. 21:8-9.

**Old Testament:** See under MATT. 21:8-9.

**Perplexing:** See under MATT. 21:8-9.

11:11 - JESUS ENTERED JERUSALEM AND THE TEMPLE; WHEN HE HAD LOOKED UPON ALL THINGS, EVENTIDE WAS COME; HE WENT UNTO BETHANY WITH THE TWELVE.

**Contradictions:**
MATT. 21:10-12 - When he was come into Jerusalem.... Jesus went into the temple of God, cast out all that sold and bought in the temple, overthrew the tables of the moneychangers, and the seats of them that sold doves.
LUKE 19:45 - [When Jesus came to Jerusalem from Jericho] He went into the temple, and began to cast out them that sold therein, and them that bought.
[Did Jesus go into the temple and then return to Bethany, before casting out the merchants the next day in MARK 11:15, or did he cast out the merchants from the temple before spending the night in Bethany?]
See also under MATT. 21:12-13.

**Perplexing:**
What happened to all the people who had been following Jesus?

11:12-14 - ON THE MORROW, WHEN THEY WERE COME FROM BETHANY, HE WAS HUNGRY; SEEING A FIG TREE...WHEN HE CAME TO IT, HE FOUND NOTHING BUT LEAVES, FOR THE TIME OF FIGS WAS NOT YET. JESUS SAID, "NO MAN EAT OF THEE HEREAFTER FOREVER." HIS DISCIPLES HEARD IT.

**Contradictions:**
MATT. 21:12-19 - Jesus cursed the fig tree after having cast the merchants out of the temple.
[Did Jesus curse the fig tree before, or after ejecting merchants from the temple? (It is not until MARK 11:15 that Jesus casts out the merchants.)]
See also under MATT. 21:17-19.

**Perplexing:**
Why did Jesus fail to know that it was not yet the season for figs? Why did the Son of God curse a fig tree for complying with nature and not bearing fruit out of season? The fig tree was doing what it had to do — obey the law established for it by God. Why did Jesus not bless the tree to bear fruit all year?
See also under MATT. 21:17-19.

**Old Testament:** See under MATT. 21:17-19.

11:15-16 - THEY COME TO JERUSALEM; JESUS WENT INTO THE TEMPLE, AND BEGAN TO CAST OUT THEM THAT SOLD AND BOUGHT IN THE TEMPLE, AND OVERTHREW THE TABLES OF THE MONEYCHANGERS, AND THE SEATS OF THEM THAT SOLD DOVES; AND WOULD NOT SUFFER THAT ANY MAN SHOULD CARRY ANY VESSEL THROUGH THE TEMPLE.

**Contradictions:** See under 11:11 and under MATT. 21:12-13.

**Perplexing:** See under MATT. 21:12-13.

**History:** See under MATT. 21:12-13.

11:17 - HE TAUGHT, SAYING, "IS IT NOT WRITTEN, 'MY HOUSE SHALL BE CALLED OF ALL NATIONS THE HOUSE OF PRAYER? BUT YE HAVE MADE IT A DEN OF THIEVES.'"

**Old Testament:** See under MATT. 21:12-13.

**Contradiction:** See under MATT. 21:12-13.

11:18 - THE SCRIBES AND CHIEF PRIESTS HEARD IT, AND SOUGHT HOW THEY MIGHT DESTROY HIM, FOR THEY FEARED HIM, BECAUSE ALL THE PEOPLE WAS ASTONISHED AT HIS DOCTRINE.

**Perplexing:**
Why would the scribes and priests want to destroy Jesus, someone who could perform amazing miracles - heal the blind, deaf, and lame, cure leprosy and other afflictions, and even raise the dead? Why did they not want to befriend him and have him perform miracles to help them and their families? Why were they not fearful of doing anything to offend someone who had miraculous powers?
See also under MATT. 12:14.

11:22-23 - JESUS SAITH, "HAVE FAITH IN GOD. WHOSOEVER SHALL SAY UNTO THIS MOUNTAIN, 'BE THOU REMOVED, AND BE THOU CAST INTO THE SEA,' AND SHALL NOT DOUBT IN HIS HEART, BUT SHALL BELIEVE THAT THOSE THINGS WHICH HE SAITH SHALL COME TO PASS, HE SHALL HAVE WHATSOEVER HE SAITH."

**Perplexing:** See under MATT. 21:21.

11:24 - JESUS: "WHAT THINGS YE DESIRE, WHEN YE PRAY, BELIEVE THAT YE RECEIVE THEM, AND YE SHALL HAVE THEM."

**Perplexing:** See under MATT. 21:22.

**Pagan concept:** See under MATT. 21:22.

11:27 - ...AS HE WAS WALKING IN THE TEMPLE, THERE COME TO HIM THE CHIEF PRIESTS SCRIBES, AND ELDERS.

**Contradiction:**
MATT. 21:23 - When he was come into the temple, the chief priests and elders of the people came unto him as he was teaching....
LUKE 20:1 - On one of those days, as he taught the people in the temple and preached the gospel, the chief priests and scribes came upon him with the elders.
[Was Jesus walking, or teaching in the temple when the priests, scribes, and elders came to him?]

**Perplexing:**
Why did the priests and others permit Jesus to again enter the temple and walk around unimpeded so soon after his violent outburst against the merchants, especially if they wanted to destroy him?
See also under MATT. 21:23.

11:29-33 - JESUS SAID UNTO THEM, ".... THE BAPTISM OF JOHN, WAS IT FROM HEAVEN, OR OF MEN?" .... THEY ANSWERED, "WE CANNOT TELL."....

**Perplexing:** See under MATT. 21:25-27.

**Pagan concept:** See under MATT. 3:5-6.

**History:** See under MATT. 3:5-6.

**Old Testament:** See under MATT. 3:5-6.

12:1-3 - HE BEGAN TO SPEAK BY PARABLES. "A MAN PLANTED A VINEYARD, SET AN HEDGE ABOUT IT, DIGGED A PLACE FOR A WINEFAT, BUILT A TOWER, LET IT OUT TO HUSBANDMEN, AND WENT INTO A FAR COUNTRY. AT THE SEASON HE SENT A SERVANT, THAT HE MIGHT RECEIVE FROM THE HUSBANDMEN THE FRUIT OF THE VINEYARD. THEY BEAT HIM AND SENT HIM AWAY EMPTY."

**Contradictions:**
MATT. 21:33-35 - Jesus: "A householder planted a vineyard...and let it out to husbandmen, and went into a far country; when the time of the fruit drew near, he sent his servants, that they might receive the fruits of it. The husbandmen beat one, killed another, and stoned another."
[Did Jesus say that the vineyard owner sent one servant, or three servants?]
See also under MATT. 21:33-36.

**Old Testament:** See under MATT. 21:33-36.

12:4-5 - JESUS: "HE SENT ANOTHER SERVANT; AT HIM THEY CAST STONES, WOUNDED HIM IN THE HEAD, AND SENT HIM AWAY. .... HE SENT ANOTHER; HIM THEY KILLED, AND MANY OTHERS, BEATING SOME, AND KILLING SOME."

**Contradiction:**
LUKE 20:11-12 - Jesus: "He sent another servant; they beat him...and sent him away empty. He sent a third; they wounded him, and cast him out.
[Did Jesus say that two more servants, one after the other, were sent, followed by many others, or that only two more servants were sent?]

12:8 - JESUS: "THEY TOOK HIM [THE OWNER'S SON], KILLED HIM, AND CAST HIM OUT OF THE VINEYARD."

**Contradiction:**
MATT. 21:39 - Jesus: "They caught him, cast him out of the vineyard, and slew him."
LUKE 20:15 - Jesus: "They cast him out of the vineyard, and killed him...."
[Did Jesus say that the son was killed before, or after being cast out of the vineyard?]

12:10-11 - JESUS: "HAVE YE NOT READ THIS SCRIPTURE: 'THE STONE WHICH THE BUILDERS REJECTED IS BECOME THE HEAD OF THE CORNER; THIS WAS THE LORD'S DOING, AND IT IS MARVELLOUS IN OUR EYES.'"

**Old Testament:** See under MATT. 21:42.

12:13 - THEY [CHIEF PRIESTS AND SCRIBES] SEND UNTO HIM CERTAIN OF THE PHARISEES AND HERODIANS, TO CATCH HIM IN HIS WORDS.

**Contradictions:** See under 3:6.

**History:** See under MATT. 22:15-16.

**Perplexing:** See under MATT. 22:15-16.

12:14-17 - THEY SAY, "...IS IT LAWFUL TO GIVE TRIBUTE UNTO CAESAR, OR NOT? ...." HE...SAID, "...BRING ME A PENNY, THAT I MAY SEE IT." THEY BROUGHT IT. HE SAITH, "WHOSE IS THIS IMAGE AND SUPERSCRIPTION?" THEY SAID, CAESAR'S." JESUS SAID, "RENDER TO CAESAR THE THINGS THAT ARE CAESAR'S, AND TO GOD, THE THINGS THAT ARE GOD'S." ....

**Perplexing:** See under 22:17-21.

**History:** See under MATT. 22:17-21.

12:18-19 - COME THE SADDUCEES, WHICH SAY THERE IS NO RESURRECTION, SAYING, "MASTER, MOSES WROTE, 'IF A MAN'S BROTHER DIE, LEAVE HIS WIFE BEHIND HIM, AND NO CHILDREN, HIS BROTHER SHOULD TAKE HIS WIFE, AND RAISE UP SEED UNTO HIS BROTHER.'"

**Old Testament:** See under MATT. 22:23-28.

**History:** See under MATT. 3:7

12:20-25 - THE SADDUCEES ASKED JESUS WHOSE WIFE A WOMAN WOULD BE IN THE RESURRECTION, IF SHE HAD SEVEN HUSBANDS AND NO CHILDREN BY ANY OF THEM. JESUS SAID, "WHEN THEY RISE FROM THE DEAD, THEY NEITHER MARRY, NOR ARE GIVEN IN MARRIAGE, BUT ARE AS THE ANGELS IN HEAVEN."

**Contradictions:** See under MATT. 22:30.

**Perplexing:** See under MATT. 22:23-28 and 30.

12:26 - JESUS: "...HAVE YE NOT READ IN THE BOOK OF MOSES, HOW IN THE BUSH GOD SPAKE UNTO HIM, SAYING, 'I AM THE GOD OF ABRAHAM, ISAAC, AND JACOB?'"

**Old Testament:** See under MATT. 22:31-32.

**History:** See under MATT. 22:31-32.

**Perplexing:** See under MATT. 22:31-32.

**Botany:** See under MATT. 22:31-32.

12:28-30 - ONE OF THE SCRIBES...ASKED, "WHICH IS THE FIRST COMMANDMENT OF ALL?" JESUS ANSWERED, "THE FIRST OF ALL THE COMMANDMENTS IS, 'HEAR O ISRAEL; THE LORD OUR GOD IS ONE LORD, AND THOU SHALT LOVE THE LORD THY GOD WITH ALL THY HEART, ALL THY SOUL, ALL THY MIND, AND WITH ALL THY STRENGTH'; THIS IS THE FIRST COMMANDMENT."

**Contradictions:**
MATT. 22:35-36 - One of them [Pharisees], a lawyer, asked, "Which is the great commandment in the law?"
[Did a scribe, or a Pharisee ask Jesus about the commandment?]
See also under MATT. 22:35-38.

**Old Testament:** See under MATT. 22:35-38.

**Perplexing:** See under MATT. 22:35-38.

**History:** See under MATT. 22:35-38.

12:31 - JESUS: "THE SECOND IS, 'THOU SHALT LOVE THY NEIGHBOUR AS THYSELF.' THERE IS NONE OTHER COMMANDMENT GREATER THAN THESE."

**Old Testament:** See under MATT. 22:39.

**Contradictions:** See under MATT. 22:39.

**Perplexing:** See under MATT. 22:39.

**History:** See under MATT. 22:39.

**Pagan parallel:** See under MATT. 22:39.

12:35-37 - JESUS SAID WHILE HE TAUGHT IN THE TEMPLE, "HOW SAY THE SCRIBES THAT CHRIST IS THE SON OF DAVID? DAVID HIMSELF SAID BY THE HOLY GHOST, 'THE LORD SAID TO MY LORD, "SIT THOU ON MY RIGHT RAND, TILL I MAKE THINE ENEMIES THY FOOTSTOOL."' DAVID THEREFORE HIMSELF CALLETH HIM LORD; AND WHENCE IS HE THEN HIS SON?"

**Old Testament:** See under MATT. 22:42-45.

**Contradictions:** See under MATT. 1:18.

**Perplexing:**
How was Jesus able to teach in the temple after his hostile encounters with the Pharisees and Sadducees, and his violent actions against the merchants? Why would the high priest or chief priests have given him permission to teach in the temple? Why did Jesus refer to the Holy Ghost? It was not mentioned in the Old Testament verse (PS. 110:1) referred to by Jesus.
See also under MATT. 22:42-45 and 46.

**Judaism:** See under MATT. 22:42-45.

12:41-44 - JESUS SAT OVER AGAINST THE TREASURY, AND BEHELD HOW THE PEOPLE CAST MONEY INTO THE [TEMPLE] TREASURY.... THERE CAME A POOR WIDOW; SHE THREW IN TWO MITES [SMALL COPPER COINS], WHICH MAKE A FARTHING. HE CALLED HIS DISCIPLES, AND SAITH, "THIS POOR WIDOW HATH CAST MORE IN, THAN ALL THEY WHICH HAVE CAST INTO THE TREASURY; THEY DID CAST IN OF THEIR ABUNDANCE, BUT SHE OF HER WANT DID CAST IN ALL THAT SHE HAD, EVEN ALL HER LIVING."

**Perplexing:**
How did Jesus know that the woman was a widow? Why did not Jesus or his disciples help the poor widow by giving her some money? Why did Jesus not perform a miracle to alleviate her poverty? Why did Jesus lack compassion for the woman? Did Jesus require people to come to him and beg for assistance? Why did Jesus not eliminate poverty?

**Pagan parallel:**
The Hindu epic, the Mahabharata, stated, "Just heaven is not so pleased with costly gifts, offered in hope of future recompense, as with the merest trifle set apart from honest gains, and sanctified by faith."

13:1 - AS HE WENT OUT OF THE TEMPLE, ONE OF HIS DISCIPLES SAITH, "MASTER, SEE WHAT MANNER OF STONES AND BUILDINGS ARE HERE?"

**Contradictions:**
MATT. 24:1 - Jesus departed from the temple, and his disciples came to shew him the buildings of the temple.
[Did one disciple question Jesus about the temple, or did his disciples show him the temple buildings?]
MATT. 24:1 - The incident at the temple occurred after Jesus gave a lengthy discourse through MATT. 22 and 23 including condemnation of the Pharisees and scribes.
[Did Jesus go to and leave the temple shortly after seeing the widow throw two mites into the temple treasury, or after denouncing the Pharisees and scribes?]

13:2 - JESUS SAID, "SEEST THOU THESE GREAT BUILDINGS? THERE SHALL NOT BE LEFT ONE STONE UPON ANOTHER, THAT SHALL NOT BE THROWN DOWN."

**History:** See under MATT. 24:1-2.

13:3-4 - AS HE SAT UPON THE MOUNT OF OLIVES OVER AGAINST THE TEMPLE, PETER, JAMES, JOHN, AND ANDREW ASKED, "WHEN SHALL THESE THINGS BE? WHAT SHALL BE THE SIGN WHEN ALL THESE THINGS SHALL BE FULFILLED?"

**Contradiction:**
MATT. 24:3 - ...the disciples came, saying, "When shall these things be? What shall be the sign of thy coming, and the end of the world?"
[Did four disciples, or all the disciples ask Jesus about when the temple would be destroyed?]

**History:**
The Mount of Olives was about three miles from the temple.

13:5-29 - JESUS RESPONDED BY GIVING THEM NUMEROUS SIGNS INCLUDING DISASTERS AND THEN SAID (13.29), "WHEN YE SHALL SEE THESE THINGS COME TO PASS, KNOW THAT IT IS NIGH, EVEN AT THE DOORS."

**Contradictions:** See under MATT. 24:3-7.

**Perplexing:** See under MATT. 24:3-7

**Pagan parallel:** See under MATT. 24:3-7.

13:6 - JESUS: "MANY SHALL COME IN MY NAME, SAYING, 'I AM CHRIST,' AND SHALL DECEIVE MANY."

**Perplexing:** See under MATT. 24:11.

13:7-8 - JESUS: "WHEN YE SHALL HEAR OF WARS AND RUMOURS OF WARS...THE END SHALL NOT BE YET. NATION SHALL RISE AGAINST NATION, KINGDOM AGAINST KINGDOM, AND THERE SHALL BE EARTHQUAKES IN DIVERS PLACES, FAMINES, AND TROUBLES; THESE ARE THE BEGINNINGS OF SORROWS."

**Perplexing:** See under MATT. 24:3-7.

13:9 - JESUS: "...THEY SHALL DELIVER YOU UP TO COUNCILS; IN THE SYNAGOGUES YE SHALL BE BEATEN, AND YE SHALL BE BROUGHT BEFORE RULERS AND KINGS FOR MY SAKE, FOR A TESTIMONY AGAINST THEM."

**History:** See under MATT. 24:9.

**Perplexing:** See MATT. 24:9.

13:10 - JESUS: "THE GOSPEL MUST FIRST BE PUBLISHED AMONG ALL NATIONS."

**Contradictions:** See under MATT. 24:14.

**Perplexing:** See under MATT. 24:14.

13:14 - JESUS: "WHEN YE SHALL SEE THE ABOMINATION OF DESOLATION, SPOKEN OF BY DANIEL THE PROPHET, STANDING WHERE IT OUGHT NOT...THEN LET THEM TIIAT BE IN JUDAEA FLEE TO THE MOUNTAINS."

**Old Testament:** See under MATT. 24:15-16.

**History:** See under MATT. 24:15-16.

**Perplexing:** See under MATT. 24:15-16.

13:18 - JESUS: "PRAY THAT YOUR FLIGHT BE NOT IN THE WINTER."

**Perplexing:** See under MATT. 24:20.

13:19 - JESUS: "IN THOSE DAYS SHALL BE AFFLICTION, SUCH AS WAS NOT SINCE THE BEGINNING OF THE CREATION WHICH GOD CREATED UNTIL THIS TIME...."

**Old Testament:** See under MATT. 24:21.

**Perplexing:** See under MATT. 24:21.

13:20 - JESUS: "...NO FLESH SHOULD BE SAVED, BUT FOR THE ELECT'S SAKE, WHOM HE HATH CHOSEN...."

**Perplexing:** See under MATT. 24:22.

13:24-25 - JESUS: "IN THOSE DAYS AFTER THAT TRIBULATION, THE SUN SHALL BE DARKENED; THE MOON SHALL NOT GIVE HER LIGHT; THE STARS SHALL FALL, AND THE POWERS THAT ARE IN HEAVEN SHALL BE SHAKEN."

**Old Testament:** See under MATT. 24:29.

**Perplexing:** See under MATT. 24:29.

13:26-27 - JESUS: "THEN SHALL THEY SEE THE SON OF MAN COMING IN THE CLOUDS WITH GREAT POWER AND GLORY. THEN SHALL HE SEND HIS ANGELS, AND GATHER TOGETHER HIS ELECT FROM THE FOUR WINDS, FROM THE UTTERMOST PART OF THE EARTH TO THE UTTERMOST PART OF HEAVEN."

**Old Testament:** See under MATT. 8:20.

**Language:** See under MATT. 8:20.

**History:** See under MATT. 8:20.

**Perplexing:** See under MATT. 8:20 and 24:30-31.

13:29-30 - JESUS: "WHEN YE SHALL SEE THESE THINGS COME TO PASS, KNOW THAT IT IS NIGH, EVEN AT THE DOORS. THIS GENERATION SHALL NOT PASS, TILL ALL THESE THINGS BE DONE."

**Contradiction:** See under MATT. 24:3-7.

**Perplexing:** See under MATT. 24:30-31 and 33-34.

**Old Testament:** See under MATT. 16:28.

13:31 - JESUS: “HEAVEN AND EARTH SHALL PASS AWAY.”

**Pagan parallel:** See under MATT. 24:35.

**Contradiction:** See under MATT. 24:35.

**Old Testament:** See under MATT. 24:35.

13:32 - JESUS: “OF THAT DAY AND THAT HOUR KNOWETH NO MAN; NO, NOT THE ANGELS WHICH ARE IN HEAVEN, NEITHER THE SON, BUT THE FATHER.”

**Perplexing:** See under MATT. 24:36.

13:33 - JESUS: “TAKE HEED, WATCH AND PRAY, FOR YE KNOW NOT WHEN THE TIME IS.”

**Perplexing:** See under MATT. 24:44.

14:1 - AFTER TWO DAYS WAS THE FEAST OF PASSOVER, AND OF UNLEAVENED BREAD. THE CHIEF PRIESTS AND SCRIBES SOUGHT HOW THEY MIGHT TAKE HIM BY CRAFT AND PUT HIM TO DEATH.

**History:** See under MATT. 26:2.

**Perplexing:** See under MATT. 26:3-4.

14:3 - BEING IN BETHANY IN THE HOUSE OF SIMON THE LEPER...THERE CAME A WOMAN HAVING AN ALABASTER BOX OF OINTMENT OF SPIKENARD VERY PRECIOUS; SHE...POURED IT ON HIS HEAD.

**Contradictions:** See under MATT. 26:6-7.

**Perplexing:** See under MATT. 26:6-7.

**Pagan parallel:** See under MATT. 26:6-7.

14:4-5 - THERE WERE SOME THAT HAD INDIGNATION AND SAID, “WHY WAS THIS WASTE OF THE OINTMENT MADE? IT MIGHT HAVE BEEN SOLD FOR MORE THAN 300 PENCE, AND HAVE BEEN GIVEN TO THE POOR.”

**Contradictions:** See under MATT. 26:8-9.

14:7 - JESUS: “YE HAVE THE POOR WITH YOU ALWAYS; WHENSOEVER YE WILL YE MAY DO THEM GOOD, BUT ME YE HAVE NOT ALWAYS.”

**Contradiction:**
MATT. 28:20 - Jesus: “...I have commanded you, and I am with you alway [sic], even unto the end of the world.”

[Did Jesus say that he would not always be with the disciples, or that he would always be with them?]

**Perplexing:**
Why did Jesus fail to use his miraculous powers to eliminate poverty?
See also under 12:41-44.

**Old Testament:**
DEUT. 15:11 - Moses: "The poor shall never cease out of the land...."

14:9 - JESUS: "WHERESOEVER THIS GOSPEL SHALL BE PREACHED THROUGHOUT THE WHOLE WORLD, THIS THAT SHE HATH DONE SHALL BE SPOKEN OF FOR A MEMORIAL OF HER."

**Perplexing:** See under MATT. 26:13.

14:10 - JUDAS ISCARIOT, ONE OF THE TWELVE, WENT UNTO THE CHIEF PRIESTS, TO BETRAY HIM UNTO THEM.

**Perplexing:** See under MATT. 26:14-16.

14:11 - WHEN THEY HEARD IT, THEY WERE GLAD, AND PROMISED TO GIVE HIM MONEY. HE SOUGHT HOW HE MIGHT CONVENIENTLY BETRAY HIM.

**Perplexing:** See under MATT. 26:3-4 and 14-16.

14:12 - THE FIRST DAY OF UNLEAVENED BREAD, WHEN THEY KILLED THE PASSOVER, HIS DISCIPLES SAID, "WHERE WILT THOU THAT WE PREPARE...THE PASSOVER?"

**History:** See under MATT. 26:2.

14:13-14 - HE SENDETH FORTH TWO OF HIS DISCIPLES, AND SAITH, "GO YE INTO THE CITY, AND THERE SHALL MEET YOU A MAN BEARING A PITCHER OF WATER; FOLLOW HIM. WHERESOEVER HE SHALL GO IN, SAY TO THE GOODMAN OF THE HOUSE, 'THE MASTER SAITH, "WHERE IS THE GUESTCHAMBER, WHERE I SHALL EAT THE PASSOVER WITH MY DISCIPLES?"'"

**Contradiction:**
MATT. 26:18-19 - Jesus [to his disciples]: "Go into the city to such a man, and say, 'The Master saith, "My time is at hand; I will keep the passover at thy house with my disciples."'" The disciples did as Jesus had appointed them.
[Did Jesus send two disciples to meet and follow a man bearing a pitcher of water, or did he send all the disciples to a specific owner of a house?]

14:17-18 - IN THE EVENING HE COMETH WITH THE TWELVE. AS THEY SAT AND DID EAT, JESUS SAID, "ONE OF YOU WHICH EATETH WITH ME SHALL BETRAY ME."

**Contradictions:** See under MATT. 26:19-21.

**Perplexing:** See under MATT. 26:14-16.

**Pagan parallel:** See under MATT. 26:19-21.

14:19 - THEY BEGAN TO BE SORROWFUL, AND TO SAY ONE BY ONE, "IS IT I?"

**Contradictions:** See under MATT. 26:22.

14:20 - HE SAID, "IT IS ONE OF THE TWELVE, THAT DIPPETH WITH ME IN THE DISH."

**Contradictions:** See under MATT. 26:23.

14:21 - JESUS: "...WOE TO THAT MAN BY WHOM THE SON OF MAN IS BETRAYED! GOOD WERE IT FOR THAT MAN IF HE HAD NEVER BEEN BORN."

**Contradictions:** See under MATT. 26:24.

**Perplexing:** See under MATT. 26:24.

14:22-24 - AS THEY DID EAT, JESUS TOOK BREAD, BLESSED, AND BRAKE IT, GAVE TO THEM, AND SAID, "EAT; THIS IS MY BODY." HE TOOK THE CUP AND WHEN HE HAD GIVEN THANKS, GAVE IT TO THEM; THEY ALL DRANK OF IT. HE SAID, "THIS IS MY BLOOD OF THE NEW TESTAMENT WHICH IS SHED FOR MANY."

**Contradiction:**
MATT. 26:28 - Jesus: "This is my blood of the new testament which is shed for many for the remission of sins."
[Is Jesus' blood shed for many, or for many for the remission of sins?]
See also under MATT. 26:25-28.

**Judaism:** See under MATT. 26:25-28.

**History:** See under MATT. 26:25-28.

**Pagan concept:** See under MATT. 26:25-28.

**Pagan parallels**: See under MATT. 26:25-28.

**Perplexing:** See under MATT. 26:25-28.

**Old Testament:** See under MATT. 26:25-28.

14:25 - JESUS: "I WILL DRINK NO MORE OF THE FRUIT OF THE VINE, UNTIL THAT DAY THAT I DRINK IT NEW IN THE KINGDOM OF GOD."

**Perplexing:** See under MATT. 26:29.

14:26 - WHEN THEY HAD SUNG AN HYMN, THEY WENT OUT INTO THE MOUNT OF OLIVES.

**Contradiction:** See under MATT. 26:30.

**Old Testament:** See under MATT. 26:30.

**Perplexing:** See under MATT. 26:30.

14:27 - JESUS SAITH, "...IT IS WRITTEN, 'I WILL SMITE THE SHEPHERD, AND THE SHEEP SHALL BE SCATTERED.'"

**Old Testament:** See under MATT. 26:31.

**Pagan parallel:** See under MATT. 26:31.

14:28 - JESUS: "AFTER I AM RISEN, I WILL GO BEFORE YOU INTO GALILEE."

**Contradictions:** See under MATT. 26:32.

**Perplexing:** See under MATT. 26:32.

14:30 - JESUS SAITH UNTO HIM [PETER], "THIS DAY, EVEN IN THIS NIGHT, BEFORE THE COCK CROW TWICE, THOU SHALT DENY ME THRICE."

**Contradictions:**
MATT. 26:34 - Jesus said, "Before the cock crow, thou shalt deny me thrice."
[Did Jesus say that Peter would deny him before the cock crowed twice, or before the cock crowed?]
See also under MATT. 26:34.

**History:** See under MATT. 26:34.

14:32 - THEY CAME TO A PLACE NAMED GETHSEMANE; HE SAITH, "SIT HERE, WHILE I SHALL PRAY."

**Contradiction:** See under MATT. 26:36.

**Perplexing:** See under MATT. 14:22-23.

14:33-35 - HE TAKETH PETER, JAMES, AND JOHN, AND BEGAN TO BE SORE AMAZED, AND VERY HEAVY, AND SAITH, "MY SOUL IS EXCEEDING SORROWFUL UNTO DEATH; TARRY HERE, AND WATCH." HE WENT FORWARD A LITTLE, FELL ON THE GROUND, AND PRAYED THAT IF POSSIBLE THE HOUR MIGHT PASS FROM HIM.

**Contradictions:** See under MATT. 26:37-39.

**Perplexing:** See under MATT. 26:37-39.

14:36 - HE SAID, "ABBA, FATHER, ALL THINGS ARE POSSIBLE UNTO THEE; TAKE AWAY THIS CUP FROM ME; NEVERTHELESS NOT WHAT I WILL, BUT WHAT THOU WILT."

**Contradictions:** See under MATT. 19:26.

**Language:**
"Abba" is Aramaic for "father." The Greek translated as "Father," is "Ho Pater."

**History:**
The term, "Abba, Ho Pater," came into use after the establishment of Greek Christian communities.

**Perplexing:**
Why did MARK use a term for God that had not yet come into vogue at the time of Jesus? Why did Jesus again pray that he not go through with his mission? By praying for the "cup" to be taken away from him, Jesus was exhibiting fear, an attribute not in keeping with a divine being. Why?
See also under MATT. 26:37-39.

14:37-38 - HE FINDETH THEM SLEEPING, AND SAITH UNTO PETER, "SLEEPEST THOU? COULDEST NOT THOU WATCH ONE HOUR? WATCH AND PRAY, LEST YE ENTER INTO TEMPTATION."

**Contradictions:**
LUKE 22:45-46 - ...he found them sleeping for sorrow, and said unto them, "Why sleep ye? Rise and pray, lest ye enter into temptation."
[Did Jesus ask Peter why he slept and tell him to pray to avoid temptation, or did he ask all the disciples why they slept and tell them all to pray to avoid temptation?]
See also under MATT. 26:37-39 and 41.

**Perplexing:** See under MATT. 26:40 and 41.

14:39 - AGAIN HE WENT AWAY AND PRAYED SPEAKING THE SAME WORDS.

**Perplexing:** See under MATT. 26:37-39.

14:41 - HE COMETH THE THIRD TIME [VV. 37, 40, AND 41] AND SAITH, "SLEEP ON NOW; TAKE YOUR REST...THE SON OF MAN IS BETRAYED INTO THE HANDS OF SINNERS."

**Contradiction:** See under MATT. 26:43.

**Perplexing:** See under MATT. 26:40.

14:43 - ...COMETH JUDAS, ONE OF THE TWELVE, AND WITH HIM A GREAT MULTITUDE WITH SWORDS AND STAVES, FROM THE CHIEF PRIESTS, SCRIBES, AND ELDERS.

**Contradictions:**
MATT. 26:47 - ...Judas came with a great multitude...from the chief priests and elders.
[Did the multitude come from the chief priests, scribes, and elders, or from the chief priests and elders?]
See also under MATT. 26:47.

**Old Testament:** See under MATT. 26:30.

**Perplexing:** See under MATT. 26:30 and 47.

14:44-45 - HE THAT BETRAYED HIM HAD GIVEN THEM A TOKEN, SAYING, "WHOMSOEVER I SHALL KISS, THAT SAME IS HE; TAKE HIM AND LEAD HIM AWAY SAFELY." ...HE GOETH STRAIGHTWAY TO HIM, AND SAITH, "MASTER, MASTER," AND KISSED HIM."

**Contradictions:** See_under MATT. 26:48-49.

**Perplexing:** See under MATT. 26:48-49.

14:46 - THEY LAID THEIR HANDS ON HIM AND TOOK HIM.

**Contradictions:** See under MATT. 26:50.

**Perplexing:** See under MATT. 26:14-16.

14:47-50 - ONE OF THEM THAT STOOD BY DREW A SWORD, SMOTE A SERVANT OF THE HIGH PRIEST, AND CUT OFF HIS EAR. JESUS SAID, ".... I WAS DAILY WITH YOU IN THE TEMPLE TEACHING...." THEY ALL FORSOOK HIM AND FLED.

**Contradictions:** See under MATT. 26:51, 55, and 56.

**Perplexing:** See under MATT. 26:51, 55, and 56.

14:51-52 - THERE FOLLOWED HIM A YOUNG MAN, HAVING A LINEN CLOTH ABOUT HIS NAKED BODY; THE YOUNG MEN LAID HOLD ON HIM; HE LEFT THE LINEN CLOTH, AND FLED FROM THEM NAKED.

**Old Testament:**
AMOS 2:16 - "He that is courageous among the mighty shall flee away naked in that day," saith the LORD.

**Perplexing:**
Why was the naked man with Jesus and the disciples? Why did the men try to seize him, but not the disciples? Why was he wearing only an easily cast off linen cloth? Was he and Jesus or his disciples engaged in homosexual activity? Why did the other gospels not report this incident? Who were the young men who laid hold on him?
See also under 10:21.

14:53 - THEY LED JESUS TO THE HIGH PRIEST; WITH HIM WERE ASSEMBLED ALL THE CHIEF PRIESTS, ELDERS, AND SCRIBES.

**Contradictions:** See under MATT. 26:57.

**Perplexing:** See under MATT. 26:57.

14:54 - PETER FOLLOWED HIM AFAR OFF, INTO THE PALACE OF THE HIGH PRIEST; HE SAT WITH THE SERVANTS AND WARMED HIMSELF AT THE FIRE.

**Contradictions:** See under MATT. 26:58.

**Perplexing:** See under MATT. 26:58.

14:55 - THE CHIEF PRIESTS AND ALL THE COUNCIL SOUGHT WITNESS AGAINST JESUS TO PUT HIM TO DEATH, AND FOUND NONE.

**Contradiction:** See under MATT. 26:59-60.

**History:** See under MATT. 26:59-60.

**Perplexing:** See under MATT. 26:59-60.

14:56 - MANY BARE FALSE WITNESS AGAINST HIM, BUT THEIR WITNESS AGREED NOT TOGETHER.

**Perplexing:** See under MATT. 26:59-60.

14:60-61 - THE HIGH PRIEST ASKED JESUS, "ANSWEREST THOU NOTHING? WHAT THESE WITNESS AGAINST THEE?" HE ANSWERED NOTHING. THE HIGH PRIEST ASKED, "ART THOU THE CHRIST, THE SON OF THE BLESSED."

**Contradictions:** See under MATT. 26:63.

**Judaism:** See under MATT. 26:63.

**Perplexing:** See under MATT. 26:63.

**Language**: See under MATT. 1:1.

14:62 - JESUS: "I AM, AND YE SHALL SEE THE SON OF MAN SITTING ON THE RIGHT HAND OF POWER, AND COMING IN THE CLOUDS OF HEAVEN."

**Contradiction:** See under MATT. 26:64.

**Perplexing:** See under MATT. 26:64.

14:63-64 - THE HIGH PRIEST RENT HIS CLOTHES, AND SAITH, ".... YE HAVE HEARD THE BLASPHEMY; WHAT THINK YE?" THEY ALL CONDEMNED HIM TO BE GUILTY OF DEATH.

**History:** See under MATT. 26:59-60 and 66.

**Perplexing:** See under MATT. 26:65 and 66.

14:65 - SOME BEGAN TO SPIT ON HIM, TO COVER HIS FACE, TO BUFFET HIM, AND TO SAY, "PROPHESY"; AND THE SERVANTS DID STRIKE HIM WITH THE PALMS OF THEIR HANDS.

**Contradictions:** See under MATT. 26:67-68.

**Perplexing:** See under MATT. 26:67-68.

14:66-67 - AS PETER WAS BENEATH IN THE PALACE, THERE COMETH ONE OF THE MAIDS OF THE HIGH PRIEST; WHEN SHE SAW PETER WARMING HIMSELF, SHE LOOKED UPON HIM, AND SAID, "THOU ALSO WAST WITH JESUS OF NAZARETH."

**Contradictions:**
MATT. 26:69 - Peter sat without in the palace; a damsel came unto him, saying, "Thou also wast with Jesus of Galilee."
[Did a woman say that Peter was with Jesus of Nazareth, or that he was with Jesus of Galilee?]
See also under MATT. 26:69.

**Perplexing:** See under MATT. 26:69.

14:68 - HE DENIED, SAYING, "I KNOW NOT, NEITHER UNDERSTAND WHAT THOU SAYEST." HE WENT OUT INTO THE PORCH, AND THE COCK CREW.

**Contradiction:**
MATT. 26:70-71 - He denied before them all, saying, "I know not what thou sayest." When he was gone out into the porch.... [The cock did not crow.]
[Did, or did not a cock crow after Peter denied knowing Jesus?]
See also under MATT. 26:70-72.

**Perplexing:** See under MATT. 26:70-72.

**History:** See under MATT. 26:34.

14:69 - A MAID SAW HIM AGAIN, AND BEGAN TO SAY TO THEM THAT STOOD BY, "THIS IS ONE OF THEM."

**Contradictions:** See under MATT. 26:70-72.

14:70-72 - HE DENIED IT AGAIN. A LITTLE AFTER, THEY THAT STOOD BY SAID, "SURELY THOU ART ONE OF THEM; THOU ART A GALILEAN; THY SPEECH AGREETH THERETO." HE BEGAN TO CURSE AND SWEAR, SAYING, "I KNOW NOT THIS MAN OF WHOM YE SPEAK." THE SECOND TIME THE COCK CREW. ....

**Contradictions:**
MATT. 26:73-74 - ...the cock crew [for the first time].
[Did the cock crow for the second time, or the first time?]
See also under MATT. 26:73-74.

**Perplexing:** See under MATT. 26:73-74.

14:72 - .... PETER CALLED TO MIND THAT JESUS SAID, "BEFORE THE COCK CROW TWICE, THOU SHALT DENY ME THRICE."

**Contradictions:**
MATT. 26:75 - Peter remembered the word of Jesus, "Before the cock crow, thou shalt dent me thrice." ....
LUKE 22:61 - The Lord turned, and looked upon Peter. And Peter remembered the word of the Lord, "Before the cock crow, thou shalt deny me thrice."
[Did Jesus say that Peter would deny him three times before the cock crowed twice, or once?]

15:1 - STRAIGHTWAY IN THE MORNING THE CHIEF PRIESTS HELD A CONSULTATION WITH THE ELDERS, SCRIBES, AND THE WHOLE COUNCIL, AND BOUND JESUS...AND DELIVERED HIM TO PILATE.

**Contradictions:** See under MATT. 27:1-2.

**History:** See under MATT. 27:1-2.

**Perplexing:** See under MATT. 27:1-2.

**Old Testament:** See under MATT. 27:1-2.

15:2 - PILATE ASKED HIM, "ART THOU KING OF THE JEWS?" HE SAID, "THOU SAYEST IT."

**Language**: See under MATT. 26:64 and 27:11.

**Contradiction:** See under MATT. 27:11.

**History:** See under MATT. 27:11.

**Perplexing:** See under MATT. 27:11.

15:4 - PILATE ASKED, "ANSWEREST NOTHING? BEHOLD HOW MANY THINGS THEY WITNESS AGAINST THEE."

**Perplexing:** See under MATT. 27:13.

15:6 - AT THAT FEAST HE RELEASED UNTO THEM ONE PRISONER, WHOMSOEVER THEY DESIRED.

**Contradiction:** See under MATT. 27:15.

**History:** See under MATT. 27:15.

**Perplexing:** See under MATT. 27:15.

15:7 - THERE WAS ONE NAMED BARABBAS, WHICH LAY BOUND WITH THEM THAT HAD MADE INSURRECTION WITH HIM, WHO HAD COMMITTED MURDER IN THE INSURRECTION.

**Contradictions:**
MATT. 27:16 - They had a notable prisoner called Barabbas.
[Was Barabbas a murderer, or was he notable?]
JOHN 18:40 - .... Barabbas was a robber.
[Was Barabbas a murderer, or a robber?]

**Language**: See under MATT. 27:16.

15:9 - PILATE ANSWERED, "WILL YE THAT I RELEASE UNTO YOU THE KING OF THE JEWS?"

**Contradiction:**
MATT. 27:17 - - ...Pilate: "Whom will ye that I release unto you? Barabbas, or Jesus which is called Christ?"
[Did Pilate refer to Jesus as, "The King of the Jews," or "Christ?"

**History:** See under MATT. 27:17.

**Perplexing:** See under MATT. 27:17.

15:11 - THE CHIEF PRIESTS MOVED THE PEOPLE, THAT HE SHOULD RELEASE BARABBAS.

**Perplexing:** See under MATT. 27:20.

**History:** See under MATT. 27:17 and 21.

15:12 - PILATE SAID AGAIN, "WHAT WILL YE THAT I SHALL DO UNTO HIM WHOM YE CALL THE KING OF THE JEWS?"

**Contradiction:**
MATT. 27:22 - Pilate: "What shall I do with Jesus which is called Christ?"
[Did Pilate refer to Jesus as, "the King of the Jews," or as, "Christ?"]

**Perplexing:**
Why did Pilate say that the people called Jesus, "the King of the Jews?" Until now, in MARK, only Pilate had referred to Jesus by that title.
See also under MATT. 27:22.

15:14-15 - PILATE SAID, "WHAT EVIL HATH HE DONE?" THEY CRIED OUT, "CRUCIFY HIM." PILATE, WILLING TO CONTENT THE PEOPLE, RELEASED BARABBAS, AND DELIVERED JESUS, WHEN HE HAD SCOURGED HIM, TO BE CRUCIFIED.

**History:**
Pilate had the authority to release anyone he deemed to be innocent. If he thought that Jesus was innocent

of any wrongdoing, he would have released him without regard to what a group of Jews may have wanted. [See comments under MATT. 27:17; Pilate would not have cared about pleasing Jews.] By saying that he was a king, however, without sanction by the Roman Emperor, Jesus admitted being guilty of treason against Rome. Consequently, Pilate had no alternative but to hold and execute Jesus.
See also under MATT. 27:22.

**Contradictions:** See under MATT. 27:26.

**Perplexing:** See under MATT. 27:15, 22, and 26.

**Pagan parallel:** See under MATT. 27:26.

15:16-17 - THE SOLDIERS.... THEY CLOTHED HIM WITH PURPLE, AND PLATTED A CROWN OF THORNS, AND PUT IT ABOUT HIS HEAD.

**Contradictions:**
MATT. 27:27-28 - The soldiers.... They stripped him, and put on him a scarlet robe.
[Did the soldiers clothe Jesus in purple, or did they strip him and put a scarlet robe on him?]
See also under MATT. 27:28 and 29.

**History:** See under MATT. 27:28.

15:19 - THEY [THE SOLDIERS] SMOTE HIM ON THE HEAD WITH A REED....

**Contradictions:** See under MATT. 27:30.

**Pagan parallel:** See under MATT. 27:30.

15:21 - THEY COMPEL SIMON A CYRENIAN, WHO PASSED BY...TO BEAR HIS CROSS.

**Contradiction:** See under MATT. 27:32.

**History:** See under MATT. 27:32.

15:22 - THEY BRING HIM UNTO THE PLACE GOLGOTHA, WHICH IS, "THE PLACE OF A SKULL."

**Language**: See under MATT. 27:33.

**History:** See under MATT. 27:33.

15:23 - THEY GAVE HIM TO DRINK WINE MINGLED WITH MYRRH, BUT HE RECEIVED IT NOT.

**Contradictions:**
MATT. 27:34 - They gave him vinegar mingled with gall; when he tasted thereof, he would not drink.
[Was Jesus given wine mingled with myrrh, or vinegar mingled with gall?]
[Did Jesus refuse it, or did he taste it?]

15:24 - WHEN THEY HAD CRUCIFIED HIM, THEY PARTED HIS GARMENTS, CASTING LOTS UPON THEM, WHAT EVERY MAN SHOULD TAKE.

**Contradictions:** See under MATT. 27:35.

**Old Testament:** See under MATT. 27:35.

**History:** See under MATT. 27:35.

**Perplexing:** See under MATT. 27:35.

**Language**: See under MATT. 27:35.

15:25 - IT WAS THE THIRD HOUR, AND THEY CRUCIFIED HIM.

**Contradictions:**
JOHN 19:14-18 - It was the preparation of the passover and about the sixth hour.... .... They took Jesus and led him away. ...into the place of a skull, called in the Hebrew "Golgotha," where they crucified him....
[Was Jesus crucified during the third hour, or after the sixth hour?]
[Was the crucifixion after the day of the preparation of Passover (MARK 14:12; MATT. 24:17; LUKE 22:8), or was it on the preparation day? That is, was the crucifixion on Passover day, or was it the day before?]
[Did the third hour come after Jesus had been taken to Golgotha (MARK 15:22), or did the sixth hour come before Jesus had been taken to Golgotha?]

**Perplexing:**
Why is there uncertainty about the day and time of the crucifixion?

15:26 - THE SUPERSCRIPTION OF HIS ACCUSATION WAS WRITTEN OVER, "THE KING OF THE JEWS."

**Contradictions:**
MATT. 27:37 - Set up over his head his accusation written, "THIS IS JESUS THE KING OF THE JEWS."
LUKE 23:38 - A superscription was written over him in Greek, Latin, and Hebrew, "THIS IS THE KING OF THE JEWS."
JOHN 19:19 - Pilate wrote a title, and put it on the cross: "JESUS OF NAZARETH THE KING OF THE JEWS."
[Was the superscription reported in MARK, MATT., LUKE, or JOHN written over Jesus?]

**Perplexing:**
If each of the gospel writers had been with Jesus and had seen the cross, why did they each report seeing a different inscription on it?
See also under MATT. 27:37-38.

**History:** See under MATT. 27:35.

15:27 - WITH HIM THEY CRUCIFY TWO THIEVES....

**Pagan parallel:** See under MATT. 27:38.

15:28 - THE SCRIPTURE WAS FULFILLED, WHICH SAITH, "HE WAS NUMBERED WITH THE TRANSGESSORS."

**Old Testament:**

ISA. 53:12 - "...he was numbered with the transgressors...."

15:29 - THEY THAT PASSED BY RAILED ON HIM....

**Old Testament:** See under MATT. 27:39.

**Pagan parallel:** See under MATT. 27:39.

**Perplexing:** See under MATT. 27:39.

15:31-32 - THE CHIEF PRIESTS MOCKING SAID WITH THE SCRIBES ".... LET CHRIST THE KING OF ISRAEL DESCEND NOW FROM THE CROSS, THAT WE MAY SEE AND BELIEVE." THEY THAT WERE CRUCIFIED WITH HIM REVILED HIM.

**Contradictions:**
MATT. 27:41-42 - The chief priests mocking him, with the scribes and elders, said, "...if he be the King of Israel, let him now come down from the cross, and we will believe him."
[Did the chief priests and others refer to Jesus as, "Christ the King of Israel," or did they say, "if he be the King of Israel?"
See also under MATT. 27:41-42 and 44.

**Perplexing:** See under MATT. 27:41-42.

15:33 - WHEN THE SIXTH HOUR WAS COME, THERE WAS DARKNESS OVER THE WHOLE LAND UNTIL THE NINTH HOUR.

**History:** See under MATT. 27:45.

**Perplexing:** See under MATT. 27:45.

**Pagan parallels**: See under MATT. 27:45.

15:34 - AT THE NINTH HOUR JESUS CRIED WITH A LOUD VOICE, "ELOI, LAMA SA-BACHTHA-NI?" WHICH IS, "MY GOD, MY GOD, WHY HAST THOU FORSAKEN ME?"

**Language:**
The words spoken by Jesus are in Aramaic.

**Old Testament:** See under MATT. 27:46.

**Contradictions:**
MATT. 27:46 - About the ninth hour Jesus cried, "Eli, Eli, lama sa-bachtha-ni?" That is, "My God, my God, why hast Thou forsaken me?"
[Did Jesus use the Aramaic, "Eloi," meaning, "God," or did he use, "Eli," the Greek transliteration of the Hebrew in the PS. 22:1 verse (see Old Testament under MATT. 27:46)?]
See also Under MATT. 27:46.

**Perplexing:** See under MATT. 27:46.

**History:** See under MATT. 27:35.

15:39 - WHEN THE CENTURION...SAW THAT HE CRIED OUT, AND GAVE UP THE GHOST, HE SAID, "TRULY THIS WAS THE SON OF GOD."

**Contradictions:**
MATT. 27:51-54 - The veil of the temple was rent in twain...the earth did quake, and the rocks were rent. .... When the centurion and they with him watching Jesus, saw the earthquake, and those things that were done, they feared greatly saying, "Truly this was the Son of God."
[Did the centurion say that Jesus was the Son of God when he saw Jesus cry out, or did he and others say it after seeing an earthquake?]
See also under MATT. 27:50 and 54.

**Perplexing:**
Why did the centurion say that Jesus was the Son of God after seeing (hearing) him ask why God had forsaken him?
See also under MATT. 27:54.

**History:** See under MATT. 8:29.

15:40 - THERE WERE ALSO WOMEN LOOKING ON AFAR OFF; AMONG WHOM WAS MARY MAGDALENE, AND MARY THE MOTHER OF JAMES THE LESS AND OF JOSES, AND SALOME."

**Contradictions:** See under MATT. 27:55-56.

**Pagan concept:** See under MATT. 27:55-56.

**Perplexing:** See under MATT. 27:55-56.

15:42-43 - WHEN EVEN WAS COME...JOSEPH OF ARIMATHAEA...WENT BOLDLY UNTO PILATE, AND CRAVED THE BODY OF JESUS.

**Contradiction:**
MATT. 27:57-58 - Joseph...went to Pilate and begged the body of Jesus. ....
LUKE 23:52 - This man [Joseph] went unto Pilate, and begged the body of Jesus.

JOHN 19:38 - Joseph besought Pilate that he might take the body of Jesus.
[Did Joseph go boldly to Pilate and crave Jesus' body, or did he go to Pilate and beg for Jesus' body?]

**Perplexing:** See under MATT. 27:57-58.

15:44-45 - PILATE...CALLING THE CENTURION, ASKED WHETHER HE HAD BEEN ANY WHILE DEAD. WHEN HE KNEW IT, HE GAVE THE BODY TO JOSEPH.

**Contradictions:**
MATT. 27:58 - ...Pilate commanded the body to be delivered.
[Did Pilate, after speaking with a centurion, give Jesus' body to Joseph, or did he command that it be given to him without first speaking with a centurion?]
LUKE 23:53 - He [Joseph] took it down [after speaking with Pilate, but without Pilate being reported to have given him authorization to do so.]
[Did Pilate, after speaking with a centurion, give Jesus' body to Joseph, or did Joseph take down Jesus' body?]
JOHN 19:38 - ...Pilate gave him leave. He came and took the body of Jesus.
[Did Pilate speak with the centurion before giving Jesus' body to Joseph, or did he give Joseph permission to take the body?]
See also under MATT. 27:57-58.

15:46 - HE BOUGHT FINE LINEN, TOOK HIM DOWN, WRAPPED HIM IN THE LINEN, AND LAID HIM IN A SEPULCHRE WHICH WAS HEWN OUT OF A ROCK, AND ROLLED A STONE UNTO THE DOOR.

**Contradictions:** See under MATT. 27:59-60.

**Perplexing:** See under MATT. 27:59-60.

**Pagan parallel:** See under MATT. 27:59-60.

15:47 - MARY MAGDALENE AND MARY THE MOTHER OF JOSES BEHELD WHERE HE WAS LAID.

**Contradiction:**
MATT. 27:61 - There was Mary Magdalene and the other Mary, sitting over against the sepulchre.
[Did Mary the mother of Joses, or the other Mary see where Jesus was interred?]
See also under MATT. 27:61.

**Perplexing:** See under MATT. 27:61.

16:1-2 - WHEN THE SABBATH WAS PAST, MARY MAGDALENE, MARY THE MOTHER OF JAMES, AND SALOME, HAD BOUGHT SWEET SPICES, THAT THEY MIGHT ANOINT HIM. VERY EARLY IN THE MORNING THE FIRST DAY OF THE WEEK, THEY CAME UNTO THE SEPULCHRE AT THE RISING OF THE SUN.

**Contradictions:**
MATT. 28:1 - In the end of the sabbath, as it began to dawn toward the first day of the week, came Mary Magdalene and the other Mary to see the sepulchre.
[Did three women come to anoint Jesus' body, or did two women come to see the sepulchre?]
See also under MATT. 28:1.

**Perplexing:**
Why did Jewish women come to the sepulchre to anoint a corpse, when according to Jewish belief, touching a sepulchre or dead body would make them "unclean?"
See also under MATT. 28:1.

16:4-5 - ...THEY SAW THAT THE STONE WAS ROLLED AWAY, FOR IT WAS VERY GREAT. ENTERING INTO THE SEPULCHRE, THEY SAW A YOUNG MAN SITTING ON THE RIGHT SIDE, CLOTHED IN A LONG WHITE GARMENT; THEY WERE AFFRIGHTED.

**Contradictions:**
MATT. 28:2-4 - There was a great earthquake; the angel of the Lord descended from heaven, rolled back the stone from the door, and sat upon it. His countenance was like lightning, and his raiment white as snow. For fear of him the keepers [guards] did shake, and became as dead men.
[Did the women see that the stone was rolled away and a young man sitting in the sepulchre, or was there an earthquake, after which the women saw an angel roll away the stone and sit on it?]
[Did, or did not the women enter the sepulchre?]
See also under MATT. 28:2-4.

**Pagan parallel:** See under MATT. 28:2-4.

**Old Testament:** See under MATT. 28:2-4.

16:6-7 - HE SAITH, "BE NOT AFFRIGHTED; YE SEEK JESUS OF NAZARETH, WHICH WAS CRUCIFIED; HE IS RISEN; HE IS NOT HERE; BEHOLD THE PLACE WHERE THEY LAID HIM. GO, TELL HIS DISCIPLES AND PETER THAT HE GOETH BEFORE YOU INTO GALILEE; THERE SHALL YE SEE HIM, AS HE SAID UNTO YOU."

**Contradictions:**
MATT. 28:7-10 - The angel: "Tell his disciples that he is risen from the dead, and he goeth before you into Galilee; there shall ye see him." .... As they went to tell his disciples, Jesus met them.... Said Jesus, "Go tell my brethren that they go into Galilee, and there shall they see me."
[Did a young man (an angel?) instruct the women to tell the disciples that Jesus would meet them in Galilee, or did both an angel and the resurrected Jesus instruct them to do so?]
See also under MATT. 28:5-7.

**Perplexing:**
Why did the young man say, "Behold the place where they laid him?" when, according to MARK, only one man, Joseph, placed Jesus' body in the sepulchre? Why did the young man lie to the women by telling them that Jesus was going to Galilee and would meet the disciples there? In MARK 16:14, Jesus, actually, met with the disciples in Jerusalem, not in Galilee.
See also under MATT. 28:5-7.

**Pagan parallels:** MATT. 28:5-7.

16:8 - THEY WENT OUT QUICKLY, AND FLED FROM THE SEPULCHRE; THEY TREMBLED AND WERE AMAZED; NEITHER SAID THEY ANY THING TO ANY MAN, FOR THEY WERE AFRAID.

**Contradictions:**
MATT. 28:8 - They departed quickly from the sepulchre with fear and great joy, and did run to bring his disciples word.
[Were three women afraid to say anything, or did two women with fear and great joy run to the disciples?]
LUKE 24:9 - [Several women] returned from the sepulchre, and told these things unto the eleven, and all the rest.
[Were three women afraid to say anything, or did several women run to and speak to the disciples?]
JOHN 20:2 - She [Mary Magdalene] runneth, and cometh to Simon Peter, and the disciple, whom Jesus loved, and saith, "They have taken away the Lord out of the sepulchre...."
[Were three women afraid to say anything, or did Mary Magdalene alone tell two disciples that Jesus' body was missing?]

**History:**
Many, perhaps most, biblical scholars believe that the above was the last verse in the original Gospel of MARK, and that the following verses were added at a later date.

16:9 - WHEN JESUS WAS RISEN EARLY THE FIRST DAY OF THE WEEK, HE APPEARED FIRST TO MARY MAGDALENE....

**Contradictions:**
MATT. 28:9 - As they went to tell his disciples, Jesus met them, saying, "All hail." They held him by the feet, and worshipped him.
[Did the resurrected Jesus first appear to Mary Magdalene, or to Mary Magdalene and the other Mary?]
See also under MATT. 28:9-10.

**History:** See under MATT. 28:9-10.

**Pagan parallel:** See under MATT. 28:9-10.

16:10 - SHE WENT AND TOLD THEM THAT HAD BEEN WITH HIM, AS THEY MOURNED AND WEPT.

**Contradiction:**
LUKE 24: 10 - It was Mary Magdalene, Joanna, Mary the mother of James, and other women with them, which told these things unto the apostles.
[Did Mary Magdalene alone tell the disciples what had happened, or did she with several other women tell them?]

**Perplexing:**
Why were the disciples mourning, when Jesus had repeatedly informed them that he would rise from the dead? Why did they not believe him?

16:11 - WHEN THE DISCIPLES HEARD THAT HE WAS ALIVE, AND HAD BEEN SEEN BY HER, THEY BELIEVED NOT.

**Perplexing:**
Why did the disciples refuse to believe Mary?
See also under 16:10.

16:12-13 - HE APPEARED IN ANOTHER FORM UNTO TWO OF THEM [DISCIPLES], AS THEY WALKED INTO THE COUNTRY. THEY TOLD IT UNTO THE RESIDUE; NEITHER BELIEVED THEY THEM.

**Contradictions:**
MATT. 28:16-17 - The eleven disciples went into Galilee, into a mountain where Jesus had appointed them. When they saw him, they worshipped him, but some doubted.
[Did the resurrected Jesus appear to two disciples in the country, or to eleven disciples in Galilee?]
JOHN 20:19-24 - Jesus appeared to the disciples; Thomas, one of the twelve was not with them when Jesus came.
[Did Jesus appear first to two disciples in the country, or did he appear to the eleven disciples in Jerusalem?]
[Did Jesus appear in another form, or as himself?]
See also under MATT. 28:17.

**Perplexing:**
Why did Jesus appear in another form? How did the two disciples recognize Jesus if he was in another form? What was his other form? Why did the other disciples refuse to believe that the two met Jesus?
See also under 16:10, and MATT. 28:17.

16:14 - AFTERWARD HE APPEARED UNTO THE ELEVEN AS THEY SAT AT MEAT, AND UPBRAIDED THEM...BECAUSE THEY BELIEVED NOT THEM WHICH HAD SEEN HIM AFTER HE WAS RISEN.

**Contradictions:**
MATT. 28:16-17 - Jesus appeared to the 11 disciples on a mountain in Galilee.
LUKE 24:33-44 - Jesus appeared to the eleven disciples (plus the two with whom he spoke in LUKE 24:13-31) in Jerusalem. He spoke to them, showed them his hands and feet, and ate with them.
JOHN 20:19-26 - Jesus appeared to all the disciples in Jerusalem eight days after having appeared to all of them except Thomas.
[Did Jesus first appear to the 11 disciples in Jerusalem, or in Galilee?]
[Did Jesus first appear to two disciples and then to all of them, or did he wait eight days after his initial meeting, at which Thomas was absent, to meet with all of the disciples?]
[Did Jesus upbraid them for not believing that he had risen, or did he converse in a friendly manner with them and eat with them?]
See also under MATT. 28:17.

**Perplexing:**
Jesus told his disciples in MARK 14:28, "After I am risen, I will go before you into Galilee." Why did he tell the disciples that he would precede them to Galilee, but then remain in Jerusalem where he met with them? Did Jesus deliberately lie to his disciples? In MARK 16:7, the young man in the sepulchre told the

women, “Tell the disciples and Peter that he goeth before you into Galilee; there shall ye see him.” Why did Jesus fail to know that the disciples would not believe that he had risen from the dead?
See also under MATT. 28:17.

**History:** See under MATT. 28:17.

16:15 - HE SAID UNTO THEM, “GO YE INTO ALL THE WORLD, AND PREACH THE GOSPEL TO EVERY CREATURE.”

**Contradictions:**
MATT. 10:5-6 - These twelve Jesus sent forth and commanded them, “Go not into the way of the Gentiles, and into any city of the Samaritans enter ye not, but go rather to the lost sheep of Israel.”
MATT. 10:23 - Jesus (to the disciples): “.... Ye shall not have gone over the cities of Israel, till the Son of man be come.”
MATT. 15:24-26 - Jesus (to a woman of Canaan): “I am not sent but unto the lost sheep of the house of Israel. .... It is not meet to take the children’s bread, and cast it to dogs.”
MARK 7:27 - Jesus (to a Greek woman): “Let the children first be filled, for it is not meet to take the children’s bread, and cast it unto the dogs.”
[Did Jesus tell the disciples to go into all the world, or just to the “lost sheep of Israel?”]
MATT. 28:19-20 - Jesus: “Go and teach all nations, baptizing them in the name of the Father, the Son, and the Holy Ghost, teaching them to observe all things whatsoever I have commanded you.”
[Did Jesus tell his disciples to preach the gospel, or to teach, baptize, and observe his commands?]
LUKE 24:47-49 - [Jesus said] that repentance and remission of sins should be preached in his name among all nations, beginning at Jerusalem. .... “I send the promise of my Father upon you, but tarry ye in the city of Jerusalem, until ye be endued with power from on high.”
[Did Jesus say to preach the gospel, or to preach repentance and the remission of sins?]
[Did Jesus tell the disciples to go out into the world, or to remain in Jerusalem until they were endowed with power from on high?]
JOHN 20 and 21 - Jesus did not instruct the disciples to go into the world and preach.
[Did, or did not Jesus tell the disciples to go out into the world and preach?]

**Perplexing:**
After having told the disciples in MATT. 10:23, “Ye shall not have gone over the cities of Israel, till the Son of man come, why did Jesus tell the disciples to preach all over the world? How could Jesus have expected the disciples to go all over the world, (1) when most of the world was not yet known to the people of the Middle East; (2) when they lacked the ability to traverse the oceans, of which they were ignorant; and (3) how would they have been able to travel over deserts, jungles, and arctic areas, all of which they were also ignorant?

16:16 - JESUS: “HE THAT BELIEVETH AND IS BAPTIZED SHALL BE SAVED, BUT HE THAT BELIEVETH NOT SHALL BE DAMNED.”

**Contradiction:**
JOHN 20:29 - Jesus saith [to Thomas], “Blessed are they that have not seen, and yet have believed.”
[Did Jesus say that those who believe and are baptized are saved, or that those who believe without seeing are blessed?]
See also under MATT. 19:17-19 (for obtaining eternal life).

**Perplexing:**
If baptism is essential for salvation, why is there no report about the disciples having been baptized? Were they baptized? When? Where? By whom? (JOHN 4:2 said that Jesus baptized not....) Why was baptism, an ancient pagan rite deemed to be important by Jesus? (See under MATT. 3:5-6 - Pagan concept, and History.) Why would the God of the entire universe be so insecure as to be concerned about something as trivial as whether or not mere mortals believed in His existence or that of Jesus? Why would God resort to inciting fear by threats of damnation, rather than offering irrefutable, unquestionable proof of His and Jesus' existence? Why would He damn anyone for refusing to believe that He is as evil and ignorant as He is portrayed in the Bible?
In JOHN 6:44, Jesus said, "No man can come to me, except the Father which hath sent me draw him...." If people cannot be saved unless God has so decided, does He have the moral right to damn those who He decided should not be saved? Is He not responsible for their unbelief?
See also under 4:11-12.

**Pagan parallel:**
If one has faith in the Hindu god Rama, all of one's sins will be remitted, and those who worship him at the time of their death will be forgiven.

16:17-18 - JESUS: "THESE SIGNS SHALL FOLLOW THEM THAT BELIEVE; IN MY NAME SHALL THEY CAST OUT DEVILS; THEY SHALL SPEAK WITH NEW TONGUES; THEY SHALL TAKE UP SERPENTS; AND IF THEY DRINK ANY DEADLY THING, IT SHALL NOT HURT THEM; THEY SHALL LAY HANDS ON THE SICK, AND THEY SHALL RECOVER."

**History:**
In approximately two millennia since Jesus' time, no one has demonstrated the ability to cast out any devils; no one has demonstrated the ability to drink deadly poisons and survive; and no one has walked through hospital wards touching and healing the patients.

**Perplexing:**
Since no one has yet been able to do all the things that Jesus said believers would be able to do, does this mean that no one really believes? or does it mean that Jesus lied? Why do the other gospels not report that Jesus made these statements?

**Pagan concept:** See under 6:5.

16:19 - AFTER THE LORD HAD SPOKEN UNTO THEM, HE WAS RECEIVED UP INTO HEAVEN. AND SAT AT THE RIGHT HAND OF GOD.

**Contradictions:**
MATT. 28:20 - [Jesus said (in Galilee)], "...I am with you alway [sic], even unto the end of the world."
[Did Jesus ascend to heaven from Jerusalem, after speaking with the disciples and saying what those who believed could do, or did he tell the disciples that he would always be with them?]
LUKE 24:50-51 - He led them out [from Jerusalem] as far as to Bethany; he lifted up his hands, and blessed them. While he blessed them, he was parted from them, and carried up into heaven.
[Before ascending to heaven, did Jesus tell the disciples what believers would be able to do, or did he bless them?]
[Did Jesus ascend from Jerusalem, or from Bethany?]

ACTS 1:8-12 - Jesus: "Ye shall receive power; after that the Holy Ghost is come upon you, and ye shall be witnesses unto me in Jerusalem, Judaea, Samaria, and unto the uttermost part of the earth." When he had spoken these things, he was taken up, and a cloud received him out of their sight. ...two men stood by them in white apparel, which said, "...Jesus, which is taken up from you into heaven shall come as ye have seen him go into heaven." They returned unto Jerusalem from the mount called Olivet, a sabbath day's journey.
[Before ascending to heaven, did Jesus tell the disciples what believers would be able to do, or did he instruct them to wait for the Holy Ghost?]
[Did he ascend to heaven from Jerusalem, or Mount Olivet?]
[Were there, or were there not two men (angels?) who spoke to the disciples at the Ascension?]
JOHN 21:21-22 - Jesus' last reported words were to Peter, and were, "If I will that he tarry until I come, what is that to thee? Follow thou me."
[Were Jesus' last reported words given to all the disciples, or just to Peter?]
[Did Jesus ascend to heaven, or did he stay on the earth?]
JOHN 20:14 - 21:23 - Jesus was on earth for at least ten days after his resurrection.
[Did Jesus ascend to heaven on the same day as his resurrection, or after being on the earth for at least ten days?]
ACTS 1:2-3 - Unto the apostles whom he had chosen, he showed himself alive, after his passion by many infallible proofs, being seen of them 40 days.
[Did Jesus ascend to heaven on the same day as his resurrection, or did he remain on earth for 40 days?]

**Perplexing:**
Why did MATT. AND JOHN not consider the Ascension important enough to mention? How did Jesus ascend? Why did Jesus not make his ascension in public for historians, prominent figures, the priests, and others to see? Such would have proved his divinity and spared humanity centuries of religious atrocities and horrors.
Why is there a discrepancy about how long Jesus remained on the earth between his resurrection and ascension?

**Pagan parallel:**
The Hindu deities Krishna and Rama, in human form, ascended into heaven. Similarly, Buddha, Hercules, and Zoroaster ascended bodily into heaven. The concept was later incorporated into Islam with Muhammad said to have ascended into heaven.

**Old Testament:**
GEN. 5:24 - Enoch walked with God, and he was not; God took him.
2 KINGS 2:11-12 - ...there appeared a chariot of fire, and horses of fire...and Elijah went up by a whirlwind into heaven. Elisha saw it....

16:20 - THEY WENT FORTH, AND PREACHED EVERYWHERE, THE LORD WORKING WITH THEM, AND CONFIRMING THE WORD WITH SIGNS FOLLOWING.

**Contradictions:**
LUKE 24:53 - [The disciples] were continually in the temple, praising and blessing God.
[Did the disciples go forth preaching everywhere, or did they remain continually in the temple in Jerusalem?]
JOHN 21:1-25 - The disciples went fishing on the sea of Tiberias, met with Jesus a third time, ate and spoke with him. They are not said to have gone elsewhere.
[Did the disciples preach everywhere, or did they go fishing and stay in Galilee?]

ACTS 1:13 - 8:1 - The original disciples are not reported to have traveled or preached outside of Jerusalem. [Did the disciples go forth preaching, or did they remain in Jerusalem?]

**History:**

There is no secular evidence that any signs (miracles) followed the disciples, that they performed any miracles, or that they preached anywhere.

**Perplexing:**

Where did the disciples preach? What were the signs that followed them? Why is there no record of these signs or the disciples? Why did an almighty God require piddling, short-lived, imperfect humans to speak for Him? Why does He not speak for Himself?

# CHAPTER THREE

## THE GOSPEL ACCORDING TO ST. LUKE

1:1-4 - AS MANY HAVE TAKEN IN HAND TO SET FORTH IN ORDER A DECLARATION OF THOSE THINGS WHICH ARE MOST SURELY BELIEVED AMONG US, AS THEY DELIVERED THEM UNTO US, WHICH FROM THE BEGINNING WERE EYEWITNESSES, AND MINISTERS OF THE WORD; IT SEEMED GOOD TO ME ALSO...TO WRITE UNTO THEE IN ORDER, MOST EXCELLENT THEOPHILUS, THAT THOU MIGHTEST KNOW THE CERTAINTY OF THOSE THINGS, WHEREIN THOU HAST BEEN INSTRUCTED.

**History:**
From A.D. 169-177, Theophilus was the Bishop of Antioch. If this was the Theophilus cited by LUKE (and the title, "most excellent," would imply that such was the case), he would have written his gospel during the second century. (See also under Language, below.) Consequently, he could not have been an eyewitness to any of the events he described.

**Perplexing:**
Who were the "many" to whom LUKE referred? What did they write? Were they the other gospel writers? Why did LUKE imply that he was now writing because the previous writings were unacceptable to him?

**Language:**
"Theophilus," in Greek, means "lover of God." (Some Christians, therefore, have suggested that LUKE was addressing the Christian community, rather than an individual.)

1:5 - THERE WAS IN THE DAYS OF HEROD, KING OF JUDAEA, A PRIEST NAMED ZACHARIAS, OF THE COURSE OF ABIA, AND HIS WIFE WAS OF THE DAUGHTERS OF AARON; HER NAME WAS ELISABETH.

**History:** See under MATT. 2:1-2.

**Contradiction:**
LUKE 2:2 - Cyrenius was governor of Syria. [Cyrenius became governor in A.D. 6.]
[Was Zacharias in the days of Herod the King, during or prior to 4 B.C., or when Cyrenius was governor of Syria, during or after A.D. 6?]

**Old Testament:**
1 CHRON. 3:10 - Solomon's son was Rehoboam, Abia his son....
(Some Bibles use "Abijah," in lieu of "Abia." In 1 CHRON. 24:1-10, Abijah was identified as a priest descended from Aaron.)

1:6 - THEY WERE BOTH RIGHTEOUS BEFORE GOD, WALKING IN ALL THE COMMANDMENTS AND ORDINANCES OF THE LORD BLAMELESS.

**Contradiction:**
ROM. 3:10 - Paul: "...there is none righteous, no, not one."
[Were, or were not Zacharias and Elisabeth righteous?]

**Old Testament:**
GEN. 26:5 - The LORD: "Abraham obeyed My voice, kept My charge, commandments, statutes, and laws."

1:7 - THEY HAD NO CHILD, BECAUSE ELISABETH WAS BARREN, AND THEY BOTH WERE NOW WELL STRICKEN IN YEARS.

**Old Testament:**
GEN. 11:30 - Sarai [Sarah] was barren; she had no child.
GEN. 18:11 - Abraham and Sarah were old and well stricken in age; and it ceased to be with Sarah after the manner of women.

**Perplexing:**
Since having children was deemed desirable at the time, why did God punish these righteous people by keeping them childless?

1:9 - ACCORDING TO THE CUSTOM OF THE PRIEST'S OFFICE, HIS LOT WAS TO BURN INCENSE WHEN HE WENT INTO THE TEMPLE OF THE LORD.

**History:**
The privilege of burning incense in the temple came only once or twice in a priest's lifetime.

**Old Testament:**

EX. 30:7 - Aaron shall burn thereon sweet incense every morning [before the ark of the testimony]....

**Pagan concept:**
Incense was believed to ward off evil or demons.

1:13 - THE ANGEL: "FEAR NOT, ZACHARIAS, FOR THY PRAYER IS HEARD; THY WIFE ELISABETH SHALL BEAR THEE A SON, AND THOU SHALT CALL HIS NAME JOHN"

**Perplexing:**
When did Zacharias pray for a son? If recently, why would Zacharias, who with his wife, was well stricken in years, pray to have a child? Why would he want to be burdened in his old age with a baby? Why did LUKE not report that he had prayed for Elisabeth to become pregnant? Could he possibly have prayed many years ago when they were both much younger? If so, why did God fail to answer his prayer then? The angel did not say that Zacharias would be the child's father; did this mean that the angel or the Lord would be the father? Why was the name "John" selected?
See also under MATT. 1:20 (about angels).

**Old Testament:**
GEN. 18:10 - He [the LORD] said, "...Sarah thy wife shall have a son."
JUDG. 13:2-3 - ...Manoah; his wife was barren. The angel of the LORD appeared unto the woman, and said, "Thou art barren, and bearest not, but thou shalt conceive, and bear a son."
See also under MATT. 28:5-7.

**Language:**
"John" may be derived from the Sumerian, "gan-nu," meaning "red."
In Greek, "John," is "Oannes," which is also the Greek name for the Sumerian water god, "Ea." (Was he to be given this name because of his later association with water - baptism?)

1:15 - THE ANGEL: "HE SHALL BE GREAT IN THE SIGHT OF THE LORD, AND SHALL DRINK NEITHER WINE NOR STRONG DRINK; HE SHALL BE FILLED WITH THE HOLY GHOST, EVEN FROM HIS MOTHER'S WOMB."

**Contradiction:**
JOHN 7:39 - ...the Holy Ghost was not yet given, because Jesus was not yet glorified.
[Was, or was not John filled with the Holy Ghost before Jesus was glorified or even born?]

**Old Testament:**
NUM. 6:2-3 - The LORD: "...when either man or woman shall separate themselves to vow a vow of a Nazarite, to separate themselves unto the LORD, he shall separate himself from wine and strong drink...."
JUDG. 13:4-5 - [An angel instructed Manoah's wife] "Drink not wine nor strong drink...for thou shalt conceive and bear a son [Samson]...the child shall be a Nazarite unto God from the womb...."

**Perplexing:**
Was the angel telling Zacharias that his son would be a Nazarite?

**History:**
Nazarites were people who devoted themselves to the spiritual life in ancient Israel. They were comparable to Christian monks.

1:16 - THE ANGEL: "MANY OF THE CHILDREN OF ISRAEL SHALL HE TURN TO THE LORD THEIR GOD."

**Perplexing:**
Why did the angel say that the children of Israel would be turned to "the Lord their God?" Did he mean that the Lord was the God for only the Israelites? Did he mean that other people had different gods?

**History:**
Polytheism was a widespread belief throughout the Middle East and elsewhere prior to and during the time Jesus is said to have lived.

**Old Testament:**
GEN. 17:7 - God: "I will establish My covenant between Me and thee and thy seed...in their generations for an everlasting covenant, to be a God unto thee, and to thy seed after thee."

MIC. 4:5 - “All people will walk every one in the name of his god, and we will walk in the name of the LORD our God forever.”
[The above verses and numerous others citing the LORD as the God only of the Israelites illustrate the belief that different people had different gods. In the Old Testament, the LORD frequently referred to Himself and was referred to as the God of the Israelites, not the God of all humanity.]
EX. 20:2-3 - God: “I am the LORD thy God, Which brought you out of Egypt, out of bondage. Thou shalt have no other gods before Me.”
[Here, God specifically identifies Himself as the God of the Israelites (Hebrews) who He brought out of Egypt, not the God of any other people? This is the first of the ten commandments of EX. 20; the first sentence of the commandment, however, is almost always ignored.]

1:17 - THE ANGEL: “HE SHALL GO BEFORE HIM IN THE SPIRIT AND POWER OF ELIAS [ELIJAH]...TO MAKE READY A PEOPLE PREPARED FOR THE LORD.”

**Contradiction:** See under MATT. 11:13-14.

**Old Testament:**
MAL. 3:1 - The LORD: “I will send My messenger, and he shall prepare the way before Me....”
See also under MATT. 11:13-14.

**Judaism:** See under MATT. 11:13-14.

**Perplexing:**
If John was to make the people ready for the Lord, why did the Lord allow Herod Antipas to kill him (MATT. 14:10; MARK 6:16; LUKE 9:9)?

1:18 - ZACHARIAS SAID: “WHEREBY SHALL I KNOW THIS? I AM AN OLD MAN, AND MY WIFE WELL STRICKEN IN YEARS.”

**Old Testament:**
GEN. 17:17 - Abraham said in his heart, “Shall a child be born unto him that is 100 years old? Shall Sarah, that is 90 years old bear?”

**Perplexing:**
If Zacharias had prayed as the angel said in v.13, would he not have thanked God and the angel for answering his prayer, rather than showing surprise and disbelief?

**Pagan concept:**
Gods used lower level deities as messengers to convey their words to mortals. For example, in the Greek pantheon, Hermes (Mercury) served in this capacity.

1:19-20 - THE ANGEL SAID, “I AM GABRIEL...AND AM SENT TO SPEAK UNTO THEE, AND SHEW THEE THESE GLAD TIDINGS. THOU SHALT BE DUMB, AND NOT ABLE TO SPEAK, UNTIL THE DAY THAT THESE THINGS SHALL BE PERFORMED, BECAUSE THOU BELIEVEST NOT MY WORDS....”

**Old Testament:**
DAN. 10:15 - Daniel: "When he [Gabriel) had spoken unto me...I became dumb."
Gabriel was also mentioned in DAN. 8:16 and 9:21.

**Perplexing:**
Why was Zacharias punished for asking a legitimate question? If he and his wife were aged, and she had been barren, was he not justified in doubting that she would now become pregnant? Why did the angel not respond by saying that it was God's will, or something similar? Was striking Zacharias dumb, what one would expect from a merciful God? Why did God and the angel fail to know that he would be puzzled by the angel's prophecy? Why did God not speak directly to Zacharias, rather than sending an angel to speak for Him?

1:24-25 - HIS WIFE ELISABETH CONCEIVED, AND HID HERSELF FIVE MONTHS, SAYING, "THUS HATH THE LORD DEALT WITH ME IN THE DAYS WHEREIN HE LOOKED ON ME, TO TAKE AWAY MY REPROACH AMONG MEN."

**Old Testament:**
GEN. 30:22-23 - God remembered Rachel...and opened her womb. She conceived...and said, "God hath taken away my reproach."
In addition to Rachel, Sarah, and Manoah's wife cited under 1:13, biblical women past child-bearing age or who were barren but later had children were: Rebekah (GEN. 25:21); Leah (GEN. 30:9-17); Hannah (1 SAM. 2-20); and an unidentified woman (2 KINGS 4:14-17).

**Perplexing:**
Why did she hide herself? Was she embarrassed to be pregnant at her age?

1:26-27 - IN THE SIXTH MONTH THE ANGEL GABRIEL WAS SENT FROM GOD UNTO NAZARETH TO A VIRGIN ESPOUSED TO A MAN WHOSE NAME WAS JOSEPH, OF THE HOUSE OF DAVID; THE VIRGIN'S NAME WAS MARY.

**Perplexing:**
Why did God wait six months before sending Gabriel to Mary?
Why did LUKE note that Joseph was "of the house of David, " something that was immaterial if God was to be Jesus' Father?
See also under MATT. 1:20.

**Pagan concept:** See under MATT. 1:18.

**History:** See under MATT. 1:18.

1:28 - THE ANGEL CAME IN UNTO HER, AND SAID, "HAIL, THOU THAT ART HIGHLY FAVOURED, THE LORD IS WITH THEE; BLESSED ART THOU AMONG WOMEN."

**Perplexing:**
Why did the Lord highly favor Mary, an espoused (married) woman?

1:31 - GABRIEL: "THOU SHALT CONCEIVE IN THY WOMB, AND BRING FORTH A SON, AND SHALL CALL HIS NAME JESUS."

**Contradictions:**

MATT. 1:20-21 - ...the angel of the Lord appeared unto him in a dream, saying,"Joseph, thou son of David, fear not to take unto thee Mary thy wife, for that which is conceived in her is of the Holy Ghost. She shall bring forth a son, and thou shalt call his name JESUS...."

[Did the angel order Mary, or Joseph to name the child, "Jesus?"]

[Did the angel inform Mary, or Joseph that Mary would bear a son? Neither MATT., nor LUKE say that the angel spoke to both of them.]

**Language:** See under MATT. 1:1.

1:32-33 - THE ANGEL: "HE SHALL BE GREAT, AND THE SON OF THE HIGHEST; THE LORD GOD SHALL GIVE UNTO HIM THE THRONE OF HIS FATHER DAVID; HE SHALL REIGN OVER THE HOUSE OF JACOB FOREVER; AND OF HIS KINGDOM THERE SHALL BE NO END."

**Contradictions:**

JOHN 18:36 - Jesus answered, "My kingdom is not of this world...."

[Was Jesus to reign over the house of Jacob, or was his kingdom not of this world?]

LUKE 21:33 - Jesus: "Heaven and earth shall pass away...."

HEB. 1:11 - Paul: "They [the earth and heavens] shall perish...."

2 PET. 3:10 - Peter: "...the heavens shall pass away...the earth also...."

REV. 21:1 - John: "...the first heaven and the first earth were passed away...."

[Will Jesus reign over the house of Jacob forever, or will heaven and earth perish?]

See also under MATT. 1:21.

**Perplexing:**

Why did the angel say that Jesus will be called "The Son of the Highest?" Jesus was not referred to by that specific title throughout the Bible. If Jesus was the Son of God, how could David be his father (ancestor)? The Jews only recognized a paternal genealogy; maternal genealogies were not recognized or kept, so his lineage could not be traced back to David or anyone else through Mary. [Mary, however, as a cousin of Elisabeth (1:36) who was descended from Aaron (1:5), would have been from the tribe of Levi, not from the tribe of Judah—David's tribe—and consequently, not descended from David.]

Why did the angel say that Jesus would reign over the house of Jacob (the Jews) forever, when they did not recognize him then or now as their king or ruler? The angel implied that Jesus would reign some time after his birth; he did not say that Jesus would be killed, resurrected, and then return at some unspecified time in the future to begin his reign. Why was the angel not truthful with Mary? If Jesus' kingdom is not of this world, how could he reign over the house of Jacob which is of this world?

**Old Testament:**

2 SAM. 7:12-13 - Nathan (quoting the LORD): "...I will set up thy seed...out of thy bowels, and will establish his kingdom. ...and I will establish the throne of his kingdom forever."

2 CHRON. 7:17-18 - The LORD (to Solomon]: "As for thee, If thou wilt walk before me, as David thy father walked, and do all that I commanded...then will I establish the throne of thy kingdom, as I have covenanted with David, there shall not fail thee a man to be ruler over Israel." [The LORD is saying that the future king of Israel will be descended from David through Solomon.]

**History:**
The Kingdom of Israel ended over 2000 years ago, without Jesus ever having reigned over it. Modern Israel is a democracy, not a kingdom.

**Dead Sea Scrolls:**
A scroll identified as 4Q246 mentions a figure who will appear during a time of tribulation and who will be called, "the son of God" and "son of the Most high"; he will be obeyed by all nations. The text, however, implies that he is a villain who usurps the place of God, but who is eventually overthrown.

1:34 - SAID MARY, "HOW SHALL THIS BE, SEEING I KNOW NOT A MAN?"

**Perplexing:**
Why was Mary, who is married, puzzled about the probability of becoming pregnant?
(In the Koran, Mary is the unmarried sister of Aaron and Moses.)

**History:** See under MATT. 1:18.

1:35 - THE ANGEL SAID, "THE HOLY GHOST SHALL COME UPON THEE, AND THE POWER OF THE HIGHEST SHALL OVERSHADOW THEE; THEREFORE THAT HOLY THING WHICH SHALL BE BORN OF THEE SHALL BE CALLED THE SON OF GOD."

**Perplexing:**
Did Mary understand what the angel meant by the Holy Ghost? It is not a Jewish concept.
See also under MATT. 1:18.

**Contradictions:** See under MATT. 1:18.

**Pagan concept**: See under MATT. 1:18 and 22-23.

**Dead Sea Scrolls:** See under MATT. 4:3.

**History:** See under MATT. 1:22-23.

1:36 - GABRIEL: "THY COUSIN ELISABETH, HATH CONCEIVED A SON IN HER OLD AGE, AND THIS IS THE SIXTH MONTH WITH HER WHO WAS CALLED BARREN."

**Old Testament:**
EX. 6:23 - Aaron [Miriam's brother] took Elisheba to wife.
["Miriam" is the Hebrew equivalent of "Mary," and "Elisheba" is the Hebrew equivalent of "Elizabeth."]

1:37 - GABRIEL: "WITH GOD NOTHING SHALL BE IMPOSSIBLE."

**Old Testament:** See under MATT. 19:26.

**Contradictions:** See under MATT. 19:26.

**Perplexing:** See under MATT. 19:26.

1:41 - WHEN ELISABETH HEARD THE SALUTATION OF MARY, THE BABE LEAPED IN HER WOMB, AND ELISABETH WAS FILLED WITH THE HOLY GHOST.

**Contradiction:**
JOHN 7:39 - ...the Holy Ghost was not yet given, because Jesus was not yet glorified.
[Was Elisabeth filled with the Holy Ghost, or was it not yet given?]

**Perplexing:**
Since Mary and Elisabeth were cousins (v.36), John and Jesus also would be cousins. Why then did he and Jesus never acknowledge, greet, or speak with each other as relatives? And, if John, developing in utero, recognized that Mary was present with the embryonic Jesus, why in LUKE 7:19, did John send two of his disciples to ask Jesus, "Art thou he that should come? or do we look for another?"

1:42 - SHE [ELISABETH] SPAKE WITH A LOUD VOICE, "BLESSED ART THOU AMONG WOMEN, AND BLESSED IS THE FRUIT OF THY WOMB."

**Perplexing:**
How did Elisabeth know that Mary was pregnant? She had only recently become so, therefore, her condition would not have been apparent. How did she know that Mary was "blessed" among women? Mary was not reported to have told her anything about what the angel said.

1:43 - ELISABETH: "WHENCE IS THIS TO ME, THAT THE MOTHER OF MY LORD SHOULD COME TO ME?"

**Perplexing:**
How did Elisabeth know that Mary was pregnant with "her Lord?" The angel is said to have told only Mary.

**Pagan concept:**
In many pre-Christian religions, virgins who gave birth to gods were called, "Mother of God," or "Mother of Gods." Some examples are: Ishtar, Isis, Cybele, and Hathor.

1:45 - ELISABETH: "BLESSED IS SHE...THERE SHALL BE A PERFORMANCE OF THOSE THINGS WHICH WERE TOLD HER FROM THE LORD."

**Perplexing:**
How did Elisabeth know what was told to Mary?

1:56 - ...MARY RETURNED TO HER OWN HOUSE.

**Perplexing:**
Why did Mary not return to Joseph? Where was her house? Did she live with anyone, such as her parents, or did she live alone? Where was Joseph? How did Mary travel from the hill country of Juda (v.39) to Nazareth in Galilee (v.26), a distance of at least 50 miles?

1:58-59 - HER [ELISABETH'S] NEIGHBORS AND COUSINS.... ON THE EIGHTH DAY THEY CAME TO CIRCUMCISE THE CHILD; THEY CALLED HIM ZACHARIAS, AFTER THE NAME OF HIS FATHER.

**Judaism:**
Jews, especially those who are religious, tend not to name a child after a living father.

**Perplexing:**
Why did religious Jews (they were relatives and friends of Zacharias, a priest in the temple) want to contravene Jewish custom and name the child after Zacharias? Was LUKE unfamiliar with Jewish customs, or did he make a mistake?

**Old Testament:**
GEN. 17:12 - The LORD: "He that is eight days old shall be circumcised...."

**History:**
Although the origins and reasons for circumcision are lost in antiquity, it is known that at least as far back as 2500 B.C., the Egyptians practiced it. The procedure, however, does not appear to have been emphasized by the Hebrews or made into a religious rite until the time of the Babylonian Exile (6th century B.C.).

1:60 - HIS MOTHER SAID, "NOT SO; HE SHALL BE CALLED JOHN."

**Language**: See under 1:13.

**Perplexing:**
Since it was Zacharias who had been told by the angel to name the baby "John" and who had been struck dumb by the angel, how did Elisabeth learn that the baby was to be named "John?" It is not until 1:63 that Zacharias, still dumb, wrote that the baby's name is "John."

1:67 - HIS FATHER ZACHARIAS WAS FILLED WITH THE HOLY GHOST....

**Contradictions:**
JOHN 7:39 -...the Holy Ghost was not yet given, because Jesus was not yet glorified.
[Was Zacharias filled with the Holy Ghost, or had it not yet been given?]
See also under 1:41.

1:68 - ZACHARIAS: "BLESSED BE THE LORD GOD OF ISRAEL...."

**Old Testament:** See under MATT. 15:31.

**Perplexing:**
Did Zacharias believe that The Lord is only the God of Israel, and that there are different gods for other people? Was Zacharias expressing his belief in the prevailing concept of polytheism?
See also under MATT. 15:31.

**Pagan concept:**
People contemporary with the ancient Israelites were polytheistic, and believed that different groups of people or nationalities had different gods.

1:70-71 - ZACHARIAS: "HE [GOD] SPAKE BY THE MOUTH OF HIS HOLY PROPHETS...THAT WE SHOULD BE SAVED FROM OUR ENEMIES, AND FROM THE HAND OF ALL THAT HATE US."

**Perplexing:**
Why did God's prophecy, as cited by Zacharias, fail? Over the centuries the Jews have been subjected to persecution, violence, and atrocities into modern times.

1:72 - ZACHARIAS: "[GOD SPAKE]...TO REMEMBER HIS HOLY COVENANT."

**Old Testament:**
GEN. 15:18 - The LORD made a covenant with Abram, saying, "Unto thy seed have I given this land, from the river of Egypt unto the Euphrates."
GEN. 17:7-11 - The LORD [to Abraham]: "I will establish My covenant between Me, thee, and thy seed for an everlasting covenant, to be a God unto thee, and to thy seed. I will give unto thee, and thy seed...all the land of Canaan, for an everlasting possession, and I will be their God. .... This is My covenant, which ye shall keep, between Me, you, and thy seed. Every man child among you shall be circumcised. ...it shall be a token of the covenant betwixt Me and you."

**Perplexing:**
Why did God fail to remember and keep His holy covenant?

1:73-75 - ZACHARIAS: "THE OATH WHICH HE [GOD] SWARE TO OUR FATHER ABRAHAM, THAT HE WOULD GRANT UNTO US, THAT WE BEING DELIVERED OUT OF THE HAND OF OUR ENEMIES MIGHT SERVE HIM WITHOUT FEAR, IN HOLINESS AND RIGHTEOUSNESS ALL THE DAYS OF OUR LIFE."

**Contradiction:**
GEN. 22:16-18 - "By Myself have I sworn," saith the LORD, "because thou...hast not withheld thy son, thine only son, I will bless thee, and I will multiply thy seed as the stars of the heaven, and the sand upon the seashore; thy seed shall possess the gate of his enemies. In thy seed shall all the nations of the earth be blessed, because thou hast obeyed My voice."
[Did the Lord swear to Abraham that He would deliver the Hebrews out of the hand of their enemies, and that they would serve Him, or did He swear to multiply Abraham's descendants and say that they would possess the gate of their enemies?]

1:76 - ZACHARIAS: "THOU, CHILD SHALL BE CALLED THE PROPHET OF THE HIGHEST; THOU SHALL GO BEFORE THE FACE OF THE LORD TO PREPARE HIS WAYS."

**Perplexing:**
Why was John never referred to as "the Prophet of the Highest" by any gospel writer?
See also under 1:17.

**Old Testament:** See under MATT 3:3 and 11:10.

1:80 - THE CHILD GREW, WAXED STRONG IN SPIRIT, AND WAS IN THE DESERTS TILL THE DAY OF HIS SHEWING UNTO ISRAEL.

**Perplexing:**
When and at what age did John leave home to live in the desert? Why did he go into the desert? How long was he on the desert? How did he survive and support himself? What did he do? What happened to his

parents, Zacharias and Elisabeth? Why were they not mentioned again? Were they invented by LUKE to give John a miraculous birth? Why was his relationship to Jesus not reported again?

2:1-2 - IN THOSE DAYS THERE WENT OUT A DECREE FROM CAESAR AUGUSTUS, THAT ALL THE WORLD SHOULD BE TAXED. (THIS TAXING WAS FIRST MADE WHEN CYRENIUS WAS GOVERNOR OF SYRIA.)

**Contradiction:**

LUKE 1: 5 - There was in the days of Herod, the king of Judaea, a certain priest names Zacharias....
[Were these the days of Herod the King who died in 4 B.C. or the days of Cyrenius who became governor in A.D. 6?]

**History:**

The first census for taxing purposes took place in A.D. 6-7, after the Romans deposed Archelaus the Tetrarch of Judea, and transferred Judea from Herodian to Roman control. Cyrenius (Quirinius) was named governor in A.D. 6. Taxation by Rome, would not have been possible while Judea was under Herodian rule by King Herod or Archelaus. The first Galilean census did not take place until between A.D. 44-49.
Augustus was Caesar from 27 B.C. - A.D. 14.

**Perplexing:**

Why did LUKE fail to know that the taxing occurred ten years after the death of King Herod, and that it did not affect "all the world," but only Judea?

2:3 - ALL WENT TO BE TAXED, EVERY ONE INTO HIS OWN CITY.

**History:**

The Romans did not require people to travel around the land to the town of their birth to be counted. They required that individuals be registered and taxed in the community in which they were residing.
See also under 2:1-2.

2:4-5 - JOSEPH WENT FROM GALILEE, OUT OF NAZARETH INTO JUDAEA, UNTO THE CITY OF DAVID, WHICH IS CALLED BETHLEHEM; (BECAUSE HE WAS OF THE HOUSE AND LINEAGE OF DAVID) TO BE TAXED WITH MARY HIS ESPOUSED WIFE, BEING GREAT WITH CHILD.

**History:**

The census affected only the residents of Judea, not the residents of Galilee. (See above under 2:1-2.) Thus there was no need for anyone currently residing in Galilee to return to a birthplace in Judea. An order to force people to return to the city of their birth just to sign a tax form would have been difficult to enforce. (Furthermore, the ill, infirm, and elderly would not have been able to travel, and their homes might no longer be in existence or might be owned by others.)
See also under 2:3.

**Perplexing:**

Why did LUKE again emphasize that Joseph was of the house and lineage of David, when God, not he, was reported to be Jesus' father? As Jesus' step-father, his lineage would be irrelevant. LUKE did not say that Mary was of Davidic lineage (see also under 1:32-33); it also would not matter, because Jews did not

maintain or recognize matriarchal lineages. Why did Joseph have Mary travel about 90 miles over exceedingly rough terrain, presumably by ass, during the last days of her pregnancy? Why did God select Joseph to be Jesus' step-father?
See also under 1:26-27.

2:6-7 - WHILE THEY WERE THERE, THE DAYS WERE ACCOMPLISHED THAT SHE SHOULD BE DELIVERED. SHE BROUGHT FORTH HER FIRSTBORN SON, WRAPPED HIM IN SWADDLING CLOTHES, AND LAID HIM IN A MANGER, BECAUSE THERE WAS NO ROOM FOR THEM IN THE INN.

**Contradiction:**
MATT. 2:11 - The wise men found the newly born Jesus in a house.
[Was Jesus born in a manger, or in a house?]

**History:** See under MATT. 2:11.

**Perplexing:**
Why did almighty God fail to provide a better birthplace for His Son?
Why could He not have performed a miracle so that Mary could have given birth under better circumstances?
Why was no date given for Jesus' birth? (See below under 2:8 - History.)

**Pagan parallels:**
The Hindu deity Krishna was born when his father traveled to another city to pay taxes. The Greek gods Hermes and Dionysus at birth were each said to have been wrapped in swaddling clothes and placed in a manger basket. The Egyptian goddess Isis could not find accommodations in a town she was visiting, so she had to give birth to her son, the god Horus, on a bed of reeds.

2:8 - THERE WERE IN THE SAME COUNTRY SHEPHERDS ABIDING IN THE FIELD, KEEPING WATCH OVER THEIR FLOCK BY NIGHT.

**History:**
Shepherds stayed with their flocks which they kept out at night during the warm months of the year. They did not do so in December. Therefore, contrary to the Christian tradition, established by Pope Liberius (352-366), Jesus' birth—Christmas—could not have been in December. The December 25 date was selected so as to make Jesus birthday coincide with that of many pagan deities of the time.
The Orthodox Church, however, opted to decree January 6th as Jesus birth date to coincide with the Egyptian celebration of the birth of one of the incarnations of Osiris.

**Pagan parallels:**
Mithra, Bacchus, a number of Egyptian gods, and sun-gods, most of whom, if not all, had virgin mothers, were born on December 25. It is also the first day after the winter solstice when the days begin to be perceptibly longer, hence the belief that it was the birthday of the sun (and sun-gods) or that the sun had been born again.

2:9-12 - THE ANGEL OF THE LORD CAME UPON THEM, AND THE GLORY OF THE LORD SHONE ROUND ABOUT THEM. THEY WERE AFRAID. THE ANGEL SAID, "FEAR NOT; I BRING GOOD TIDINGS OF GREAT JOY, WHICH SHALL BE TO ALL PEOPLE. UNTO YOU IS

BORN THIS DAY IN THE CITY OF DAVID A SAVIOUR, CHRIST THE LORD. YE SHALL FIND THE BABE WRAPPED IN SWADDLING CLOTHES, LYING IN A MANGER."

**Contradiction:**
MATT. 2:8-11 - He [Herod] sent them [an unspecified number of wise men] to Bethlehem, and said, "Go and search diligently for the young child.... ...they departed...the star went before them, till it stood over where the young child was. .... When they were come into the house, they saw the young child....
[Did an angel announce Jesus' birth to some anonymous shepherds and send them to Bethlehem, or did Herod send some wise men who followed a star to Bethlehem?]

**Perplexing:**
Why did the angel appear to and notify some unidentified shepherds about Jesus' birth, rather than making the announcement to public officials, historians, scholars, or other educated people who could have verified and documented the event? How many shepherds were there? Why were they not identified? Why did the angel lie by saying that the birth of Jesus would bring good tidings of great joy to all people? (The birth of Jesus has led to untold, misery, suffering, persecution, slavery, atrocities, violence, wanton killing, and wars being inflicted on humanity in his name by people professing to be Christians; it gave rise to such abominable horrors as the Crusades, the Inquisition, witch burnings, pogroms, the slaughter of American Indians, and the Holocaust, among other evils. Thus, the vast majority of people did not experience joy, but, suffered terribly because of Jesus' birth.) Why is there no historical record of this meeting between the angels and the shepherds, although, in v.18, the shepherds publicized the event?
See also under MATT. 2:8.

**History:**
Egyptian pharoahs, Roman emperors, and a number of pagan deities were called "saviors." When Caesar Augustus was born, it was written that he had been sent "to us and to our offspring to be a savior, destined to make every war cease...the birthday of this god is become the beginning of glad tidings regarding him for the world."

**Old Testament:** See under MATT. 28:5-7.

2:13-14 - THERE WAS WITH THE ANGEL A MULTITUDE OF THE HEAVENLY HOST PRAISING GOD, AND SAYING, "GLORY TO GOD IN THE HIGHEST, AND ON EARTH PEACE, GOOD WILL TOWARD MEN."

**Perplexing:**
Why does an almighty God in control of a universe enormous beyond comprehension need to be praised? Does this God who gives the world religious hate and violence, wars, terrorism, crime, poverty, starvation, pestilence, floods, earthquakes, etc., and a plethora of diseases including cancer, arthritis, diabetes, leprosy, venereal diseases, AIDS, among others, deserve to be praised? Could the devil have inflicted worse calamities on humanity?
See also under MATT. 1:20 (for angels).

**Pagan parallels:**
Celestial beings sang praises upon the birth of Buddha and said that he was born to give joy and peace to men. When the Hindu god Krishna was born, spirits and nymphs of heaven danced and sang.

**Language:**
Some Bible translations have, "peace to men of good will," or "peace to men favored by God," or similar words, in lieu of "good will toward men."

2:15-16 - AS THE ANGELS WERE GONE INTO HEAVEN, THE SHEPHERDS SAID ONE TO ANOTHER, "LET US NOW GO UNTO BETHLEHEM, AND SEE THIS THING WHICH IS COME TO PASS...." THEY CAME WITH HASTE, AND FOUND MARY, JOSEPH, AND THE BABE LYING IN A MANGER.

**Contradiction:**
MATT. 2:11 - When they [the wise men] were come into the house, they saw the young child with Mary his mother, and fell down, worshipped him, and presented unto him gifts....
[Did shepherds find Jesus in a manger, or did wise men find him in a house?]
See also under 2:6-7, and under MATT. 2:11.

**Pagan parallel:**
Shepherds were the first people reported to have visited the newborn god Mithra.

**Perplexing:**
How did the angels return to heaven? How were the shepherds able to find the manger with Jesus? Why was it not necessary for them to be guided by a star as were MATT.'s wise men? What did they say or do when they saw the infant Jesus?
Did Joseph pay his taxes while in Bethlehem?
See also under MATT. 2:11.

2:17 - WHEN THEY HAD SEEN IT, THEY MADE KNOWN ABROAD THE SAYING WHICH WAS TOLD THEM CONCERNING THIS CHILD.

**Perplexing:**
To how many people did the shepherds tell the news? Why was there no historical record of the shepherds or Jesus' birth? Did God not believe that the birth of His Son was important enough to have documented?
See also under MATT. 2:8.

2:21 - WHEN EIGHT DAYS WERE ACCOMPLISHED FOR THE CIRCUMCISING OF THE CHILD, HIS NAME WAS CALLED JESUS....

**Old Testament:**
GEN. 17:12 - God: "He that is eight days old shall be circumcised...."

**History:** See under 1:58-59.

**Language:** See under MATT. 1:1

2:22 - WHEN THE DAYS OF HER PURIFICATION ACCORDING TO THE LAW OF MOSES WERE ACCOMPLISHED, THEY BROUGHT HIM TO JERUSALEM, TO PRESENT HIM TO THE LORD.

**Contradiction:**
MATT. 2:13 - When they [the wise men] departed, the angel of the Lord appeareth to Joseph in a dream, saying, "Take the young child and his mother, and flee into Egypt...for Herod will seek to destroy him." [After his birth, was Jesus taken to the temple in Jerusalem (where Herod resided), or was he taken to Egypt to escape Herod?]

**Perplexing:**
If Herod wanted to kill Jesus, as MATT. wrote, why did Mary and Joseph take Jesus to Jerusalem where Herod resided? Where did Joseph, Mary, and Jesus stay during Mary's time of purification? Did they remain in the manger?

**Old Testament :**
LEV. 12:2-4 - The LORD: "...if a woman...have born a man child she shall be unclean seven days.... .... She shall then continue in...her purifying 33 days; she shall touch no hallowed thing, nor come into the sanctuary...."

**History:**
In the fifth century, the Catholic Church adopted the concept of "Immaculate Conception" - that Mary had been conceived without original sin. (If so, and if Jesus was similarly conceived as God's Son, why did God not exempt her from undergoing the purification ritual?)

2:24 - AND TO OFFER A SACRIFICE ACCORDING TO THAT WHICH IS SAID IN THE LAW OF THE LORD, A PAIR OF TURTLEDOVES, OR TWO YOUNG PIGEONS.

**Old Testament:**
LEV. 12:6-8 - The LORD: "When the days of her purification are fulfilled...she shall bring a lamb of the first year for a burnt offering, and a young pigeon, or a turtledove, for a sin offering, unto the door of the tabernacle, unto the priest, who shall offer it before the LORD, and make atonement for her, and she shall be cleansed from the issue of her blood. .... If she be not able to bring a lamb, she shall bring two turtles, or two young pigeons, one for a burnt offering, the other for a sin offering; the priest shall make an atonement for her, and she shall be clean.

**Perplexing:**
If, as some Christians contend, Mary bore God's Son and remained a virgin, why did she have to undergo purification, make a sin offering, and need the priest to make an atonement for her? MATT. 1:25 stated that Joseph had sexual relations with Mary after Jesus was born, by writing, "Joseph...knew her not till she had brought forth her firstborn son...." How, therefore, could she have remained a virgin?

**History:** See under MATT. 1:22-23.

2:25 - THERE WAS A MAN IN JERUSALEM, WHOSE NAME WAS SIMEON...WAITING FOR THE CONSOLATION OF ISRAEL, AND THE HOLY GHOST WAS UPON HIM.

**Contradiction:**
JOHN 7:39 - The Holy Ghost was not yet given, because Jesus was not yet glorified.
[Was the Holy Ghost upon Simeon, or was it not yet given? (The Holy Ghost did not even descend onto Jesus until later in 3:22.)]

**Perplexing:**
Why did the Holy Ghost come upon Simeon? Why had it not yet come upon Jesus?

2:27-28 - HE CAME BY THE SPIRIT INTO THE TEMPLE, AND WHEN THE PARENTS BROUGHT IN THE CHILD JESUS...TOOK HE HIM UP IN HIS ARMS, AND BLESSED GOD.

**Perplexing:**
Why did LUKE refer to both Joseph and Mary as Jesus' parents? Joseph could not be Jesus' parent, if God was his father. (Is it possible that in LUKE's original gospel, Joseph was Jesus' real father? Note that in 2:4, LUKE points out that Joseph "was of the house and lineage of David"; there would have been no need for this statement, if LUKE did not view Joseph as Jesus' father.)
Why would an almighty God need or want to be blessed by a mere human? Of what benefit would such a blessing be to God?

2:29-33 - SIMEON: "LORD...MINE EYES HAVE SEEN THY SALVATION, WHICH THOU HAST PREPARED BEFORE THE FACE OF ALL PEOPLE; A LIGHT TO LIGHTEN THE GENTILES, AND THE GLORY OF THY PEOPLE ISRAEL." JOSEPH AND HIS MOTHER MARVELLED AT THOSE THINGS WHICH WERE SPOKEN OF HIM.

**Perplexing:**
Why were Mary and Joseph surprised at Simeon's words? Mary was told about Jesus' divine nature by the angel (1:28-35), and Joseph was told in MATT. 1:20-22. Did they forget? Did LUKE forget? Is it possible that the angel and virgin accounts were not in LUKE's original gospel, but were added at a later date?

2:36-37 - THERE WAS ONE ANNA, A PROPHETESS...A WIDOW OF ABOUT FOURSCORE AND FOUR YEARS, WHICH DEPARTED NOT FROM THE TEMPLE, BUT SERVED GOD WITH FASTINGS AND PRAYERS NIGHT AND DAY.

**Perplexing:**
Why does God need or want to be served by fasting and prayers? Why would He not prefer people to be helpful and kind to their fellow humans? How could humanity survive if all people spent their life in a temple praying and fasting?

2:39 - WHEN THEY HAD PERFORMED ALL THINGS ACCORDING TO THE LAW OF THE LORD, THEY RETURNED INTO GALILEE, TO THEIR OWN CITY NAZARETH.

**Contradiction:**
MATT. 2:19-23 - When Herod was dead, an angel of the Lord appeared in a dream to Joseph in Egypt, saying, "Take the young child and his mother, and go into Israel, for they are dead which sought the young child's life." He took the young child and his mother into Israel. ...he turned into Galilee, and dwelt in a city called Nazareth....
[Did Joseph, Mary, and Jesus go to Nazareth from Jerusalem, or did they go to Nazareth from Egypt bypassing Jerusalem?]

2:41 - HIS PARENTS WENT TO JERUSALEM EVERY YEAR AT THE FEAST OF THE PASSOVER.

**Perplexing:**
Why did LUKE again refer to both Joseph and Mary as Jesus' parents? By so doing, he again implied that Joseph was Jesus' father.
See also under 2:27-28.

2:42-45 - WHEN HE WAS TWELVE YEARS OLD, THEY WENT TO JERUSALEM.... ...AS THEY RETURNED, THE CHILD JESUS TARRIED BEHIND IN JERUSALEM; JOSEPH AND HIS MOTHER KNEW NOT OF IT. THEY, SUPPOSING HIM TO BE IN THE COMPANY, WENT A DAY'S JOURNEY; THEY SOUGHT HIM AMONG THEIR KINSFOLK AND ACQUAINTANCE. WHEN THEY FOUND HIM NOT, THEY TURNED BACK TO JERUSALEM, SEEKING HIM.

**Perplexing:**
Why did they not make sure that the child Jesus was with them before they left Jerusalem? By what means did they travel that they did not know that Jesus was missing? Why did they let a 12-year old child wander away from them? Why did they wait a day before looking for him? How many people were traveling with them?

2:46 - AFTER THREE DAYS THEY FOUND HIM IN THE TEMPLE, SITTING IN THE MIDST OF THE DOCTORS, BOTH HEARING THEM, AND ASKING THEM QUESTIONS.

**Perplexing:**
Why did Jesus fail to ask Mary and Joseph for permission to remain in Jerusalem? Why did he lack the courtesy to inform them that he would stay in Jerusalem? Why did he cause them to worry and spend three days trying to locate him? Why did he cause them anguish? How and where did the 12-year old Jesus find shelter and food in Jerusalem for three days? Why did an angel not inform Mary and Joseph that Jesus was safe and where he could be found?

**History:**
Josephus, writing about himself, claimed that at the age of 14 years, the high priests and principal men of the city came frequently to him to obtain his opinion about the accurate understanding of the law. (Josephus wrote the account of his life shortly after A.D. 93 or shortly after 100. LUKE is believed to have been written some time between 80 and 180. Therefore, LUKE, if he wrote near the end of the first century or in the second century may have been familiar with Josephus' self praise, and decided to attribute something very similar to Jesus.)

2:48 - WHEN THEY SAW HIM THEY WERE AMAZED; HIS MOTHER SAID, "SON, WHY HAST THOU THUS DEALT WITH US? THY FATHER AND I HAVE SOUGHT THEE SORROWING."

**Perplexing:**
Why were Mary and Joseph amazed? Why did Mary refer to Joseph as Jesus' father? Had Mary forgotten about the angel and what he told her - that Jesus was the Son of God (1:35)? Did she forget about the Holy Ghost and about Elisabeth's words to her? Why did Jesus not correct the reference to Joseph as his father?

2:49-50 - HE SAID, "HOW IS IT THAT YE SOUGHT ME? WIST YE NOT THAT I MUST BE ABOUT MY FATHER'S BUSINESS?" THEY UNDERSTOOD NOT THE SAYING WHICH HE SPAKE UNTO THEM.

**Contradiction:**
MATT. 19:19 - Jesus: "Honour thy father and mother...."
MARK 10:19 - Jesus: "...honour thy father and mother."
[Did, or did not, Jesus believe in honoring his mother? He caused her and Joseph sorrow, made them search for him, and did not respond courteously to them.]

**Perplexing:**
Why did they not understand Jesus? Did Mary forget the angel's words? (See above under 2:48.) Were the accounts of the angel, the virgin birth, and Elisabeth added to LUKE's original gospel by later writers? Why did Jesus speak disrespectfully to his mother, and not answer her question? Why did he fail to apologize to Mary and Joseph for causing them worry?

2:51 - HE WENT WITH THEM, TO NAZARETH, AND WAS SUBJECT UNTO THEM, BUT HIS MOTHER KEPT ALL THESE SAYINGS IN HER HEART.

**Perplexing:**
Why did Jesus leave with Mary and Joseph? Did he f inish with his Father's business? Did he go willingly? Did they drag him out of the temple? How were Mary and Joseph able to control him in Nazareth? What kind of child support did God give to them?

2:52 - JESUS INCREASED IN WISDOM AND STATURE, AND IN FAVOUR WITH GOD AND MAN.

**Perplexing:**
If Jesus was the Son of God, how could his wisdom increase? Was he not born with all the wisdom he needed? What additional wisdom was there for him to acquire? How could his favor with God increase? Did he ever return to the temple to continue his Father's business? Did Mary and Joseph ever take him to Jerusalem again? What did Jesus do as he grew up in Nazareth?

**Old Testament:**
1 SAM. 2:26 - The child Samuel grew on, and was in favour both with the LORD, and with men.

3:1 - IN THE 15TH YEAR OF THE REIGN OF TIBERIUS CAESAR, PONTIUS PILATE BEING GOVERNOR OF JUDAEA, AND HEROD BEING TETRARCH OF GALILEE....

**History:**
Tiberius was Caesar from A.D. 14-37. The 15th year of his reign, therefore, was A.D. 29. Pontius Pilate was governor from A.D. 26-36. Some biblical scholars believe that LUKE originally began with 3:1 and that the two preceding chapters were added by another writer at a later date.
See also under MATT. 2:1-2.

**Perplexing:**
According to MATT. 2:1 - Jesus was born...in the days of Herod the king.... LUKE 1:5 - In the days of Herod, the king of Judaea.... LUKE 2:2 - ...Cyrenius was governor of Syria; and LUKE 3:23 - Jesus began to be about 30 years of age.... [If Jesus was about 30 years old when Tiberius was in the 15th year of his reign (A.D. 29), Jesus would have had to be born around 1 B.C., three years after the death of King Herod in 4 B.C., and seven years before Cyrenius became governor in A.D. 6.] How could Jesus have been about 30 in the 15th year of Tiberius' reign and have been born either before 4 B.C. or after A.D. 6?

3:2 - ANNAS AND CAIAPHAS BEING THE HIGH PRIESTS, THE WORD OF GOD CAME UNTO JOHN...IN THE WILDERNESS.

**Contradiction:**
JOHN 18:13 - ...Annas was father-in-law to Caiaphas the high priest that year.
[Was Annas a high priest the same time as Caiaphas, or was he the father-in-law of the high priest Caiaphas?]

**History:**
Caiaphas served as high priest during A.D. 18-36; Annas served as the high priest from A.D. 6-15. Another Annas was high priest in A.D. 48. (Therefore, Caiaphas and Annas could not have been high priests at the same time.)
Thereis no historical verification that Annas was Caiaphas' father-in-law.

**Perplexing:**
If John was filled with the Holy Ghost from his mother's womb (1:15), why did the word of God just now come to him in the wilderness? Did the Holy Ghost fail to imbue him with God's word?
See also under 1:80.

3:3 - HE [JOHN] CAME INTO ALL THE COUNTRY ABOUT JORDAN, PREACHING THE BAPTISM OF REPENTANCE FOR THE REMISSION OF SINS.

**Pagan concept:** See under MATT. 3:5-6.

**History:** See under MATT. 3:5-6.

**Old Testament:** See under MATT. 3:5-6.

**Perplexing:**
Why did John preach baptism, a pagan, not a Jewish, custom, for the repentance of sins? Christianity which adopted the this pagan custom was not yet in existence. In LUKE 1:16, the angel said that John would turn many of the children of Israel to the Lord their God. How could he do so by preaching a non-Jewish pagan ritual? How did John travel? From where did he obtain funds for food and lodging?
See also under MATT. 3:5-6.

**Contradiction:**
MATT. 3:5 - Then went out to him Jerusalem, all Judaea, and all the region round about Jordan.
[Did John travel into all the country preaching, or did people from all over the region come to him?]

3:4 - IT IS WRITTEN IN THE BOOK OF THE WORDS OF ESAIAS [ISAIAH] THE PROPHET, "THE VOICE OF ONE CRYING IN THE WILDERNESS, 'PREPARE YE THE WAY OF THE LORD; MAKE HIS PATHS STRAIGHT.'"

**Old Testament:** See under MATT. 3:3.

**History:** See under MATT. 3:3.

**Perplexing:** See under MATT. 3:3.

3:5-6 - "EVERY VALLEY SHALL BE FILLED, AND EVERY MOUNTAIN AND HILL SHALL BE BROUGHT LOW; THE CROOKED SHALL BE MADE STRAIGHT, AND THE ROUGH WAYS SHALL BE MADE SMOOTH; ALL FLESH SHALL SEE THE SALVATION OF GOD."

**Old Testament:**
ISA. 40:4-5 - "Every valley shall be exalted, and every mountain and hill shall be made low; the crooked shall be made straight, and the rough places plain; the glory of the LORD shall be revealed, and all flesh shall see it together; the mouth of the LORD hath spoken it."
[Note that LUKE added the "salvation" phrase.]

**History:** See under MATT. 3:3.

**Perplexing:** See under MATT. 3:3.

3:7 - SAID HE TO THE MULTITUDE THAT CAME TO BE BAPTIZED OF HIM, "O GENERATION OF VIPERS, WHO HATH WARNED YOU TO FLEE FROM THE WRATH TO COME?"

**Contradiction:**
MATT. 3:7 - When he saw many of the Pharisees and Sadducees come to his baptism, he said, "O generation of vipers, who hath warned you to flee from the wrath to come?"
[Did John call the multitude that came to be baptized "vipers," or did he just call Pharisees and Sadducees, "vipers?"]

**Perplexing:**
The word "multitude" implied that a large number of people were involved; it may be assumed, therefore, that many were Jews. Why did they come to be baptized, when baptism was not a Jewish custom? Why did John call those who came to be baptized, "vipers?"
Why did John imply that the "wrath to come" was to befall the multitude that came to be baptized?

3:10-11 - THE PEOPLE ASKED, "WHAT SHALL WE DO?" HE SAID, "HE THAT HATH TWO COATS, LET HIM IMPART TO HIM THAT HATH NONE; HE THAT HATH MEAT, LET HIM DO LIKEWISE."

**Perplexing:**
Did any of the people obey John? Why have few if any Christians or Jews followed John's order?

3:14 - THE SOLDIERS DEMANDED OF HIM, "WHAT SHALL WE DO?" HE SAID, "DO VIOLENCE TO NO MAN, NEITHER ACCUSE FALSELY, AND BE CONTENT WITH YOUR WAGES."

**Perplexing:**
How many soldiers came to John? Why did the soldiers, who were Roman, come to a Jew to be baptized? Why did they ask John what they should do? Why did their commanding officers allow them to go? Why did John tell them to be satisfied with their wages? Did he want to ingratiate himself with the Roman officials?

3:16 - JOHN ANSWERED, "I BAPTIZE YOU WITH WATER, BUT ONE MIGHTIER THAN I COMETH, THE LACHET OF WHOSE SHOES I AM NOT WORTHY TO UNLOOSE; HE SHALL BAPTIZE YOU WITH THE HOLY GHOST AND WITH FIRE."

**Contradictions:** See under MATT. 3:11 and MARK 1:7.

**Perplexing:**
Since the Holy Ghost was not a Jewish concept, how did the Jews know about what John was speaking?

3:19-20 - HEROD [ANTIPAS] THE TETRARCH, BEING REPROVED BY HIM FOR HERODIAS HIS BROTHER PHILIP'S WIFE, AND FOR ALL THE EVILS WHICH HEROD HAD DONE, ADDED THIS ABOVE ALL, HE SHUT UP JOHN IN PRISON.

**History:** See under MATT. 14: 3-4.

**Old Testament:** MATT. 14:3-4.

3:21 - WHEN ALL THE PEOPLE WERE BAPTIZED, IT CAME TO PASS, THAT JESUS ALSO BEING BAPTIZED, AND PRAYING, THE HEAVEN WAS OPENED.

**Contradictions:**
MATT. 3:13-16 - Jesus was baptized by John, before John was imprisoned in MATT. 4:12.
MARK 1:9 - Jesus was baptized by John, before John's imprisonment and death were reported in MARK 6:16-17.
[Was Jesus baptized before or after John's imprisonment?]
See also under MATT. 3:13.

**Perplexing:**
If John was already in prison (3:20), who baptized Jesus?
Some biblical scholars contend that Jesus was of human ancestry and that it was after his baptism that he became God's adopted Son.
See also under MATT. 3:13 and 14:22-23 (for praying).

**History:** See under MATT. 3:13.

3:22 - THE HOLY GHOST DESCENDED IN A BODILY SHAPE LIKE A DOVE UPON HIM, AND A VOICE CAME FROM HEAVEN WHICH SAID, "THOU ART MY BELOVED SON; IN THEE I AM WELL PLEASED."

**Perplexing:** See under MATT. 3:16 and 3:17.

**Contradictions:** See under MATT. 1:18.

**Old Testament:** See under MATT. 3:17.

**Pagan parallels**: See under MATT. 1:18 and 3:17.

3:23 - JESUS HIMSELF BEGAN TO BE ABOUT 30 YEARS OF AGE, BEING (AS WAS SUPPOSED) THE SON OF JOSEPH, WHICH WAS THE SON OF HELI.

**History:** See under LUKE 3:1.

**Contradictions:**
MATT. 1: 16 - Jacob begat Joseph the husband of Mary, of whom was born Jesus....
[Was Joseph the son of Heli, or of Jacob? (Some theologians contend that Heli was actually Mary's father, thereby, making him Joseph's father-in-law. There is, however, no biblical or other evidence to support such a claim; and as the Jews of biblical times did not maintain matriarchal genealogical records, the contention cannot be considered valid. Since Mary also was a Levite (see under 1:32-33 -Perplexing), she was not descended from David; hence, a genealogy through Mary is meaningless).]
See also under MATT. 1:16.

**Perplexing:**
If Joseph was not Jesus' father, why did LUKE, like MATT., deem Joseph's father to be so important that he was not only identified, but a genealogy given for Jesus through him.
See also under 3:1.

**Pagan parallel:**
Zoroaster (between 1000 - 600 B.C.) was about 30 years of age when he was tempted by the evil god Ahriman.
See also under MATT. 4:3.

3:23-34 - A GENEALOGY CONTAINING 56 GENERATIONS (INCLUDING JESUS), FROM JOSEPH BACK TO ABRAHAM, IS GIVEN FOR JESUS.

**Contradictions:**
MATT. 1:2-16 - a genealogy for Jesus was given that contained 41 different generations (including Jesus, and citing Jechonias twice) from Abraham to Joseph.
[Were there 56, or 41 generations in Jesus' human genealogy?]
See also under MATT. 1:2-16.

**Perplexing:** See under MATT. 1:2-16.

**History:** See under MATT. 1:2-16.

3:27 - ...RHESA, WHICH WAS THE SON OF ZOROBABEL, WHICH WAS THE SON OF SALATHIEL, WHICH WAS THE SON OF NERI.

**Contradictions:**
1 CHRON. 3:19-20 - The sons of Pedaiah were, Zerubbabel [Zorobabel] the sons of Zerubbabel: Meshullam, Hananiah, Shelomith their sister, Hashubah, Ohel, Berechiah, Hasadiah, Jushabhesed....
[Was, or was not Rhesa a son of Zorobabel?]
[Was Zorobabel the son of Salathiel, or of Pedaiah?]
1 CHRON. 3:17 - The sons of Jechoniah, Assir, Salathiel....
MATT. 1:12 - ...Jechonias begat Salathiel, and Salathiel begat Zorobabel.
[Was Salathiel the son of Neri, or of Jechonias?]

3:35-36 - ...SALA, WHICH WAS THE SON OF CAINAN, THE SON OF ARPHAXAD....

**Contradictions:**
GEN. 10:24; 11:12; 1 CHRON. 1:18 - Arphaxad begat Salah [Sala; Shelahl - his only cited son.]
[Was Sala the son of Cainan, or Arphaxad?]
[Was, or was not Cainan a son of Arphaxad?]

4:1-2 - JESUS FULL OF THE HOLY GHOST...WAS LED BY THE SPIRIT INTO THE WILDERNESS, BEING 40 DAYS TEMPTED OF THE DEVIL. IN THOSE DAYS HE DID EAT NOTHING; WHEN THEY WERE ENDED, HE AFTERWARD HUNGERED.

**Contradiction:**
MARK 1:12 - The spirit driveth him into the wilderness.
[Was Jesus led, or driven into the wilderness?]
MATT. 4:2-3 - When he had fasted 40 days and 40 nights, he hungered. When the tempter came, he said, " If thou be the Son of God, command that these stones be made bread."
[Did Jesus fast for 40 days while being tempted by the devil, or did he fast for 40 days before the tempter came?]
MARK 1: 13 - He was there in the wilderness 40 days, tempted by Satan; angels ministered unto him.
[Did Jesus fast and become hungry, or did angels take care of him?]

**Perplexing:** See also under MATT. 4:1-2 and 3.

**Old Testament:** See under MATT. 4:1-2.

**Pagan concept:** See under MATT. 4:1-2

4:3 - THE DEVIL SAID, "IF THOU BE THE SON OF GOD, COMMAND THIS STONE THAT IT BE MADE BREAD."

**Contradiction:**
MATT. 4:3 - The tempter said, "If thou be the Son of God, command that these stones be made bread."
[Did the devil tell Jesus to convert one stone into bread, or did he command Jesus to turn all the stones into bread?]

**Perplexing:** See under MATT. 4:3.

**Pagan parallels:** See under MATT. 4:3.

**Dead Sea Scrolls:** See under MATT. 4:3.

4:4 - JESUS ANSWERED, "IT IS WRITTEN, THAT MAN SHALL NOT LIVE BY BREAD ALONE, BUT BY EVERY WORD OF GOD."

**Old Testament:** See under MATT. 4:4.

4:5 - THE DEVIL, TAKING HIM UP INTO AN HIGH MOUNTAIN, SHEWED UNTO HIM ALL THE KINGDOMS OF THE WORLD IN A MOMENT OF TIME.

**Contradiction:**
MATT. 4:5 - [After having asked Jesus to convert stones to bread] The devil taketh him into the holy city, and sitteth him on a pinnacle of the temple.
[After the incident with the stone, did the devil take Jesus to a high mountain to show him the world's kingdoms, or did he take him to a pinnacle on the temple in Jerusalem?]

**Perplexing:** See under MATT. 4:8.

4:6-7 - THE DEVIL SAID, "ALL THIS POWER WILL I GIVE THEE, AND THE GLORY OF THEM, FOR THAT IS DELIVERED UNTO ME, AND TO WHOMSOEVER I WILL GIVE IT. IF THOU THEREFORE WILT WORSHIP ME, ALL SHALL BE THINE."

**Perplexing:**
When and why were the power, and glory of the kingdoms delivered to the devil?
See also under MATT. 4:9.

4:8 - JESUS SAID, "GET THEE BEHIND ME, SATAN"; IT IS WRITTEN, 'THOU SHALT WORSHIP THE LORD THY GOD, AND HIM ONLY SHALT THOU SERVE.'"

**Language**: See under MATT. 4:10.

**Old Testament:** See under MATT. 4:10.

**Pagan parallel:** See under MATT. 4:10.

**Perplexing:** See under MATT. 4:10.

4:9-11 - HE [SATAN] BROUGHT HIM TO JERUSALEM, SET HIM ON A PINNACLE OF THE TEMPLE, AND SAID, "IF THOU BE THE SON OF GOD, CAST THYSELF DOWN FROM HENCE, FOR IT IS WRITTEN, 'HE SHALL GIVE HIS ANGELS CHARGE OVER THEE, TO KEEP THEE; IN THEIR HANDS THEY SHALL BEAR THEE UP, LEST AT ANY TIME THOU DASH THY FOOT AGAINST A STONE.'"

**Contradiction:**
MATT. 4:5-8 - The incident occurred before the devil took Jesus to a high mountain.
[Did Satan take Jesus from a high mountain to the pinnacle, or did he take Jesus first to the pinnacle then to the high mountain?]

**Old Testament:** See under MATT. 4:5-6.

**Perplexing:** See under MATT. 4:5-6.

4:12 - JESUS SAID, "IT IS SAID, 'THOU SHALT NOT TEMPT THE LORD THY GOD.'"

**Old Testament:** See under MATT. 4:7.

**Perplexing:** See under MATT. 4:7.

4:13-14 - WHEN THE DEVIL HAD ENDED ALL THE TEMPTATION, HE DEPARTED FOR A SEASON. JESUS RETURNED IN THE POWER OF THE SPIRIT INTO GALILEE; THERE WENT OUT FAME OF HIM THROUGH ALL THE REGION.

**Contradictions:**

MATT. 4:11-12 - The devil leaveth him [from the mountain], and angels came and ministered unto him. When Jesus heard that John was cast into prison, he departed into Galilee.

MARK 1: 13-14 - He was...with the wild beasts, and angels ministered to him. After John was put in prison, Jesus came into Galilee....

[Did the devil depart from the pinnacle, or from the mountain?]

[Did Jesus return to Galilee in the power of the Spirit, or did he need angels to minister to him before he went to Galilee?]

[Did Jesus go to Galilee long after John's imprisonment (in LUKE 3:20), or immediately after learning about John's imprisonment?]

JOHN 1:28-49 - In Bethabara beyond Jordan, John the Baptist and his disciples saw Jesus; two of John's disciples, one of whom was Andrew, followed Jesus; Andrew brought Peter to Jesus. The next day Jesus went to Galilee where he found Philip and Nathanael.

[Did Jesus go to Galilee after being tempted by the devil, or after acquiring his first disciples (Andrew and Peter).]

See also under MATT. 4:12.

**Perplexing:**

If Jesus' fame had spread throughout the region, why is there no reference to him in secular historical, political, or other records?

(Some individuals cite two very brief references to Jesus by Josephus. These, however, make no mention of his accomplishments, and did not appear in the Josephus' documents until after they were rewritten by Eusebius in the 4th century.)

4:15 - HE TAUGHT IN SYNAGOGUES, BEING GLORIFIED OF ALL.

**Contradiction:**

MATT. 4:13-23 - ...he dwelt in Capernaum.... Jesus began to preach, "Repent ye, for the kingdom of heaven is at hand." Jesus walking by the sea of Galilee saw and acquired Simon called Peter, Andrew, James, and John as disciples. Then Jesus went about all Galilee preaching in synagogues, preaching the gospel of the kingdom, and healing all manner of sickness and disease.

MARK 1:14-21 - ...Jesus came into Galilee preaching the gospel of the kingdom of God, saying, "The time is fulfilled; the kingdom of God is at hand; repent ye...." He walked by the sea and saw and acquired Simon, Andrew, John, and James as disciples before teaching in a synagogue in Capernaum.

[Did Jesus teach in synagogues before, or after obtaining disciples?]

[Did he begin teaching in synagogues when he entered Galilee, or did he first travel around Galilee preaching that the kingdom of God/heaven was at hand and that one should repent?]

JOHN 1:43-45 - [After acquiring Andrew and Peter as disciples] Jesus would go into Galilee, findeth Philip, and saith, "Follow me." Philip findeth Nathanael....

[Did Jesus go to Galilee and teach in synagogues, or did he go and meet Philip and Nathnanael there before teaching in synagogues?]

**Perplexing:**
How was Jesus able to obtain permission from the presiding priests to teach in the synagogues?

4:17-19 - THERE WAS DELIVERED UNTO HIM THE BOOK OF ESAIAS [ISAIAH]. ...HE FOUND THE PLACE WHERE IT WAS WRITTEN, "THE SPIRIT OF THE LORD IS UPON ME, BECAUSE HE HATH ANOINTED ME TO PREACH THE GOSPEL TO THE POOR; HE HATH SENT ME TO HEAL THE BROKENHEARTED, TO PREACH DELIVERANCE TO THE CAPTIVES, AND RECOVERING SIGHT TO THE BLIND, TO SET AT LIBERTY THEM THAT ARE BRUISED, TO PREACH THE ACCEPTABLE YEAR OF THE LORD."

**Old Testament:**
ISA. 61:1-3, Isaiah: "The spirit of the Lord God is upon me, because the LORD hath anointed me to preach good tidings unto the meek; He hath sent me to bind up the brokenhearted, to proclaim liberty to the captives, and the opening of the prison to them that are bound; to proclaim the acceptable year of the LORD, and the day of vengeance of our God; to comfort all that mourn; to appoint unto them that mourn in Zion, to give unto them beauty for ashes, the oil of joy for mourning, the garment of praise for the spirit of heaviness, that they might be called trees of righteousness, the planting of the LORD, that He might be glorified."

**Perplexing:**
Why did Jesus add to the verse the phrases about being anointed and the blind recovering their sight? Why did Jesus fail to recite the verses in their entirety?

4:21 - HE BEGAN TO SAY, "THIS DAY IS THIS SCRIPTURE FULFILLED IN YOUR EARS."

**Perplexing:**
The words in ISA. were spoken by Isaiah referring to himself. Why did Jesus apply the words to himself, thereby, equating himself with Isaiah?

4:22 - ALL BEAR HIM WITNESS, AND WONDERED AT THE GRACIOUS WORDS.... THEY SAID, "IS NOT THIS JOSEPH'S SON?"

**Perplexing:**
Why did the people fail to correct Jesus' reading of ISA.? Why did they fail to ask him why he was equating himself with Isaiah? When and where did Jesus learn to read? Who taught him?

4:23 - HE SAID, "YE WILL SURELY SAY UNTO ME THIS PROVERB, 'PHYSICIAN HEAL THYSELF; WHATSOEVER WE HAVE HEARD DONE IN CAPERNAUM, DO ALSO HERE IN THY COUNTRY.'"

**Perplexing:**
Why did Jesus expect people to say to him, "Physician heal thyself?" Did Jesus have an obvious infirmity—deformity, blemish, or visible illness?
Why did LUKE fail to report what Jesus did in Capernaum or that he even had been in Capernaum?

**History:**
Early Christian leaders: Origin, Tertullian, Clement of Alexandria, and Cyril of Alexandria wrote that Jesus was ugly with numerous imperfections. For examples, Tertullian (c. 160-230) said that Jesus' body was not of honest human shape; Clement of Alexandria (c. 150-215) and Cyril of Alexandria (5th century) said that Jesus had an ugly countenance; Origin (c. 185-253) commenting on reports of Jesus' bodily imperfections wrote that nonetheless he had the stamp of divinity. None of these Christians, however, lived during the time of Jesus. (The descriptions, therefore, may have been derived from ISA. 53:1-12—which many Christians believe refer to the Messiah—".... ...he hath no form or comeliness...there is no beauty that we should desire him.")

4:27 - JESUS: "MANY LEPERS WERE IN ISRAEL IN THE TIME OF ELISEUS [ELISHA] THE PROPHET; NONE WAS CLEANSED, SAVING NAAMAN THE SYRIAN."

**Old Testament:**
2 KINGS 5:1-14 - Naaman, captain of the host of the king of Syria...was a leper. .... Elisha sent a messenger unto him, saying, "Go and wash in Jordan seven times...and thou shalt be clean." .... Went he, and dipped seven times in Jordan...and he was clean. [Naaman was healed after the king of Syria requested that the king of Israel have Naaman healed; Elisha then volunteered to heal him.]

4:31 - HE CAME TO CAPERNAUM, A CITY OF GALILEE, AND TAUGHT ON THE SABBATH DAYS.

**Contradictions:**
MARK 1:16-21 - Jesus went to Capernaum from the Sea of Galilee with Simon, Andrew, James, and John.
[Did Jesus go to Capernaum alone, or with four disciples?]
[Did Jesus go to Capernaum from Nazareth (4:10), or from the Sea of Galilee?]
JOHN 2:1-12 - Jesus went to Capernaum from Cana with disciples, brethren, and his mother.
[Did Jesus go to Capernaum alone, or with disciples, brethren, and his mother?]
[Did Jesus go to Capernaum from Nazareth, or from Cana?]
[Did Jesus go to Capernaum before, or after acquiring disciples?]

4:33-34 - IN THE SYNAGOGUE THERE WAS A MAN, WHICH HAD A SPIRIT OF AN UNCLEAN DEVIL, AND CRIED OUT, "LET US ALONE; WHAT HAVE WE TO DO WITH THEE, THOU JESUS OF NAZARETH? ART THOU COME TO DESTROY US? I KNOW WHO THOU ART: THE HOLY ONE OF GOD."

**Contradictions:**
1 JOHN 4:2 - "Hereby know ye the Spirit of God; every spirit that confesseth that Jesus Christ is come in the flesh is of God."
[Was the spirit in the man unclean, or was it of God because it acknowledged that Jesus was the Holy One of God?]
MARK 1:23-24 - [After acquiring four disciples, Jesus went into a synagogue] There was in their synagogue a man with an unclean spirit, saying, ".... I know who thou art, the Holy One of God."
[Did Jesus encounter the man with an unclean spirit in the synagogue before, or after acquiring disciples?]
See also under MATT. 4:23.

**History:** See under MATT. 4:23 and 8:29.

**Perplexing:** See under MATT. 4:24-25, 8:29, and 12:43-45.

**Pagan concept:** See under MATT. 4:24-25.

4:35 - JESUS REBUKED HIM, SAYING, "HOLD THY PEACE, AND COME OUT OF HIM." WHEN THE DEVIL HAD THROWN HIM IN THE MIDST, HE CAME OUT, AND HURT HIM NOT.

**Contradiction:**
MARK 1:25-26 - ....When the unclean spirit had torn him he came out of him.
[Did the unclean spirit leave without hurting the man, or did it tear him before leaving?]

4:37 - THE FAME OF JESUS WENT OUT INTO EVERY PLACE OF THE COUNTRY ROUND ABOUT.

**History:** See under MATT. 4:24-25.

**Perplexing:** See under MATT. 4:24-25.

4:38-39 - HE AROSE OUT OF THE SYNAGOGUE, AND ENTERED INTO SIMON'S HOUSE. SIMON'S WIFE'S MOTHER WAS TAKEN WITH A GREAT FEVER; THEY BESOUGHT HIM FOR HER. HE STOOD OVER HER, REBUKED THE FEVER; IT LEFT HER, AND IMMEDIATELY SHE AROSE AND MINISTERED UNTO THEM.

**Contradictions:**
MATT. 8:14-15 - [After Simon and others became his disciples] Jesus was come into Peter's house, he saw his wife's mother sick of a fever. He touched her hand, and the fever left her.... [The incident occurred after Jesus delivered his "Sermon on the Mount" in MATT. 5:1 - 7:29.]
MARK 1:29-31 - When they [Jesus and four disciples] were come out of the synagogue, they entered the house of Simon and Andrew.... Simon's wife's mother lay sick of a fever.... He took her by the hand, lifted her up, and the fever left her....
[Did Jesus go to Simon's house before, or after Simon and others became his disciples?]
[Did Jesus go to Simon's house before delivering his "Sermon" (in LUKE 6:17-49)], or after doing so?]
[Did he eliminate the fever by rebuking it, or by touching the woman's hand?]

**Perplexing:**
Why did Jesus enter Simon's house? It is not until LUKE 5:11 that Simon becomes a follower of Jesus. Why did MATT. and MARK say that Jesus already had disciples, whereas according to LUKE, Jesus did not acquire them until later in Chapter 5?
See also under MATT. 8:14-15.

4:40 - ALL THAT HAD ANY SICK WITH DIVERS DISEASES BROUGHT THEM UNTO HIM; HE LAID HIS HANDS ON EVERY ONE OF THEM, AND HEALED THEM.

**Contradictions:**
MATT. 8:16 - ...they brought unto him many that were possessed with devils; he cast out the spirits with his word, and healed all that were sick.

[Did Jesus use his hands, or his word to heal people?]
MARK 1:32-34 - ...they brought unto him all that were diseased, and them possessed with devils. ...he healed many that were sick of divers diseases....
[Did Jesus heal all who were sick, or did he heal many who were sick?]

**Perplexing:** See under MATT. 4:24-25.

**Pagan parallels**: See under MATT. 4:23 and MARK 5:23.

4:41 - DEVILS CAME OUT OF MANY, SAYING, "THOU ART CHRIST THE SON OF GOD." HE REBUKING THEM SUFFERED THEM NOT TO SPEAK, FOR THEY KNEW THAT HE WAS CHRIST.

**Contradictions:**
1 JOHN 4:2 - "Hereby know ye the Spirit of God; every spirit that confesseth that Jesus Christ is come in the flesh is of God."
[Were these actually devils, or were they of God because they acknowledged Jesus to be Christ?]
MARK 1:34 - He...suffered not the devils to speak, because they knew him.
[Did the devils identify Jesus as the Son of God before being ordered not to speak, or were they ordered not to speak before they had a chance to say anything?]

**Language**: See under MATT. 1:1.

**Perplexing:**
Why was Jesus referred to as "Christ" ("Anointed One") when he had not yet been anointed?

**History:** See under MATT. 1:1 and 8:29.

**Pagan concept:** See under MATT. 1:1.

4:42 - WHEN IT WAS DAY, HE DEPARTED AND WENT INTO A DESERT PLACE; THE PEOPLE SOUGHT HIM, CAME, AND STAYED HIM, THAT HE SHOULD NOT DEPART FROM THEM.

**Contradictions:**
MATT. 8:16-18 - When the even was come.... .... When Jesus saw great multitudes about him, he gave commandment to depart unto the other side.
[Did Jesus depart alone when it was day, or did he depart with his disciples in the evening?]
MARK 1:35-38 - In the morning, rising up a great while before day, he went out, and departed into a solitary place and prayed. Simon and they that were with him followed after him.... He said, "Let us go into the next towns, that I may preach there...."
[Did Jesus depart alone when it was day, or did he depart with his disciples in the morning before day?]
[Did people follow Jesus and ask him to remain, or did he tell his disciples that he would go to preach in the next towns?]

4:43 - HE SAID UNTO THEM [THE PEOPLE], "I MUST PREACH THE KINGDOM OF GOD TO OTHER CITIES, FOR THEREFORE AM I SENT."

**Contradiction:**
MARK 1:38 - He said unto them [his disciples], "Let us go into the next towns, that I may preach there, for therefore came I forth."
[Did Jesus tell the people listening to him, or his disciples, that he had to preach in other cities?]

4:44 - JESUS PREACHED IN THE SYNAGOGUES OF GALILEE [BEFORE HE OBTAINED ANY DISCIPLES].

**Contradictions:**
MATT. 8:23 - When he was entered into a ship, his disciples followed him.
[Did Jesus preach in the synagogues of Galilee, or did he enter a ship with his disciples?]
MARK 1:39 - He preached in their synagogues throughout all Galilee, and cast out devils. [His disciples were with him.]
[Did Jesus preach in synagogues in Galilee before, or after acquiring disciples?]

5:1-2 - AS THE PEOPLE PRESSED UPON HIM TO HEAR THE WORD OF GOD, HE STOOD BY THE LAKE OF GENNESARET [SEA OF GALILEE], AND SAW TWO SHIPS STANDING BY THE LAKE, BUT THE FISHERMEN WERE GONE OUT OF THEM, AND WERE WASHING THEIR NETS.

**Contradictions:**
MATT. 4:18 - Jesus, walking by the sea of Galilee, saw two brethren, Simon called Peter, and Andrew, casting a net into the sea, for they were fishers. [This occurred shortly after the incident with Satan (4:1-11) and long before Jesus healed Simon's mother-in-law (8:15).]
MARK 1:16 - As he walked by the sea of Galilee, he saw Simon and Andrew his brother casting a net into the sea, for they were fishers. [This occurred shortly after the Satan incident (1:13) and before Simon's mother-in-law was healed (1:31).]
[Was Jesus standing by the sea preaching the word of God to a crowd of people, or was he just walking by the sea?]
[Did he see two empty ships and fishermen washing nets, or did he see Simon and Andrew casting a net?]
[Did the event take place before, or after Jesus healed Simon's mother-in-law?]

5:3 - HE ENTERED INTO ONE OF THE SHIPS, WHICH WAS SIMON'S, AND PRAYED HIM THAT HE WOULD THRUST OUT A LITTLE FROM THE LAND. HE SAT DOWN AND TAUGHT THE PEOPLE OUT OF THE SHIP.

**Contradictions:**
MATT. 4:19-20 - He saith [to Simon and Andrew], "Follow me; I will make you fishers of men." They straightway left their nets and followed him.
MARK 1:17-18 - Jesus said [to Simon and Andrew], "Come ye after me; I will make you fishers of men." Straightway they forsook their nets, and followed him.
[Did Jesus board Simon's ship and teach people from it, or did he remain on land and call Andrew and Simon to follow him?]
JOHN 1:28-42 - Jesus was in Bethabara beyond Jordan when two of John's disciples, one of whom was Andrew, followed him, after John pointed him out. Andrew then brought his brother Simon to Jesus.
[Was Jesus by the Sea of Galilee, or in Bathabara beyond Jordan when he encountered Simon and Andrew?]
[Did Jesus go onto Simon's ship, or did he remain on land where Andrew first followed him and then brought Simon to him?]

**Perplexing:**

Why did Jesus have to go onto a ship to teach the people? Why did he not walk on the water as he will do in MATT. 14:25-26 and MARK 6:48-49? Would not standing on the water have made a greater impact on the people and established Jesus' divinity beyond doubt?

5:4-9 - WHEN HE HAD LEFT SPEAKING, HE SAID UNTO SIMON, "LAUNCH OUT INTO THE DEEP, AND LET DOWN YOUR NETS." SIMON SAID, "MASTER, WE HAVE TOILED ALL NIGHT, AND HAVE TAKEN NOTHING. NEVERTHELESS I WILL LET DOWN THE NET." ...THEY INCLOSED A GREAT MULTITUDE OF FISHES, AND THEIR NET BRAKE... THEIR PARTNERS WERE IN THE OTHER SHIP.... THEY CAME, AND FILLED BOTH SHIPS SO THAT THEY BEGAN TO SINK. SIMON PETER FELL AT JESUS' KNEES, SAYING, "DEPART FROM ME; I AM A SINFUL MAN, O LORD."

**Contradictions:**

MATT. 4:20 and MARK 1:18 - They straightway left their nets and followed Jesus [without going fishing]. [Did Jesus go fishing with Simon and fill two ships with fish, or did Jesus, Simon, and Andrew remain on land, without going fishing?]

JOHN 1:42 - .... Jesus said, "Thou art Simon... "Thou shalt be called Cephas." [They did not go fishing.] [Did Jesus go fishing on Simon's boat, or did he tell Simon that he will be called Cephas, while on land and without going fishing?]

**Perplexing:**

Why did LUKE use the name, "Simon Peter," here, before Jesus gives the name "Peter" to Simon in 6:14?
Why did Jesus allow the net to break?
What did they do with all the fish? There is no report of the fish being sold, given away, or eaten.
Why did Simon say that he was a sinful man?
Why did LUKE mention Simon but not Andrew?

5:10-11 - JAMES, AND JOHN, THE SONS OF ZEBEDEE, WERE PARTNERS WITH SIMON. JESUS SAID UNTO SIMON, "FEAR NOT; FROM HENCEFORTH THOU SHALT CATCH MEN." WHEN THEY BROUGHT THEIR SHIPS TO LAND, THEY FORSOOK ALL, AND FOLLOWED HIM.

**Contradictions:**

MATT. 4:18-22 and MARK 1:16-20 - While walking with Simon and Andrew, Jesus saw two brethren, James the son of Zebedee, and John his brother, in a ship with Zebedee their father, mending their nets. He called them, and they immediately left the ship and their father, and followed him.

[Were James and John partners with Simon, or were they encountered later on a ship repairing nets?]

[Were James and John fishing with Jesus and Simon, or were they with their father mending nets?]

[Were Jesus' first disciples Simon, James, and John, or Simon, Andrew, James, and John?]

JOHN 1:43 - The day following [the meeting with Andrew and Simon] Jesus would go forth into Galilee, and findeth Philip, and saith, "Follow me."

[Were Jesus' first three disciples (according to LUKE) Simon, James, and John, or Andrew, Simon, and Philip (according to JOHN)?]

[Was Jesus in Galilee when he acquired his first three disciples (in LUKE), or did he obtain his first two in Bethabara (JOHN 1:28-42) and his third disciple in Galilee?]

**Perplexing:**
Why would fishermen forsake their livelihood and family to follow a stranger who called them? Why did they not question Jesus before following him? Why did Jesus take the fishermen away from their families? How could their families including parents, wives, and children manage to survive without them?

5:12-13 - ...IN A CERTAIN CITY, A MAN FULL OF LEPROSY, SEEING JESUS FELL ON HIS FACE, SAYING, "LORD, IF THOU WILT, THOU CANST MAKE ME CLEAN." HE PUT FORTH HIS HAND, AND TOUCHED HIM, SAYING, "I WILL; BE THOU CLEAN." IMMEDIATELY THE LEPROSY DEPARTED FROM HIM.

**Contradictions:**
MATT. 8:1-3 - When he was come down from the mountain [after having given his "Sermon on the Mount" and before healing Simon's mother-in-law in v.8:15] a leper worshipped him saying, "Lord, if thou wilt, thou canst make me clean." Jesus put forth his hand, and touched him, saying, "I will; be thou clean." Immediately his leprosy was cleansed.
[Did Jesus heal the leper shortly after obtaining three disciples (Simon, James, and John), or when he descended from a mountain after giving the "Sermon on the Mount?"]
[Did the leper come to Jesus after, or before he healed Simon's mother-law?]
MARK 1:40-42 - [After returning from a solitary place and preaching throughout Galilee (vv. 1:35-39)] There came a leper to him , kneeling down, and saying, "If thou wilt, thou canst make me clean." Jesus, moved with compassion, put forth his hand, touched him, and saith, "I will; be thou clean." ...immediately the leprosy departed from him, and he was cleansed.
[Did Jesus heal the leper shortly after acquiring three disciples, or after he returned from a solitary place and went preaching in Galilee?]
See also under MATT. 8:1-3.

**Perplexing:** See under MATT. 8:1-3.

**Old Testament:** See under MATT. 8:1-3.

**Language**: See under MATT. 8:1-3.

**Pagan parallels**: See under MATT. 4:23.

5:15 - SO MUCH THE MORE WENT THERE A FAME ABROAD OF HIM; GREAT MULTITUDES CAME TOGETHER TO HEAR, AND TO BE HEALED BY HIM OF THEIR INFIRMITIES.

**Perplexing:**
Why did no one in the multitudes who heard Jesus or was healed by him leave any written account of Jesus' achievements? Why did not the Roman soldiers, or the Greek and other merchants give an account of Jesus when they returned home?

**History:** See under MATT. 4:24-25.

5:16 - HE WITHDREW HIMSELF INTO THE WILDERNESS, AND PRAYED.

**Contradiction:**
MATT. 8:5-6 - [After healing the leper] When Jesus was entered into Capernaum, there came a centurion, saying, "Lord, my servant lieth at home sick of the palsy...."
[After healing the leper, did Jesus go into the wilderness to pray, or did he go to Capernaum where a centurion came to him?]
MARK 1:45 - 2:1 - [After healing the leper] He went...in desert places.... And he entered into Capernaum....
[After curing the leper, did Jesus go into the wilderness and pray, or did he go into the desert then to Capernaum?]

**Perplexing:** See under MATT. 14:22-23.

5:18-19 - MEN BROUGHT IN A BED A MAN TAKEN WITH A PALSY; THEY SOUGHT TO BRING HIM IN, AND LAY HIM BEFORE HIM. ...THEY WENT UPON THE HOUSETOP, AND LET HIM DOWN THROUGH THE TILING, WITH HIS COUCH INTO THE MIDST BEFORE JESUS.

**Contradictions:**
MATT. 9:2 - They brought to him a man sick of the palsy, on a bed....
[The incident occurred after Jesus cast devils into a herd of swine (in 8:31-32). The incident with the swine is not reported by LUKE until 8:32-33.]
[Was the man with palsy brought to Jesus before, or after Jesus cast devils into a herd of swine?]
[Was the palsy victim brought to Jesus through the roof, or was he brought directly to Jesus?]

5:22 - WHEN JESUS PERCEIVED THEIR THOUGHTS, HE SAID, "WHAT REASON YE IN YOUR HEARTS?"

**Contradictions:** See under MATT. 9:4.

5:27-28 - ...HE WENT FORTH, SAW A PUBLICAN, NAMED LEVI, SITTING AT THE RECEIPT OF CUSTOM, AND SAID UNTO HIM, "FOLLOW ME." HE LEFT ALL, AND FOLLOWED HIM.

**Contradictions:** See under MARK 2:14.

**Perplexing:** See under MATT. 9:9.

5:30 - SCRIBES AND PHARISEES MURMURED AGAINST HIS DISCIPLES, SAYING, "WHY DO YE EAT AND DRINK WITH PUBLICANS AND SINNERS?"

**Contradictions:**
MATT. 9:11 - When the Pharisees saw it, they said unto his disciples, "Why eateth your master with publicans and sinners?"
MARK 2:16 - Scribes and Pharisees...said unto his disciples, "How is it that he eateth and drinketh with publicans and sinners?"
[Did scribes and Pharisees, or just Pharisees speak to the disciples?]
[Did the Scribes and Pharisees (or only the Pharisees) ask the disciples why they ate with sinners, or did they ask them why Jesus ate with publicans and sinners?]

5:32 - JESUS: "I CAME NOT TO CALL THE RIGHTEOUS, BUT SINNERS TO REPENTANCE."

**Contradictions:** See under MATT. 9:13.

**Perplexing:** See under MATT. 9:13.

5:33 - THEY [SCRIBES AND PHARISEES] SAID UNTO HIM, "WHY DO THE DISCIPLES OF JOHN FAST OFTEN, AND MAKE PRAYERS, AND LIKEWISE THE DISCIPLES OF THE PHARISEES, BUT THINE EAT AND DRINK?"

**Contradiction:**
MATT. 9:14 - Then came to him the disciples of John, saying, "Why do we and the Pharisees fast oft, but thy disciples fast not?"
[Did scribes and Pharisees, or the disciples of John ask Jesus why the disciples of John and the Pharisees fast but his do not?]

6:1 - ON THE SECOND SABBATH AFTER THE FIRST, HE WENT THROUGH THE CORN FIELDS; HIS DISCIPLES PLUCKED THE EARS OF CORN, AND DID EAT, RUBBING THEM IN THEIR HANDS [BEFORE JESUS GAVE HIS "SERMON" (IN LUKE 6:17-49)].

**Contradiction:** See under MATT. 12:1.

**Perplexing:**
What did LUKE mean by "the second sabbath after the first?"
See also under MATT. 12:1.

**History:** See under MATT. 12:1.

6:2 - CERTAIN OF THE PHARISEES SAID UNTO THEM, "WHY DO YE THAT WHICH IS NOT LAWFUL TO DO ON THE SABBATH DAYS.?"

**Perplexing:** See under MATT. 12:2.

**Old Testament:** See under MATT. 12:2.

6:3-4 - JESUS SAID, "HAVE YE NOT READ WHAT DAVID DID, WHEN HIMSELF WAS AN HUNGERED, AND THEY WHICH WERE WITH HIM, HOW HE WENT INTO THE HOUSE OF GOD, AND DID TAKE AND EAT OF THE SHEWBREAD, AND GAVE ALSO TO THEM THAT WERE WITH HIM, WHICH IT IS NOT LAWFUL TO EAT BUT FOR THE PRIESTS ALONE?"

**Contradiction:** See under MATT. 12:3-4.

**Perplexing:** See under MATT. 12:3-4.

**Judaism:** See under MATT. 12:3-4.

6:6-7 - ON ANOTHER SABBATH, HE ENTERED INTO A SYNAGOGUE AND TAUGHT; THERE WAS A MAN WHOSE RIGHT HAND WAS WITHERED. THE SCRIBES AND PHARISEES WATCHED HIM, WHETHER HE WOULD HEAL ON THE SABBATH DAY, THAT THEY MIGHT FIND AN ACCUSATION AGAINST HIM.

**Contradiction:** See under MARK 3:1-2.

**History:** See under MATT. 12:9-10.

**Perplexing:** See under MATT. 12:9-10.

6:10-11 - LOOKING UPON THEM ALL, HE SAID UNTO THE MAN, "STRETCH FORTH THY HAND." HE DID SO, AND HIS HAND WAS RESTORED. THEY WERE FILLED WITH MADNESS, AND COMMUNED ONE WITH ANOTHER WHAT THEY MIGHT DO TO JESUS.

**Old Testament:** See under MATT. 12:13.

**Perplexing:**
Why were they filled with madness? Their laws permitted healing on the sabbath.
See also under MATT. 12:13 and 14.

**Contradiction:** See under MATT. 12:14.

6:12 - ...HE WENT OUT INTO A MOUNTAIN TO PRAY, AND CONTINUED ALL NIGHT IN PRAYER TO GOD.

**Contradiction:**
MATT. 12:15 - When Jesus knew it, he withdrew from thence; great multitudes followed him, and he healed them all.
MARK 3:7 - Jesus withdrew with his disciples to the sea; a great multitude from Galilee followed, and from Judaea.
[Did Jesus go onto a mountain to pray all night, or did he depart followed by a great multitude?]

**Perplexing:**
Why did Jesus pray all night? See also under MATT. 14: 22-23.

6:13 - WHEN IT WAS DAY, HE CALLED HIS DISCIPLES; AND OF THEM HE CHOSE TWELVE, WHOM HE NAMED APOSTLES.

**Contradictions:**
MATT. 12:22 - [After healing the man with the withered hand] Then was brought unto him one possessed with a devil, blind, and dumb, and he healed him....
[After healing the man with the withered hand, did Jesus select twelve disciples, or was a blind and dumb man brought to him?]
MARK 3:9 - [After healing the man with the withered hand] He spake to his disciples, that a small boat should wait on him because of the multitude....
[After healing the man with the withered hand, did Jesus select twelve disciples, or did he request a small

boat?]
MATT. 10:1 - [Before healing the man with the withered hand and before going through the cornfield (in 12:1)] Jesus called unto him his twelve disciples....
[Did Jesus select his twelve disciples after, or before going through the cornfield and healing the man's withered hand?]

**Perplexing:**
How many disciples did Jesus have before selecting the twelve apostles?
See also under MATT. 10:1.

**Language:** See under MATT. 10:2-4.

**History:** See under MATT. 10:1.

**Old Testament:** See under MATT. 10:1.

**Pagan parallels**: See under MATT. 10:1.

**Dead Sea Scrolls:** See under MATT. 10:1.

6:14-16 - SIMON (WHOM HE NAMED PETER), ANDREW HIS BROTHER, JAMES, JOHN, PHILIP, BARTHOLOMEW, MATTHEW, THOMAS, JAMES THE SON OF ALPHAEUS, SIMON CALLED ZELOTES, JUDAS THE BROTHER OF JAMES, AND JUDAS ISCARIOT, THE TRAITOR.

**Contradictions:**
MATT. 10:3 - "Lebbaeus, whose surname was Thaddaeus," is cited, instead of "Judas the brother of James," as one of the twelve.
MARK 3:18 - "Thaddaeus" is cited, instead of "Judas the brother of James."
[Was Judas the brother of James, or was Thadaeus one of the twelve disciples?]
See also under MATT. 10:2-4.

**Perplexing:** See under MATT. 10:2-4.

**Language:** See under MATT. 10:2-4.

**History:** See under MATT. 10:2-4.

6:17-19 - HE CAME DOWN WITH THEM AND STOOD IN THE PLAIN, AND HIS DISCIPLES, AND A GREAT MULTITUDE OUT OF ALL JUDAEA, JERUSALEM, TYRE, AND SIDON, TO HEAR HIM, AND TO BE HEALED OF THEIR DISEASES.... ...THERE WENT VIRTUE OUT OF HIM, AND HEALED THEM ALL.

**Contradiction:**
MATT. 4:24 - 5:1 - His fame went throughout all Syria, and they brought unto him sick people...and he healed them. There followed him great multitudes from Galilee, Decapolis, Jerusalem, Judaea, and beyond Jordan. Seeing the multitude, he went up into a mountain; when he was set, his disciples came unto him.
[Did Jesus come down from the mountain and stand in the plain to give his "Sermon," or did he go up onto

a mountain and deliver his "Sermon"?]

**Perplexing:** See under MATT. 4:24-25.

**History:** See under MATT. 4:24-25.

6:20 - ...JESUS: "BLESSED BE YE POOR, FOR YOURS IS THE KINGDOM OF GOD."

**Contradictions:**
MATT. 5:3 - Jesus; "Blessed are the poor in spirit, for theirs is the kingdom of heaven."
[Did Jesus say that the poor, or the poor in spirit would receive the kingdom of God/heaven?]
See also under MATT. 5:3.

6:22-23 - JESUS: "BLESSED ARE YE, WHEN MEN SHALL HATE YOU... REPROACH YOU, CAST OUT YOUR NAME AS EVIL, FOR THE SON OF MAN'S SAKE. ...YOUR REWARD IS GREAT IN HEAVEN...."

**Perplexing:** See under MATT. 5:11-12.

6:24 - JESUS: "WOE UNTO YOU THAT ARE RICH! YE HAVE RECEIVED YOUR CONSOLATION."

**Perplexing:**
Why do most Christians, especially the clergy, ignore this statement by Jesus, and endeavor to amass as much wealth as possible?

6:27-28 - JESUS: "LOVE YOUR ENEMIES; DO GOOD TO THEM THAT HATE YOU. BLESS THEM THAT CURSE YOU; PRAY FOR THEM WHICH DESPITEFULLY USE YOU."

**Old Testament:** See under MATT. 5:44.

**Judaism:** See under MATT. 5:44.

**Perplexing:** See under MATT. 5:44.

6:29-30 - JESUS: "UNTO HIM THAT SMITETH THEE ON ONE CHEEK OFFER THE OTHER; AND HIM THAT TAKETH AWAY THY CLOAK FORBID NOT TO TAKE THY COAT. GIVE TO EVERY MAN THAT ASKETH OF THEE, AND OF HIM THAT TAKETH AWAY THY GOODS ASK THEM NOT AGAIN."

**Old Testament:** See under MATT. 5:39-40.

**Judaism:** See under MATT. 5:39-40.

**Perplexing:** See under MATT. 5:39-40.

6:31 - JESUS: "AS YE WOULD THAT MEN SHOULD DO TO YOU, DO YE ALSO TO THEM LIKEWISE."

**Judaism:** See under MATT. 7:12.

**Pagan parallel:** See under MATT. 7:12.

**Perplexing:** See under MATT. 7:12.

**Old Testament:** See under MATT. 5:44.

6:35 - JESUS: "LOVE YOUR ENEMIES; DO GOOD; LEND HOPING FOR NOTHING, AND YOUR REWARD SHALL BE GREAT; YE SHALL BE THE CHILDREN OF THE HIGHEST; HE IS KIND UNTO THE UNTHANKFUL AND THE EVIL."

**Contradictions:**
PS. 9:17 - "The wicked shall be turned into hell...."
PS. 11:6 - "Upon the wicked He shall rain snares, fire, brimstone, and an horrible tempest...."
PS. 34:16 - "The face of the LORD is against them that do evil, to cut off the remembrance of them from the earth."
PS. 37:9 - "Evildoers shall be cut off...."
PS. 37:20 - "The wicked shall perish...."
PROV. 21:12 - "...God overthroweth the wicked for their wickedness."
MATT. 13:41-42 - Jesus: "The Son of man shall send his angels, and they shall gather...them which do iniquity, and cast them into a furnace of fire...."
MATT. 13:49-50 - Jesus: "...the angels shall come forth, and sever the wicked from the just, and cast them into the furnace of fire...."
[Is God kind to the evil, or does He punish them?]

**Old Testament:** See under MATT. 5:44.

**Judaism:** See under MATT. 5:44.

**Perplexing:**
Why did Jesus say that God is kind unto the evil?
See also under MATT. 5:44.

6:36 - JESUS: "BE YE MERCIFUL, AS YOUR FATHER IS MERCIFUL."

**Contradictions:** See under MATT. 19:17-19 (for God being good).

6:37 - JESUS: "JUDGE NOT, AND YE SHALL NOT BE JUDGED...."

**Contradiction:** See under MATT. 7:1-2.

**Perplexing:** See under MATT. 7:1-2.

**Judaism:** See under MATT. 7:1-2.

6:39 - HE SPAKE A PARABLE UNTO THEM....

**History:** See under MATT. 13:1-9.

**Pagan parallel:** See under MATT. 13:1-9.

7:1-3 - WHEN HE HAD ENDED HIS SAYINGS IN THE AUDIENCE OF THE PEOPLE, HE ENTERED CAPERNAUM. A CENTURION'S SERVANT WAS SICK AND READY TO DIE. WHEN HE HEARD OF JESUS, HE SENT ELDERS OF THE JEWS, BESEECHING HIM TO COME AND HEAL HIS SERVANT.

**Contradictions:**
MATT. 8:5-6 - When Jesus was entered into Capernaum, there came unto him a centurion, saying, "Lord, my servant lieth at home sick of the palsy, grievously tormented."
[Did the centurion send elders to tell Jesus about the sick servant, or did he tell Jesus?]
[Was the servant ready to die, or was he just grievously tormented?]

7:6-7 - JESUS WENT WITH THEM. ...THE CENTURION SENT FRIENDS TO HIM SAYING, "LORD, TROUBLE NOT THYSELF, FOR I AM NOT WORTHY THAT THOU SHOULDEST ENTER UNDER MY ROOF, WHEREFORE NEITHER THOUGHT I WORTHY TO COME UNTO THEE...."

**Contradiction:**
MATT. 8:8 - The centurion said, "Lord I am not worthy that thou shouldest come under my roof...."
[Did the centurion send friends to tell Jesus that he was not worthy, or did he, himself, tell Jesus?]

7:9 - WHEN JESUS HEARD THESE THINGS, HE MARVELLED....

**Perplexing:** See under MATT. 8:10.

7:11-12 - THE DAY AFTER, HE WENT INTO A CITY CALLED NAIN; MANY OF HIS DISCIPLES WERE WITH HIM, AND MUCH PEOPLE. WHEN HE CAME NIGH TO THE GATE OF THE CITY, THERE WAS A DEAD MAN CARRIED OUT, THE ONLY SON OF A WIDOW....

**History:**
The city of Nain never had a wall; consequently, it did not have a gate.

**Contradiction:**
MATT. 8:14 - [After healing the centurion's servant] Jesus was come into Peter's house; he saw his wife's mother sick of a fever.
[After healing the centurion's servant, did Jesus go to Nain, or to Peter's house?]

7:13-15 - WHEN THE LORD SAW HER, HE HAD COMPASSION ON HER.... HE TOUCHED THE BIER...AND SAID, "YOUNG MAN, ARISE." HE THAT WAS DEAD SAT UP, AND BEGAN TO SPEAK.

**Contradictions:**
ACTS 26:23 - Paul: "Christ...should be the first that should rise from the dead...."
REV. 1:5 - Jesus Christ...the first begotten of the dead....

[Did the young man rise from the dead prior to Jesus' resurrection, or was Jesus the first to be resurrected?]

**Old Testament:** See under MATT. 9:25.

**Pagan parallels**: See under MATT. 9:25.

7:17 - THIS RUMOUR OF HIM WENT THROUGHOUT ALL JUDAEA, AND THE REGION ROUND ABOUT.

**History:**
There is no secular documentation for this miracle.

**Perplexing:**
If word of what Jesus had done circulated throughout the region, why is there no historical or corroborating report of the miracle? Why did the other gospel writers also fail to report this resurrection miracle?

7:19 - JOHN CALLING TWO OF HIS DISCIPLES SENT THEM TO JESUS, SAYING, "ART THOU HE THAT SHOULD COME? OR LOOK WE FOR ANOTHER?"

**Contradictions:**
MATT. 11:2-3 - [After Jesus had sent his disciples to preach (in 10:5)] John sent his two disciples to Jesus. [Did John send his disciples to Jesus after Jesus resurrected a dead man in Nain and shortly after he healed the centurion's servant, or after Jesus sent his disciples to preach and long after he healed the centurion's servant (8:18)?]
See also under MATT. 11:2-3.

**Perplexing:** See under MATT. 11:2-3.

7:22 - JESUS SAID, "...TELL JOHN WHAT THINGS YE HAVE SEEN AND HEARD: THE BLIND SEE, THE LAME WALK, LEPERS ARE CLEANSED, THE DEAF HEAR; THE DEAD ARE RAISED; TO THE POOR THE GOSPEL IS PREACHED."

**Contradictions:** See under 7:13-15.

**Perplexing:** See under MATT. 9:35.

**Old Testament:** See under MATT. 11:5.

7:27 - JESUS: "THIS IS HE [JOHN] OF WHOM IT IS WRITTEN, 'BEHOLD, I SEND MY MESSENGER BEFORE THY FACE, WHICH SHALL PREPARE THY WAY BEFORE THEE.'"

**Old Testament:** See under MATT. 11:10.

**History:** See under MATT. 11:10.

**Perplexing:** See under MATT. 10:11.

7:34-35 - JESUS: "THE SON OF MAN IS COME EATING AND DRINKING, AND YE SAY, 'BEHOLD A GLUTTONOUS MAN, AND A WINEBIBBER BUT WISDOM IS JUSTIFIED OF ALL HER CHILDREN."

**Old Testament:** See under MATT. 8:20 and 11:19.

**Perplexing:** See under MATT. 8:20 and 11:19.

**Pagan parallels**: See under MATT. 11:19.

7:36-38 - ONE OF THE PHARISEES DESIRED THAT HE WOULD EAT WITH HIM. HE WENT INTO THE PHARISEE'S HOUSE, AND SAT DOWN TO MEAT. A WOMAN WHICH WAS A SINNER...BROUGHT AN ALABASTER BOX OF OINTMENT, STOOD AT HIS FEET BEHIND HIM WEEPING, AND BEGAN TO WASH HIS FEET WITH TEARS, WIPE THEM WITH THE HAIRS OF HER HEAD, KISSED HIS FEET, AND ANOINTED THEM WITH OINTMENT. [THE INCIDENT OCCURRED LONG BEFORE JESUS SENT HIS DISCIPLES FORTH TO PREACH (IN 9:1-2), AND BEFORE HE CAME TO BETHANY (IN 19:29).]

**Contradictions:**
MATT. 26:6-7 - When Jesus was in Bethany, in the house of Simon the leper, there came a woman having an alabaster box of very precious ointment, and poured it on his head, as he sat at meat.
MARK 14:3 - Being in Bethany in the house of Simon the leper, as he sat at meat, there came a woman having an alabaster box of ointment of spikenard very precious; she brake the box, and poured it on his head.
[Was Jesus in the house of Simon the Pharisee (7:43), or the house of Simon the leper?]
[Was the ointment poured onto Jesus' head, or his feet?]
[Did the event take place before, or after Jesus sent forth his disciples to preach?]
JOHN 12:1-3 - Jesus six days before Passover came to Bethany, where Lazarus was...whom he raised from the dead. They made him a supper; Martha served.... Then took Mary a pound of ointment of spikenard, very costly, anointed the feet of Jesus, and wiped his feet with her hair....
[Was Jesus in the house of Simon the Pharisee, or the house of Lazarus, Martha, and Mary?]
[Did the event take place before, or after Jesus reached Bethany?]
[Was the woman a sinner, or the sister of Martha and Lazarus?]
[Did she wipe Jesus' feet with her hair before, or after anointing them?]
[Did she wash Jesus' feet first with her tears before wiping them, or did she anoint them without first washing them with tears?]

**Perplexing:**
Why did Jesus accept an invitation to eat with a Pharisee after he had said that Pharisees were "vipers" and "evil" (MATT. 12:34) and had denounced them in many other verses (see under MATT. 5:20 - Contradictions)?
Why did a Pharisee invite someone who was so hostile into his home to eat with him?
Why would the Son of God allow a woman to degrade herself by washing his feet with her tears, drying them with her hair, and kissing them?
See also under MATT. 26:6-7.

**Pagan parallel:** See under MATT. 26:6-7.

7:44 - HE...SAID UNTO SIMON, "...I ENTERED INTO THINE HOUSE; THOU GAVEST ME NO WATER FOR MY FEET, BUT SHE HATH WASHED MY FEET WITH TEARS, AND WIPED THEM WITH THE HAIRS OF HER HEAD."

**Perplexing:**
As it was customary for a host to provide water to guests so that they could wash their feet, why did Simon fail to do so, especially since Pharisees were meticulous about cleanliness?
Why would anyone, especially the Son of God, boast about a woman washing his feet with tears and wiping them with her hair? Why did he allow her to do so? Why would he even want to have his feet washed with tears? Was not this event degrading, and depraving both for the woman and for Jesus? Could the account be considered blasphemous?

**Old Testament:**
GEN. 18:4 - Abraham: "Let a little water, I pray you, be fetched, and wash your feet...."

7:45 - JESUS: "THOU GAVEST ME NO KISS, BUT THIS WOMAN SINCE I CAME IN HATH NOT CEASED TO KISS MY FEET."

**Perplexing:**
Why would Jesus want to be kissed by a Pharisee?
Why did Jesus allow the woman to degrade herself by constantly kissing his feet? Did he enjoy it so much that he could not tell her to stop?
Was Jesus' action what one would expect from the Son of God?
See also under 7:44.

7:46 - JESUS: "...THIS WOMAN HATH ANOINTED MY FEET WITH OINTMENT."

**Contradiction:**
MATT. 26:7 - ...a woman...poured it on his head....
MARK 14:3 - ...a woman...poured it on his head.
[Were Jesus' feet, or head anointed?]

7:48 - HE SAID UNTO HER, "THY SINS ARE FORGIVEN."

**Perplexing:**
Why was it necessary for the woman to wash Jesus' feet with tears and kiss them to have her sins forgiven?

7:49 - THEY THAT SAT AT MEAT WITH HIM....

**Perplexing:**
Who else besides the Pharisee and the woman were present with Jesus?

7:50 - HE SAID TO THE WOMAN, "THY FAITH HATH SAVED THEE...."

**Perplexing:**
Would the woman's faith have saved her, if she had not washed Jesus, feet with her tears and kissed them?

8:1 - ...HE WENT THROUGHOUT EVERY CITY AND VILLAGE, PREACHING AND SHEWING THE GLAD TIDINGS OF THE KINGDOM OF GOD; THE TWELVE WERE WITH HIM.

**Contradictions:**

MATT. 26:17 - [After being anointed by the woman] The first day of the feast of unleavened bread, the disciples came to Jesus, saying, "Where wilt thou that we prepare to eat the Passover?"
MARK 14:12 - [After being anointed by the woman] The first day of unleavened bread, when they killed the Passover, his disciples said, "Where wilt thou that we go and prepare the Passover?"
[After being anointed, did Jesus go preaching, or did his disciples ask where they should prepare the Passover?]
JOHN 12:12 - [After being anointed by Mary] The next day much people were come to the feast, when they heard that Jesus was coming to Jerusalem.
[After being anointed, did Jesus go preaching, or did people come to the feast in Jerusalem when they heard that he was going to be there?]

**History:**

There is no secular record of Jesus traveling and preaching throughout the region? There is no record of what he said, or what questions people may have asked him.

**Perplexing:**

Why is there no secular record of Jesus' travels and his preaching? How did he and the disciples travel? How much time was spent traveling? Where did they stop and spend nights while traveling? How did they obtain funds for food, lodging, and clothes, etc.?

8:2-3 - WOMEN, WHICH HAD BEEN HEALED OF EVIL SPIRITS AND INFIRMITIES, MARY MAGDALENE...JOANNA THE WIFE OF CHUZA HEROD'S STEWARD, SUSANNA, AND MANY OTHERS, MINISTERED UNTO HIM OF THEIR SUBSTANCE.

**Perplexing:**

Did the women travel with Jesus and his disciples? How were the women able to take time away from their homes and families to travel around with them? Did these women have sexual relations with Jesus and the disciples? Did their husbands know that they were using their substance (money?) to minister to them?

8:4-8 - WHEN MUCH PEOPLE WERE GATHERED TOGETHER, OUT OF EVERY CITY, HE SPAKE BY A PARABLE ABOUT A SOWER.

**Contradictions:**

MATT. 13:1-9 and MARK 4:1-9 - Jesus sat by the seaside; great multitudes were gathered; he went into a ship, spoke in parables, and recited the parable of the sower to the multitude on the shore. [In both of these instances the event occurred prior to Jesus going to Simon the leper's home and prior to being anointed by a woman (in MATT. 26:6-7 and MARK 14:3).]
[Did Jesus recite the parable while on land (traveling through cities and villages), or to multitudes from a ship?]
[Did Jesus speak the parable after, or before being anointed with ointment by a woman?]

**History:** See under MATT. 13:1-9.

**Pagan parallel:** See under MATT. 13:1-9.

8:9-10 - HIS DISCIPLES ASKED, "WHAT MIGHT THIS PARABLE BE?" HE SAID, "UNTO YOU IS GIVEN TO KNOW THE MYSTERIES OF THE KINGDOM OF GOD; BUT TO OTHERS IN PARABLES, THAT SEEING THEY MIGHT NOT SEE, AND HEARING THEY MIGHT NOT UNDERSTAND."

**Contradictions:** See under MATT. 13:10-13.

**Perplexing:** See under MATT. 13:10-13

**Pagan concept:** See under MATT. 13:10-13.

8:12 - JESUS: "THOSE BY THE WAYSIDE ARE THEY THAT HEAR; THEN COMETH THE DEVIL AND TAKETH AWAY THE WORD OUT OF THEIR HEARTS, LEST THEY SHOULD BELIEVE AND BE SAVED."

**Perplexing:** See under MARK 4:15.

8:19 - [AFTER JESUS EXPLAINED THE PARABLE OF THE SOWER TO HIS DISCIPLES] THEN CAME TO HIM HIS MOTHER AND BRETHREN, AND COULD NOT FOR THE PRESS.

**Contradiction:**
In MATT. 12:46 - [After speaking about unclean spirits, and before reciting the parable of the sower (in MATT. 13:1-9)] While he yet talked, his mother and brethren stood without, desiring to speak with him.
MARK 3:31 - [After speaking about blasphemy, and before reciting the parable of the sower (in MARK 4:1-9)] There came his brethren and his mother, and standing without, sent unto him, calling him.
[Did Jesus' mother and brethren try to come to him after, or before he recited the parable of the sower?]

8:20-21 - IT WAS TOLD HIM, "THY MOTHER AND BRETHREN STAND WITHOUT, DESIRING TO SEE THEE." HE SAID, "MY MOTHER AND BRETHREN ARE THESE WHICH HEAR THE WORD OF GOD, AND DO IT."

**Perplexing:** See under MATT. 12:46-50.

8:22 - [AFTER JESUS' MOTHER AND BRETHREN TRIED TO SPEAK WITH HIM] HE WENT INTO A SHIP WITH HIS DISCIPLES, AND SAID, "LET US GO OVER TO THE OTHER SIDE OF THE LAKE." THEY LAUNCHED FORTH.

**Contradictions:**
MATT. 13:1-2 - [After his mother and brethren tried to speak with him] The same day Jesus went out of the house and sat by the seaside. Great multitudes were gathered unto him....
MARK 4:1 - [After his mother and brethren tried to speak with him] He began to teach by the seaside; there was gathered unto him a great multitude....
[After Jesus' mother and brethren attempted to contact him, did he go onto a ship to cross the lake, or did he go to the seaside and teach?]
MATT. 8:18-23 - [Before Jesus' mother and brethren attempted to contact him] When Jesus saw great multitudes about him, he gave commandment to depart unto the other side. .... When he entered a ship, his disciples followed him.
[Did Jesus enter the ship after, or before his mother and brethren tried to speak with him?]

8:23-24 - AS THEY SAILED HE FELL ASLEEP; THERE CAME A STORM OF WIND; THEY WERE FILLED WITH WATER, AND WERE IN JEOPARDY. THEY AWOKE HIM...HE AROSE, REBUKED THE WIND AND THE RAGING OF THE WATER; THEY CEASED, AND THERE WAS CALM.

**Contradictions:**
MATT. 8:23-26 - The incident is reported to have occurred prior to Jesus having done such things as: healing a man's withered hand (12:13); speaking with two disciples sent by John (11:2-3); reciting the parable of the sower (13:3-8); and being anointed by a woman with an ointment (26:7).]
MARK 4:36-39 - The incident is reported to have occurred prior to such things as: sending forth his disciples to preach (6:7-12); and being anointed by a woman with an ointment (14:3).
[Did Jesus calm the storm after, or before healing a withered hand, speaking with John's disciples, reciting the parable of the sower, and being anointed?]
See also under MATT. 8:24-25.

**Perplexing:** See under MATT. 8:24-25.

**Old Testament:** See under MATT. 8:24-25 and 26.

8:25 - .... THEY BEING AFRAID WONDERED, SAYING ONE TO ANOTHER , "WHAT MANNER OF MAN IS THIS! HE COMMANDETH EVEN THE WINDS AND WATER, AND THEY OBEY HIM."

**Perplexing:** See under MATT. 8:27.

8:26 - THEY ARRIVED AT THE COUNTRY OF THE GADARENES....

**Contradiction:**
MATT. 8:28 - He was come into the country of the Gergesenes....
[Did they arrive at the country of the Gadarenes or Gergesenes?]

8:27 - WHEN HE WENT FORTH, THERE MET HIM A MAN, WHICH HAD DEVILS LONG TIME, AND WARE NO CLOTHES, NEITHER ABODE IN ANY HOUSE, BUT LIVED IN THE TOMBS.

**Contradictions:**
MATT. 8:28 - ...there met him two possessed with devils, coming out of the tombs, exceeding fierce so that no man might pass.
[Was Jesus met by a naked man who had devils, or by two people possessed by devils?]
MARK 5:2 - When he was out of the ship, immediately there met him out of the tombs a man with an unclean spirit.
[Was Jesus met by a naked man possessed by devils, or by a man with an unclean spirit?]

**Perplexing:** See under MATT. 4:24-25.

8:28 - WHEN HE SAW JESUS, HE CRIED OUT, FELL DOWN BEFORE HIM, AND SAID, "WHAT HAVE I TO DO WITH THEE, JESUS, THOU SON OF GOD MOST HIGH? I BESEECH THEE, TORMENT ME NOT."

**Contradictions:**
MATT. 8:29 - They cried out, "What have we to do with thee, Jesus, thou Son of God? Art thou come to torment us before the time?"
[Did one man worship and speak to Jesus, or did two men speak to Jesus?]
[Did the devils in one man beg Jesus not to torment them, or did they ask Jesus if he had come to torment them?]
1 JOHN 4:2 - "Hereby know ye the Spirit of God; every spirit that confesseth that Jesus Christ is come in the flesh is of God."
[Were these devils, or were they Spirits of God because they acknowledged Jesus as the Son of God?]
See also under MATT. 1:18.

**Perplexing:** See under MATT. 8:29.

**History:** See under MATT. 8:29.

8:30 - JESUS ASKED, "WHAT IS THY NAME?" HE SAID, "LEGION," BECAUSE MANY DEVILS WERE ENTERED INTO HIM.

**History:**
Many ancient people tended to believe that by knowing the name of a spirit or demon it could be driven out of an afflicted person.
See also under MATT. 4:23.

**Perplexing:**
This is the only time that Jesus had to know the name of an unclean spirit or devil before he could drive it out of an individual. Why was it unnecessary all other times for him to know a devil's name before casting it out of a person? Why did Jesus encourage belief in devils/unclean spirits rather than instructing people about the nature, causes, and prevention of diseases?
See also under MATT. 4:24-25.

8:31 - THEY BESOUGHT HIM THAT HE WOULD NOT COMMAND THEM TO GO OUT INTO THE DEEP.

**Contradiction:**
MARK 5:10 - He besought him that he would not send them out of the country.
[Did the devils ask not to be sent into the deep, or not to be sent out of the country?]

8:32-33 - THERE WAS AN HERD OF MANY SWINE FEEDING ON THE MOUNTAIN; THEY BESOUGHT HIM THAT HE WOULD SUFFER THEM TO ENTER THEM. HE SUFFERED THEM. THEN WENT THE DEVILS OUT OF THE MAN, AND ENTERED THE SWINE; THE HERD RAN DOWN A STEEP PLACE INTO THE LAKE, AND WERE CHOKED.

**Perplexing:** See under MATT. 8:30-32.

8:34-37 - WHEN THEY THAT FED THEM SAW WHAT WAS DONE, THEY FLED, AND TOLD IT IN THE CITY AND COUNTRY. THEY WENT OUT TO SEE WHAT WAS DONE...AND FOUND THE MAN OUT OF WHOM THE DEVILS WERE DEPARTED, SITTING AT THE FEET OF

JESUS CLOTHED, IN HIS RIGHT MIND.... .... THE WHOLE MULTITUDE...BESOUGHT HIM TO DEPART...HE WENT INTO THE SHIP, AND RETURNED BACK AGAIN.

**Perplexing:** See under MATT. 8:33-34.

8:38-39 - THE MAN OUT OF WHOM THE DEVILS WERE DEPARTED.... ... HE PUBLISHED THROUGHOUT THE WHOLE CITY THE GREAT THINGS THAT JESUS HAD DONE UNTO HIM.

**Contradiction:**
MARK 5:20 - The man published in Decapolis the great things that Jesus had done for him....
[Did the man publicize what Jesus had done for him in the city, or in the territory of Decapolis?]

**History:** See under MATT. 4:24-25.

8:40-42 - WHEN JESUS RETURNED.... THERE CAME A MAN NAMED JAIRUS, A RULER OF A SYNAGOGUE; HE FELL AT JESUS' FEET, AND BESOUGHT HIM THAT HE WOULD COME INTO HIS HOUSE; HE HAD ONE DAUGHTER, ABOUT TWELVE YEARS OF AGE; SHE LAY DYING....

**Contradictions:** See under MARK 5:21-22 and 5:23.

**Language:** See under MARK 5:21-22.

8:43-45 - A WOMAN WHO HAD AN ISSUE OF BLOOD TWELVE YEARS...CAME BEHIND HIM, TOUCHED HIS GARMENT, AND IMMEDIATELY HER ISSUE OF BLOOD STANCHED. JESUS SAID, "WHO TOUCHED ME?" All DENIED....

**Contradictions:**
MATT. 9:20-22 - A woman diseased with an issue of blood twelve years, came behind him, and touched the hem of his garment.... .... Jesus turned, and when he saw her, said, "...thy faith hath made thee whole." The woman was made whole from that hour.
[Did Jesus ask who touched him, or did he turn and see the woman who touched him without first asking?]
See also under MARK 5:25-34.

**Perplexing:** See under MARK 5:25-34.

8:48 - HE SAID UNTO HER, "...THY FAITH HATH MADE THEE WHOLE...."

**History:** See under MATT. 9:20-22.

8:49 - ...THERE COMETH ONE FROM THE RULER OF THE SYNAGOGUE'S HOUSE, SAYING, "THY DAUGHTER IS DEAD, TROUBLE NOT THE MASTER."

**Contradictions:** See under MARK 5:35.

8:51 - WHEN HE CAME INTO THE HOUSE, HE SUFFERED NO MAN TO GO IN, SAVE PETER, JAMES, JOHN, AND THE FATHER AND MOTHER OF THE MAIDEN.

**Contradiction:** See under MARK 5:37.

**Perplexing:** See under MARK 5:37.

8:54-55 - ...HE TOOK HER BY THE HAND, SAYING, "MAID, ARISE." HER SPIRIT CAME AGAIN, AND SHE AROSE....

**Contradictions:** See under MATT. 9:25 and MARK 5:39-42.

**Pagan parallels**: See under MATT. 9:25.

**Old Testament:** See under MATT. 9:25.

8:56 - ...HE CHARGED THEM [THE GIRL'S PARENTS] THAT THEY SHOULD TELL NO MAN WHAT WAS DONE.

**Perplexing:** See under MARK 5:43.

9:1 - HE CALLED HIS TWELVE DISCIPLES TOGETHER, AND GAVE THEM POWER AND AUTHORITY OVER ALL DEVILS, AND TO CURE DISEASES.

**Contradictions:**
MATT. 9:27-38 - [After resurrecting the dead girl] When Jesus departed thence, two blind men followed him; he healed them; a dumb man possessed with a devil was brought to him; he cast out the devil, and then went about all cities and villages, teaching in synagogues and healing every sickness and disease among the people.
[After resurrecting the dead girl, did Jesus call his disciples together and give them power, or did he encounter and heal two blind men and a dumb man, and then travel around all cities teaching in synagogues?]
MARK 6:1-2 - [After resurrecting the dead girl] He went out from thence, came into his own country.... ...he began to teach in the synagogues.
[After resurrecting the dead girl, did Jesus call his disciples together and give them power, or did he return to his own country and begin teaching in synagogues?]
MATT. 10:1-8 - When he called his twelve disciples, he gave them power against unclean spirits, to heal sickness and disease. .... ...raise the dead....
[Did, or did not Jesus give the disciples power to raise the dead?]
MARK 3:14-15 - He ordained twelve...to have power to heal sickness and to cast out devils. [This was done prior to resurrecting the dead girl in MARK 5:42.]
[Did Jesus give his disciples power after, or before he brought a dead girl back to life?]
See also under MATT. 10:1 and MARK 3:14-19.

**History:** See under MATT. 10:1.

**Old Testament:** See under MATT. 10:1.

**Perplexing:** See under MATT. 10:1.

**Pagan parallels:** See under MATT. 10:1.

9:3 - JESUS: "TAKE NOTHING FOR YOUR JOURNEY, NEITHER STAVES, NOR SCRIP, NEITHER BREAD, NEITHER MONEY, NEITHER HAVE TWO COATS APIECE."

**Contradictions:**
MATT. 10:9-10 - Jesus: "Provide neither gold, silver, nor brass in your purses, nor scrip, neither two coats, shoes, nor staves...."
[Did, or did not Jesus prohibit the disciples from taking bread?]
MARK 6:8-9 - [Jesus] commanded that they should take nothing, save a staff only, no scrip, no bread, no money, but be shod with sandals, and not put on two coats.
[Did, or did not Jesus prohibit the disciples from taking a staff (staves)?]
[Did not, or did Jesus prohibit the disciples from taking sandals (shoes)?]
See also under MARK 6:7-9.

**Perplexing:** See under MATT. 10:9.

**History:** See under MATT. 10:9.

9:6 - THEY DEPARTED, WENT THROUGH THE TOWNS, PREACHING THE GOSPEL AND HEALING EVERYWHERE.

**History:** See under MARK 6:12-13.

**Perplexing:** See under MARK 6:12-13.

9:7 - HEROD THE TETRARCH HEARD OF ALL THAT WAS DONE BY HIM; HE WAS PERPLEXED, BECAUSE IT WAS SAID OF SOME, THAT JOHN [THE BAPTIST] WAS RISEN FROM THE DEAD.

**Contradictions:**
MATT. 11:2-3 - When John had heard in the prison the works of Christ, he sent two of his disciples unto him....
[Was John dead, or was he still alive?]
MATT. 14:1-2 - Herod the tetrarch heard of the fame of Jesus, and said..."This is John the Baptist; he is risen from the dead; therefore, mighty works do shew forth in him."
MARK 6:14-16 - King Herod heard of him...and said, "John the Baptist was risen from the dead, and therefore mighty works do shew forth in him." .... Herod said, "It is John, whom I beheaded; he is risen from the dead."
[Did some say that John was risen from the dead, or did Herod say that John had risen?]
See also under MARK 6:14.

**Perplexing:** See under MATT. 14:1 and 14:2.

9:9 - HEROD SAID, "JOHN HAVE I BEHEADED, BUT WHO IS THIS, OF WHOM I HEAR SUCH THINGS?" HE DESIRED TO SEE HIM.

**Contradiction:**
MATT. 14:2; MARK 6:14 and 16 - Herod said that it is John the Baptist risen from the dead.
[Did Herod say that John was dead and that he wanted to know "who is this," or did he say that John had risen from the dead?]

9:10 - THE APOSTLES WHEN THEY RETURNED, TOLD ALL THAT THEY HAD DONE. HE TOOK THEM PRIVATELY INTO A DESERT PLACE BELONGING TO THE CITY CALLED BETHSAIDA.

**Contradictions:**
MATT. 12:1- At that time Jesus went on the Sabbath day through the corn; his disciples were an hungered, and began to pluck the ears of corn to eat.
[When the disciples returned, did Jesus take them to a desert place, or through a cornfield?]
MATT. 14:13 When Jesus heard of it [John's death], he departed by ship into a desert place; the people followed him.
[Did Jesus go to the desert place when his disciples returned, or after learning about John's death?]
See also under MATT. 12:1.

**Perplexing:** See under MATT. 12:1 and MARK 6:30.

9:11 - PEOPLE...FOLLOWED HIM; HE SPAKE UNTO THEM OF THE KINGDOM OF GOD, AND HEALED THEM THAT HAD NEED OF HEALING.

**Perplexing:** See under MATT. 14:14 and MARK 6:34.

9:12-13 - WHEN DAY BEGAN TO WEAR AWAY, CAME THE TWELVE, AND SAID, "SEND THE MULTITUDE AWAY SO THAT THEY MAY GO INTO THE TOWNS AND COUNTRY, LODGE, AND GET VICTUALS...." HE SAID, "GIVE THEM TO EAT." THEY SAID, "WE HAVE BUT FIVE LOAVES AND TWO FISHES...."

**Contradictions:** See under MATT. 14:15-17.

**Perplexing:** See under MATT. 14:15-17.

**Pagan concept:** See under MATT. 14:15-17.

9:14-15 - THEY WERE ABOUT 5000 MEN. HE SAID TO HIS DISCIPLES, "MAKE THEM SIT DOWN BY FIFTIES IN A COMPANY." ...THEY MADE THEM ALL SIT DOWN.

**Contradictions:**
MATT. 14:19 - He commanded the multitude to sit down....
[Did Jesus tell his disciples to make the people sit down, or did he command them to sit?]
MARK 6:39-40 - He commanded them to make all sit down by companies.... They sat down in ranks, by hundreds, and by fifties.

[Did the people sit down by fifties, or by hundreds and fifties?]
MATT. 14:21 - There were about 5000 men, beside women and children.
[Were there just about 5000 men, or about 5000 men plus an unspecified number of women and children?]

**Perplexing:** See under MATT. 14:19.

9:16 - HE TOOK THE FIVE LOAVES AND TWO FISHES...AND GAVE TO THE DISCIPLES TO SET BEFORE THE MULTITUDE.

**Old Testament:** See under MATT. 14:19.

**Perplexing:** See under MATT. 14:19.

9:17 - THEY DID EAT, AND WERE FILLED; THERE WAS TAKEN UP OF FRAGMENTS THAT REMAINED TWELVE BASKETS.

**History:** See under MATT. 14:21.

**Perplexing:** See under MATT. 14:20 and 21.

9:18 - AS HE WAS ALONE PRAYING, HIS DISCIPLES WERE WITH HIM, HE ASKED THEM, "WHOM SAY THE PEOPLE THAT I AM?"

**Contradictions:**
MATT. 14:22-23 - Jesus constrained his disciples to get into a ship, and go before him unto the other side, while he sent the multitudes away. When he had sent the multitudes away, he went up into a mountain to pray; when even was come, he was there alone.
MARK 6:45-47 - He constrained his disciples to get into the ship, and go to the other side before unto Bethsaida, while he sent away the people When he had sent them away, he departed into a mountain to pray. When even was come...he was alone on the land.
[After feeding the people, did Jesus and his disciples remain together, or did the disciples depart by ship while he remained to send the people away?]
[Did Jesus pray while his disciples were with him, or did he pray after they had left?]
JOHN 6:14-17 - Those men, when they had seen the miracle, said, "This is that prophet that should come into the world. When Jesus perceived that they would take him by force, to make him a king, he departed into a mountain alone. When even was come, his disciples entered a ship and went over the sea toward Capernaum. It was now dark, and Jesus was not come to them.
[Was Jesus with his disciples, or had they departed?]
[Did, or did not, people want to seize him to make him a king?]

**Perplexing:** See under MATT. 14:22-23.

9:20-21 - JESUS: "WHOM SAY YE THAT I AM?" PETER SAID, "THE CHRIST OF GOD." HE COMMANDED THEM TO TELL NO MAN THAT THING."

**Perplexing:** See under MATT. 16:20.

**Old Testament:** See under MATT. 16:20.

9:22 - JESUS: "THE SON OF MAN MUST...BE SLAIN, AND BE RAISED THE THIRD DAY."

**Contradictions:** See under MATT. 16:21.

**Old Testament:** See under MATT. 12:40.

9:23 - HE SAID, "IF ANY MAN WILL COME AFTER ME, LET HIM DENY HIMSELF, TAKE UP HIS CROSS, AND FOLLOW ME."

**Perplexing:**
What did Jesus mean by "Let him deny himself?" Did he mean that his followers should forgo material comforts and the accumulation of wealth? If so, why do few modern Christians adhere to this teaching?

**History:** See under MATT. 10:38.

9:27 - JESUS: "I TELL YOU OF A TRUTH, THERE BE SOME STANDING HERE, WHICH SHALL NOT TASTE OF DEATH, TILL THEY SEE THE KINGDOM OF GOD."

**Perplexing:** See under MATT. 16:28.

**Old Testament:** See under MATT. 16:28.

9:28 - ABOUT EIGHT DAYS AFTER THESE SAYINGS, HE TOOK PETER, JOHN, AND JAMES, AND WENT UP INTO A MOUNTAIN TO PRAY.

**Contradiction:**
MATT. 17:1 and MARK 9:2 - After six days Jesus taketh Peter, James, and John his brother up into a high mountain.
[Did Jesus and the three disciples go onto the mountain after about eight days, or after six days?]

**Perplexing:** See under MATT. 14:22-23 and 17:1.

9:29 - AS HE PRAYED, THE FASHION OF HIS COUNTENANCE WAS ALTERED, AND HIS RAIMENT WAS WHITE AND GLISTENING.

**Old Testament:** See under MATT. 17:2.

**Pagan parallel:** See under MATT. 17:2.

**Perplexing:** See under MATT. 17:2.

9:30-33 - THERE TALKED WITH HIM TWO MEN, MOSES AND ELIAS, WHO APPEARED IN GLORY, AND SPAKE OF HIS DECEASE AT JERUSALEM. PETER AND THEY WITH HIM WERE HEAVY WITH SLEEP; WHEN THEY WERE AWAKE, THEY SAW HIS GLORY, AND THE TWO MEN WITH HIM. AS THEY DEPARTED FROM HIM, PETER SAID, "MASTER LET US MAKE THREE TABERNACLES: ONE FOR THEE, ONE FOR MOSES, AND ONE FOR ELIAS."

**Perplexing:** See under MATT. 17:3-4.

9:34-35 - WHILE HE SPAKE, THERE CAME A CLOUD, AND OVERSHADOWED THEM.... THERE CAME A VOICE OUT OF THE CLOUD SAYING, "THIS IS MY BELOVED SON; HEAR HIM."

**Contradiction:** See under MATT. 17:5.

**Old Testament:** See under MATT. 17:5.

**Pagan parallel:** See under MATT. 3:17.

**Perplexing:** See under MATT. 17:5.

**History:** See under MATT. 1:20.

9:38-40 - A MAN CRIED OUT, "MASTER, I BESEECH THEE; LOOK UPON MY SON A SPIRIT TAKETH HIM, AND HE CRIETH OUT; IT TEARETH HIM THAT HE FOAMETH, AND BRUISING HIM HARDLY DEPARTETH FROM HIM. I BESOUGHT THY DISCIPLES TO CAST HIM OUT; THEY COULD NOT."

**Contradictions:**
MATT. 17:14-16 - ...a man came...saying, "Lord, ...my son is a lunatick and sore vexed; he falleth into fire and oft into water. I brought him to thy disciples; they could not cure him."
[Did the man say that his son was taken by a spirit that tore and bruised him, or that he was a lunatic who fell into fire and into water?]
See also under MATT. 17:16.

**Perplexing:** See under MATT. 4:24-25 and 17:16.

9:42 - .... JESUS REBUKED THE UNCLEAN SPIRIT, HEALED THE CHILD, AND DELIVERED HIM TO HIS FATHER.

**Contradiction:** See under MATT. 17:18.

**Perplexing:** See under MATT. 17:18.

9:46-47 - THERE AROSE A REASONING AMONG THEM [THE DISCIPLES], WHICH OF THEM SHOULD BE GREATEST. JESUS PERCEIVING THE THOUGHT OF THEIR HEART, TOOK A CHILD AND SET HIM BY HIM.

**Contradictions:**
MATT. 18:1-2 - [After returning to Capernaum (17:24) ] Came the disciples unto Jesus, saying, "Who is the greatest in the kingdom of heaven?" Jesus called a little child unto him, and set him in the midst of them.
MARK 9:33-36 - He came to Capernaum, and asked them, "What was it ye disputed among yourselves by the way?" They held their peace, for they had disputed among themselves, who should be the greatest.

.... He took a child, and set him in the midst of them....
[Did the disciples dispute about which of them should be the greatest, or who is the greatest in heaven?]
[Did Jesus perceive their thoughts, or did he ask them what they had disputed?]
[Did the incident occur shortly after Jesus healed a boy of an unclean spirit, or after they returned to Capernaum?]
See also under MATT. 9:4.

9:49-50 - JOHN SAID, "MASTER, WE SAW ONE CASTING OUT DEVILS IN THY NAME; WE FORBAD HIM, BECAUSE HE FOLLOWETH NOT WITH US." JESUS SAID, "FORBID HIM NOT, FOR HE THAT IS NOT AGAINST US IS FOR US."

**Perplexing:**
How can one cast out devils without receiving power to do so from Jesus? In ACTS 19:13-16, people were unable to exorcise evil spirits by means of Jesus' name.

9:52 - [JESUS] SENT MESSENGERS BEFORE HIS FACE; THEY ENTERED INTO A VILLAGE OF THE SAMARITANS, TO MAKE READY FOR HIM.

**Perplexing:**
In MATT. 10:5 - Jesus commanded them, "Go not...into any city of the Samaritans...." Why did Jesus change his mind and now decide to enter a Samaritan village? Why did Jesus send messengers ahead of him?

**History:**
Samaritan beliefs were very similar to those of the Jews. They differed by contending that their temple on Mt. Garizim, not the temple in Jerusalem, was the only legitimate place for worship. This difference led to extreme hostility between the two groups. (It may also be the reason that Jesus, a Jew, prohibited the disciples from going into Samaritan cities in MATT. 10:5.)

9:53 - THEY DID NOT RECEIVE HIM, BECAUSE HIS FACE WAS AS THOUGH HE WOULD GO TO JERUSALEM.

**Perplexing:**
Why did Jesus, a Jew, not know that the Samaritans would be hostile to him? According to JOHN 18:4, he knew all the things that would happen to him. Why, therefore, did he waste time by going into the Samaritan village?

9:54 - WHEN HIS DISCIPLES JAMES AND JOHN SAW THIS, THEY SAID, "LORD, WILT THOU THAT WE COMMAND FIRE TO COME DOWN FROM HEAVEN, AND CONSUME THEM, EVEN AS ELIAS DID?"

**Old Testament:**
2 KINGS 1:10-15 - Elijah called down fire from heaven on three occasions to destroy Samaritan soldiers.

**Perplexing:**
Why did James and John believe that they had the power to call down fire from heaven as did Elijah?

9:56 - JESUS: "THE SON OF MAN IS NOT COME TO DESTROY MEN'S LIVES, BUT TO SAVE THEM." ....

**Contradictions:**
MATT. 10: 34 - Jesus: "Think not that I am come to send peace on earth; I came not to send peacc, but a sword."
[Did Jesus come to save lives, or to bring a sword not peace to the earth?]
MATT. 10:35 - Jesus: "I am come to set a man at variance against his father, the daughter against her mother, and the daughter-in-law against her mother-in-law."
[Did Jesus come to save lives, or to incite family strife and dissension?]
LUKE 12:49 - Jesus: "I am come to send fire on the earth...."
[Did Jesus come to save lives, or to send fire onto the earth?]
LUKE 12:51 - Jesus: "Suppose ye that I am come to give peace on earth? Nay, but rather division."
[Did Jesus come to save lives, or to cause division?]

**Perplexing:**
If Jesus came to save lives, why did he not prove conclusively to everyone who he was and, thereby, save the lives of countless millions of people who have been killed in his name in religious wars and religious slaughters over the ensuing centuries?

9:59-60 - .... HE [A MAN] SAID, "LORD, SUFFER ME FIRST TO GO AND BURY MY FATHER." JESUS SAID, "LET THE DEAD BURY THEIR DEAD; GO THOU AND PREACH THE KINGDOM OF GOD."

**Perplexing:** See under MATT. 8:21-22.

**Contradiction:**
MATT. 8:21-22 - The above incident occurred prior to Jesus and the disciples walking through a cornfield (12:1).
[Did Jesus say, "Let the dead bury their dead," before, or after walking through a cornfield?]

**Language:** See under MATT. 8:21-22.

9:61-62 - ANOTHER SAID, "LORD, I WILL FOLLOW THEE, BUT LET ME FIRST GO BID THEM FAREWELL, WHICH ARE IN MY HOUSE." JESUS: "NO MAN. HAVING PUT HIS HAND TO THE PLOUGH, AND LOOKING BACK, IS FIT FOR THE KINGDOM OF GOD."

**Contradiction:** See under MATT. 19:29.

**Perplexing:**
Why did Jesus lack the compassion to allow the man to say good-by to his family? Why did Jesus not take into consideration the concern and worry that his family would have when the man failed to return home? Why did he fail to have any feeling about whether or not the man's family would be able to survive without him? Why is a man who has regard for his family, not fit for the kingdom of heaven? Does God really want a man to desert his family?
See also under MATT. 19:29.

10:1 - THE LORD APPOINTED OTHER 70, AND SENT THEM TWO AND TWO BEFORE HIS FACE INTO EVERY CITY WHITHER HE HIMSELF WOULD COME.

**Perplexing:**
Who were these 70? Were the twelve named in 6:14-16 among them? Why are they not reported by the other gospels? Why at this time did Jesus need 70 disciples to precede him into every city? [Some Bibles say, "72," instead of "70."]

**History:**
In the Book of Enoch, generally believed to be a Pharisee document, the LORD sent forth 70 shepherds to care for His sheep (people).

10:9 - JESUS: "...SAY, 'THE KINGDOM OF GOD IS COME NIGH UNTO YOU.'"

**Perplexing:**
Why did Jesus want them to say that the kingdom of God is near? Why did he not know that 2000 years later it still would not have come? Jesus, by informing these disciples that the kingdom is near, was saying that it had not yet arrived. Thus, he discredited the claim by some individuals that his transfiguration was the arrival of the kingdom (see comments under MATT. 16:28).

10:10-12 - JESUS: "INTO WHATEVER CITY YE ENTER, AND THEY RECEIVE YE NOT, GO YOUR WAYS...AND SAY, 'BE SURE OF THIS, THAT THE KINGDOM OF GOD IS COME NIGH UNTO YOU.' IT SHALL BE MORE TOLERABLE FOR SODOM, THAN FOR THAT CITY."

**Judaism:**
According to Jewish tradition, Sodom was destroyed because its people were inhospitable to strangers. (Jesus, here, accepted Jewish tradition and equated any city's inhospitality to his disciples with Sodom's hostility to visitors. In Christian tradition, Sodom was destroyed because of homosexuality.)

10:13-15 - JESUS: "WOE UNTO THEE, CHORAZIN! WOE UNTO THEE, BETHSAIDA! .... IT SHALL BE MORE TOLERABLE FOR TYRE AND SIDON AT THE JUDGMENT, THAN FOR YOU. AND THOU, CAPERNAUM, WHICH ARE EXALTED TO HEAVEN, SHALT BE THRUST DOWN TO HELL."

**Contradictions:** See under MATT. 11:20-23.

**Perplexing:** See under MATT. 11:20-23.

**Old Testament:** See under MATT. 11:20-23.

**Language**: See under MATT. 5:22.

**Pagan concept:** See under MATT. 5:29-30.

10:17 - THE 70 RETURNED WITH JOY, SAYING, "LORD EVEN THE DEVILS ARE SUBJECT UNTO US THROUGH THY NAME."

**Perplexing:**
How long did it take for these 70 to preach in "every city and place" (10:1)? What happened to them after they returned to Jesus? What did they do? Why are they not mentioned again? Why are they ignored by the other gospels?

10:19 - JESUS: "I GIVE YOU POWER TO TREAD ON SERPENTS AND SCORPIONS, AND OVER ALL THE POWER OF THE ENEMY; NOTHING SHALT BY ANY MEANS HURT YOU."

**Perplexing:**
If Jesus had given his followers power over "the enemy" (interpreted as meaning Satan), why do so many modern Christians fear Satan? Do they not believe Jesus—that he has given them power over Satan? Why do Christians still fear poisonous (and other) snakes, scorpions, venomous creatures, etc.? Do they not believe Jesus when he said that they cannot be hurt by such creatures? Why do they not believe Jesus? In fact, why are Christians as susceptible as non-Christians to harm and death from such creatures, as well as to being hurt? Why did Jesus lie to his followers?
See also under MARK 16:17-18.

**History:** See under MARK 16:17-18.

10:25-28 - A LAWYER STOOD UP...SAYING, "WHAT SHALL I DO TO INHERIT ETERNAL LIFE?" HE [JESUS] SAID, "WHAT IS WRITTEN IN THE LAW?" HE SAID, "THOU SHALT LOVE THE LORD THY GOD WITH ALL THY SOUL, STRENGTH, AND WITH ALL THY MIND; AND THY NEIGHBOUR AS THYSELF." HE SAID, "THOU HAST ANSWERED RIGHT; THIS DO, AND THOU SHALT LIVE."

**Contradictions:**
MATT. 19:16-21 - One said, "Good Master, what good thing shall I do, that I may have eternal life?" .... Jesus: "...keep the commandments." .... "Thou shalt do no murder; thou shalt not commit adultery; thou shalt not steal; thou shalt not bear false witness; honour thy father and mother, and thou shalt love thy neighbour as thyself." The man saith, "All these things have I kept from my youth; what lack I?" Jesus: "If thou wilt be perfect," go and sell that thou hast, and give to the poor...."
[Did Jesus say that one must love God and one's neighbor, or just obey certain commandments to obtain eternal life?]
See also under MATT. 19:17-19 (for obtaining eternal life).

**Old Testament:**
LEV. 19:18 - "...thou shalt love thy neighbour as thyself; I am the LORD."
DEUT. 6:5 - Moses: "Thou shalt love the LORD thy God with all thine heart, all thy soul, and with all thy might."
(The Old Testament, however, does not say that by doing the above one will obtain eternal life. Eternal life is not a Jewish concept.)

**Perplexing:**
Why would almighty God want people to love Him? Why would almighty God care whether or not people loved Him? Is God so lonely, insecure, or egotistical, as Jesus and Moses seem to imply, that He needs to be loved by mere, puny mortals? If loving God is so important, why was it not included among the first ten

commandments cited by EX. 20 and EX. 34? What does eternal life mean or entail? Why would anyone want it? Why did Jesus say that loving God would give one eternal life? Was the commandment meant to make people feel important—that almighty God needed their love?
See also under MATT. 19:16 and 17-19 (for obtaining eternal life).

**Pagan concept:** See under MATT. 19:16.

11:1 - AS HE WAS PRAYING IN A CERTAIN PLACE, WHEN HE CEASED, ONE OF HIS DISCIPLES SAID, "LORD. TEACH US TO PRAY...."

**Perplexing:** See under MATT. 14:22-23.

11:2-4 - HE SAID, "WHEN YE PRAY, SAY, 'OUR FATHER WHICH ART IN HEAVEN, HALLOWED BE THY NAME.... .... ...LEAD US NOT INTO TEMPTATION, BUT DELIVER US FROM EVIL.'" [THIS OCCURRED AFTER JESUS HAD TAKEN HIS DISCIPLES THROUGH A CORNFIELD (6:1) AND AFTER HE HAD SENT THEM FORTH TO PREACH (9:2).]

**Contradictions:**
MATT. 6:9-13 - [After delivering the "Sermon on the Mount," and before sending the disciples forth to preach (10:5) and before taking them through a cornfield (12:1)] Jesus [without anyone asking him] said, "After this manner therefore pray ye, 'Our Father which art in heaven, hallowed be Thy name.... ...deliver us from evil.'"
[Did a disciple ask Jesus how to pray, or did Jesus, without being asked, instruct the disciples how to pray?]
[Did Jesus recite the prayer after having sent forth his disciples to preach, or before sending them out to preach?]
[Did Jesus recite the prayer after, or before going through a cornfield?]
See also under MATT. 6:13.

**Perplexing:** See under MATT. 6:13.

11:9-10 - I SAY, "ASK, AND IT SHALL BE GIVEN YOU; SEEK AND YE SHALL FIND.... EVERYONE THAT ASKETH RECEIVETH, AND HE THAT SEEKETH FINDETH...."

**Perplexing:** See under MATT. 7:7-8 and 21:22.

11:14-15 - HE WAS CASTING OUT A DEVIL, AND IT WAS DUMB. ...WHEN THE DEVIL WAS GONE, THE DUMB SPAKE, AND THE PEOPLE WONDERED. SOME OF THEM SAID, "HE CASTETH OUT DEVILS THROUGH BEELZEBUB THE CHIEF OF THE DEVILS."

**Pagan concept:** See under MATT. 4:24-25 and 10:25.

**Old Testament:** See under MATT. 10:25.

**Perplexing:** See under MATT. 4:24-25.

11:24-26 - JESUS: "WHEN THE UNCLEAN SPIRIT IS GONE OUT OF A MAN, HE WALKETH...SEEKING REST; FINDING NONE, HE SAITH, "I WILL RETURN UNTO MY HOUSE WHENCE I CAME OUT.' .... HE TAKETH SEVEN SPIRITS MORE WICKED THAN

HIMSELF, AND ENTER...AND THE LAST STATE OF THAT MAN IS WORSE THAN THE FIRST."

**Perplexing:** See under MATT. 4:24-25.

**Pagan parallel:** See under MATT. 12:43-45.

11:29 - WHEN PEOPLE WERE GATHERED TOGETHER, HE BEGAN TO SAY, "THIS IS AN EVIL GENERATION; THEY SEEK A SIGN; THERE SHALL NO SIGN BE GIVEN IT, BUT THE SIGN OF JONAS THE PROPHET."

**Contradictions:**
MARK 8:12 - Jesus saith, "Why doth this generation seek after a sign?" There shall no sign be given unto this generation."
[Did Jesus say that the sign of Jonah, or no sign would be given?]
See also under MATT. 12:40.

11:34 - JESUS: "...WHEN THINE EYE IS EVIL, THY BODY IS FULL OF DARKNESS."

**Pagan concept:** See under MATT. 6:23.

**Perplexing:** See under MATT. 6:23.

11:37 - ...A PHARISEE BESOUGHT HIM TO DINE WITH HIM; HE WENT, AND SAT DOWN TO MEAT.

**Perplexing:** See under 7:36-38.

11:38 - THE PHARISEE SAW THAT JESUS HAD NOT FIRST WASHED BEFORE DINNER.

**History:** See under MATT. 15:1-2.

**Perplexing:**
Why did Jesus not have the courtesy to wash his hands?
See also under MATT. 15:11.

11:40 - JESUS: "YE FOOLS...."

**Perplexing:** See under MATT. 23:17.

11:44 - JESUS: "WOE UNTO YOU, SCRIBES AND PHARISEES, HYPOCRITES!...."

**Contradiction:** See under MATT. 15:7-9.

11:47-48 - JESUS: "WOE UNTO YOU! YE BUILD THE SEPULCHRES OF THE PROPHETS, AND YOUR FATHERS KILLED THEM. .... THEY INDEED KILLED THEM...."

**Old Testament:** See under MATT. 23:30-31.

**Perplexing:** See under MATT. 23:30-31.

11:49 - JESUS: "SAID THE WISDOM OF GOD, 'I WILL SEND THEM PROPHETS AND APOSTLES, AND SOME OF THEM THEY SHALL SLAY AND PERSECUTE.'"

**Contradiction:**
MATT. 23:34 - Jesus: "I send unto you prophets, wise men, and scribes, and some of them ye shall kill and crucify...."
[Did the wisdom of God say that prophets and apostles would be sent, or did Jesus say that he would send prophets, wise men, and scribes?]

**Old Testament:**
The statement does not appear in the Old Testament. Why did Jesus say that the "wisdom of God," rather than God, made the statement? Why would God send prophets and apostles to be killed?

**Perplexing:**
What did Jesus mean by, "Said the wisdom of God?" Did he mean that this "wisdom" was distinct from "God?"
Who were the prophets and apostles that were sent? Which were slain?
See also under MATT. 23:34.

**History:** See under MATT. 23:34.

**Pagan concept:**
In some ancient religions, "wisdom" ("Sophia," in Greek) was a goddess, usually a virgin, who created the world and/or all things.

11:50-51 - JESUS: "THE BLOOD OF ALL THE PROPHETS, WHICH WAS SHED FROM THE FOUNDATION OF THE WORLD...FROM THE BLOOD OF ABEL UNTO THE BLOOD OF ZACHARIAS, WHICH PERISHED BETWEEN THE ALTAR AND THE TEMPLE, SHALL BE REQUIRED OF THIS GENERATION."

**Contradictions:** See under MATT. 23:35.

**Perplexing:**
Why would the blood be required of Jesus' generation for something that he said happened centuries earlier?
See also under MATT. 23:35.

**History:** See under MATT. 23:35.

12:1 - ...WHEN THERE WERE GATHERED TOGETHER AN INNUMERABLE MULTITUDE OF PEOPLE...HE BEGAN TO SAY UNTO HIS DISCIPLES, "BEWARE YE OF THE LEAVEN OF THE PHARISEES, WHICH IS HYPOCRISY."

**Contradictions:**
MATT. 16:6 - Jesus said unto them [his disciples], "Take heed and beware of the leaven of the Pharisees and Sadducees." [The incident occurred long before Jesus spoke about the killing of prophets.]
[Did Jesus warn his disciples about the leaven of the Pharisees, or about the leaven of the Pharisees and Sadducees?]
[Did Jesus speak about the leaven after, or before speaking about the killing of prophets?]
[Was there, or was there not an innumerable multitude present when he spoke to his disciples?]
See also under MATT. 15:7-9 and 16:6-12.

**Perplexing:**
If an innumerable multitude was present, why was there no secular account of Jesus in the literature or records of that time?

12:5 - JESUS: "...FEAR HIM, WHICH AFTER HE HATH KILLED HATH POWER TO CAST INTO HELL; FEAR HIM."

**Contradictions:** See under MATT. 10:28.

**Perplexing:** See under MATT. 10:28.

12-9 - JESUS: "HE THAT DENIETH ME BEFORE MEN SHALL BE DENIED BEFORE THE ANGELS OF GOD."

**Perplexing:**
Why would Jesus and/or God care whether or not people believed in Jesus? Does not God have anything more important with which to be concerned?

12:10 - JESUS: "WHOSOEVER SHALL SPEAK A WORD AGAINST THE SON OF MAN, IT SHALL BE FORGIVEN, BUT HIM THAT BLASPHEMETH AGAINST THE HOLY GHOST SHALL NOT BE FORGIVEN."

**Perplexing:** See under MATT. 12:31-32.

12:19 - JESUS: "[A MAN SAID] '...TAKE THINE EASE; EAT, DRINK, AND BE MERRY.'"

**Old Testament:**
ECCL. 8:15 - "I commended mirth, because a man hath no better thing under the sun, than to eat, drink, and be merry...."

12:20 - JESUS: "GOD SAID UNTO HIM, 'THOU FOOL....'"

**Perplexing:**
In MATT. 5:22, Jesus said, "...whosoever shall say, 'Thou fool,' shall be in danger of hell fire."
Is God, then, in danger of hell fire?

12:22 - JESUS: "TAKE NO THOUGHT FOR YOUR LIFE, WHAT YE SHALL EAT; NEITHER FOR THE BODY, WHAT YE SHALL PUT ON."

**Contradiction:** See under MATT. 6:25.

**Perplexing:** See under MATT. 6:25.

12:24 - JESUS: "CONSIDER THE RAVENS; THEY NEITHER SOW NOR REAP...AND GOD FEEDETH THEM; HOW MUCH MORE ARE YE BETTER THAN THE FOWLS?"

**Perplexing:** See under MATT. 6:26.

12:29-31 - JESUS: "SEEK NOT WHAT YE SHALL EAT, OR DRINK, NEITHER BE OF DOUBTFUL MIND.... ...YOUR FATHER KNOWETH THAT YE HAVE NEED OF THESE THINGS. RATHER SEEK THE KINGDOM OF GOD, AND ALL THESE THINGS SHALL BE ADDED UNTO YOU."

**Perplexing:**
If God knows what one needs and will provide it, why do believers still have to work and worry about obtaining enough money to purchase such things as food, clothes, shelter, and medical care?
See also under MATT. 6:25.

12:33 - JESUS: "SELL THAT YE HAVE, AND GIVE ALMS...."

**Perplexing:** See under MATT. 19:21.

12:46-48 - JESUS [DISCUSSING SERVANTS WHO WERE NOT OBEDIENT TO THEIR MASTER]: "THE LORD OF THAT SERVANT...WILL CUT HIM IN SUNDER.... AND THAT SERVANT, WHICH KNEW HIS LORD'S WILL, AND...NEITHER DID ACCORDING TO HIS WILL SHALL BE BEATEN WITH MANY STRIPES. BUT HE THAT KNEW NOT, AND DID THINGS WORTHY OF STRIPES, SHALL BE BEATEN WITH FEW STRIPES...."

**Contradictions:**
MATT. 6:14 - Jesus: "If ye forgive men their trespasses, your heavenly Father will forgive you."
[Did Jesus advocate punishing individuals for their transgressions, or did he advocate forgiving them?]
MATT. 19:18 - .... Jesus said, "Thou shalt do no murder...."
MARK 10:19 and LUKE 18:20 - Jesus: "...Do not kill...."
[Did Jesus believe that a disobedient servant should be killed, or that one should not kill or commit murder?]

**Perplexing:**
Why did Jesus countenance the killing and beating of servants? Why did he not order more humane treatment or disciplining of wayward servants? Why did he not believe that firing the servants would be adequate punishment? Why did Jesus fail to show compassion for servants? Why did he not mitigate his comments with orders to treat servants decently, mercifully, and compassionately? Did Jesus condone capital punishment when he approved of a servant being killed ("cut him in sunder")?
If the parable was meant to mean that the "lord" referred to Jesus or to God, why are they exempt from the commandment not to kill?

12:49 - JESUS: "I AM COME TO SEND FIRE ON THE EARTH...."

**Contradictions:**

MATT. 1:21 - An angel: "...he [Jesus] shall save his people from their sins."
[Did Jesus come to send fire on the earth, or to save people from their sins?]
MARK 10:45 - Jesus: "The Son of man came...to give his life a ransom for many."
[Did Jesus come to send fire on the earth, or to give his life for many?]
LUKE 2:11 - An angel: "Unto you is born this day in the city of David a Saviour, Christ the Lord."
LUKE 9:56 - Jesus: "The Son of man is not come to destroy men's lives, but to save them." ....
JOHN 3:17 - "God sent not his Son into the world to condemn the world, but that the world through him might be saved."
1 JOHN 4:14 - "We have seen and do testify that the Father sent the Son to be the Saviour of the world."
[Did Jesus come to send fire on earth, or to be a savior?]
LUKE 5:32 - Jesus: "I came not to call the righteous, but sinners to repentance."
[Did Jesus come to send fire on earth, or to call sinners to repentance?]
JOHN 10:10 - Jesus: "The thief cometh to steal, kill, and destroy; I come that they [his followers] might have life, and have it more abundantly."
[Did Jesus come to send fire onto the earth, or to give life?]
ACTS 10:36 - Peter: "The word which God sent unto the children of Israel, preaching peace by Jesus Christ"....
[Did Jesus come to send fire on the earth, or to preach peace?]
1 JOHN 3:8 - "The Son of God was manifested, that he might destroy the works of the devil."
[Did Jesus come to send f ire on the earth, or to destroy the works of the devil?]
See also under MATT. 1:21.

12:51 - JESUS: "SUPPOSE YE THAT I HAVE COME TO GIVE PEACE ON EARTH? I TELL YOU, NAY, BUT RATHER DIVISION."

**Contradictions:**

ACTS 10:36 - Peter: "The word which God sent unto the children of Israel preaching peace by Jesus Christ."
[Did Jesus come to give division, or peace on earth?]
See also under 12:49.

13:1 - ...SOME TOLD HIM OF THE GALILEANS, WHOSE BLOOD PILATE HAD MINGLED WITH THEIR SACRIFICES.

**History:**

Although there is no evidence to support the above verse, Pilate did massacre at least hundreds of Jews and looted the Jerusalem Temple. His atrocities were eventually too much even for Rome to tolerate, and he was removed from office. Nonetheless, he was canonized by at least two Christian denominations: the Coptic and Ethiopian (Abyssinian) Churches. The Coptic and Greek Orthodox Churches also canonized his wife, Claudia Procula.

13:10 - JESUS WAS TEACHING IN ONE OF THE SYNAGOGUES ON THE SABBATH.

**Perplexing:**

How was Jesus able to walk into a synagogue and teach? Why would the Pharisee or Sadducee priests give him permission to teach on the Sabbath after he had shown hostility towards them? Would they allow someone who denounced them to usurp their role in a synagogue?

13:11-14 - THERE WAS A WOMAN WHICH HAD A SPIRIT OF INFIRMITY 18 YEARS, WAS BOWED, AND COULD NOT LIFT UP HERSELF. WHEN JESUS SAW HER, HE SAID, "WOMAN, THOU ART LOOSENED FROM THY INFIRMITY." HE LAID HANDS ON HER; IMMEDIATELY SHE WAS MADE STRAIGHT.... THE RULER OF THE SYNAGOGUE ANSWERED WITH INDIGNATION, BECAUSE JESUS HEALED ON THE SABBATH DAY....

**History:**

Jews did not object to healing on the Sabbath. Healing was not deemed to be a violation of the prohibition against working on the Sabbath.

See also under MATT. 12:9-10.

**Perplexing:**

Since Jews permitted healing to take place on the Sabbath, why was the ruler of the synagogue angry at Jesus for healing someone? Why did the other Jews fail to inform the ruler that healing on the Sabbath was permitted? Were the gospel writers unaware of this fact, or were they endeavoring to incite hostility towards the Jews?

See also under MATT. 12:9-10.

13:27 - JESUS: "HE SHALL SAY...DEPART FROM ME, ALL YE WORKERS OF INIQUITY."

**Old Testament:**

PS. 6:8 - "Depart from me, all ye workers of iniquity, for the LORD hath heard the voice of my weeping."

13:28 - JESUS: "THERE SHALL BE WEEPING AND GNASHING OF TEETH, WHEN YE SHALL SEE ABRAHAM, ISAAC, JACOB, AND ALL THE PROPHETS, IN THE KINGDOM OF GOD, AND YOU THRUST OUT."

**Perplexing:**

How are those outside the kingdom of God able to see anyone in the kingdom? How are they able to recognize Abraham and the others? Was Jesus a failure as the Savior, if some people cannot qualify for admittance to the kingdom? Was Jesus' death, therefore, in vain?

13:31 -THERE CAME CERTAIN PHARISEES, SAYING, "GET THEE OUT; DEPART HENCE, FOR HEROD WILL KILL THEE."

**Contradiction:**

LUKE 23:8 - When Herod saw Jesus, he was exceeding glad; he was desirous to see him of a long season, because he had heard many things of him, and he hoped to have seen some miracle done by him.

[Did Herod want to kill Jesus, or was he glad to see him?]

**Perplexing:**

Why did Pharisees want to protect Jesus from Herod? In MARK 3:6, the Pharisees and the Herodians conspired to kill Jesus, and in MATT. 12:14, the Pharisees plotted to destroy him. He also had been vehemently hostile towards the Pharisees.

13:34 - JESUS: "O JERUSALEM, JERUSALEM, WHICH KILLEST THE PROPHETS, AND STONEST THEM THAT ARE SENT UNTO THEE...."

**Old Testament:** See under MATT. 23:30-31.

**Perplexing:** See under MATT. 23:30-31.

13:35 - JESUS: "...WHEN YE SHALL SAY, 'BLESSED IS HE THAT COMETH IN THE NAME OF THE LORD.'"

**Old Testament:** See under MATT. 21:8-9.

14:1 - HE WENT INTO THE HOUSE OF ONE OF THE CHIEF PHARISEES TO EAT BREAD ON THE SABBATH DAY....

**Perplexing:** See under 7:36-38.

14:2-4 - THERE WAS A MAN BEFORE HIM WHICH HAD DROPSY. JESUS SPAKE UNTO THE LAWYERS AND PHARISEES, "IS IT LAWFUL TO HEAL ON THE SABBATH DAY?" THEY HELD THEIR PEACE. HE HEALED HIM....

**History:** See under 13:11-14 and MATT. 12:9-10.

**Perplexing:**
Why did Jesus not know that the Jews permitted healing on the Sabbath? Why did the Pharisees hold their peace? Why did they fail to inform Jesus that such healing was lawful?
See also under 13:11-14 and under MATT. 12:9-10.

14:13-14 - JESUS: "WHEN THOU MAKEST A FEAST, CALL THE POOR, THE MAIMED, THE LAME, THE BLIND, AND THOU SHALT BE BLESSED...THOU SHALT BE RECOMPENSED AT THE RESURRECTION OF THE JUST."

**Perplexing:**
Why did Jesus imply that one would be recompensed for doing good? Why should one not do good for the sake of doing so without expecting a reward?

14:15 - ONE OF THEM THAT SAT AT MEAT WITH HIM...SAID, "BLESSED IS HE THAT SHALL EAT BREAD IN THE KINGDOM OF GOD."

**Perplexing:**
Does one eat in the kingdom of God? If so, why? Is anything other than bread available? If so, what? From where does the f ood come? Are there farms and ranches, etc., in the kingdom? Is the food cooked? Does one have a choice of what to eat? Who prepares and serves it? Are lavatory facilities also needed and available?
See also under MATT. 26:29.

14:26 - JESUS: “IF ANY MAN COME TO ME, AND HATE NOT HIS FATHER, MOTHER, WIFE, CHILDREN, BRETHREN, SISTERS, AND HIS OWN LIFE ALSO, HE CANNOT BE MY DISCIPLE.”

**Contradictions:**
LEV. 19:17 - God: “Thou shalt not hate thy brother in thine heart.”
[Should one hate one’s brother, as Jesus commanded, or not hate one’s brother as God commanded?]
MATT. 19:19, MARK 10:19, and LUKE 18:20 - Jesus: “Honour thy father and mother.”
EX. 20:12 [One of the ten commandments of EX. 20 and DEUT. 5:16] - God: “Honour thy father and thy mother.”
[Should one hate one’s father and mother, or honor them?]
1 JOHN 3:15 - “Whosoever hateth his brother is a murderer, and ye know that no murderer hath eternal life abiding in him.”
[Did Jesus say one must hate one’s brethren to become his disciple, or is one who hates his brethren a murderer?]
MATT. 10:37 - Jesus: “He that loveth father or mother more than me is not worthy of me; he that loveth son or daughter more than me is not worthy of me.”
[Should one hate one’s parents and children, or should one just love Jesus more than one’s parents and children?]

**Perplexing:**
Why did Jesus want people who followed him to reject their families, probably leaving them without a means of support? Why could he not allow them to love their families and still follow him? Is a command to hate, what is to be expected from the Son of a loving God?
See also under MATT. 19:29.

**History:**
The Jewish sect, the Essenes, advocated repudiating and hating family members who did not belong to the sect. (Some modern Christian cults do the same.)

14:27 - JESUS: “WHOSOEVER DOTH NOT BEAR HIS CROSS, AND COME AFTER ME, CANNOT BE MY DISCIPLE.”

**History:** See under MATT. 10:38.

**Perplexing:** See under MATT. 10:38.

14:31 - JESUS: “WHAT KING GOING TO WAR AGAINST ANOTHER KING....”

**Perplexing:**
Why did Jesus fail to condemn war? Why did he fail to tell people how to prevent war? Why did he not eliminate war?
Jesus referred to kings here and in other places. Why did he fail to speak about the development of governments other than kingdoms?

14:33 - JESUS: “WHOSOEVER HE BE OF YOU THAT FORSAKETH NOT ALL THAT HE HATH, CANNOT BE MY DISCIPLE.”

**Perplexing:**
How can one give up everything that one has and still survive? Why do modern Christians ignore this statement by Jesus? Is it because it is impossible to obey? If it is impossible, does it mean that no one is or can be a disciple of Jesus?
See also under MATT. 19:21 and 23-24.

**History:** See under MATT. 19:23-24.

**Pagan concept:** See under MATT. 19:23-24.

14:34 - JESUS: "SALT IS GOOD...."

**Perplexing:** See under MARK 9:50.

15:7 - JESUS: "JOY SHALL BE IN HEAVEN OVER ONE SINNER THAT REPENTETH, MORE THAN 99 JUST PERSONS, WHICH NEED NO REPENTANCE."

**Perplexing:**
Why does a person who repents after having led a life of crime that may have included murder, torture, and the causing of immense suffering elicit more joy in heaven that a person who has done good and brought happiness into the world? How does a criminal's repentance benefit his or her victim(s)? What happens to murder victims who do not have the opportunity to repent? How is anyone benefited by the last minute repentance of a fiend? Why did Jesus imply that it is acceptable to lead a sinful life or a life of crime and then repent, rather than to lead as righteous a life as possible? Why does God allow criminals to inflict suffering on innocent people? If someone murders your young children and then says that he repents, would you be joyful and reward the murderer? Why not, if God does so?

16:9 - JESUS [AFTER RELATING A PARABLE IN WHICH A DISHONEST STEWARD IS REWARDED BY HIS LORD FOR HIS DISHONESTY]: "MAKE TO YOURSELVES FRIENDS OF THE MAMMON OF UNRIGHTEOUSNESS, THAT, WHEN YE FALL, THEY MAY RECEIVE YOU INTO EVERLASTING HABITATIONS."

**Perplexing:**
Why did Jesus want his disciples to be "friends of the mammon of unrighteousness?" How could his disciples become friends of the unrighteous? Why did he want them to be received into their habitations, rather than into those of the righteous? Jesus said, "when ye fall," but how and why would his disciples fall? Why did Jesus approve of rewarding dishonesty? Was Jesus advocating dishonesty? Can one really depend on unrighteous individuals to help you after your money is gone or if you should you encounter difficulties?

**Language**: See under MATT. 6:24.

16:11 - JESUS: "IF, THEREFORE, YE HAVE NOT BEEN FAITHFUL IN THE UNRIGHTEOUS MAMMON, WHO WILL COMMIT TO YOUR TRUST THE TRUE RICHES?"

**Perplexing:**
Why must one be faithful to the unrighteous mammon to be trusted with "the true riches?" What are "the true riches?"

16:13 - JESUS: ".... YE CANNOT SERVE GOD AND MAMMON."

**Perplexing:** See under MATT. 6:19 and MATT. 6:24.

16:17 - JESUS: "IT IS EASIER FOR HEAVEN AND EARTH TO PASS, THAN ONE TITTLE OF THE LAW TO FALL."

**Contradictions:** See under MATT. 5:17-18 and 31-32..

16:18 - JESUS: "WHOSOEVER PUTTETH AWAY HIS WIFE, AND MARRIETH ANOTHER, COMMITTETH ADULTERY, AND WHOSOEVER MARRIETH HER THAT IS PUT AWAY FROM HER HUSBAND COMMITTETH ADULTERY."

**Old Testament:** See under MATT. 5:31-32.

**Contradictions:** See under MATT. 5:31-32.

**History:** See under MATT. 5:31-32.

16:19-31 - JESUS RECITED THE STORY OF A RICH MAN AND A BEGGAR. THE BEGGAR DIED, AND WAS CARRIED BY ANGELS TO "ABRAHAM'S BOSOM" [HEAVEN]. THE RICH MAN DIED, WENT TO HELL, LOOKED UP, AND SAW ABRAHAM AND THE BEGGAR [IN HEAVEN]. HE SPOKE WITH ABRAHAM WHO INFORMED HIM THAT ONE CANNOT PASS ACROSS THE GULF BETWEEN HEAVEN AND HELL.

**Perplexing:**
Can people in heaven and hell recognize, see, and speak with one another? Does this mean that their appearance is the same as it was on the earth when they were near the end of their life? How was the rich man able to recognize Abraham? The beggar is not said to have had faith, believed in Jesus, been baptized or born again, or have done good works. Why then was he admitted to heaven? Was he able to enter just because he was poor? What did the rich man do to deserve being sent to hell? What did he do, or not do, to deserve eternal torment? Was he sent to hell just for being rich? Was Jesus exhibiting an anti-rich prejudice? Do people go to either heaven or hell directly after death without waiting for a judgment day?

17:6 - THE LORD SAID, " IF YE HAD FAITH AS A GRAIN OF MUSTARD SEED, YE MIGHT SAY UNTO THIS SYCAMINE [MULBERRY] TREE, 'BE THOU PLUCKED UP BY THE ROOT, AND BE THOU PLANTED IN THE SEA,' AND IT SHOULD OBEY YOU."

**Contradictions:**
MARK 6:5 - He [Jesus] there could do no mighty work....
MARK 11:13-14 - Jesus could not cause a fig tree to bear fruit out of season.
[Did, or did not Jesus have a mustard seed's worth of faith?]

**Perplexing:**
Why, in about two millennia, has no follower of Jesus been able to make a tree move itself? Did no one even have as much faith as a grain of mustard seed? Are all those who profess faith in Jesus lying?
See also under MATT. 17:19-21.

17:12-13 - AS HE ENTERED A VILLAGE, THERE MET HIM TEN MEN THAT WERE LEPERS...THEY SAID, "JESUS, MASTER, HAVE MERCY ON US."

**History:**
Lepers were forbidden from wandering near populated areas. They had to remain confined in isolated areas (leper colonies).

**Perplexing:**
If lepers were prohibited from entering villages, how could Jesus have encountered them in a village? How were the lepers able to recognize Jesus? Why did Jesus fail to explain the nature of leprosy, so its victims would not be forced to live away from populated areas? Why did he fail to denounce the practice of persecuting lepers?
See also under MATT. 8:1-3.

17:14 - ...HE SAID, "GO SHEW YOURSELVES UNTO THE PRIESTS." AS THEY WENT THEY WERE CLEANSED.

**Old Testament:** See under MATT. 8:1-3.

**Pagan parallels**: See under MATT. 4:23.

17:20 - WHEN HE WAS DEMANDED OF THE PHARISEES, WHEN THE KINGDOM OF GOD SHOULD COME, HE ANSWERED, "THE KINGDOM OF GOD COMETH NOT WITH OBSERVATION."

**Contradictions:**
MATT. 12:38-40 - Jesus told the Pharisees that the sign will be "the sign of the prophet Jonas [Jonah]; for as Jonas was three days and three nights in the whale's belly, so shall the Son of man be three days and three nights in the heart of the earth."
[Will there be no observable sign, or will the only sign be that of Jonah?]
MATT. 24:3-34, MARK 13:4-30, and LUKE 21:7-32 - The disciples asked Jesus "what shall be the sign of thy coming, and of the end of the world"; he responded by citing numerous things that will take place including wars, the coming of false prophets, a great tribulation, that the sun and moon will be darkened, and that the stars will fall. He said, "When ye shall see all these things, know that it is near, even at the doors."
[Will there be no observable sign, or many signs?]

**History:** See under MATT. 12:38-39.

17:34 - JESUS: "IN THAT NIGHT THERE SHALL BE TWO MEN IN ONE BED; THE ONE SHALL BE TAKEN, AND THE OTHER SHALL BE LEFT."

**Perplexing:**
Was Jesus referring to homosexuals? Was he saying that some homosexuals will enter the kingdom of God?

18:7-8 - JESUS: "SHALL NOT GOD AVENGE HIS OWN ELECT, WHICH CRY DAY AND NIGHT UNTO HIM, THOUGH HE BEAR LONG WITH THEM? I TELL YOU THAT HE WILL AVENGE THEM SPEEDILY. ...."

**Contradiction:**
PS. 22:1-2 - "My God, my God, why hast Thou forsaken me? Why art Thou so far from helping me, and from the words of my roaring? O my God, I cry in the daytime, but Thou hearest not, and in the night season, and am not silent."
[Does God avenge people speedily, or does He ignore them?]

**Perplexing:**
Why does God allow "His own elect" to be placed in situations requiring vengeance? If God avenges one speedily, why do so many who pray for assistance for years die without having been avenged or helped by God? If God knows what one needs before it is prayed for (MATT. 6:8), why does He allow people to pray for aid that He knows He will not provide?

18:18-19 - A CERTAIN RULER ASKED HIM, "GOOD MASTER, WHAT SHALL I DO TO INHERIT ETERNAL LIFE?" JESUS SAID, "WHY CALLEST THOU ME GOOD? NONE IS GOOD, SAVE ONE, THAT IS, GOD."

**Contradictions:** See under MATT. 19:17-19 (for God being good).

**Perplexing:** See under MATT. 19:16 and 17-19 (for God being good).

**Pagan concept:** See under MATT. 19:16.

18:20 - JESUS: "THOU KNOWEST THE COMMANDMENTS: DO NOT COMMIT ADULTERY; DO NOT KILL; DO NOT BEAR FALSE WITNESS; HONOUR THY FATHER AND MOTHER."

**Contradictions:** See under MATT. 19:17-19 (for obtaining eternal life).

**Perplexing:** See under MATT 19:17-19 (for obtaining eternal life).

**Old Testament:** See under MATT. 18:20.

**Pagan parallels**: See under MATT. 19:17-19.

18:22 - JESUS...SAID, "...SELL ALL THAT THOU HAST, AND DISTRIBUTE UNTO THE POOR, AND THOU SHALT HAVE TREASURE IN HEAVEN; FOLLOW ME."

**Perplexing:** See under MATT. 19:21.

18:24-25 - WHEN JESUS SAW THAT HE WAS VERY SORROWFUL, HE SAID, "HOW HARDLY SHALL THEY THAT HAVE RICHES ENTER INTO THE KINGDOM OF GOD! IT IS EASIER FOR A CAMEL TO GO THROUGH A NEEDLE'S EYE, THAN FOR A RICH MAN TO ENTER INTO THE KINGDOM OF GOD."

**Perplexing:** See under MATT, 19:23-24.

**History:** See under MATT. 19:23-24.

**Pagan concept:** See under MATT. 19:23-24.

18:29-30 - HE SAID, "THERE IS NO MAN THAT HATH LEFT HOUSE, PARENTS, BRETHREN, WIFE, OR CHILDREN, FOR THE KINGDOM OF GOD'S SAKE. WHO SHALL NOT RECEIVE MANIFOLD MORE IN THIS PRESENT TIME, AND IN THE WORLD TO COME LIFE EVERLASTING."

**Contradictions:** See under MATT. 19:17-19 (for obtaining eternal life) and 19:29.

**Perplexing:** See under MATT. 19:29.

18:31 - HE TOOK THE TWELVE, AND SAID, "...ALL THINGS ARE WRITTEN BY THE PROPHETS CONCERNING THE SON OF MAN SHALL BE ACCOMPLISHED."

**Perplexing:**
To which prophets did Jesus refer?

18:32-33 - JESUS: "HE SHALL BE DELIVERED UNTO THE GENTILES...AND THEY SHALL...PUT HIM TO DEATH; THE THIRD DAY HE SHALL RISE AGAIN."

**Contradictions:** See under MATT. 16:21.

**Perplexing:** See under MATT. 20:18-19.

**Old Testament:** See under MATT. 12:40.

18:35 - AS HE WAS COME NIGH UNTO JERICHO, A BLIND MAN SAT BY THE WAYSIDE BEGGING.

**Contradictions:**
MATT. 20:29-30 - As they departed from Jericho.... Two blind men sitting by the wayside, when they heard that Jesus passed by, cried out....
MARK 10:46 - ...as he went out of Jericho with his disciples...blind Bartimaeus, sat by the highway side begging.
[Was Jesus entering, or leaving Jericho?]
[Was there one blind man, or were there two?]

**Old Testament:** See under MATT. 20:29.

**Perplexing:** See under MATT. 20:29.

18:38 - HE CRIED, "JESUS, THOU SON OF DAVID...."

**Perplexing:** See under MATT. 9:27.

18:41 - JESUS: "WHAT WILT THOU THAT I SHOULD DO UNTO THEE?" HE SAID, "LORD, THAT I MAY RECEIVE MY SIGHT."

**Contradiction:** See under MATT. 20:32.

**Perplexing:** See under MATT. 20:32.

18:42 - JESUS SAID, "RECEIVE THY SIGHT; THY FAITH HATH SAVED THEE."

**Contradictions:** See under MATT. 20:33-34.

**Perplexing:** See under MATT. 20:33-34.

**History:** See under MATT. 20:33-34.

**Pagan parallels**: See under MATT. 4:23.

19:2-5 - A MAN NAMED ZACCHAEUS...WAS RICH. HE SOUGHT TO SEE JESUS WHO HE WAS.... HE CLIMBED UP INTO A SYCOMORE TREE TO SEE HIM. WHEN JESUS CAME, HE LOOKED UP, SAW HIM, AND SAID, "ZACCHAEUS, COME DOWN FOR TODAY I MUST ABIDE AT THY HOUSE."

**Perplexing:**
Since Zacchaeus had not seen Jesus before, how did Jesus know him by sight and by name? Why did Jesus want to stay with him, a rich man? Why did Jesus invite himself to stay at Zacchaeus' house?

**Language:**
Zacchaeus is the Greek form of the Aramaic word, "zakkai," meaning "righteous."
Sycomore is a translation of the Greek word, "sukomorea," meaning "fig-mulberry."

19:8-9 - ZACCHAEUS SAID, "LORD, HALF OF MY GOODS I GIVE TO THE POOR, AND IF I HAVE TAKEN ANYTHING FROM ANY MAN BY FALSE ACCUSATION, I RESTORE HIM FOURFOLD." JESUS SAID, "THIS DAY IS SALVATION COME TO THIS HOUSE...."

**Contradictions:** See under MATT. 19:17:19 (for obtaining eternal life).

**Perplexing:**
Prior to giving salvation to Zacchaeus, why did Jesus not ask him if he had been baptized, "born again," eaten Jesus' flesh and drunk his blood, forsaken his family, obeyed the commandments he had previously cited, or even if he had kept all of Jesus' sayings? Why did Jesus decide now that one need only give half of one's possessions to the poor to obtain salvation?

19:11 - ...HE SPAKE A PARABLE, BECAUSE HE WAS NIGH TO JERUSALEM, AND BECAUSE THEY THOUGHT THAT THE KINGDOM OF GOD SHOULD IMMEDIATELY APPEAR.

**Perplexing:**

Why had Jesus mislead his followers by giving them the impression that the kingdom of God was imminent? Why did he fail to tell them the truth, that the kingdom, if it exists and ever comes, would not arrive for centuries, even millennia, into the future?

19:12-23 - JESUS RECITED A LENGTHY PARABLE IN WHICH A NOBLEMAN PRIOR TO GOING ON A TRIP GAVE A SUM OF MONEY TO EACH OF TEN SERVANTS. ALL EXCEPT ONE USED THE MONEY TO MAKE MORE MONEY FOR THE NOBLEMAN. ONE SERVANT, HOWEVER, RETURNED THE SAME AMOUNT OF MONEY AS HE HAD RECEIVED. THE NOBLEMAN SAID TO HIM, "GAVEST NOT THOU MY MONEY INTO THE BANK, THAT AT MY COMING I MIGHT HAVE REQUIRED MY OWN WITH USERY?"

**Perplexing:**

Would a nobleman entrust money with servants while he was away? Would he want them to speculate, gamble, or loan his money thereby risking its loss? Why was the nobleman angry with the servant who was honest and did not risk losing the money? Why did Jesus relate a parable supporting gambling and usury, while rejecting honesty? What did LUKE mean by "bank," since banks did not come into existence until the 17th century?

19:27 - [IN JESUS' PARABLE, THE NOBLEMAN SAID:] "THOSE MINE ENEMIES, WHICH WOULD NOT THAT I SHOULD REIGN OVER THEM, BRING HITHER, AND SLAY THEM BEFORE ME."

**Contradictions:**

EX. 20:13 - God: "Thou shalt not kill."
[Should one kill, or not kill?]
MATT. 5:44 - Jesus: "Love your enemies"; bless them that curse you; do good to them that hate you...."
[Should one kill one's enemies, or love, bless, and do good for them?]
MATT. 6:14 - Jesus: "If ye forgive men their trespasses, your heavenly Father will also forgive you."
[Should one forgive men their trespasses, or kill them?]
MATT. 10:16 - Jesus: "...be ye...harmless as doves."
[Should one engage in killing, or be as harmless as doves?]
MARK 10:19; LUKE 18:20 - Jesus: "Do not kill."
MATT. 19:18 - Jesus: "Thou shalt do no murder."
[Did Jesus support, or oppose killing (murder)?]

**Perplexing:**

Why did Jesus recite a parable in which he justified killing? Why did Jesus not recite a parable about loving one's enemies? Why was Jesus hypocritical by supporting killing in some verses, but opposing it in other verses? Does this parable show that Jesus supported capital punishment? In MATT. 24:51, he also recited a parable in which a servant is cut asunder for misdeeds.
See also under 12:46-48.

19:29-30 - WHEN HE WAS COME NIGH TO BETHPHAGE AND BETHANY, AT THE MOUNT OF OLIVES, HE SENT TWO DISCIPLES, SAYING, "GO INTO THE VILLAGE, WHICH AT YOUR ENTERING YE SHALL FIND A COLT TIED, WHEREUPON NEVER MAN SAT; BRING HIM HITHER."

**Contradiction:** See under MATT. 21:1-2 and MARK 11:1-2.

**Perplexing:** See under MATT. 21:1-2.

19:31 - JESUS: "IF ANY MAN ASK YOU, 'WHY DO YOU LOOSE HIM?'...."

**Perplexing:** See under MATT. 21:3.

19:32 - THEY WENT, AND FOUND AS HE HAD SAID UNTO THEM.

**Contradiction:** See under MARK 11:4.

19:33 - AS THEY WERE LOOSING THE COLT, THE OWNERS SAID, "WHY LOOSE YE THE COLT?"

**Contradiction:**
MARK 11: 5 - Certain of them that stood there said, "What do ye, loosing the colt?"
[Did the owners of the colt, or certain people standing around question the disciples?]

19:35 - THEY BROUGHT HIM TO JESUS, CAST THEIR GARMENTS UPON THE COLT, AND SET JESUS THEREON.

**Contradictions:** See under MATT. 21:6-7 and MARK 11:7.

**Perplexing:** See under MARK 11:7.

**Old Testament:** See under MATT. 21:6-7.

19:37-38 - WHEN HE WAS COME NIGH AT THE DESCENT OF THE MOUNT OF OLIVES, THE WHOLE MULTITUDE OF DISCIPLES BEGAN TO REJOICE AND...SAYING, "BLESSED BE THE KING THAT COMETH IN THE NAME OF THE LORD; PEACE IN HEAVEN, AND GLORY IN THE HIGHEST."

**Contradictions:**
MATT. 21:9 - Multitudes that went before, and that followed, cried, "Hosanna to the Son of David; Blessed is he that cometh in the name of the Lord; Hosanna in the highest."
MARK 11:9-10 - They that went before, and that followed, cried, "Hosanna; Blessed is he that cometh in the name of the Lord; Blessed be the kingdom of our father David, that cometh in the name of the Lord, Hosanna in the highest."
JOHN 12:12-13 - People that...heard that Jesus was coming to Jerusalem...went to meet him, cried, "Hosanna; Blessed is the King of Israel that cometh in the name of the Lord." [This occurred before Jesus found the young ass in JOHN 12:14.]
[Did just the disciples, or a multitude of people speak?]
[Did the people say what LUKE, or MATT., or MARK, or JOHN reported?]
[Did the people speak after, or before Jesus rode on an ass or colt?]
See also under MATT. 21:8-9.

**Language**: See under MATT. 21:8-9.

**Old Testament:** See under MATT. 21:8-9.

19:39 - SOME OF THE PHARISEES FROM AMONG THE MULTITUDE SAID, "MASTER...."

**Perplexing:**
If the Pharisees were hostile to Jesus, why were they in the multitude welcoming him? Why did they call Jesus, "Master?"

19:45 - HE WENT INTO THE TEMPLE, AND BEGAN TO CAST OUT THEM THAT SOLD THEREIN, AND THEM THAT BOUGHT.

**Contradictions:**
MARK 11:11 - Jesus entered...the temple, looked around, and went to Bethany.
[Did Jesus go directly into the temple and throw out those who bought and sold, or did he just look around and return to Bethany?]
MARK 11: 12-15 - On the morrow.... .... Jesus went into the temple, and began to cast out them that sold and bought....
[Did Jesus cast the merchants out of the temple the first day he entered, or did he do it on the second day after just looking around the temple on the first day?]
JOHN 2:13-15 - Passover was at hand, and Jesus went to Jerusalem, and found in the temple those that sold oxen, sheep, and doves, and the changers of money...he drove them all out of the temple.... [This occurred at the start of his ministry shortly after acquiring disciples, and long before he entered Jerusalem riding on an ass.]
[Was it, or was it not yet Passover, when Jesus threw the merchants out of the temple?]
[Did he throw out the merchants near the end of his ministry, or near the beginning?]
See also under MATT. 21:12-13.

**Perplexing:** See under MATT. 21:12-13.

19:46 - JESUS: "IT IS WRITTEN, 'MY HOUSE IS THE HOUSE OF PRAYER, BUT YE HAVE MADE IT A DEN OF THIEVES.'"

**Old Testament:** See under MATT. 21:12-13.

19:47 - HE TAUGHT DAILY IN THE TEMPLE. THE CHIEF PRIESTS, THE SCRIBES, AND THE CHIEF OF THE PEOPLE SOUGHT TO DESTROY HIM.

**Perplexing:**
Why did the priests who wanted to destroy Jesus allow him to teach daily in the temple? Why did they want to destroy him, when he had not violated any Jewish law requiring capital punishment? If they wanted to destroy Jesus, why, in 13:31, did they urge him to flee when Herod wanted to kill him?
See also under MATT. 21:23.

20:1-2 - ...AS HE TAUGHT IN THE TEMPLE...THE CHIEF PRIESTS, AND SCRIBES CAME WITH THE ELDERS, SAYING, "BY WHAT AUTHORITY DOEST THOU THESE THINGS? OR WHO IS HE THAT GAVE THEE THIS AUTHORITY?"

**Contradiction:** See under MATT. 21:23.

**Perplexing:**
Why did the priests not stop Jesus from entering and teaching in the temple?
See also under 19:47.

20:4-7 - JESUS: "THE BAPTISM OF JOHN, WAS IT FROM HEAVEN, OR OF MEN?".... THEY ANSWERED THAT THEY COULD NOT TELL.

**Perplexing:** See under MATT. 21:25-27.

**Pagan concept:** See under MATT. 3:5-6.

**History:** See under MATT. 3:5-6.

**Old Testament:** See under MATT. 3:5-6.

20:9-12 - BEGAN HE TO SPEAK THIS PARABLE; "A MAN LEFT A VINEYARD IN THE CARE OF HUSBANDMEN. THE MAN ON THREE SEPARATE OCCASIONS SENT A SERVANT TO OBTAIN SOME OF THE FRUIT FROM THE HUSBANDMEN. EACH SERVANT WAS BEATEN AND FORCED TO RETURN EMPTY."

**Contradictions:**
MATT. 21:34-36 - Three servants were initially sent; one was beaten, one was killed, and another was stoned. Additional servants were then sent, but they were treated in the same manner.
[Did Jesus say that the man sent a servant on three separate occasions, or that three were sent together, followed by additional servants?]
MARK 12:1-5 - On three separate occasions a servant was sent; two were beaten and one was killed. Many others were then sent; some were beaten and some were killed.
[Did Jesus say that a servant was sent on three separate occasions, or that many servants were sent after a servant had been sent on three separate occasions?]
[Were the three servants who were sent individually beaten, or was one or more killed?]
[Were three, or more than three servants sent?]

20:13-15 - JESUS: " SAID THE LORD OF THE VINEYARD, 'I WILL SEND MY BELOVED SON....' WHEN THE HUSBANDMEN SAW HIM, THEY REASONED, 'THIS IS THE HEIR; LET US KILL HIM, THAT THE INHERITANCE MAY BE OURS.' THEY CAST HIM OUT OF THE VINEYARD, AND KILLED HIM. WHAT SHALL THE LORD OF THE VINEYARD DO UNTO THEM?"

**Contradiction:** See under MATT. 21:37-39.

20:16 - JESUS: "HE SHALL COME AND DESTROY THESE HUSBANDMEN, AND SHALL GIVE THE VINEYARD TO OTHERS." THE PEOPLE SAID, "GOD FORBID."

**Contradictions:**
MATT. 21:41 - They say unto Jesus, "He will miserably destroy those wicked men, and will let out his

vineyard unto other husbandmen, which shall render him the fruits in their seasons."
[Did Jesus, or the people say that the owner would destroy the husbandmen?]
[Did the people say, "God forbid," or did they say that the owner would destroy the husbandmen?]

**Perplexing:**
Jesus again sanctioned killing for criminal activity.
Why did Jesus not have the man follow his teachings, and forgive, bless, and do good for the husbandmen? See also under 12:46-48 and 19:27.

20:17-18 - JESUS: "WHAT IS THIS THAT IS WRITTEN, 'THE STONE WHICH THE BUILDERS REJECTED, IS BECOME THE HEAD OF THE CORNER? WHOSOEVER SHALL FALL UPON THAT STONE SHALL BE BROKEN; BUT ON WHOMSOEVER IT SHALL FALL, IT WILL GRIND TO POWDER.'"

**Contradiction:**
MATT. 21:42 - Jesus saith, "Did ye never read in the scriptures, 'The stone which the builders rejected, is become the head of the corner; this is the Lord's doing, and it is marvellous in our eyes?'"
MARK 12:10:11 - Jesus: "Have ye not read this scripture, 'The stone which the builders rejected is become the head of the corner; this was the Lord's doing, and it is marvellous in our eyes?'"
[Did Jesus speak about someone falling on the stone and the stone falling on someone, or did he say that according to scripture it was the Lord's doing and is marvelous?]

**Old Testament:** See under MATT. 21:42.

**Perplexing:**
Why did the people, especially the priests, fail to point out that Jesus misquoted the scripture?

20:21-25 - THEY ASKED HIM, "...IS IT LAWFUL FOR US TO GIVE TRIBUTE UNTO CAESAR?" HE...SAID, "...? SHEW ME A PENNY. WHOSE IMAGE AND SUPERSCRIPTION HATH IT?" THEY SAID, "CAESAR'S." HE SAID, "RENDER UNTO CAESAR THE THINGS WHICH BE CAESAR'S, AND UNTO GOD THE THINGS WHICH BE GOD'S."

**Perplexing:** See under MATT. 22:17-21.

**History:** See under MATT. 22:17-21.

20:27-28 - CAME TO HIM CERTAIN SADDUCEES, WHICH DENY THAT THERE IS ANY RESURRECTION, SAYING, "MASTER, MOSES WROTE, IF ANY MAN'S BROTHER DIE WITHOUT CHILDREN, HIS BROTHER SHOULD TAKE HIS WIFE AND RAISE UP SEED UNTO HIS BROTHER."

**Old Testament:** See under MATT. 22:23-28.

**Perplexing:** See under MATT. 22:23-28.

20:35-36 - JESUS: "THEY WHICH SHALL BE ACCOUNTED WORTHY TO OBTAIN THAT WORLD, AND THE RESURRECTION FROM THE DEAD, NEITHER MARRY, NOR ARE GIVEN IN MARRIAGE...FOR THEY ARE EQUAL UNTO THE ANGELS, AND ARE THE CHILDREN OF GOD...."

**Contradiction:** See under MATT. 22:30.

**Perplexing:** See under MATT. 22:30.

20:37 - JESUS: "...MOSES SHEWED AT THE BUSH, WHEN HE CALLETH THE LORD THE GOD OF ABRAHAM, THE GOD OF ISAAC, AND THE GOD OF JACOB."

**Contradictions:**
EX. 3:6 - [At the bush] He [God] said, "I am the God of thy father, the God of Abraham, the God of Isaac, and the God of Jacob."
[Did Moses call God, "The God of Abraham, Isaac, and Jacob," or did God make the statement?]
MARK 12:26 - Jesus: "...have ye not read in the book of Moses, how in the bush God spake, 'I am the God of Abraham, Isaac, and Jacob?'"
[Did Jesus say that Moses called God the God of Abraham, Isaac, and Jacob, or did he say that God so referred to Himself?]

**History:** See under MATT. 22:31-32.

**Perplexing:**
Why did Jesus misquote the scripture? Why did the Jews not correct him?
See also under MATT. 22:31-32.

20:41-44 - JESUS: "HOW SAY THEY THAT CHRIST IS DAVID'S SON? DAVID SAITH IN THE BOOK OF PSALMS, 'THE LORD SAID UNTO MY LORD, "SIT THOU ON MY RIGHT HAND, TILL I MAKE THINE ENEMIES THY FOOTSTOOL."' DAVID THEREFORE CALLETH HIM 'LORD'; HOW IS HE THEN HIS SON?"

**Old Testament:** See under MATT. 22:42-45.

**Contradictions:** See under MATT. 1:18.

**Judaism:** See under MATT. 22:42-45.

**Perplexing:** See under MATT. 22:42-45.

20:46-47 - JESUS: "BEWARE OF THE SCRIBES...THE SAME SHALL RECEIVE GREATER DAMNATION."

**Contradictions:**
MATT. 5:20 - Jesus: "That except your righteousness shall exceed the righteousness of the scribes and Pharisees, ye shall in no case enter into the kingdom of heaven."
[Were the scribes doomed to damnation, or were they righteous?]
See also under Matt. 15:7-9.

**Perplexing:** See under MATT. 23:14.

21:1-4 - HE SAW RICH MEN CASTING THEIR GIFTS INTO THE TREASURY. HE SAW A POOR WIDOW CASTING IN TWO MITES [SMALL COINS]. HE SAID, "THIS POOR WIDOW HATH CAST IN MORE THAN THEY; ALL THESE OF THEIR ABUNDANCE CAST OFFERINGS, BUT SHE CAST IN ALL THE LIVING THAT SHE HAD."

**Perplexing:** See under MARK 12:41-44.

**Pagan parallel:** See under MARK 12:41-44.

21:5-6 - AS SOME SPAKE OF THE TEMPLE...HE SAID, "...THE DAYS WILL COME, IN WHICH THERE SHALL NOT BE LEFT ONE STONE THAT SHALL NOT BE THROWN DOWN."

**History:** See under MATT. 24:1-2.

21:7 - THEY ASKED, "MASTER, WHEN SHALL THESE THINGS BE? WHAT SIGN WILL THERE BE WHEN THESE THINGS SHALL COME TO PASS?"

**Contradictions:**
MATT. 24:3 - As he sat upon the mount of Olives, the disciples came unto him privately, saying, "When shall these things be? What shall be the sign of thy coming?
MARK 13:3-4 - As he sat upon the mount of Olives, over against the temple [the Mount of Olives was about three miles from the temple], Peter, James, John, and Andrew asked him privately, "When shall these things be? What shall be the sign? What shall be the sign when all these things shall be fulfilled?"
[Was Jesus at the temple, or at the Mount of Olives, when he was asked about the sign?]
[Was he asked openly, or privately?]
[Did all the disciples, or just four disciples ask Jesus about the sign?]

21:8-27 - JESUS IDENTIFIED NUMEROUS SIGNS THAT WILL PRECEDE HIS RETURN. THESE INCLUDED FALSE CHRISTS, WARS, EARTHQUAKES, FAMINES, PESTILENCE, FEARFUL SIGHTS AND GREAT SIGNS FROM HEAVEN, PERSECUTION, AND OTHER DISASTERS. "THEN SHALL THEY SEE THE SON OF MAN COMING IN A CLOUD WITH POWER AND GREAT GLORY."

**Contradictions:** See under MATT. 24:3-7.

**Perplexing:** See under MATT. 24:3-7, 9, and 11.

**Pagan parallel:** See under MATT. 24:3-7.

21:12-17 - JESUS: "BEFORE ALL THESE, THEY SHALL PERSECUTE YOU, DELIVERING YOU TO SYNAGOGUES, AND INTO PRISONS.... .... SOME OF YOU SHALL BE PUT TO DEATH. YE SHALL BE HATED FOR MY NAME'S SAKE."

**Perplexing:** See under MATT. 24:9.

**History:** See under MATT. 24:9.

21:18 - JESUS: "THERE SHALL NOT AN HAIR OF YOUR HEAD PERISH."

**Perplexing:**
Was Jesus referring only to those listening to him, or to everyone who believed him? What persecution did those listening to him experience? Did all those who listened to him survive the persecution and killing? If he meant everyone who believed in him, why did his prophecy fail? Beginning with ACTS 7:58-60, when Stephen was killed, through the killing of Christians by the Romans under Nero, the later slaughter by Muslims, and the religious wars into modern times, some Christians have not been spared persecution even by other Christians. Why did Jesus mislead his adherents?

21:24 - JESUS: "THEY [THE RESIDENTS OF JUDAEA] SHALL FALL BY THE EDGE OF THE SWORD, AND SHALL BE LED AWAY CAPTIVE INTO ALL NATIONS; AND JERUSALEM SHALL BE TRODDEN DOWN OF THE GENTILES, UNTIL THE TIMES OF THE GENTILES BE FULFILLED."

**Perplexing:**
Why did Jesus fail to tell people about the future invention of guns and other weapons? When did the residents of Judaea fall by the edge of the sword? When were they led away captive into all nations? As swords are rarely used in wars now, and since Judaea no longer exists, how can Jesus' prophecy ever materialize?
Since the Gentiles no longer control Jerusalem, has the time of the Gentiles come, or is this another failed prophecy? Why were these prophecies not cited in the other gospels?

21:27-28 - JESUS: "THEN SHALL THEY SEE THE SON OF MAN COMING IN A CLOUD WITH POWER AND GREAT GLORY. AND WHEN THESE THINGS BEGIN TO PASS, THEN LOOK UP, AND LIFT UP YOUR HEADS, FOR YOUR REDEMPTION DRAWETH NIGH."

**Perplexing:** See under MATT. 24:30-31.

**Old Testament:** See under MATT. 24:30-31.

21:31-32 - JESUS: "WHEN YE SEE THESE THINGS COME TO PASS, KNOW THAT THE KINGDOM OF GOD IS NIGH AT HAND. THIS GENERATION SHALL NOT PASS AWAY, TILL ALL BE FULFILLED."

**Contradiction:** See under MATT. 24:3-7.

**Perplexing:**
Why did Jesus tell his listeners that they will observe the happenings that he was prophesying? Why did he deceive them into believing that the events would occur during their lifetime? Why was Jesus' prophecy not fulfilled? In MATT. 17:11-12 and MARK 9:12-13, Jesus said that Elias (Elijah) must come first, and that he had already come. If he had come, why is the world still waiting for the kingdom?
See also under MATT. 24:3-7 and 30-31.

21:33 - JESUS: “HEAVEN AND EARTH SHALL PASS AWAY, BUT MY WORDS SHALL NOT PASS AWAY.”

**Contradiction:** See under MATT. 24:35.

**Old Testament:** See under MATT. 24:35.

**Pagan parallel:** See under MATT. 24:35.

21:37-38 - IN THE DAYTIME HE WAS TEACHING IN THE TEMPLE.... ALL THE PEOPLE CAME EARLY IN THE MORNING TO THE TEMPLE TO HEAR HIM.

**Perplexing:**
Considering the animosity that existed between Jesus and the Pharisees and the chief priests, how was he able to obtain permission to teach in the temple? Why did the priests allow him into the temple after his tantrum there (when he attacked the merchants - MATT. 21:12, MARK 11:15-16, LUKE 19:45, and JOHN 2:14-15)? Why did people want to listen to him?

22:2 - THE CHIEF PRIESTS AND SCRIBES SOUGHT HOW THEY MIGHT KILL HIM, FOR THEY FEARED THE PEOPLE.

**Perplexing:**

Why did the priests and scribes not arrange to have someone kill Jesus? They knew when he came and went from the temple; they could have had him watched and followed. Why did they fear the people? Later no one will come to defend Jesus after his arrest. They could also have relied on the Roman authorities to squelch any protests or riots.
See also under MATT. 26:3-4.

22:3-6 - ENTERED SATAN INTO JUDAS ISCARIOT; HE WENT, AND COMMUNED WITH THE CHIEF PRIESTS AND CAPTAINS, HOW HE MIGHT BETRAY HIM UNTO THEM IN THE ABSENCE OF THE MULTITUDE. [JESUS AND THE DISCIPLES HAD NOT YET PARTAKEN OF THE “LAST SUPPER.”]

**Contradictions:**
JOHN 13:1-27 - After the meal and sop on the day before passover, Satan entered Judas.
[Did Satan enter Judas before, or after the meal?]
[Was the meal the feast of Passover, or a supper the day before Passover?]

**Perplexing:**
Why was it necessary for Satan to cause Judas to betray Jesus? If Satan instigated Jesus’ betrayal, arrest, crucifixion, and resurrection, is Satan then responsible for Christianity? If Satan had not induced Judas to betray Jesus, would Christianity have come into existence? Should Christians thank Satan for having given them their religion(s)?
See also under MATT. 26:14-16.

22:7-9 - CAME THE DAY OF UNLEAVENED BREAD WHEN THE PASSOVER MUST BE KILLED. HE SENT PETER AND JOHN, SAYING, "GO AND PREPARE THE PASSOVER." THEY SAID, "WHERE WILT THOU THAT WE PREPARE?"

**Contradiction:**
MATT. 26:17 - The first day of the feast of unleavened bread, the disciples came to Jesus, saying, "Where wilt thou that we prepare to eat the Passover?"
MARK 14:12 - The first day of unleavened bread, when they killed the Passover, his disciples said, "Where wilt thou that we prepare the Passover?"
[Did Jesus send Peter and John to prepare the Passover, or did the disciples come to him and ask where they should prepare it?]

**History:** See under MATT. 26:2.

22:10-12 - HE SAID, "WHEN YE ARE ENTERED INTO THE CITY, THERE SHALL A MAN MEET YOU, BEARING A PITCHER OF WATER; FOLLOW HIM INTO THE HOUSE WHERE HE ENTERETH. YE SHALL SAY UNTO THE GOODMAN OF THE HOUSE, 'THE MASTER SAITH, WHERE IS THE GUESTCHAMBER, WHERE I SHALL EAT THE PASSOVER WITH MY DISCIPLES?' HE SHALL SHEW YOU A LARGE ROOM FURNISHED; THERE MAKE READY."

**Contradictions:**
MATT. 26:18 - He said, "Go into the city to such a man, and say, 'The Master saith, "My time is at hand; I will keep the Passover at thy house with my disciples."'"
[Did Jesus tell the disciples to meet and follow a man carrying a pitcher of water to a house where they will speak to the house owner about a room for Passover,, or did he tell them to go directly to a certain house and speak to the owner?]
See also under MATT. 26:17-18.

**Perplexing:**
If Jesus had already made arrangements for a water carrier to meet the disciples, why could he not also have made the Passover arrangements?

22:14-15 - WHEN THE HOUR WAS COME, HE SAT DOWN, AND THE TWELVE APOSTLES WITH HIM. HE SAID, "I HAVE DESIRED TO EAT THIS PASSOVER WITH YOU BEFORE I SUFFER."

**History:** See under MATT. 26:2.

**Perplexing:**
Why did Jesus fail to inform his disciples that in about 300 years the Roman Emperor Constantine would prohibit Christians from celebrating Passover, and instead require them to observe the pagan Easter celebrating the resurrection of pagan deities around the time of the vernal equinox? Why have almost all Christians since then continued to observe the pagan Easter, rather than Passover which was observed by Christians into the fourth century?

**Pagan parallel:** See under MATT. 26:19-21.

22:16 - JESUS: "I WILL NOT ANYMORE EAT THEREOF, UNTIL IT BE FULFILLED IN THE KINGDOM OF GOD."

**Contradiction:**
LUKE 24:42-43 - They gave him [Jesus] a piece of a broiled fish and of an honeycomb. He took it and did eat before them.
JOHN 21:13 - Jesus cometh, and taketh bread...and fish.
[Did not, or did Jesus eat again on earth?]

**Perplexing:**
Was Jesus saying that people eat in the kingdom of God? If so, what food is available? Is there meat, bread, etc. in God's kingdom? If so, how is the food obtained? Are there regular meal times? Does everyone there eat at the same time? Who does the cooking and cleaning up? What vegetables are there? Who grows them? What meat is available? Who raises and kills the animals? If Jesus eats, does this mean that God and the Holy Ghost also eat? Do people get hungry in heaven? Does anyone get indigestion? Since eating implies the existence of a digestive tract and excretory systems, what type of rest room facilities are available? Why would food and drink be needed in the kingdom?
See also under 14:15 and under MATT. 26:29.

**Pagan parallels:**
A number of pre-Christian pagan religions such as those involved with the worship of Mithra, and Serapis, among others, believed in celestial/heavenly banquets.

22:17-20 - HE TOOK THE CUP, GAVE THANKS, AND SAID, "TAKE THIS, AND DIVIDE IT AMONG YOURSELVES; I WILL NOT DRINK OF THE FRUIT OF THE VINE, UNTIL THE KINGDOM OF GOD SHALL COME." HE TOOK BREAD, GAVE THANKS, BRAKE IT, AND GAVE UNTO THEM, SAYING, "THIS IS MY BODY WHICH IS GIVEN FOR YOU; THIS DO IN REMEMBRANCE OF ME." LIKEWISE, THE CUP AFTER SUPPER, SAYING, "THIS CUP IS THE NEW TESTAMENT IN MY BLOOD, WHICH IS SHED FOR YOU."

**Contradictions:**
MATT. 26:26-27 - As they were eating, Jesus took bread.... He took the cup....
MARK 14:22-23 - As they did eat, Jesus took bread.... He took the cup....
[Did Jesus take the cup, or the bread first?]
MATT. 26:28 - Jesus: "This is my blood of the new testament, which is shed for many for the remission of sins."
[Did Jesus say that his blood is shed for his disciples, or for many for the remission of sins?]
MARK 14:24 - He said, "This is my blood of the new testament, which is shed for many."
[Did Jesus say that his blood is shed for the disciples, or for many?]

**Judaism:** See under MATT. 26:25-28.

**Pagan concept:** See under MATT. 26:25-28.

**Pagan parallels**: See under MATT. 26:25-28.

**History:** See under MATT. 26:25-28.

**Perplexing:** See also under MATT. 26:25-28 and 26:29.

**Old Testament:** See under MATT. 26:25-28.

22:21 - JESUS: "THE HAND OF HIM THAT BETRAYETH ME IS ON THE TABLE."

**Contradictions:**
MATT. 26:21 - As they did eat [Prior to Jesus referring to his body and his blood], he said, "One of you shall betray me."
MARK 14:18 - As they sat and did eat [Before Jesus referred to his body and his blood] he said, "One of you which eateth with me shall betray me."
[Did Jesus say that he would be betrayed by one who was at the table after, or before speaking about his body and blood?]
JOHN 13:18 - [At the end of a supper the day before the feast of Passover, without speaking of his body and blood, but after washing the disciples' feet] Jesus: "...He that eateth bread with me hath lifted up his heel against me."
[Did Jesus tell the disciples at the Passover meal that he would be betrayed, or at a meal the night before Passover?]
See also under MATT. 26:19-21.

22:22 - JESUS: "...WOE UNTO THAT MAN BY WHOM HE IS BETRAYED!"

**Contradiction:** See under MATT. 26:24.

**Perplexing:** See under MATT. 26:24.

22:23-24 - THEY BEGAN TO INQUIRE AMONG THEMSELVES, WHICH OF THEM SHOULD DO THIS THING. THERE WAS ALSO A STRIFE AMONG THEM, WHICH OF THEM SHOULD BE ACCOUNTED THE GREATEST.

**Contradictions:**
MATT. 26:22 - They were exceeding sorrowful, and began every one of them to say, "Lord is it I?"
MARK 14:19 - They began to be sorrowful, and to say unto him one by one, "Is it I?"
[Did the disciples inquire among themselves, or did they ask Jesus who would betray him?]
See also under MATT. 26:22.

**Perplexing:**
Why did the disciples quickly forget about the betrayal and argue about which one of them is the greatest? Why did they not question Jesus further about the betrayal?

22:29-30 - JESUS: "I APPOINT UNTO YOU A KINGDOM, AS MY FATHER HATH APPOINTED UNTO ME, THAT YE MAY EAT AND DRINK AT MY TABLE IN MY KINGDOM, AND SIT ON THRONES JUDGING THE TWELVE TRIBES OF ISRAEL."

**Contradictions:** See under MATT. 19:28.

**History:** See under MATT. 19:28.

**Perplexing:**
In 22:22, Jesus said, "...woe unto that man by whom he [Jesus] is betrayed!" Why now, then, did he promise Judas along with the other disciples a place in his kingdom eating, drinking, and judging the Israelite tribes?
See also under 14:15, 22:16, and under MATT. 19:28

**Pagan concept:** See under 22:16

22:32 - JESUS [TO SIMON]: "I HAVE PRAYED FOR THEE, THAT THY FAITH FAIL NOT; AND WHEN THOU ART CONVERTED, STRENGTHEN THY BRETHREN."

**Perplexing:**
Why did Jesus have to pray for Peter? He said in MATT. 6:8, "Your Father knoweth what things ye have need of, before ye ask Him." If Jesus is part of the Trinity, to which part does he pray? If he is one with his Father, as he said in JOHN 10:30, was he praying to himself? How could Peter's faith fail after he had witnessed so may of Jesus' miracles including the resurrection of the dead? Why was Peter not yet converted? Why did the other disciples have to be strengthened? Why could Jesus not prevent Peter's faith from failing without having to pray for him? Why could Jesus not strengthen the other disciples?

22:34 - HE SAID "PETER, THE COCK SHALL NOT CROW THIS DAY, BEFORE THOU SHALT THRICE DENY THAT THOU KNOWEST ME." [THIS OCCURRED BEFORE THEY WENT TO THE MOUNT OF OLIVES (22:39).]

**Contradictions:**
MATT. 26:30-34 - When they had sung an hymn, they went into the Mount of Olives. .... Jesus said, "... this night before the cock crow, thou shalt deny me thrice."
MARK 14:26-30 - When they had sung an hymn, they went into the Mount of Olives. .... Jesus saith, "This night, before the cock crow twice, thou shalt deny me thrice."
[Did Jesus say that Peter would deny him three times before, or after they went to the Mount of Olives?]
See also under MATT. 26:34.

**History:** See under MATT. 26:34.

22:36 - SAID HE, "...HE THAT HATH NO SWORD, LET HIM SELL HIS GARMENT, AND BUY ONE."

**Contradictions:**
MATT. 10:16 - Jesus: "I send you forth as sheep in the midst of wolves; be ye therefore wise as serpents, and harmless as doves."
[Should one carry a sword, or be as harmless as a dove?]
MATT. 26:52 - Said Jesus, "Put up thy sword into his place, for all that take the sword shall perish with the sword."
[Should one buy a sword, or should one not use (have) a sword?]
ACTS 10:36 - Peter: "The word which God sent unto the children of Israel, preaching peace by Jesus Christ...."

[Did Jesus want his disciples to have swords, or did he preach peace?]

**Perplexing:**
If Jesus opposed the use of swords, and wanted his followers to be as harmless as doves, why did he tell his disciples to buy swords? Instead of telling them to obtain swords, why did Jesus not instruct them to pray for protection? Why would anyone having faith in God need a sword? Did not Jesus believe that he or his Father could protect them? Does the need for or use of a sword demonstrate a lack of faith in the ability of God to provide protection? In LUKE 10:19, Jesus said, "I give you power...and nothing shall by any means hurt you." If nothing can hurt the disciples, why do they need swords?
See also under MATT. 26:51.

22:37 - JESUS: "THIS THAT IS WRITTEN MUST YET BE ACCOMPLISHED IN ME, 'HE WAS RECKONED AMONG THE TRANSGRESSORS....'"

**Old Testament:**
ISA. 53:12 - "...he was numbered with the transgressors...."

22:38 - THEY SAID, "LORD, HERE ARE TWO SWORDS." HE SAID, "IT IS ENOUGH."

**Contradictions:** See under 22:36.

**Perplexing:** See under 22:36.

22:39 - HE WENT TO THE MOUNT OF OLIVES, AS HE WAS WONT; HIS DISCIPLES FOLLOWED HIM.

**Contradictions:** See under 22:34 and under MATT. 26:30.

**Old Testament:** See under MATT. 26:30.

**Perplexing:** See under MATT. 26:30.

22:40 - ...HE SAID, "PRAY THAT YE ENTER NOT INTO TEMPTATION." [THIS WAS SAID BEFORE HE FOUND THE DISCIPLES ASLEEP (22:45).]

**Contradictions:**
MATT. 26:41 - [After finding the disciples asleep in 26:40] Jesus: "Watch and pray, that ye enter not into temptation."
MARK 14:38 - [After finding the disciples asleep in 14:37] Jesus: "Watch and pray, lest ye enter into temptation."
[Did Jesus tell the disciples to pray that they enter not into temptation before, or after he found them asleep?]
See also under MATT. 26:41.

**Perplexing:** See under MATT. 26:41.

22:41 - HE WAS WITHDRAWN FROM THEM ABOUT A STONE'S CAST, KNEELED DOWN, AND PRAYED.

**Contradictions:**

MATT. 26:36-39 - Cometh Jesus with them unto a place called Gethsemane.... .... He went a little further, fell on his face, and prayed....

MARK 14:32-35 - They came to a place named Gethsemane.... .... He went forward a little, fell on the ground, and prayed....

[Did Jesus pray at the Mount of Olives (22:39), or in Gethsemane?]

[Did Jesus pray after, or before telling the disciples to pray to avoid temptation?]

**Perplexing:** See under MATT. 14:22-23.

22:42-46 - JESUS: "FATHER, IF THOU BE WILLING, REMOVE THIS CUP FROM ME; NEVERTHELESS NOT MY WILL, BUT THINE BE DONE." AN ANGEL STRENGTHENED HIM. BEING IN AGONY HE PRAYED MORE EARNESTLY; HIS SWEAT WAS AS GREAT DROPS OF BLOOD FALLING TO THE GROUND. HE ROSE, AND WAS COME TO HIS DISCIPLES; HE FOUND THEM SLEEPING, AND SAID, "...RISE AND PRAY LEST YE ENTER INTO TEMPTATION."

**Contradictions:**

MATT. 26:39-44 and MARK 14:35-41 - He...prayed three separate times; after each time he found the disciples asleep; after the first prayer he told them to pray to avoid temptation.

[Did Jesus pray two, or three times?]

[Did Jesus find the disciples asleep once, or three times?]

[Did Jesus tell the disciples to pray to avoid temptation after praying the second time, or after the first prayer?]

[Did Jesus tell the disciples to pray to avoid temptation twice (22:40 and 22:46), or just once as in MATT. and MARK?]

See also under MATT. 26:36 and 37-39.

**Perplexing:**

Why did Jesus, a divine being, who claimed to be one with God in JOHN 10:30, need to be strengthened? How could the Son of God become so weak as to require an angel to strengthen him? How did the angel strengthen Jesus? Why did the other gospels not report the angel? Why did Jesus behave like a terrified human being? Why was he in agony? Why could he not control his emotions? Why did he not act like an immortal divine being? As the Son of God, he need not even feel pain; he will be resurrected, and will be in heaven with his Father. Why was he not joyful about the prospect of returning to his Father? Why did the immortal Jesus sweat blood? Why did the other gospels not report this event?

See also under MATT. 4:11, 26:37-39, 40, and 45-46.

**Medical condition:**

Sweating blood is known as hematidrosis.

22:47 - ...A MULTITUDE, AND JUDAS, WENT BEFORE THEM, AND DREW NEAR JESUS TO KISS HIM.

**Perplexing:** See under MATT. 26:47.

22:48 - JESUS: "JUDAS, BETRAYEST THOU THE SON OF MAN WITH A KISS?"

**Contradictions:**
MATT. 26:48-50 - [Judas] gave them a sign, saying,"Whomsoever I shall kiss, is he...." He came to Jesus, and said, "Hail, master," and kissed him. Jesus said, "Friend, wherefore art thou come?"
[Did Jesus say that Judas was betraying him with a kiss, or did he call Judas, "friend," and ask him why he had come?]
MARK 14:44-45 - [Judas] had given them a token, saying, "Whomsoever I shall kiss, is he...." He goeth to him, and saith, "Master, master," and kissed him.
[Did Judas attempt to kiss Jesus without first speaking to him, or did he greet Jesus before kissing him?]
[Did, or did not Jesus speak to Judas?]
JOHN 18:3-5 - Judas having received a band of men and officers...cometh with lanterns, torches, and weapons. Jesus...said, "Whom seek ye?"
[Did Jesus ask Judas why he was betraying him with a kiss, or did he ask the people for whom they were looking?]
See also under MATT. 26:48-49.

**Perplexing:** See under MATT. 26:47 and 26: 48-49

22:50-51 - ONE OF THEM [WITH JESUS] SMOTE THE SERVANT OF THE HIGH PRIEST, AND CUT OFF HIS RIGHT EAR. .... HE TOUCHED HIS EAR, AND HEALED HIM. [THIS OCCURRED BEFORE JESUS WAS SEIZED IN 22:54.]

**Contradictions:**
MATT. 26:50-51 - .... They laid hands on Jesus and took him. One of them with Jesus drew his sword, and struck a servant of the high priest's, and smote off his ear.
MARK 14:46-47 - They laid hands on him, and took him. One of them that stood by drew a sword, and smote a servant of the high priest, and cut off his ear.
[Was the servant's ear cut off before, or after Jesus was seized by the people?]
[Did, or did not Jesus heal the servant's ear?]

**Perplexing:** See under MATT. 26:51.

**Language**: See under MATT. 26:51.

22:52-54 - JESUS SAID UNTO THE CHIEF PRIESTS, CAPTAINS OF THE TEMPLE, AND ELDERS, "BE YE COME OUT, AS AGAINST A THIEF, WITH SWORDS AND STAVES? WHEN I WAS DAILY WITH YOU IN THE TEMPLE, YE STRETCHED FORTH NO HANDS AGAINST ME...." THEN TOOK THEY HIM....

**Contradictions:**
MATT. 26:50-55 - .... Came they, laid hands on Jesus, and took him. .... Said Jesus to the multitudes, "Are ye come out as against a thief...? I sat daily with you teaching in the temple, and ye laid no hold on me."
MARK 14:46-49 - They laid hands on him and took him. .... Jesus said, "Are ye come out as against a thief...? I was daily with you in the temple teaching, and ye took me not...."

[Did Jesus remind the people that he had been with them in the temple before, or after he was seized?]
[Did Jesus speak to the chief priests, captains, and elders, or to the multitudes?]

**Perplexing:** See under MATT. 26:55.

22:54 - THEY TOOK JESUS INTO THE HIGH PRIEST'S HOUSE. PETER FOLLOWED AFAR OFF.

**Contradictions:** See under MATT. 26:57.

**Old Testament:** See under MATT. 26:30.

**Perplexing:** See under MATT. 26:57.

**History:** See under MATT. 26:57.

22:55 - WHEN THEY HAD KINDLED A FIRE IN THE MIDST OF THE HALL, AND WERE SET DOWN TOGETHER, PETER SAT AMONG THEM.

**Contradictions:**
MATT. 26:58 - Peter followed...unto the high priest's palace, went in, and sat with the servants....
MARK 14:54 - Peter followed...into the palace of the high priest, and sat with the servants.
[Did Peter sit with the people who brought Jesus, or with the servants?]
See also under MATT. 26:58.

**Perplexing:** See under MATT. 26:58.

22:56 - A MAID BEHELD HIM AS HE SAT BY THE FIRE, AND SAID, "THIS MAN WAS ALSO WITH HIM." [THIS OCCURRED BEFORE JESUS WAS QUESTIONED BY THE PRIESTS AND OTHERS.]

**Contradictions:**
MATT. 26:69 - [After Jesus was questioned in 26:62-64] Peter sat without in the palace, and a damsel came, saying, "Thou also wast with Jesus of Galilee."
[Did the woman refer to Jesus as "him," or as "Jesus of Galilee?]
MARK 14:66-67 - [After Jesus was questioned in 14:60] As Peter was beneath in the palace, cometh one of the maids of the high priest; when she saw Peter, she looked, and said, "Thou also wast with Jesus of Nazareth."
[Did the woman refer to Jesus as "him," or as "Jesus of Nazareth"?]
JOHN 18:16-17 - Peter stood at the door.... Saith the damsel that kept the door unto Peter, "Art not thou also one of this man's disciples?" ....
[Did a woman speak to Peter before, or after Jesus was questioned?]
[Was the woman who spoke to Peter a maid, or a doorkeeper?]
[Did the woman refer to Jesus as "him," or as "this man"?]
[Did the woman ask Peter if he was with Jesus, or if he was a disciple of Jesus?]
[Was Peter sitting in the palace, or standing by the palace door when he was pointed out as being a follower of Jesus?]
See also under MATT. 26:69.

**Perplexing:** See under MATT. 26:69.

22:57 - PETER: "WOMAN, I KNOW HIM NOT."

**Contradictions:**
MATT. 26:70 - Peter: "I know not what thou sayest."
MARK 14:68 - Peter: "I know not, neither understand what thou sayest"; ...and the cock crew.
[Did Peter say that he did not know Jesus, or that he did not know what the woman was saying?]
[Did, or did not the cock crow?]
JOHN 18:17 - .... He saith, "I am not."
[Did Peter say that he did not know Jesus, or that he was not one of Jesus' disciples?]

**Perplexing:**
Peter had seen Jesus' power in performing remarkable miracles including raising the dead; he also had stated that Jesus was "The Christ of God" (LUKE 9:20). Why then was he now afraid to say that he knows Jesus? Why was he not proud to say that he was associated with someone who could perform miracles and who is "The Christ"?
See also under MATT. 26:70-72.

22:58 - AFTER A LITTLE WHILE ANOTHER SAW HIM AND SAID, "THOU ART ALSO OF THEM." PETER SAID, "MAN, I AM NOT."

**Contradictions:**
MATT. 26:71-72 - When he was gone out onto the porch, another maid saw him, and said unto them that were there, "This fellow was also with Jesus of Nazareth." He denied with an oath, "I do not know the man."
[Did a man ask Peter if he was one of Jesus' disciples, or did a maid speaking to nearby people say that he was with Jesus of Nazareth?]
[Was Peter still by the fire, or had he gone onto the porch?]
MARK 14:69-70 - A maid saw him again, and began to say to them that stood by, "This is one of them." He denied it again. ....
[Did a man ask Peter if he was one of Jesus' disciples, or did a maid speaking to nearby people say that he was one of Jesus' disciples?]
JOHN 18:25 - Peter stood and warmed himself. They said, "Art not thou also one of his disciples?" He said, "I am not." [This occurred after Jesus was questioned by the high priest.]
[Did a man ask Peter if he was one of Jesus' disciples, or did those around him ask whether he was one of Jesus' disciples?]
[Did the incident take place before, or after Jesus was questioned?]

**Perplexing:** See under 22:57, and under MATT. 26:69.

22:59 - ABOUT THE SPACE OF ONE HOUR AFTER ANOTHER AFFIRMED, "THIS FELLOW ALSO WAS WITH HIM, FOR HE IS GALILAEAN."

**Contradictions:**
MATT. 26:73 - After a while, they that stood by, said, "Thou also art one of them, for thy speech betrayeth thee."

MARK 14:70 - .... A little after, they that stood by said, "Thou art one of them, for thou art a Galilaean; thy speech agreeth thereto."
[Did one unidentified person, or a group of people identify Peter as a Galilean?]
JOHN 18:26 - One of the servants of the high priest, being his kinsman whose ear Peter cut off, saith, "Did not I see thee in the garden with him?"
[Was Peter identified as a Galilean, or did a servant say that he saw Peter with Jesus?]

22:60 - PETER SAID, "MAN, I KNOW NOT WHAT THOU SAYEST." IMMEDIATELY, WHILE HE SPOKE, THE COCK CREW. [JESUS HAD NOT YET BEEN QUESTIONED BY THE CHIEF PRIESTS, SCRIBES, AND ELDERS.]

**Contradictions:**
MATT. 26:74 - Then began he to curse and swear, saying, "I know not the man." Immediately the cock crew. [Jesus had been questioned in 26:62-64.]
MARK 14:71-72 - He began to curse and swear, saying, "I know not this man of whom ye speak." The second time the cock crew. .... [Jesus had been questioned in 14:60-62.]
[Did not, or did Peter curse and swear?]
[Did the cock crow for the first, or second time?]
JOHN 18:27 - Peter denied again; immediately the cock crew. [Jesus had been questioned in 18:19-22.]
[Did Peter say that he did not understand what was said, or did he deny having been with Jesus?]
[Did the cock crow after Peter denied knowing Jesus for the third time, and before, or after Jesus had been questioned?]

**Perplexing:** See under MATT. 26:73-74.

**History:** See under MATT. 26:34.

22:61 - THE LORD TURNED, AND LOOKED UPON PETER....

**Perplexing:**
How could Jesus see Peter, if Jesus was inside the house waiting to be questioned, and Peter was out in a hall (22:55), or beneath the palace (MARK 14:66), or out on the porch (MATT. 26:71)?

22:63-64 - THE MEN THAT HELD JESUS MOCKED, AND SMOTE HIM. WHEN THEY HAD BLINDFOLDED HIM, THEY STRUCK HIM ON THE FACE, SAYING, "PROPHESY, WHO SMOTE THEE?"

**Contradictions:**
MATT. 26:67-68 - [After responding to the high priest] They spit in his face, and buffeted him; others smote him with their hands, saying, "Prophesy, who smote thee?"
MARK 14:65 - [After respondinq to the high priest] Some began to spit on him, cover his face, buffet him and say, "Prophesy"; the servants did strike him with their hands.
[Was Jesus struck before being asked if he was the Christ (later in 22:67), or after being asked (in MATT. 26:63 and MARK 14:61)?]
[Was, or was not Jesus blindfolded before being asked to prophesy?]
[Was Jesus told to prophesy who struck him, or just to prophesy?]

JOHN 18:22 - [After responding to the high priest] When he had thus spoken, one of the officers which stood by struck Jesus with the palm of his hand, saying, "Answerest thou the high priest so?"
[Was Jesus struck before being asked if he was the Christ, or after responding to the high priest's questions about his disciples and doctrine (in JOHN 18:19)?]
[Was Jesus struck by men, or by one officer?]
MATT. 26:74, MARK 14:68, and JOHN 18:27 - ...the cock crew [after Jesus had been struck].
[Did the cock crow (22:60) before, or after Jesus was struck?]

**Perplexing:**
Jesus' ability to perform amazing miracles including raising the dead were said to have been witnessed and heard about by multitudes. Why then were these men not afraid of antagonizing someone who possessed such awesome power?
See also under MATT. 26:67-68.

22:66-67 - AS SOON AS IT WAS DAY, THE ELDERS, CHIEF PRIESTS, AND SCRIBES CAME TOGETHER, AND LED HIM INTO THEIR COUNCIL, SAYING, "ART THOU THE CHRIST?" HE SAID, "IF I TELL YOU, YE WILL NOT BELIEVE."

**Contradictions:**
MATT. 26:63-64 - ...the high priest said, "...tell us whether thou be the Christ, the Son of God" [before Jesus was struck]. Jesus saith, "Thou hast said...."
MARK 14:61-62 - ...the high priest said, "Art thou the Christ, the Son of the Blessed [before Jesus was struck]. Jesus: "I am...."
[Did the elders, chief priests, and scribes ask Jesus if he was Christ, or did the high priest ask him?]
[Was Jesus asked only if was the Christ, or if he was the Christ, the Son of God (the Blessed)?]
JOHN 18:19-23 - The high priest asked Jesus of his disciples, and his doctrine [before he was struck]. Jesus answered, "I spake openly to the world...."
[Was Jesus struck before, or after being questioned?]
[Was Jesus asked if he was the Christ, or about his disciples and doctrine?]
MATT. 27:1 and MARK 15:1 - The morning came after Jesus was questioned.
[Was Jesus interrogated as soon as it became day, or during the night of his arrest before it became morning?]

**History:**
The Passover day begins at sundown with the evening Passover meal and continues until sundown the next day. It is a Jewish High Holy Day. During such a holiday, Jews, especially those who are religious, do not hold or attend councils, meetings, trials. or engage in any business activities. To do so would be a violation of Jewish law and unthinkable. They would be in synagogues or the temple. Jews also did not leave their homes before the morning following the Passover meal.

**Old Testament:** See under MATT. 26:30.

**Perplexing:**
Why were the priests and other Jews violating Jewish law by attending a council during Passover when they were supposed to be at home preparing for services in the temple? How many people were present in the council? Why were they not sleepy after being awake all night? Was LUKE ignorant of Jewish law pertaining to Passover? Could the described events actually have taken place, or are they fiction?
See also under MATT. 26:67-68.

**Language**: See under MATT. 1:1.

**Pagan parallels**: See under MATT. 1:1.

22:69 - JESUS: "HEREAFTER SHALL THE SON OF MAN SIT ON THE RIGHT HAND OF THE POWER OF GOD."

**Contradiction:**
MATT. 26:64 - Jesus saith, "...hereafter shall ye see the Son of man sitting on the right hand of power, and coming in the clouds of heaven."
MARK 14:62 - Jesus said, "...ye shall see the Son of man sitting on the right hand of power, and coming in the clouds of heaven."
[Did Jesus say only that he would sit on the right hand of the power of God, or did he also say that the high priest and the others would be alive to see him coming in the clouds on the right hand of power?]

**Perplexing:** See under MATT. 26:64.

22:70 - THEN SAID THEY ALL, "ART THOU THEN THE SON OF GOD?" HE SAID, "YE SAY THAT I AM."

**Judaism:** See under MATT. 26:63.

**Perplexing:** See under MATT. 26:63.

**Language:** See under MATT. 26:64.

23:1-2 - THE MULTITUDE LED HIM UNTO PILATE. ...SAYING, "WE FOUND THIS FELLOW PERVERTING THE NATION, AND FORBIDDING TO GIVE TRIBUTE TO CAESAR, SAYING, THAT HE IS CHRIST A KING."

**History:**
Jews referred to their kings as "The Anointed," or "The Anointed One," because they were anointed with oil or a special liquid during their coronation ritual. Therefore, one would expect the Jews to refer to someone alleged to be a king as "The Anointed" ("Christ"). See also under MATT. 1:1, 27:1-2, and 11.

**Contradiction:** See under MATT. 27:1-2.

**Perplexing:** See under MATT. 27:1-2 and 27:11.

23:3 - PILATE ASKED HIM, "ART THOU THE KING OF THE JEWS?" HE ANSWERED, "THOU SAYEST IT."

**Contradiction:** See under MATT. 27:11.

**History:** See under MATT. 27:11.

**Language**: See under MATT. 26:64.

**Perplexing:** See under MATT. 27:11.

23:4 - SAID PILATE TO THE CHIEF PRIESTS AND PEOPLE, "I FIND NO FAULT IN THIS MAN."

**Contradiction:**
MATT. 27:13 - Said Pilate unto him, "Hearest not how many things they witness against thee?"
MARK 15:4 - Pilate asked, "Answerest thou nothing? Behold how many things they witness against thee."
[Did Pilate say that he finds no fault in Jesus, or did he ask Jesus if he heard the accusations against him?]

**History:**
Under Roman law, anyone claiming to be a king without authorization by Rome was guilty of treason and subject to execution. A governor, Pilate, in this case, did not have the authority to declare such a person innocent without being, himself, subject to a charge of treason and being executed. Additionally, Pilate was vehemently anti-Jewish; he had already ordered the massacre of hundreds of Jews and had looted the Jerusalem Temple. It is, therefore, highly unlikely that he would have taken the time to meet with and listen to a group of Jews, much less interview a Jew (Jesus).
See also under MATT. 27:11.

**Perplexing:**
Since it was illegal and considered to be treason for anyone to claim to be a king without first obtaining approval from the Roman Emperor, how could Pilate legitimately say that he found no fault with Jesus after Jesus acknowledged being a king? Why did Pilate ask Jesus only one question?

23:7 - ...HE SENT HIM TO HEROD, WHO WAS IN JERUSALEM AT THAT TIME.

**Perplexing:**
Why did Pilate send Jesus to be questioned by Herod? Pilate did not take orders from Herod, and Pilate was in charge of trying Jesus. Why did the other gospels not report that Pilate had sent Jesus to Herod?

23:8 - WHEN HEROD SAW JESUS, HE WAS EXCEEDING GLAD; HE WAS DESIROUS TO SEE HIM OF A LONG SEASON, BECAUSE HE HAD HEARD MANY THINGS OF HIM, AND HOPED TO HAVE SEEN SOME MIRACLE DONE BY HIM.

**Contradiction:**
LUKE 13:31 - ...there came Pharisees, saying unto him, "...depart hence, for Herod will kill thee."
[Was Herod glad to see Jesus, or did he want to kill him?]

**Perplexing:**
It was Passover day, when Jews attended services in synagogues and the temple. Why was Herod not in the temple?

23:11 - HEROD WITH HIS MEN OF WAR MOCKED JESUS, ARRAYED HIM IN A GORGEOUS ROBE, AND SENT HIM AGAIN TO PILATE.

**Contradictions:**
MATT. 27:27-28 - The soldiers of the governor.... They stripped him, and put on him a scarlet robe.
[Did Herod's men put a gorgeous robe on Jesus, or did Pilate's soldiers put a scarlet robe on him?]
MARK 15:16-17 - The soldiers [from Pilate].... They clothed him with purple....
JOHN 19:2 - The soldiers [from Pilate]...put on him a purple robe.
[Did Herod's men put a gorgeous robe on Jesus, or did Pilate's soldiers put a purple robe on Jesus?]
See also under MATT. 27:26 and 28.

**History:** See under MATT. 27:28.

23:13 - PILATE WHEN HE HAD CALLED TOGETHER THE CHIEF PRIESTS, RULERS, AND PEOPLE,

**Perplexing:**
Why were the chief priests, rulers, and people not in the synagogues and temple this Passover day? Why would the vehemently anti-Jewish Pilate bother meeting with Jews, especially to discuss Jesus, a Jew? See also under 22:66-67, and under MATT. 27:11.

**History:** See under 22:66-67, and MATT. 27:11.

23:14-15 - [PILATE] SAID, "YE HAVE BROUGHT THIS MAN TO ME...I HAVING EXAMINED HIM...HAVE FOUND NO FAULT IN THIS MAN...NOR HEROD...NOTHING WORTHY OF DEATH IS DONE UNTO HIM."

**Perplexing:**
If Pilate believed that Jesus was not guilty of any crime, he had the authority to release him. Why did he not do so? Jesus, however, had stated that he was King of the Jews. Making this claim without Rome's approval was tantamount to rejecting the rule of the Roman Emperor; consequently, under Roman law, he was guilty of treason. In 23:38; MATT. 27:37; and MARK 15:26, the sign on Jesus' cross said that he was King of the Jews; in JOHN 19:19, Pilate, himself, is said to have written the sign on the cross saying that Jesus was King of the Jews. How could Pilate then say that he found no fault in Jesus? Could Pilate be expected to risk his own life by releasing a Jew who claimed to be a king?
See also under 22:66-67 and 23:4

**History:** See under 23:4

23:16 - PILATE: "I WILL THEREFORE CHASTISE HIM, AND RELEASE HIM."

**Perplexing:**
If Pilate found no fault with Jesus, why did he want to chastise him? How could he consider releasing someone guilty of treason under Roman law?

23:17 - (OF NECESSITY HE MUST RELEASE ONE UNTO THEM AT THE FEAST.)

**Contradiction:**
MATT. 27:15 - At that feast the governor was wont to release unto the people a prisoner, whom they

would.
JOHN 18:39 - Pilate: "Ye have a custom, that I should release unto you one at the Passover...."
[Was Pilate required to release a prisoner during Passover, or was it a custom for such to be done?]

**History:** See under MATT. 27:15.

23:18-19 - THEY CRIED OUT, "AWAY WITH THIS MAN, AND RELEASE UNTO US BARABBAS, (WHO FOR A CERTAIN SEDITION MADE IN THE CITY, AND FOR MURDER WAS CAST INTO PRISON).

**Contradictions:** See under MATT. 27:16 and MARK 15:7.

**Language**: See under MATT. 27:16.

**Perplexing:** See under MATT. 27:20.

23:20 - PILATE WILLING TO RELEASE JESUS, SPAKE AGAIN T0 THEM.

**History:** See under MATT. 27:21.

23:21 - THEY CRIED, "CRUCIFY HIM, CRUCIFY HIM."

**History:** See under MATT. 27:22.

**Perplexing:** See under MATT. 27:22.

23:22 - HE SAID, "...WHAT EVIL HATH HE DONE? I HAVE FOUND NO CAUSE OF DEATH IN HIM; I WILL THEREFORE CHASTISE HIM, AND LET HIM GO."

**Perplexing:** See under 23:14-15, 16, and MATT. 27:22.

23:23-24 - THEY WERE WITH LOUD VOICES, REQUIRING THAT HE MIGHT BE CRUCIFIED. THE VOICES OF THEM AND THE CHIEF PRIESTS PREVAILED. PILATE GAVE SENTENCE THAT IT SHOULD BE AS THEY REQUIRED.

**Perplexing:**
Where were the people who had benefited from Jesus' miracles? Why were they not present to defend Jesus? Why did Pilate not ignore the Jews, and release Jesus, if he deemed him not to be guilty of a capital. offense?
See also under MATT. 27:20.

**History:**
Had Pilate released anyone accused of sedition, he would have been removed from office and executed.
See also under MATT. 27:24.

23:25 - HE RELEASED UNTO THEM HIM THAT FOR SEDITION AND MURDER WAS CAST INTO PRISON, WHOM THEY HAD DESIRED, BUT DELIVERED JESUS TO THEIR WILL.

**Contradictions:**
MATT. 27:26-31 - ...he delivered him to be crucified. The soldiers of the governor took Jesus.... .... ...and led him away to crucify him.
MARK 15:15-20 - Pilate...delivered Jesus...to be crucified. The soldiers led him away.... .... ...and led him out to be crucified.
[Did Pilate deliver Jesus to the Jews, or to the soldiers to be crucified?]
See also under MATT. 27:26.

**History:** See under 23:23-24, under MATT. 27:15 and 17.

**Perplexing:** See under MATT. 27:26.

**Pagan parallel:** See under MATT. 27:26.

23:26 - AS THEY LED HIM AWAY, THEY LAID HOLD UPON ONE SIMON, A CYRENIAN, AND ON HIM THEY LAID THE CROSS, THAT HE MIGHT BEAR IT AFTER JESUS.

**Contradiction:** See under MATT. 27:32.

**History:** See under MATT. 27:32.

**Language:** See under MATT. 27:35.

23:27 - THERE FOLLOWED HIM A GREAT COMPANY OF PEOPLE, AND WOMEN WHICH BEWAILED AND LAMENTED HIM.

**Perplexing:**
Where were these people when Jesus was on trial? Why did they not come to his defense? Why did this great company of people fail to come to Jesus' assistance and rescue him? How did they learn about Jesus' pending execution?

23:30 - JESUS: "THEN SHALL THEY BEGIN TO SAY TO THE MOUNTAINS, 'FALL ON US'; AND TO THE HILLS, 'COVER US.'"

**Old Testament:**
HOS. 10:8 - Hosea: "The high places of Aven, the sin of Israel, shall be destroyed; the thorn and thistle shall come up on their altars, and say to the mountains, 'Cover us'; and to the hills, 'Fall on us.'"

23:33 - WHEN THEY WERE COME TO THE PLACE, WHICH IS CALLED CALVARY, THERE THEY CRUCIFIED HIM, AND THE MALEFACTORS, ONE ON THE RIGHT, THE OTHER ON THE LEFT.

**Contradictions:** See under MATT. 27:35.

**History:** See under MATT. 27:35.

**Perplexing:** See under MATT. 27:35.

**Language:**
"Calvary" is Latin for "skull"; in MATT. 27:33, the Aramaic and Hebrew word, "Golgotha," also meaning "skull," was used.

23:34 - SAID JESUS, "FATHER, FORGIVE THEM, FOR THEY KNOW NOT WHAT THEY DO." THEY PARTED HIS GARMENTS AND CAST LOTS.

**Perplexing:**
Why did Jesus ask his Father to forgive them? His executioners were doing what they were ordained by God to do. If Jesus had not died, there would have been no resurrection, and, consequently, no Christianity. The entire event was preordained, and Jesus, himself, knew what was to occur. Why did Jesus not thank the people for complying with his Father's will and allowing him to fulfill his mission on earth?

**History:** See under MATT. 27:35.

**Old Testament:** See under MATT. 27:35.

23:36 - THE SOLDIERS...COMING TO HIM, AND OFFERING HIM VINEGAR.

**Contradictions:**
MATT. 27:34 - They gave him vinegar to drink mingled with gall; when he had tasted, he would not drink [before he was crucified]. (In MATT. 27:48, he was given vinegar after he was on the cross.)
MARK 15:23 - They gave him to drink wine mingled with myrrh, but he received it not [before being crucified]. (In MARK 15:36, he was given vinegar after he was on the cross.)
[Was Jesus given a vinegar drink after he was on the cross, or both before and after he was on the cross?]
See also under MATT. 27:34.

**Old Testament:** See under MATT. 27:34.

23:38 - A SUPERSCRIPTION WAS WRITTEN OVER HIM IN LETTERS OF GREEK, LATIN, AND HEBREW, "THIS IS THE KING OF THE JEWS."

**Contradictions:**
MATT. 27:37 - Set up over his head his accusation written, "THIS IS JESUS KING OF THE JEWS."
MARK 15:26 - The superscription of his accusation was written, "THE KING OF THE JEWS."
JOHN 19:19 - Pilate wrote a title, and put it on the cross. The writing was, "JESUS OF NAZARETH THE KING OF THE JEWS."
[Was the inscription on the cross that of LUKE, or MATT., or MARK, or JOHN?]

**Perplexing:** See under MATT. 27:37-38.

**History:** See under MATT. 27:35.

23:39-41 - ONE OF TWO MALEFACTORS WHICH WERE HANGED RAILED, SAYING, "IF THOU BE CHRIST, SAVE THYSELF AND US." THE OTHER REBUKED HIM, SAYING, ".... WE JUSTLY RECEIVE THE REWARD OF OUR DEEDS, BUT THIS MAN HATH DONE NOTHING AMISS."

**Contradiction:**
MATT. 27:44 - The thieves, which were crucified with him, cast the same in his teeth.
MARK 15:32 - They that were crucified with him reviled him.
[Did one, or both of the criminals revile Jesus?]

**Perplexing:** See under MATT. 27:41-42.

23:42-43 - HE SAID, "LORD, REMEMBER ME WHEN THOU COMEST INTO THY KINGDOM." JESUS SAID, TODAY SHALT THOU BE WITH ME IN PARADISE."

**Contradictions:**
MATT. 28:16-17 - [After his resurrection] Jesus appeared to his disciples in Galilee.
MARK 16:9-19 - [After his resurrection] Jesus appeared to Mary Magdalene, two disciples, then to the eleven, before ascending to heaven.
LUKE 24:15-51 - [After his resurrection] Jesus appeared to two disciples, then to the eleven, before ascending to heaven.
JOHN 20:17 - [After his resurrection] Jesus said to Mary Magdalene, "Touch me not, for I am not yet ascended to my Father...."
ACTS 1:3 - He shewed himself alive after his passion...being seen forty days....
1 COR. 15:5-8 - [After his resurrection] Paul said that Jesus was seen by the disciples and over 500 other people.
[Did Jesus ascend to his kingdom with the malefactor on the day of their crucifixion, or did he remain on earth for some time after the crucifixion and resurrection, before ascending to heaven?]

**Perplexing:**
The criminal was not reported to have been baptized or born again, two of Jesus' many stated requirements for obtaining eternal life; and as a criminal he had not obeyed one or more of the Lord's commandments. Additionally, he was not reported to have repented. Why, therefore, did Jesus promise him a place in paradise? Can one lead a life of crime and still be admitted to Jesus' kingdom? If a criminal, the last minute, decides to have faith in Jesus, and, thus is saved, what incentive is there for a person to lead a good moral life until facing death? Furthermore, are the victims of murder by such criminals sentenced to hell because they may have been deprived of the opportunity to live long enough to decide to believe in Jesus? Is this not discrimination against decent people who at the time of their murder did not happen to believe in Jesus? Is this not injustice - rewarding criminals and punishing their victims?
Why did Jesus break his promise to the criminal about being in paradise with him that same day?

23:44 - IT WAS ABOUT THE SIXTH HOUR, AND THERE WAS A DARKNESS OVER ALL THE EARTH UNTIL THE NINTH HOUR.

**History:** See under MATT. 27:45.

**Perplexing:** See under MATT. 27:45.

**Pagan parallel:** See under MATT. 27:45.

23:45 - THE SUN WAS DARKENED....

**Perplexing:**
If the sun had stopped shining for three hours, the environmental temperature would have dropped to well-below freezing resulting in the death of most plants and animals including people. Why were no consequences of the darkened sun reported? How did the people keep from freezing? Was LUKE ignorant of what would happen if the earth was deprived of the sun's light and heat?
See also under MATT. 27:45.

23:46 - WHEN JESUS HAD CRIED WITH A LOUD VOICE, "FATHER, INTO THY HANDS I COMMEND MY SPIRIT," HE GAVE UP THE GHOST.

**Contradictions:**
MATT. 27:46 - About the ninth hour Jesus cried with a loud voice, "Eli, Eli, lama sabachthani?" That is, "My God, my God, why hast Thou forsaken me?"
MATT. 27:50 - Jesus, when he had cried again with a loud voice, yielded up the ghost.
MARK 15:34 - At the ninth hour Jesus cried with a loud voice, "Eloi, Eloi, lama sabachthani." which is, "My God, my God, why hast thou forsaken me?"
MARK 15:37 - Jesus cried with a loud voice, and gave up the ghost.
[Did Jesus say that he commends his spirit to his Father, or did he ask God why He had forsaken him?]
[Did Jesus cry out once, or twice before dying?]
See also under MATT. 27:50.

**Old Testament:**
PS. 31:5 - "Into Thine hand I commit my spirit; Thou hast redeemed me...."

**Perplexing:**
Why did Jesus commend his spirit to God, when according to JOHN 10:30, he and his Father are one?

**History:** See under MATT. 27:35.

23:49 - ALL HIS ACQUAINTANCE, AND THE WOMEN THAT FOLLOWED HIM FROM GALILEE, STOOD AFAR OFF, BEHOLDING THESE THINGS.

**Contradiction:** See under MATT. 27:55-56.

**Perplexing:** See under MATT. 27:55-56.

**Pagan concept:** See under MATT. 27:55-56.

26:50-51 - A MAN NAMED JOSEPH, A COUNSELLOR...(THE SAME HAD NOT CONSENTED TO THE COUNSEL AND DEED OF THEM), WAS OF ARIMATHAEA...WHO WAITED FOR THE KINGDOM OF GOD.

**Contradictions:**
MATT. 27:57 - ...there came a rich man of Arimathaea, named Joseph, who was Jesus' disciple.
[Was Joseph a counsellor, or a rich man?]
JOHN 19:38 - ...Joseph of Arimathaea, being a disciple of Jesus, but secretly....
[Was Joseph a counsellor, or a secret disciple?]

23:52 - THIS MAN WENT UNTO PILATE, AND BEGGED THE BODY OF JESUS.

**Contradiction:**
MARK 15:43 - Joseph of Arimathaea...went in boldly unto Pilate, and craved the body of Jesus.
[Did Joseph beg for Jesus' body, or did he crave it boldly?]

**Perplexing:** See under MATT. 27:57-58.

23:53 - HE TOOK IT DOWN, WRAPPED IT IN LINEN, AND LAID IT IN A SEPULCHRE HEWN IN STONE, WHEREIN NEVER MAN BEFORE WAS LAID.

**Contradictions:** See under MATT. 27:57-58 and 59-60.

**Perplexing:** See under MATT. 27:59-60.

**Pagan parallel:** See under MATT. 27:59-60.

23:54 - THAT DAY WAS THE PREPARATION, AND THE SABBATH DREW ON.

**History:**
The Jewish sabbath is Saturday, but it is considered to begin at sundown Friday evening.

23:55 - THE WOMEN WHICH CAME WITH HIM FROM GALILEE, FOLLOWED AFTER, AND BEHELD THE SEPULCHRE, AND HOW HIS BODY WAS LAID.

**Contradiction:**
MATT. 27:61 - There was Mary Magdalene, and the other Mary, sitting over against the sepulchre.
MARK 15:47 - Mary Magdalene and Mary the mother of Joses beheld where he was laid.
[Did several women from Galilee see where Jesus was interred, or did only two women named Mary see the interment?]

**Perplexing:**
Why were women waiting around when Joseph took down Jesus' body? How many women were there? What were they doing? Were they just staring at Jesus on the cross?
See also under MATT. 27:61.

23:56 - THEY RETURNED, AND PREPARED SPICES AND OINTMENTS, AND RESTED THE SABBATH DAY ACCORDING TO THE COMMANDMENT.

**Pagan concept:**
The use of spices and ointments on a corpse was believed to give the body life in the "underworld."

**Perplexing:**
If the women were from Galilee, where were they able to stay in the Jerusalem area?
See also under MATT. 27:55-56.

**Old Testament:**
EX. 20:8-11 (The fourth commandment): "Remember the sabbath day, to keep it holy. .... The seventh day is the sabbath of the LORD thy God; in it thou shalt not do any work...."
EX. 34:21 (The fifth commandment): "...on the seventh day thou shalt rest...."

24:1 - THE FIRST DAY OF THE WEEK, VERY EARLY IN THE MORNING, THEY CAME UNTO THE SEPULCHRE, BRINGING THE SPICES WHICH THEY HAD PREPARED, AND CERTAIN OTHERS WITH THEM.

**Contradictions:**
MATT. 28:1 - As it began to dawn toward the first day of the week, came Mary Magdalene and the other Mary to see the sepulchre.
[Did several women bring spices and ointments to the sepulchre, or did two Marys come to see the sepulchre?]
MARK 16:1-2 - When the sabbath was past, Mary Magdalene, and Mary the mother of James, and Salome, had bought sweet spices, that they might come and anoint him. Very early in the morning the first day of the week, they came unto the sepulchre at the rising of the sun.
[Did several women, or just three women bring spices to the sepulchre?]
JOHN 20:1 - The first day of the week cometh Mary Magdalene early, when it was yet dark, unto the sepulchre....
[Did several women come with spices to the sepulchre, or did Mary Magdalene come alone to visit the sepulchre?]
[Did women come to the sepulchre when it was very early in the morning, or did Mary Magdalene come alone when it was still dark?]

**Perplexing:**
Why did these women bring spices with them to the sepulchre, when, according to JOHN 19:39-40, Nicodemus and Joseph had already wrapped Jesus' body in linen with spices? How many women were there?
See also under MATT. 28:1 and MARK 16:1-2.

24:2 - THEY FOUND THE STONE ROLLED AWAY FROM THE SEPULCHRE.

**Contradictions:**
MATT. 28:2 - There was a great earthquake, and an angel descended from heaven, rolled back the stone from the door, and sat on it.
[Did the women find that the stone had been rolled away, or find the stone rolled away by an angel after an earthquake?]
JOHN 20:1 - Mary Magdalene...seeth the stone taken away from the sepulchre.
[Did several women, or only Mary Magdalene see that the stone had been moved?]

**Pagan parallel:** See under MATT. 28:2-4.

**Perplexing:**
Why was it necessary for the stone to be moved from the tomb's entrance? Since according to JOHN 20:19, Jesus could pass through closed doors, why could he not pass through the walls of the sepulchre or the stone without it having to be moved?

24:3-4 - THEY ENTERED, AND FOUND NOT THE BODY OF THE LORD JESUS. AS THEY WERE MUCH PERPLEXED, TWO MEN STOOD BY THEM IN SHINING GARMENTS.

**Contradictions:**

MATT. 28:3-4 - His [the angel that sat on the stone] countenance was like lightning, and his raiment white as snow. [The women did not enter the tomb.]

[Did the women enter, or not enter the sepulchre?]

[Were there two men in shining garments in the sepulchre, or one angel in white raiment outside?]

MARK 16:5 - Entering into the sepulchre, they saw a young man sitting on the right side, clothed in a long white garment.

[Did two men in shining garments stand by the women in the sepulchre, or was one young man sitting in the sepulchre?]

JOHN 20:2-12 - Mary Magdalene, after having spoken with two disciples who also visited the sepulchre, returned to the sepulchre; she looked into it and saw two angels in white sitting...where the body of Jesus had lain.

[Did Mary Magdalene with one or more women visit the sepulchre, or did she make two trips alone to the tomb?]

[Did only women go to the sepulchre, or did two disciples also go there after speaking with Mary Magdalene?]

[Were there two men standing with the women inside the sepulchre, or did Mary Magdalene on her second trip to the sepulchre look inside and see two angels sitting?]

[Were there two men in shining garments, or two angels in white?]

See also under MATT. 28:2-4.

**Perplexing:**

Who were these men? Were they angels?

**Old Testament:** See under MATT. 28:2-4.

24:5-6 - THEY WERE AFRAID...THEY [THE TWO MEN] SAID, "WHY SEEK YE THE LIVING AMONG THE DEAD? HE IS NOT HERE, BUT IS RISEN...."

**Contradictions:**

MATT. 28:5-6 - The angel said, "Fear not; I know that ye seek Jesus which was crucified. He is not here, for he is risen.... Come see the place where the Lord lay."

[Did the men in the sepulchre, or an angel outside the sepulchre say that Jesus is risen?]

MARK 16:6 - He saith, "Be not affrighted; ye seek Jesus of Nazareth, which was crucified; he is risen; he is not here; behold the place where they laid him."

[Did two men in the sepulchre, or a young man in the sepulchre say that Jesus is risen?]

JOHN 20:13 - They [two angels] say unto her [Mary Magdalene], "Woman, why weepest thou?" She saith, "Because they have taken away my Lord...."

[Did two men in the sepulchre say that Jesus is risen, or did two angels ask Mary Magdalene why she was weeping?]

[Did not, or did Mary Magdalene speak to angels?]

See also under MATT. 28:5-7.

**Perplexing:** See under MATT. 28:5-7.

**History:** See under MATT. 28:5-7.

**Pagan parallel:** See under MATT. 28:5-7.

**Old Testament:** See under MATT. 28:5-7.

24:6-7 - THE TWO MEN: “HE...IS RISEN; REMEMBER HE SPAKE UNTO YOU WHEN HE WAS IN GALILEE, SAYING, ‘THE SON OF MAN MUST BE DELIVERED INTO THE HANDS OF SINFUL MEN, BE CRUCIFIED, AND THE THIRD DAY RISE AGAIN.’”

**Contradictions:**
MATT. 28:7 - The angel: “Go quickly, and tell his disciples that he is risen from the dead, and, he goeth before you into Galilee; there shall ye see him....”
MARK 16:7 - The young man: “Go your way; tell his disciples and Peter that he goeth before you into Galilee; there shall ye see him, as he said unto you.”
[Were the women told that Jesus would rise on the third day, or were they told to inform the disciples that Jesus was going to Galilee where they will see him?”]
MATT. 12:40 - Jesus: “As Jonas was three days and three nights in the whale’s belly, so shall the Son of man be three days and three nights in the heart of the earth.”
[Did Jesus say that he would rise on the third day (after one and a half days and two nights in the stone sepulchre near the surface of the earth), or after spending three days and three nights in the heart of the earth?]
MARK 8:31 - Jesus: “...the Son of man must...be killed, and after three days rise again.”
[Did Jesus say that he would rise the third day, or after three days?]

**History:** See under MATT. 28:5-7.

**Perplexing:**
When did Jesus tell the women that he would be crucified and then rise on the third day?
See also under MATT. 28:5-7.

**Pagan parallels**: See under MATT. 28:5-7.

**Old Testament:** See under MATT. 12:40.

24:9-10 - [THE WOMEN] RETURNED FROM THE SEPULCHRE, AND TOLD ALL THESE THINGS UNTO THE ELEVEN, AND TO ALL THE REST. IT WAS MARY MAGDALENE, JOANNA, MARY THE MOTHER OF JAMES, AND OTHER WOMEN WHICH TOLD THESE THINGS TO THE APOSTLES.

**Contradictions:**
MATT. 28:8-9 - They departed quickly from the sepulchre.... As they went to tell the disciples, Jesus met them....
[Did Mary Magdalene and several other women tell the disciples what happened, or did Mary Magdalene and the other Mary encounter Jesus while on their way to the disciples?]
MARK 16:8-9 - They went out quickly from the sepulchre...neither said they anything to any man, for they

were afraid. Jesus...appeared first to Mary Magdalene....
[Did the several women tell the disciples what occurred, or were Mary Magdalene and two other women afraid to reveal to anyone what had happened?]
[Did the several women together speak to the disciples, or did Mary Magdalene meet Jesus and then alone inform the disciples (MARK 16:10) about what had occurred?]
JOHN 20:2 - She [Mary Magdalene] cometh to Peter, and the disciple whom Jesus loved, and saith, "They have taken away the Lord out of the sepulchre, and we know not where they have laid him."
JOHN 20:18 - Mary Magdalene told the disciples that she had seen the Lord, and that he had spoken these things unto her.
[Did the several women speak to the eleven disciples, or did Mary Magdalene alone speak first to only two disciples, then after meeting Jesus (in JOHN 20:13-17) speak to the others?]
See also under MATT. 28:8.

24:11-12 - ...THEY [THE DISCIPLES] BELIEVED THEM NOT. PETER RAN UNTO THE SEPULCHRE; STOOPING DOWN, HE BEHELD THE LINEN CLOTHES LAID BY THEMSELVES, AND DEPARTED, WONDERING AT THAT WHICH WAS COME TO PASS.

**Contradictions:**
MATT. 28:16 - The eleven disciples went into Galilee, into a mountain where Jesus had appointed them .
[Did the disciples refuse to believe the women and remain in Jerusalem, or did they believe and go to Galilee?]
MARK 16:10-11 - She told them that had been with him, as they mourned and wept. When they had heard that he was alive, and had been seen of her believed not.
[Did the disciples refuse to believe the several women who spoke to them, or did they refuse to believe Mary Magdalene who alone spoke to them?]
JOHN 20:3-8 Peter went and that other disciple, came to the sepulchre. ...he [the other disciple] looking in...went not in. Peter went into the sepulchre.... .... Then went in that other disciple....
[Did Peter go alone to the sepulchre, or did Peter and another disciple go to the sepulchre?]

**Perplexing:**
Why did the disciples not believe that Jesus had risen, after he had on a number of occasions told them that he would do so? If Jesus' clothes were left behind, what did he wear when he left the sepulchre? Was he naked? If not, how and from where did he obtain replacement clothes?

24:13-31 - TWO OF THEM WENT THAT SAME DAY TO EMMAUS FROM JERUSALEM.... .... WHILE THEY COMMUNED, JESUS WENT WITH THEM. BUT...THEY SHOULD NOT KNOW HIM.... ONE WAS CLEOPAS.... .... AS HE SAT AT MEAT WITH THEM.... .... THEY KNEW HIM, AND HE VANISHED.

**Contradictions:**
MATT. 28:9 - As they [Mary Magdalene and the other Mary] went to tell the disciples, Jesus met them, saying, "All hail." They held him by the feet, and worshipped him.
[Did the resurrected Jesus appear first to Cleopas and another disciple, or to Mary Magdalene and the other Mary?]
MARK 16:9 - When Jesus was risen early the first day of the week, he appeared first to Mary Magdalene....
JOHN 20:15-16 - Jesus saith unto her [Mary Magdalene], "Why weepest thou?".... Jesus saith, "Mary." She saith, "Rabboni"....
[Did the resurrected Jesus appear first to two disciples, or to Mary Magdalene?]

1 COR. 15:4-5 - Paul: "...he [Jesus] was buried, and rose the third day...and was seen of Cephas [another name for Peter - see JOHN 1:42], then of the twelve."
[Was the risen Jesus seen first by Cleopas and another disciple, or by Cephas (Peter)?]

**Perplexing:**
Why did the two disciples walk about seven miles to Emmaus? What did they do there? How long did the trip there and back take? Why did Jesus appear first to these two men, rather than to his eleven disciples? Why did Jesus disappear? Where did he go?
To whom did the resurrected Jesus first appear? Was it to two disciples, to Mary Magdalene and the other Mary, to Mary Magdalene alone, or to Cephas? Why did the gospel writers and also Paul disagree about who first encountered the resurrected Jesus?

**History:** See under MATT. 28:9-10.

**Pagan parallel:**
In Greek mythology, Aristeas died and his body vanished, but later he was met by travelers.

24:25 - HE SAID UNTO THEM [THE TWO MEN], "O FOOLS, AND SLOW OF HEART TO BELIEVE ALL THAT THE PROPHETS HAVE SPOKEN."

**Perplexing:** See under MATT. 23:17.

24:33-34 - THEY [CLEOPAS AND THE OTHER MAN] RETURNED TO JERUSALEM, FOUND THE ELEVEN AND THEM THAT WERE WITH THEM, SAYING, "THE LORD IS RISEN, AND HATH APPEARED TO SIMON."

**Perplexing:**
Who is the cited Simon? Was he the man with Cleopas? If so, why did they not say that Jesus appeared to both of them?

24:36 - AS THEY THUS SPOKE, JESUS HIMSELF STOOD IN THE MIDST OF THEM, AND SAID, "PEACE BE UNTO YOU."

**Contradictions:**
MATT. 28:16-18 - The eleven disciples went into Galilee, into a mountain where Jesus had appointed them. When they saw him, they worshipped him, but some doubted. Jesus spake, "All power is given me in heaven and in earth."
[Did the resurrected Jesus first appear to the disciples in Jerusalem, or on a mountain in Galilee?]
MARK 16:12-14 - He appeared in another form unto two of them, as they walked into the country. .... Afterward he appeared unto the eleven as they sat at meat, and upbraided them with their unbelief...because they believed not them which had seen him after he was risen.
[Did the resurrected Jesus say, "Peace be unto you," to the disciples, or did he upbraid them for their unbelief?]
JOHN 20:19-24 - The same evening, the first day of the week...the disciples were assembled...came Jesus in the midst, and saith, "Peace be unto you. .... Thomas, one of the twelve, was not with them.
[Did the resurrected Jesus meet with all of his eleven disciples, or was Thomas missing from the group?]
1 COR. 15:5 - He was seen by Cephas, then of the twelve.

[Did the resurrected Jesus appear to two disciples, then to the eleven disciples, or did he appear first to Cephas before appearing to the twelve?]

24:37 - THEY WERE TERRIFIED AND AFFRIGHTED, AND SUPPOSED THAT THEY HAD SEEN A SPIRIT.

**Contradictions:**
MATT. 28:17 - When they saw him, they worshipped him, but some doubted.
[Were the disciples terrified when they saw Jesus, or did they worship him while some doubted?]
JOHN 20:20 - ...he showed them his hands and his side. Then were the disciples glad, when they saw the Lord.
[Were the disciples terrified and affrighted, or were they glad after he showed them his hands and side?]

**Perplexing:**
Why were the disciples terrified and frightened? Jesus had told them that he would rise from the dead. Did they not believe him?

24:39-41 - JESUS: "BEHOLD MY HANDS AND FEET; IT IS I; HANDLE ME, AND SEE; A SPIRIT HATH NOT FLESH AND BONES...." .... WHILE THEY BELIEVED NOT FOR JOY, AND WONDERED, HE SAID, "HAVE YE HERE ANY MEAT?"

**Contradictions:**
MARK 16:14 - He upbraided them for their unbelief....
[Did Jesus tell the disciples that he was flesh and bones and ask for meat, or did he upbraid them for their unbelief?]
JOHN 20:22-28; 21:1-14 - ...he breathed on them, and saith, "Receive ye the Holy Ghost." .... After eight days his disciples were within, Thomas with them; came Jesus...and said, "Peace be unto you." .... Thomas said, "My Lord and my God." .... After these things, Jesus showed himself to the disciples at the sea of Tiberias [where they were fishing].... .... This is the third time that Jesus showed himself to his disciples, after he was risen from the dead.
[Did Jesus demonstrate that he was not a spirit, and then ask for food, or did he visit the disciples minus Thomas and give them the Holy Ghost, visit a second time when Thomas was present and convince him to believe, and later make a third visit to seven of them while they fished?]
[Did Jesus show himself to the disciples once, or three times?]
See also under 24:36.

**Perplexing:**
Why was Jesus hungry? Why did the disciples hesitate to believe?
See also under 24:11-12.

24:42-43 - THEY GAVE HIM A PIECE OF A BROILED FISH, AND OF AN HONEYCOMB. HE TOOK IT AND DID EAT BEFORE THEM.

**Contradictions:**
JOHN 21:13-14 - Jesus cometh, taketh bread, and fish likewise. This is the third time that Jesus showed himself to his disciples, after he was risen from the dead.
[Did Jesus eat fish and a honeycomb during his first and only meeting with the disciples in Jerusalem, or on

his third visit did he take bread and fish with seven of them by the Sea of Tiberias in Galilee?]
LUKE 22:16 - Jesus: "I will not anymore eat thereof, until it be fulfilled in the kingdom of God."
[Did Jesus ask for food, or did he say that he would not eat again on the earth?]

24:44 - HE SAID, "...ALL THINGS MUST BE FULFILLED, WHICH WERE WRITTEN IN THE LAW OF MOSES, IN THE PROPHETS, AND IN THE PSALMS, CONCERNING ME."

**Perplexing:**
To what written items did Jesus refer?
See also under 18:31.

24:46 - [JESUS] SAID, "IT IS WRITTEN, AND THUS IT BEHOVED CHRIST TO SUFFER, AND TO RISE FROM THE DEAD THE THIRD DAY."

**Contradictions:** See under MATT. 16:21.

**Old Testament:** See under MATT. 12:40.

24:47 - JESUS: "REPENTANCE AND REMISSION OF SINS SHOULD BE PREACHED IN HIS [JESUS'] NAME AMONG ALL NATIONS, BEGINNING AT JERUSALEM."

**Contradictions:**
MATT. 10:5-8 - These twelve Jesus sent forth, saying, "Go not into the way of the Gentiles, and into any city of the Samaritans enter not; go rather to the lost sheep of the house of Israel. And as ye go, preach, 'The kingdom of heaven is at hand.' Heal the sick; cleanse the lepers; raise the dead; cast out devils; freely ye have received; freely give."
[Did Jesus order the disciples to preach repentance and remission of sins, or that the kingdom of heaven is at hand?]
[Did Jesus instruct the disciples to preach to all nations, or just to the lost sheep of the house of Israel?]
MATT. 10:23 - Jesus: "...ye shall not have gone over the cities of Israel, till the Son of man be come."
[Did Jesus instruct the disciples to preach to all nations, or did he tell them that he would return before they went over all the cities of Israel?]
MATT. 28:19-20 - Jesus: "Teach all nations, baptizing them in the name of the Father, the Son, and the Holy Ghost, teaching them to observe all things whatsoever I have commanded you...."
[Did Jesus instruct the disciples to preach repentance and the remission of sins, or everything that he had commanded them?]
MARK 13:10 - Jesus: "The gospel must first be published among all nations."
MARK 16:15-18 - He said, "Go into all the world, and preach the gospel to every creature. He that believeth and is baptized shall be saved; but he that believeth not shall be damned. These signs shall follow them that believe; in my name shall they cast out devils; they shall speak with new tongues; they shall take up serpents, and if they drink any deadly thing, it shall not hurt them; they shall, lay hands on the sick, and they shall recover."
[Did Jesus instruct his disciples to preach repentance and the remission of sins, or to preach the gospel, believe and be baptized, and that they would not be harmed, etc.?]
See also under MATT. 28:18-20.

**Perplexing:** See under MATT. 28:18-20.

24:49 - JESUS: "...TARRY YE IN THE CITY OF JERUSALEM, UNTIL YE BE ENDUED WITH POWER FROM ON HIGH."

**Contradictions:**
MATT. 28:16-20 - Jesus [in Galilee]: "Go ye, and teach all nations...."
[Was Jesus in Jerusalemt or Galilee when he instructed the disciples for the last time?]
MARK 16:15 - He said unto them, "Go into all the world, and preach the gospel to every creature."
[Did Jesus instruct the disciples to remain in Jerusalem until they received power from on high, or to go out and teach/preach?]
See also under 24:47.

24:50-51 - HE LED THEM AS FAR AS BETHANY, LIFTED UP HIS HANDS, BLESSED THEM, WAS PARTED FROM THEM, AND CARRIED UP TO HEAVEN.

**Contradictions:**
MATT. 28:20 - Jesus [in Galilee): "...I am with you alway [sic], even unto the end of the world." [No ascension was reported.]
[Was Jesus carried up to heaven, or did he say that he would be with the disciples until the end of the world?]
MARK 16:19 - After the Lord had spoken unto them [in Jerusalem], he was received up into heaven, and sat on the right hand of God.
[Did Jesus ascend to heaven from Bethany, or from Jerusalem?]
JOHN 21:22 - Jesus [in Galilee] saith unto him [Peter] "...follow thou me."
[Were Jesus' last words spoken to all the disciples, or just to Peter?]
ACTS 1:9-12 - ...he was taken up, and a cloud received him out of their sight. While they looked toward heaven as he went up, two men in white apparel said, "...this same Jesus, which is taken up from you into heaven, shall so come in like manner as ye have seen him go into heaven." Returned they unto Jerusalem from the mount called Olivet....
[Did Jesus ascend from Bethany, or Mount Olivet?]
ACTS 1:3 - ...he shewed himself alive after his passion...being seen forty days....
[Did Jesus spend one day on the earth between his resurrection and ascension (LUKE 24:6-51 and MARK 16:6-19), or 40 days (ACTS 1:3)?]
JOHN 20:2 - 21:23 - Jesus remained on earth at least ten days after his resurrection [no ascension was reported] meeting the disciples twice in Jerusalem and once in Galilee.
[Did Jesus spend one day on earth between his resurrection and ascension, or at least ten days on the earth?]
[Did the resurrected Jesus meet the disciples once in Jerusalem, or on two different occasions in Jerusalem and then once in Galilee?]
See also under MARK 16:19.

**Perplexing:** See under MARK 16:19.

**Pagan parallels**: See under MARK 16:19.

**Old Testament:** See under MARK 16:19.

24:52-53 - THEY WORSHIPPED HIM, RETURNED TO JERUSALEM WITH GREAT JOY, AND WERE CONTINUALLY IN THE TEMPLE, PRAISING AND BLESSING GOD.

**Contradictions:**

MARK 16:20 - They went forth, preaching everywhere, and the Lord working with them and confirming the word with signs following.

[Did they remain continually in the temple, or did they go forth and preach?]

JOHN 21:1-3 - After Jesus' first two appearances, the disciples went fishing in Galilee.

[Did the disciples remain continually in the temple in Jerusalem, or did they go fishing in Galilee?]

ACTS 1:13-14 - They [the disciples] went into an upper room.... These all continued in prayer and supplication with the women, and Mary the mother of Jesus, and with his brethren.

[Did the disciples remain continually in the temple in Jerusalem, or go to an upper room where they prayed with women and Jesus' mother and brethren?]

**Perplexing:**

Why did the disciples believe that God needed their praises and blessings? Of what use were their praises and blessings to God?

Why did they fail to obey Jesus' commands in MATT. 28:19 to go and teach all nations, and in MARK 16:15 to go into all the world preaching to every creature?

See also under 2:13-14.

# *Chapter Four*

## THE GOSPEL ACCORDING TO ST. JOHN

1:1 - IN THE BEGINNING WAS THE WORD, AND THE WORD WAS WITH GOD, AND THE WORD WAS GOD.

**Pagan parallels:**
The Greek sun-god Apollo (fifth century B.C.) was referred to as "the Word." The Zoroastrian god Mithra (sixth century B.C. or earlier) was considered to be a manifestation of "the Word."

**Pagan concept:**
The concept of a divine "word" creating the universe is also found in ancient Egyptian and Hindu beliefs.

**History:**
The belief that the voice or word of a god could act as a distinct entity can be traced back to the third millennium B.C.

**Language:**
The Greek word, "Sophia," translated as "Word," also means "Wisdom."

**Perplexing:**
In ISA. 43:10, ...saith the LORD, " ...before Me there was no God formed, neither shall there be after Me." If no God existed before God, what did exist? What, therefore, preceded the beginning (God and the Word)? What will exist after Him? What will happen when God ceases to exist?
Why did God decide to create anything? Why did He need a material universe, much of which appears to be uninhabited? What did God do before the creation? How did God and the Word come into existence? Of what are God and the Word composed? If God and the Word could have existed eternally without having been created, why could not the material universe have been in existence eternally, in one form or another, without having been created?

1:2 - THE SAME WAS IN THE BEGINNING WITH GOD.

**Old Testament:**
PROV. 8:23 - Wisdom: "I was set up from everlasting, from the beginning, or ever the earth was."

**History:**
The Church councils in Nicea (A.D. 325) and Constantinople (A.D. 381) proclaimed Jesus to be "God from God," "true God of true God," "begotten but not created," and "of one substance with the Father."

1:3 - ALL THINGS WERE MADE BY HIM; WITHOUT HIM WAS NOT ANYTHING MADE.

**Perplexing:** See under 1:1.

**Old Testament:**
GEN. 1:1 - In the beginning God created the heaven and the earth.
PS. 33:6 - "By the word of the LORD were the heavens made, and all the rest of them by the breath of His mouth."

**Language:**
The Hebrew word in GEN. 1:1, translated as "created," is "bara," meaning to fashion something out of an existing material. (The writer, therefore, did not envision a creation out of nothing.)

**Pagan parallels:**
The Hindu god Krishna said that he created the universe, and that those with spiritual wisdom worship him. Mithra and numerous other pre-Christian pagan deities were also credited with creating the universe. In Sumerian mythology, all things were created by the word of the water-god Enki (Ea).
See also under 1:1.

**Pagan concept:**
The idea of a divine "word" creating the universe is found in Egyptian mytholgy.
See also under 1:1.

1:4-5 - IN HIM WAS LIFE, AND THE LIFE WAS THE LIGHT OF MEN. THE LIGHT SHINETH IN DARKNESS, AND THE DARKNESS COMPREHENDED IT NOT.

**Pagan parallels:**
The Greek god Apollo was known as the "God of Radiance." The Zoroastrian god Ahura Mazda (Ormazd) was a deity of light and goodness.

**Old Testament:**
PS. 27:1 - "The LORD is my light and salvation...."
PS. 36:9 - "...in Thy light shall we see light."
PS. 104:2 - "Who coverest Thyself with light as with a garment...."
PS. 119:130 - "The entrance of Thy words giveth light...."
HAB. 3:4 - "His [God's] brightness was as the light...."

1:6 - THERE WAS A MAN SENT FROM GOD, WHOSE NAME WAS JOHN.

**Perplexing:**
Why did God select John? Why was it necessary for any man to be sent? Why did God, Himself, not appear to prove to the world that He really exists and thereby eliminate any doubts about His existence? Why did this gospel fail to give any background information about the miraculous birth of John as reported by LUKE?

1:10 - HE WAS IN THE WORLD; THE WORLD WAS MADE BY HIM, AND THE WORLD KNEW HIM NOT.

**Contradictions:**
GEN. 1:1 - In the beginning God ["Elohim," in the Hebrew] created the heaven and the earth.
[Did the Word, or did God ("Elohim," meaning "Gods," in Hebrew) create the world?]

PROV. 3:19 - "The LORD by wisdom hath founded the earth; by understanding hath He established the heavens."
[Did the Word create the world, or were the earth and heavens created by the LORD by wisdom, and understanding?]

**Language**: See under 1:3.

**Perplexing:**
Why did he make the world? Who created him? Why?
See also under 1:1.

1:11 - HE CAME UNTO HIS OWN, AND HIS OWN RECEIVED HIM NOT.

**Perplexing:**
In LUKE 1:33, an angel told Mary that Jesus "shall reign over the house of Jacob forever." If he was not received by his own, how could he reign over them?

**Pagan parallel:**
Krishna said, "Deluded men despise me when I take human form."

1:13 - WHICH WERE BORN, NOT OF BLOOD, NOR OF THE WILL OF THE FLESH, NOR OF THE WILL OF MAN, BUT OF GOD.

**Contradictions:**
MATT. 1:1-16 presented a human mother and a human genealogy for Jesus traced back to Abraham - "Jesus Christ, the son of David, the son of Abraham."
LUKE 3:23-38 presented a human mother and a human genealogy for Jesus traced back to Adam.
MATT. 1:25 and LUKE 2:7 - Mary brought forth her firstborn son, Jesus.
[Was Jesus not born of blood and the will of the flesh and man, or was he a human descendant of Adam and Abraham?]
See also under MATT. 1:18.

1:14 - THE WORD WAS MADE FLESH, AND DWELT AMONG US, (AND WE BEHELD HIS GLORY, THE GLORY AS THE ONLY BEGOTTEN OF THE FATHER,) FULL OF GRACE AND TRUTH.

**Contradictions:**
ACTS 2:22 - Peter: "...Jesus of Nazareth, a man approved of God among you by miracles, wonders, and signs, which God did by him in the midst of you."
[Was Jesus the Word made flesh, the only begotten of God, or was he a human man born of a woman and of whom God approved?]
See also under 1:13 and MATT. 1:18.

**Pagan parallel:**
Buddha was also referred to as "the Only Begotten."

1:18 - NO MAN HATH SEEN GOD AT ANY TIME....

**Contradictions:**

GEN. 12:7 - The LORD appeared unto Abram....
GEN. 17:1 - ...the LORD appeared to Abram....
GEN. 18:1 - The LORD appeared unto him [Abraham]....
GEN. 26:2 - The LORD appeared unto him [Isaac]....
GEN. 26:24 - The LORD appeared unto him [Isaac]....
GEN. 32:30 - ..."I [Jacob] have seen God face to face, and my life is preserved."
GEN. 35:1 - God said to Jacob, "...make there an altar unto God, that appeared unto thee...."
GEN. 35:9 - God appeared unto Jacob again....
EX. 4:4-5 - The LORD said unto Moses, ".... ...the God of Abraham, the God of Isaac, and the God of Jacob, hath appeared unto thee."
EX. 4:24 - ...the LORD met him [Moses], and sought to kill him.
EX. 6:3 - God: "I appeared unto Abraham, unto Isaac, and unto Jacob...."
EX. 24:9-10 - Moses, Aaron, Nadab, Abihu, and 70 elders of Israel saw the God of Israel; there was under His feet as it were a paved work of sapphire stone, and as it were the body of heaven in His clearness.
EX. 24:11 - The nobles of the children of Israel ... saw God....
EX. 33:11 - The LORD spake unto Moses face to face, as a man speaketh unto his friend. ....
EX. 33:23 - The LORD: "...thou shalt see My back parts...."
NUM. 14:14 - Moses: "...they have heard that Thou LORD art among this people, that Thou LORD art seen face to face...."
NUM. 23:4 - God met Balaam....
NUM. 23:15-16 - He [Balaam] said unto Balak, "Stand here...while I meet the LORD yonder." The LORD met Balaam....
DEUT. 5:4 - Moses: "The LORD talked with you [Israelites] face to face in the mount...."
DEUT. 34:10 - ...Moses whom the LORD knew face to face.
1 SAM. 3:21 - The LORD appeared again in Shiloh....
2 SAM. 22:11 - David: "He [the LORD]...was seen upon the wings of the wind."
1 KINGS 11:9 - ...the LORD God of Israel, which had appeared unto him (Solomon) twice.
1 KINGS 22:19 - Micaiah: "I saw the LORD sitting on His throne, and all the host of heaven standing by Him on His right hand and His left."
2 CHRON. 1:7 - That night did God appear unto Solomon....
2 CHRON. 3:1 - ...the LORD appeared unto David....
JOB 42:5 - Job: "...now mine eye seeth Thee."
ISA. 6:1 - Isaiah: "I saw also the Lord sitting upon a throne, high and lifted up, and His train filled the temple."
EZEK. 1:28 - Ezekiel: ".... This was the appearance of the likeness of the glory of the LORD. And when I saw it, I fell upon my face."
EZEK. 3:23 - Ezekiel: "...the glory of the LORD stood there, as the glory which I saw by the river of Chebar."
EZEK, 8:4 - Ezekiel: "...the glory of the God of Israel was there...."
AMOS 9:1 - Amos: "I saw the Lord standing upon the altar...."
HAB. 3:3-4 - Habakkuk: "God came.... His brightness was as the light; He had horns coming out of His hand...."
JOHN 14:9 - Jesus: "He that hath seen me hath seen the Father."
ACTS 7:55 - ...he [Stephen]...looked up into heaven, and saw the glory of God, and Jesus on the right hand of God.
Many other verses also reported that God has been seen.

[Has God been seen, or not seen?]

**Perplexing:**
If God has not been seen, how were some people (above) able to describe His appearance?

1:21 - THEY ASKED HIM [JOHN], “ART THOU ELIAS [ELIJAH]?” HE SAITH, “I AM NOT.” “ART THOU THAT PROPHET?” HE ANSWERED, “NO.”

**Contradiction:**
LUKE 1:17 - An angel told Zacharias, “He [John] shall go before him (Jesus) in the spirit and power of Elias....”
MATT. 11:13-14 - Jesus: “All the prophets and the law prophesied until John. ...this is Elias, which was to come.”
MATT. 17:12-13 - Jesus: “Elias is come already....” The disciples understood that he spake unto them of John the Baptist.
[Was not, or was John the prophet Elijah?]

**Old Testament:** See under MATT. 11:13-14.

**Perplexing:**
If John was not Elijah, why did Jesus say that he was? If the day of the LORD has not yet come some two millennia after Jesus, John probably spoke the truth when he denied being Elijah. Why then did the angel and Jesus falsely assert that John was the prophet? Did they deliberately lie?
See also under MATT. 11:13-14 and LUKE 1:17.

1:23 - HE [JOHN] SAID, “I AM THE VOICE OF ONE CRYING IN THE WILDERNESS. ‘MAKE STRAIGHT THE WAY OF THE LORD,’ AS SAID THE PROPHET ESAIAS [ISAIAH].”

**Old Testament:** See under MATT. 3:3.

**Perplexing:**
Why did John equate himself with Isaiah?

1:25 - THEY [PHARISEES], ASKED HIM. “WHY BAPTIZEST THEN, IF THOU BE NOT CHRIST, NOR ELIAS....”

**History:** See under MATT. 3:5-6.

**Pagan concept:** See under MATT. 3:5-6.

**Perplexing:**
Why did the Pharisees question John about baptizing, since baptism was a pagan, not a Jewish ritual? If John was Jewish, why did he baptize? Why did the Pharisees not reprimand John for resorting to a pagan ritual?
See also under MATT. 3:5-6 and 21:25-27.

**Old Testament:** See under MATT. 3:5-6.

1:27 - JOHN: "HE IT IS...WHOSE SHOE'S LATCHET I AM NOT WORTHY TO UNLOOSE."

**Contradiction:** See under MARK 1:7.

1:28 - THESE THINGS WERE DONE IN BETHABARA BEYOND JORDAN, WHERE JOHN WAS BAPTIZING.

**History:** See under MATT. 3:5-6.

**Perplexing:** See under 1:25.

1:29 - ...JOHN SEETH JESUS, AND SAITH, "BEHOLD THE LAMB OF GOD, WHICH TAKETH AWAY THE SIN OF THE WORLD."

**Pagan parallel:**
Some ancient people who worshiped the sun referred to the constellation of Aries as the "Lamb of God" when the sun passed through it. They had a litany which included the following, "O Lamb of God, that taketh away the sins of the world, have mercy upon us. Grant us thy peace."

**History:**
Until the fifth century, the lamb, not the cross, was the symbol of Christianity. Early Christians rejected the cross, because it was a pagan symbol for sun-gods and also a phallic symbol.

**Perplexing:**
Why did John fail to identify Jesus as his cousin (LUKE 1:36)?

1:31 - JOHN: "I KNEW HIM NOT...THEREFORE AM I COME BAPTIZING WITH WATER."

**Perplexing:**
Why did John say that he did not know Jesus? In LUKE 1:41-44, John, in utero, recognized Mary and the embryonic Jesus. Was not JOHN aware of the account in LUKE, or did he reject it?

1:33-34 - JOHN: "I KNEW HIM NOT, BUT HE THAT SENT ME TO BAPTIZE WITH WATER, THE SAME SAID UNTO ME, 'UPON WHOM THOU SHALT SEE THE SPIRIT DESCENDING, AND REMAINING, IS HE WHICH BAPTIZETH WITH THE HOLY GHOST.' I SAW, AND BARE RECORD THAT THIS IS THE SON OF GOD."

**Contradictions:**
LUKE 1:36-44 - [The angel Gabriel said to Mary] "Thy cousin Elisabeth, hath also conceived a son...." .... When Elisabeth heard the salutation of Mary, the babe leaped in her womb.... .... [Elisabeth said to Mary] "As soon as the voice of thy salutation sounded...the babe leaped in my womb for joy."
[Did the Spirit have to identify Jesus for John, or was he Jesus' cousin who recognized him in utero?]
JOHN 5:37 - Jesus: ".... Ye have neither heard His voice at any time, nor seen His shape."
[Did John hear the voice of God, or has no one heard God's voice?]
See also under MATT. 1:18 and 11:2-3.

**History:** See under MATT. 3:17.

**Perplexing:**
Why was it necessary for the Spirit to identify Jesus? Why did God send John to baptize—a pagan ritual. See also under 1:25, 29, and 31.

1:36 - LOOKING UPON JESUS AS HE WALKED, HE [JOHN] SAITH, "BEHOLD THE LAMB OF GOD!"

**Pagan concept:** See under 1:29.

**History:** See under 1:29.

**Perplexing:**
Why did John fail to speak to or even greet his cousin Jesus?
See also under 1:29.

1:37-38 - TWO DISCIPLES [OF JOHN]...FOLLOWED JESUS. JESUS SAW THEM AND SAITH, "WHAT SEEK YE?" ....

**Contradictions:** See under MATT. 9:28-30.

**Perplexing:**
Why did John fail to follow Jesus and become one of his disciples?

1:39 - .... THEY CAME AND SAW WHERE HE [JESUS] DWELT, AND ABODE WITH HIM THAT DAY....

**Perplexing:**
According to 1:28, they were in Bethabara beyond Jordan. Where did Jesus dwell there? Why did the other gospels not mention that Jesus had a home beyond Jordan?

1:40-42 - ONE OF THE TWO WHICH...FOLLOWED HIM, WAS ANDREW, SIMON PETER'S BROTHER. HE FINDETH HIS BROTHER, AND SAITH, "WE HAVE FOUND THE MESSIAS, WHICH IS, THE CHRIST. HE BROUGHT HIM TO JESUS. ....

**Contradictions:**
MATT. 4:18-19 - Jesus, walking by the sea of Galilee, saw two brethren, Simon called Peter, and Andrew, casting a net into the sea, for they were fishers. He saith, "Follow me...."
MARK 1:16-17 - As he walked by the sea of Galilee, he saw Simon and Andrew his brother casting a net into the sea, for they were fishers. Jesus said, "Come ye after me....."
[Did Andrew see Jesus at Bethabara beyond Jordan, or by the Sea of Galilee?]
[Was Andrew a disciple of John who decided to follow Jesus, or was he a fisherman who Jesus ordered to follow him?]
[Was Andrew with John the Baptist when he saw Jesus, or was he with Peter casting a net into the sea?]
[Did Andrew bring Simon to Jesus, or were Andrew and Simon together when Jesus saw them?]
[Did Andrew bring Simon to Jesus, or was Andrew not present when Jesus encountered Simon?]
[Did Andrew go to Jesus' home beyond Jordan, or was he at the Sea of Galilee?]
[Was Andrew Jesus' first disciple, or were he and Peter jointly the first disciples?]

LUKE 5:1-11 - ...he stood by the lake Gennesaret.... He entered one of the ships, which was Simon's.... He taught the people out of the ship. [He then helped Simon, James, and John fish.] .... ...they forsook all, and followed him.
[Were Andrew and Simon Jesus' first disciples, or were Simon, James, and John jointly the first disciples?]
[Did Jesus acquire his first disciples beyond Jordan, or at the Sea of Galilee (Gennesaret)?]
MATT. 4:12-20 - When Jesus heard that John was cast into prison he departed into Galilee where he met Andrew and Simon.
MARK 1:14-18 - After John was put in prison, Jesus came into Galilee where he met Andrew and Simon....
LUKE 3:19-20 - Herod the tetrarch...shut up John in prison before Jesus met Simon, James, and John (LUKE 5:1-11).
[Was John free, or in prison when Jesus met Andrew and Simon and acquired disciples?]

**Perplexing:**
Who was the unidentified disciple with Andrew? Did he also become one of Jesus' disciples?

**Language:**
"Messias" is the Latin form of "Messiah," the English version of the Hebrew, "Mashiach. "Christ" is the English version of the Greek, "Khristos." Both mean "The Anointed" or "The Anointed One." The titles were applied to kings in the Near East, because they were anointed during their coronation ceremony. See also under MATT. 1:1.

**Judaism:**
According to Jewish belief, an individual descended paternally from David would be the "Messiah," the king, who would re-establish the Kingdom of David, rebuild the Jerusalem temple, and reinstitute the laws of the Torah.

**History:**
Jews of the first century A.D. believed that the Messiah would free them from Roman rule and establish an independent Jewish kingdom.
See also under MATT. 1:1.

1:43 - THE DAY FOLLOWING JESUS WOULD GO INTO GALILEE, FINDETH PHILIP, AND SAITH, "FOLLOW ME."

**Contradictions:**
MATT. 4:18-22 and MARK 1:14-20 - Jesus obtained his first four disciples, Andrew, Simon, James, and John in Galilee.
LUKE 5:1-10 - Jesus obtained his first three disciples, Simon, James, and John in Galilee.
[Was Philip the first disciple that Jesus obtained in Galilee, or did he acquire three or four before him in Galilee?]
[Was Philip one of Jesus' first three disciples, or did Jesus acquire three disciples before Philip?]

**Perplexing:**
How did Jesus travel from beyond Jordan to Galilee? How long did the trip take?

1:45 - PHILIP FINDETH NATHANAEL, AND SAITH, "WE HAVE FOUND HIM, OF WHOM MOSES IN THE LAW, AND THE PROPHETS DID WRITE, JESUS OF NAZARETH, THE SON OF JOSEPH."

**Perplexing:**
Why did Philip call Jesus "the son of Joseph," rather than the "Son of God," "the Christ," or the "son of David?" JOHN had not mentioned Joseph or anything about Jesus' birth. Who was Nathanael? Why did the other gospels fail to mention him?

1:46 - NATHANAEL SAID, "CAN ANY GOOD THING COME OUT OF NAZARETH?" ....

**Perplexing:**
Why did Nathanael doubt that anything good could come from Nazareth?

1:49 - NATHANAEL SAITH, "RABBI, THOU ART THE SON OF GOD; THOU ART THE KING OF ISRAEL."

**Perplexing:**
According to JOHN 21:2, Nathanael had become one of Jesus' disciples. Why did the other gospels fail to identify him as a disciple? Why did Nathanael refer to Jesus as the Son of God, after Philip said that he was the son of Joseph? Why did he refer to Jesus as the King of Israel? Did Jesus at this time consider himself to be the King of Israel?
See also under MATT. 27:37.

**Language:**
"Rabbi," in Hebrew means "teacher" or "master."

**History:** See under MATT. 3:17.

1:51 - HE [JESUS] SAITH UNTO HIM, "HEREAFTER YE SHALL SEE HEAVEN OPEN, AND THE ANGELS OF GOD ASCENDING AND DESCENDING UPON THE SON OF MAN."

**Perplexing:**
Why did Jesus refer to himself as "the Son of man," after Nathanael has called him "the Son of God?" Why did Jesus tell Nathanael that he will see angels ascending and descending on him? Why did Jesus' prophecy to Nathanael fail to materialize?
See also under MATT. 8:20.

**Language**: See under MATT. 8:20.

**History:** See under MATT. 8:20.

**Old Testament:** See under MATT. 8:20.

2:1 - THE THIRD DAY THERE WAS A MARRIAGE IN CANA OF GALILEE; THE MOTHER OF JESUS WAS THERE.

**Perplexing:**
JOHN 1:13 said that Jesus was born, not of blood, nor of the will of the flesh, nor of the will of man. If so, how could he have a mother? What did "the third day mean—the third day after what?" Who was getting married? Why did JOHN fail to provide the name of Jesus' mother?

2:2 - BOTH JESUS WAS CALLED, AND HIS DISCIPLES, TO THE MARRIAGE.

**Contradictions:**
MATT. 4:23 - [After having acquired his first four disciples] Jesus went about all Galilee teaching in synagogues, preaching the gospel, and healing all manner of sickness and disease.
[After having acquired his first disciples, did Jesus go to Cana, or travel around Galilee teaching and healing?]
MARK. 1:21 - [After having acquired his first four disciples] Jesus went into Capernaum; on the Sabbath day he entered the synagogue, and taught.
[After acquiring his first disciples, did Jesus go to a wedding in Cana, or to a synagogue in Capernaum?]
LUKE 5:12-13 - [After having acquired his first three disciples] He was in a city; a man full of leprosy ... besought him, saying, "Lord...thou canst make me clean." He touched him.... Immediately the leprosy departed from him.
[After having acquired his first disciples, did Jesus go to a wedding Cana, or did he heal a leper?]

**Perplexing:**
Why did the other gospels fail to mention Cana or the marriage? How was Jesus located and called? How many disciples did he have at this time? How did they travel to Cana?

2:3-4 - ...THE MOTHER OF JESUS SAITH UNTO HIM, "THEY HAVE NO WINE." JESUS SAITH, "WOMAN, WHAT HAVE I TO DO WITH THEE?...."

**Old Testament:**
1 KINGS 17:18 - She [a widow] said unto Elijah, "What have I to do with thee...?"

**Perplexing:**
Why was Jesus not courteous to his mother?
See also under 2:1.

2:6-11 - THERE WERE SIX WATERPOTS...CONTAINING TWO OR THREE FIRKINS APIECE. JESUS SAITH [TO SERVANTS], "FILL THE WATERPOTS WITH WATER." THEY FILLED THEM UP TO THE BRIM. .... ...THE WATER THAT WAS MADE WINE.... ...THIS BEGINNING OF MIRACLES DID JESUS IN CANA OF GALILEE...AND HIS DISCIPLES BELIEVED ON HIM.

**Contradictions:**
MATT. 4:23 - [After acquiring disciples] Jesus' first miracles were healing all manner of sickness and disease in all Galilee.
[Was Jesus' first miracle converting water into wine, or healing all manner of sickness and disease?]
MARK 1:23-26 - [After having acquired disciples] Jesus' first miracle was driving an unclean spirit out of a man in a synagogue [in Capernaum (4:21)].
LUKE 4:33-35 - [Before acquiring any disciples] Jesus' first miracle was driving an unclean spirit out of a man in a synagogue [in Capernaum (4:31)].

[Was Jesus' first miracle converting water into wine, or healing a man of an unclean spirit?]
[Did Jesus perform his first miracle after or before acquiring disciples?]

**Language:**
A firkin was 20-30 gallons. (Jesus, therefore converted about 120-180 gallons of water into wine.)

**Perplexing:**
Why was the water into wine miracle not reported by the other gospels? Why did the disciples believe now? Nathanael had already said that Jesus was the Son of God (1:49).
Why did Jesus produce an additional 120-180 gallons of wine for people who had exhausted the existing supply and were probably intoxicated? Why did he not teach moderation in drinking, rather than encouraging drunkenness?

**Pagan parallel:**
The Greek god Dionysus converted water into wine.

2:12 - AFTER THIS HE WENT TO CAPERNAUM, AND HIS MOTHER, BRETHREN, AND DISCIPLES; THEY CONTINUED THERE NOT MANY DAYS. [JOHN THE BAPTIST WAS NOT YET CAST INTO PRISON (3:24).]

**Contradictions:**
MATT. 4:13 - [Before performing any miracles or obtaining disciples, Jesus] Leaving Nazareth, came and dwelt in Capernaum....
[Did Jesus go to Capernaum from Nazareth, or from Cana?]
[Did Jesus spend some days in Capernaum, or did he dwell there?]
MARK 1:21 - [From the Sea of Galilee and before performing any miracles] They [Jesus with Simon. Andrew, James, and John] went into Capernaum ....
[Did Jesus go to Capernaum from Cana, or from the Sea of Galilee?]
[Did Jesus go to Capernaum with his mother, brethren, and disciples, or just with four disciples?]
[Did Jesus go to Capernaum after, or before performing his first miracle?]
LUKE 4:14-23 - [After leaving the wilderness and before acquiring disciples] Jesus returned into Galilee .... .... He came to Nazareth.... .... He said, "Ye will say, '...whatsoever we have heard done in Capernaum, do here....'"
[Did Jesus go to Capernaum from Cana, or from the wilderness?]
LUKE 4:31 - [Before obtaining disciples, Jesus leaving Nazareth] came to Capernaum [for the second time].
[Did Jesus go to Capernaum after acquiring disciples, or did he make two trips there before acquiring disciples?]
[Did Jesus go to Capernaum with his mother, brethren, and disciples, or alone?]
MATT. 4:12; MARK 1:14; LUKE 3:20 - John the Baptist was imprisoned before Jesus traveled to Capernaum.
[Did Jesus go to Capernaum prior to, or after John's imprisonment?]

2:13 - THE JEWS' PASSOVER WAS AT HAND, AND JESUS WENT TO JERUSALEM.

**Contradictions:**
MATT. 4:18 - [After leaving Capernaum before acquiring any disciples] Jesus walking by the sea of Galilee, saw two brethren, Simon called Peter, and Andrew, casting a net into the sea.... [Passover was not mentioned].
[After leaving Capernaum, did Jesus go to Jerusalem, or for a walk by the Sea of Galilee?]
LUKE 4:42 - [After leaving Capernaum] When it was day, he departed and went into a desert place.... [Passover was not mentioned.]
[After departing Capernaum, did Jesus go to Jerusalem, or to a desert place?]
[Was it, or was it not Passover?]
MARK 1:35-36 - [After leaving Capernaum] In the morning...he departed into a solitary placc.... Simon and they that were with him followed. [Passover was not mentioned.]
[After departing Capernaum, did Jesus go to Jerusalem, or to a solitary place with his disciples?]
LUKE 2:42 - When he was 12 years old, they [he and his parents] went to Jerusalem after the custom of the feast [Passover].
[Was Jesus an adult who had acquired disciples and converted water into wine, or was he a 12 year old boy when he went with his parents to Jerusalem for Passover for the first time ?]
MATT. 21:10 and MARK 11:11 - Jesus made his first trip to Jerusalem for Passover after going through Jericho.
[Did Jesus make his first trip to Jerusalem from Capernaum, or via Jericho?]
LUKE 2:39-42 - Jesus made his first reported trip to Jerusalem for Passover from Nazareth.
[Did Jesus go to Jerusalem the first time for Passover from Capernaum, or from Nazareth?]

**Perplexing:**
Why did JOHN say, "The Jews' Passover?" Was he writing for Gentile readers unfamiliar with Jewish holidays? If he was writing for Jews, there would have been no need to specify that it was a Jewish holiday.

2:14-15 - [JESUS] FOUND IN THE TEMPLE THOSE THAT SOLD OXEN, SHEEP, AND DOVES, AND THE CHANGERS OF MONEY SITTING; WHEN HE HAD MADE A SCOURGE OF SMALL CORDS, HE DROVE THEM ALL OUT OF THE TEMPLE...POURED OUT THE CHANGERS' MONEY, AND OVERTHREW THE TABLES.

**Contradictions:**
LUKE 2:46 - ...[Jesus was] in the temple, sitting in the midst of the doctors, hearing them, and asking them questions.
[At his first visit to the temple, did Jesus find and drive merchants out of the temple, or did he sit and speak with the doctors?]
MARK 11:11 - [Near the end of his ministry] Jesus entered Jerusalem, and the temple; when he had looked round upon all things...he went to Bethany with the twelve.
[At his first visit to the temple, did Jesus cast out the merchants from the temple, or did he just look around and leave?]
MATT. 21:12 - [Near the end of his ministry] Jesus went into the temple, and cast out all that sold and bought in the temple, and overthrew the tables of the moneychangers....
[Did Jesus drive the merchants out of the temple at the start, or near the end of his ministry?]
MARK 11:15 - [During his second visit to the temple on the next day]...Jesus went into the temple, and began to cast out them that sold and bought in the temple, and overthrew the tables of the moneychangers....
LUKE 19:45 - [Near the end of his ministry, when Jesus went to the temple for the second time, but the first time as an adult] He went into the temple, and began to cast out them that sold therein, and them that

bought.
[Did Jesus cast out the merchants during his first, or second visit to the temple?]
See also under MATT. 21:12-13.

**Perplexing:** See under MATT. 21:12-13.

**History:** See under MATT. 21:12-13.

2:16 - [JESUS] SAID UNTO THEM THAT SOLD DOVES, "TAKE THESE THINGS HENCE; MAKE NOT MY FATHER'S HOUSE AN HOUSE OF MERCHANDISE."

**Contradictions:**
MATT. 21:13 - [Jesus] Said unto them, "It is written, 'My house shall be called the house of prayer,' but ye have made it a den of thieves."
MARK 11:17 - He taught, saying unto them, "Is it not written, 'My house shall be called of all nations the house of prayer?' But ye have made it a den of thieves."
LUKE 19:46 - [Jesus] saying unto them, "It is written, 'My house is the house of prayer,' but ye have made it a den of thieves."
[Did Jesus speak only to the sellers of doves, or to all the merchants?]
[Did Jesus tell the dove sellers not to make the temple a house of merchandise, or did he tell all the merchants that it was a house of prayer that they had converted into a den of thieves?]

**Old Testament:** See under MATT. 21:12-13.

2:17 - THE DISCIPLES REMEMBERED THAT IT WAS WRITTEN, "THE ZEAL OF THINE HOUSE HATH EATEN ME UP."

**Old Testament:**
PS. 69:9 - "The zeal of thine house hath eaten me up...."

2:18-19 - JEWS SAID UNTO HIM, "WHAT SIGN SHEWEST THOU UNTO US, SEEING THAT THOU DOEST THESE THINGS?" JESUS SAID, "DESTROY THIS TEMPLE, AND IN THREE DAYS I WILL RAISE IT UP."

**Contradictions:**
MATT. 12:38-40 - Certain scribes and Pharisees answered, "Master, we would see a sign from thee." He said, "...there shall no sign be given, but the sign of the prophet Jonas; as Jonas was three days and three nights in the whale's belly, so shall the Son of man be three days and three nights in the heart of the earth."
[Did Jesus say that the sign would be the raising of the "temple" in three days, or the sign of Jonah - that he would spend three days and three nights in the earth?]
MARK 8:11-12 - Pharisees came...seeking a sign.... He saith, "There shall no sign be given unto this generation."
[Did Jesus say that the sign would be the raising of the "temple" in three days, or that there would be no sign?]

2:20 - SAID THE JEWS, "FORTY AND SIX YEARS WAS THIS TEMPLE IN BUILDING, AND WILT THOU REAR IT UP IN THREE DAYS?"

**History:** See under MATT. 24:1-2.

**Perplexing:**
Why did the Jews say that the temple was 46 years in building? If they were counting from 19 B.C. when Herod began rebuilding the temple, the year would now be A.D. 27. If Jesus had been born during the reign of Herod the King (MATT. 2:1) , he would have been about 31 years old, as Herod died in 4 B.C.; if, however, he had been born when Cyrenius became governor of Syria (LUKE 2:2) during A.D. 6, he would have been about 21 years old. In JOHN 8:57, however, Jews said to him, "Thou art not yet 50 years old...." How old was Jesus at this time?

2:21-22 - HE SPAKE OF THE TEMPLE OF HIS BODY. WHEN HE WAS RISEN FROM THE DEAD, HIS DISCIPLES REMEMBERED THAT HE HAD SAID THIS UNTO THEM; THEY BELIEVED THE SCRIPTURE, AND THE WORD WHICH JESUS HAD SAID.

**Contradiction:**
JOHN 20:9 - As yet they [the disciples] knew not the scripture, that he must rise again from the dead.
[Did the disciples remember Jesus' words and believe Scripture, or were they ignorant of Scripture and that Jesus would rise from the dead?]

2:23 - WHEN HE WAS IN JERUSALEM AT THE PASSOVER, MANY BELIEVED IN HIS NAME, WHEN THEY SAW THE MIRACLES WHICH HE DID.

**Contradiction:**
JOHN 4:49-54 - [After having healed a nobleman's son] This is the second miracle that Jesus did, when he was come out of Judaea into Galilee.
[Had Jesus performed miracles seen by people, or was healing the nobleman's son after Passover only his second miracle?] (The verse might, however, be interpreted by some to mean that the miracle was Jesus' second in Galilee, not just the second miracle that he performed.)

**Perplexing:**
What were these miracles? How many were there? Where were they performed? Why were they not specified? Why is there no record of them?

3:1-2 - A MAN OF THE PHARISEES, NAMED NICODEMUS...CAME TO JESUS BY NIGHT....

**Perplexing:**
How did Nicodemus know where to find Jesus? How was he able to locate him at night? Why was neither he, nor the ensuing discourse mentioned by the other gospels?

3:3-5 - JESUS SAID, "EXCEPT A MAN BE BORN AGAIN, HE CANNOT SEE THE KINGDOM OF GOD." .... "EXCEPT A MAN BE BORN OF WATER AND OF THE SPIRIT, HE CANNOT ENTER INTO THE KINGDOM OF GOD."

**Pagan parallel:**
Followers of the goddess Cybele (also known as the Mother of Gods), at least as early as the seventh century B.C., referred to themselves as "born again" after they had washed in the blood of a ram (lamb) or bull.

**Perplexing:**
Why was JOHN the only gospel to say that it is necessary to be born again?

**Contradictions:** See under MATT. 19:17-19 (for obtaining eternal life).

3:13 - JESUS: "NO MAN HATH ASCENDED UP TO HEAVEN, BUT HE THAT CAME DOWN FROM HEAVEN, EVEN THE SON OF MAN WHICH IS IN HEAVEN."

**Contradictions:**
GEN. 5:24 - Enoch walked with God, and he was not, for God took him.
HEB. 11:5 - Paul: "By faith Enoch was translated that he should not see death, and was not found, because God had translated him; ...he pleased God."
2 KINGS 2:11 - ...Elijah went up by a whirlwind into heaven.
[Was Jesus the only man to ascend to heaven, or did Enoch and Elijah ascend?]

3:14 - JESUS: "MOSES LIFTED UP THE SERPENT IN THE WILDERNESS...."

**Old Testament:**
NUM. 21:9 - Moses made a serpent of brass, and put it upon a pole....
[Note that brass was not yet in existence at the time Moses is said to have done this. Some Bibles use "bronze" or "copper," instead of "brass."]

3:15 - JESUS: "WHOSOEVER BELIEVETH IN HIM [JESUS] SHOULD NOT PERISH, BUT HAVE ETERNAL LIFE."

**Contradictions:** See under MATT. 19:17-19 (for obtaining eternal life).

**Perplexing:** See under MATT. 19:16 and 17-19 (for eternal life).

**Pagan concept:** See under MATT. 19:16.

3:16 - GOD SO LOVED THE WORLD THAT HE GAVE HIS ONLY BEGOTTEN SON, THAT WHOSOEVER BELIEVETH IN HIM SHOULD NOT PERISH, BUT HAVE EVERLASTING LIFE.

**Contradictions:** See under 1:13, and under MATT 1:18, and 19:17-19 (for obtaining eternal life).

**Perplexing:**
If God loves the world why does He allow suffering, disease, crime, war, poverty, etc. to exist? Why does he not appear Himself, rather than ask people to believe that He had a Son through adultery who He sent into the world to die? Why has He allowed belief in His son to contribute to religious hate, persecution, violence, murders, and wars? Why should belief in His son be a prerequisite for eternal life? Do not those who are sentenced to hell also have eternal life, albeit a life of punishment? If not, what happens to them? If God loved the world, why did He create hell, eternal torment, and evil (see ISA. 45:7)?
If God wanted people to believe in Him, Jesus, and the Bible, why did he fail to produce an easily understood, unambiguous Bible, and unquestionable proof of His and His Son's existence? By not doing so, is He not morally responsible for all the suffering, hate, persecution, violence, murders, wars, etc. perpetrated in His

name and the name of His Son? Could the devil have wrought more destruction and misery on humanity? If God is omniscient, why did He not know who would or would not believe in His Son and in Him, without having to send His Son to die and bring untold calamities over the centuries upon the earth? Why did He fail to create people, all of whom would believe in Jesus?
In JOHN 6:44, Jesus said, "No man can come to me, except the Father which sent me draw him; I will raise him up at the last day." Then in JOHN 17:12, Jesus said, "...those that Thou gavest me I have kept...." Therefore, if God has already decided who will be saved, what was the purpose of sending Jesus? What is the point of being born again or believing in Jesus or trying to adhere to any of the criteria Jesus specified for obtaining eternal life?
See also under MATT. 19:17-19 (for obtaining eternal life).

**History:**
There is disagreement among theologians about whether verses 3:15-21 should be attributed to Jesus or to the gospel writer.

3:17 - GOD SENT NOT HIS SON INTO THE WORLD TO CONDEMN THE WORLD, BUT THAT THE WORLD THROUGH HIM MIGHT BE SAVED.

**Contradictions:**
MATT. 10:34 - Jesus: "Think not that I am come to send peace on earth; I came not to send peace, but a sword."
[Was Jesus sent to save the world, or to bring a sword?]
LUKE 12:49 - Jesus: "I am come to send fire on the earth....."
[Was Jesus sent to save the world, or to send fire onto the earth?]
LUKE 12:51 - Jesus: "Suppose ye that I have come to give peace on earth? I tell you, nay, but rather division."
[Was Jesus sent to save the world, or to bring division?]
1 JOHN 3:8 - "The Son of God was manifested that he might destroy the works of the devil."
[Was Jesus sent to save the world, or to destroy the works of the devil?]
MARK 4:11-12 - Jesus: "Unto you it is given to know the mystery of the kingdom of God; but unto them that are without, all these things are done in parables, that seeing they...may not perceive...and not understand, lest at any time they should be converted, and their sins should be forgiven them."
[Was Jesus sent to save the world, or to speak in parables to prevent people from having their sins forgiven?]
EPH. 2:8 - Paul: "By grace ye are saved through faith, and that not of yourselves; it is the gift of God."
[Did God send Jesus to save the world, or is salvation a gift through the grace of God?]
See also under MATT. 1:18.

**Perplexing:**
Why could God not save the world without sending His Son? Why did He fail to create a world that did not need to be saved?
See also under 3:16.

3:18 - HE THAT BELIEVETH ON HIM IS NOT CONDEMNED, BUT HE THAT BELIEVETH NOT IS CONDEMNED ALREADY, BECAUSE HE HATH NOT BELIEVED IN THE NAME OF THE ONLY BEGOTTEN SON OF GOD.

**Contradictions:** See under MATT. 19:17-19 (for obtaining eternal life).

**Perplexing:**
Why does God require one to believe in Jesus to be saved? Why is unbelief so terrible that a person must be condemned for it, regardless of how good that person may otherwise be? Why is God afraid of unbelief? Why is belief so important that a believer, no matter how bad, will be saved? Why did God create people who would not believe in Jesus and, therefore, have to be condemned? Why did God not know that some people would not believe in Jesus? Why did Jesus or the gospel writer try to induce belief through fear - fear of being condemned and whatever that entails, rather than using reason?
See also under 3:16, and under MARK 16:16.

**Pagan parallel:** See under 1:14, and under MARK 16:16

3:19 - ...MEN LOVED DARKNESS RATHER THAN LIGHT, BECAUSE THEIR DEEDS WERE EVIL.

**Perplexing:**
Why did God fail to create people who would not perpetrate evil deeds? Why does God allow evil to exist? Can He really be a god, if He is incapable of preventing evil?

3:22 - AFTER THESE THINGS CAME JESUS AND HIS DISCIPLES INTO JUDAEA; THERE HE TARRIED WITH THEM, AND BAPTIZED.

**Contradiction:**
JOHN 4:2 - Jesus himself baptized not, but his disciples.
[Did, or did not Jesus do any baptizing?]

**Perplexing:**
When did Jesus leave Jerusalem and Judaea? The temple was in Jerusalem in Judaea. Where was Jesus before he went to Judaea ? Where in Judaea did he now go? Why were the disciples not reported to have been baptized? Were they? By whom? When? How did Jesus baptize? John (in 1:33, and MARK 1:8) said that Jesus would baptize with the Holy Ghost; in MATT. 3:11 and LUKE 3:16, he said that Jesus would baptize with the Holy Ghost and fire. Did Jesus baptize anyone with the Holy Ghost (and fire?)? If so, who did he baptize? Why did Jesus and his disciples practice baptism, a pagan purification ritual?

**Pagan concept:** See under MATT. 3:5-6.

**History:** See under MATT. 3:5-6.

**Old Testament:** See under MATT. 3:5-6.

3:23-24 - JOHN ALSO WAS BAPTIZING IN AENON NEAR SALIM .... JOHN WAS NOT YET CAST INTO PRISON.

**Contradiction:**
MATT. 4:12-20; MARK 1:14-18; LUKE 3:20-5:11 - John was imprisoned before Jesus had any disciples. [Did John continue to baptize after Jesus obtained disciples, or was he imprisoned before Jesus acquired his first disciples?]

**Perplexing:**
Why was John still baptizing, rather than following Jesus and becoming one of his disciples? In 1:29, John saw Jesus and said, "Behold the Lamb of God which taketh away the sin of the world"; and in 1:34, that Jesus "is the Son of God."
See also under 1:37-38.

3:25 - THERE AROSE A QUESTION BETWEEN SOME OF JOHN'S DISCIPLES AND THE JEWS ABOUT PURIFYING.

**Perplexing:**
Why did John still have disciples? Why did he not tell them all to follow Jesus? If John's disciples were not Jews, of what religion were they? If they were Jews,why were they said to argue with "the Jews?"

3:26 - THEY CAME UNTO JOHN, AND SAID, "HE THAT WAS WITH THEE BEYOND JORDAN, TO WHOM THOU BAREST WITNESS, BAPTIZETH, AND ALL COME TO HIM."

**Contradiction:** See under 3:22.

3:30 - JOHN: "HE MUST INCREASE, BUT I MUST DECREASE."

**Perplexing:**
Why did John say that he must decrease, rather than say that he will cease and become a disciple of Jesus?

**History:**
Theologians disagree about whether the following verses, 3:31-36, should be attributed to John or to the gospel writer.

3:35 - THE FATHER LOVETH THE SON....

**Perplexing:**
In JOHN 10:30, Jesus said, "I and my Father are one." If so, was JOHN saying that Jesus loved himself?

3:36 - HE THAT BELIEVETH ON THE SON HATH EVERLASTING LIFE; HE THAT BELIEVETH NOT THE SON SHALL NOT SEE LIFE; THE WRATH OF GOD ABIDETH ON HIM.

**Contradictions:** See under MATT. 19:17-19 (for obtaining eternal life).

**Perplexing:**
Why did God fail to provide evidence to prove that Jesus is His Son? Why does He want people to believe without any supporting evidence? Why does He try to coerce people to believe by threatening them?
See also under 3:18, and under MARK 16:16.

4:1-2 - ...JESUS MADE AND BAPTIZED MORE DISCIPLES THAN JOHN, (THOUGH JESUS HIMSELF BAPTIZED NOT, BUT HIS DISCIPLES).

**Contradictions:**
JOHN 3:22 - Came Jesus and his disciples into Judaea, and there he tarried with them and baptized.

[Did Jesus' disciples but not Jesus baptize, or did Jesus and his disciples baptize?]
JOHN 3:26 - They [John's disciples] came unto John, and said, "Rabbi, he that was with thee beyond Jordan...baptizeth, and all men come to him."
[Did not, or did Jesus baptize?]

**Perplexing:**
Why were John and Jesus competing for disciples? Why was John still trying to obtain disciples? Why did John fail to become a disciple of Jesus?
See also under 3:23-24 and 25.

4:5-6 - THEN COMETH HE TO A CITY OF SAMARIA, SYCHAR, NEAR TO THE PARCEL OF GROUND THAT JACOB GAVE TO HIS SON JOSEPH. JACOB'S WELL WAS THERE. JESUS BEING WEARIED...SAT ON THE WELL....

**Contradiction:**
GEN. 33:18-20 - Jacob came to Shalem.... He bought a parcel of a field ... at the hand of the children of Hamor, Shechem's father....He erected there an altar.... [This was the only parcel of land that Jacob was reported to have purchased; Joseph and a well were not mentioned.]
[Did Jacob own a parcel of ground in Sychar which he gave to Joseph, or did he buy a parcel of ground in Shalem and build an altar?]

**Perplexing:**
How could a divine being, a Son of God, be wearied even when in the guise of a man? How did Jesus travel? Did he walk? How long did the trip take? If Jesus was by the Jordan close to Samaria or in the Jerusalem area, the distance would have been about 30 miles.

4:7-8 - THERE COMETH A WOMAN OF SAMARIA TO DRAW WATER; JESUS SAITH, "GIVE ME TO DRINK." (HIS DISCIPLES WERE GONE UNTO THE CITY TO BUY MEAT.)

**Perplexing:**
Why did Jesus demand a drink, rather than asking for it politely? Why did Jesus request a drink, instead of taking it himself? Why did a divine being require a drink? Why did Jesus not perform a miracle to get the drink? Why did Jesus fail to perform a miracle to provide food for himself and the disciples, rather than have them travel to a city to buy it? Why were the disciples not so weary as to need a rest? Why did they not also need a drink?

**Old Testament:**
GEN. 24:11-17 - One of Abraham's servants sat by a well and asked a woman for a drink.
GEN. 29:1-10 - Jacob waited by a well where he met Rachel.
EX. 2:15-16 - Moses sat by a well where he met the daughters of Midian.
1 KINGS 17:10 - Elijah asked a widow for a little water to drink.

**Pagan parallel:**
Ananda, a disciple of Buddha, after a long walk, met a low cast woman at a well and asked her for a drink.

4:9 - SAITH THE WOMAN OF SAMARIA, "HOW IS IT THAT THOU, A JEW, ASKETH DRINK OF ME, A WOMAN OF SAMARIA?" THE JEWS HAVE NO DEALINGS WITH THE SAMARITANS.

**Perplexing:**
In MATT. 10:5, Jesus said, "Go not into the way of the Gentiles, and into any city of the Samaritans enter ye not." Why then did he take his disciples into Samaria?

**Pagan parallel:**
A woman told Ananda that she could not approach him, because she was of a low caste. Ananda responded that he was asking for water, not about her caste.

**History:** See under MATT. 10:5-6.

4:10 - JESUS SAID, "IF THOU KNEWEST THE GIFT OF GOD, AND WHO IT IS THAT SAITH TO THEE, 'GIVE ME TO DRINK,' THOU WOULDST HAVE ASKED OF HIM, AND HE WOULD HAVE GIVEN THEE LIVING WATER."

**Old Testament:**
JER. 2:13 - The LORD: "My people...have forsaken me the fountain of living waters...."
ZECH. 14:8 - Zechariah: "It shall be in that day [the day of the LORD], that living waters shall go out from Jerusalem...."

4:12 - THE WOMAN: "...OUR FATHER JACOB, WHICH GAVE US THE WELL...."

**Old Testament:**
There is no record of Jacob having given a well to the Samaritans or to anyone else.

4:14 - JESUS: "WHOSOEVER DRINKETH OF THE WATER THAT I SHALL GIVE HIM SHALL BE IN HIM A WELL OF WATER SPRINGING UP INTO EVERLASTING LIFE."

**Pagan parallel:**
The Sumerian gods Anu and Enki maintained and offered the water of eternal life. In a Sumerian myth, Enki used the water of life to resurrect the goddess Inanna.

**Dead Sea Scrolls:**
The Teacher of Righteousness equated himself with a "fountain of living waters." ("Thou, O my God, hast put into my mouth...a spring of living waters.")

4:17-18 - THE WOMAN SAID, "I HAVE NO HUSBAND." JESUS SAID, "...THOU HAST HAD FIVE HUSBANDS, AND HE WHOM THOU NOW HAST IS NOT THY HUSBAND...."

**Perplexing:**
Why did Jesus not rebuke her for living with a man to whom she was not married? Was she a concubine? Had she been divorced and/or widowed five times? If she was divorced and remarried at any time, why did Jesus not say that she was guilty of adultery? In MATT. 5:32, MARK 10:12, and LUKE 16:18, he said that a divorced person who remarries commits adultery.

4:21 - JESUS SAITH, "WOMAN, THE HOUR COMETH, WHEN YE SHALL NEITHER IN THIS MOUNTAIN, NOR AT JERUSALEM, WORSHIP THE FATHER."

**Perplexing:**
Why did Jesus imply that the "hour" would come in the woman's lifetime? Why, about two millennia later has it failed to come?

4:22 - JESUS: "SALVATION IS OF THE JEWS."

**Perplexing:**
If "salvation is of the Jews," why have Christians in the name of Jesus engaged in the persecution, torture, killing, and mass murder of Jews over the ensuing centuries? If Jesus is a Jew, will he look kindly on those who kill his people even though they do not believe in him? Jesus is not reported to have ordered his followers to kill anyone. In MATT. 10:16, he said, "...be ye...harmless as doves." Why do many (most?) Christians disobey this command by Jesus?

4:23 - JESUS: "THE HOUR COMETH, AND NOW IS, WHEN THE TRUE WORSHIPPERS SHALL WORSHIP THE FATHER IN SPIRIT AND IN TRUTH, FOR THE FATHER SEEKETH SUCH TO WORSHIP HIM."

**Perplexing:**
Why does God seek people to worship Him? Why does Almighty God, creator of the universe care whether or not puny, short-lived humans worship Him? Was Jesus saying that God is so insecure or such an egomaniac that He needs to have His ego boosted by the worship of piddling human beings? Did He create people just so they would worship Him?
Why did Jesus tell the woman that the hour is now here, when about 2000 years later it still has not arrived?"

4:24 - JESUS: "GOD IS A SPIRIT...."

**Perplexing:**
How did the spirit of which God is composed come into existence? When did God come into existence? Why? How? Was He created by a superior being? If God is a spirit, why does He take the shape of a man in numerous verses such as GEN. 18:1-33?
See also under 1:1 and 1:3.

4:25-26 - THE WOMAN SAITH, "I KNOW THAT MESSIAS COMETH, WHICH IS CALLED CHRIST; ...." JESUS SAITH, "I THAT SPEAK UNTO THEE AM HE."

**History:**
The Samaritans and the Jews believed in the coming of a Messiah.

**Perplexing:**
Why did Jesus tell this one Samaritan woman that he was the Messiah? Why did he not publicly say it to all people?

**Contradiction:**
JOHN 8:40 - Jesus: "Ye seek to kill a man that hath told you the truth, which I have heard of God...."
[Did Jesus say that he was the Messiah (Christ), or that he was a man who heard the truth from God?]

**Language**: See under MATT. 1:1.

4:28 - THE WOMAN THEN LEFT HER WATERPOT, AND WENT INTO THE CITY....

**Perplexing:**
Did the women give Jesus the drink he had requested?

4:43 - AFTER TWO DAYS HE DEPARTED THENCE, AND WENT INTO GALILEE.

**Perplexing:**
Where did Jesus and the disciples lodge for two days in Samaria?

4:46-54 - JESUS CAME AGAIN INTO CANA OF GALILEE.... THERE WAS A NOBLEMAN, WHOSE SON WAS SICK AT CAPERNAUM. ...HE ...BESOUGHT HIM THAT HE WOULD HEAL HIS SON, FOR HE WAS AT THE POINT OF DEATH. .... JESUS SAITH, "THY SON LIVETH." .... ...SERVANTS MET HIM, SAYING, "THY SON LIVETH." .... THIS IS THE SECOND MIRACLE THAT JESUS DID, WHEN HE WAS COME OUT OF JUDAEA INTO GALILEE.

**Contradictions:**
MATT. 4:23 - Jesus went about all Galilee...healing all manner of sickness and diseases among the people.
[These healings included Jesus' second miracle.]
[Was Jesus' second miracle in Galilee the healing of a nobleman's son, or healing all manner of sickness and diseases?]
MARK 1:30-31 and LUKE 4:38-39 - Jesus' second miracle in Galilee was curing Simon's mother-in-law's fever.
[Was Jesus' second miracle in Galilee the healing of a nobleman's son, or curing Simon's mother-in-law's fever?]

5:1 - AFTER THIS THERE WAS A FEAST OF THE JEWS, AND JESUS WENT TO JERUSALEM.

**Perplexing:**
Why did JOHN not identify the feast?
Why did JOHN say, "a feast of the Jews," as though he was writing for a non-Jewish audience?

5:2-4 - THERE IS AT JERUSALEM...A POOL, CALLED IN HEBREW BETHESDA, HAVING FIVE PORCHES. IN THESE LAY A GREAT MULTITUDE OF IMPOTENT FOLK, BLIND, HALT, WITHERED, WAITING FOR THE MOVEMENT OF THE WATER, FOR AN ANGEL WENT DOWN AT A CERTAIN SEASON INTO THE POOL, AND TROUBLED THE WATER; WHOSOEVER FIRST AFTER THE TROUBLING OF THE WATER STEPPED IN WAS MADE WHOLE....

**Perplexing:**
Why was only one person—the fastest into the pool—healed?

**History:**
There is no evidence for the described pool, angel, and healing.

5:6 - WHEN JESUS SAW HIM [AN INFIRM MAN]...HE SAITH, "WILT THOU BE MADE WHOLE?"

**Contradictions:** See under MATT. 9:28-30.

**Perplexing:**
Why did Jesus ask the man if he wanted to be healed? Why did he not know that an infirm person would want to be healed, especially if he had come to a pool where miraculous healings were supposed to take place? Why did Jesus ask only this one man? Why did Jesus go to the pool?

5:7-8 - THE MAN ANSWERED, "SIR, I HAVE NO MAN, WHEN THE WATER IS TROUBLED, TO PUT ME INTO THE POOL; WHILE I AM COMING, ANOTHER STEPPETH DOWN BEFORE ME." JESUS SAITH, "RISE; TAKE UP THY BED, AND WALK."

**Perplexing:**
If the man's infirmity was so bad that he needed someone to put him into the pool, how was he able to travel to the pool while taking a bed with him? Why did he come to the pool if he knew that he would not be the first person into it?

5:9 - IMMEDIATELY THE MAN WAS MADE WHOLE, TOOK UP HIS BED, AND WALKED. THE DAY WAS THE SABBATH.

**Perplexing:**
Why did Jesus select this particular one man to heal? Why did Jesus not ask the man if he had faith? Why did Jesus fail to heal everyone by the pool?

5:14 - AFTERWARD JESUS FINDETH HIM IN THE TEMPLE, AND SAID, "THOU ART MADE WHOLE; SIN NO MORE, LEST A WORSE THING COME UNTO THEE."

**Perplexing:**
Why did Jesus not know whether or not the man would sin again? Why did Jesus imply that the man's infirmity was due to a sin? Why was this man afflicted because of a sin, whereas countless numbers of people worldwide were and are not afflicted for sinning? Why did the other gospels fail to report this incident at Bethesda?

5:15 - THE MAN DEPARTED, AND TOLD THE JEWS THAT JESUS MADE HIM WHOLE.

**Perplexing:**
Why did JOHN say that the man "told the Jews," when the man was a Jew? Why did JOHN not say that he "told the people?"
See also under 2:13 and 3:25.

5:16 - THEREFORE DID THE JEWS PERSECUTE JESUS, AND SOUGHT TO SLAY HIM, BECAUSE HE HAD DONE THESE THINGS ON THE SABBATH DAY.

**Perplexing:**
How did the Jews persecute Jesus? Why did he not perform a miracle to prevent the persecution? Why would the Jews want to persecute and slay Jesus for healing someone on the Sabbath, since it was legal to do so under Jewish law? Why would they want to harm someone who could heal people miraculously? If healing had not been permitted, why did an angel heal anyone, and why did people come to the pool on the Sabbath to be healed?
See also under MATT. 12:14.

**History:**
There is no secular evidence that the Jews or anyone else persecuted or intended to kill Jesus.
See also under MATT. 12:9-10.

**Contradictions:**
JOHN 7:14 - About the midst of the feast Jesus went into the temple and taught.
JOHN 8:2 - ...he came again into the temple...and taught them.
JOHN 8:20 - ...he taught in the temple....
[Did Jews want to kill Jesus, or did they allow him to teach them in the temple?]
JOHN 7:19-20 - Jesus: ".... Why go ye about to kill me?" The people said, "Thou hast a devil; who goeth about to kill thee?"
[Did Jews want to kill Jesus, or did they not want to kill him?]
JOHN 8:4 - They [scribes and Pharisees] say, "Master, this woman was taken in adultery...."
[Did the Jews want to kill Jesus, or did they call him, "Master," and converse with him?]

5:17-18 - JESUS ANSWERED, "MY FATHER WORKETH HITHERTO, AND I WORK." THEREFORE THE JEWS SOUGHT THE MORE TO KILL HIM, BECAUSE HE NOT ONLY HAD BROKEN THE SABBATH, BUT SAID THAT GOD WAS HIS FATHER, MAKING HIMSELF EQUAL WITH GOD.

**History:** See under 5:16.

**Contradictions:** See under 5:16.

**Pagan concept:**
The belief that a deity could be both god and son was in existence long before the time of Christianity.
See also under MATT. 28:18-20.

5:22 - JESUS: "THE FATHER JUDGETH NO MAN, BUT HATH COMMITTED ALL JUDGMENT UNTO THE SON."

**Contradictions:**
PS. 7:11 - "God judgeth the righteous...."
PS. 9:8 - "He [the LORD] shall judge the world in righteousness; He shall minister judgment to the people...."
PS. 96:13 - "... He [the LORD] cometh to judge the earth; He shall judge the world with righteousness, and the people with His truth."
PS. 98:9 - "...He [the LORD] cometh to judge the earth; with righteousness shall He judge the world, and the people with equity."
ECCL. 12:14 - "God shall bring every work into judgment...."

EZEK. 7:8 - The LORD God: "...I will judge thee according to thy ways...."
EZEK. 7:27 - "...according to their deserts will I judge them; and they shall know that I am the LORD."
EZEK. 18:30 - "I will judge you, O house of Israel, everyone according to his ways," saith the LORD God, "...."
JOHN 8:50 - Jesus: "...there is One [God] who seeketh and judgeth."
HEB. 12:23 - Paul: "...God the Judge of all...."
HEB. 13:4 - Paul: "...whoremongers and adulterers God will judge."
[Will Jesus, or God do the judging?]
MATT. 19:28 - Jesus said unto them [his twelve disciples], "...ye also shall sit upon 12 thrones, judging the twelve tribes of Israel."
LUKE 22:29-30 - Jesus: "I appoint unto you a kingdom...that ye may...sit on thrones judging the twelve tribes of Israel."
[Will Jesus do the judging, or will his disciples (including Judas Iscariot) judge the Israelite tribes?]
JOHN 8:15 - Jesus: "...I judge no man."
JOHN 12:47 - Jesus: "...I came not to judge the world, but to save the world."
[Will or, will not Jesus do the judging?]
1 COR. 6:2 - Paul: "Do ye not know that saints shall judge the world?...."
[Will Jesus, or saints do the judging?]

**Perplexing:**
Who is to do the judging, God, Jesus, the disciples, or the saints? Why is judgment needed, since God presumably knows beforehand who He will save?

**Pagan parallel:**
The Egyptian god Osiris sat in judgment of the souls of the dead. Osiris was also part of a trinity - Osiris, Isis, and Horus. In Zoroastrianism, Mithra is to judge the world after the resurrection of the dead. The concept of a judgment also existed in other pre-Christian pagan religions.

5:24 - JESUS: "HE THAT HEARETH MY WORD, AND BELIEVETH ON HIM THAT SENT ME, HATH EVERLASTING LIFE, AND SHALL NOT COME INTO CONDEMNATION, BUT IS PASSED FROM DEATH UNTO LIFE."

**Contradictions:**
JOHN 3:15 - Whosoever believeth in him [the Son] should not perish, but have eternal life.
JOHN 3:36 - He that believeth on the Son hath everlasting life; he that believeth not the Son shall not see life, but the wrath of God abideth on him.
[To obtain everlasting life, must one believe in God, or in Jesus?]
See also under MATT. 19:17-19 (for obtaining eternal life).

**Perplexing:**
In JOHN 6:37, Jesus said, "All that the Father giveth me shall come to me...." Therefore, if only those that God selected can come to Jesus, does God have the moral right to condemn those that He did not send to Jesus?
See also under MATT. 19:16 and 17-19 (for obtaining eternal life).

**Pagan concept:** See under MATT. 19:16.

**Old Testament:**
ISA. 45:22 - God: "Look unto Me, and be saved, all the ends of the earth, for I am God, and there is none else."
JOEL 2:32 - "Whosoever shall call on the name of the LORD shall be delivered and in the remnant whom the LORD shall call."
AMOS 5:4 - "Saith the LORD unto the house of Israel, '...seek ye me, and ye shall live.'"

5:25 - JESUS: "THE HOUR IS COMING, AND NOW IS, WHEN THE DEAD SHALL HEAR THE VOICE OF THE SON OF GOD, AND THEY THAT HEAR SHALL LIVE."

**Contradictions:** See under 4:21 and under MATT. 19:17-19 (for obtaining eternal life).

**Perplexing:**
Why did Jesus say that the hour is now?" Why about two millennia later, has the hour not yet arrived? Why did Jesus misinform his listeners? If he was wrong about this, could he have been wrong about other things?
See also under 4:23.

5:27 - JESUS: "AND (THE FATHER] HATH GIVEN HIM [JESUS] AUTHORITY TO EXECUTE JUDGMENT...."

**Contradictions:** See under 5:22.

**Perplexing:** See under 5:22.

5:28-29 - JESUS: "...THE HOUR IS COMING, IN WHICH ALL THAT ARE IN THE GRAVES SHALL HEAR HIS VOICE, AND SHALL COME FORTH; THEY THAT HAVE DONE GOOD, UNTO THE RESURRECTION OF LIFE; AND THEY THAT HAVE DONE EVIL, UNTO THE RESURRECTION OF DAMNATION."

**Contradictions:**
JOB 14:12 - "Man lieth down , and riseth not; till the heavens be no more, they shall not awake, nor be raised out of their sleep."
[Will those in graves come forth, or will they never be raised?]
ECCL. 9:5 - "...the dead know not anything, neither have they anymore a reward...."
[Will the dead be rewarded with life, or will they have no reward?]
See also under MATT. 19:17-19 (for obtaining eternal life).

**Perplexing:**
What will happen to those dead who are not in graves? For examples, those who were devoured by animals or cannibals; those who were burned to death or cremated, or killed by dismemberment?
Why did God create people who do evil? Why cannot God prevent or eliminate evil?
See also under 5:25.

**Old Testament:**
DAN. 12:2 - "Many of them that sleep in the dust of the earth shall awake, some to everlasting life, and some to shame and everlasting contempt."

5:30 - JESUS: "...AS I HEAR, I JUDGE, AND MY JUDGMENT IS JUST, BECAUSE I SEEK NOT MINE OWN WILL, BUT THE WILL OF THE FATHER...."

**Contradictions:** See under 5:22.

**Perplexing:** See under 5:22.

5:31 - JESUS: "IF I BEAR WITNESS OF MYSELF, MY WITNESS IS NOT TRUE."

**Contradiction:**
JOHN 8:14 Jesus: "Though I bear record of myself, yet my record is true...."
JOHN 8:18 Jesus: "I am one that bear witness of myself...."
[Did Jesus bear, or not bear a true witness of himself?]

**Old Testament:**
DEUT. 19:15 - Moses: "...at the mouth of two witnesses, or three witnesses, shall the matter established."

5:37 - JESUS: "THE FATHER WHICH HATH SENT ME, HATH BORN WITNESS OF ME. YE HAVE NEITHER HEARD HIS VOICE AT ANY TIME, NOR SEEN HIS SHAPE."

**Contradictions:**
See under 1:18 - God was seen.
In many of the verses in which God was seen, His voice was also heard. There are numerous additional verses in the Old Testament in which God spoke, but was not seen.
In the New Testament, the following verses report God speaking and being heard:
MATT. 3:17 - Lo a voice from heaven saying, "This is My beloved Son, in whom I am well pleased."
MARK 1:11 - There came a voice from heaven, saying, "Thou art My beloved Son, in whom I am well pleased."
LUKE 3:22 - ...a voice came from heaven, which said, "Thou art My beloved Son; in thee I am well pleased."
MATT. 17:5 - ...a voice out of the cloud said, "this is My beloved Son, in whom I am well pleased; hear him."
MARK 9: 7 - ...a voice came out of the cloud, saying, "This is My beloved Son, hear him."
LUKE 9:35 - There came a voice out of the cloud, saying, "This is My beloved Son, hear him."
JOHN 1:33 - John: " He that sent me to baptize with water, the same said unto me, 'Upon whom thou shalt see the Spirit descending, and remaining on him, the same is he which baptizeth with the Holy Ghost.'"
[Have people seen, or not seen God?]
[Have people heard, or not heard the voice of God?]

5:40 - JESUS: "YE WILL NOT COME TO ME THAT YE MIGHT HAVE LIFE."

**Perplexing:**
How can people come to Jesus unless his Father sends them (6:37)?
See also under 5:24.

5:45 - JESUS: "DO NOT THINK THAT I WILL ACCUSE YOU TO THE FATHER; THERE IS ONE THAT ACCUSETH YOU, MOSES, IN WHOM YE TRUST."

**Perplexing:**
Why would anyone have to make an accusation to the Father, when the Father already knows (or should know) who will or will not believe in Jesus?

5:46 - JESUS: "HE [MOSES] WROTE OF ME."

**Perplexing:**
Where did Moses write about Jesus? What did he write? In what language did he write, as ancient written Hebrew did not come into existence until the tenth or eleventh century B.C.? On what and with what did Moses write?

6:1-4 - ...JESUS WENT OVER THE SEA OF GALILEE.... A GREAT MULTITUDE FOLLOWED HIM.... JESUS WENT UP A MOUNTAIN, AND SAT WITH HIS DISCIPLES. PASSOVER, A FEAST OF THE JEWS, WAS NIGH.

**Contradiction:**
MATT. 14:13 - Jesus...departed by ship into a desert place...they [the people] followed.
MARK 6:32-33 - They [Jesus and his disciples] departed into a desert place by ship. The people...came together unto him.
LUKE 9: 10-11 - .... He took them [his disciples] into a desert place.... The people followed him....
[Did Jesus and his disciples go onto a mountain, or did they go to a desert place?]

**Perplexing:**
How did the multitude (about 5000 men according to 6:10) follow Jesus? Did they travel by boat? Were there enough boats to carry 5000 people? How many boats were needed? How long did it take 5000 men to board the boats? How long did it take for all the boats to dock and for 5000 people to disembark? How large an area was needed for the people to be able to spread out after disembarking? Did they come by land? If so, how far did they have to travel? How did they travel? How long would it have taken 5000 people to travel over narrow roads and/or open fields? How could they all have arrived at the same time, considering that they would have formed long processions, that people walk at different speeds, and that some would have needed to spend time resting? Why did the Romans allow such a mass movement of people to clog the roads?
Why did John report that Jesus participated in two Passovers prior to the Passover at the end of his ministry? By so doing, JOHN, stated that Jesus' ministry lasted three yearsf rather than the one year of the other gospels.
See also under 2:13, and under MATT. 14:13.

6:5 - WHEN JESUS...SAW A GREAT COMPANY COME UNTO HIM, HE SAITH UNTO PHILIP, "WHENCE SHALL WE BUY BREAD, THAT THESE MAY EAT?"

**Contradiction:**
MATT. 14:15-16 - ...his disciples came, saying, "This is a desert place...send the multitude away, that they may go into the villages, and buy victuals." Jesus: "They need not depart; give them to eat."
MARK 6:35-37 - ...his disciples said, "This is a desert place...send them away,that they may go into the country and villages, and buy themselves bread, for they have nothing to eat." He said, "Give ye them to eat."
LUKE9:12-13 - ...the twelve said, "Send the multitude away, that they may go into the towns and country, lodge, and get victuals, for we are in a desert place." He said, "Give ye them to eat." ....

[Did Jesus ask Philip where to buy bread, or did Jesus tell the disciples to feed the people?]

6:6 - JESUS SAID THIS TO PROVE HIM, FOR HE HIMSELF KNEW WHAT HE WOULD DO.

**Perplexing:**
Why did Jesus want "to prove" Philip? According to 18:4, Jesus knew all things that should come upon him.

6:7 - PHILIP ANSWERED, "TWO HUNDRED PENNYWORTH OF BREAD IS NOT SUFFICIENT FOR THEM...."

**Contradiction:**
MARK 6:37 - .... They [disciples] say, "Shall we go and buy 200 pennyworth of bread, and give them to eat?"
[Did Philip say that 200 pennyworth of bread would not be sufficient, or did the disciples ask whether they should buy 200 pennyworth of bread?]

6:8-9 - ANDREW, PETER'S BROTHER, SAITH, "THERE IS A LAD HERE, WHICH HATH FIVE BARLEY LOAVES, AND TWO SMALL FISHES...."

**Contradictions:**
MATT. 14:17 - They [disciples] say, "We have here but five loaves, and two fishes."
MARK 6:38 - He saith, "How many loaves have ye? Go and see." When they knew, they say, "Five, and two fishes."
LUKE 9:13 - They said, "We have no more but five loaves and two fishes, except we go and buy meat for all this people."
[Did Andrew say that a lad has five loaves of bread and two fish, or did the disciples say that they have five loaves and two fishes?]
[Did Andrew mention the lad with bread and fishes after hearing Jesus speak to Philip, or did Jesus ask the disciples how many loaves they had?]

6:10 - JESUS SAID, "MAKE THE MEN SIT DOWN." THERE WAS MUCH GRASS IN THE PLACE. THE MEN SAT DOWN, IN NUMBER ABOUT 5000.

**Contradictions:**
MATT. 14:13 - Jesus departed ... into a desert place...they[the people] followed him....
MARK 6:32-33 - They departed into a desert place.... The people...came together unto him.
LUKE 9:10-11 - .... He took them [the disciples]...into a desert place.... The people followed him.
[Did Jesus and the people go to a grassy area, or to a desert place?]
See also under MATT. 14:19 and MARK 6:41-44.

**Perplexing:** See under MATT. 14:13 and 19.

6:11 - JESUS TOOK THE LOAVES AND WHEN HE HAD GIVEN THANKS. DISTRIBUTED TO THE DISCIPLES, AND THE DISCIPLES TO THEM THAT WERE SET DOWN; LIKEWISE THE FISHES....

**Perplexing:**
In JOHN 10:30, Jesus said that he is one with his Father. Why then did he give thanks? Was he thanking himself?
See also under MATT. 14:19.

**Old Testament:** See under MATT. 14:19.

6:12-13 - WHEN THEY WERE FILLED, HE SAID UNTO HIS DISCIPLES, "GATHER UP THE FRAGMENTS THAT REMAIN THAT NOTHING BE LOST." THEY FILLED 12 BASKETS WITH THE FRAGMENTS OF THE FIVE BARLEY LOAVES, WHICH REMAINED....

**Perplexing:** See under MATT. 14:20.

6:14 - THOSE MEN WHEN THEY HAD SEEN THE MIRACLE THAT JESUS DID, SAID, "THIS IS THAT PROPHET THAT SHOULD COME INTO THE WORLD."

**Contradiction:**
JOHN 6:24-30 - The people took ships to Capernaum seeking Jesus. When they found him, he reminded them of the food miracle, but they said, "What sign shewest thou then, that we may see and believe? What dost thou work?"
[After eating, did the people say that Jesus is the "prophet that should come," or did they follow him to Capernaum and ask him to show them a sign so that they might believe him?]

6:15 - WHEN JESUS PERCEIVED THAT THEY WOULD COME AND TAKE HIM BY FORCE, TO MAKE HIM A KING, HE DEPARTED AGAIN INTO A MOUNTAIN ALONE.

**Contradictions:**
JOHN 18:4 - Jesus knowing all things that should come upon him....
[Did Jesus not know beforehand, or did he know that the people would want to make him a king?]
MATT. 14:23 - When he had sent the multitudes away, he went up into a mountain to pray; when the evening was come, he was there alone.
MARK 6:45-46 - ...he sent away the people. When he had sent them away, he departed into a mountain to pray.
LUKE 9:18 - ...he was alone praying....
[Did Jesus flee to a mountain to avoid being seized by the people, or did he send the people away and go onto a mountain to pray?]

**Perplexing:**
Why did Jesus flee? Why did he fail to perform a miracle to discourage the people from wanting to make him a king?

6:16-17 - WHEN EVEN WAS COME, HIS DISCIPLES WENT DOWN UNTO THE SEA, ENTERED A SHIP, AND WENT OVER THE SEA TOWARD CAPERNAUM. IT WAS NOW DARK....

**Contradictions:**
MATT. 14:22 - Straightway Jesus constrained his disciples to get into a ship, and to go before him unto the other side, while he sent the multitudes away.

MARK 6:45 - Straightway Jesus constrained his disciples to get into the ship, and go to the other side before unto Bethsaida, while he sent away the people.
[Did the disciples go onto a ship after Jesus went onto a mountain, or before Jesus went onto a mountain (6:15)?]
[Was the ship going to Capernaum, or to Bethsaida?]
LUKE 9:18-28 - As he was alone praying, his disciples were with him. He spoke with them, then took Peter, James, and John up into a mountain where the transfiguration occurred. [A ship was not mentioned.]
[Did the disciples enter a ship, or remain on land where Jesus took three of them to a mountain to see his transfiguration?]

6:18-19 - THE SEA AROSE BY REASON OF A GREAT WIND THAT BLEW. WHEN THEY HAD ROWED ABOUT 25-30 FURLONGS, THEY SEE JESUS WALKING ON THE SEA, AND DRAWING NIGH UNTO THE SHIP; THEY WERE AFRAID.

**Contradictions:**
LUKE 9:18-28 - [The disciples did not board a ship, and Jesus did not walk on the sea] - He spoke with the disciples and took three of them to a mountain.
[Did Jesus walk on the sea to the ship carrying his disciples, or did they all remain on land where he took three disciples to a mountain?]
See also under MATT. 14:25.

**Old Testament:** See under MATT. 14:25.

**Pagan parallel:** See also under MATT. 14:25.

**Perplexing:**
How was Jesus able to go from the mountain (6:15) to the sea and escape the people who wanted to make him a king?
See also under MATT. 14:25 and 26.

6:21 - THEY WILLINGLY RECEIVED HIM INTO THE SHIP, AND IMMEDIATELY THE SHIP WAS AT THE LAND WHITHER THEY WENT.

**Contradictions:**
MATT. 14:28-34 - Peter left the ship and walked on the sea, but became afraid and started to sink; Jesus saved him and they both boarded the ship. Those on the ship worshiped Jesus and said, "Thou art the Son of God." They came into the land of Gennesaret.
[Did Jesus board the ship when he reached it, or did Peter leave the ship, join him, and then the two of them board the ship?]
MARK 6:48-53 - Jesus would have passed by the ship, but the disciples cried out; he spoke with them and went up into the ship. They came into the land of Gennesaret.
[Did Jesus find the ship on his own, or did the disciples have to cry out as he walked past them?]
[Did the ship arrive at Capernaum (6:17, 24), or at Gennesaret?]

6:22-25 - THE DAY FOLLOWING...WHEN THE PEOPLE SAW THAT JESUS WAS NOT THERE...THEY TOOK SHIPPING, AND CAME TO CAPERNAUM, SEEKING FOR JESUS. WHEN THEY FOUND HIM, THEY SAID, "RABBI, WHEN CAMEST THOU HITHER?"

**Contradictions:**
MATT. 14:22-23 - ...he sent the multitudes away. ...he was there alone.
MARK 6:46 - When he had sent them away...and he alone on the land.
[Did the people remain where they had eaten, then the next day follow Jesus across the sea and find him in Capernaum, or did they depart from the area of the miracle leaving him there alone?]
LUKE 9:18 - It came to pass, as he was alone praying, his disciples with him, he asked, "Whom say people that I am?"
[Did Jesus go to Capernaum after the feeding miracle, or did he remain where the miracle took place and speak with his disciples?]

**Perplexing:**
Where did 5000 men find lodging and meals for the night at the site of the miracle? Where did they find washing and sanitary facilities? Did they all have enough money to pay for transportation to Capernaum? Why did they not go home? How did the men know that Jesus had gone to Capernaum? How many ships were needed to take the 5000 men to Capernaum? How may trips had to be made? From where did these ships come? How long did it take for all the people to reach Capernaum?

6:30 - THEY SAID, "WHAT SIGN SHEWEST THOU THEN, THAT WE MAY SEE, AND BELIEVE THEE? WHAT DOST THOU WORK?"

**Perplexing:**
Why did the people ask Jesus for a sign and what he can do? They already saw and participated in the feeding miracle the day before. Did they forget so soon? Did JOHN forget?

6:33 - JESUS: "THE BREAD OF GOD IS HE WHICH COMETH DOWN FROM HEAVEN, AND GIVETH LIFE UNTO THE WORLD."

**Contradictions:** See under MATT. 1:18 (did Jesus come down from heaven, or was he a human descendant of David?).

6:35 - JESUS SAID, "I AM THE BREAD OF LIFE...."

**Pagan concept:**
The Sumerian god Anu was the keeper of the "Bread of Eternal Life."
See also under 4:14 and under MATT. 28:18-20

6:37 - JESUS: "...HIM THAT COMETH TO ME I WILL IN NO WISE CAST OUT."

**Contradiction:**
MATT. 7:22-23 - Jesus: "Many will say to me, "Lord, Lord, have we not prophesied in thy name? And in thy name have cast out devils? And in thy name done many wonderful works?' Then will I profess unto them, I never knew you, depart from me, ye that work iniquity."
[Did Jesus say that he will not cast out those who come to him, or did he say that he will disown many who come to him?]

6:38 - JESUS: "I CAME DOWN FROM HEAVEN...."

**Contradictions:**
See under MATT. 1:18 (Did Jesus come down from heaven, or was he a human descended from David?)

6:39 - JESUS: "...OF ALL WHICH HE [THE FATHER] HATH SENT ME I SHOULD LOSE NOTHING...."

**Contradiction:**
JOHN 6:66 - From that time many of his disciples went back, and walked no more with him."
JOHN 17:12 - Jesus; "...those that Thou gavest me I have kept, and none of them is lost, but the son of perdition...."
1 TIM. 4:1 - Paul: "The Spirit speaketh, that...some shall depart from the faith, giving heed to seducing spirits, and doctrines of devils."
[Did Jesus keep all who were sent to him by his Father, or did he lose one or more disciples?]

6:4O - JESUS: "THIS IS THE WILL OF HIM THAT SENT ME, THAT EVERYONE WHICH SEETH THE SON, AND BELIEVETH ON HIM, MAY HAVE EVERLASTING LIFE...."

**Contradictions:** See under MATT. 19:17-19 (for obtaining eternal life).

**Perplexing:**
Was Jesus saying that to obtain everlasting life one must not only believe on him, but also, see (have seen) him?
See also under MATT. 19:16 and 17-19 (for obtaining eternal life).

**Pagan concept:** See under MATT. 19:16.

6:42 - THEY [JEWS] SAID, "IS NOT THIS JESUS, THE SON OF JOSEPH, WHOSE FATHER AND MOTHER WE KNOW?...."

**Perplexing:**
If they knew Jesus' father and mother, why did they not say so when he performed the food miracle? Why did they refer to him as, "That prophet that should come into the world" (6:14)? Did they believe that the "prophet" should be a human being, as Jews expected the Messiah to be?

6:44 - JESUS: "NO MAN CAN COME TO ME, EXCEPT THE FATHER WHICH HATH SENT ME DRAW HIM...."

**Contradictions:**
JOHN 6:70 - Jesus answered, "Have not I chosen you twelve...."
[Did the Father send the disciples to Jesus, or did Jesus select them?]
JOHN 14:6 - "...no man cometh unto the Father, but by me."
[Does one come to Jesus by way of the Father, or does one come to the Father by way of Jesus?]

**Perplexing:**
Was Jesus saying that only those who are selected by God to come to him can be saved - that God has predetermined who is to be saved (predestination)? If so, what was the point of Jesus coming to the earth? Of what use then are missionaries and prayers? What is the point of trying to convert people? Note that

JOHN 6:64 says that Jesus knew from the beginning who they were that believed not. Consequently, does God have a right to punish those who do not believe in Jesus if He is responsible for their unbelief? Why did God not send everyone to Jesus? How did God decide who He would send to Jesus?

**Dead Sea Scrolls:**
"Before they [people] existed He established their whole design, and when, as ordained for them, they come into their being, it is in accord with His glorious plan that they fulfill their work"; and before creating them Thou knowest all their works. ...the wicked Thou didst create."

6:45 - JESUS: "IT IS WRITTEN IN THE PROPHETS, 'THEY SHALL ALL BE TAUGHT OF GOD.'"

**Old Testament:**
ISA. 54:13 - "All thy children shall be taught of the LORD...."

6:46 - JESUS: "NOT THAT ANY MAN HATH SEEN THE FATHER, SAVE HE WHICH IS OF GOD; HE HATH SEEN THE FATHER."

**Contradictions:** See under 1:18.

6:47 - JESUS: "HE THAT BELIEVETH ON ME HATH EVERLASTING LIFE."

**Contradictions:**
JOHN 5:24 - Jesus: "He that heareth my word, and believeth on Him that sent me, hath everlasting life...."
[Must one believe in Jesus, or in Him who sent Jesus to receive everlasting life?]
See also under MATT. 19:17-19 (for obtaining eternal life).

**Perplexing:** See under MATT. 19:16 and 17-19 (for obtaining eternal life).

**Pagan concept:** See under MATT. 19:16.

6-48 - JESUS: "I AM THAT BREAD OF LIFE."

**Pagan concept:** See under 6:35.

6:51-56 - JESUS: "I AM THE LIVING BREAD WHICH CAME DOWN FROM HEAVEN. IF ANY MAN EAT OF THIS BREAD, HE SHALL LIVE FOREVER; AND THE BREAD THAT I WILL GIVE IS MY FLESH...." .... "WHOSO EATETH MY FLESH, AND DRINKETH MY BLOOD, HATH ETERNAL LIFE.... FOR MY FLESH IS MEAT INDEED, AND MY BLOOD IS DRINK INDEED. HE THAT EATETH MY FLESH, AND DRINKETH MY BLOOD, DWELLETH IN ME, AND I IN HIM."

**Contradictions:** See under MATT. 19:17-19 (for obtaining eternal life).

**Pagan concept:** See under 6:35, and under 19:16 and 26:25-28.

**Perplexing:**
Why is the act of symbolical theophagy necessary for obtaining eternal life?

See also under MATT. 19:16, 17-19 (for eternal obtaining life), and 26:25-28.

**History:** See under MATT. 26:25-28.

**Old Testament:** See under MATT. 26:25-28.

6:58 - JESUS: "THIS IS THE BREAD WHICH CAME DOWN FROM HEAVEN...HE THAT EATETH OF THIS BREAD SHALL LIVE FOREVER."

**Contradictions:** See under MATT. 19:17-19 (for obtaining eternal life).

**Pagan concept:** See under 6:35, and under MATT. 19:16.

6:63 - JESUS: "IT IS THE SPIRIT THAT QUICKENETH; THE FLESH PROFITETH NOTHING...."

**Pagan concept:**
Orphic doctrines, in existence as early as the sixth century B.C., held that the spirit was imprisoned in the body; therefore, the flesh was viewed as evil. Orphism also introduced the concept of sin, recognized a trinity (Jupiter, Juno, and Minerva), and believed that pure spirits would go to a place in the sky where they would have eternal life.

6:64 - JESUS: "THERE ARE SOME OF YOU THAT BELIEVE NOT." JESUS KNEW FROM THE BEGINNING WHO THEY WERE THAT BELIEVED NOT, AND WHO SHOULD BETRAY HIM.

**Perplexing:** See under 5:24 and 6:44.

6:65 - HE SAID, "...NO MAN CAN COME UNTO ME, EXCEPT IT WERE GIVEN UNTO HIM OF MY FATHER."

**Contradictions:** See under 6:44.

**Perplexing:** See under 5:24 and 6:44.

6:66 - FROM THAT TIME MANY OF THE DISCIPLES WENT BACK, AND WALKED NO MORE WITH HIM.

**Contradiction:**
JOHN 6:39 - Jesus: "This is the Father's will which hath sent me, that of all which He hath given me I should lose nothing...."
JOHN 10:27-28 - Jesus: "My sheep...follow me. I give them eternal life; they shall never perish, neither shall any man pluck them out of my hand."
JOHN 18:9 - Jesus: "That the saying might be fulfilled...'Of them which Thou gavest me have I lost none.'"
[Did Jesus lose some disciples, or did he lose no one?]

6:69 - PETER: "WE BELIEVE AND ARE SURE THAT THOU ART THAT CHRIST, THE SON OF THE LIVING GOD."

**Contradictions:**

ACTS 2:22 - Peter: "...Jesus of Nazareth, a man approved of God among you by miracles, wonders, and signs, which God did by him...."

[Did Peter say that Jesus was the Son of God, or a man through whom God performed miracles?]

ACTS 2:30 - Peter: "...God had sworn with an oath to him [David], that of the fruit of his loins, according to the flesh, He would raise up Christ to sit on his throne."

[Did Peter say that Jesus was the Son of God, or a descendant of David?]

ACTS 2:36 - Peter: "...God hath made that same Jesus, whom ye have crucified, both Lord and Christ."

[Did Peter say that Jesus was the Son of God, or a man who God made Lord and Christ?]

ACTS 10:38 - Peter: "God anointed Jesus of Nazareth with the Holy Ghost and power, who went doing good, and healing...for God was with him."

[Did Peter say that Jesus is the Son of God, or a man who God anointed with the Holy Ghost and power, and who was able to do healing?]

**Judaism:**

In Jewish belief, the Messiah (Christ) was to be a human descended from David, not a son of God.

**Perplexing:**

Why did Peter, a Jew, refer to Jesus as "Christ [the Messiah], the Son of God," when such was not in keeping with the Jewish belief that the Messiah would be a man descended from David?

6:70-71 - JESUS ANSWERED, "HAVE NOT I CHOSEN YOU TWELVE, AND ONE OF YOU IS A DEVIL?" HE SPOKE OF JUDAS ISCARIOT...FOR HE IT WAS THAT SHOULD BETRAY HIM.

**Perplexing:**

Why did JOHN fail to identify all of the twelve disciples? Why did Jesus refer to Judas as a "devil," since by betraying Jesus, he was complying with God's will, thereby enabling Jesus to fulfill his mission on earth? Why could Jesus not have died and been resurrected without the betrayal? Why did Jesus select a "devil" to judge the twelve tribes of Israel (MATT. 19:28 and LUKE 22:29-30)? Why in MATT. 26:50 did Jesus call Judas "friend?"

See also under MATT. 26:14-16 and LUKE 22:3-6.

**Contradiction:**

JOHN 6:44 - Jesus; "No man can come to me, except the Father which hath sent me draw him...."

JOHN 17:12 - Jesus, those that Thou gavest me I have kept, and none of them is lost, but the son of perdition....

[Did Jesus select the disciples, or were they given to him by God?]

7:1 - JESUS WALKED IN GALILEE; HE WOULD NOT WALK IN JEWRY [JUDEA], BECAUSE THE JEWS SOUGHT TO KILL HIM.

**Contradiction:**

JOHN 7:14-15 - ...Jesus went into the temple [in Judea] and taught. The Jews marvelled....

[Did the Jews seek to kill Jesus, or did they allow him to enter and teach in the temple, and listen to him?]

**Perplexing:**
Were there no Jews in Galilee? Why would the Jews want to kill him? Why was he fearful? Why could he not perform a miracle to protect himself? Why did he not let himself be killed so that he could be publicly resurrected and, thereby, convince everyone of his divinity? Why did he want to wait to be killed by the Romans and be resurrected secretly?
How was Jesus able to obtain permission to teach in the temple? If the Jews wanted to kill Jesus why did they permit him to teach in the temple? Would it not also have been relatively easy for the Jews to have killed Jesus if they wanted to do so?
See also under MATT. 12:14.

**History:** See under 5:16.

7:2 - NOW THE JEWS' FEAST OF TABERNACLES WAS AT HAND.

**Old Testament:**
LEV. 23:34 - The LORD: ".... The 15th day of this seventh month shall be the feast of tabernacles for seven days unto the LORD."
DEUT. 16:13 - Moses: "Thou shalt observe the feast of tabernacles seven days, after that thou hast gathered in thy corn and wine."
DEUT. 16:16 - Moses: "Three times in a year shalt all thy males appear before the LORD thy God...and in the feast of tabernacles."

**Perplexing:**
Why did JOHN specify that the feast of tabernacles was Jewish? Jews would have known this. Was JOHN writing for non-Jewish readers?
See also under 2:13.

7:5 - NEITHER DID HIS BRETHREN BELIEVE IN HIM.

**Perplexing:**
Why did Jesus' brethren not believe in him? Did not their mother Mary tell them what the angel told her about Jesus? Were they ignorant of Jesus' miracles? Does their failure to believe in him mean they will not receive eternal life, but will face damnation?

7:7 - JESUS: "THE WORLD CANNOT HATE YOU, BUT ME IT HATETH, BECAUSE I TESTIFY OF IT, THAT THE WORKS THEREOF ARE EVIL."

**Perplexing:**
Why did God create a world the works of which are evil? What moral right did Jesus have to condemn the world for its evil works, since his Father created it that way? Should he not, instead, have condemned his Father for creating the evil? If God created evil, how does He differ from the devil? How can He then be called "good?" If Jesus' Father cannot eliminate evil, can He really be God?
See also under MATT. 13:38-39 and 19:17-19 (for God being good).

**Contradictions:** See under MATT. 19:17-19 (for God being good).

7:10-11 - ...WENT HE UNTO THE FEAST, NOT OPENLY, BUT AS IT WERE IN SECRET. THE JEWS...SAID, "WHERE IS HE?"

**Contradictions:**

JOHN 7:14 - About the midst of the feast Jesus went into the temple and taught.
[Did Jesus go to the feast secretly, or did he appear and teach openly in the temple?]
See also under 5:16.

**Perplexing:**

How was Jesus able to enter the temple and teach without obtaining authorization from the priests? If he obtained permission, why did the priests give it if they sought to kill him (7:1)? Why did the Jews allow him to teach rather than attack him, if they really wanted to kill him?
See also under MATT. 12:14.

7:13 - NO MAN SPOKE OPENLY OF HIM FOR FEAR OF THE JEWS.

**Perplexing:**

Since all of the people at the feast were Jews, how could they be afraid of "the Jews?"

7:14 - ABOUT THE MIDST OF THE FEAST JESUS WENT INTO THE TEMPLE, AND TAUGHT.

**Contradictions:**

JOHN 5:16 - Therefore did the Jews persecute Jesus, and sought to slay him....
JOHN 5:18 - The Jews sought to kill him....
JOHN 7:1 - Jesus...would not walk in Jewry, because the Jews sought to kill him....
[Did Jesus enter and teach in the temple without being attacked by the Jews, or did the Jews try to kill him?]
JOHN 7:10 - ...Jesus went unto the feast, not openly, but as it were in secret.
[Did Jesus teach openly in the temple during the feast, or did he go to the feast secretly?]

**Perplexing:** See under 7:10-11.

7:15 - THE JEWS MARVELLED, SAYING, "HOW KNOWETH THIS MAN LETTERS, HAVING NEVER LEARNED?"

**Perplexing:**

How did the Jews know, or why did they believe, that Jesus never learned "letters?"
Why did JOHN continually say "Jews," rather than "people?"

7:19-20 - JESUS: "DID NOT MOSES GIVE YOU THE LAW, AND YET NONE OF YOU KEEPETH THE LAW? WHY GO YE ABOUT TO KILL ME?" THE PEOPLE SAID, "THOU HAST A DEVIL; WHO GOETH ABOUT TO KILL THEE?"

**Contradictions:**

EX. 20 - 23 and 34 - The LORD, not Moses, gave the law. [Note the different sets of "Ten Commandments" given in EX. 20 and EX. 34; it is only in EX. 34:28, however, that the term "Ten Commandments" is used, and it refers to the immediately preceding commandments, not to those in EX. 20 which are generally cited

as the “Ten Commandments”.]
ACTS 7:53 - Paul: “Who [Jews] received the law by the disposition of angels, and have not kept it.”
[Did Moses, or the LORD, or angels give the law?]

**Perplexing:**
In what way had the Jews failed to keep the law? Why did they not question him about it? If Jesus believed that the Jews wanted to kill him, why did he go among them in the temple? Was Jesus wrong about the Jews wanting to kill him, since they deny it? If they really wanted to kill him, why did they not do so before he entered or after he departed from the temple? Why did Jesus fail to attribute the Law to God?

7:22 - JESUS: “MOSES GAVE UNTO YOU CIRCUMCISION (NOT BECAUSE IT IS OF MOSES, BUT OF THE FATHERS), AND YE ON THE SABBATH DAY CIRCUMCISE A MAN.”

**Contradiction:**
GEN. 17:9-10 - God said unto Abraham.... “This is My covenant, which ye shall keep and thy seed after thee; every man child among you shall be circumcised.”
[Was circumcision a law given by the fathers, or by God to Abraham as His covenant?]

**History:** See under LUKE 1:58-59.

7:23 - JESUS: “IF A MAN ON THE SABBATH DAY RECEIVE CIRCUMCISION, THAT THE LAW OF MOSES SHOULD NOT BE BROKEN, ARE YE ANGRY AT ME, BECAUSE I HAVE MADE A MAN EVERY WHIT WHOLE ON THE SABBATH DAY?”

**History:** See under MATT. 12:9-10 (Jews did not oppose healing on the Sabbath).

**Perplexing:**
Why would the Jews be angry with Jesus for doing something of which they approved? Why did Jesus and/ or JOHN not know that the Jews allowed healing on the Sabbath?
See also under MATT. 12:9-10.

7:24 - JESUS: “JUDGE NOT ACCORDING TO THE APPEARANCE, BUT JUDGE RIGHTEOUS JUDGMENT.”

**Contradiction:**
MATT. 7:1 - Jesus: “Judge not, that ye be not judged.”
[Did Jesus tell people to judge, or not to judge?]

**Perplexing:**
What is righteous judgment?

7:25 - THEN SAID SOME OF THEM OF JERUSALEM, “IS NOT THIS HE, WHOM THEY SEEK TO KILL?”

**Perplexing:**
Since all of the people present were Jews, who was meant by “they”?

7:30 - THEN THEY SOUGHT TO TAKE HIM....

**Perplexing:**
Who are the "they" that JOHN said sought to take him?

7:31-32 - MANY OF THE PEOPLE...SAID, "WHEN CHRIST COMETH, WILL HE DO MORE MIRACLES THAN THIS MAN HATH DONE?" ...THE PHARISEES AND CHIEF PRIESTS SENT OFFICERS TO TAKE HIM.

**Perplexing:** See under MATT. 12:14.

7:35 - THEN SAID THE JEWS AMONG THEMSELVES, "WHITHER WILL HE GO, THAT WE SHALL NOT FIND HIM? WILL HE GO UNTO THE DISPERSED AMONG THE GENTILES...?"

**History:**
Reference to the dispersal is an anachronism; the dispersal of the Jews took place in the years following the destruction of the Jerusalem Temple in A.D. 70. (Consequently, this is evidence that JOHN was written long after Jesus' crucifixion; it is usually dated to some time between A.D. 90 and 125.)

**Perplexing:**
How could the people have referred to the dispersal at this time when it had not yet occurred? Was JOHN unaware that the dispersal did not take place until after A.D. 70?

7:38 - JESUS: "HE THAT BELIEVETH ON ME, AS THE SCRIPTURE HATH SAID, 'OUT OF HIS BELLY SHALL FLOW RIVERS OF LIVING WATER.'"

**Old Testament:**
ISA. 58: 11 - "The Lord shall...satisfy thy soul in drought...and thou shalt be like a watered garden, and like a spring of water, whose waters fail not."
See also under 4:10.

**Pagan parallel:** See under 4:14.

7:39 - (THIS SPAKE HE OF THE SPIRIT, WHICH THEY THAT BELIEVE ON HIM SHOULD RECEIVE, FOR THE HOLY GHOST WAS NOT YET GIVEN, BECAUSE JESUS WAS NOT YET GLORIFIED.)

**Contradictions:**
MATT. 1:18 - ...his mother Mary espoused to Joseph...was found with child of the Holy Ghost.
MARK 12:36 - Jesus: "David himself said by the Holy Ghost...."
LUKE 1:13-15 - An angel said unto him, "Fear not, Zacharias...thy wife Elisabeth shall bear thee a son John. .... ...and he shall be filled with the Holy Ghost, even from his mother's womb."
LUKE 1:35 - The angel said unto her [Mary], "The Holy Ghost shall come upon thee...."
LUKE 1:41 - ...Elisabeth was filled with the Holy Ghost.
LUKE 1:67 - His father Zacharias was filled with the Holy Ghost...."
LUKE 2:25 - ...the Holy Ghost was upon him [Simeon].
[Was the Holy Ghost not yet given, or had some people (e.g., David, John, Mary, Elisabeth, Zacharias, and

Simeon) already received the Holy Ghost before Jesus was glorified?]
MATT. 3:11, MARK 1:8, and LUKE 3:16 - John: "...he [Jesus] shall baptize you with the Holy Ghost...."
[Was the Holy Ghost not yet given, or did Jesus baptize with the Holy Ghost?]

7:41-42 - OTHERS SAID, "THIS IS THE CHRIST." SOME SAID, "SHALL CHRIST COME OUT OF GALILEE? HATH NOT SCRIPTURE SAID, THAT CHRIST COMETH OF THE SEED OF DAVID, AND OUT OF BETHLEHEM WHERE DAVID WAS?"

**Old Testament:**
2 SAM. 7:12-13 - The LORD: "...I will set up thy [David's] seed...and I will establish his kingdom. I will establish the throne of his kingdom forever."
2 CHRON. 7:18 - The LORD [to Solomon]: "Then will I establish the throne of thy kingdom, according as I have covenanted with David thy father, 'There shall not fail thee a man to be ruler in Israel.'"
MIC. 5: 2 - Micah: "Thou, Bethlehem Ephratah, though thou be little among the thousands of Judah, out of thee shall he come forth unto Me that is to be ruler in Israel.

**Judaism:**
Jewish belief is that the Messiah (Christ) will be descended from David and be from David's city Bethlehem. The descent would also have to be paternal, as Jews did not recognize a maternal genealogy. Additionally, the Messiah was to reestablish the kingdom of Israel.

**Perplexing:**
Why did MARK (1:9) say that Jesus came from Nazareth, not Bethlehem; and JOHN (1:45) refer to him as "Jesus of Nazareth? Why did neither of these gospels cite Bethlehem as Jesus' birthplace? If the Jews in v.42 above are correct, how could Jesus be the Messiah (Christ) if he came out of Nazareth?
See also under 1:46, and under MATT. 1:1.

**Contradictions:** See under MATT. 1:1 (If Jesus was the Son of God, not paternally descended from David, how could he be the Messiah/Christ?).

**Language**: See under MATT. 1:1.

**History:** See under MATT. 1:1.

**Pagan parallels**: See under MATT. 1:1.

7:52 - THEY [PHARISEES] SAID, ".... ...OUT OF GALILEE ARISETH NO PROPHET."

**Contradiction:**
2 KINGS 14:25 - ...Jonah...the prophet was of Gathhepher [in Galilee].
NAH. 1:1 - .... ...Nahum the Elkoshite. [The location of Elkosh is not known, but some scholars believe that it was in Galilee and may have been another name for Capernaum.]
[Did not, or did at least one prophet come out of Galilee?]

**Perplexing:**
Why did the Pharisees, well-versed in and authorities on the Old Testament, erroneously say that no prophet arose in Galilee? Did JOHN misquote the Pharisees?

8:2 - EARLY IN THE MORNING, HE CAME AGAIN INTO THE TEMPLE; ALL THE PEOPLE CAME UNTO HIM, AND HE SAT DOWN, AND TAUGHT THEM.

**Contradictions:** See under 7:14.

**Perplexing:** See under 7:10-11.

**History:**
Some biblical scholars do not believe that verses 8:1-11 are genuine; consequently, they are not included in a number of Bibles.

8:3-4 - THE SCRIBES AND PHARISEES BROUGHT UNTO HIM A WOMAN TAKEN IN ADULTERY ...THEY SAY, "MASTER, THIS WOMAN WAS TAKEN IN ADULTERY, IN THE VERY ACT."

**Perplexing:**
Considering the hostility of the Pharisees towards Jesus and that they had sent officers to seize him (7:32) and even wanted to kill him, why did they come to him and call him "Master?" Why did they not use this opportunity to attack him? Why was the man with whom she had the adulterous affair not brought to Jesus with her?
See also under 7:10-11.

8:5 - SCRIBES AND PHARISEES: "MOSES IN THE LAW COMMANDED US, THAT SUCH SHOULD BE STONED, BUT WHAT SAYEST THOU?"

**History:**
The Sanhedrin had abolished the death penalty for adultery before Jesus' time.

**Perplexing:**
Why did the scribes and Pharisees not know that the death penalty for adultery had been abolished? Why did Jesus not point out that adultery was no longer a capital crime? Did he not know? Did JOHN not know that the death penalty for adultery had been abolished? Did JOHN misquote the scribes and Pharisees?

**Old Testament:**
LEV. 20:10 - The LORD: "...the adulterer and the adulteress shall surely be put to death."
DEUT. 22:22 - Moses: "If a man be found lying with a woman married to an husband, they shall both die...."

8:6 - .... JESUS STOOPED DOWN, AND WITH HIS FINGER WROTE ON THE GROUND, AS THOUGH HE HEARD THEM NOT.

**Perplexing:**
What did Jesus write? In what script did he write? Why is there no record of what he wrote? If he could write, why did he fail to put his teachings into writing? Why did Jesus not know that his failure to do so would lead to confusion, to a proliferation of Christian sects with different interpretations of these teachings, to religious hate, to violence, and to wars?

8:7 - ...HE SAID, "HE THAT IS WITHOUT SIN AMONG YOU, LET HIM CAST A STONE AT HER."

**Perplexing:**
Did Jesus approve of adultery? In 4:18, Jesus did not condemn a woman for having had five husbands and for living with a man to whom she was not married.
See also under 4:17-18 and 8:5.

**History:** See under 8:5.

8:8 - AGAIN HE STOOPED DOWN, AND WROTE ON THE GROUND.

**Perplexing:** See under 8:6.

8:9-11 - THEY WHICH HEARD IT...WENT OUT.... JESUS...SAID UNTO HER, "WHERE ARE THINE ACCUSERS? HATH NO MAN CONDEMNED THEE?" SHE SAID, "NO MAN, LORD." JESUS SAID, "NEITHER DO I CONDEMN THEE; GO, AND SIN NO MORE."

**Perplexing:**
In MATT. 19:18 - ...Jesus said, "...Thou shalt not commit adultery...." In MARK 10:19 and LUKE 18:20 - Jesus said, "...Do not commit adultery...." If Jesus opposed adultery, why did he not condemn the woman? Did Jesus condone adultery? Did he not consider adultery to be a serious violation of the commandment against it? Did he view it only as a minor infraction of the law, not to be taken seriously? Why was this story of the adulteress and Jesus' writing not reported by the other gospels?

8:12 - THEN SPAKE JESUS AGAIN UNTO THEM: "I AM THE LIGHT OF THE WORLD; HE THAT FOLLOWETH ME SHALL NOT WALK IN DARKNESS, BUT SHALL HAVE THE LIGHT OF LIFE."

**Contradiction:**
MATT. 5:14 - Jesus: "Ye [his disciples] are the light of the world. ...."
[Was Jesus the light of the world, or were his disciples the light of the world?]

**History:**
The "Dark Ages," (a time of feudalism, ignorance, superstition, religious massacres, and epidemics) not light, existed when Christianity was in total control of Europe.

**Perplexing:**
To whom was Jesus speaking? The scribes and Pharisees had left (see 8:9-11).
If Jesus was the "light of the world," why, when Europe was dominated by the Church, was humanity afflicted with the "Dark Ages?" Why has belief in him brought suffering, misery, and violence into the world?

**Pagan parallels:**
The Hindu god Krishna said, "I am the light ... the light of lights."
Agni, another Hindu deity, is referred to as the "Great Light" and as shining forth with a "high light."
See also under 1:4-5.

**Old Testament:** See under 1:4-5.

8:13 - THE PHARISEES SAID, "THOU BEAREST RECORD OF THYSELF; THY RECORD IS NOT TRUE."

**Old Testament:** See under 5:31.

**Perplexing:**
Why did the Pharisees speak to Jesus, instead of seizing or killing him?

8:14 - JESUS SAID, "THOUGH I BEAR RECORD OF MYSELF, YET MY RECORD IS TRUE...."

**Contradiction:**
JOHN 5:31 - Jesus: "If I bear witness of myself, my witness is not true."
[Was Jesus' record of himself true, or not true?]

8:15 - JESUS: "...I JUDGE NO MAN."

**Contradiction:**
JOHN 5:22 - Jesus: "The Father judgeth no man, but hath committed all judgment unto the Son?"
JOHN 5:30 - Jesus: "...as I hear, I judge, and my judgment is just...."
JOHN 8:26 - Jesus: "I have many things to say and to judge of you...."
JOHN 9:39 - Jesus: "For judgment I am come into the world...."
ACTS 10:42 - Peter: "He commanded us to preach, and to testify that it is he [Jesus] which was ordained of God to be the judge of the quick and the dead."
2 TIM. 4:1 - Paul: "...the Lord Jesus Christ, who shall judge the quick and the dead...."
[Did Jesus say that he will not judge, or that he will do judging?]

8:17 - JESUS: "IT IS WRITTEN IN YOUR LAW THAT THE TESTIMONY OF TWO MEN IS TRUE."

**Old Testament:** See under 5:31.

**Perplexing:**
Why did Jesus (a Jew) say, "your law" to the Pharisees (Jews), rather than "our law?" Did JOHN forget that Jesus is a Jew?

8:18 - JESUS: "I AM ONE THAT BEARETH WITNESS OF MYSELF, AND THE FATHER THAT SENT ME BEARETH WITNESS OF ME."

**Perplexing:**
How and when did "the Father" bear witness of Jesus?

8:20 - THESE WORDS SPAKE JESUS IN THE TREASURY, AS HE TAUGHT IN THE TEMPLE; NO MAN LAID HANDS ON JESUS, FOR HIS HOUR WAS NOT YET COME.

**Perplexing:**
How was Jesus able to continue speaking in the temple, if the Pharisees and other Jews were hostile to him and supposedly wanted to kill him? If Jesus' hour has not yet come, why in 7:1 did He flee to Galilee and later in 7:10 return to Judea secretly? Why did Jesus need a special hour?
See also under 7:10-11.

8:24 - JESUS: "...IF YE BELIEVE NOT THAT I AM HE, YE SHALL DIE IN YOUR SINS."

**Perplexing:**
Why did Jesus resort to threats and fear to induce people to believe in him? Why did he fail to offer incontrovertible proof of who he was? Was he an egomaniac? Why did he condemn people for something as trivial as not believing in him? In JOHN 6:44, Jesus said, "No man can come to me, except the Father which hath sent me draw him"; and according to ACTS 13:48, those who "were ordained to eternal life believed." How then can one believe in Jesus if not so ordained by God? Did Jesus have a moral right to condemn people who were not sent to him by God? Why did Jesus assume that all people sinned?
See also under 6:44.

**Dead Sea Scrolls:** See under 6:44.

8:26 - JESUS: "I HAVE MANY THINGS TO SAY AND TO JUDGE OF YOU...."

**Contradictions:** See under 5:22.

8:29 - JESUS: "...I DO ALWAYS THOSE THINGS THAT PLEASE HIM [THE FATHER]."

**Perplexing:**
If Jesus did what pleased God, why in MATT. 27:46 and MARK 15:34 did he say, "My God, why hast Thou forsaken me?" In JOHN 10:30, Jesus said, "I and my Father are one." Was Jesus, therefore, saying that he did those things that pleased himself?

8:31-37 - SAID JESUS TO THOSE JEWS WHICH BELIEVED ON HIM.... .... "I KNOW THAT YE ARE ABRAHAM'S SEED, BUT YE SEEK TO KILL ME, BECAUSE MY WORD HATH NO PLACE IN YOU."

**Contradictions:** See under MATT. 5:16.

**Perplexing:**
Why did Jesus accuse Jews who believed in him of seeking to kill him?
See also under 7:19-20.

**History:** See under 5:16.

8:40 - JESUS: "NOW YE SEEK TO KILL ME, A MAN THAT HATH TOLD YOU THE TRUTH, WHICH I HAVE HEARD OF GOD...."

**Contradictions:**
JOHN 4:25-26 - The woman said, "I know Messias cometh, which is called Christ...." Jesus saith, "I that speak unto thee am he."
[Did Jesus say that he was a man who heard from God, or that he was Christ?]
See also under 5:16; and under MATT. 1:1.

**Perplexing:**
Why did Jesus identify himself as "a man" to whom God had conveyed "the truth?" Why did he not

identify himself as Christ as he did to the Samaritan woman in 4:25-26?
See also under 7:19-20 and 8:31-37.

8:42 - JESUS SAID, "...I PROCEEDED FORTH FROM GOD...HE SENT ME."

**Contradictions:** See under MATT. 1:18.

8:44 - JESUS: "YE ARE OF YOUR FATHER THE DEVIL.... HE WAS A MURDERER FROM THE BEGINNING.... HE IS A LIAR...."

**Pagan concept:** See under MATT. 4:1-2.

**Perplexing:**
Why did Jesus accuse people who do not believe in him of having the devil as their father, when they could not believe in him unless God sent them to him (6:44)? Why did Jesus try to incite hatred against those who do not accept him? Why did Jesus not show tolerance, compassion, and mercy? Why did he not pray for these people?
If God created the devil, is not then God the devil's Father? Are not then the devil's children also God's children?
Who did the devil murder? What lies did he tell? Why did God create him? By creating the devil, does not God bear responsibility for the devil's actions? Why does God permit the devil to exist? Was Jesus unaware of the murders committed by God (see under MATT. 13:38-39)?
Was Jesus also unaware of God's lies? For examples: in GEN. 15:5 and 26:4, He lied to Abraham by telling him that his progeny will be as numerous as the stars; in GEN. 15:18, He lied by telling Abraham that He will give his descendants the land from the river of Egypt to the Euphrates; in GEN. 18:18, He lied by saying that Abraham will become a great and mighty nation; in NUM. 14:34, He told the Israelites, "... ye shall know my breach of promise"; in 1 KINGS 21:29, He said that He will not bring evil to Ahab in his days, but in 1 KINGS 22:20-35, He sent a lying spirit to lure Ahab to his death; in PS. 89:35-37, He lied by saying, "I will not lie to David. ...his throne.... It shall be established forever"; in HOS. 1:10, He erroneously claimed that, "The number of the children of Israel shall be as the sand of the sea, which cannot be measured nor numbered." See also under MATT. 19:17-19 (for God being good).

**History:**
Gnostics believed that the biblical God was an evil deity - the equivalent of the Christian devil. Their belief was based on the numerous biblical verses in which the biblical God perpetrated atrocities and in which He acknowledged having created evil.

8:48 - THE JEWS SAID, "SAY WE NOT WELL THAT THOU ART A SAMARITAN, AND HAST A DEVIL?"

**History:**
The word, "Samaritan," was used derogatorily by Jews for individuals believed to be demented.
See also under MATT. 10:5-6.

8:51 - JESUS: "IF A MAN KEEP MY SAYINGS, HE SHALL NEVER SEE DEATH."

**Contradictions:** See under 5:24, and under MATT. 19:17-19 (for obtaining eternal life).

**Perplexing:** See under MATT. 19:16, and 17-19 (for obtaining eternal life).

**Pagan concept:** See under MATT. 19:16.

8:56 - JESUS: "YOUR FATHER ABRAHAM REJOICED TO SEE MY DAY, AND HE SAW IT, AND WAS GLAD."

**Perplexing:**
When and where did Abraham rejoice to see Jesus' day?

**History:**
There is no evidence that the biblical Abraham existed.

8:57 - SAID THE JEWS, "THOU ART NOT YET 50 YEARS OLD, AND HAST THOU SEEN ABRAHAM?"

**Perplexing:**
Why did the Jews say that Jesus was not yet 50, when according to LUKE 3:23, he was about 30 years of age? If Jesus was about 30, why did the Jews not say that he was not yet 35 or 40? By saying that Jesus is "not yet 50," they were implying that he was in his late forties. How old was Jesus at this time?
See also under 2:20.

**History:**
Some early Christians (Docetists, for example) refused to believe that Jesus was crucified and resurrected; they asserted that Jesus lived to be about 50 years of age before dying a natural death.

8:58 - JESUS SAID, "...BEFORE ABRAHAM WAS, I AM."

**Old Testament:**
EX. 3:14 - God said unto Moses, "I AM THAT I AM...I AM...."

8:59 - THEN TOOK THEY UP STONES TO CAST AT HIM, BUT JESUS HID HIMSELF.....

**Perplexing:**
Why did Jesus hide himself? Why did he not let them hurl stones at him, so they could see that he was not harmed by them? Why did JOHN here depict Jesus as a fearful human? Why did God not ordain the stone throwers to believe in Jesus?
See under 6:44.

9:1-2 - JESUS SAW A MAN BLIND FROM BIRTH. HIS DISCIPLES ASKED, "WHO DID SIN, THIS MAN, OR HIS PARENTS, THAT HE WAS BORN BLIND?"

**Perplexing:**
How did the disciples know that the man was blind from birth? Why did they believe that blindness was the result of sin? If the man was born blind, how could he have sinned before being born? What sin would

cause God to punish someone with blindness? Why are not murderers and those who commit heinous crimes punished with blindness? Why do so many such individuals seem to go unpunished?
See also under 5:14.

9:3 - JESUS ANSWERED, "NEITHER HATH THIS MAN SINNED, NOR HIS PARENTS, BUT THAT THE WORKS OF GOD SHOULD BE MADE MANIFEST IN HIM."

**Perplexing:**
Why would God make an innocent man blind from birth just so His works could be made manifest in him? Why did Jesus not refer the disciples to EZEK. 18:20 - "The son shall not bear the iniquity of the father?" Why did Jesus fail to explain the natural/actual causes of physical infirmities and diseases as well as their prevention and treatment?

9:4 - JESUS: "I MUST WORK THE WORKS OF HIM THAT SENT ME, WHILE IT IS DAY; THE NIGHT COMETH, WHEN NO MAN CAN WORK."

**Perplexing:**
Why could Jesus not work miracles at night? Why did Jesus fail to prophesy the future invention of electric lights that would enable people to work at night?

**Contradiction:**
MATT. 14:25 - In the fourth watch of the night, Jesus went unto them, walking on the sea.
MARK 6:48 - ...about the fourth watch of the night he cometh unto them, walking upon the sea....
JOHN 6:17-19 - .... It was now dark.... .... ...they see Jesus walking on the sea....
[Could not, or could Jesus perform miracles at night?]

9:5 - JESUS: "...I AM THE LIGHT OF THE WORLD."

**Contradiction:** See under 8:12.

**Pagan parallels**: See under 8:12.

**History:** See under 8:12.

**Perplexing:** See under 8:12.

9:6-7 - HE SPAT ON THE GROUND, MADE CLAY OF THE SPITTLE, ANOINTED THE EYES OF THE BLIND MAN WITH THE CLAY. AND SAID, "GO, WASH IN THE POOL OF SILOAM" .... HE WENT, WASHED, AND CAME SEEING.

**Perplexing:**
Why did Jesus not heal the man immediately to manifest the works of God (9:3)? Why did Jesus have to resort to saliva, clay, and the water of a pool to heal the man? Why did Jesus not ask the man to have faith? Why in MARK 8:23-25 could Jesus heal a blind man by spitting on and touching his eyes? Why in MATT. 20:34 were two blind men able to see when Jesus touched their eyes? Why in MARK 10:51-52 and LUKE 18:41-43 did faith alone enable a blind man to see? How could the man, blind from birth, find his way to the pool of Siloam? Did he walk to the pool with the clay over his eyes?

**History:**
In ancient Egypt and the Near East, saliva was believed to have healing properties. It was considered to be magical, and stories of its use in healing the blind were common.
The pool of Siloam, in Jerusalem, was the outlet of an underground aqueduct constructed by King Hezekiah between 710 -701 B.C. The pool's water was used in special temple rites.

**Pagan parallel:**
Asclepius (Aesculapius), the Greek god of healing, restored sight to a blind soldier. (Asclepius was known as "the Son of God" and "the Savior"; he was also killed, but rose from the dead.)

9:22 - ...HIS PARENTS...FEARED THE JEWS, FOR THE JEWS HAD AGREED, THAT IF ANY MAN CONFESS THAT HE [JESUS] WAS CHRIST, HE SHOULD BE PUT OUT OF THE SYNAGOGUE.

**History:**
The policy of being put out of the synagogue (excommunication) did not begin until A.D. 90. Thus, this verse is an anachronism.
See also under 7:35.

**Perplexing:**
How could the Jews agree to do something that was not in existence during Jesus' time? Was JOHN ignorant of Jewish history and customs? Why did JOHN write as though the man's parents were not Jewish, by saying that they "feared the Jews?" Was JOHN using "Jews" as a synonym for "priests?"

9:34 - THEY SAID UNTO HIM [THE FORMER BLIND MAN], "THOU WAST BORN IN SINS...." THEY CAST HIM OUT [OF THE SYNAGOGUE].

**History:**
The concept of being born in sin was Christian. Such a concept did not exist in Judaism. It did not come into existence until after the followers of Jesus broke away from Judaism and established their own theology.
See also under 9:22.

**Perplexing:**
How could the Jews use a non-Jewish, Christian term which had not yet come into existence? (Jesus, and his disciples at this time were Jewish.) Was JOHN ignorant of history and Jewish beliefs?

9:35-37 - JESUS HEARD THAT THEY HAD CAST HIM OUT; WHEN HE FOUND HIM, HE SAID, "DOST THOU BELIEVE ON THE SON OF GOD?" HE SAID, "WHO IS HE...?" JESUS SAID, "... IT IS HE THAT TALKETH WITH THEE."

**Contradictions:** See under 4:25-26; 6:69, and under MATT. 9:28-30.

**History:** See under 9:22.

**Perplexing:**
Why did Jesus fail to tell historians, scholars, and all people that he is the Son of God? Why did he reveal it to an unidentified formerly blind man? If Jesus knew people's thoughts (see under MATT. 9:28-30 -

Contradictions), why did he have to ask the man whether he believed in the Son of God?
See also under 4:25-26.

9:38 - HE SAID, "LORD, I BELIEVE." HE WORSHIPPED HIM.

**Perplexing:**
Since the concept of a "Son of God" is not Jewish, why did the man so quickly accept Jesus as this "Son," without questioning him about what it meant?

9:39 - JESUS SAID, "FOR JUDGMENT I AM COME INTO THIS WORLD...."

**Contradictions:**
JOHN 12:47 - Jesus: "...I came not to judge the world, but to save the world."
[Did Jesus come into the world to judge, or not to judge?]
See also under 5:22.

**Perplexing:** See under 5:22.

**Pagan parallel:** See under 5:22.

10:6 - THIS PARABLE [ABOUT A SHEPHERD AND SHEEP] SPAKE JESUS UNTO THEM, BUT THEY UNDERSTOOD NOT WHAT THINGS THEY WERE WHICH HE SPAKE UNTO THEM.

**Perplexing:** See under MATT. 13:10-13 and MARK 4:11-12.

**History:** See under MATT. 13:1-9.

**Pagan concept:** See under MATT. 13:10-13.

**Pagan parallel:** See under MATT. 13:1-9.

10:11 - JESUS: "I AM THE GOOD SHEPHERD; THE GOOD SHEPHERD GIVETH HIS LIFE FOR THE SHEEP."

**Pagan parallel:**
Zoroaster (some time between 1000 - 600 B.C.) referred to himself as a shepherd, and his followers as sheep.

10:13 - JESUS: "THE HIRELING FLEETH, BECAUSE HE IS AN HIRELING, AND CARETH NOT FOR THE SHEEP."

**Perplexing:**
Why did Jesus speak disparagingly about hired help? Why did he imply that employees are not really interested in their work and will not protect property with which they are entrusted? Why did he seem to be unaware that workers would lose their jobs and livelihood if they were not conscientious and competent?

10:14 - JESUS: "I AM THE GOOD SHEPHERD, AND KNOW MY SHEEP...."

**Pagan parallel:** See under 10:11.

10:16 - JESUS: "OTHER SHEEP I HAVE WHICH ARE NOT OF THIS FOLD; THEM ALSO I MUST BRING; THEY SHALL HEAR MY VOICE; AND THERE SHALL BE ONE FOLD, AND ONE SHEPHERD."

**History:**
The sheep - the followers of Jesus - have not formed into one fold. They have done the opposite; they have fractionated into dozens of sects and have persecuted and killed one another for about two millennia.

**Perplexing:**
Why did Jesus not realize that failure to put his teachings into writing would result in the development of a multiplicity of conflicting interpretations of his teachings? Why did his prophecy of "one fold" fail to materialize?

**Old Testament:**
EZEK. 34:23 - The LORD: "I will set up one shepherd over them (Israelites), and he shall feed them, even My servant David; he shall feed them, and he shall be their shepherd."

10:17 - JESUS: "THEREFORE DOTH MY FATHER LOVE ME, BECAUSE I LAY DOWN MY LIFE, THAT I MIGHT TAKE IT AGAIN."

**Contradiction:**
JOHN 10:30 - Jesus; "I and my Father are one."
[Does Jesus' Father love him, or are he and his Father one?]

**Perplexing:**
If Jesus and his Father are one, was Jesus saying that he loves himself?
Why does Jesus have to lay down his life? Why could Jesus not have fulfilled his mission without sacrificing himself? How can an immortal being give up his life?

10:22 - IT WAS AT JERUSALEM THE FEAST OF THE DEDICATION, AND IT WAS WINTER.

**History:**
The feast of the dedication became the Jewish holiday of Hanukkah. It commemorated the rededication of the Jerusalem Temple in December 165 B.C., following a victory by the Jews over the Syrians. The Syrian king Antiochus IV Epiphanes had desecrated the temple three years earlier.

10:23 - JESUS WALKED IN THE TEMPLE IN SOLOMON'S PORCH.

**History:**
Solomon's porch or portico was a covered walkway by the eastern side of the court which surrounded the temple.

**Contradictions:** See under 7:14.

10:28 - JESUS [TO JEWS]: "I GIVE THEM [HIS FOLLOWERS] ETERNAL LIFE, AND THEY SHALL NEVER PERISH, NEITHER SHALL ANY MAN PLUCK THEM OUT OF MY HAND."

**Contradictions:**
ECCL. 9:5 - "...the dead know not anything, neither have they anymore a reward, for the memory of them is forgotten."
[Is there eternal life, or do the dead have no reward?]
See also under 6:39.

**Perplexing:** See under MATT. 19:16.

**Pagan concept:** See under 6:63 and under MATT. 19:16.

10:29 - JESUS: "MY FATHER, WHICH GAVE THEM TO ME, IS GREATER THAN ALL; NO MAN IS ABLE TO PLUCK THEM OUT OF MY FATHER'S HAND."

**Contradiction:** See under 6:39.

10:30 - JESUS: "I AND MY FATHER ARE ONE."

**Contradictions:**
MATT. 19:17 and MARK 10:18 - Jesus: "Why callest thou me good? There is none good but one, that is God...."
LUKE 18:19 - Jesus: "Why callest thou me good? None is good save one, that is, God."
[Did Jesus claim to be one with God, or did he deny it by asserting that God, not he, is good?]
JOHN 8:40 - Jesus; "Ye seek to kill me, a man that hath told you the truth...."
[Was Jesus one with God, or a man who told the truth?]
ACTS 2:22 - Peter: "...Jesus of Nazareth, a man approved of God among you by miracles and wonders and signs, which God did by him in the midst of you...."
ACTS 10:38 - Peter: "God anointed Jesus of Nazareth with the Holy Ghost and power, who went about doing good, and healing all that were oppressed of the devil, for God was with him."
ACTS 17:30-31 - Paul: "...God...will judge the world in righteousness by that man whom He hath ordained ...He hath raised him from the dead."
[Is Jesus one with God, or is he a man of whom God approved, anointed, ordained, and raised from the dead?]
See also under MATT. 1:1 for verses claiming that Jesus is the Son of God.
See also under MATT. 1:18 for verses claiming that Jesus is descended from David.
[Is Jesus one with God, or is he the Son of God?]
[Is Jesus one with God, or is he a descendant of David?]
MATT. 14:23 - ...[Jesus] went up into a mountain to pray....
MATT. 26:39 - ...[Jesus] prayed, "If it be possible, let this cup pass from me...."
MARK 1:35 - ...[Jesus] departed into a solitary place and prayed.
LUKE 5:16 - [Jesus] withdrew into the wilderness and prayed.
There are also additional verses in which Jesus is reported to have prayed.
[Is Jesus one with God, or did he have to pray to God?]
JOHN 14:28 - Jesus: "...my Father is greater than I."
[Is Jesus one with God, or is God greater than Jesus?]

MATT. 26:64 - Jesus saith, "...Hereafter shall ye see the Son of man sitting on the right hand of power...."
MARK 14:62 - Jesus said, "...ye shall see the Son of man sitting on the right hand of power...."
LUKE 22:69 - Jesus: "Hereafter shall the Son of man sit on the right hand of the power of God."
[Is Jesus one with God, or will he sit on God's right hand?]
16:28 - Jesus: "I came forth from the Father, and I leave the world and go to the Father."
[Is Jesus one with God, or did he come from and return to God?]
MATT. 27:46 and MARK 15:34 - Jesus cried, "My God, my God, why hast Thou forsaken me?"
[Is Jesus one with God, or is he someone who God has forsaken?]

**Perplexing:**
How could Jesus be one with God, be His son, and be a man selected by God? If Jesus is one with God, was he praying to himself when he prayed? If he is one with God, how could he sit on God's right hand, come from God, and be forsaken by Him? If he is one with God, how can God be greater than he?
See also under MATT. 19:17-19 (for God being good).

10:33 - THE JEWS ANSWERED, "FOR A GOOD WORK WE STONE THEE NOT, BUT FOR BLASPHEMY; AND BECAUSE THOU, BEING A MAN, MAKEST THYSELF GOD."

**Judaism:**
Blasphemy refers to a perceived attack on the uniqueness of God denigrating God.

**Perplexing:**
Why is blasphemy a capital crime? If blasphemy is a terrible crime, why does God not punish the blasphemer directly? Why does God need humans to do the killing for Him? Where were Jesus' disciples?
See also under MATT. 9:3, 12:31-32, and 26:65.

**Old Testament:**
LEV. 24:16 - The LORD: "He that blasphemeth the name of the LORD, shall be put to death...the congregation shall stone him...."

10:34 - JESUS ANSWERED, "IS IT NOT WRITTEN IN YOUR LAW, I SAID, 'YE ARE GODS?'"

**Old Testament:**
PS. 82:6 - "I have said, 'Ye are gods, and all of you are children of the most High.'"

**Perplexing:**
Since Jesus cited the Old Testament, why did he say, "your law," rather than "our law?" Why did Jesus refer to a verse in PS. as the "law," when Jews consider only the Torah - the first five books of the Old Testament - to be the law? Why did Jesus and/or JOHN not know this? Why did the Jews fail to correct him?
See also under 8:17.

10:36 - JESUS: "SAY YE...'THOU BLASPHEMEST,' BECAUSE I SAID, 'I AM THE SON OF GOD?'"

**Contradictions:**
JOHN 10:30 - Jesus: "I and my Father are one."
[Is Jesus the son of God, or God?]
See also under 10:30, and under MATT. 1:18.

**Perplexing:** See under MATT. 26:65.

**Judaism:** See under 10:33.

10:38 - JESUS: "...THE FATHER IS IN ME, AND I IN HIM."

**Contradictions:** See under 10:30.

10:39 - THEY SOUGHT AGAIN TO TAKE HIM, BUT HE ESCAPED OUT OF THEIR HAND.

**Perplexing:**
How did Jesus escape? Why did he have to escape? Why did he fail to perform a miracle to convert them, or perform a miracle that would persuade them to believe in him? Where were his disciples?

10:40 - [JESUS] WENT AWAY AGAIN BEYOND JORDAN INTO THE PLACE WHERE JOHN AT FIRST BAPTIZED [BETHABARA (1:28)], AND THERE HE ABODE.

**Perplexing:**
How long did it take Jesus to travel the approximately 75 miles involved? Did he travel by foot? Did the disciples travel with him? If not, where were they? Why did he go to this particular place? How long did he remain there? Where did he stay? What did he do? Why did he opt to abide beyond Jordan?

11:2 - (IT WAS MARY WHICH ANOINTED THE LORD WITH OINTMENT AND WIPED HIS FEET WITH HER HAIR, WHOSE BROTHER LAZARUS WAS SICK.)

**Perplexing:**
JOHN did not report the anointing by Mary until 12:3. Why then did JOHN write as though the anointing had already taken place?

11:3 - HIS SISTERS SENT UNTO HIM, SAYING, "LORD, BEHOLD, HE WHOM THOU LOVEST IS SICK."

**Perplexing:**
How did the sisters (in Bethany according to 11:1) know where to reach Jesus? How were they able to get a message to him? How long did it take for the message to reach Jesus? How was the message delivered? Why did Jesus not know that Lazarus was sick before being so informed? Who was Lazarus? Why did Jesus love him? Why was he not mentioned previously by JOHN or by the other gospels?

**Pagan parallel:**
The Egyptian sisters Isis and Nephthys bewailed the death of their brother Osiris and sent for Horus (Isis' son) to resurrect him.

11:4 - WHEN JESUS HEARD, HE SAID, "THIS SICKNESS IS NOT UNTO DEATH, BUT FOR THE GLORY OF GOD, THAT THE SON OF GOD MIGHT BE GLORIFIED THEREBY."

**Contradictions:**
JOHN 11:14 - Said Jesus, "Lazarus is dead."

[Did Jesus say that Lazarus would not die from his sickness, or did he say that Lazarus is dead?]
See also under MATT. 1:18.

**Perplexing:**
Why did God need glory? Why did the Son of God need to be glorified? Why must someone become sick and suffer just so God and His Son can be glorified? Why did Jesus not know that Lazarus would die?

11:5 - JESUS LOVED MARTHA, HER SISTER, AND LAZARUS.

**Perplexing:**
Why did the other gospels fail to report that Jesus loved these women and Lazarus? Why is this the first time that Jesus is said to have loved any women?

11:6 - WHEN HE HAD HEARD THAT HE WAS SICK, HE ABODE TWO DAYS STILL IN THE SAME PLACE WHERE HE WAS.

**Perplexing:**
Why did Jesus not rush to his beloved Lazarus? Why could he not perform a long distance miracle to cure him? (In MATT. 8:5-13, Jesus healed a centurion's servant from a distance.)

11:8 - HIS DISCIPLES: "MASTER, THE JEWS OF LATE SOUGHT TO STONE THEE...."

**Perplexing:**
Why did the disciples, who were Jews, say, "the Jews," as if they, themselves were not Jewish? Did JOHN forget that they also were Jews?

11:14 - SAID JESUS, "LAZARUS IS DEAD."

**Perplexing:**
Why in 11:4 did Jesus say that Lazarus' sickness "is not unto death?" How did he now know that Lazarus was dead? Why did the disciples not ask Jesus how he knew that Lazarus was dead? Did Jesus delay his departure for two days so that Lazarus would die? Why did Jesus show no concern or compassion for the heartache that Lazarus' death would bring to his sisters Martha and Mary?

11:15 - JESUS: "I AM GLAD FOR YOUR SAKES THAT I WAS NOT THERE, TO THE INTENT YE MAY BELIEVE...."

**Perplexing:**
Was Jesus saying that his disciples still did not believe in him, after all the miracles he had worked and after they had listened to his teachings? If so, why did they not yet believe? JOHN 2:11 says, "his disciples believed on him."

11:16 - SAID THOMAS, WHICH IS CALLED DIDYMUS, UNTO HIS FELLOW DISCIPLES, "LET US ALSO GO, THAT WE MAY DIE WITH HIM."

**Language:**
In Greek, "Didymus," means "twin." "Thomas," in Aramaic,"Thomish," also means "twin." The name "Thomas Didymus," therefore, means "Twin Twin."

**Perplexing:**
Why did Thomas say that they should go to the dead Lazarus so that the disciples "may die with him?" Why was Thomas identified as a twin? Whose twin was he?

11:17 - WHEN JESUS CAME, HE FOUND THAT LAZARUS HAD LAIN IN THE GRAVE FOUR DAYS.

**Perplexing:**
If they departed two days after Lazarus' death, and arrived four days after his death, the trip would have taken two days. How did they travel? JOHN did not say that they rode on asses, horses, camels, or in any conveyance. Why could Jesus not perform a miracle to arrive in Bethany instantaneously?

11:26 - JESUS: "WHOSOEVER LIVETH AND BELIEVE IN ME SHALL NEVER DIE. BELIEVEST THOU THIS?"

**Contradictions:** See under MATT. 5:3, 19:17-19 (for obtaining eternal life), and 9:28-30.

**Perplexing:** See under MATT. 19:16, and 17-19 (for obtaining eternal life).

**Pagan concept:** See under MATT. 19:16.

11:27 - SHE [MARTHA] SAITH, "YEA, LORD, I BELIEVE THAT THOU ART THE CHRIST, THE SON OF GOD, WHICH SHOULD COME INTO THE WORLD."

**Perplexing:**
Why did Martha, a Jewish woman, use a Christian term, "the Son of God," when referring to Jesus? Jews do not believe that Jesus or anyone else is the Son of God. [The Muslim holy book, the Koran, erroneously claims that Jews believe that someone named Ezra (perhaps the biblical Ezra) is the son of God.] Jews believe that the Messiah (Christ) will be descended paternally from David.

**Language**: See under MATT. 1:1.

**History:** See under MATT. 1:1 and 8:29.

**Pagan parallel:** See MATT. 1:1.

11:33 - WHEN JESUS SAW HER [MARY] AND THE JEWS WITH HER WEEPING, HE GROANED IN THE SPIRIT, AND WAS TROUBLED.

**Perplexing:**
Why did Jesus fail to show any compassion for his beloved friend and his sisters until now? Why did he not realize that people would be sorrowful over Lazarus' death? Why did the Jews who JOHN asserted wanted to kill Jesus show no hostility towards him?

**Pagan parallel:**
At the death of Osiris, his two sisters and other people wept.

11:34 - JESUS: “WHERE HAVE YE LAID HIM?” THEY SAID, “LORD, COME AND SEE. “

**Contradictions:**
JOHN 18:4 - Jesus knew all things that should come upon him.
[Did Jesus know, or not know all things that were to happen in relation to himself?]
MATT. 9:4; 12:25; LUKE 5:22; 6:8; 9:47; 11:17 - Jesus read minds - he knew people’s thoughts.
[Did Jesus have to ask where Lazarus was buried, or could he read people’s minds?]
See also under MATT. 9:28-30.

**Perplexing:**
Why did Jesus not amaze the people by going directly to the tomb without having to ask for its location?

11:35 - JESUS WEPT.

**Perplexing:**
Why did Jesus weep now? Why did he not weep when he learned about Lazarus’ death? Why did he weep when he knew that he would resurrect him?

11:37 - SOME OF THEM SAID, “COULD NOT THIS MAN, WHICH OPENED THE EYES OF THE BLIND, HAVE CAUSED THAT EVEN THIS MAN SHOULD NOT HAVE DIED?”

**Perplexing:**
Why were the Jews not hostile to Jesus as they were previously reported to have been?

11:38-39 - JESUS GROANING TO HIMSELF COMETH TO THE GRAVE. IT WAS A CAVE; A STONE LAY UPON IT. JESUS SAID, “TAKE YE AWAY THE STONE.” MARTHA SAITH, “LORD, BY THIS TIME HE STINKETH, FOR HE HATH BEEN DEAD FOUR DAYS.”

**Perplexing:**
Why did Jesus command that the stone be moved? Why did he not help move it? Why did he not perform a miracle to move it?

**Pagan parallel:**
Osiris had been dead four days when Horus arrived to bring him back to life.

11:41-42 - THEN THEY TOOK AWAY THE STONE.... JESUS LIFTED UP HIS EYES, AND SAID, “FATHER, I THANK THEE THAT THOU HAST HEARD ME. I KNEW THAT THOU HEAREST ME ALWAYS, BUT BECAUSE OF THE PEOPLE WHICH STAND BY I SAID IT, THAT THEY MAY BELIEVE THAT THOU HAST SENT ME.”

**Contradiction:**
JOHN 10:30 - Jesus: “I and my Father are one.”
[Did Jesus thank God and say that God sent him, or was he one with God?]

**Perplexing:**
If Jesus and God are the same, was Jesus thanking himself?

11:43-44 - ...HE CRIED WITH A LOUD VOICE, "LAZARUS COME FORTH." HE THAT WAS DEAD CAME FORTH, BOUND HAND AND FOOT WITH GRAVECLOTHES; HIS FACE WAS BOUND ABOUT WITH A NAPKIN. JESUS SAITH, "LOOSE HIM, AND LET HIM GO."

**Contradiction:**
ACTS 26:23 - Paul: "...he (Christ) should be the first that should rise from the dead...."
REV. 1:5 - Jesus Christ is the first begotten of the dead...."
[Was Lazarus resurrected from the dead before Jesus was resurrected, or was Jesus the first to be resurrected?]

**Perplexing:**
How could Lazarus come forth if he was bound hand and foot with graveclothes? How badly was he decomposed? How much of an odor did he exude? Were there many maggots eating away at his body? Were not the people afraid to go near him? Why was this amazing resurrection of a four-day old corpse not mentioned in the other gospels? Why was this resurrection, witnessed by many people, not recorded anywhere else? News of such a monumental event, if it occurred, would have been circulated throughout the region and even to Greece and Rome. Did Lazarus, after returning to life, regain his pre-death features, or did he walk around looking like a decaying cadaver? How long afterwards did he live? What did he do? Why did he fail to appear later to defend Jesus before the high priest and Pilate?
See also under MATT. 9:26.

**Old Testament:** See under MATT. 9:25.

**Pagan parallels:**
Horus ordered the dead Osiris to "go forth and wake up." Osiris then rose from the dead. A dead man was also resurrected by the Greek god Asclepius (depicted as a benevolent, bearded man, who was himself killed and then resurrected).
See also under MATT. 9:25.

**History:**
Bishop origin (185-253) conceded that some biblical passages are not true, but are absurd and impossible.

11:46-48 - SOME WENT TO THE PHARISEES, AND TOLD THEM WHAT THINGS JESUS HAD DONE. THEN GATHERED THE CHIEF PRIESTS AND PHARISEES A COUNCIL, AND SAID, "WHAT DO WE? THIS MAN DOETH MANY MIRACLES. IF WE LET HIM THUS ALONE, ALL MEN WILL BELIEVE ON HIM, AND THE ROMANS SHALL COME AND TAKE AWAY BOTH OUR PLACE AND NATION."

**Perplexing:**
Why were the Pharisees not curious about the miracle? Why did they not investigate to determine whether it actually occurred? Why were they perturbed about Jesus? Why were they not fearful and in awe of Jesus, especially since he could bring back to life a four-day old corpse? Why did they not want to be friendly with him and try to have him perform miracles to help them and their families? Why did they not ask him to perform a miracle to free the Jews from Roman rule (as the Messiah was expected to do)?

11:49 - ONE OF THEM, CAIAPHAS, BEING THE HIGH PRIEST THAT YEAR, SAID, "YE KNOW NOTHING AT ALL."

**History:**
Joseph Caiaphas was the high priest from A.D. 18-36. Caiaphas was also the title of a functionary in the high priest's office who conducted interrogations.

11:50-53 - CAIAPHAS: "CONSIDER THAT IT IS EXPEDIENT FOR US, THAT ONE MAN SHOULD DIE FOR THE PEOPLE, THAT THE WHOLE NATION PERISH NOT." ...HE PROPHESIED THAT JESUS SHOULD DIE FOR THAT NATION. ... THAT ALSO HE SHOULD GATHER TOGETHER THE CHILDREN OF GOD THAT WERE SCATTERED ABROAD. FROM THAT DAY FORTH THEY TOOK COUNSEL TOGETHER TO PUT HIM TO DEATH.

**History:** See under 7:35.

**Perplexing:**
Why did the high priest and the others want to kill someone who could bring the dead back to life and perform other miracles? Why were they not afraid of such a person?
See also under 7:35 and 11:46-48.

11:54 - JESUS WALKED NO MORE OPENLY AMONG THE JEWS; HE WENT INTO A COUNTRY NEAR THE WILDERNESS, INTO A CITY CALLED EPHRAIM, WITH HIS DISCIPLES.

**Perplexing:**
Ephraim was about 12 miles from Bethany. Were there no Jews there?
Why did Jesus not perform a miracle to dissuade the Pharisees and other Jews from wanting to kill him before his designated time of death? Why did he not perform a miracle to drive the Romans out of Judea?
Why did JOHN depict Jesus as fearful?
See also under 7:1.

**History:** See under 5:16.

11:55 - THE JEWS' PASSOVER WAS NIGH AT HAND....

**Contradiction:**
JOHN now reported the third Passover in Jesus' ministry. The other gospels reported only one Passover, and that occurred at the end of his ministry (MATT. 26:2; MARK 14:1; LUKE 22:1. LUKE 2:41 cited an additional Passover when Jesus was a child.)
[Were there three Passovers, or only one during Jesus' ministry?]

**Perplexing:** See under JOHN 2:13.

12:1-3 - JESUS SIX DAYS BEFORE PASSOVER CAME TO BETHANY.... THERE THEY MADE HIM A SUPPER; MARTHA SERVED; LAZARUS SAT WITH HIM. THEN TOOK MARY A POUND OF OINTMENT OF SPIKENARD, VERY COSTLY, ANOINTED THE FEET OF JESUS, AND WIPED HIS FEET WITH HER HAIR....

**Contradictions:**
MATT. 26:2-7 - Jesus: "...after two days is the feast of Passover.... .... When Jesus was in Bethany, in the house of Simon the leper, a woman having very precious ointment poured it on Jesus' head, as he sat at

meat.
[Was Jesus anointed in the home of Lazarus and his sisters, or in the home of Simon the leper?]
MARK 14:1-3 - After two days was the feast of Passover, and unleavened bread.... .... Being in Bethany in the house of Simon the leper, as he sat at meat, came a woman having ointment of spikenard very precious; she poured it on his head.
[Was Jesus anointed six days, or two days before Passover?]
[Was Jesus anointed by Mary, or by an unidentified woman?]
[Were Jesus feet anointed, or was the ointment poured on his head?]
LUKE 7:36-39 - .... He went into the Pharisee's house and sat down to meat. A woman, which was a sinner ...brought ointment...and began to wash his feet with tears, and wipe them with the hairs of her head, kissed his feet, and anointed them with the ointment. [Passover was not mentioned.]
[Was Jesus anointed in the home of Lazarus and his sisters, the or in home of a Pharisee?]
[Was Jesus anointed by Mary, or by a woman who was a sinner?]
[Were Jesus' feet anointed with ointment before Mary wiped them with her hair, or were they first washed with tears, wiped with hair, and kissed before being anointed?]
See also under MATT. 26:6-7.

**Perplexing:**
Why did Jesus permit Mary, whom he loved (11:5), to degrade herself by anointing his feet and wiping them with her hair? Why was he not afraid now to return to Bethany, from where he fled, because the Pharisees wanted to kill him?
What was Lazarus' appearance? JOHN did not say that Jesus repaired whatever decay occurred to his body externally, internally, and mentally?
See also under MATT. 26:6-7.

**Pagan concept:** See under MATT. 26:2.

**Pagan parallel:** See under MATT. 26:6-7.

12:4-5 - SAITH JUDAS ISCARIOT, SIMON'S SON... "WHY WAS NOT THIS OINTMENT SOLD FOR 300 PENCE, AND GIVEN TO THE POOR?"

**Contradictions:**
MATT. 26:8-9 - When his disciples saw it, they had indignation, saying, "To what purpose is this waste?" This ointment might have been sold for much and given to the poor."
[Did Judas, or the disciples say that the ointment could have been sold and the proceeds given to the poor?]
MARK 14:4-5 - There were some that had indignation within themselves, and said, "Why was this waste of the ointment made? It might have been sold for more than 300 pence, and have been given to the poor."
[Did Judas, or some unidentified people say that the ointment could have been sold for 300 pence with the proceeds given to the poor?]
LUKE 7:39 - When the Pharisee saw it, he spake within himself, "This man, if he were a prophet, would have known who and what manner of woman this is that toucheth him, for she is a sinner."
[Did Judas say that the ointment should have been sold, or did a Pharisee say that the woman was a sinner?]

**Perplexing:**
Why did Jesus not suggest that the ointment be sold and the proceeds given to the poor?
Why was Judas identified as Simon's son? Who was this Simon?

12:6 - ...HE WAS A THIEF, AND HAD THE BAG [WITH THE DISCIPLES' MONEY]....

**Perplexing:**

If Judas was a thief, why did Jesus allow him to handle the group's money? Why did Jesus select a thief to be one of his disciples? In MATT. 19:28 and LUKE 22:30, Jesus promised the twelve disciples including Judas that they would sit on thrones judging the tribes of Israel. Why would Jesus allow a thief to sit in judgment of others? How did Jesus and the disciples acquire money? Did they work? If so, at what? When? Did they solicit contributions like modern Christian clergy? Did they beg?

12:8 - JESUS: "THE POOR ALWAYS YE HAVE WITH YOU; BUT ME YE HAVE NOT ALWAYS."

**Contradiction:**

MATT. 28:20 - Jesus: " ...I am with you alway [always], even unto the end of the world."
[Did Jesus say that he will not, or will always be with his disciples?]

**Perplexing:**

Why did Jesus fail to eliminate poverty or show humanity how to do so?

12:9 - MUCH PEOPLE OF THE JEWS...CAME, NOT ONLY FOR JESUS' SAKE, BUT THAT THEY MIGHT ALSO SEE LAZARUS....

**Perplexing:**

Why was Jesus no longer afraid of being among Jews? Why were the Jews, who were reported to have wanted to kill Jesus, not hostile to him? They did not threaten or attack him, but just wanted to see him.

12:10 - THE CHIEF PRIESTS CONSULTED HOW THEY MIGHT PUT LAZARUS ALSO TO DEATH.

**Perplexing:**

Why were the chief priests not in awe and fearful of someone who had returned to life after being interred for four days? Why did they want to kill Lazarus?

**Pagan parallel:**

Asclepius and the man he resurrected were killed by Zeus.
See also under 11:43-44.

12:12-13 - THE NEXT DAY MUCH PEOPLE ... TOOK BRANCHES OF PALM TREES, WENT FORTH TO MEET HIM, AND CRIED, "HOSANNA; BLESSED IS THE KING OF ISRAEL THAT COMETH IN THE NAME OF THE LORD."

**Contradictions:**

MATT. 21:8-9 - A very great multitude spread their garments in the way; others cut down branches, and strawed them in the way. The multitude ... cried, "Hosanna to the Son of David. Blessed is he that cometh in the name of the Lord; Hosanna in the highest."
[Was Jesus called, "the King of Israel," or "the Son of David?"]

MARK 11:8-10 - Many spread their garments in the way; others cut down branches, and strawed them in the way. They ...cried, "Hosanna; Blessed is he that cometh in the name of the Lord; Blessed be the kingdom of our father David, that cometh in the name of the Lord; Hosanna in the highest."
[Was Jesus called, "the King of Israel," or "he that cometh in the name of the Lord?"]
LUKE 19:37-38 - ...the whole multitude of disciples began to rejoice and praise God...saying "Blessed be the King that cometh in the name of the Lord; peace in heaven, and glory in the highest."
[Did a great multitude of people cry out, or did just the disciples speak?]
[Was Jesus called "the King of Israel," or "the King that cometh in the name of the Lord?"]

**Perplexing:**
Why were people who reportedly wanted to kill Jesus now cheering him and calling him the King of Israel?

**Language:** For "Hosanna," see under MATT. 21:8-9.

**Old Testament:** See under MATT. 21:8-9.

12:14 - JESUS, WHEN HE HAD FOUND A YOUNG ASS, SAT THEREON....

**Contradictions:**
MATT. 21:6-7 - The disciples...brought the ass, and colt, and put on them their clothes, and set him thereon [before people shouted, "Hosanna," etc., in 21:8-9].
[Did Jesus find an ass, or did the disciples find and bring an ass and colt to Jesus?]
[Did Jesus sit on the ass, or did the disciples place him on an ass and colt?]
MARK 11:7 - They brought the colt to Jesus, cast their garments on him, and he sat upon him [before people shouted, "Hosanna, etc., in 11:8-10].
LUKE 19:35 - They brought him [the colt] to Jesus, cast their garments upon the colt, and set Jesus thereon.
[Did Jesus find an ass, or did the disciples find and bring a colt to him?]
[Did Jesus sit on an ass, or a colt?]
[Did Jesus sit on one or two animals after, or before the people shouted, "Hosanna, etc.?]
See also under MATT. 21:1-2 and 6-7.

**Old Testament:** See under MATT. 21:6-7.

12:14-15 - ...AS IT IS WRITTEN, "FEAR NOT, DAUGHTER OF SION; BEHOLD, THY KING COMETH, SITTING ON AN ASS'S COLT."

**Contradiction:**
MATT. 21:4-5 - All this was done that it might be fulfilled which was spoken by the prophet, "Tell ye the daughter of Sion, 'Behold, thy King cometh unto thee, meek, and sitting upon an ass, and a colt the foal of an ass.'"
[Was the King to come riding on an ass' colt, or on an ass and an ass' colt? (See below under Language.)]

**Old Testament:** See under MATT. 21:4-5.

**Language**: See under MATT. 21:4-5 - Old Testament.

12:17 - THE PEOPLE THAT WAS WITH HIM WHEN HE CALLED LAZARUS OUT OF HIS GRAVE, AND RAISED HIM FROM THE DEAD, BARE RECORD.

**Perplexing:**
How did they bear record? Where is any record of the occurrence? Why is there no historical record of this fantastic miracle - returning a four-day old corpse to life? Why did Roman, Greek, and other foreign merchants and soldiers not report the event when they returned to their homes? Why did no one but JOHN mention this resurrection? Why did MATT., MARK, and LUKE not deem it important enough to cite? Did they not know about it? If not, why not? Why did people not come to Jesus and ask him to resurrect their dead loved ones?

12:18 - FOR THIS CAUSE PEOPLE ALSO MET HIM, FOR THEY HEARD THAT HE HAD DONE THIS MIRACLE.

**Perplexing:**
If many people were aware of the miracle, why did not any of them publicize and write about it?
See also under 12:17.

12:23 - JESUS ANSWERED, "THE HOUR IS COME, THAT THE SON OF MAN SHOULD BE GLORIFIED."

**Perplexing:** See under 11:4.

12:25 - JESUS: "...HE THAT HATETH HIS LIFE IN THIS WORLD SHALL KEEP IT UNTO LIFE ETERNAL.

**Contradictions:** See under MATT. 19:17-19 (for obtaining eternal life).

**Perplexing:**
Why would anyone who hates his life want eternal life?
See also under MATT. 19:16 and 17-19 (for obtaining eternal life).

12:27 - JESUS: "NOW IS MY SOUL TROUBLED; WHAT SHALL I SAY? FATHER SAVE ME FROM THIS HOUR, BUT FOR THIS CAUSE CAME I UNTO THIS HOUR."

**Contradictions:**
MATT. 26:39 - He...prayed, "O my father, if it be possible, let this cup pass from me; nevertheless not as I will, but as Thou wilt."
MARK 14:35-36 - He [Jesus]...prayed.... He said, "Father, all things are possible unto Thee; take away this cup from me; nevertheless not what I will, but what Thou wilt."
LUKE 22:41-42 - He [Jesus]...prayed, "Father, if Thou be willing, remove this cup from me; nevertheless not my will, but Thine be done."
[Did Jesus say that for this hour he came, or that he would prefer to have the "cup" taken away from him?]
JOHN 10:30 - Jesus: "I and my Father are one."
[Was Jesus so distinct from God that he considered asking God to save him, or is he one with God, thus, asking himself about saving himself?]

**Perplexing:**
Why was Jesus' soul troubled? Why was he troubled about returning to his Father? How could the Son of God, or God, be troubled? Was he not above feeling pain, suffering, and permanent death? Even in the guise of a human, he had nothing to fear.

12:28 - JESUS: "FATHER, GLORIFY THY NAME." THEN CAME A VOICE FROM HEAVEN SAYING, "I HAVE BOTH GLORIFIED IT, AND WILL GLORIFY IT AGAIN."

**Perplexing:**
Why does an almighty God of the universe need to have His name glorified for or by ignorant, puny, short-lived, humans on a small, obscure planet circling a small, obscure star (the sun), on the fringe of a small, obscure galaxy? Why is He obsessed with impressing and being adored by these humans? Why is not the universe that He created adequate glory for Him? How does God benefit by having His name glorified? Is He an egomaniac or an insecure deity? If so, why?

12:29 - THE PEOPLE THAT STOOD BY, AND HEARD IT, SAID THAT IT THUNDERED; OTHERS SAID, "AN ANGEL SPAKE TO HIM."

**Perplexing:**
If the people heard God's voice and words, why did they not immediately become believers in and followers of Jesus? If God's voice could be heard, why did He not command them to accept Jesus as His Son and thereby avoid the crucifixion, the resurrection, and centuries of religious hate, persecution, violence, and war?

12:31 - JESUS: "NOW IS THE JUDGMENT OF THIS WORLD; NOW SHALL THE PRINCE OF THIS WORLD BE CAST OUT."

**Contradiction:**
JOHN 14:30 - Jesus: "...the prince of this world cometh...."
[Was the prince of this world cast out, or is he still around?]

**Perplexing:**
Why did Jesus tell his listeners that the judgment of the world is "now?" About two millennia later it still has not come. Why did he say that "now" "the prince of this world" (a synonym for Satan) will "be cast out?" About two millennia later, according to Christian clergy, Satan is still here? Why did Jesus fail to keep these promises? Why did God fail to cast out Satan? Did Jesus deliberately lie to the people?

12:32-33 - JESUS: "I, IF I BE LIFTED UP FROM THE EARTH, WILL DRAW ALL MEN UNTO ME." THIS HE SAID, SIGNIFYING WHAT DEATH HE SHOULD DIE.

**Perplexing:**
Why did Jesus say, "If I be lifted up from the earth" (meaning the crucifixion), when he knew that it would occur? Why did Jesus' prophecy that all men will be drawn to him at the time of the crucifixion fail? Why during about two millennia has it continued to fail?
Did Jesus mean that God would draw all people to him?

12:34 - THE PEOPLE ANSWERED, "WE HAVE HEARD OUT OF THE LAW THAT CHRIST ABIDETH FOREVER; HOW SAYEST THOU, 'THE SON OF MAN MUST BE LIFTED UP?' WHO IS THIS SON OF MAN?"

**Perplexing:**
Why did Jesus not answer the people, and say that he is "the Son of man?"
See also under MATT. 8:18.

**Language**: See under MATT. 8:18.

**History:** See under MATT. 8:18.

**Old Testament:** See under MATT. 8:18.

12:36 - JESUS: "WHILE YE HAVE LIGHT, BELIEVE IN THE LIGHT, THAT YE MAY BE THE CHILDREN OF LIGHT." ... JESUS DEPARTED AND DID HIDE HIMSELF FROM THEM.

**Contradiction:** See under 8:12.

**Pagan parallels**: See under 1:4-5 and 8:12.

**History:** See under 8:12.

**Perplexing:**
Why did Jesus hide?

12:37 - THOUGH HE HAD DONE SO MANY MIRACLES BEFORE THEM, YET THEY BELIEVED NOT ON HIM.

**Contradiction:**
JOHN 2:11 - The beginning of miracles did Jesus in Cana...and his disciples believed on him.
[Did his disciples not believe, or did they believe on Jesus?]

**Perplexing:**
Why did they refuse to believe on Jesus? Not only had he worked miracles including bringing the dead back to life, but they had also heard the voice of God (12:28-29). Why did Jesus fail to perform a miracle to cause them to believe?
See also under 11:15.

12:38-40 - THAT THE SAYING OF ESAIAS [ISAIAH] THE PROPHET MIGHT BE FULFILLED, "LORD, WHO HATH BELIEVED OUR REPORT? TO WHOM HATH THE ARM OF THE LORD BEEN REVEALED?" .... "HE HATH BLINDED THEIR EYES, AND HARDENED THEIR HEART, THAT THEY SHOULD NOT SEE WITH THEIR EYES, NOR UNDERSTAND WITH THEIR HEART, AND BE CONVERTED, AND I SHOULD HEAL THEM."

**Old Testament:**
ISA. 6:10 - The Lord [to Isaiah]: "Make the heart of this people fat, and make their ears heavy, and shut

their eyes, lest they see with their eyes, and hear with their ears, and understand with their heart, and convert, and be healed." [These verses taken out of context were part of a prophecy made by God pertaining to the Israelites. In the ensuing verses, God stated that the cities would be destroyed and be without inhabitants, and the land made desolate.]

**Perplexing:**
Why does God want to prevent people from being converted? By doing so, God, is responsible for the refusal of some people to believe in Jesus. Does He then have the right to punish such people with damnation (MARK 16:16)?
See also under MATT. 13:10-13.

12:41 - THESE THINGS SAID ESAIAS [ISAIAH], WHEN HE SAW HIS GLORY, AND SPAKE OF HIM.

**Perplexing:**
As Isaiah was quoting a prophecy made by God in reference to the Israelites, how could he have seen Jesus' glory and spoken of him?
See under 12:38-40 - Old Testament.

12:42 - AMONG THE CHIEF RULERS MANY BELIEVED ON HIM, BUT BECAUSE OF THE PHARISEES THEY DID NOT CONFESS HIM, LEST THEY SHOULD BE PUT OUT OF THE SYNAGOGUE.

**History:** See under 9:22.

**Perplexing:** See under 9:22.

12:43 - THEY LOVED THE PRAISE OF MEN MORE THAN THE PRAISE OF GOD.

**Perplexing:**
When, how, and why does God praise anyone?

12:44 - JESUS SAID, "HE THAT BELIEVETH ON ME, BELIEVETH NOT ON ME, BUT ON HIM THAT SENT ME."

**Perplexing:**
In JOHN 10:30, Jesus said, "I and my Father are one." Therefore, if Jesus is one with God, did he send himself?

12:45 - JESUS: "HE THAT SEETH ME SEETH HIM THAT SENT ME."

**Perplexing:**
Was Jesus saying that he looked like God? In LUKE 4:23, Jesus said to people, "Ye will surely say unto me this proverb, 'Physician, heal thyself.'" Did this mean that Jesus and, therefore, God have physical imperfections?
See also under LUKE 4:23.

**History:** See under LUKE 4:23.

12:46 - JESUS: "I AM COME A LIGHT INTO THE WORLD, THAT WHOSOEVER BELIEVETH ON ME SHOULD NOT ABIDE IN DARKNESS."

**Contradiction:** See under 8:12.

**History:** See under 8:12.

**Pagan parallels**: See under 1:4-5 and 8:12.

**Perplexing:** See under 8:12.

12:47 - JESUS: "IF ANY MAN HEAR MY WORDS, AND BELIEVE NOT, I JUDGE HIM NOT, FOR I CAME NOT TO JUDGE THE WORLD, BUT TO SAVE THE WORLD."

**Contradictions:** See under 3:17 and 8:15.

12:48 - JESUS: "HE THAT REJECTETH ME, AND RECEIVETH NOT MY WORDS, HATH ONE THAT JUDGETH HIM; THE WORD THAT I HAVE SPOKEN, THE SAME SHALL JUDGE HIM IN THE LAST DAY."

**Contradictions:** See under 8:15.

12:49-50 - JESUS: "...THE FATHER WHICH SENT ME, GAVE ME A COMMANDMENT, WHAT I SHOULD SAY, AND SPEAK. ...WHATSOEVER I SPEAK THEREFORE, AS THE FATHER SAID UNTO ME; SO I SPEAK."

**Perplexing:**
In JOHN 10: 30 - Jesus: "I and my Father are one." If Jesus is one with his Father, was Jesus saying that he tells himself what to say?

13:1-2 - BEFORE THE FEAST OF THE PASSOVER, WHEN JESUS KNEW THAT HIS HOUR WAS COME THAT HE SHOULD DEPART OUT OF THIS WORLD UNTO THE FATHER.... SUPPER BEING ENDED, THE DEVIL PUT INTO THE HEART OF JUDAS ISCARIOT, SIMON'S SON, TO BETRAY HIM.

**Contradictions:**
MATT. 26:14-17 - ...Judas Iscariot, went unto the priests, and said, "What will ye give me, and I will, deliver him unto you?" .... The first day of the feast of unleavened bread, the disciples came to Jesus, saying, "Where wilt thou that we prepare for thou to eat the Passover?"
MARK 14:10-12 - Judas Iscariot went to the chief priests, to betray him to them. They were glad.... The first day of unleavened bread, when they killed the Passover, his disciples said, "Where wilt thou that we prepare that thou mayest eat the Passover?"....
LUKE 22:3-8 - Then entered Satan into Judas Iscariot.... He went and communed with the chief priests and captains, how he might betray him. They were glad.... .... Then came the day of unleavened bread, when the Passover must be killed. He [Jesus] sent Peter and John, saying, "Go and prepare the Passover, that we

may eat."
[Was Jesus' last supper prior to the feast of Passover, or was it the Passover meal?]
[Did the devil induce Judas to betray Jesus after, or before the supper?]

**Pagan concept:** See under MATT. 4:3.

**Pagan parallel:** See under MATT. 4:3 and 26:19-21.

**History:** See under MATT. 26:2.

**Perplexing:** See under LUKE 22:3-6.

13:3 - JESUS KNOWING...THAT HE WAS COME FROM GOD, AND WENT TO GOD.

**Contradictions:** See under 1:14, and under MATT. 1:18.

13:5 - HE POURETH WATER INTO A BASIN, BEGAN TO WASH THE DISCIPLES' FEET, AND WIPE THEM WITH THE TOWEL WHEREWITH HE WAS GIRDED.

**Pagan parallel:**
The Hindu god Krishna washed the feet of Brahmins (priests and members of the highest Hindu caste).

**Perplexing:**
Why did not the other gospels report this incident?
Was the washing of feet meant to be a form of baptism? The disciples were never reported to have been baptized. Was the ritual meant to be a form of anointing? In LUKE 7:38, a woman washed Jesus' feet.

13:11 - HE KNEW WHO SHOULD BETRAY HIM....

**Contradiction:**
MATT. 26:50 - Jesus said unto him [Judas Iscariot,] "Friend, wherefore art thou come?"
[Did Jesus know who would betray him, or did he believe that Judas was a friend?]

**Perplexing:**
If Jesus knew that Judas would betray him, why did he greet him as "friend," and ask him why he had come?
Why in MATT. 19:28 and LUKE 22:30 did Jesus say that he will give each of the disciples, including Judas, a throne and have them sit in judgment of the twelve tribes of Israel? Did Jesus not know at the time that Judas would betray him?
See also under 12:6.

13:18 - JESUS: "...I KNOW WHOM I HAVE CHOSEN, THAT THE SCRIPTURE MAY BE FULFILLED, 'HE THAT EATETH BEAD WITH ME HATH LIFTED UP HIS HEEL AGAINST ME.'"

**Old Testament:**
PS. 41:9 - "Mine own familiar friend, in whom I trusted, which did eat of my bread, hath lifted up his heel against me."

**Contradiction:** See under 6:70-71.

**Language:**
Some scholars contend that the term, "lifted up his heel against me," is a translation error, and that the correct term should be, "betrayed me."

13:21 - JESUS...WAS TROUBLED IN SPIRIT...AND SAID, "...ONE OF YOU SHALL BETRAY ME."

**Perplexing:**
Why was Jesus troubled in spirit? If he was one with God or the Son of God, he knew what was to occur and he knew that he really could not be harmed. He also knew that Judas was doing what he was ordained by God to do.
See also under 12:27, and under LUKE 22:3-6.

13:23 - THERE WAS LEANING ON JESUS' BOSOM ONE OF HIS DISCIPLES, WHOM JESUS LOVED.

**Contradiction:**
JOHN 13:34 - Jesus: "A new commandment I give unto you, that ye love one another; as I have loved you, that ye also love one another."
JOHN 15:12 - Jesus: "This is my commandment, that ye love one another, as I have loved you."
[Did Jesus love just one disciple, or did he love them all?]

**Perplexing:**
Why was the beloved disciple not identified?

**Pagan parallel:**
The Hindu god Krishna had a beloved disciple (Arjuna).

13:24-25 - SIMON PETER BECKONED TO HIM, THAT HE SHOULD ASK OF WHOM HE SPAKE. HE LYING ON JESUS' BREAST SAITH, "LORD, WHO IS IT?"

**Contradictions:**
MATT. 26:22 - They...began every one of them to say unto him, "Lord, is it I?"
MARK 14:19 - They began ... to say unto him one by one, "Is it I?"
[Did Peter tell the beloved disciples to ask Jesus who would betray him, or did each of the disciples ask Jesus?]
[Did only the beloved disciple speak to Jesus, or did each disciple speak to him?]
LUKE 22:23 - They began to inquire among themselves, which of them it was that should do this thing.
[Did Peter tell the beloved disciple to ask Jesus who would betray him, or did the disciples ask each other?]
[Did the beloved disciples ask Jesus, or did none of the disciples ask him?]

13:26 - JESUS ANSWERED, "HE IT IS, TO WHOM I SHALL GIVE A SOP.... WHEN HE HAD DIPPED THE SOP, HE GAVE IT TO JUDAS ISCARIOT, THE SON OF SIMON."

**Contradictions:**
MATT. 26:25 - Judas...said, "Master, is it I?" He said, "Thou hast said."
[Did Jesus say that it was the man to whom he will give a sop, or did Judas ask him if he was the one?]
[Did Jesus give the sop to Judas, or did he tell Judas that he was the betrayer?]
MARK 14:20 - He said, "It is one of the 12, that dippeth with me in the dish."
[Did Jesus say that it was the man to whom he will give a sop, or that it was one of them that dipped into the dish with him?]
LUKE 22:21 - Jesus: "The hand of him that betrayeth me is with me on the table."
[Did Jesus say that it was the man to whom he will give a sop, or that the hand of the betrayer is with him at the table?]

**Perplexing:**
Why did JOHN again identify Judas as Simon's son?

**History:**
Some scholars have pointed out that the stories of the betrayal by Judas did not come into existence until around the end of the second century.

13:27 - AFTER THE SOP SATAN ENTERED INTO HIM.... ....

**Contradiction:**
JOHN 13:2 - Supper being ended, the devil...put into the heart of Judas Iscariot, Simon's son, to betray him.
[Did the devil/Satan incite Judas to betray Jesus after, or before he received the sop?]

**Perplexing:** See under LUKE 22:3-6.

13:31-32 - ...JESUS SAID, "NOW IS THE SON OF MAN GLORIFIED, AND GOD IS GLORIFIED IN HIM. IF GOD BE GLORIFIED IN HIM, GOD SHALL ALSO GLORIFY HIM IN HIMSELF, AND SHALL STRAIGHTWAY GLORIFY HIM."

**Perplexing:** See under 11:4 and 12:28.

13:33 - JESUS: ".... ...AS I SAID UNTO THE JEWS...."

**Perplexing:**
Why did Jesus use the phrase, "unto the Jews," as though he and his disciples were not Jewish?

13:34-35 - JESUS: "A NEW COMMANDMENT I GIVE UNTO YOU, THAT YE LOVE ONE ANOTHER; AS I HAVE LOVED YOU, THAT YE ALSO LOVE ONE ANOTHER. BY THIS SHALL ALL MEN KNOW THAT YE ARE MY DISCIPLES, IF YE HAVE LOVE ONE TO ANOTHER."

**Contradiction:**
JOHN 13:23 - There was leaning on Jesus' bosom one of his disciples, whom Jesus loved.

[Did Jesus love all of his disciples, or just one?]

**Perplexing:**
Why have not the vast majority of Christians followed this commandment? Followers of Jesus have not only hated one another, but have engaged in violence and wars against one another.

13:38 - JESUS ANSWERED HIM [PETER], ".... THE COCK SHALL NOT CROW, TILL THOU HAST DENIED ME THRICE."

**Contradictions:**
MATT. 26:30-34 - [After the Passover meal]...they went out into the mount of Olives. .... Jesus said unto him [Peter], "This night, before the cock crow, thou shalt deny me thrice."
MARK 14:26-30 - [After the Passover meal]...they went out into the mount of olives. .... Jesus saith unto him [Peter], "...this night, before the cock crow twice, thou shalt deny me thrice."
[Did Jesus tell Peter that he will deny him three times before the cock crows once, or twice?]
[Did Jesus speak to Peter indoors at a meal, or outdoors at the mount of olives?]
LUKE 22:34 - [After the Passover meal] Jesus said, "I tell thee, Peter, the cock shall not crow this day, before that thou shall thrice deny that thou knowest me."
[Did Jesus speak to Peter at a meal prior to Passover, or after the Passover meal?]

**History:** See under MATT. 26:34

14:1-2 - JESUS: "... YE BELIEVE IN GOD; BELIEVE ALSO IN ME. IN MY FATHER'S HOUSE ARE MANY MANSIONS. I GO TO PREPARE A PLACE FOR YOU."

**Contradiction:**
JOHN 10:30 - Jesus: "I and my Father are one."
[Are God and Jesus separate entities, or are they one?]

**Perplexing:**
If God and Jesus are one (10:30), how can a person believe in one, but not the other? What did Jesus mean by "mansions?" Are they places in heaven where people reside? If so, what are they like? Are they private, or do groups of people live together in them? What kind of furniture and other facilities do they have? Are the disciples to have special places in heaven?

14:3 - JESUS [TO HIS DISCIPLES]: "...I WILL COME AGAIN, AND RECEIVE YOU UNTO MYSELF...."

**Contradiction:**
JOHN 16:10 - Jesus: " I go to my Father, and ye see me no more."
[Will Jesus come again, or will he be seen no more?]

**Perplexing:**
Why have about two millennia passed without Jesus returning? Why did he imply to the disciples that his return would be relatively soon?
See also under MATT. 16:28.

14:6 - JESUS SAITH UNTO HIM [THOMAS], "I AM THE WAY, THE TRUTH, AND THE LIFE; NO MAN COMETH UNTO THE FATHER, BUT BY ME."

**Contradiction:**
JOHN 6:44 - Jesus: "No man can come to me, except the Father which sent me draw him...."
[Does one come to the Father through Jesus, or does one come to Jesus through the Father?]

**Perplexing:**
How can someone reach the Father unless sent by Jesus, if the person cannot reach Jesus unless sent by the Father?
See also under 6:44.

**Pagan parallel:**
Krishna said that he was the way and the refuge, also the sustainer of the world, its friend, and Lord.

14:7 - JESUS: "IF YE HAD KNOWN ME, YE SHOULD HAVE KNOWN MY FATHER ALSO; FROM HENCEFORTH YE KNOW HIM, AND HAVE SEEN HIM."

**Perplexing:** See under 12:45, and under LUKE 4:23..

**History:** See under LUKE 4:23.

14:9 - JESUS SAITH, ".... HE THAT HATH SEEN ME HATH SEEN THE FATHER...?"

**Perplexing:** See under 12:45, and under LUKE 4:23.

**History:** See under LUKE 4:23.

14:12 - JESUS: "HE THAT BELIEVETH ON ME, THE WORKS THAT I DO SHALL HE DO ALSO; AND GREATER WORKS THAN THESE SHALL HE DO, BECAUSE I GO UNTO MY FATHER."

**Contradiction:**
JOHN 10:30 - Jesus: "I and my Father are one."
[Is Jesus one with his Father, or is his Father a being to whom he goes?]

**Perplexing:**
If one who believes on Jesus can do even greater works than he did, why, in about two millennia, have his believers failed to perform miracles to heal the blind, deaf, lame, infirm, and diseased, raise the dead, or even walk on water, or feed large numbers of people with two fishes and five loaves? Why cannot believers perform any of these miracles? Does the failure of believers to have even equaled Jesus' works mean that no one really believes on him? Does it mean that Jesus lied? If the believers were to perform the miracles, they would have no difficulty converting everyone to belief in Jesus' divinity.
See also under MATT. 17:19-21 and 21:21, MARK 16:17-18, and LUKE 17:6.

**History:** See under MARK 16:17-18.

14:13 - JESUS: "WHATEVER YE SHALL ASK IN MY NAME, THAT WILL I DO, THAT THE FATHER MAY BE GLORIFIED IN THE SON."

**Contradictions:** See under MATT. 1:18.

**Perplexing:**
Does Jesus do whatever a believer asks in his name? If so, why have none been able to duplicate any of his miracles, or convert the world to Christianity?
Has no one asked for a mass worldwide conversion to Christianity? If not, why not? Did Jesus lie?
See also under 12:28.

14:14 - JESUS: "IF YE ASK ANYTHING IN MY NAME, I WILL DO IT."

**Perplexing:** See under 14:12 and 13, MARK 16:17-18, and LUKE 17:6.

14:16-17 - JESUS: "I WILL PRAY THE FATHER, AND HE SHALL GIVE YOU ANOTHER COMFORTER, THAT HE MAY ABIDE WITH YOU FOREVER, EVEN THE SPIRIT OF TRUTH ... HE DWELLETH WITH YOU, AND SHALL BE IN YOU."

**Contradictions:**
JOHN 14:26 - Jesus: "The Comforter, which is the Holy Ghost...."
[Is the Comforter the Spirit of truth, or the Holy Ghost?]
JOHN 15:26 - Jesus: "When the Comforter is come, whom I will send to you from the Father, even the Spirit of truth, which proceedeth from the Father...."
JOHN 16:7 - Jesus: " I will send him (the Comforter) unto you."
[Will the Father send the Comforter, or will Jesus do so?]

**Perplexing:**
Why was another Comforter needed? Did the Comforter ever arrive? If so, why did the gospels fail to report the event? What did he do? What happened to him? How could the Comforter abide with the disciples forever? Why could not Jesus and the Comforter be present together?
What is "the Spirit of truth?"

**Dead Sea Scrolls:**
The "spirit of truth," is reported to mean "a pious state of mind." The "spirit" also is said to make one compassionate, good, righteous, humble, and trust in God's mercy.

14:18 - JESUS: "I WILL NOT LEAVE YOU COMFORTLESS; I WILL COME TO YOU."

**Perplexing:**
Why did Jesus say that he would come to them? Why did he fail to come? Why has he still failed to come?

14:21 - JESUS: "...HE THAT LOVETH ME SHALL BE LOVED OF MY FATHER...."

**Perplexing:**
Why does Jesus want to be loved? Why does he need to be loved by mere humans? What kind of divine being would want people to love him?

14:22 - JUDAS SAITH, NOT ISCARIOT, "LORD...."

**Contradictions:**
MATT. 10:2-4 and MARK 3:14-19 - No disciple named Judas, other than Judas Iscariot, was cited.
[Was there, or was there not another disciple, other than Iscariot, named Judas?]
See also under MATT. 10:2-4.

**History:**
In third and fourth century Coptic versions, the "not Iscariot" does not appear. According to these versions, the cited Judas is Iscariot.

14:23 - JESUS: "IF A MAN LOVE ME...."

**Perplexing:** See under 14:21.

14:26 - THE COMFORTER, WHICH IS THE HOLY GHOST, WHOM THE FATHER WILL SEND IN MY NAME, SHALL TEACH YOU ALL THINGS, AND BRING ALL THINGS TO YOUR REMEMBRANCE, WHATSOEVER I HAVE SAID UNTO YOU."

**Contradictions:**
JOHN 14:16-17 - Jesus: "...[the] Comforter...[is]the Spirit of truth...."
JOHN 16: 7-13 - Jesus: "...the Comforter...I will send unto you. .... When the Spirit of truth, is come...."
[Is the Comforter the Holy Ghost, or the Spirit of truth?]
See also under 14:16-17.

**Perplexing:**
If the Comforter came, did he teach all things?
See also under 14:16-17.

14:28 - JESUS: "...I SAID, I GO AWAY, AND COME AGAIN UNTO YOU. GO UNTO THE FATHER, FOR MY FATHER IS GREATER THAN I."

**Contradictions:**
JOHN 10:30 - Jesus: "I and my Father are one?"
[Is Jesus' Father greater than he, or is he one with his Father?]
[Is the Father a Being to which Jesus will go, or is he one with the Father?]
See also under 14:1-2 and 3.

**Perplexing:**
[If Jesus is one with his Father, is he going to himself?]
See also under 14:3.

14:30 - JESUS: "...THE PRINCE OF THIS WORLD COMETH, AND HATH NOTHING IN ME."

**Contradiction:**
JOHN 12:31 - "Now is the judgment of this world; now shall the prince of this world be cast out."
[Is the prince of this world coming, or was he cast out?]

**Perplexing:** See under 12:31.

14:31 - JESUS: "...I LOVE THE FATHER.... ...."

**Perplexing:**
If Jesus and his Father are one, as stated in 10:30, was Jesus saying that he loves himself?
See also under 10:17.

15:1 - JESUS: "I AM THE TRUE VINE, AND MY FATHER IS THE HUSBANDMAN."

**Contradiction:**
JOHN 10:30 - Jesus: "I and my Father are one."
[Is Jesus the vine, and his Father the husbandman, or is Jesus one with his father and therefore both vine and husbandman?]

15:5 - JESUS: "...HE THAT ABIDETH IN ME, AND I IN HIM, BRINGETH FORTH MUCH FRUIT, FOR WITHOUT ME YE CAN DO NOTHING."

**Perplexing:**
What did Jesus mean by "fruit?" Did he mean personal accomplishments, creating, building, discovering, contributing to human welfare, etc.? Did he mean making converts? If one can do nothing without Jesus, why have most of the scientific and medical discoveries, among others, been made by people who do not abide in, believe in, or take him seriously? Why have believers failed to contribute much to the betterment of human life?

15:6 - JESUS: "IF A MAN ABIDE NOT IN ME, HE IS CAST FORTH AS A BRANCH, IS WITHERED, AND MEN GATHER THEM, CAST THEM INTO THE FIRE, AND THEY ARE BURNED."

**Perplexing:**
Why did Jesus resort to inciting fear, the threat of being consumed by fire, to coerce people into accepting him? Why did he fail to use reason or logic to persuade people to believe in him? Why did he assert that people cannot be productive without him? Why did he not accept people for the way they are if thy are good people?
See also under 15:5, and under MARK 16:16.

15:7 - JESUS: "IF YE ABIDE IN ME, AND MY WORDS ABIDE IN YOU, ASK WHAT YE WILL AND IT SHALL BE DONE UNTO YOU."

**Perplexing:** See under 14:12 and 13 (apparently no one abides in Jesus, and his words do not abide in anyone).

15:8 - JESUS: "HEREIN IS MY FATHER GLORIFIED, THAT YE BEAR MUCH FRUIT...."

**Perplexing:** See under 12:28 and 15:5.

15:9 - JESUS: "AS THE FATHER HAS LOVED ME, SO HAVE I LOVED YOU; CONTINUE IN MY LOVE."

**Contradictions:** See under 10:17, 13:23, and 34-35.

**Perplexing:** See under 10:17.

15:10 - JESUS: "IF YE KEEP MY COMMANDMENTS, YE SHALL ABIDE IN MY LOVE; I HAVE KEPT MY FATHER'S COMMANDMENTS, AND ABIDE IN HIS LOVE."

**Contradiction:** See under 10:17, 13:34-35, 14:31, and 15:9.

15:12 - JESUS: "THIS IS MY COMMANDMENT: LOVE ONE ANOTHER, AS I HAVE LOVED YOU."

**Contradiction:** See under 13:34-35.

**Perplexing:** See under 13:34-35.

15:15 - JESUS: "...ALL THINGS THAT I HAVE HEARD OF MY FATHER I HAVE MADE KNOWN UNTO YOU."

**Contradiction:**
JOHN 10:30 - Jesus: "I and my Father are one."
[Did Jesus hear things from his Father, or did he hear things from himself?]

**Perplexing:**
Where and how did Jesus hear things of his Father? What things did he hear?
Why did Jesus' Father fail to tell him how to help humans create a world free of disease, infirmities, poverty, crime, war, and other calamities? By failing to do so, is He not responsible for the evils that afflict humanity?

15:16 - JESUS: "...I HAVE CHOSEN YOU...THAT YE SHOULD GO AND BRING FORTH FRUIT... THAT WHATSOEVER YE SHALL ASK OF THE FATHER IN MY NAME, HE MAY GIVE IT YOU."

**Contradictions:**
JOHN 14:13-14 - Jesus: "Whatsoever ye shall ask in my name, that will I do.... If ye shall ask anything in my name, I will do it."
[If you ask for something in Jesus' name, will His Father give it, or will Jesus do it?]
See also under 6:70-71 and 14:6.

**Perplexing:** See under 14:12, 13, and MARK 16:17-18.

15:18 - JESUS: "IF THE WORLD HATE YOU, YE KNOW THAT IT HATED ME BEFORE IT HATED YOU."

**Perplexing:**
Why could Jesus or his Father not perform a miracle to prevent the world from hating him and the disciples?
See also under MATT. 24:9.

15:19 - JESUS: "...I HAVE CHOSEN YOU OUT OF THE WORLD; THEREFORE THE WORLD HATETH YOU."

**Contradiction:** See under 6:70-71 and 14:6.

**Perplexing:**
Why was there no reference in the gospels of any hate directed at the disciples? Why would the world hate them? Why could not Jesus perform a miracle to make the world love, rather than hate his disciples?
See also under 15:18.

15:20 - JESUS: ".... IF THEY HAVE PERSECUTED ME, THEY WILL ALSO PERSECUTE YOU...."

**Perplexing:**
Why could not Jesus perform a miracle to prevent him and his disciples from being persecuted? Why did Jesus fail to say that in the future centuries, his followers would be the ones who would do the persecuting and murdering of countless millions of people in his name?
See also under 5:16, and MATT. 24:9.

**History:**
Although there is evidence that in Rome some Christians were persecuted, there is no documentation to show that any of the 12 disciples were persecuted. There is also no evidence to show that the disciples named in the gospels ever existed.
See also under MATT. 24:9.

15:24 - JESUS: "... NOW HAVE THEY SEEN AND HATED BOTH ME AND MY FATHER."

**Contradiction:**
JOHN 10:30 - Jesus: "I and my Father are one."
[Are Jesus and his Father both seen and hated, or is only Jesus, as one with his Father, seen and hated?]

**Perplexing:**
When were both Jesus and his Father seen? When were they hated? Was Jesus equating unbelief with hate? If so, why? Why did Jesus not realize that one may refuse to believe someone without hating that person? Why did he fail to teach his disciples to be tolerant of others? Why did Jesus fail to say that many of his followers would hate people of other religions? Would the victims of Christian persecution and violence be justified in hating the followers of Jesus for all the suffering inflicted upon them?

15:25 - JESUS: "...THAT THE WORD MIGHT BE FULFILLED THAT IS WRITTEN IN THEIR LAW, 'THEY HATED ME WITHOUT A CAUSE.'"

**Old Testament:**
PS. 35:19 - [In a plea to the LORD, David said] "Let not them that are mine enemies wrongfully rejoice over me; neither let them wink with the eye that hate me without a cause."
PS. 69:1-4 - [David said] "Save me, O God.... They that hate me without a cause are more than the hairs of mine head...."

**Perplexing:**
Why did Jesus take verses attributed to David out of context and use them for himself?
See also under 10:34.

15:26 - JESUS: "WHEN THE COMFORTER IS COME, WHOM I WILL SEND UNTO YOU FROM THE FATHER, EVEN THE SPIRIT OF TRUTH, WHICH PROCEEDETH FROM THE FATHER, HE SHALL TESTIFY OF ME."

**Contradiction:**
JOHN 14:16 - Jesus: "I shall pray the Father, and He shall give you another Comforter...."
[Will Jesus, or the Father send the Comforter?]
See also under 14:16-17 and 26.

**Perplexing:**
Why did Jesus need the Comforter to testify of him? When, if ever, did the Comforter testify of Jesus? Why did the gospels and the rest of the New Testament not mention anything about a Comforter having come to the disciples?
See also under 14:16-17.

16:2 - JESUS: "THEY SHALL PUT YOU OUT OF THE SYNAGOGUES; YEA, THE TIME COMETH, THAT WHOSOEVER KILLETH YOU WILL THINK THAT HE DOETH GOD SERVICE."

**Contradiction:**
JOHN 9:22 - ...the Jews had agreed already, that if any man did confess that he was Christ, he should be put out of the synagogue.
[Were the disciples already put out of the synagogues for accepting Jesus as Christ, or were they not yet put out?]

**History:** See under 9:22.

**Perplexing:**
Why did Jesus fail to say that over the centuries to come Christians would kill countless millions of innocent people while claiming to be doing a service for God and for him? Why did or could God not prevent the killing? Does God enjoy having people killed in His service? Why would Jesus be unable to protect his followers from being killed? When were the disciples put out of synagogues? In ACTS, the disciples were still going to synagogues and to the temple.

16:7 - JESUS: "...IF I GO NOT AWAY, THE COMFORTER WILL NOT COME UNTO YOU; BUT IF I DEPART, I WILL SEND HIM UNTO YOU."

**Contradictions:** See under 15:26.

**Perplexing:**
Why cannot Jesus and the Comforter be present at the same time with the disciples?
See also under 14:16-17 and 15:26.

16:8 - JESUS: "WHEN HE IS COME, HE WILL REPROVE THE WORLD OF SIN, AND OF RIGHTEOUSNESS, AND OF JUDGMENT."

**Perplexing:**
Did the Comforter come and reprove the world of sin, righteousness, and judgment? When? If not, why not? If not, why did Jesus mislead the disciples by telling them that he would be sent to them?
See also under 14:16-17 and 15:26.

16:9 - JESUS: "OF SIN, BECAUSE THEY BELIEVE NOT ON ME."

**Perplexing:**
According to Jesus, "sin" is merely not believing on him. Why did Jesus consider something as trivial as unbelief a sin? Why does almighty God even care whether or not anyone believes on Jesus? How can it be a sin, when according to JOHN 6:44 people cannot believe in Jesus unless God so ordains them? Consequently, a person's unbelief is due to God's will. Does the fact that billions of people do not believe on Jesus, mean that the Comforter did not arrive? Does it mean that he failed? Did Jesus lie to the disciples? Why did Jesus fail to perform a miracle to convert everyone to him? Why have Christians failed to pray for the conversion of the world to Jesus? If they have so prayed, why has Jesus and/or God failed to answer their prayer affirmatively?
See also under 6:44.

16:10 - JESUS: "...I GO TO MY FATHER, AND YE SEE ME NO MORE."

**Contradictions:**
JOHN 14:3 - Jesus: "I will come again, and receive you unto myself."
JOHN 16:16 - Jesus: "A little while, and ye shall not see me, and again a little while, and ye shall see me, because I go to the Father."
[Did Jesus say that the disciples would see him no more, or that they would see him?]
JOHN 20:19-29 and 21:1-22 - Jesus was seen by he disciples on three occasions after his resurrection.
[Did the disciples see, or not see, Jesus again?]
See also under 14:28.

**Perplexing:** See under 14:28.

16:11 - JESUS: "OF JUDGMENT, BECAUSE THE PRINCE OF THIS WORLD IS JUDGED."

**Contradiction:**
JOHN 12:31 - Jesus: "Now is the judgment of this world; now shall the prince of this world be cast out."
[Did Jesus say that the prince of the world is yet to be judged, or that he is judged and cast out "now?"]

**Perplexing:**
Why is the prince of the world judged? When? Since he was created by God to do whatever he does, is God or Jesus justified in judging him?
See also under 12:31.

16:13 - JESUS: "WHEN HE, THE SPIRIT OF TRUTH, IS COME, HE WILL GUIDE YOU INTO ALL TRUTH...AND HE WILL SHEW YOU THINGS TO COME."

**Contradiction:** See under 14:16-17.

**Perplexing:**
Did the Spirit of truth come to the disciples and guide them in truth and show them things to come? If so, when? If not, why not?
See also under 14:16-17 and 26.

**Dead Sea Scrolls:** See under 14:16-17.

16:14 - JESUS: "HE SHALL GLORIFY ME...."

**Perplexing:** See under 11:4 and 12:28.

16:16 - JESUS: "A LITTLE WHILE, AND YE SHALL NOT SEE ME, AND AGAIN, A LITTLE WHILE, AND YE SHALL SEE ME, BECAUSE I GO TO THE FATHER."

**Contradictions:** See also under 14:3 and 16:10.

**Perplexing:** See under 16:10.

16:22 - JESUS: "...I WILL SEE YOU AGAIN...."

**Contradiction:** See under 16:10.

16:23 - JESUS: ".... WHATSOEVER YE SHALL ASK THE FATHER IN MY NAME, HE WILL GIVE IT YOU."

**Contradiction:** See under 15:16.

**Perplexing:** See under 14:13, MATT. 7:7, and 21:22.

16:24 - JESUS: "...IN MY NAME ASK, AND YE SHALL RECEIVE...."

**Contradiction:** See under 15:16.

**Perplexing:** See under 14:13, and MATT. 7:7-8, and 21:22.

16:25 - JESUS: "...I SHALL SHEW YOU PLAINLY OF THE FATHER."

**Perplexing:**
Did Jesus show the disciples "plainly of the Father?" If so, when?

16:26 - JESUS: "...I WILL PRAY THE FATHER FOR YOU."

**Contradiction:**
JOHN 10:30 - Jesus: "I and my Father are one."
[Does Jesus have to pray to his Father who is a separate entity, or is Jesus one with his Father?]

**Perplexing:** See under MATT. 6:8 and 14:22-23.

16:30-31 - THE DISCIPLES: "NOW ARE WE SURE THAT THOU KNOWEST ALL THINGS...BY THIS WE BELIEVE THAT THOU CAMEST FORTH FROM GOD." JESUS ANSWERED, "DO YE NOW BELIEVE?"

**Contradictions:**
ACTS 2:22 - Peter: "... Jesus of Nazareth, a man approved of God among you by miracles...which God did by him...."
ACTS 2:30 - Peter: "...God had sworn with an oath to him [David], that of the fruit of his loins, according to the flesh, he would raise up Christ...."
[Did the disciples believe that Jesus came forth from God, or did at least one disciple, Peter, believe that Jesus was a man descended from David and of whom God approved?]
ACTS 13:23 - Paul: "Of this man's [David's] seed hath God according to his promise raised unto Israel a Saviour, Jesus."
ACTS 17:31 - Paul: "...he will judge the world...by that man whom He hath ordained...that He hath raised from the dead."
2 TIM. 2:8 - Paul: "Remember that Jesus Christ of the seed of David was raised from the dead...."
[Did the disciples believe that Jesus came forth from God, or did Paul believe that Jesus was a man descended from David and who God raised from the dead?]

**Perplexing:**
Jesus had told them on numerous occasions either that he was from God or was one with God. Why did they not believe him before now? Why were they not convinced by Jesus' miracles including his ability to raise Lazarus and others from the dead?

16:33 - JESUS: ".... IN THE WORLD YE SHALL HAVE TRIBULATION...."

**Perplexing:**
Why could not Jesus prevent tribulation, especially for his disciples?

17:1 - THESE WORDS SPAKE JESUS, LIFTED UP HIS EYES TO HEAVEN, AND SAID, "FATHER, THE HOUR IS COME; GLORIFY THY SON, THAT THY SON ALSO MAY GLORIFY THEE."

**Contradictions:** See under 10:30, and MATT. 1:18.

**Perplexing:** See under 11:4 and 12:28.

17:2 - JESUS: "THOU HAST GIVEN HIM [JESUS] POWER OVER ALL FLESH, THAT HE SHOULD GIVE ETERNAL LIFE TO AS MANY AS THOU HAST GIVEN HIM."

**Contradictions:** See under 6:44, and under MATT. 19:17-19 (for obtaining eternal life).

**Perplexing:**
If God has predetermined (6:44) who He is going to give to Jesus to receive eternal life, were not Jesus and his followers wasting their time trying to convert everyone to belief in Jesus? Were they not deceiving people by doing so, if God has already made a decision about them? What then was the point of the

crucifixion and resurrection?
See also under 6:44, 14:6, and MATT. 19:16.

**Pagan concept**: See under MATT. 19:16.

17:3 - JESUS: "...THAT THEY MIGHT KNOW THEE THE ONLY TRUE GOD AND JESUS CHRIST, WHOM THOU SENT."

**Contradiction:** See under 12:44.

**Perplexing:**
What is meant by "true God?" Is not a "true god" any god in which a person believes? Meanwhile, a god in whom one does not believe is not "true."

17:4 - JESUS: "I HAVE GLORIFIED THEE ON THE EARTH; I HAVE FINISHED THE WORK WHICH THOU GAVEST ME TO DO."

**Perplexing:**
What work did God give Jesus to do? Jesus said:
in MATT. 10:34, "I came not to send peace, but a sword";
in MATT. 10-35, "I am come to set a man at variance against his father, and the daughter against her mother, and the daughter-in-law against her mother-in-law";
in MARK 10:45, "The Son of man came ... to give his life a ransom for many";
in LUKE 5:32, "I came not to call the righteous, but sinners to repentance";
in LUKE 9:56, "The Son of man is not come to destroy men's lives, but to save them";
in LUKE 12:49, "I am come to send fire on the earth";
in LUKE 12:51, "Suppose ye that I have come to give peace on earth? I tell you, nay, but rather division";
in LUKE 19:10, "The Son of man is come to seek and to save that which was lost."
in 1 JOHN 3:8, John said: "The Son of God was manifested, that he might destroy the works of the devil."
What work did Jesus finish?
According to many Christian clergy, the devil is still around doing his work, so, destroying the works of the devil is one job that Jesus failed to finish.
If Jesus meant that his work was to bring a sword, fire, and division to the earth, one may conclude that indeed he successfully completed his work.
Did he succeed in giving his life as a ransom for many, calling sinners to repentance, saving men's lives, and saving that which was lost?
See also under 11:4 and 12:28.

17:5 - JESUS: "O FATHER, GLORIFY ME WITH THINE OWN SELF WITH THE GLORY WHICH I HAD WITH THEE BEFORE THE WORLD WAS."

**Contradictions:**
JOHN 10:30 - Jesus: "I am one with my Father."
[Is Jesus one with his Father, or is he with his Father as a separate entity?]
See also under 1:13, and MATT. 1:18.

**Perplexing:**
What kind of glory did Jesus have prior to the creation of the world? Why did he need glory in heaven? In ISA. 43:10, God said, "...before Me there was no God formed, neither shall there be after Me." What existed before the world? How was it created? Why was the world created? Who or what created Jesus and his Father? What existed before God?
See also under 11:4.

17:9 - JESUS: "I PRAY FOR THEM; I PRAY NOT FOR THE WORLD, BUT FOR THEM WHICH THOU HAST GIVEN ME, FOR THEY ARE THINE."

**Contradiction:** See under 6:44.

**Perplexing:**
Why did Jesus pray for his followers? For what did he pray? In 16:27, Jesus said that his Father loved them. Was not God's love sufficient for them? Why did Jesus not pray for the world - for God to love all the people of the earth? Did not the world need God's love at least as much as did the disciples? See also under MATT. 14:22-23.

17:10 - JESUS: "ALL MINE ARE THINE, AND THINE ARE MINE, AND I AM GLORIFIED IN THEM."

**Perplexing:** See under 11:4.

17:11 - JESUS: "...I COME TO THEE. HOLY FATHER, KEEP THROUGH THINE OWN NAME THOSE WHOM THOU HAST GIVEN ME, THAT THEY MAY BE ONE AS WE ARE."

**Contradictions:** See under 10:30.

**Perplexing:**
If Jesus is one with his Father, how can he come to Him, and how can his followers be one with Him? See also under 6:44.

17:12 - JESUS: "WHILE I WAS WITH THEM IN THE WORLD, I KEPT THEM...THOSE THAT THOU GAVEST ME; NONE OF THEM IS LOST, BUT THE SON OF PERDITION, THAT THE SCRIPTURE MIGHT BE FULFILLED."

**Contradictions:**
JOHN 6:66 - From that time many of his disciples went back, and walked no more with him.
1 TIM. 4:1 - Paul: "...some shall depart from the faith...."
[Did Jesus lose only one disciple, or many disciples?]
JOHN 18:9 - Jesus: "Of them which Thou gavest me have I lost none."
[Did Jesus lose one disciple, or no disciples?]
See also under 6:44.

**Perplexing:** Why did Jesus have to lose one disciple? To which Scripture verses did he refer? Why was Judas referred to as "the son of perdition," when he was doing God's will - leading to Jesus' resurrection and the creation of Christianity?

17:14 - JESUS: "...THE WORLD HATH HATED THEM...."

**Perplexing:**
How did the world hate them? What hate had been directed against the disciples? Why did JOHN not report any hateful actions directed towards them?
See also under 15:18, 19, 24, and under MATT. 24:9.

17:15 - JESUS: "I PRAY NOT THAT THOU SHOULDEST TAKE THEM OUT OF THE WORLD, BUT THAT THOU SHOULDEST KEEP THEM FROM THE EVIL."

**Perplexing:**
Why did Jesus have to pray that his disciples be protected from the evil? How can evil afflict those who God loves (16:27)?
Why did Jesus and/or his Father fail to eliminate evil?
See also under MATT. 14:22-23 and 19:17-19 (under God being good).

17:20 - JESUS: "NEITHER PRAY I FOR THESE ALONE, BUT FOR THEM ALSO WHICH SHALL BELIEVE ON ME THROUGH THEIR WORD."

**Contradiction:**
JOHN 6:44 - Jesus: "No man can come to me, except the Father which hath sent me draw him...."
[Will people believe on Jesus because of the disciples' word, or because the Father draws them to Jesus?]

**Perplexing:** See under MATT. 14:22-23.

17:21 - JESUS: "THEY ALL MAY BE ONE, AS THOU FATHER ART IN ME, AND I IN THEE, THAT THEY ALSO MAY BE ONE IN US, THAT THE WORLD MAY BELIEVE THAT THOU HAST SENT ME."

**Contradictions:** See under 10:30.

**Perplexing:**
If God wanted the world to believe that He sent Jesus, why did He not tell it to the world directly, or have Jesus prove it by showing himself publicly to have been resurrected after the crucifixion?
See also under 17:11.

17:22 - JESUS: "THE GLORY WHICH THOU GAVEST ME I HAVE GIVEN THEM, THAT THEY MAY BE ONE, EVEN AS WE ARE ONE."

**Contradictions:** See under 10:30.

**Perplexing:** See under 11:4.

17:23 - JESUS: "I IN THEM, AND THOU IN ME, THAT THEY MAY BE MADE PERFECT IN ONE, THAT THE WORLD MAY KNOW THAT THOU HAST SENT ME, AND HAST LOVED THEM, AS THOU HAST LOVED ME."

**Contradiction:** See under 10:17.

**Perplexing:** See under 10:17.

17:24 - JESUS: "FATHER, I WILL THAT THEY WHOM THOU HAST GIVEN ME, BE WITH ME WHERE I AM, THAT THEY MAY BEHOLD MY GLORY, WHICH THOU HAST GIVEN ME, FOR THOU LOVEDST ME BEFORE THE FOUNDATION OF THE WORLD."

**Contradiction:** See under 10:17.

**Perplexing:**
Why is Jesus obsessed with showing off his glory, especially to mere humans?
See also under 10:17, 11:4, and 17:5.

17:25 - JESUS: "...THOU HAST SENT ME."

**Contradictions:** See under 10:30.

17:26 - JESUS: "...THOU HAST LOVED ME...."

**Contradictions:** See under 15:9.

18:1 - ...HE WENT FORTH WITH HIS DISCIPLES OVER THE BROOK CEDRON, WHERE WAS A GARDEN, INTO WHICH HE ENTERED, AND HIS DISCIPLES.

**Contradiction:**
MATT. 26:30, MARK 14:26, and LUKE 22:39 - Jesus and the disciples went to the mount of Olives.
[Did Jesus and the disciples go to a garden past the brook Cedron, or to the mount of Olives?]

18:3 - JUDAS, HAVING RECEIVED A BAND OF MEN AND OFFICERS FROM THE CHIEF PRIESTS AND PHARISEES, COMETH THITHER WITH LANTERNS, TORCHES, AND WEAPONS.

**Language:**
The Greek translated as "a band" means "a cohort"; a Roman cohort consisted of from 200 - 600 men.

**Contradictions:**
MATT. 26:47 - ...Judas came with a great multitude with swords and staves, from the chief priests and elders of the people.
[Did Judas come with a band of men from the chief priests and Pharisees, or with a great multitude from the chief priests and elders?]
MARK 14:43 - ...cometh Judas with a great multitude with swords and staves, from the chief priests, scribes, and elders.
[Did Judas come with a band of men from the chief priests and Pharisees, or with a great multitude from the chief priests, scribes, and elders?]
LUKE 22:47-52 - ...a multitude, and Judas drew near unto Jesus.... .... Then Jesus said unto the chief priests, captains of the temple, and the elders which were come to him....

[Did Judas come with a band of men from the chief priests and Pharisees, or with the chief priests, temple captains, and elders?]

**Perplexing:**
How could the chief priests and Pharisees provide Judas with a band (cohort) when they did not have troops, especially Roman troops or police, at their disposal? What qualifications did Judas have to command a cohort of Roman troops? Why would anti-Jewish Pilate put a Jew in command of Romans? Why would he even permit Roman soldiers to go out to arrest someone who had not been charged yet with any crime against Rome? Why was it necessary to send 200 - 600 men to arrest one person? Why would the chief priests and Pharisees want to arrest, rather than befriend, someone who could perform miracles including raising the dead?

18:4 - JESUS KNOWING ALL THINGS THAT SHOULD COME UPON HIM, SAID UNTO THEM, "WHOM SEEK YE?"

**Contradictions:**
MATT. 26:48-50 - ...[Judas]: "Whomsoever I shall kiss, that same is he; hold him fast." He came to Jesus, said, "Hail, Master," and kissed him. Jesus said, "Friend, wherefore art thou come?"....
MARK 14:44-45 - ...[Judas]: "Whomsoever I shall kiss, that same is he; take him, and lead him away safely." As soon as he was come, he goeth to him, and saith, "Master, master," and kissed him.
LUKE 22:47-48 - ...[Judas]...drew near unto Jesus to kiss him. Jesus said, "Judas, betrayest thou the Son of man with a kiss?"
[Did Jesus speak to the men, or to Judas?]
[Did Jesus ask the men who they wanted, or did Judas kiss Jesus to identify him?]
[Did Jesus know all things that were to happen to him, or did he have to ask who the men wanted, address Judas as "friend" and ask him why he had come?]
MATT. 9:4, 12:25, MARK 2:8, LUKE 5:22, 6:8, 9:47, and 11:17 - Jesus knew people's thoughts.
[Did Jesus have to ask the men who they wanted, or did he know their thoughts?]

**Perplexing:**
If Jesus knew all things that were to happen to him, why did he have to ask the men who they sought? Why did he not identify himself and voluntarily offer to go with them?

18:5-6 - THEY ANSWERED, "JESUS OF NAZARETH." JESUS SAID, "I AM HE." .... THEY WENT BACKWARD, AND FELL TO THE GROUND.

**Contradictions:**
MATT. 26:50 and MARK 14:46 - [After Judas kissed Jesus]...they laid hands on Jesus, and took him.
[Did the men fall down after he identified himself, or did they seize him after he was kissed by Judas?]
LUKE 22:50-54 - [After Judas approached Jesus to kiss him].... One of them smote the servant of the high priest, and cut off his right ear.... He [Jesus] touched his ear, and healed him. Jesus said to the chief priests, captains of the temple, and the elders... "Be ye come out, as against a thief, with swords and staves? When I was daily in the temple, ye stretched forth no hands against me.... They took him....
[Did the men fall down after Jesus identified himself, or did Jesus speak to the chief priests, temple captains, and elders before they seized him?]

**Perplexing:**
Since 200 - 600 men would cover a sizable area, how could they all have heard Jesus identify himself? Why did they ask for Jesus of Nazareth, rather than Jesus of Galilee, or Jesus of Bethlehem? Why did they fall down?

**Pagan concept:**
Many primitive people believed that names had magical powers; that they possessed the power of the named person.
See also under MARK 5:8-9.

18:7-8 - ASKED HE AGAIN, "WHOM SEEK YE?" THEY SAID, "JESUS OF NAZARETH." JESUS ANSWERED, "I TOLD YOU THAT I AM HE; IF THEREFORE YE SEEK ME, LET THESE GO THEIR WAY."

**Contradictions:** See under 18:4 and 5-6.

**Perplexing:**
Why did Jesus again ask them who they wanted, after they said, "Jesus of Nazareth?" Why did he imply that he did not know who they wanted? JOHN 18:4 stated that he knew "all things that should come upon him." Why did the men not fall down when Jesus identified himself the second time?

18:9 - THAT THE SAYING MIGHT BE FULFILLED, WHICH HE SPAKE, "OF THEM WHICH THOU GAVEST ME HAVE I LOST NONE."

**Contradiction:** See under 6:39.

**Perplexing:**
From where did Jesus obtain the saying that he cited? It is not in the Old Testament.

18:10 - SIMON PETER HAVING A SWORD, SMOTE THE HIGH PRIEST'S SERVANT, AND CUT OFF HIS RIGHT EAR. THE SERVANT'S NAME WAS MALCHUS.

**Language**: See under MATT. 26:51.

**Contradictions:** See under LUKE 22:36 and 22:50-51.

**Perplexing:** See under MATT. 26:51 and LUKE 22:36.

18:11 - SAID JESUS, "PUT UP THY SWORD INTO THE SHEATH; THE CUP WHICH MY FATHER HATH GIVEN ME, SHALL I NOT DRINK?"

**Perplexing:** See under MATT. 26:51 and LUKE 36.

18:12 - THE BAND, CAPTAINS, AND OFFICERS OF THE JEWS TOOK JESUS AND BOUND HIM.

**Contradictions:**
MATT. 26:49-50 and MARK 14:45-46 - He [Judas]...kissed him. .... Then they laid hands on Jesus, and took him.

[Was Jesus seized after speaking to the men (18:4-8) and after the ear cutting incident, or immediately after Judas kissed him before the ear cutting incident (18:10)?]
See also under 18:3.

**Perplexing:**
Why was Peter not seized for having attacked the high priest's servant?
See also under 18:3.

**Language**: See under 18:3.

18:13 - [THE BAND] LED HIM AWAY TO ANNAS FIRST; HE WAS FATHER-IN-LAW TO CAIAPHAS, THE HIGH PRIEST THAT YEAR.

**Contradictions:**
MATT. 26:57 - They that had laid hold on Jesus led him away to Caiaphas the high priest....
MARK 14:53 - They led Jesus away to the high priest....
LUKE 22:54 - They...brought him into the high priest's house. ....
[Was Jesus brought to Annas, or to the high priest?]
LUKE 3:2 - Annas and Caiaphas being the high priests....
[Was Annas the father-in-law of Caiaphas, or was he a high priest along with Caiaphas?]
ACTS 4:6 - Annas the high priest, and Caiaphas...were at Jerusalem.
[Was Caiaphas, or Annas the high priest?]

**History:** See under LUKE 3:2.

18:15 - SIMON PETER FOLLOWED JESUS, AND SO DID ANOTHER DISCIPLE KNOWN TO THE HIGH PRIEST, AND WENT IN WITH JESUS INTO THE PALACE OF THE HIGH PRIEST.

**Contradictions:**
MATT. 26:58 - Peter followed him afar off unto the high priest's palace, and went in....
MARK 14:54 - Peter followed him afar off, into the palace of the high priest....
LUKE 22:54 - They brought him [Jesus] into the high priest's house, and Peter followed afar off.
[Did Peter and another disciple follow Jesus into the high priest's palace, or did Peter alone follow and enter the palace?]
[Did Peter and another disciple enter the palace with Jesus, or did they follow afar off and enter after Jesus?]

**Perplexing:**
Who was the other disciple? Why was he not identified? How well was he known by the high priest? How did the high priest come to know this disciple? Did JOHN invent this disciple to explain how Peter was able to enter the palace?

18:16 - PETER STOOD AT THE DOOR WITHOUT. THEN WENT OUT THAT OTHER DISCIPLE ... SPAKE UNTO HER THAT KEPT THE DOOR, AND BROUGHT IN PETER.

**Contradiction:**
MATT. 26:58 - Peter...went in....

MARK 14:54 - Peter followed...into the palace....
LUKE 22:54 - Peter followed afar off [and into the high priest's house].
[Did the other disciple have to speak to the doorkeeper to allow Peter to enter, or did Peter enter alone on his own?]

18:17 - SAITH THE DAMSEL THAT KEPT THE DOOR UNTO PETER, "ART NOT THOU ALSO ONE OF THIS MAN'S DISCIPLES?" HE SAITH, "I AM NOT."

**Contradictions:**
MATT. 26:69-70 - Peter sat without in the palace; a damsel came unto him saying, "Thou also wast with Jesus of Galilee." He denied before them all [servants], saying, "I know not what thou sayest."
[Was Peter asked if he is one of Jesus' disciples, or was he accused of being with Jesus of Galilee?]
MARK 14:66-68 - As Peter was beneath in the palace [with the servants], there cometh one of the maids of the high priest...and said, "Thou also wast with Jesus of Nazareth." He denied, saying, "I know not, neither understand I what thou sayest." He went out into the porch, and the cock crew.
[Was Peter asked if he is one of Jesus' disciples, or was he accused of being with Jesus of Nazareth?"]
[Was Peter questioned by the doorkeeper, or by a damsel/maid?]
[Did not, or did a cock crow?]
LUKE 22:56-57 - A maid beheld Peter as he sat by the fire [with the men who had brought Jesus], earnestly looked upon him, and said, "This man was also with him." He denied, saying, "Woman, I know him not."
[Was Peter questioned at the door by the doorkeeper, or after he had entered the palace did a maid say that he had been with Jesus?]
[Was Peter alone, or with the servants when a woman spoke to him?]
See also under MATT. 26:69.

**Perplexing:**
Where was the other disciple? Why was he not identified as having been with Jesus?
See also under 18:15, and under MATT. 26:69, 70-72.

18:18 - THE SERVANTS AND OFFICERS STOOD THERE, MADE FIRE, FOR IT WAS COLD, AND THEY WARMED THEMSELVES; PETER STOOD WITH THEM....

**Contradictions:**
MATT. 26:58 - Peter...sat with the servants to see the end [before a damsel spoke to him].
MARK 14:54 - Peter...sat with the servants, and warmed himself at the fire [before a maid spoke to him].
LUKE 22:55 - When they had kindled a fire...Peter sat down among them in the hall [before a maid spoke to him].
[Did Peter stand with the servants and officers, or did he sit with the servants and/or "them"?]
[Was Peter with the servants after, or before he was accused of having been with Jesus?]
See also under MATT. 26:58.

**Perplexing:**
Why did the servants and officers allow Peter to sit with them after he had cut off the ear of one of the servants? Why did the affected servant not demand that Peter be arrested? Why was the other disciple not questioned?

18:19 - THE HIGH PRIEST ASKED JESUS OF HIS DISCIPLES, AND OF HIS DOCTRINE.

**Contradictions:**
JOHN 18:24 - Now Annas had sent him bound unto Caiaphas the high priest.
[Was Jesus questioned by Caiaphas the high priest, or by Annas (18:13) who then sent him to Caiaphas?]
MATT. 26:59-63 - The chief priests, elders, and all the council, sought false witness against Jesus.... At last came two false witnesses, and said, "This fellow said, 'I am able to destroy the temple of God, and to build it in three days.'" The high priest said, "Answerest thou nothing what these witness against thee?" Jesus held his peace. The high priest said, "I adjure thee by the living Gcd, that thou tell us whether thou be the Christ, the Son of God."
MARK 14:55-61 - The chief priests and council sought witness against Jesus.... .... Certain bare false witness, saying, "We heard him say, 'I will destroy this temple that is made with hands, and within three days I will build another made without hands.'" .... The high priest asked Jesus, "Answerest thou nothing what these witness against thee?" He answered nothing. The high priest asked, "Art thou the Christ, the Son of the Blessed?"
[Were not, or were false witnesses sought?]
[Did not, or did false witnesses testify against Jesus?]
[Was Jesus asked about his disciples and doctrine, or to respond to false witnesses and to say whether he was the Christ?]
LUKE 22:66-67 - As soon as it was day, the elders of the people, chief priests, and scribes said, "Art thou the Christ?"
[Was Jesus questioned at night after being brought to the high priest's palace, or when it was day?]
[Was Jesus questioned by the high priest, or by the elders, chief priests, and scribes?]
[Was Jesus asked about his disciples and doctrine, or only whether he was the Christ?]

18:20-21 - JESUS ANSWERED, "I SPAKE OPENLY TO THE WORLD; I EVER TAUGHT IN THE SYNAGOGUE, AND IN THE TEMPLE, WHITHER THE JEWS ALWAYS RESORT, AND IN SECRET HAVE I SAID NOTHING. WHY ASKETH THOU ME? ASK THEM WHICH HEARD ME, WHAT I HAVE SAID...."

**Contradictions:**
MATT. 26:64 - Jesus saith, "Thou hast said; nevertheless, I say unto you, hereafter shall ye see the Son of man sitting on the right hand of power, and coming in the clouds of heaven."
MARK 14:62 - Jesus said, "I am; and ye shall see the Son of man sitting on the right hand of power, and coming in the clouds of heaven."
LUKE 22:67-70 - .... He said, "If I tell you, ye will not believe; if I also ask you, ye will not answer me, nor let me go. Hereafter shall the Son of man sit on the right hand of the power of God." They said, "Art thou then the Son of God?" He said, "Ye say that I am."
[Did Jesus tell the high priest that he spoke openly and taught in the synagogue and temple, and that the high priest should ask those who heard him, or did he acknowledge that he was the Christ, the Son of God, that he would sit on God's right hand, and that the high priest would see him coming in the clouds of heaven?]
MATT. 13:11-13 - He [Jesus] said, "It is given unto you to know the mysteries of the kingdom of heaven, but to them it is not given. .... Speak I to them in parables, because they seeing see not, and hearing they hear not, neither do they understand."
MARK 4:11-12 - He [Jesus] said, "Unto you it is given to know the mystery of the kingdom of God; but unto them that are without, all these things are done in parables, that seeing they may see, and not perceive,

and hearing they may hear, and not understand, lest at any time they should be converted, and their sins should be forgiven them."
[Did Jesus speak openly to the world, or did he speak in parables so that people would not know what he meant, and, therefore, would not convert and have their sins forgiven?]

18:22 - WHEN HE HAD SPOKEN, ONE OF THE OFFICERS STRUCK JESUS WITH THE PALM OF HIS HAND, SAYING, "ANSWEREST THE HIGH PRIEST SO?"

**Contradictions:**

MATT. 26:67-68 - Then did they spit in his face, and buffeted him; others smote him with the palms of their hands, saying, "Prophesy unto us, thou Christ: Who is he that smote thee?"
[Did one officer strike Jesus, or did several people strike him?]
MARK 14:65 - Some began to spit on him, cover his face, buffet him, and say, "Prophesy"; and the servants did strike him with the palms of their hands.
[Did one officer, or servants strike Jesus?]
LUKE 22:63-64 - The men that held Jesus mocked, and smote him. They struck him on the face, and asked him, "Prophesy, who smote thee?"
[Did one officer, or the men who held Jesus strike him?]
[Was he asked about how he spoke to the high priest, or was he told to prophesy who struck him?]

**Perplexing:**

In 18:13, Jesus was brought to Annas, the high priest's father-in-law; he was not reported to have been sent to Caiaphas the high priest until 18:24. Why then did the officer refer to Annas as the high priest?
Why was the officer not afraid to strike someone who could perform miracles including resurrecting the dead?

18:23 - JESUS ANSWERED, "IF I HAVE SPOKEN EVIL, BEAR WITNESS OF THE EVIL; IF WELL, WHY SMITEST THOU ME?"

**Contradiction:**

JOHN 18:4 - Jesus knowing all things that should come upon him....
[Did Jesus not know, or did he know why the officer struck him?]

18:24 - NOW ANNAS HAD SENT HIM BOUND UNTO CAIAPHAS THE HIGH PRIEST.

**Contradictions:**

MATT. 26:57 - They that had laid hold on Jesus led him away to Caiaphas....
MARK 14:53 - They [those who had seized Jesus] led Jesus away to the high priest [MARK did not identify the high priest]....
LUKE 22:54 - Took they [those who had seized Jesus] him, into the high priest's house [LUKE 3:2 said that both Annas and Caiaphas were the high priests].
[Did the people who seized Jesus take him to the high priest, or did Annas send him to the high priest?]
See also under 18:13.

**Perplexing:**

In 18:19, the high priest questioned Jesus, and in 18:22, an officer struck Jesus for the way he spoke to the high priest. Was Jesus first sent to the high priest by Annas now, or was he with him previously?
See also under 18:22.

18:25 - SIMON PETER STOOD AND WARMED HIMSELF. THEY SAID, "ART NOT THOU ALSO ONE OF HIS DISCIPLES?" HE DENIED IT, AND SAID, "I AM NOT."

**Contradictions:**
MATT. 26:71-72 - When he was gone out into the porch, another maid saw him, and said unto them that were there, "This fellow was also with Jesus of Nazareth." He denied with an oath, "I do not know the man."
[Did the people standing around Peter ask him if he was one of Jesus' disciples, or did a maid tell people that he had been with Jesus of Nazareth?]
[Was Peter standing around the fire warming himself, or was he out on the porch?]
MARK 14:69-70 - A maid saw him again, and began to say to them that stood by, "This is one of them." He denied it again....
[Did the people with Peter ask him if he was one of Jesus' disciples, or did a maid tell people that he "is one of them?"]
LUKE 22:58 - After a while another saw him, and said, "Thou art also of them." Peter said, "Man, I am not."
[Did people question Peter, or did a man say that he was one of them?]

**Perplexing:** See under 18:17.

18:26-27 - ONE OF THE SERVANTS OF THE HIGH PRIEST, BEING HIS KINSMAN WHOSE EAR PETER CUT OFF, SAITH, "DID NOT I SEE THEE IN THE GARDEN WITH HIM?" PETER DENIED AGAIN, AND IMMEDIATELY THE COCK CREW.

**Contradictions:**
MATT. 26:73-74 - After a while came unto him they that stood by, and said, "Surely thou also art one of them, for thy speech betrayeth thee." Then began he to curse and swear, saying, "I know not the man," and immediately the cock crew.
MARK 14:70-72 - .... A little after, they that stood by said, "Surely thou art one of them, for thou art a Galilean, and thy speech agreeth thereto." He began to curse and swear, saying, "I know not this man of whom ye speak." And the second time the cock crew.
[Did a relative of the servant whose ear Peter cut off ask Peter if he had been in the garden with Jesus, or did people standing by say that he was one of them because of his speech?]
[Did the cock crow after the servant spoke to Peter, or after the nearby people spoke to him?]
[Did the ccck crow for the first and only time, or for the second time?]
LUKE 22:59 -61 - About the space of one hour after another confidently affirmed, "Of a truth this fellow also was with him, for he is a Galilean." Peter said, "Man, I know not what thou sayest." Immediately, while he yet spake, the cock crew. The Lord turned, and looked upon Peter. ....
[Was Peter questioned by a relative of the servant whose ear he cut off, or did a man say that Peter was a Galilean?]
[Did the cock crow after Peter was questioned by a relative of the servant whose ear he cut off, or after a man said that he was a Galilean?]

**Perplexing:**
Why did the other disciple not remain with Peter? Where did he go? What did he do? Why has he disappeared from the account? Why was Peter not pointed out as the one who cut off the servant's ear, especially, if the servant's relative was in the garden at the time?

**History:** See under MATT. 26:34.

18:28-29 - THEN LED THEY JESUS FROM CAIAPHAS UNTO THE HALL OF JUDGMENT; IT WAS EARLY; THEY THEMSELVES WENT NOT INTO THE HALL, LEST THEY SHOULD BE DEFILED, BUT THAT THEY MIGHT EAT THE PASSOVER. PILATE WENT OUT UNTO THEM, AND SAID, "WHAT ACCUSATION BRING YE AGAINST THIS MAN?"

**Contradictions:**

MATT. 26:19-21 - The disciples made ready the Passover. When the even was come, he sat down with the twelve. They did eat. [Then] In MATT. 27:1-2 - When morning was come...they had bound him, led him away, and delivered him to Pontius Pilate the governor.

MARK 14:16-18 - His disciples made ready the Passover. In the evening he cometh with the twelve. They did sit down and eat. [Then] In MARK 15:1 - In the morning...[they] bound Jesus and delivered him to Pilate.

LUKE 22:13-15 - They made ready the Passover. When the hour was come he sat down, and the twelve apostles with him. He said, "I have desired to eat this Passover meal with you before I suffer." [Then] In LUKE 23:1 - the whole multitude led him unto Pilate.

[Was Jesus taken to Pilate before he had a chance to eat the Passover meal, or after he and his disciples partook of it?]

[Was Jesus taken to Pilate the day before Passover, or on Passover day?]

See also under MATT. 27:1-2.

**History:**

Jews believed that they would be defiled for seven days by entering a pagan residence. This belief, however, did not exist among Jews at the time the reported incident is said to have occurred. There is no non-biblical record of Jews taking Jesus to Pilate.

See also under MATT. 27:1-2.

**Perplexing:**

Would the historical, vehemently anti-Jewish Pilate have inconvenienced himself and condescended to meet with a group of Jews outside the hall in deference to their religious belief (especially when that belief had not yet come into existence)?

See also under MATT. 27:1-2.

18:30 - THEY SAID, "IF HE WERE NOT A MALEFACTOR, WE WOULD NOT HAVE DELIVERED HIM UP UNTO THEE."

**Contradictions:**

MARK 15:3 - The chief priests accused him of many things [after Pilate asked him in 15:2, if he is the King of the Jews]....

[Was Jesus accused of being a malefactor, or accused of many things?]

[Was Jesus accused before, or after being questioned by Pilate?]

LUKE 23:2 - They began to accuse him, saying, "We found this fellow perverting the nation, and forbidding to give tribute to Caesar, saying that he himself is Christ a King."

[Was Jesus accused of being a malefactor, or of perverting the nation, forbidding the giving of tribute to Caesar, and calling himself a king?]

18:31 - SAID PILATE, "TAKE HIM, AND JUDGE HIM ACCORDING TO YOUR LAW." THE JEWS SAID, "IT IS NOT LAWFUL FOR US TO PUT ANY MAN TO DEATH."

**Perplexing:**
Why would the Jews want Jesus put to death? He was not said to have committed any crime for which Jewish law would require capital punishment.

**History:** See under MATT. 26:59-60.

18:33 - PILATE ENTERED INTO THE JUDGMENT HALL AGAIN, CALLED JESUS, AND SAID, "ART THOU THE KING OF THE JEWS?"

**Perplexing:**
Why did Pilate ask Jesus if he was King of the Jews? In JOHN, the Jews did not accuse Jesus of calling himself a king; they referred to him only as a malefactor (18:30).
Why did the anti-Jewish Pilate acquiesce to a group of Jews and bother to take Jesus into the judgment hall for questioning? Did he suspect Jesus of being involved in some type of anti-Roman activity?
Why did Pilate not ask Jesus about the miracles he performed? Why did he appear to be ignorant of Jesus' miraculous works including raising the dead?
See also under MATT. 27:11.

**History:**
If Jesus had declared himself to be a king without first obtaining approval from Rome to do so, he would have been in violation of Roman law and, hence, subject to interrogation by Pilate. There is, however, no record of Jesus having appeared before or having been questioned by Pilate. There is no mention of Jesus in Pilate's existing court documents.
See also under MATT. 27:11.

18:34 - JESUS ANSWERED, "SAYEST THIS THING OF THYSELF, OF, DID OTHERS TELL IT THEE?"

**Contradiction:**
MATT. 27:11, MARK 15:2, and LUKE 23:3 - Jesus: "Thou sayest."
[Did Jesus ask Pilate if he said it himself or heard it, or did he concur that he was King of the Jews?]

18:35 - PILATE ANSWERED, "AM I A JEW? THINE OWN NATION AND THE CHIEF PRIESTS HAVE DELIVERED THEE UNTO ME; WHAT HAST THOU DONE?"

**Contradictions:**
MATT. 27:13 - Pilate said, "Hearest thou not how many things they witness against thee?"
MARK 15:4 - Pilate asked, "Behold how many things they witness against thee."
[Did Pilate ask Jesus what he had done, or say that many things were witnessed against him?]
LUKE 23:4 - Pilate said to the chief priests and people, "I find no fault in this man."
[Did Pilate ask Jesus what he had done, or did he say that he found no fault in Jesus?]

**Perplexing:**
Why did Pilate ask Jesus, rather that the priests, what he had done? Did the priests fail to specify the crimes of which they were accusing Jesus, other than calling him a "malefactor?"

18:36 - JESUS ANSWERED, "MY KINGDOM IS NOT OF THIS WORLD; IF MY KINGDOM WERE OF THIS WORLD, THEN WOULD MY SERVANTS FIGHT, THAT I SHOULD NOT BE DELIVERED TO THE JEWS, BUT NOW IS MY KINGDOM NOT FROM HENCE."

**Contradictions:**
MATT. 27:14 - He answered him never a word; the governor marvelled greatly.
MARK 15:5 - Jesus answered nothing, so that Pilate marvelled.
[Did Jesus say that his kingdom is not of this world, or did he say nothing?]
LUKE 23:5 - They said, "He stirreth up the people, teaching throughout all Jewry, beginning from Galilee to this place."
[Did Jesus say that his kingdom is not of this world, or did the priests say that he stirred up the people?]
MATT. 27:11, MARK 15:2, and LUKE 23:3 - Jesus concurred with the claim that he is King of the Jews.
[Did Jesus say that his kingdom is not of this world, or did he claim to be King of the Jews?]
LUKE 1:32-33 - [The angel Gabriel told Mary] "...the Lord God shall give him the throne of his father David, and he shall reign over the house of Jacob forever...."
[Is Jesus' kingdom not of this world, or is he to sit on David's throne reigning over the house of Jacob on earth?]

**Perplexing:**
Why did Jesus use the phrase, "delivered to the Jews," when he too was a Jew?

18:37 - PILATE SAID, "ART THOU A KING THEN?" JESUS: "THOU SAYEST THAT I AM A KING. TO THIS END WAS I BORN, AND FOR THIS CAUSE CAME I INTO THE WORLD, THAT I SHOULD BEAR WITNESS UNTO THE TRUTH. EVERYONE THAT IS OF THE TRUTH HEARETH THY VOICE."

**Contradictions:**
JOHN 18:36 - Jesus: "My kingdom is not of this world."
[Did Jesus come into the world to be a king, or is his kingdom not of this world?]
MATT. 27:14 and MARK 15:5 - Jesus did not answer Pilate.
[Did Jesus engage in a discourse with Pilate, or did he remain silent?]

**History:** See under MATT. 27:11.

18:38 - PILATE SAITH, "WHAT IS TRUTH?" WHEN HE HAD SAID THIS, HE WENT OUT AGAIN UNTO THE JEWS, AND SAITH, "I FIND IN HIM NO FAULT AT ALL."

**Perplexing:**
Why did Pilate say that he found no fault in Jesus, after Jesus claimed to be a king in violation of Roman law? Why did Jesus not respond to Pilate's question about truth? Would the vehemently anti-Jewish Pilate have inconvenienced himself again by going out to speak to a group of Jews? If Pilate really found no fault in Jesus, he could have freed him. Why did he not do so?
See also under LUKE 23:4.

**History:**
Pilate would have been arrested and possibly executed for freeing a person who committed what was a capital crime (treason) under Roman law. Although there is no evidence for the meeting between Pilate and Jesus, the pagan Pilate was canonized by the Coptic and Abyssinian Churches for the statement that he found no fault in Jesus. (The later assertions in 19:1 that he scourged Jesus and in 19:18 that he had him crucified are ignored by these Churches. One may wonder whether they would have canonized Pilate had he released Jesus.)
The oldest known fragment of the Gospel of JOHN consists of verses 37 and 38; it was found in Egypt and has been dated to between A.D. 100 - 120.
See also under MATT. 27:11 and LUKE 23:4

18:39 - PILATE: "YE HAVE A CUSTOM, THAT I SHOULD RELEASE UNTO YOU ONE AT THE PASSOVER; WILL YE THAT I RELEASE UNTO YOU THE KING OF THE JEWS?"

**Contradictions:**
LUKE 23:6-7 - [After Pilate said that he found no fault in Jesus]...he asked whether the man [Jesus] were a Galilean. As soon as he knew that he belonged unto Herod's jurisdiction, he sent him to Herod, who was at Jerusalem at that time.
[Did Pilate ask the people about releasing Jesus, or did he send Jesus to Herod?]
See also under MARK 15:9.

**History:** See under 18:38, and MATT. 27:11, 15, 17, 21, and 22.

**Perplexing:** See under MATT. 27:17.

18:40 - THEN CRIED THEY ALL, "NOT HIS MAN, BUT BARABBAS." BARABBAS WAS A ROBBER.

**Contradictions:**
MATT. 27:16 - They had a notable prisoner, called Barabbas.
[Was Barabbas a robber, or a notable prisoner?]
MARK 15:7 - There was one named Barabbas, which lay bound with them that had made insurrection with him, who had committed murder in the insurrection.
LUKE 23:18-19 - Barabbas (who for a certain sedition made in the city, and for murder, was cast into prison).
[Was Barabbas a robber, or a murderer and rebel?]
ACTS 3:14 - Peter: "Ye denied the Holy One and the Just, and desired a murderer to be granted unto you."
[Was Barabbas a robber, or a murderer?]

**Perplexing:** See under MATT. 27:20.

**Language**: See under MATT. 27:16.

19:1 - PILATE TOOK JESUS AND SCOURGED HIM.

**Perplexing:** See under MATT. 27:26.

19:2 - THE SOLDIERS PLATTED A CROWN OF THORNS, PUT IT ON HIS HEAD, AND THEY PUT ON HIM A PURPLE ROBE.

**Contradictions:** See under MARK 15:16-17.

**Perplexing:**
Why was the meeting between Jesus and Herod not reported by the other gospels?

**History:** See under MATT. 27:28.

19:4 - PILATE WENT FORTH AGAIN, AND SAITH, "I BRING HIM TO YOU, THAT YE MAY KNOW THAT I FIND NO FAULT IN HIM."

**Perplexing:** See under 18:38, and under LUKE 23:4.

**History:** See under 18:38, and under LUKE 23:4.

19:6 - THE CHIEF PRIESTS AND OFFICERS CRIED OUT, "CRUCIFY HIM; CRUCIFY HIM." PILATE SAITH, "TAKE HIM, AND CRUCIFY HIM, FOR I FIND NO FAULT IN HIM."

**Perplexing:**
Since crucifixion was a Roman, not a Jewish, means of execution, why did Pilate tell the Jews to crucify Jesus, especially after the Jews told him (in 18:31), "It is not lawful for us to put any man to death?" Where were the multitudes of people that Jesus had healed or those, such as Lazarus, he had resurrected? Why did none of these people come to be witnesses for Jesus?
See also under 18:38, and under MATT. 27:22.

**History:** See under 18:38.

19:7 - THE JEWS ANSWERED, "WE HAVE A LAW, AND BY OUR LAW HE OUGHT TO DIE, BECAUSE HE MADE HIMSELF THE SON OF GOD."

**Contradictions:**
MARK 15:3 - The chief priests accused him of many things....
[Did the Jews accuse Jesus of making himself the Son of God, or did they accuse him of many things?]
LUKE 23:2 - They [the Jews] began to accuse him saying, "We found this fellow perverting the nation, forbidding tribute to be given to Caesar, saying that he is Christ a King."
[Did the Jews accuse Jesus of making himself the Son of God, or of crimes against Rome including calling himself a king?]
JOHN 18:30 - They said, "If he were not a malefactor, we would not have delivered him to thee."
[Did the Jews accuse Jesus of making himself the Son of God, or of being a malefactor?]

**History:**
The Jews had no law requiring a person to be killed for calling himself a Son of God. Under Jewish law such a claim was not considered to be blasphemy. The death penalty for blasphemy also was no longer in existence. If a person had committed a capital offense, execution under Jewish law would have been by stoning, not by crucifixion. See also 18:31 - at this time the Jews did not execute people.

See also under MATT. 26:59-60.

**Perplexing:** See under 18:31, and MATT. 26:65.

**Judaism:** See under MATT. 26:63.

19:8 - WHEN PILATE HEARD THAT SAYING, HE WAS THE MORE AFRAID.

**History:**
Pilate, as governor, had hundreds, if not thousands, of Roman troops available. He did not hesitate to use them to massacre Jews when they publicly opposed his actions.

**Perplexing:**
Why was Pilate, with Roman troops at his command, afraid of a group of Jews? Why was Pilate afraid of a Jew who called himself a Son of God, when he as a Roman did not believe in the Jewish God?

19:11 - JESUS ANSWERED [PILATE], "...HE THAT DELIVERED ME UNTO THEE HATH THE GREATER SIN."

**Perplexing:**
To whom did Jesus refer? Was it to Caiaphas, or to Judas Iscariot? Why was turning Jesus over to Pilate a sin? Was it not God's will? Should not whoever did it be commended for being obedient to God and for contributing to the creation of Christianity? Since the entire affair was designed by God, was Jesus accusing God of sinning?

19:12 - FROM THENCEFORTH PILATE SOUGHT TO RELEASE HIM, BUT THE JEWS CRIED OUT, SAYING, "IF THOU LET THIS MAN GO, THOU ART NOT CAESAR'S FRIEND; WHOSOEVER MAKETH HIMSELF A KING SPEAKETH AGAINST CAESAR."

**Contradictions:**
JOHN 19:7 - The Jews answered, "...he ought to die, because he made himself the Son of God."
[Did Jews claim that Jesus spoke against Caesar by making himself a king, or did they say that he ought to die because he made himself the Son of God?]
See under 19:7.

**Perplexing:**
Pilate had the authority to release Jesus if he wanted, and he had the military to support him. Why then did he not do so? Why did the Jews have to point out to Pilate what he should have known - that calling oneself a king is treason, and that by releasing such an individual Pilate would be placing himself in a very precarious situation risking arrest and possible execution?
See also under MATT. 27:24.

**History:**
Pilate did not take orders from Jews, nor did he ask them what actions he should take in any matter.
See also under 18:33, and under MATT. 27:11, 17, and 24.

19:14 - IT WAS THE PREPARATION OF THE PASSOVER, AND ABOUT THE SIXTH HOUR; HE SAITH UNTO THE JEWS, "BEHOLD YOUR KING."

**Contradictions:**

MATT. 27:33-45 - Jesus was taken to Golgotha and crucified prior to the sixth hour; there was darkness from the sixth to the ninth hour.

MARK 15:22-33 - Jesus was taken to Golgotha and it was the third hour and they crucified him; there was darkness from the sixth to the ninth hour.

LUKE 23:33-44 - Jesus was taken to Calvary and crucified prior to the sixth hour; there was darkness from about the sixth to the ninth hour.

[Was Jesus not yet crucified by the sixth hour, or was he crucified prior to the sixth hour?]

MATT. 26:17-21, MARK 14:12-18, and LUKE 22:7-15 - Jesus' disciples prepared the Passover; he ate the Passover meal with them.

[Was it the time of the preparation of the Passover, or had Jesus and his disciples already partaken of the Passover?]

**Perplexing:**

Why did JOHN not mention the amazing phenomenon of the darkness reported by the other gospels?

19:15 - THEY CRIED OUT, "AWAY WITH HIM, CRUCIFY HIM." PILATE SAITH, "SHALL I CRUCIFY YOUR KING?" THE CHIEF PRIESTS ANSWERED, "WE HAVE NO KING BUT CAESAR."

**History:**

The Jews were violently opposed to Roman rule and engaged in periodic rebellions; they did not recognize any Caesar as their king. There is no evidence that Pilate discussed Jesus' fate with the Jews, or that he even met Jesus. If Pilate viewed Jesus as being a king without Rome's approval, he would have been obligated to have him executed.

See also under 18:33, 38, and MATT. 27:11.

**Perplexing:**

Why did Pilate refer to Jesus as the Jews' king, when they never acknowledged him as a king? Why did the anti-Jewish Pilate ask Jews what he should do about someone he believed to be a king without Roman authorization?

19:16 - DELIVERED HE HIM THEREFORE UNTO THEM TO BE CRUCIFIED. THEY TOOK JESUS AND LED HIM AWAY.

**History:**

The Jews did not hold trials or executions during the time of Passover. Jews did not believe in execution by crucifixion. By referring to Jesus as a king, Pilate acknowledged that Jesus was guilty of a crime against Rome and would not have turned Jesus over to Jews for execution.

See also under 19:7.

**Contradictions:**

JOHN 18:31 - The Jews said to Pilate, "It is not lawful for us to put any man to death."

[Did the Jews take Jesus away to crucify him, or had they taken Jesus to Pilate because it was not lawful for

them to execute anyone?]
See also under LUKE 23:25.

19:17 - HE BEARING HIS CROSS WENT FORTH INTO A PLACE CALLED THE PLACE OF A SKULL, WHICH IS CALLED IN THE HEBREW, "GOLGOTHA."

**Contradiction:**
MATT. 27:32 - ...they found a man of Cyrene, Simon by name; him they compelled to bear his cross.
MARK 15:21 - They compel one Simon a Cyrenian...to bear his cross.
LUKE 23:26 As they led him away, they laid hold upon one Simon, a Cyrenian...on him they laid the cross, that he might bear it after Jesus.
[Did Jesus, or Simon bear the cross?]

**Language**: See under MATT. 27:33.

**History:** See under MATT. 27:32 and 33.

19:18 - THEY CRUCIFIED HIM, AND TWO OTHER WITH HIM, ON EITHER SIDE ONE, AND JESUS IN THE MIDST.

**Contradictions:** See under MATT. 27:35.

**Perplexing:** See under MATT. 27:35.

**History:** See under MATT. 27:33 and 35.

**Pagan parallels**: See under MATT. 27:26 and 37-38.

**Language**: See under MATT. 27:35.

19:19-20 - PILATE WROTE A TITLE, AND PUT IT ON THE CROSS: "JESUS OF NAZARETH THE KING OF THE JEWS." ...IT WAS WRITTEN IN HEBREW, GREEK, AND LATIN.

**Contradictions:**
MATT. 27:37 - Set up over his head his accusation written, "THIS IS JESUS THE KING OF THE JEWS."
MARK 15:26 -The superscription of his accusation was written over, "THE KING OF THE JEWS."
LUKE 23:38 - A superscription was written over him in letters of Greek, Latin, and Hebrew, "THIS IS THE KING OF THE JEWS."
[Did the sign on the cross over Jesus read as stated by JOHN, or MATT., or MARK, or LUKE?]

**History:** See under MATT. 27:35.

**Perplexing:** See under MATT. 27:37-38.

19:21 - SAID THE CHIEF PRIESTS TO PILATE: "WRITE NOT, 'THE KING OF THE JEWS,' BUT THAT HE SAID, 'I AM KING OF THE JEWS.'"

**Contradictions:**
MATT. 27:42 - [The chief priests, scribes, and elders]: "...if he be the King of Israel, let him now come down from the cross, and we will believe him."
[Did the chief priests speak to Pilate, or did the chief priests, scribes, and elders speak among themselves?]
MARK 15:32 - [The chief priests and scribes]: "Let Christ the King of Israel descend now from the cross, that we may see and believe."....
[Did the chief priests speak to Pilate, or did the chief priests and scribes speak among themselves?]
LUKE 23:37 - [Soldiers]: "If thou be the king of the Jews, save thyself."
[Did the chief priests speak to Pilate, or did the soldiers speak to Jesus?]
See also under MATT. 27:41-42.

**Perplexing:**
If it was the day, now late afternoon or evening, for the preparation of the Passover, how could Jews be away from their homes, rather than preparing for the Passover? Why would Jews be attending a Roman execution at this time? If it was already Passover as the other gospels assert, they would have been home with their families, in synagogues, or in the temple.
See also under MATT. 27:41-42.

19:24 - THEY [SOLDIERS]: "LET US NOT REND IT [JESUS' COAT], BUT CAST LOTS FOR IT, WHOSE IT SHALL BE," THAT THE SCRIPTURE MIGHT BE FULFILLED, WHICH SAITH, "THEY PARTED MY RAIMENT AMONG THEM, AND FOR MY VESTURE THEY DID CAST LOTS."....

**Old Testament:** See under MATT. 27:35.

19:25 - THERE STOOD BY THE CROSS OF JESUS HIS MOTHER, HIS MOTHER'S SISTER, MARY THE WIFE OF CLEOPHAS, AND MARY MAGDALENE.

**Contradictions:**
MATT. 27:55-56 - Many women were there beholding afar off, which followed Jesus from Galilee, among which was Mary Magdalene, Mary the mother of James and Joses, and the mother of Zebedee's children.
MARK 15:40-41 - There were women looking afar off, among whom was Mary Magdalene, and Mary the mother of James the less and Joses, and Salome...and many other women which came up with him unto Jerusalem.
LUKE 23:49 - All his acquaintance, and the women that followed him from Galilee, stood afar off, beholding these things.
[Were women by the cross, or far off?]
[Was Mary Magdalene by the cross, or far off?]
[Was, or was not Jesus' mother by the cross?]

**Perplexing:**
Why did JOHN not identify Jesus' mother by name? JOHN, however, according to some scholars, identified her sister as being named Mary.
If Jesus' mother was named Mary as the other gospels said, could her sister also have been named Mary?
See also under 2:3-4, and MATT. 27:55-56.

**Pagan concept:** See under MATT. 27:55-56.

**History:** See under MATT. 27:35.

19:26 - WHEN JESUS SAW HIS MOTHER, AND THE DISCIPLE STANDING BY, WHOM HE LOVED, HE SAITH UNTO HIS MOTHER, "WOMAN, BEHOLD THY SON!"

**Contradictions:**
JOHN 13:34 - Jesus: "...love one another, as I have loved you...."
JOHN 15:9 - Jesus: "...I loved you...."
JOHN 15:12 - Jesus: "...love one another as I have loved you."
[Did Jesus love only one of his disciples, or all of them?]
See also under 19:25, and MATT. 27:55-56.

**Perplexing:**
Why is the beloved disciple not identified? Why did the other gospels not report that Jesus spoke to his mother, and mention the presence of a beloved disciple? Why did not Jesus' mother speak to him?
Why did Jesus refer to himself as the son of his mother, rather than the Son of God? Why was Joseph not present?

19:27 - SAITH HE TO THE DISCIPLE, "BEHOLD THY MOTHER!" FROM THAT HOUR THAT DISCIPLE TOOK HER INTO HIS OWN HOME.

**Perplexing:**
Who was the disciple's mother? Was she both Jesus' and the disciple's mother? Were Jesus and the disciple brothers? Why did the other gospels fail to report this incident?

19:28-30 - AFTER THIS, JESUS KNOWING THAT ALL THINGS WERE NOW ACCOMPLISHED, THAT THE SCRIPTURE MIGHT BE FULFILLED, SAITH, "I THIRST." ... THEY FILLED A SPUNGE WITH VINEGAR, PUT IT UPON HYSSOP, AND PUT IT TO HIS MOUTH. WHEN JESUS HAD RECEIVED THE VINEGAR, HE SAID, "IT IS FINISHED." HE BOWED HIS HEAD AND GAVE UP THE GHOST.

**Contradictions:**
MATT. 27:46-50 and MARK 15:34-37 - ...Jesus cried, "...My God, my God, why hast Thou forsaken me?" .... One of them ran, took a spunge, filled it with vinegar, put it on a reed and gave him to drink. .... Jesus, when he had cried again with a loud voice, yielded up the ghost.
[Did Jesus say that he was thirsty and "It is finished," or did he say, "My God, why hast Thou forsaken me?]
[Was Jesus given the vinegar before, or after he uttered his final words?]
LUKE 23:46 - When Jesus had cried with a loud voice, he said, "Father, into Thy hands I commend my spirit"; having said thus, he gave up the ghost.
[Did Jesus say that he was thirsty and, "It is finished," or did he commend his spirit to God?]

**Perplexing:**
Why did Jesus thirst? Why could he, a divine being, not control his thirst? Why did he fail to perform a miracle that would convince everyone there and the rest of the world who he was? Is Jesus, by his failure to prove who he was, morally responsible for all the suffering, violence, persecution, torture, murders, and wars done over the centuries in his name?

**Old Testament:**
PS. 69:21 - "...in my thirst they gave me vinegar to drink."

19:31-33 - THE JEWS, BECAUSE IT WAS THE PREPARATION, THAT THE BODIES SHOULD NOT REMAIN UPON THE CROSS ON THE SABBATH DAY (FOR THE SABBATH WAS A HIGH DAY), BESOUGHT PILATE THAT THEIR LEGS MIGHT BE BROKEN, AND THAT THEY MIGHT BE TAKEN AWAY. THE SOLDIERS BREAK THE LEGS OF THE FIRST, AND THE OTHER CRUCIFIED WITH HIM. WHEN THEY CAME TO JESUS, AND SAW THAT HE WAS DEAD ALREADY, THEY BREAK NOT HIS LEGS.

**History:**
It was a Roman custom to break the legs of crucifixion victims to hasten death.

**Perplexing:**
How did the Jews have ready access to speak with Pilate? Why did the intensely anti-Jewish governor care if it was a Jewish holy day and comply with a request by the Jews? Why were not these Jews home preparing for the Passover, as it was getting late in the day? Why did not the other gospels report the leg breaking incident? Why is there no historical documentation for Jesus' crucifixion?

**Contradictions:** See under 19:14.

19:34 - ONE OF THE SOLDIERS WITH A SPEAR PIERCED HIS SIDE, AND FORTHWITH CAME THERE OUT BLOOD AND WATER.

**Perplexing:**
Why did the soldier pierce Jesus? Why is the incident not reported by the other gospels?

**Pagan parallels:**
The pre-Christian, Scandinavian god Odin was pierced by a spear when he was hanging on a tree. The Babylonian deity Tammuz has also been depicted with a wound in one side of his body.

19:35 - HE THAT SAW IT BARE RECORD, AND HIS RECORD IS TRUE....

**Perplexing:**
Who saw and recorded the event? When? Where is the record? Was the writer of JOHN referring to himself and to his gospel? If it was recorded, why do none of the other gospel writers or historians mention it?

19:36 - THESE THINGS WERE DONE, THAT THE SCRIPTURE SHOULD BE FULFILLED, "A BONE OF HIM SHALL NOT BE BROKEN."

**Old Testament:**
EX. 12:46 - "...neither shall ye break a bone thereof [the Passover lamb]." [JOHN may be equating Jesus with the Passover lamb, although the EX. verse is a command from God, not a prophecy as in JOHN.]
PS. 34:20 - "He [the righteous] keepeth all his bones; not one of them is broken."

19:37 - AGAIN ANOTHER SCRIPTURE SAITH, "THEY SHALL LOOK ON HIM WHOM THEY PIERCED."

**Old Testament:**

ZECH. 12:10 - The LORD: "...they [inhabitants of Jerusalem] shall look upon Me whom they have pierced."

19:38 - AFTER THIS JOSEPH OF ARIMATHAEA, BEING A DISCIPLE OF JESUS, BUT SECRETLY FOR FEAR OF THE JEWS, BESOUGHT PILATE THAT HE MIGHT TAKE AWAY THE BODY OF JESUS; PILATE GAVE HIM LEAVE. HE CAME THEREFORE, AND TOOK THE BODY OF JESUS.

**Contradictions:**

MATT. 27:57-59 - When even was come, a rich man of Arimathaea, named Joseph, who was Jesus' disciple, went to Pilate, and begged the body of Jesus. Pilate commanded the body to be delivered. When Joseph had taken the body, he wrapped it in a clean linen cloth.
[Did Pilate give Joseph permission to take Jesus' body, or did he have the body delivered to Joseph?]
MARK 15:43-45 - Joseph of Arimathaea, an honourable counsellor, which also waited for the kingdom of God, came, went boldly unto Pilate, and craved the body of Jesus. Pilate calling the centurion asked whether he had been any while dead. When he knew it of the centurion, he gave the body to Joseph.
[Did Joseph beseech Pilate for Jesus' body, or did he boldly crave Jesus' body?]
[Did not, or did Pilate first ask a centurion whether Jesus was dead?]
ACTS 13:29 - Paul: "...they [the Jews who turned Jesus over to Pilate] took him down from the tree, and laid him in a sepulchre."
[Did Joseph take Jesus body down from the cross, or did Jews take Jesus' body down from a tree?]

**Perplexing:**

How was Joseph, a Jew, able to quickly get to speak with the vehemently, anti-Jewish Pilate? Why was Pilate readily available to meet with a Jew and acquiesce to a Jew's request? The Jews had asked that the crucified bodies be taken down from the crosses, because of the Passover holiday. Where, therefore, was Jesus' body? Was it still on the cross, or was it lying on the ground? If Jesus was still on the cross, how was Joseph able to take the body down by himself?

19:39 - THERE CAME ALSO NICODEMUS, WHICH AT THE FIRST CAME TO JESUS BY NIGHT, AND BROUGHT A MIXTURE OF MYRRH AND ALOES, ABOUT 100-POUND WEIGHT.

**Contradiction:**

MARK 16:1 - ...Mary Magdalene, Mary the mother of James, and Salome brought sweet spices, that they might come and anoint him.
LUKE 24:1 - ...they [women from Galilee] came unto the sepulchre, bringing the spices which they had prepared, and certain others with them.
[Did Nicodemus bring the spices, or did women bring them?]

**Perplexing:**

How was Nicodemus able to obtain and transport 100 pounds of myrrh and aloes? How did he know that Joseph had obtained Jesus' body? Why was such a large quantity needed? Why did the other gospels not mention Nicodemus' presence?

19:40 - THEN TOOK THEY THE BODY OF JESUS, AND WOUND IT IN LINEN CLOTHES WITH THE SPICES, AS THE MANNER OF THE JEWS IS TO BURY.

**Contradiction:**

MATT. 27:59 - When Joseph had taken the body, he wrapped it in a clean linen cloth.
MARK 15:46 - He [Joseph] bought fine linen, and took him down, and wrapped him in the linen....
LUKE 23:53 - He [Joseph] took it [Jesus' body] down, and wrapped it in linen....
[Did Joseph and Nicodemus wrap Jesus' body in linen with spices, or did Joseph alone wrap Jesus' body without spices?]

19:41-42 - IN THE PLACE WHERE HE WAS CRUCIFIED THERE WAS A GARDEN, AND IN THE GARDEN A NEW SEPULCHRE WHEREIN WAS NEVER MAN YET LAID. THERE LAID THEY JESUS THEREFORE BECAUSE OF THE JEWS' PREPARATION DAY; THE SEPULCHRE WAS NIGH AT HAND.

**Contradictions:**

MATT. 27:60 - [Joseph] laid it in his own new tomb, which he had hewn out in the rock....
MARK 15:46 - ...[Joseph] laid him in a sepulchre which was hewn out of a rock....
LUKE 23:53 - ...[Joseph] laid it in a sepulchre that was hewn in stone, where never man before was laid.
[Did Joseph and Nicodemus place Jesus in a sepulchre, or did Joseph alone do it?]
ACTS 13:29 - Paul: "...they [that dwell at Jerusalem]...laid him in a sepulchre."
[Did Joseph and Nicodemus place Jesus in a sepulchre, or did people from Jerusalem do it?]
See also under 19:14.

**Perplexing:**

Why did Paul in 1 COR. 15:4 say only that Jesus was buried? Why did he not mention Joseph, Nicodemus, or the stone sepulchre?

20:1 - THE FIRST DAY OF THE WEEK COMETH MARY MAGDALENE EARLY, WHEN IT WAS YET DARK, UNTO THE SEPULCHRE, AND SEETH THE STONE TAKEN AWAY.

**Contradictions:**

MATT. 28:1-2 - ...as it began to dawn toward the first day of the week, came Mary Magdalene and the other Mary to see the sepulchre. There was a great earthquake; the angel of the Lord descended from heaven, and rolled back the stone from the door, and sat upon it.
[Did Mary Magdalene come to the sepulchre alone, or with the other Mary?]
[Was not, or was an angel sitting on the stone?]
MARK 16:1-4 - When the Sabbath was past, Mary Magdalene, Mary the mother of James, and Salome, bought sweet spices, that they might anoint him. Very early in the morning the first day of the week, they came unto the sepulchre at the rising of the sun. .... They saw that the stone was rolled away....
[Did Mary Magdalene come to the sepulchre alone, or did she come with Mary the mother of James, and Salome?]
[Did not, or did Mary Magdalene bring spices to the sepulchre?]
LUKE 24:1-2 - Upon the first day of the week, very early in the morning, they [women from Galilee] came unto the sepulchre, bringing spices.... They found the stone rolled away from the sepulchre.
[Did Mary Magdalene come to the sepulchre alone, or did women from Galilee come bringing spices to the sepulchre?]

[Was there not, or was there a great earthquake?]
See also under MATT. 12:40.

**Perplexing:**
How did Mary know that Jesus' body had been placed in the sepulchre? Why did she go to the sepulchre while it was still dark? How did she find her way in the dark? Why was the stone rolled away? Why could not Jesus have left without the stone being moved? (In JOHN 20:19, he appeared in a closed room without opening the door.) Would it not have been more remarkable if the stone had still been in place, but Jesus' body was gone?
See also under MATT. 12:40 and 28:2-4.

**Pagan parallel:** See under MATT. 28:2-4.

20:2 - THEN SHE RUNNETH TO SIMON PETER AND TO THE DISCIPLE, WHOM JESUS LOVED, AND SAITH, "THEY HAVE TAKEN AWAY THE LORD OUT OF THE SEPULCHRE, AND WE KNOW NOT WHERE THEY HAVE LAID HIM."

**Contradictions:**
MATT. 28:5-8 - The angel said, "Fear not; I know that ye seek Jesus.... He is not here; he is risen.... Come, see the place where the Lord lay. Go quickly, and tell his disciples that he is risen from the dead, and goeth into Galilee; there shall ye see him." They departed from the sepulchre...and did run to bring his disciples word.
[Did Mary Magdalene run to Peter and the beloved disciple and tell them that Jesus' body was missing, or did an angel tell her and the other Mary that Jesus was risen and that they should go to and so inform the disciples?]
MARK 16:5-8 - Entering into the sepulchre, they saw a young man sitting.... He saith, "... ye seek Jesus of Nazareth ... he is risen ... behold the place where they laid him. Go, tell the disciples and Peter that he goeth before you into Galilee; there shall ye see him...." They went out quickly, and fled from the sepulchre ... neither said they anything to any man, for they were afraid.
[Did Mary Magdalene run to Peter and the beloved disciple and tell them that Jesus' body was missing, or did a young man tell her, Mary the mother of Joses, and Salome that Jesus was risen and that they should so inform the disciples, but they fled and did not say anything to any man?]
LUKE 24:3-10 - They entered in, and found not the body of the Lord Jesus. ...two men stood by them in shining garments...they said, "Why seek ye the living among the dead? He is not here, but is risen...." They...returned from the sepulchre, and told these things unto the eleven, and to all the rest. It was Mary Magdalene, Joanna, Mary the mother of James, and women that were with them, which told these things unto the apostles.
[Did Mary Magdalene tell Peter and the beloved disciple that Jesus' body was missing, or did two men tell her, Mary the mother of James, Joanna, and other women that Jesus had risen, and they then so informed the disciples?]
[Did Mary Magdalene look into the sepulchre, or enter into it?]
[Did Mary Magdalene see no one, an angel, a young man, or two men inside the sepulchre?]
See also under MATT. 28:2-4, 5-7, and 8.

**Perplexing:**
Why did Jesus rise secretly? Why did he not wait until Mary with or without other women came to witness his resurrection?

See also under MATT. 28:5-7.

**Pagan parallels**: See under MATT. 28:5-7.

**History:** See under MATT. 28:5-7.

20:3-8 - PETER AND THE OTHER DISCIPLE CAME TO THE SEPULCHRE. ...THE OTHER DISCIPLE ...CAME FIRST TO THE SEPULCHRE. HE STOOPING DOWN, AND LOOKING IN, SAW THE LINEN CLOTHES.... COMETH SIMON PETER, AND WENT INTO THE SEPULCHRE, AND SEETH THE LINEN CLOTHES.... THEN WENT IN THAT OTHER DISCIPLE...HE SAW AND BELIEVED.

**Contradictions:**
MATT. 28:16 - The eleven disciples went into Galilee....
[Did Peter and the other disciple go to the sepulchre, or did the eleven disciples go to Galilee?]
MARK 16:9-11 - Jesus...appeared first to Mary Magdalene.... She told them that had been with him.... When they heard that he was alive, and had been seen by her, believed not.
[Did Peter and the other disciple go to the sepulchre after being informed by Mary Magdalene that Jesus' body was missing, or did Jesus appear to her, but the disciples refuse to believe it when she told them?]
LUKE 24:11-12 - Their [the women's] words seemed to them as idle tales, and they believed them not. Then Peter ran unto the sepulchre...he beheld the linen clothes, departed, wondering at that which was come to pass.
[Did Peter and the other disciple enter the sepulchre and see the linen clothes, or did Peter go alone to the sepulchre and just look in?]

20:9 - AS YET THEY [THE DISCIPLES] KNEW NOT THE SCRIPTURE, THAT HE MUST RISE FROM THE DEAD.

**Contradictions:**
MATT. 16:21 - From that time forth began Jesus to shew unto his disciples, how that he must go to Jerusalem...be killed, and be raised again the third day.
MATT. 17:9 - ...Jesus: "Tell the vision to no man, until the Son of man be risen again from the dead."
MATT. 20:18-19 - Jesus: "...the Son of man shall be betrayed...they shall condemn him to death...and the third day he shall rise again."
MARK 8:31 - He began to teach them, that the Son of man must suffer many things...be killed, and after three days rise again.
MARK 9:31 - He taught his disciples, "The Son of man...after he is killed, shall rise the third day."
MARK 10:33-34 - Jesus: "We go to Jerusalem...the Gentiles...shall kill him, and the third day he shall rise again."
[Did the disciples not know, or had Jesus taught them that he would rise from the dead?]
JOHN 2:19-22 - Jesus: "Destroy this temple, and in three days I will raise it up." .... He spake of the temple of his body. When therefore he was risen from the dead, his disciples remembered that he had said this unto them, and they believed the scripture.
[Did the disciples not know the Scripture, or did they believe it?]

20:10 - THEN THE DISCIPLES WENT AWAY AGAIN UNTO THEIR OWN HOME.

**Contradictions:**
MATT. 28:16 - The eleven disciples went away into Galilee, into a mountain where Jesus had appointed them.
[Did the disciples go to their home, or did they gc to a mountain in Galilee?]
MARK 16:12-14 - He appeared unto two of them [in] the country. .... He appeared unto the eleven as they sat at meat [in Jerusalem]....
LUKE 24:15-36 - Jesus appeared to two disciples who were walking between Emmaus and Jerusalem then to the eleven in Jerusalem.
ACTS 1:2-4 - ...unto the apostles whom he had chosen, he shewed himself alive after his passion...and being assembled with them in Jerusalem, commanded that they should not depart from Jerusalem....
[Did the disciples go home, or remain together in Jerusalem?]

**Perplexing:**
Did only Peter and the other disciple, or all the disciples go home? Where were their homes? Did they all live together in one house? Why did they fail to go forth and teach/preach as Jesus commanded them to do in MATT. 28:20 and MARK 16:15?

20:11-13 - MARY STOOD WITHOUT AT THE SEPULCHRE WEEPING; AS SHE WEPT, SHE STOOPED DOWN, LOOKED INTO THE SEPULCHRE, AND SEETH TWO ANGELS SITTING, ONE AT THE HEAD, AND THE OTHER AT THE FEET, WHERE THE BODY OF JESUS HAD LAIN. THEY SAY, "WHY WEEPEST THOU?" SHE SAITH, "BECAUSE THEY HAVE TAKEN MY LORD, AND I KNOW NOT WHERE THEY HAVE LAID HIM."

**Contradictions:**
MATT. 28:2-5 - An angel of the Lord rolled back the stone, sat upon it, and spoke to Mary Magdalene and the other Mary during their only visit to the sepulchre. He said that Jesus had risen.
[Did Mary Magdalene during her second visit to the sepulchre look in and see two angels or did she and the other Mary see one angel outside the sepulchre during their only visit to the sepulchre?]
[Did two angels ask Mary Magdalene why she wept, or did one angel tell her and the other Mary that Jesus had risen?]
MARK 16:1-6 - Mary Magdalene, Mary the mother of James, and Salome entered the sepulchre where a young man [an angel?], sitting on the right side, spoke to them during their only visit to the sepulchre. He said that Jesus had risen.
[Did Mary Magdalene during her second visit to the sepulchre look in and see two angels, or did she and two other women enter the sepulchre and see a young man during their only visit to the sepulchre?]
[Did two angels ask Mary Magdalene why she wept, or did a young man tell her and two other women that Jesus had risen?]
LUKE 24:3-10 - Mary Magdalene, and several other women entered the sepulchre where two men [angels?] stood and spoke to them during their only visit to the sepulchre. They said that Jesus had risen.
[Did Mary Magdalene during her second visit to the sepulchre look in and see two angels, or did she and several women enter the sepulchre and see two men during their only visit to the sepulchre?]
[Did the angels ask Mary Magdalene why she wept, or did they tell her and several other women that Jesus had risen?]
[Were two angels sitting, or standing?]
[Did Mary Magdalene make one, or two trips to the sepulchre?]

**Perplexing:**
Why were the angels not present the first time Mary went to the sepulchre? Why did the other gospels report only one visit by Mary to the sepulchre? Why did they not report the conversation between Mary and the angels? Why did the angels fail to tell her that Jesus has risen? If the angels did not inform Mary that Jesus had risen, why were they there? Why did the angels not know why Mary was weeping?

20:14 - ...SHE TURNED HERSELF BACK, SAW JESUS STANDING, AND KNEW NOT THAT IT WAS JESUS.

**Contradictions:**
MATT. 28:9 - As they [Mary Magdalene and the other Mary] went to tell the disciples, Jesus met them, saying, "All hail." They came and held him by the feet, and worshipped him.
[Did the resurrected Jesus appear first to Mary Magdalene alone, or to Mary Magdalene and the other Mary?]
[Did Mary fail to recognize Jesus, or did she and the other Mary recognize him, hold him by the feet, and worship him?]
LUKE 24:13-31 - Jesus appeared first to two disciples on their way to Emmaus.
[Did the resurrected Jesus appear first to Mary Magdalene, or to two disciples walking to Emmaus?]
[Did Jesus first appear by the sepulchre, or on the way to Emmaus?]
[Did Jesus appear after, or before the disciples had been informed of his resurrection or the disappearance of his body?]
1 COR. 15:4-5 - Paul: "...he rose the third day...and was seen of Cephas, then the twelve."
[Did the risen Jesus appear first to Mary Magdalene, or to Cephas (Peter; see 1:42)?]

**Perplexing:**
How could Mary fail to recognize Jesus, especially, if she had seen and worshiped him as claimed by MATT. 28:9?

**History:** See under MATT. 28:9-10.

**Pagan parallel:** See under MATT. 28:9-10.

20:15-17 - JESUS SAITH, "WOMAN WHY WEEPEST THOU? WHOM SEEKEST THOU?" SHE, SUPPOSING HIM TO BE THE GARDENER, SAITH, "SIR, IF THOU HAVE BORNE HIM HENCE, TELL ME WHERE...." JESUS SAITH, "MARY." SHE SAITH, "RABBONI," WHICH IS TO SAY, "MASTER." JESUS SAITH, "TOUCH ME NOT, FOR I AM NOT YET ASCENDED TO MY FATHER; TELL MY BRETHREN, I ASCEND UNTO MY FATHER, AND YOUR FATHER, AND TO MY GOD, AND YOUR GOD."

**Contradictions:**
MATT. 28:9 - ...Jesus met them [Mary Magdalene and the other Mary].... ...they held him by the feet, and worshipped him.
[Did Jesus tell Mary not to touch him, or did he allow her and the other Mary to hold his feet?]
JOHN 20:27 - Saith he [Jesus after his resurrection] to Thomas, "Reach hither thy finger, and behold my hands; reach hither thy hand, and thrust it into my side...."
[Could not Jesus be touched because he was not yet ascended, or could he be touched?]
LUKE 23:43 - Jesus said unto him [one of the criminals being crucified with him], "Today shalt thou be

with me in paradise."
[Did Jesus remain on the earth, or did he ascend to paradise with the criminal on the day of crucifixion?]

**Perplexing:**
Why did Mary suppose Jesus to be a gardener? Was he wearing a gardener's attire? If so, from where did he obtain it? Why did Jesus tell Mary not to touch him because he had not yet ascended, when, in MATT. 28:9 he voiced no objection to her touching (holding) him? Why did Jesus allow one of his disciples to touch him (JOHN 20:27)? Why had Jesus not yet ascended? Why did he instruct Mary to tell the disciples, "I ascend to my Father," rather than notify them that he was going to stay around and meet them? Did Jesus deliberately mislead Mary? Why did Jesus ask Mary why she wept and for whom she was seeking [see under MATT. 9:28-30 - Contradictions]?

**History:**
The Roman Emperor Domitian (A.D. 81-86) demanded that he be addressed as, "My master and my god." Since the Gospel of JOHN is generally believed to have been written between A.D. 90 - 140, it is possible that the author was familiar with Domitian's demand and incorporated it into his gospel.

20:18 - MARY MAGDALENE CAME AND TOLD THE DISCIPLES THAT SHE HAD SEEN THE LORD, AND THAT HE HAD SPOKEN THESE THINGS UNTO HER.

**Contradictions:**
MATT. 28:9 - They [Mary Magdalene and the other Mary] went to tell his disciples....
[Did Mary Magdalene tell the disciples that she had seen Jesus, or did she and the other Mary go to tell the disciples?]
LUKE 24: 10 - It was Mary Magdalene, Joanna, Mary the mother of James, and other women that were with them, which told these things unto the apostles.
[Did Mary Magdalene tell the disciples about Jesus, or did she and several other women tell them that Jesus had risen?]

20:19 - THE SAME DAY AT EVENING, THE FIRST DAY OF THE WEEK, WHEN THE DOORS WERE SHUT WHERE THE DISCIPLES [EXCEPT THOMAS (JOHN 20:24)] WERE ASSEMBLED FOR FEAR OF THE JEWS, CAME JESUS AND STOOD IN THE MIDST, AND SAITH, "PEACE BE UNTO YOU."

**Contradictions:**
MATT. 28:16-18 - The eleven disciples went into Galilee, into a mountain where Jesus had appointed them. When they saw him, they worshipped, but some doubted. Jesus spake, "All power is given unto me in heaven and earth."
[Did Jesus appear to his disciples in a closed room in Jerusalem, or on a mountain in Galilee?]
[Did Jesus say, "Peace be unto you," or that all power in heaven and earth is given to him?]
MARK 16:12-14 - He appeared in another form unto two of them as they went into the country. Afterward he appeared unto the eleven as they sat at meat [in Jerusalem], and upbraided them with their unbelief....
[Did Jesus appear to the disciples in a room, or did he appear first to two disciples as they walked in the country, then to the rest while they were eating?]
[Did Jesus say, "Peace be with you," or did he upbraid them for their unbelief?]
LUKE 24:13-36 - Jesus appeared to two disciples as they walked to Emmaus; he then appeared in the midst of the disciples, and saith, "Peace be unto you."

[Did Jesus appear to all the disciples in a room, or two disciples walking to Emmaus, then to the others in Jerusalem?]

**Perplexing:**
Why did JOHN say that the disciples were in fear of the Jews? He had not reported that any Jews had attacked or even threatened the disciples.

20:22 - ...HE BREATHED ON THEM, AND SAITH, "RECEIVE YE THE HOLY GHOST."

**Contradictions:**
ACTS 1:8 - Jesus: "Ye shall receive power, after the Holy Ghost is come upon you...."
[Did the disciples, except Thomas, receive the Holy Ghost, or did they still have to wait to receive the Holy Ghost?]
ACTS 2:3-4 - [After Jesus ascended] There appeared unto them cloven tongues as of fire, and it sat upon each of them. And they were filled with the Holy Ghost....
[Did the disciples, except Thomas, receive the Holy Ghost when Jesus breathed on them, or when they were touched by tongues as of fire?]
[Did the disciples receive the Holy Ghost before, or after Jesus' ascension?]

20:24 - THOMAS, ONE OF THE TWELVE, CALLED DIDYMUS. WAS NOT WITH THEM WHEN JESUS CAME.

**Contradiction:**
MATT. 28:16-17 - The eleven disciples went into Galilee.... When they saw him, they worshipped, but some doubted.
MARK 16:14 - He appeared unto the eleven....
LUKE 24:33-36 - ...the eleven gathered together.... .... Jesus stood in the midst of them....
[Was Thomas not with the disciples when Jesus first appeared to them, or was he present with them, as indicated by MATT., MARK, and LUKE?]

**Language**: See under 11:16.

**Perplexing:**
As Thomas was not present when Jesus breathed the Holy Ghost onto the other disciples, did he ever receive the Holy Ghost from Jesus? Why was Thomas not referred to as "Didymus" by the other gospels? Why did JOHN refer to "the twelve?" Was JOHN saying that Judas Iscariot was still one of the disciples? Why did JOHN fail to identify all twelve disciples?
See also under 11:16.

20:25 - .... HE [THOMAS] SAID, "EXCEPT I SHALL SEE IN HIS HANDS THE PRINT OF THE NAILS, PUT MY FINGER INTO THE PRINT OF THE NAILS, AND THRUST MY HAND INTO HIS SIDE, I WILL NOT BELIEVE."

**Contradiction:**
MATT. 28:17 - When they saw him, they worshipped him, but some doubted.
[Was Thomas the only disciple who doubted, or did "some" of them doubt?]

**History:**
Nails were placed through the wrists, not the hands, of crucifixion victims. The hands were not strong enough to sustain the weight of the body.

**Perplexing:**
Why did Thomas doubt that Jesus had returned from the dead? Did he not believe Jesus' claims that he would be resurrected?
How did Thomas know that Jesus' side had been pierced?

20:26 - AFTER EIGHT DAYS AGAIN HIS DISCIPLES WERE WITHIN, AND THOMAS WITH THEM; THEN CAME JESUS...AND STOOD IN THE MIDST....

**Contradictions:**
MARK 16:19 - After the Lord had spoken to them [later on the day of his resurrection], he was received up into heaven, and sat on the right hand of God.
LUKE 24:50-51 - He led them as far as Bethany [later on the day of his resurrection], and blessed them. ... while he blessed them, he was...carried up into heaven.
[Was Jesus still on earth with his disciples at least eight days after his resurrection, or did he ascend to heaven on the day of his resurrection?]
[Did Jesus visit the disciples a second time after his resurrection, or did he meet with them only once before his ascension?]

**Perplexing:**
Why in 20:17 did Jesus instruct Mary Magdalene to tell his disciples that he was ascending to his Father? Why did Jesus not ascend as he said he would? Why did he remain on the earth? What did he do during the eight days? What did the disciples do during that time?
See also under 20:15-17.

20:27 - SAITH HE TO THOMAS, "REACH HITHER THY FINGER; BEHOLD MY HANDS; REACH HITHER THY HAND, AND THRUST IT INTO MY SIDE...."

**Contradiction:**
JOHN 20:17 - Jesus told Mary, "Touch me not, for I am not yet ascended to my father."
[Could, or could not Jesus be touched prior to his ascension?]

20:28 - THOMAS SAID, "MY LORD AND MY GOD."

**History:** See under 20:15-17.

20:30 - MANY OTHER SIGNS DID JESUS IN THE PRESENCE OF HIS DISCIPLES, WHICH ARE NOT WRITTEN IN THE BOOK.

**History:**
There are no secular records of anything done by Jesus.

**Perplexing:**
What did Jesus do? Why is there no historical record of his achievements?

20:31 - THESE ARE WRITTEN THAT YE MIGHT BELIEVE THAT JESUS IS THE CHRIST, THE SON OF GOD, AND BY BELIEVING YE MIGHT HAVE LIFE THROUGH HIS NAME.

**Contradictions:** See under MATT. 1:18 and 19:17-19 (for obtaining eternal life).

**Perplexing:** See under MATT. 19:16 and 17-19 (for obtaining eternal life)

21:1 - AFTER THESE THINGS JESUS SHEWED HIMSELF AGAIN TO THE DISCIPLES AT THE SEA OF TIBERIAS....

**Contradiction:**
MARK 16:19 - After the Lord had spoken to them [on the day of his resurrection] he was received up into heaven, and sat on the right hand of God.
LUKE 24:50-51 - He led them as far as Bethany, blessed them, was parted from them, and carried up into heaven [on the day of his resurrection].
[Did the resurrected Jesus remain on earth for an unspecified length of time and visit the disciples on three separate occasions, or did he ascend to heaven during the day of his resurrection?]

**Perplexing:**
How long did Jesus remain on earth after his resurrection? What did he do during this time? Why did MARK and LUKE imply that Jesus ascended to heaven the same day as his resurrection? Why was it necessary for Jesus to make a third visit to the disciples?

21:2 - THERE WERE TOGETHER SIMON PETER, THOMAS CALLED DIDYMUS, NATHANAEL OF CANA IN GALILEE, THE SONS OF ZEBEDEE, AND TWO OTHER OF HIS DISCIPLES.

**Contradiction:**
MATT. 10:2-4, MARK 3:14-19, and LUKE 6:13-16 - Nathanael was not listed as one of the twelve disciples.
[Was, or was not Nathanael one of Jesus' disciples?]

**Perplexing:**
Where were the other disciples? Who were the two unnamed disciples?
See also under 1:49

21:3 - SIMON PETER SAITH, "I GO A FISHING." THEY SAY, "WE GO WITH THEE." THEY WENT, AND ENTERED A SHIP IMMEDIATELY; THAT NIGHT THEY CAUGHT NOTHING.

**Contradictions:**
MARK 16:20- They went forth, and preached everywhere, the Lord working with them, and confirming the word with signs following.
[Did the disciples go fishing, or did they go preaching everywhere?]
LUKE 24:52-53 - ...they returned to Jerusalem with great joy, and were continually in the temple, praising and blessing God.
[Did the disciples go fishing, or did they go to the temple where they continually praised God?]
ACTS 1:12-13 - Returned they unto Jerusalem from the mount called Olivet [after Jesus' ascension].... When they were come, they went into an upper room [where the eleven disciples abode].
[Did the disciples go fishing, or go to an upper room where they lived?]

**Perplexing:**
Why did the disciples, after meeting with the resurrected Jesus twice and after he breathed the Holy Ghost on them, go fishing as if nothing out of the ordinary had occurred? Why did they speak about fishing, rather than the amazing events that they had witnessed? Why did they not go out preaching as Jesus commanded in MATT. 28:19 ("Go ye therefore, and teach all nations, baptizing them in the name of the Father, the Son, and the Holy Ghost."), MARK 16:15 ("Go ye into all the world, and preach the gospel to every creature."), and LUKE 24:47 ("...repentance and remission of sins should be preached in his name among all nations, beginning at Jerusalem.")? Was JOHN unaware of the commands that Jesus had given the disciples in the other gospels?

21:4-6 - WHEN MORNING WAS COME, JESUS STOOD ON THE SHORE, BUT THE DISCIPLES KNEW NOT THAT IT WAS JESUS. THEN JESUS SAITH, "CHILDREN, HAVE YE ANY MEAT?" THEY ANSWERED, "NO." HE SAID, "CAST THE NET ON THE RIGHT SIDE OF THE SHIP, AND YE SHALL FIND." THEY CAST AND WERE NOT ABLE TO DRAW IT FOR THE MULTITUDE OF FISHES.

**Contradictions:**
MARK 16:19 - After the Lord had spoken unto them, he was received up into heaven, and sat on the right hand of God [on the day of his resurrection].
LUKE 24:51 - ...he was parted from them, and carried up into heaven [on the day of his resurrection].
[Did the risen Jesus remain on the earth, visit the disciples three times, and help them fish, or ascend to heaven on the day of his resurrection after meeting with the disciples once?]
ACTS 1:9 - ...while they beheld, he was taken up, and a cloud received him out of their sight [after being on the earth 40 days (1:3)].
[Did the risen Jesus meet and speak with the disciples a third time and help them fish, several days after his resurrection, or did he remain on the earth 40 days conversing with the disciples?]

**Perplexing:**
How could the disciples fail to recognize Jesus after having recently seen and spoken with him (JOHN 20:19-30), especially when they were close enough to speak with him? If, however, they were 200 cubits [300-400 feet] from land, as stated in 21:8, how could they hear and respond to Jesus?
Why did Jesus have to ask the disciples whether they have "any meat?" Why did he not know? Why did he fail to come the day before and help them find fish? Where had he been? What did he do? Why did the other gospels not report that the resurrected Jesus visited the disciples while they were fishing? Why did Jesus not walk on the water to the ship?

21:7 - THAT DISCIPLE WHOM JESUS LOVED SAITH UNTO PETER, "IT IS THE LORD." WHEN PETER HEARD THAT IT WAS THE LORD, HE GIRT HIS FISHER'S COAT UNTO HIM (FOR HE WAS NAKED), AND DID CAST HIMSELF INTO THE SEA.

**Perplexing:**
Why was Peter naked? Were the other disciples also naked? Why did he put on a coat before jumping into the sea? (People tend to take off clothes prior to swimming.) How could he swim in the sea while wearing a coat? [This is the second reference to a naked man associated with Jesus (see MARK 14:51-52)].

21:8 - ...THEY WERE NOT FAR FROM LAND, BUT AS IT WERE 200 CUBITS....

**Perplexing:**
A cubit is believed to have been equivalent to 18 or 24 inches. The disciples, therefore, were about 300 feet (100 yards) - 400 feet off shore. Could they have spoken with Jesus on shore across that distance, but not recognize him?
See also under 21:4-6.

21:11 - SIMON PETER WENT UP, AND DREW THE NET TO LAND FULL OF GREAT FISHES, 153...YET WAS NOT THE NET BROKEN.

**Perplexing:**
Did Peter continue to wear the wet coat, or did he take it off and show himself naked again? Why did the other disciples not help him pull in the net? If Jesus did not object to naked people being around him, why are many modern Christians hostile to nudity?

21:13 - JESUS TAKETH BREAD, GIVETH THEM, AND FISH LIKEWISE.

**Perplexing:**
Were they able to eat all 153 fish? If not, what happened to the surplus? Since they did not have ice or refrigeration, the fish could not be stored very long before becoming aromatic. Did they leave the fish to rot, to dry, or did they do something else with them?

21:14 - THIS IS NOW THE THIRD TIME THAT JESUS SHOWED HIMSELF TO HIS DISCIPLES, AFTER HE WAS RISEN FROM THE DEAD.

**Contradictions:**
MATT. 28:16-20 - The resurrected Jesus met with the disciples only once - on a mountain in Galilee.
[Did the resurrected Jesus appear to disciples on three occasions, or just once?]
MARK 16:12-19 and LUKE 24:13-51 - The resurrected Jesus appeared to disciples twice before ascending to heaven: first to two disciples as they walked, then to the eleven while they ate in Jerusalem.
[Did the resurrected Jesus appear to disciples on three, or two occasions?]
1 COR. 15:4-8 - The resurrected Jesus was said to have been seen on five occasions. (It is not clear, however, whether all of these appearances involved the disciples. For example: he appeared first to Cephas, another name for Peter (JOHN 1:42); then to the twelve, presumably all of the disciples, as Paul seemed to be unaware of Judas' betrayal; then to 500 brethren who might also include the disciples; then to James, possibly one of the original disciples; then to all the apostles, presumably, including the original disciples.)
[Did the resurrected Jesus appear to his disciples on three, or five occasions?]
[Did resurrected Jesus help, or not help the disciples to fish?]

**Perplexing:**
Why did not the other gospels mention a third visit by Jesus to his disciples? How much time had elapsed between Jesus first meeting with the disciples in a closed room in Jerusalem (20:19) and his appearance at the Sea of Tiberias?

21:15-17 - WHEN THEY HAD DINED, JESUS SAITH TO SIMON PETER, "LOVEST ME MORE THAN THESE?" HE SAITH, "... I LOVE THEE." HE SAITH, "FEED MY LAMBS." HE SAITH THE SECOND TIME, "...LOVEST THOU ME?" HE SAITH, "...I LOVE THEE." HE SAITH, "FEED MY SHEEP." HE SAITH THE THIRD TIME, "...LOVEST THOU ME?" .... HE SAID,

"LORD, THOU KNOWEST ALL THINGS; THOU KNOWEST THAT I LOVE THEE." JESUS SAITH, "FEED MY SHEEP."

**Perplexing:**
Why did Jesus, a divine being, want to be loved by a mere mortal? Why should he even care whether or not anyone loved him?

**Language:**
The Greek word, "agape," was translated as "lovest," the first two times that it was used by Jesus. The third time, the word used was "philos." Peter in his three responses used, "philos." "Agape" essentially means, "to have a strong affection," whereas "philos" means, "passionate love."

**Pagan parallel:** See under MATT. 26:31.

21:19 - THIS SPAKE HE [JESUS], SIGNIFYING BY WHAT DEATH HE [PETER] SHOULD GLORIFY GOD. WHEN HE HAD SPOKEN THIS, HE SAITH UNTO HIM, "FOLLOW ME."

**Perplexing:**
Why could Jesus not protect Peter? Why would almighty God of the universe be glorified by Peter's or anyone's death?
Why does God need to be glorified? Why did Jesus say, "Follow me," when Peter was already one of his followers?
See also under 12:28.

**History:**
There is no documentation of Peter's death, just as there is no documentation outside the Bible for his life.

21:21-22 - PETER SEEING HIM [THE DISCIPLE THAT JESUS LOVED] SAITH TO JESUS, "LORD, AND WHAT SHALL THIS MAN DO?" JESUS SAITH, "IF I WILL THAT HE TARRY TILL I COME, WHAT IS THAT TO THEE? FOLLOW THOU ME."

**Perplexing:**
Why did Jesus imply that he would return while the disciple he loved was still alive? Why did he again tell Peter to follow him? Why did Jesus fail to return as he implied?

21:24 - THIS IS THE DISCIPLE WHICH TESTIFIETH OF THESE THINGS, AND WROTE THESE THINGS....

**Perplexing:**
Was the writer saying that he, John, wrote the gospel and was the disciple who Jesus loved? If so, how could a Galilean fisherman, probably illiterate, have become so proficient in written Greek, as to have composed this gospel? Why did he write in Greek rather than in the more familiar Aramaic?

21:25 - THERE ARE ALSO MANY OTHER THINGS WHICH JESUS DID, WHICH, IF THEY SHOULD BE WRITTEN EVERY ONE, I SUPPOSE THAT EVEN THE WORLD ITSELF COULD NOT CONTAIN THE BOOKS THAT SHOULD BE WRITTEN."

**History:**

There is no record in any of the historical documents of the period of any of the things Jesus was alleged to have done.

See also under 20:30.

**Perplexing:**

Why were none of the things that Jesus is said to have done recorded in any of the contemporary written documents of the time? Why did the Roman soldiers and merchants, other merchants, travelers, and political personages, all of whom would have been knowledgeable of Jesus' accomplishments, fail to write about him? Why did the people he healed of various infirmities and diseases, as well as those be brought back from the dead fail to write about him, or relate their stories to someone who could write?

Why did JOHN fail to report Jesus' ascension?

# *CHAPTER FIVE*

## THE ACTS OF THE APOSTLES

1:1 - THE FORMER TREATISE HAVE I MADE, O THEOPHILUS, OF ALL THAT JESUS BEGAN BOTH TO DO AND TEACH.

**History:**
The date when ACTS was compiled is not known, but it is generally believed to have been between A.D. 80 - 150. Some biblical scholars contend that the same person wrote LUKE and ACTS. Others claim that they each had different authors; there is also a belief that ACTS was written by two different people. Many (most?) believe that it is fictional, but with historical fragments.
See also under LUKE 1:1-4.

**Perplexing:**
What was the treatise to which the author referred? Was it LUKE? If so, why are there so many discrepancies (as will be seen) between ACTS and LUKE?

1:3 - TO WHOM [THE APOSTLES] HE SHEWED HIMSELF ALIVE AFTER HIS PASSION BY MANY INFALLIBLE PROOFS, BEING SEEN OF THEM 40 DAYS....

**Contradictions:**
MARK - 16:6-19 and LUKE 24:6-51 - Jesus showed himself to the apostles for only one day.
[Was Jesus seen by the apostles for 40 days, or for one day?]
JOHN 20:19 - 21:22 - Jesus appeared to the disciples on three different occasions during a span of at least ten days.
[Was Jesus seen by the apostles for 40 days, or on three occasions during at least a ten-day period?]

**History:**
There is no historical evidence that the resurrected Jesus appeared to anyone.

**Perplexing:**
What were the infallible proofs? Why were they not cited in the gospels? Why did Jesus fail to give infallible proof of himself to the general public or to Pilate and those responsible for his crucifixion? Why is there no record of Jesus' appearances after, or even before, his resurrection?

**Old Testament:**
The number "40" appeared numerous times in the Old Testament and may have had a mystical meaning for the ancient Hebrews that carried over into the New Testament where it appears several times.
See also under MATT. 4:1-2.

1:4 - BEING ASSEMBLED TOGETHER WITH THEM, COMMANDED THAT THEY SHOULD NOT DEPART FROM JERUSALEM, BUT WAIT FOR THE PROMISE OF THE FATHER....

**Contradictions:**

MATT. 28:16-20 - The eleven disciples went into Galilee, into a mountain where Jesus had appointed them. .... Jesus spake unto them, "..... Go ye therefore, and teach all nations, baptizing them in the name of the Father, the Son, and the Holy Ghost; teaching them to observe all things whatsoever I have commanded you...."

[Did Jesus assemble with the disciples in Jerusalem, or in Galilee?]

[Did Jesus instruct the disciples to remain in Jerusalem, or did he order them to go teaching and baptizing?]

MARK 16:15 - Jesus: "Go ye into all the world, and preach the gospel to every creature."

[Did Jesus instruct the disciples to remain in Jerusalem, or to preach the gospel?]

See also under LUKE 24:49.

1:5 - JESUS: "...YE SHALL BE BAPTIZED WITH THE HOLY GHOST NOT MANY DAYS HENCE."

**Contradiction:**

JOHN 20:22 - He breathed on them, and saith, "Receive ye the Holy Ghost."

[Did Jesus tell the apostles that they would have to wait several days before receiving the Holy Ghost, or had he already given them the Holy Ghost by breathing on them?]

1:6 - ...THEY ASKED HIM, "LORD WILT THOU AT THIS TIME RESTORE AGAIN THE KINGDOM OF ISRAEL?"

**Jewish belief:**

The Messiah was expected to drive the Romans out of Israel and re-establish the Israelite kingdom. Therefore, the disciples, who were Jewish and who believed that Jesus was the Messiah, would have expected him to free Israel from Roman occupation. The concept of the Messiah, however, did not include death and resurrection.

1:8 - JESUS: "YE SHALL RECEIVE POWER, AFTER THAT THE HOLY GHOST IS COME UPON YOU, AND YE SHALL BE WITNESSES UNTO ME IN JERUSALEM, ALL JUDAEA, SAMARIA, AND UNTO THE UTTERMOST PART OF THE EARTH."

**Contradiction:**

MATT. 10:23 - Jesus: "...Ye shall not have gone over the cities of Israel, till the Son of man be come.

[Did Jesus believe that he would not return before the disciples traveled over the earth, or did he believe that he would return before they had visited all the cities if Israel?]

**Perplexing:**

Why did the resurrected Jesus not witness for himself? Why did he need disciples to witness for him?

1:9-10 - WHEN HE HAD SPOKEN THESE THINGS, WHILE THEY BEHELD, HE WAS TAKEN UP, AND A CLOUD RECEIVED HIM OUT OF THEIR SIGHT. WHILE THEY LOOKED STEADFASTLY TOWARD HEAVEN AS HE WENT UP, TWO MEN STOOD BY THEM IN WHITE APPAREL.

**Contradictions:**

MARK 16:19 - After having told the disciples in 16:18 that they cannot be hurt by serpents or deadly drinks, and that they shall heal the sick, he was received up into heaven, and sat on the right hand of God.

LUKE 24:51 - While he blessed them, after having told them in 24:47 to preach repentance and remission of sins in his name to all nations, he was carried up into heaven.
[Were Jesus' last words those cited in 1:8, or those cited by MARK, or by LUKE?]
[Were there, or were there not two men in white with the disciples?]

**Perplexing:**
How was Jesus taken up to heaven? How far away is heaven? How long did it take him to reach heaven? Why did the gospels not report the presence of the two men (angels?) in white?

**Old Testament:** See under MARK 16:19.

**Pagan parallels**: See under MARK 16:19.

**History:**
There is no historical evidence for Jesus' ascension.

1:11 - [THE MEN] SAID, "YE MEN OF GALILEE.... JESUS, WHICH IS TAKEN UP FROM YOU INTO HEAVEN, SHALL SO COME IN LIKE MANNER AS YE HAVE SEEN HIM GO INTO HEAVEN."

**Perplexing:**
Why has Jesus not returned as the men [angels?] said? They implied that the apostles would see Jesus return. Did something happen in heaven to prevent Jesus from coming back to earth?
See also under MATT. 17:11-13.

1:12 - RETURNED THEY UNTO JERUSALEM FROM THE MOUNT CALLED OLIVET, WHICH FROM JERUSALEM IS A SABBATH DAY'S JOURNEY.

**Contradictions:**
MARK 16;14-19 - Jesus ascended from Jerusalem.
[Did Jesus ascend from Mount Olivet, or from Jerusalem?]
LUKE 24:50-51 - Jesus ascended from Bethany.
[Did Jesus ascend from Mount Olivet, or Bethany?]

**Perplexing:**
Why did MATT. and JOHN not report Jesus' ascension?

**History:**
A Sabbath day's journey was about 2/3 of a mile.

1:13-14 - WHEN THEY WERE COME IN, THEY WENT INTO AN UPPER ROOM, WHERE ABODE PETER, JAMES, JOHN, ANDREW, PHILIP, THOMAS, BARTHOLOMEW, MATTHEW, JAMES THE SON OF ALPHAEUS, SIMON ZELOTES, AND JUDAS THE BROTHER OF JAMES. THEY ALL CONTINUED WITH ONE ACCORD IN PRAYER AND SUPPLICATION WITH THE WOMEN, AND MARY THE MOTHER OF JESUS, AND WITH HIS BRETHREN.

**Contradictions:**
MARK 16:20 - They went forth, and preached everywhere, the Lord working with them, and confirming the word with signs following.
[Did the apostles go to an upper room with women and spend their time in prayer and supplication, or did they go preaching everywhere?]
LUKE 24:52-53 - They worshipped him, and returned to Jerusalem with great joy, and were continually in the temple, praising and blessing God.
[Did the apostles go to an upper room with women and spend their time in prayer and supplication, or were they continually in the temple?]
MATT. 10:2-4 - Lebbaeus Thaddaeus, not Judas the brother of James, was cited as one of the twelve disciples.
MARK 3:16-19 - Thaddaeus, not Judas the brother of James, was cited as one of the twelve disciples.
[Was Judas the brother of James, or Thaddaeus one of the twelve disciples?]
See also under MATT. 10:2-4.

**Perplexing:**
Who were the women in the room? Did they live there? Were they related to the apostles? Whose room was it? How large was it? Why did the eleven disciples all live in one room? Was the room rented? If so, who paid the rent? From where was the money obtained? Why was Joseph, Jesus' stepfather not present? Where was he? What happened to him?
See also under MATT. 10:2-4.

**History:** See under MATT. 10:2-4.

1:15 - PETER STOOD IN THE MIDST OF THE DISCIPLES...(THE NUMBER OF NAMES TOGETHER WERE ABOUT 120).

**Old Testament:**
Number "120," like the number "40," appeared numerous times in the Old Testament and may also have been of some mystical significance to the ancient Hebrews; (120 is the result of lx2x3x4x5, and 40x3; 20 is also a very frequently cited number).
A few examples of the use of "120" are:
1 CHRON. 15:5 - ...Uriel the chief, and his brethren 120;
2 CHRON. 5:12 - ...and with them 120 priests sounding with trumpets;
DAN 6:1 - It pleased Darius to set over the kingdom 120 princes....
See also under 1:3.

1:16 - PETER: "THIS SCRIPTURE MUST NEEDS HAVE BEEN FULFILLED WHICH THE HOLY GHOST BY THE MOUTH OF DAVID SPAKE BEFORE CONCERNING JUDAS, WHICH WAS A GUIDE TO THEM THAT TOOK JESUS."

**Perplexing:**
To which statement in Scripture did Peter refer?

1:18 - PETER: "THIS MAN [JUDAS ISCARIOT] PURCHASED A FIELD WITH THE REWARD OF INIQUITY, AND FALLING HEADLONG, HE BURST ASUNDER IN THE MIDST, AND ALL HIS BOWELS GUSHED OUT."

**Contradictions:**
MATT. 27:5 - He [Judas Iscariot] cast down the pieces of silver in the temple, departed, and went and hanged himself.
[Did Judas purchase a field with the money he received for betraying Jesus, or did he cast it down in the temple?]
[Did Judas fall and burst, or did he hang himself?]
MATT. 27:6-7 - The chief priests took the silver pieces and bought the potter's field to bury strangers.
[Did Judas purchase the field, or did the chief priests purchase the field?]

**Perplexing:**
Why did Judas either fall and burst or hang himself, for doing what God ordained him to do? Had he not betrayed Jesus, there would not have been a crucifixion and resurrection, and, consequently, no Christianity. Why was Judas, therefore, not commended and hailed as a hero? Why was Judas' death not reported by MARK, LUKE, JOHN, and Paul?
See also under LUKE 22:3-6.

1-19 - PETER: "IT WAS KNOWN UNTO ALL DWELLERS IN JERUSALEM, INSOMUCH AS THAT FIELD IS CALLED IN THEIR PROPER TONGUE, 'ACELDAMA,' THAT IS TO SAY, 'THE FIELD OF BLOOD.'"

**Contradiction:**
MATT. 27:6-8 - The chief priests.... ...bought the potter's field, to bury strangers. Wherefore that field was called, "The field of blood," unto this day.
[Was the field called "The field of blood," because Judas purchased it, or because the priests bought it to use as a burial place?]

**Language:**
In Aramaic, "aceldama" means "atonement," "compensation," or "food of price." The Aramaic, "khaqel dema" means, "field of blood."

1:20 - PETER: "IT IS WRITTEN IN THE BOCK OF PSALMS, 'LET HIS HABITATION BE DESOLATE, AND LET NO MAN DWELL THEREIN, AND HIS BISHOPRICK LET ANOTHER TAKE.'"

**Old Testament:**
PS. 69:25 - "Let their [my enemies' (69:19)] habitation be desolate, and let none dwell in their tents."
PS. 109:8 - "Let his [an adversary's (109:4)] days be few, and let another take his office."
[Note that Peter changed the plural "their" to the singular "his," and he changed "in their tents" to "therein." Note also that the curses in PS. are aimed at the Psalmist's adversaries, and do not comprise a prophecy about something that is to occur hundreds of years in the future.]

**Perplexing:**
Why did Peter misquote the PS. verses? Did he deliberately lie? Why did not any of the other Jews correct him?

1:21-22 - PETER: "WHEREFORE OF THESE MEN WHICH HAVE COMPANIED WITH US ALL THE TIME THAT THE LORD JESUS WENT IN AND OUT AMONG US, BEGINNING FROM THE BAPTISM OF JOHN, UNTO THE SAME DAY THAT HE WAS TAKEN UP FROM US, MUST ONE BE ORDAINED TO BE A WITNESS WITH US OF HIS RESURRECTION."

**Contradiction:**
MATT. 3:13-16 - Jesus was baptized by John before meeting Peter and acquiring his first disciples in 4:18-20.
MARK 1:9 - Jesus was baptized by John before meeting Peter and obtaining his first disciples in 1:16-18.
LUKE 3:21 - Jesus was baptized by John before meeting Peter and selecting his first disciples in 5:3-11.
[Did, or did not Jesus have disciples present when he was baptized by John?]

**Perplexing:**
Why did Peter lie by saying that he and the other disciples were with Jesus from the time he was baptized by John? Why did MATT. and JOHN fail to report that Jesus was taken (ascended) in the presence of the disciples?

1:23 - THEY APPOINTED TWO, JOSEPH CALLED BARSABAS, WHO WAS SURNAMED JUSTUS, AND MATTHIAS.

**Perplexing:**
Why was another twelfth disciple needed? Why were these two, who were not reported by the gospels as having been present at Jesus' baptism or even as having been present at any time with Jesus, selected?

1:26 - THEY GAVE FORTH THEIR LOTS, AND THE LOT FELL UPON MATTHIAS; HE WAS NUMBERED WITH THE ELEVEN APOSTLES.

**Perplexing:**
Did all of the about 120 (1:15) cast lots, or did only the original eleven disciples do so? How were the lots cast? Why was Matthias not mentioned again in the Bible? What happened to him?

**Old Testament:**
PROV. 16:33 - The lot is cast into the lap, but the whole disposing thereof is of the LORD.

2:1 - WHEN THE DAY OF PENTECOST WAS FULLY COME, THEY WERE ALL WITH ONE ACCORD IN ONE PLACE.

**History:**
Pentecost was a Jewish harvest holiday called the "Feast of Weeks," "Shabouth" ("Shavu'ot"), in Hebrew; it was probably derived from earlier pagan harvest festivals in the Canaan region.
The Essene sect believed that the last day of the 50 days after Passover was the time for a solemn renewal of the Covenant. They also believed that it was the time at which a divine manifestation might occur.

**Perplexing:**
In what place were the disciples gathered? Were all 120, or just the 12 there?

**Old Testament:**
LEV. 23:15-16 - The LORD: "Ye shall count unto you from the morrow after the sabbath [Passover]... seven sabbaths shall be complete; unto the morrow after the seventh sabbath shall ye number 50 days, and ye shall offer a new meat offering unto the LORD."

2:3-4 - THERE APPEARED UNTO THEM CLOVEN TONGUES LIKE AS OF FIRE; IT SAT UPON EACH OF THEM. THEY WERE ALL FILLED WITH THE HOLY GHOST, AND BEGAN TO SPEAK WITH OTHER TONGUES, AS THE SPIRIT GAVE THEM UTTERANCE.

**Contradictions:**
MATT. 3:16 - Jesus...saw the Spirit of God descending like a dove, and lighting upon him.
MARK 1:10 - ...he saw...the Spirit like a dove descending upon him.
LUKE 3:22 - The Holy Ghost descended in a bodily shape like a dove upon him....
[Is the Holy Ghost in the form of cloven tongues of fire, or like a dove? ]
JOHN 20:22 - he [Jesus] breathed on them, and saith, "Receive ye the Holy Ghost."
[Did the disciples have to wait until Pentecost to receive the Holy Ghost, or did they receive it when Jesus breathed on them?]

**Perplexing:**
Why in MATT. 3:11 and LUKE 3:16, did John say, "...he [Jesus] shall baptize you with the Holy Ghost and with fire"; in MARK 1:8, "...he shall baptize you with the Holy Ghost," and in JOHN 1:33, "...the same is he which baptizeth with the Holy Ghost?" Was ACTS saying that Jesus failed to baptize the disciples, or that John lied? Why did the Holy Ghost wait until Pentecost before descending upon the disciples, and why did it cause them to speak in tongues?

2:5 - THERE WERE DWELLING AT JERUSALEM JEWS, DEVOUT MEN, OUT OF EVERY NATION UNDER HEAVEN.

**Perplexing:**
Why did the writer say, "every nation under heaven," when such was not the case? Why was the writer ignorant of the fact that there were more nations than he knew about? Why was he unaware that Jews were not in every nation? Why did Jesus fail to inform his disciples and others about the size of the planet and about the existence of hundreds of different nations and peoples? Why did he allow his disciples to believe that the world consisted only of those nations and people in the Middle/Near East, the Mediterranean region, and adjacent parts of Africa? Why did he fail to educate them about the Western Hemisphere, the Far East, and the Pacific region, etc.? If the disciples were ignorant of the existence of most of the world's nations, how could they comply with his order in MATT. 28:19 to teach all nations?"

2:6-11 - WHEN THIS WAS NOISED ABROAD, THE MULTITUDE CAME TOGETHER, AND WERE CONFOUNDED, BECAUSE EVERY MAN HEARD THEM SPEAK IN HIS OWN LANGUAGE. ....PARTHIANS, MEDES, ELAMITES, DWELLERS IN MESOPOTAMIA, IN JUDAEA, AND CAPPADOCIA, PONTUS, ASIA, PHRYGIA, PAMPHYLLA, EGYPT, PARTS OF LIBYA ABOUT CYRENE, STRANGERS OF ROME, JEWS, PROSELYTES, CRETES, AND ARABIANS ..."WE HEAR THEM SPEAK IN OUR TONGUES THE WONDERFUL WORKS OF GOD."

**Perplexing:**
Did the disciples know what they were saying when they spoke in different languages? Did they understand

each other? Why did no one, so far, other than the apostles speak in tongues after receiving the Holy Ghost? Why did they not speak in tongues after Jesus breathed the Holy Ghost on to them in JOHN 20:22?

**History:**

At that time Greek was widely spoken throughout the area, although the Parthians spoke Aramaic. Consequently, to be understood by all of the cited people, the disciples need only to have spoken in Greek and Aramaic - languages they would already have known. Some ancient Israelite and pagan religious practices also involved speaking in tongues (glossolalia - the utterance of incoherent sounds) under the influence of religious ecstasy).

**Pagan parallel:**

When Buddha gave his first sermon, each of the many listeners believed that they heard him speak in their particular language.

2:13-15 - OTHERS MOCKING SAID, "THESE MEN ARE FULL OF NEW WINE." PETER ... SAID, "... THESE MEN ARE NOT DRUNKEN, AS YE SUPPOSE, SEEING IT IS BUT THE THIRD HOUR OF THE DAY."

**Perplexing:**

If the men were speaking coherently, why were they believed to be drunk? Why did Peter have to say that they were not drunk, going so far as to cite the hour of the day? Was Peter saying that the disciples tended to get drunk after the third hour? Was Paul commenting about such speaking in tongues when he said in 1 COR. 14:2, "He that speaketh in an unknown tongue speaketh not unto men, but unto God, for no man understandeth him"; then in 1 COR. 14:6, "Brethren, if I come unto you speaking with tongues, what shall I profit you, except I shall speak to you either by revelation, knowledge, prophesying, or doctrine"; and in 1 COR. 14:14, "If I pray in an unknown tongue, my spirit prayeth, but my understanding is unfruitful?" Paul added (1 COR. 14:23), "If the whole church be come together into one place, and all speak with tongues, and there come in those that are unlearned, or unbelievers, will they not say that ye are mad?" And in 1 COR. 14:27-28, "If any man speak in an unknown tongue...let one interpret. If there be no interpreter, let him keep silence in the church; let him speak to himself, and to God."

2:16-21 - PETER: "THIS IS THAT WHICH WAS SPOKEN BY THE PROPHET JOEL, 'IT SHALL COME TO PASS IN THE LAST DAYS, SAITH GOD, I WILL POUR OUT MY SPIRIT UPON ALL FLESH, AND YOUR SONS AND DAUGHTERS SHALL PROPHESY ... AND ON MY SERVANTS AND ON MY HANDMAIDENS I WILL POUR OUT IN THOSE DAYS OF MY SPIRIT, AND THEY SHALL PROPHESY ... THE SUN SHALL BE TURNED INTO DARKNESS, AND THE MOON INTO BLOOD, BEFORE THAT GREAT AND NOTABLE DAY OF THE LORD COMES; WHOSOEVER SHALL CALL ON THE NAME OF THE LORD SHALL BE SAVED.'"

**Old Testament:**

JOEL 2:27-32 - God: "Ye shall know that I am in the midst of Israel, and that I am the LORD your God, and none else, and My people shall never be ashamed. It shall come to pass afterward, that I will pour out My spirit upon all flesh, and your sons and daughters shall prophesy...and upon the servants and upon the handmaids in those days will I pour out My spirit. .... The sun shall be turned into darkness, and the moon into blood, before the great and terrible day of the LORD come. Whosoever shall call on the name of the

LORD shall be delivered, for in mount Zion and in Jerusalem shall be deliverance, and in the remnant whom the LORD shall call."
See also under MATT. 24:29.

**Perplexing:**
Why did the Jews fail to point out that Peter did not cite the verse accurately? Why did Peter equate speaking in tongues with prophesy? Did Peter really believe that he was currently living in the last days as implied by the prophecy?
See also under MATT. 24:29.

**Contradictions:** See under MATT. 19:17-19 (for obtaining eternal life).

2:22 - PETER: "YE MEN OF ISRAEL, HEAR THESE WORDS; JESUS OF NAZARETH, A MAN APPROVED OF GOD AMONG YOU BY MIRACLES, WONDERS, AND SIGNS, WHICH GOD DID BY HIM IN THE MIDST OF YOU, AS YE YOURSELVES ALSO KNOW."

**Contradictions:**
JOHN 6:69 - Peter: "We believe and are sure that thou art that Christ, the Son of the living God."
ACTS 3:26 - Peter: "Unto you first God, having raised up his Son Jesus...."
[Did Peter say that Jesus was "a man approved of God" and through whom God worked miracles, or did he say that Jesus was the Son of God?]
See also under MATT. 1:1.

**Perplexing:**
After all that Jesus had said about being the Son of God, and being one with God, why did Peter still consider him to have been just a man—a man of whom God approved? Why did Peter believe that Jesus was only a man through whom God performed His miracles? Why did Peter give credit to God, not to Jesus for the miracles worked by Jesus?

**History:**
Some of the first Christians known as Ebionites (Jewish-Christians) believed that Jesus was a man who God selected for the performance of miracles; they did not believe that Jesus was the Son of God. Jews of that period used the term, "Son of God," figuratively, as a title for Judean and Israelite kings, not in a literal sense.
See also under MATT. 3:17 and 29.

2:23 - PETER: "HIM, BEING DELIVERED BY THE DETERMINATE COUNSEL AND FOREKNOWLEDGE OF GOD, YE HAVE TAKEN, AND BY WICKED HANDS HAVE CRUCIFIED AND SLAIN."

**Contradictions:**
ACTS 5:29-30 - Peter: "The God of our fathers raised up Jesus, whom ye slew and hanged on a tree."
ACTS 10:39 - Peter: "[Jesus]...whom they slew and hanged on a tree."
[Did Peter say that Jesus was crucified, or did he say that Jesus was killed, in an unspecified manner, and then hung on a tree?]
See also under MATT. 27:35.

**History:** See under MATT. 26:59-60 and 35

**Perplexing:**
Why did the Jews fail to correct Peter by pointing out that crucifixion was not a Jewish means of execution, that at that time they did not resort to capital punishment, and that Jesus was killed by the Romans for claiming to be a king in violation of Roman law? If God had ordained Jesus to be killed, how could those responsible for his death be called "wicked?"
See also under MATT. 27:25.

**History:** See under MATT. 27:35.

2:24 - PETER: "WHOM GOD HATH RAISED UP...."

**Perplexing:**
Did God raise up Jesus the man, or did Jesus as the Son of God or as one with God resurrect himself?

2:25-28 - PETER: "DAVID SPEAKETH CONCERNING HIM [JESUS], 'I FORESAW THE LORD ALWAYS BEFORE MY FACE...THEREFORE DID MY HEART REJOICE, AND MY TONGUE WAS GLAD; MOREOVER ALSO MY FLESH SHALL REST IN HOPE, BECAUSE THOU WILT NOT LEAVE MY SOUL IN HELL, NEITHER WILT THOU SUFFER THINE HOLY ONE TO SEE CORRUPTION. THOU HAST MADE KNOWN TO ME THE WAYS OF LIFE; THOU SHALT MAKE ME FULL OF JOY WITH THY COUNTENANCE.'"

**Old Testament:**
PS. 16:8-11 - "I have set the LORD always before me.... Therefore my heart is glad, and my glory rejoiceth; my flesh also shall rest in hope.Thou wilt not leave my soul in hell; neither wilt Thou suffer Thine Holy One to see corruption. Thou wilt shew me the path of life; in Thy presence is fulness of joy; at Thy right hand there are pleasures for evermore."

**Language:**
The Hebrew reads, "...my heart rejoices and my soul is elated; my flesh, too, rests in confidence; because You will not abandon my soul to the grave, You will not allow Your devout one to witness destruction. You will make known to me the path of life, the fullness of joys in Your Presence, the delights that are in Your right hand for eternity." (From *Tanach*, the Stone edition; Ed. Rabbi Nosson Scherman, Mesorah Publications, Ltd.)
(In the Hebrew versions, David referred to himself as the LORD's "devout one," or "godly one." Thus, David was referring to himself, not to a forthcoming "Holy One." Nonetheless, in the King James and other Bible versions, the term was changed to "Holy One," and interpreted as a prophecy pertaining to Jesus, although the verses are not a prophecy.)

**Perplexing:**
Why did the Jews fail to correct Peter's misquoting of the PS. verses? Why was Peter ignorant of the Hebrew Scripture? Why did Peter interpret the PS. verses as a prophecy of a resurrection to occur centuries into the future?

2:30 - PETER: "[DAVID] BEING A PROPHET, AND KNOWING THAT GOD HAD SWORN WITH AN OATH TO HIM, THAT THE FRUIT OF HIS LOINS, ACCORDING TO THE FLESH, HE WOULD RAISE UP CHRIST TO SIT ON HIS THRONE."

**Contradictions:**
MATT. 22:42-45 - Jesus asked Pharisees, "Whose son is he [Christ]?" They said, "The Son of David." Jesus responded, "How then doth David in spirit call him 'Lord'.... If David then call him 'Lord,' how is he his son?"
LUKE 20:44 - Jesus: "David therefore calleth him [Christ] 'Lord,' how is he then his son?"
[Was Jesus a human descendant of David, or was he the Son of God?]
See also under 2:22 and MATT. 1:1.
JOHN 18:36 - Jesus: "My kingdom is not of this world."
[Was Jesus to sit on David's throne, or was his kingdom not of this world?]
See also under MATT. 1:16 and LUKE 3:23.

**History:**
The Jews of that time recognized only paternal descent; they did not recognize or keep records of matriarchal descent. Therefore, unless Jesus had a human father descended from David, he could not be considered a descendant of David.
See also under MATT. 1:1.

**Perplexing:**
Why did Peter again present Jesus as a human man, not as the Son of God?

2:31 - PETER: "HE [DAVID] SEEING THIS BEFORE SPAKE OF THE RESURRECTION OF CHRIST, THAT HIS SOUL WAS NOT LEFT IN HELL, NEITHER HIS FLESH DID SEE CORRUPTION."

**Old Testament:** See under 2:25-28.

**Language:**
The Hebrew word, "shahath," meaning, "pit" or "grave," was mistranslated as "corruption."
See also under 2:25-28.

**Perplexing:**
Since the PS. verses (16:8-11), to which Peter referred, were written in the first person, they had to pertain to the writer (presumably David). How could they, therefore,be interpreted as a prophecy of a resurrection of someone (Jesus) that is to take place hundreds of years in the future? How could Jesus' soul, if he was the Son of God, go to hell?
See also under 2:25-28.

2:32-33 - PETER: "THIS JESUS HATH GOD RAISED UP, WHEREOF WE ARE ALL WITNESSES. THEREFORE BEING BY THE RIGHT HAND OF GOD EXALTED, AND HAVING RECEIVED OF THE FATHER THE PROMISE OF THE HOLY GHOST, HE HATH SHED FORTH THIS, WHICH YE NOW SEE AND HEAR."

**Contradiction:**
MATT. 3:16 - ...Jesus...saw the Spirit of God descending like a dove, and lighting upon him.
MARK 1:10 - ...he saw...the Spirit like a dove descending upon him.
LUKE 3:22 - The Holy Ghost descended in a bodily shape like a dove upon him....
LUKE 4:1 - Jesus being full of the Holy Ghost returned....
[Did the Father promise that He would give Jesus the Holy Ghost after his resurrection, or had the Holy Ghost already descended on Jesus and filled him long before the resurrection?]

**Perplexing:**
Why did the Jews in Peter's audience fail to point out that the PS. verses did not pertain to Jesus? Why did Peter refer to Jesus as, "this Jesus?" Why did Peter continue to imply that Jesus was a man raised up by God and who was promised the Holy Ghost, rather that state that he was the Son of God? When did the Father promise Jesus the Holy Ghost?
See also under 2:22, 24, and 25-28.

2:34-35 - PETER: "DAVID...SAITH, 'THE LORD SAID UNTO MY LORD, "SIT THOU ON MY RIGHT HAND, UNTIL I MAKE THY FOES THY FOOTSTOOL."'"

**Old Testament:**
PS. 110:1-2 - "The LORD said unto my Lord ["lord," or "master," in Hebrew versions], 'Sit thou at My right hand, until I make thine enemies thy footstool.' The LORD shall send the rod of thy strength out of Zion; rule thou in the midst of thine enemies." [The verses form part of an address by God to a new king of Judea. In this instance the LORD is promising him success against his enemies.]

**Language:**
The term, "my Lord," was an ancient Hebrew way of addressing a king.

2:36 - PETER: "THEREFORE LET ALL THE HOUSE OF ISRAEL KNOW ASSUREDLY, THAT GOD HATH MADE THAT SAME JESUS, WHOM YE HAVE CRUCIFIED, BOTH LORD AND CHRIST."

**Contradictions:** See under 2:23.

**Perplexing:**
Where in the Bible is it said that God made Jesus Lord and Christ? Why did Peter make the statement? Why did Peter imply that this did not occur until after Jesus' resurrection? Why did Peter again imply that Jesus was not only distinct from God, but was not a divine being until God made him so? Why did Peter refer to Jesus as a person for whom God did things, rather than as the Son of God? Did Peter forget that in JOHN 6:68-69, he said that Jesus was the Son of the living God? Later in ACTS 3:26, he will say that Jesus is the Son of God.
See also under 2:22 and 23.

**Language**: See under MATT. 1:1.

2:37 - WHEN THEY HEARD THIS, THEY WERE PRICKED IN THEIR HEART, AND SAID UNTO PETER AND THE REST OF THE APOSTLES, "MEN AND BRETHREN, WHAT SHALL WE DO?"

**Perplexing:**
Why did the people accept Peter's comments so quickly and without either commenting on them or correcting his errors? Were the people to whom Peter was speaking actually Jewish?

2:38 - PETER SAID, "REPENT, AND BE BAPTIZED EVERYONE OF YOU IN THE NAME OF JESUS CHRIST FOR THE REMISSION OF SINS, AND YE SHALL RECEIVE THE GIFT OF THE HOLY GHOST."

**Contradiction:**
MATT. 28:19 - Jesus: "Teach all nations, baptizing them in the name of the Father, the Son, and the Holy Ghost."
[Must one be baptized "in the name of Jesus Christ for the remission of sins," or must one be baptized "in the name of the Father, the Son, and the Holy Ghost?"]

**History:**
Baptism for the remission of sins, and the Holy Ghost concept were not part of Judaism.
See also under MATT. 3:5-6.

**Pagan concept:** See under MATT. 3:5-6.

**Perplexing:**
Did Peter forget Jesus' command about how to baptize? Was Peter unaware of the Trinity? When were the disciples baptized? Did Jesus baptize them? Why did the Bible not mention their baptism? Why did Peter fail to instruct his listeners about Jesus' teachings? Why did he fail to mention even one of Jesus' teachings? Why did the Jews fail to inform Peter that baptism for the remission of sins was a pagan rite, not a Jewish custom, and that the Holy Ghost was not a Jewish belief? Why did Peter instruct Jews to engage in a non-Jewish ritual?

**Language:**
Greek versions of the Old Testament translated "Messiah," meaning one who has been anointed, as "Christos," which becomes "Christ" in English. It also became misconstrued as a name. Hence, Old Testament verses translated into Greek that contained "Christos" were interpreted as references to Jesus (Jesus Christ).
See also under MATT. 1:1.

2:41 - THEY THAT GLADLY RECEIVED HIS WORD WERE BAPTIZED; THE SAME DAY THERE WERE ADDED UNTO THEM ABOUT 3000 SOULS.

**Perplexing:**
Where and how were 3000 people baptized in one day? Who baptized them? How long did it take for all of them to be baptized? If any were Jewish, why did they so willingly engage in this pagan practice? Did they all receive the Holy Ghost? If so, how did it come upon them? Did they all then speak in tongues?

2:43 - FEAR CAME UPON EVERY SOUL, AND MANY WONDERS AND SIGNS WERE DONE BY THE APOSTLES.

**History:**
There is no secular record of any wonders or signs having been done by the apostles.

**Perplexing:**
Why did everyone become fearful? What were the many wonders and signs done by the apostles? Why is

there no historical record of what they did?

2:44 - ALL THAT BELIEVED WERE TOGETHER, AND HAD ALL THINGS COMMON.

**Perplexing:**
How were over 3000 people able to get together? How were they able to avoid eliciting suspicion and investigation by the Romans? Based on these and similar verses in ACTS, these early followers of Jesus, who held all their properties in common, would be viewed as Communists in modern times. How was this common property handled? Where was it kept? Who oversaw its use and distribution?

**History:**
Members of the Essene sect held their property in common. Anyone joining the Essenes had to give his things to be in common with the rest. Consequently, everyone's possessions were intermingled, and one individual was assigned to manage the joint holdings.

2:45 - [THEY] SOLD THEIR POSSESSIONS AND GOODS, AND PARTED THEM TO ALL MEN AS EVERY MAN HAD NEED.

**Perplexing:**
Where were the possessions and goods kept? Did they sell all of their possessions and goods, or just part of them? Did they distribute the proceeds to all those in need, or just among their fellow believers? Who decided who received what? What criteria were used? Why do not modern Christians, especially the clergy, sell their possessions to help the poor? Why are most Christians interested in accumulating wealth, rather than sharing it?

**History:**
Members of the Essene sect sold their possessions and distributed the proceeds among themselves as needed.

2:46 - THEY, CONTINUING DAILY...IN THE TEMPLE, AND BREAKING BREAD FROM HOUSE TO HOUSE, DID EAT THEIR MEAT....

**Contradictions:** See under LUKE 24:52-53.

**Perplexing:**
Who owned the houses in which they ate? Did they retain possession of their houses and the contents therein? From where did they obtain the money to buy bread and meat (food)?
See also under LUKE 24:52-53.

**Jewish tradition:**
Breaking bread is a Jewish expression for the custom of beginning a meal by blessing a loaf of bread, then giving a piece to each person present.

**History:**
The early followers of Jesus, by adhering to Jewish customs and attending prayer services in the temple, showed that they still considered themselves to be Jewish, and not intent upon starting a new religion. They were Jews who thought that the Messiah had come in the person of Jesus.

2:47 - PRAISING GOD.... THE LORD ADDED TO THE CHURCH DAILY SUCH AS SHOULD BE SAVED.

**Contradiction:** See under JOHN 14:6.

**Perplexing:**
Why did the disciples believe that God needed to be praised? Why does God need praise? Of what use is praise to almighty God of the universe? Is God so egotistical and pompous that He requires praise from humans? Does praise make God feel good? Does God really care whether or not anyone praises Him? How did the Lord decide who should be saved?
See also under LUKE 2:13-14, JOHN 6:44, and 14:6.

**Dead Sea Scrolls:** See under JOHN 6:44.

3:6 - PETER [TO A LAME MAN]: "SILVER AND GOLD HAVE I NONE, BUT SUCH AS I HAVE GIVE I THEE; IN THE NAME OF JESUS CHRIST OF NAZARETH RISE UP AND WALK."

**Perplexing:**
Why did Peter not speak to the man about Jesus or ask him to have faith? Why did Peter say, "Jesus Christ of Nazareth," rather than simply, "Jesus Christ?"

**Pagan concept:** See under JOHN 18:5-6.

3:7-9 - ...IMMEDIATELY HIS FEET AND ANKLE BONES RECEIVED STRENGTH. HE LEAPING UP STOOD, WALKED, AND ENTERED WITH THEM INTO THE TEMPLE, WALKING, LEAPING, AND PRAISING GOD. ALL THE PEOPLE SAW HIM WALKING, LEAPING, AND PRAISING GOD.

**Perplexing:**
Did God heal the man, or did Jesus' name heal him? Why did the man praise God, not Jesus, and not Peter for healing him? Why did the man praise God at all, rather than denouncing God for having caused him to suffer until now? If God healed the man, why did He wait until Peter invoked the name of Jesus to do so? In JOHN 14:12, Jesus said, "He that believeth on me, the works that I do shall he do also, and greater works than these shall he do." Why, therefore, cannot modern believers also heal the lame?
See also under 2:47, and under LUKE 2:13-14.

**History:**
There is no record of this miracle, despite the claim that people, presumably many, witnessed the occurrence.

3:13 - PETER: "THE GOD OF ABRAHAM, ISAAC, AND JACOB, THE GOD OF OUR FATHERS, HATH GLORIFIED HIS SON JESUS, WHOM YE DELIVERED UP, AND DENIED IN THE PRESENCE OF PILATE, WHEN HE WAS DETERMINED TO LET HIM GO."

**Contradictions:** See under MATT. 1:18 and JOHN 6:69.

**Perplexing:** See under MATT. 27:17, 20, 22, 24, 25, and 26.

**History:** See under MATT. 27:17, 21, 22, 24, and 25.

3:14 - PETER: "YE DENIED THE HOLY ONE AND THE JUST, AND DESIRED A MURDERER TO BE GRANTED UNTO YOU."

**Contradictions:** See under MARK 15:7.

**History:** See under MATT. 27:15.

3:15 - PETER: "[YOU] KILLED THE PRINCE OF LIFE, WHOM GOD RAISED FROM THE DEAD, WHEREOF WE ARE WITNESSES."

**Perplexing:**
Why did Peter accuse the Jews of killing Jesus when the Romans killed him for calling himself a king - a capital offense under Roman law?
See also under 2:23, 24, and MATT. 27:37-38.

**History:** See under MATT. 27:1-2, 11, 22, and 35.

3:16 - PETER: "HIS NAME THROUGH FAITH IN HIS NAME HATH MADE THIS MAN STRONG ... THE FAITH WHICH IS BY HIM HATH GIVEN HIM THIS PERFECT SOUNDNESS IN THE PRESENCE OF YOU ALL."

**Perplexing:**
Why did Peter say that it was faith in Jesus' name, not in Jesus, or in God, that healed the lame man?

**Pagan concept:** See under JOHN 18:5-6.

3:18 - PETER: "THOSE THINGS, WHICH GOD BEFORE HAD SHEWED BY THE MOUTH OF ALL HIS PROPHETS, THAT CHRIST SHOULD SUFFER, HE HATH FULFILLED."

**Language**: See under 2:38.

**Perplexing:**
Why did the Jews not question Peter about those verses in which he believed the prophets referred to Jesus?
See also under 2:16-21 and 25-28.

13:21 - PETER: "...GOD HATH SPOKEN BY THE MOUTH OF ALL HIS HOLY PROPHETS SINCE THE WORLD BEGAN."

**Perplexing:**
Why cannot God speak for Himself? Why did He need prophets to speak for Him?
See also under 3:18.

3:22-23 - PETER: "MOSES SAID UNTO THE FATHERS, 'A PROPHET SHALL THE LORD YOUR GOD RAISE UP UNTO YOU OF YOUR BRETHREN, LIKE UNTO ME; HIM SHALL YE HEAR IN ALL THINGS.... .....EVERY SOUL THAT SHALL NOT HEAR THAT PROPHET, SHALL BE DESTROYED FROM AMONG THE PEOPLE.'"

**Old Testament:**
DEUT. 18:17-22 - Moses: "The LORD said unto me, '.... I will raise up a Prophet from among their brethren, like unto thee, and will put words in his mouth, and he shall speak unto them all that I shall command him. ...whosoever will not hearken unto My words which he shall speak in My name, I will require it of him. The prophet, which shall ...speak a word in My name, which I have not commanded...or that shall speak in the name of other gods ...shall die. If thou say..."How shall we know the word which the LORD hath not spoken?" When a prophet speaketh in the name of the LORD, if the thing not come to pass that is the thing which the LORD hath not spoken...thou shalt not be afraid of him.'" [The prophet, to whom. the verses pertained, was to be a human being—"from their brethren"—whose prophecies would come to pass during the life of the people to whom Moses was speaking.] Jewish theologians tend to believe that Moses was speaking about Joshua.

**Perplexing:**
If the people, addressed by Peter, were Jewish, why did they fail to point out that he misconstrued the verses? How could the DEUT. verses written hundreds of years before Jesus be accepted as a prophecy about him? Why did Peter claim that God is so cruel that He will kill for nothing more than not listening to a prophet? Was he trying to incite fear in his listeners to cause them to believe him? Even if the prophet spoke God's words, why would God care whether or not people listened? If God wants to say something to humanity, why does He not speak directly, instead of using a prophet, especially, if He wants His words to be believed?

**Contradiction:**
ACTS 10:34-35 - Peter: "...I perceive that God is no respecter of persons...he that feareth Him, and worketh righteousness, is accepted by Him."
[Must one listen to a particular prophet to avoid being destroyed by God, or must one fear God and work righteousness?]

3:24 - PETER: "ALL THE PROPHETS FROM SAMUEL AND THOSE THAT FOLLOW AFTER, AS MANY AS HAVE SPOKEN, HAVE LIKEWISE FORETOLD OF THESE DAYS."

**Perplexing:** See under 3:18.

3:25 - PETER: "...THE COVENANT WHICH GOD MADE WITH OUR FATHERS, SAYING UNTO ABRAHAM, 'IN THY SEED SHALL ALL THE KINDREDS OF THE EARTH BE BLESSED.'"

**Old Testament:**
GEN. 12:3 - The LORD [said to Abraham], "I will bless them that bless thee, and curse him that curseth thee; in thee shall all families of the earth be blessed."

**Perplexing:**
Did the LORD lie to Abraham? How have all the kindreds (families) of the earth been blessed? [Some theologians contend that Jesus was the blessing prophesied by the LORD. By so contending, they are saying that the centuries of religious hate, violence, persecution, killings, and wars perpetrated by the followers of Jesus are blessings. Are not these deeds more like demonic curses against the kindreds of the earth than like blessings?]

3:26 - PETER: "UNTO YOU FIRST GOD, HAVING RAISED UP HIS SON JESUS, SENT HIM TO

BLESS YOU, IN TURNING AWAY EVERYONE OF YOU FROM HIS INIQUITIES."

**Contradictions:** See under MATT. 1:18, 9:13, and JOHN 6:69.

**Perplexing:**
Why did God fail to tell Abraham about Jesus or about turning people from their iniquities ? Why did Jesus fail to turn people away from their iniquities?
See also under 2:24.

4:1-2 - ...THE SADDUCEES CAME UPON THEM, BEING GRIEVED THAT THEY TAUGHT AND PREACHED THROUGH JESUS THE RESURRECTION FROM THE DEAD.

**History:** See under MATT. 3:7.

4:3 - THEY LAID HANDS ON THEM, AND PUT THEM IN HOLD UNTO THE NEXT DAY....

**Perplexing:**
Why were the Sadducees not afraid of or in awe of people who could perform a notable miracle? Why would they not want to befriend Peter and John and have them perform miracles to help them, their families, and friends?

4:4 - HOWBEIT MANY OF THEM WHICH HEARD THE WORD BELIEVED; THE NUMBER OF THE MEN WAS ABOUT 5000.

**Perplexing:**
How long did it take the 5000 men to hear about Jesus and decide to believe? Who were the people who believed? Were Jews so ignorant of their religious teachings and the Old Testament that they succumbed to Peter's misquotations, misinterpretations, and errors? Were these non-Jews who were ignorant of Judaism and the old Testament?

4:6 - ANNAS THE HIGH PRIEST, CAIAPHAS, JOHN, ALEXANDER, AND AS MANY AS WERE OF THE KINDRED OF THE HIGH PRIEST, WERE GATHERED TOGETHER AT JERUSALEM.

**Contradictions:**
MATT. 26:57, JOHN 18:13, and 24 - Caiaphas was the high priest.
[Was Annas, or Caiaphas the high priest?]
LUKE 3:2 - Annas and Caiaphas being the high priests....
[Was Annas the high priest, or were Annas and Caiaphas high priests together?]

**History:**
There was an Alexander the Alabarch, a governor of the Jews in Alexandria, and brother of the Jewish philosopher Philo, who is believed by some scholars to be the cited Alexander. Some others, however, believe that the reference is to Tiberias Alexander, a nephew of Philo.
See also under LUKE 3:2.

**Perplexing:**
Who was the high priest at the time, Annas or Caiaphas? If Annas was the high priest, was the date now

A.D. 48 (see under LUKE 3:2 - History)? Who were John and Alexander? Why were they identified by name?

4:10 - PETER: "BE IT KNOWN UNTO YOU, AND TO ALL THE PEOPLE OF ISRAEL, THAT BY THE NAME OF JESUS CHRIST OF NAZARETH, WHOM YE CRUCIFIED, WHOM GOD RAISED FROM THE DEAD, EVEN BY HIM DOTH THIS MAN [THE LAME MAN] STAND HERE BEFORE YOU WHOLE."

**Contradictions:** See under 2:23.

**Pagan concept:** See under JOHN 18:5-6.

**Perplexing:** See under 2:23, 24, and 3:6.

4:11 - PETER: "THIS IS THE STONE WHICH WAS SET AT NOUGHT OF YOU BUILDERS, WHICH IS BECOME THE HEAD OF THE CORNER."

**Old Testament:** See under MATT. 21:42.

4:12 - PETER: "...THERE IS NONE OTHER NAME UNDER HEAVEN WHEREBY WE MUST BE SAVED."

**Pagan concept:** See under JOHN 18:5-6.

**Perplexing:**
Why did not the Jews ask Peter what he meant by "saved?"
Why did Peter imply that belief in Jesus' name was more important than following Jesus' teachings to be saved?

4:13 - WHEN THEY SAW...AND PERCEIVED THAT THEY [PETER AND JOHN] WERE UNLEARNED AND IGNORANT, THEY MARVELLED....

**Perplexing:**
Why did Jesus select as his disciples unlearned and ignorant men, rather than scholars or prominent people?
If John was unlearned and ignorant, why do some theologians credit him with having written the Gospel of JOHN in fluent Greek?
Were Peter's errors about Old Testament verses due to his ignorance?
See also under JOHN 21:24.

4:16 - ANNAS AND THE OTHERS: "...THAT INDEED A NOTABLE MIRACLE HATH BEEN DONE BY THEM IS MANIFEST TO ALL THEM THAT DWELL IN JERUSALEM...."

**Perplexing:**
If the miracle was known to all the inhabitants of Jerusalem, why is there no documentation for it outside of the Bible? Did not any of the inhabitants write about it or tell it to someone who would have written about it?

4:17 - ANNAS AND THE OTHERS: "THAT IT SPREAD NO FURTHER AMONG THE PEOPLE, LET US STRAITLY THREATEN THEM, THAT THEY SPEAK HENCEFORTH TO NO MAN IN THIS NAME."

**Perplexing:**
Why did they say, "this name?" By so doing so, they implied that they had no knowledge of Jesus or the miracles that he had performed. They also did not give any indication of knowing about Jesus' resurrection? Why?
See also under 4:3.

4:25-26 - THE DISCIPLES: "[GOD] WHO BY THE MOUTH OF THY SERVANT DAVID HAST SAID, 'WHY DID THE HEATHEN RAGE, AND THE PEOPLE IMAGINE VAIN THINGS? THE KINGS OF THE EARTH STOOD UP, AND THE RULERS WERE GATHERED TOGETHER AGAINST THE LORD, AND AGAINST HIS CHRIST.'"

**Old Testament:**
PS. 2:1-2 - "Why do the heathen rage, and the people imagine a vain thing? The kings of the earth set themselves, and the rulers take counsel together against the LORD, and against His anointed." [Note how the disciples changed "His anointed," referring to the anointed king of Judea, to "Christ," referring to Jesus. The verses, therefore, pertained to the Judean king, not to Jesus or a future Messiah.]
[See under 2:38 - Language.]

**Perplexing:**
Why did Peter and now the other disciples continue to misconstrue old Testament verses? Was it because they were unlearned and ignorant? Could it be that the writer of ACTS was making the errors and attributing them to Peter and the others?

4:27 - THE DISCIPLES: "FOR OF A TRUTH AGAINST THY HOLY CHILD JESUS, WHOM THOU HAST ANOINTED, BOTH HEROD, AND PONTIUS PILATE, WITH THE GENTILES, AND THE PEOPLE OF ISRAEL WERE GATHERED TOGETHER."

**Language:**
The Greek words, "Pais Theou, " translated as "holy child," also mean "holy servant." [Many other Bibles use the term, "holy servant," instead of "holy child."]

**Old Testament:** See under 4:25-26.

**History:**
The people of Israel did not support Pontius Pilate; he was hostile to them and they viewed him as an enemy.
See also under MATT. 27:17, 24.

**Perplexing:**
If the Gentiles and the people of Israel were united against Jesus, who was supporting him?
See also under 4:25-26.

4:30 - THE DISCIPLES: "...THAT SIGNS AND WONDERS MAY BE DONE BY THE NAME OF THY HOLY CHILD JESUS."

**Contradiction:**
ACTS 2:22 - Peter: "...Jesus of Nazareth, a man approved of God among you by miracles, wonders, and signs, which God did by him...."
[Did the name of Jesus do signs and wonders, or did God do them by means of the man Jesus?]

**Language**: See under 4:27.

**Pagan concept:** JOHN 18:5-6.

4:31 - WHEN THEY HAD PRAYED, THE PLACE WAS SHAKEN...AND THEY WERE ALL FILLED WITH THE HOLY GHOST....

**Perplexing:**
In 2:4 they were filled with the Holy Ghost. Why was it necessary for them to be filled with the Holy Ghost a second time?

4:32 - ...NEITHER SAID ANY OF THEM THAT OUGHT OF THE THINGS WHICH HE POSSESSED WAS HIS OWN, BUT THEY HAD ALL THINGS IN COMMON.

**Perplexing:**
Why do not modern followers of Jesus reject private ownership of property and hold all things in common? Why do most try and obtain as many personal possessions as possible? Can one even imagine the wealthy leaders of the various Christian religions distributing their funds and properties among the members of their sects and cults?
See also under 2:44.

**History:** See under 2:44.

4:34-35 - NEITHER WAS THERE ANY AMONG THEM THAT LACKED; AS MANY AS WERE POSSESSORS OF LANDS OR HOUSES SOLD THEM, AND BROUGHT THE PRICES OF THE THINGS THAT WERE SOLD, AND LAID THEM AT THE APOSTLES FEET; DISTRIBUTION WAS MADE UNTO EVERY MAN ACCORDING AS HE HAD NEED.

**Perplexing:**
Why do not modern followers of Jesus sell their lands and houses and distribute the proceeds among themselves?
See also under 2:44, 45, and 4:32.

4:36 - JOSES, WHO BY THE APOSTLES WAS SURNAMED BARNABAS (WHICH IS, BEING INTERPRETED, "THE SON OF CONSOLATION")....

**Language:**
"Bar," in Aramaic, means "son of," and "nabas" means "encouragement." Some Bible translations, therefore, read, "Son of Encouragement." In Sumerian, "bar" meant "skin," and "nabas" meant "red with white

spots." Consequently, the name has also been interpreted to be a reference to the hallucinogenic mushroom *Amanita muscaria* which is red with white spots, the use of which was relatively common among some religious groups in the Mediterranean region. (Some scholars have suggested that Christianity originated from a cult that utilized this fungus in its religious rituals.)

5:1-3 - ANANIAS, WITH SAPPHIRA HIS WIFE SOLD A POSSESSION, AND KEPT BACK PART OF THE PRICE, HIS WIFE ALSO BEING PRIVY TO IT, AND BROUGHT A CERTAIN PART, AND LAID IT AT THE APOSTLES FEET. PETER SAID, "ANANIAS, WHY HATH SATAN FILLED THINE HEART...TO KEEP BACK PART OF THE PRICE OF THE LAND?"

**Perplexing:**

Why did Ananias and Sapphira hold back some of the proceeds? How did Peter know that they had withheld the money? Why could they not resist Satan? In LUKE 10:19, Jesus said, "I give unto you power ... over all the power of the enemy [Satan], and nothing shall by any means hurt you." Therefore, if they were believers, how could Satan have affected them? If they were not believers, why did they give any money to the apostles? If God is omniscient, why did He not know that they would hold back the funds? Why did He create them to do so? Is not God, therefore, morally responsible for their action? Why did He not make them feel pangs of conscience and, thus, cause them to turn over all the money to the apostles?

In MATT. 21:22, Jesus said, "All things, whatsoever ye shall ask in prayer, believing, ye shall receive." Why then did the apostles fail to pray for money, rather than require people to give it to them? Did they not believe Jesus? Did their prayers for money fail? Why did they not work to earn money, and reduce their dependency on contributions? Why could Peter not perform a simple miracle inducing Ananias to turn over the rest of the money? Why could he not perform a miracle that would cause money to appear as needed?

5:4 - PETER: ".... THOU HAST NOT LIED UNTO MEN, BUT UNTO GOD."

**Perplexing:**

How can one lie to God? If God is omniscient, would He not know beforehand that one is going to lie? Why does God not use His power to prevent lying?

Was not Peter a hypocrite for denouncing Ananias for lying unto God, when in MATT. 26:69-74, MARK 14:68-71, LUKE 22:56-60, and JOHN 18:17, 25-27 Peter lied about knowing Jesus? Were not Peter's lies more serious than that of Ananias? Why was Peter not punished for his prevarication?

5:5-6 - ANANIAS HEARING THESE WORDS FELL DOWN, AND GAVE UP THE GHOST; GREAT FEAR CAME ON ALL THAT HEARD THESE THINGS. THE YOUNG MEN AROSE, WOUND HIM UP, CARRIED HIM OUT, AND BURIED HIM.

**Perplexing:**

Why did Peter fail to show any compassion or forgiveness? Why did he not give Ananias an opportunity to bring the withheld funds? Why was it necessary for Ananias to die? Was the incident intended to frighten people into turning over all of their money to the apostles (and later to the Church)? Why was Ananias buried so quickly? Why were his wife and other relatives not first notified of his death, so that they could arrange for his burial and appropriate funeral service? Was this action by the apostles not unnecessarily cruel, particularly to his relatives who would wonder and worry about what happened to him? Why did God permit the apostles to do this? Was not inflicting suffering (needless worry) on Ananias' relatives and friends worse that the withholding of some funds? Did Peter forget Jesus' words in MATT. 6:14-15 - "If ye forgive men their trespasses, your heavenly Father will forgive you; but if ye forgive not men their trespasses, neither will your Father forgive you?" Why did ACTS, unlike the gospels, present the apostles as being money-hungry and heartless?

**Old Testament:**
JER. 28:11-17 - Hananiah [the Hebrew form of the Greek name Ananias], a prophet who lied, was killed by the LORD.

5:7-11 - ...THREE HOURS AFTER, WHEN HIS WIFE, NOT KNOWING WHAT WAS DONE, CAME IN.... PETER SAID, "HOW IS IT THAT YE HAVE AGREED TOGETHER TO TEMPT THE SPIRIT OF THE LORD? THE FEET OF THEM WHICH RAVE BURIED THY HUSBAND ARE AT THE DOOR, AND SHALL CARRY THEE OUT." SHE FELL DOWN AT HIS FEET, AND YIELDED UP THE GHOST; THE YOUNG MEN CAME, FOUND HER DEAD, AND BURIED HER BY HER HUSBAND. AND GREAT FEAR CAME UPON ALL THE CHURCH, AND UPON AS MANY AS HEARD THESE THINGS.

**Perplexing:**
As in the case with Ananias, why did Peter and the others fail to demonstrate forgiveness? Why did God continue to permit the apostles to be unnecessarily heartless? Was ACTS saying that God was responsible for killing Ananias and Sapphira because of money? Does money mean more to God than human life? Did the apostles, or did the writer of ACTS decide to use fear as a weapon for extracting money from believers? See also under 5-6.

5:12 - BY THE HANDS OF THE APOSTLES WERE MANY SIGNS AND WONDERS WROUGHT AMONG THE PEOPLE....

**History:**
There is no non-biblical record of any signs or wonders performed by the apostles.

**Perplexing:**
What were the signs and wonders done by the apostles? Why is there no secular documentation for their accomplishments? Why were they busy collecting money rather than teaching all nations and baptizing in the name of the Father, Son, and Holy Ghost as Jesus had commanded them to do in MATT. 28:19?

5:15-16 - THEY BROUGHT THE SICK INTO THE STREETS...THAT AT LEAST THE SHADOW OF PETER PASSING BY MIGHT OVERSHADOW SOME OF THEM. THERE CAME ALSO A MULTITUDE OUT OF THE CITIES ROUND ABOUT JERUSALEM BRINGING SICK FOLKS, AND THEM VEXED WITH UNCLEAN SPIRITS; THEY WERE HEALED EVERY ONE.

**History:**
There is no secular record of any mass healing by Peter and the apostles.

**Perplexing:**
How were the people healed? Did Peter's shadow do the healing? Were the people touched? Were they required to have faith? Was Jesus' name used? Were the sick healed, as in MARK 6:13, by being anointed with oil? If multitudes were healed, why did not anyone other than the author of ACTS report it? Why is there no secular record of the occurrence?
See also under MARK 6:12-13.

5:17-18 - THE HIGH PRIEST, AND ALL THEY THAT WERE WITH HIM (WHICH IS THE SECT OF THE SADDUCEES), WERE FILLED WITH INDIGNATION, LAID THEIR HANDS ON THE APOSTLES, AND PUT THEM IN THE COMMON PRISON.

**History:** See under MATT. 3:7.

**Perplexing:**
Why did the multitudes that the apostles healed fail to come to their aid? Why did not those still waiting to be healed and their relatives come to the aid of the apostles? Why did the apostles fail to perform a miracle to avoid being imprisoned?
See also under 4:3.

5:19-20 - THE ANGEL OF THE LORD BY NIGHT OPENED THE PRISON DOORS, BROUGHT THEM FORTH, AND SAID, "GO, STAND AND SPEAK IN THE TEMPLE TO THE PEOPLE ALL THE WORDS OF THIS LIFE."

**Perplexing:**
Why did the angel fail to prevent the apostles from being imprisoned? Why did the angel wait until night to open the prison doors and sneak out the apostles? Why did the angel not take the apostles out of prison in full view of everyone there? Why did the angel not speak to the people, instead of ordering the apostles to do so? Why did Peter not perform a miracle to release himself and the others from prison?

5:25-26 - CAME ONE AND TOLD THEM [THE HIGH PRIEST AND OTHERS], "THE MEN WHOM YE PUT IN PRISON ARE STANDING IN THE TEMPLE, AND TEACHING THE PEOPLE." THEN WENT THE CAPTAIN WITH THE OFFICERS, AND BROUGHT THEM WITHOUT VIOLENCE, FOR THEY FEARED THE PEOPLE....

**Perplexing:**
How did the apostles obtain permission to teach in the temple? Why did the people not try to protect them? Why did the angel fail to protect them? Why did the angel instruct them to go to the temple (5:20)? Did he not know that they would be arrested again?

5:28 - THE HIGH PRIEST: "DID NOT WE COMMAND YOU NOT TEACH IN THIS NAME?"....

**Perplexing:**
Why did the high priest not ask the apostles how they escaped from prison?
See also under 4:17.

5:29 - PETER AND THE OTHER APOSTLES SAID, "WE OUGHT TO OBEY GOD RATHER THAN MEN."

**Contradiction:**
I PET. 2:13-14 - Peter: "Submit yourselves to every ordinance of man for the Lord's sake, whether it be to the king, as supreme, or unto governors, as unto them that are sent by him for the punishment of evildoers, and for the praise of them that do well."
[Did Peter say that they should not obey men, or that they should submit to all ordinances of men?]

5:30 - PETER AND THE OTHER APOSTLES: "THE GOD OF OUR FATHERS RAISED UP JESUS, WHOM YE SLEW AND HANGED ON A TREE."

**Contradictions:**
MATT. 27:35, MARK 15:24, LUKE 23:33, JOHN 19:18, and REV. 11:8 - Jesus was killed by crucifixion.
[Was Jesus killed in an unspecified manner and then hung on a tree, or was he crucified?]
ACTS 2:23, 36 and 4:10 - Peter said that Jesus was crucified.
[Did Peter say that Jesus was slain and then hanged on a tree, or that he was crucified?]
MATT. 27:58-60, MARK 15:45-46, LUKE 23:52-53, and JOHN 19:38-42 -Jesus' body was placed in a sepulchre after he was killed by crucifixion.
[Was Jesus hung on a tree after he was killed, or was he placed in a sepulchre?]
See also under 2:23.

**Pagan parallels:**
The ancient Middle Eastern/Mediterranean deity Attis was believed to have been killed by hanging on a tree on March 22, entombed, and on March 24, the tomb was found empty; his resurrection was celebrated on March 25.
See also under MATT. 28:5-7.

**History:**
In one account, an Essene Jewish leader named Jesus ben Pandira was stoned to death for blasphemy and then hanged on a tree some time between 106-79 B.C. In another account, he was reported to have been the Essene "Teacher of Righteousness" who was killed by the Romans on the eve of Passover between the above dates. [Some historians believe that the biblical Jesus was derived from this Essene leader.]
See also under MATT. 27:35.

**Perplexing:**
Could Peter or the writer of ACTS have confused the biblical Jesus with Jesus ben Pandira? Why did Peter say that Jesus was killed and hanged on a tree, and at other times that he was killed by crucifixion? If he was killed, why was he then hanged on a tree?
See also under 2:23 and 2:24.

5:31 - PETER AND THE APOSTLES: "HIM HATH GOD EXALTED WITH HIS RIGHT HAND TO BE A PRINCE AND A SAVIOUR, TO GIVE REPENTANCE TO ISRAEL, AND FORGIVENESS OF SINS."

**Contradictions:**
JOHN 10:30 - Jesus: "I and my Father are one."
[Was Jesus exalted by God to be a prince, or is Jesus one with God?]
See also under MATT. 1:1, 21, and 9:13.

**Perplexing:**
If Jesus is God's Son, how could God exalt him to be a prince? Would Jesus not be at least a prince by birth?
When did God exalt Jesus to be a prince and savior? Was it after his resurrection?

5:33 - ...THEY...TOOK COUNSEL TO SLAY THEM.

**Perplexing:** See under 4:3.

5:34 - THEN STOOD UP ONE IN THE COUNCIL, A PHARISEE, NAMED GAMALIEL, A DOCTOR OF THE LAW....

**History:**
Gamaliel was a grandson of Hillel, a Jewish teacher, and a Pharisee leader until his death in c. 50.

5:36-37 - GAMALIEL: "BEFORE THESE DAYS ROSE UP THEUDAS, BOASTING HIMSELF TO BE SOMEBODY, TO WHOM A NUMBER OF MEN, ABOUT 400, JOINED THEMSELVES, WHO WAS SLAIN; AND ALL, AS MANY AS OBEYED HIM, WERE SCATTERED, AND BROUGHT TO NOUGHT. AFTER THIS MAN ROSE UP JUDAS OF GALILEE IN THE DAYS OF THE TAXING, AND DREW AWAY MUCH PEOPLE AFTER HIM; HE ALSO PERISHED; AND AS MANY AS OBEYED HIM, WERE DISPERSED."

**History:**
Theudas' rebellion occurred in A.D. 46. Judas' rebellion took place in A.D. 6, when Cyrenius became governor of Syria and a census for taxing purposes was begun. Roman troops crushed both rebellions. The reference to the Theudas' incident shows that, at least, this part of ACTS had to have been written after A.D. 46 - a decade or more after Jesus' time. (Note that contrary to ACTS, the rebellion by Judas preceded that by Theudas.)

**Perplexing:**
Why did Gamaliel make the error of stating that the A.D. 46 rebellion by Theudas preceded the A.D. 6 rebellion by Judas? Why did the council members fail to correct him? Was the error made by the writer of ACTS, not by Gamaliel?

5:40 - ...WHEN THEY HAD CALLED THE APOSTLES AND BEATEN THEM, THEY COMMANDED THAT THEY SHOULD NOT SPEAK IN THE NAME OF JESUS, AND LET THEM GO.

**Perplexing:**
Why did the angel or God allow the apostles to be beaten? Why did the angel tell them to teach in the temple so that they would be arrested again, and be subjected to a beating? Why did the angel fail to intervene and protect them?
See also under 4:17.

5:41 - THEY DEPARTED FROM THE COUNCIL, REJOICING THAT THEY WERE COUNTED WORTHY TO SUFFER SHAME FOR HIS [JESUS'] NAME.

**Perplexing:**
Why should the apostles or anyone else suffer shame for Jesus, name? Why must one be "worthy" to suffer for Jesus' name? Why would Jesus want anyone who believes in him to suffer?

5:42 - DAILY IN THE TEMPLE, AND IN EVERY HOUSE, THEY CEASED NOT TO TEACH AND PREACH JESUS CHRIST.

**Perplexing:**
Why did they preach Jesus Christ, not Jesus' teachings? Why did they remain in Jerusalem at the temple and at houses there, rather than obey Jesus' orders in MATT. 28:19-20 - "Go...teach all nations, baptizing in the name of the Father, the Son, and the Holy Ghost, teaching them to observe all things whatsoever I have commanded you"; and in MARK 16:15 - "Go ye into all the world, and preach the gospel to every creature?"

6:1 - WHEN THE NUMBER OF THE DISCIPLES WAS MULTIPLIED, THERE AROSE A MURMURING OF THE GRECIANS AGAINST THE HEBREWS, BECAUSE THEIR WIDOWS WERE NEGLECTED IN THE DAILY MINISTRATION.

**Perplexing:**
Why did Jesus and/or God allow dissension to occur among the disciples? How much time had elapsed since 4:32 when "the multitude of them that believed were of one heart and one soul"; and 4:35 - [the multitude of believers] laid them [prices of things sold] down at the apostles' feet, and distribution was made unto every man according as he had need?"

**History:**
It is generally believed that "Grecians" referred to Jews who spoke primarily Greek, and that "Hebrews" referred to Jews who spoke primarily Aramaic.

6:2 - THE TWELVE CALLED THE MULTITUDE OF THE DISCIPLES UNTO THEM, AND SAID, "IT IS NOT REASON THAT WE SHOULD LEAVE THE WORD OF GOD, AND SERVE TABLES."

**Perplexing:**
How were the apostles able to contact and speak with the multitude (over 3000 disciples according to 2:41, and about 5000 more according to 4:4)? How long did it take for all of the disciples to be contacted? Where did they meet? In what place could more than 8000 people meet? Why did such a large gathering not alarm the Romans? Why did the Romans allow this many people, especially Jews, to convene at a time when there was hostility towards them and when rebellions had been occurring? Why did the apostles believe that settling disputes, particularly ones involving the distribution of common funds, among the disciples was not within their purview?
See also under 6:1.

6:3 - THE APOSTLES: "BRETHREN, LOOK YE OUT AMONG YOU SEVEN MEN OF HONEST REPORT, FULL OF THE HOLY GHOST AND WISDOM, WHOM WE MAY APPOINT OVER THIS BUSINESS."

**Perplexing:**
Why were seven needed? Were not all of the disciples filled with the Holy Ghost? Why was it necessary to seek out seven who were honest? Were not all of those filled with the Holy Ghost honest? If they were all honest, why could not seven be chosen at random? Why did the apostles not pray to resolve the problem immediately? Did they believe or find out that they did not receive what was prayed for? How could over 8000 people hear what the apostles said?

6:4 - THE APOSTLES: "WE WILL GIVE OURSELVES CONTINUALLY TO PRAYER, AND TO THE MINISTRY OF THE WORD."

**Contradiction:**

MARK 16:20 - They [the disciples] went forth, and preached everywhere....
[Did the disciples remain in Jerusalem praying, or did they go forth and preach everywhere?]

**Perplexing:**

Did they pray for a resolution to the problem, but it did not happen? For what were they continually praying?
See also under MATT. 7:7-8 and JOHN 14:12, 13.

6:5 - ...THEY CHOSE STEPHEN...PHILIP, PROCHORUS, NICANOR, TIMON, PARMENAS, AND NICHOLAS....

**Perplexing:**

How did the more than 8000 people choose these seven men? How long did the selection process take? Why did all of those selected have non-Hebrew names? Was it because the 8000 disciples were predominantly Grecian? Could an equitable decision be reached by a predominantly, or completely, Grecian group, especially since the Grecians were the ones who were complaining?
Why were the cited seven chosen?

6:6 - WHOM [THE SEVEN] THEY SET BEFORE THE APOSTLES; WHEN THEY HAD PRAYED, THEY LAID THEIR HANDS ON THEM.

**History:**

The laying on of hands was a formal sign of appointment. It did not, however, become a Church custom or rite until much later than the time during which the reported incident is supposed to have occurred.
See also under 1:1.

**Perplexing:**

Why did the writer of ACTS claim that the apostles did something that was not a Jewish custom and had not yet become a Christian custom?

6:8 - STEPHEN, FULL OF FAITH AND POWER, DID GREAT WONDERS AND MIRACLES AMONG THE PEOPLE.

**History:**

There is no secular evidence for any wonders and miracles performed by Stephen.

**Perplexing:**

What wonders and miracles were performed by Stephen? Why is there no written documentation of them? Why is there no mention of what Stephen and the other six men did to resolve the dispute between the Grecians and the Hebrews?

6:9 - ... THE SYNAGOGUE OF THE LIBERTINES, CYRENIANS, ALEXANDRIANS, AND OF THEM OF CILICIA AND ASIA, DISPUTED WITH STEPHEN.

**Perplexing:**
Why did they dispute, rather than endeavor to befriend, someone who could perform wonders and miracles? Why did Stephen fail to pray to convert his listeners to a belief in Jesus? Did he, perhaps, pray for such, but without success? Why did Stephen dispute in synagogues, rather than try to mediate the conflict between the Grecians and the Hebrews as he had been appointed to do?

6:11 - THEY SUBURNED MEN, WHICH SAID, "WE HAVE HEARD HIM SPEAK BLASPHEMOUS WORDS AGAINST MOSES, AND AGAINST GOD."

**Perplexing:**
How could Stephen have spoken blasphemously against Moses, since Moses was not God? Why did ACTS not report what blasphemy Stephen was accused of saying? Proclaiming belief in Jesus was not blasphemy.
See also under MATT. 26:65.

6:12 - THEY STIRRED UP THE PEOPLE, THE ELDERS, AND THE SCRIBES, AND CAME UPON HIM, CAUGHT HIM, AND BROUGHT HIM TO THE COUNCIL.

**Perplexing:**
Why could not Stephen, full of power (6:8) and full of the Holy Ghost (6:3), prevent himself from being seized? Why did the Holy Ghost fail to protect him? Why did the multitude (thousands) of disciples fail to come to his assistance?
See also under 6:9.

6:15 - ALL THAT SAT IN THE COUNCIL...SAW HIS FACE AS IF IT HAD BEEN THE FACE OF AN ANGEL.

**Perplexing:**
What does an angel's face look like? Angels have always been described as men; their faces have not been described.

7:2-3 - STEPHEN: "...THE GOD OF GLORY APPEARED UNTO OUR FATHER ABRAHAM, WHEN HE WAS IN MESOPOTAMIA, BEFORE HE DWELT IN CHARRAN, AND SAID, 'GET THEE OUT OF THY COUNTRY, FROM THY KINDRED, AND COME INTO THE LAND WHICH I SHALL SHEW THEE.'"

**Contradiction:**
GEN. 11:31 - 12:1 - Terah took Abram...went from Ur of the Chaldees unto Harran (Charran). .... The LORD said unto Abram, "get thee out of thy country...unto a land that I wilt shew thee."
[Did God speak to Abraham before he dwelt in Charran, as Stephen said, or after he dwelt there, as GEN. said?]

**History:**
Harran was in northern Mesopotamia, about 600 miles north of Ur. The Chaldeans did not occupy southern Mesopotamia until after 1000 B.C. and did not control Ur until 625 B.C. The reference to Ur of the Chaldeans, therefore, is an anachronism.

**Perplexing:**
If Stephen was Jewish, why was he ignorant of what the Old Testament verses said? Why did the high priest and others to whom he was speaking, fail to correct him?

7:4 - STEPHEN: "THEN CAME HE OUT OF THE LAND OF THE CHALDEANS, AND DWELT IN CHARRAN; FROM THENCE, WHEN HIS FATHER WAS DEAD, HE REMOVED HIM INTO THIS LAND, WHEREIN YE NOW DWELL."

**Contradiction:** See under 2-3.

**History:** See under 2-3.

**Perplexing:**
Why were the writers of ACTS and GEN. ignorant of the history of the Middle East?
See also under 2-3.

**Old Testament:**
GEN. 11:26 - Terah lived 70 years, and begat Abram....In GEN. 11:32, the days of Terah were 205 years; Terah died in Haran.[Thus, Abram was 135 years old when his father died; GEN. 12:4, however, states that Abram was 75 when he departed from Haran.]

7:6-7 - STEPHEN: "GOD SPAKE...THAT HIS SEED SHOULD SOJOURN IN A STRANGE LAND, AND THAT THEY SHOULD BRING THEM INTO BONDAGE, AND ENTREAT THEM EVIL 400 YEARS. 'AND THE NATION TO WHOM THEY SHALL BE IN BONDAGE WILL I JUDGE,' SAID GOD, 'AND AFTER THAT SHALL THEY COME FORTH, AND SERVE ME IN THIS PLACE.'"

**Old Testament:**
GEN. 15:13-14 - He [God] said unto Abram, "...thy seed shall be a stranger in a land that is not theirs, and shall serve them, and they shall afflict them 400 years; also that nation, whom they shall serve, will I judge, and afterward shall they come out with great substance."

**Contradiction:**
GEN. 15:13-14 (see above) - God did not say that the descendants of Abraham will serve Him.
[Did God say that the Hebrews would serve Him, as Stephen claimed, or that they would go out with great substance as reported in GEN.?]

**History:**
There is no evidence that large numbers (thousands or the millions implied by EX.) of Hebrews were enslaved or even resided in Egypt at any time.

7:9 - STEPHEN: "THE PATRIARCHS, MOVED WITH ENVY, SOLD JOSEPH INTO EGYPT, BUT GOD WAS WITH HIM.

**Contradictions:**
GEN. 37:28 - ...Midianites...lifted Joseph out of the pit, and sold Joseph to the Ishmeelites; they brought Joseph into Egypt.

[Did the Patriarchs sell Joseph into Egypt, as Stephen claimed, or did the Ishmeelites bring him to Egypt?]
GEN. 37:36 - The Midianites sold him [Joseph] into Egypt unto Potiphar....
[Did the Patriarchs sell Joseph into Egypt, as Stephen claimed, or did the Midianites sell him?]

**History:**
There is no secular evidence for the existence of Joseph or the other Patriarchs.

7:10 - STEPHEN: "[GOD] DELIVERED HIM OUT OF ALL HIS AFFLICTIONS, AND GAVE HIM FAVOUR AND WISDOM IN THE SIGHT OF PHARAOH KING OF EGYPT; AND HE MADE HIM GOVERNOR OVER EGYPT AND ALL HIS HOUSE."

**Perplexing:**
If God delivered Joseph "out of all his afflictions," why did He allow Potiphar's wife to falsely accuse him of trying to come "in unto" her, and allow him to be imprisoned (GEN. 39:10-20) for at least two years (GEN. 41:1)? When did Joseph learn enough Egyptian to be able to satisfactorily communicate with the pharaoh and the other Egyptians?

**History:**
"Pharaoh," was the title for Egyptian kings. It was not a name, as Stephen and many other biblical verses imply by saying, "Pharaoh king." The term, "Pharaoh king," is equivalent to "King king." "Pharaoh," which is a title, should be followed by the name of a particular pharaoh (king). There is no record of any pharaoh having appointed a Hebrew as governor over Egypt. It is unlikely that any pharaoh would or could have appointed a foreigner as governor without inciting resentment and possible violence by the Egyptian people.

7:14-15 - STEPHEN: "THEN JOSEPH, CALLED HIS FATHER JACOB TO HIM, AND ALL HIS KINDRED, THREESCORE AND FIFTEEN SOULS. SO, JACOB WENT DOWN INTO EGYPT, AND DIED, HE, AND OUR FATHERS."

**Contradiction:**
GEN. 46:27 - ...all the souls of the house of Jacob which came into Egypt, were threescore and ten.
EX. 1:5 - All the souls that came out of the loins of Jacob were 70 souls, for Joseph was in Egypt already.
DEUT. 10:22 - Thy fathers went down into Egypt with threescore and ten persons.
[Did 75 people go into Egypt as claimed by Stephen, or were there 70 as stated by GEN., EX., and DEUT.?]

**Perplexing:** See under 7:2-3.

7:16 - STEPHEN: "[THEY] WERE CARRIED INTO SYCHEM, AND LAID IN THE SEPULCHRE THAT ABRAHAM BOUGHT FOR A SUM OF MONEY OF THE SONS OF EMMOR THE FATHER OF SYCHEM."

**Contradictions:**
GEN. 33:19-20 - He [Jacob] bought a parcel of a field, where he had spread his tent, at the hand of the children of Hammor, Shechem's father, for an 100 pieces of money. He erected there an altar, and called it El-e-lohe-Israel ["God is Israel's Lord"].
[Did Abraham buy a sepulchre from the sons of Emmor the father of Sychem, as claimed by Stephen, or did Jacob buy the land?]

GEN. 49:29-30 - Jacob: "...bury me with my fathers in the cave that is in the field of Ephron the Hittite, in the cave that is in the field of Machpelah...which Abraham bought...for a buryingplace."
GEN. 50:13 - His [Jacob's] sons carried him into Canaan, and buried him in the cave of the field of Machpelah, which Abraham bought with the field for a possession of a buryingplace of Ephron the Hittite. (GEN. 23:8-20 - the field and cave were purchased by Abraham from Ephron.)
[Was Jacob buried in Sychem, as claimed by Stephen, or in Machpelah as reported in GEN.?]

**Perplexing:**
Why did not the Jews (council members) who were well versed in the old Testament interrupt Stephen, point out his errors, and correct him? Did Stephen deliberately distort the Old Testament stories? Were his errors unintentional? Why did he say that "our fathers" (implying all of the Patriarchs) were carried to Sychem and buried there? JOSH. 24:32 mentioned that only Joseph was interred in Sychem (Shechem). See also under 2-3.

7:17 - STEPHEN: "...THE PEOPLE [THE HEBREWS] GREW AND MULTIPLIED IN EGYPT."

**Old Testament:**
EX. 1:7 - The children of Israel were fruitful, increased abundantly, multiplied, waxed exceeding mighty, and the land was filled with them. EX. 1:20 - ...the people multiplied, and waxed very mighty.

**History:**
There is no record of a massive Hebrew presence in Egypt, with the possible exception of the period when the Hyksos (believed to have been Hebrews) invaded, conquered, and ruled Egypt from about 1730 -1570 B.C.

7:23 - STEPHEN: "WHEN HE [MOSES] WAS 40 YEARS OLD, IT CAME INTO HIS HEART TO VISIT HIS BRETHREN THE CHILDREN OF ISRAEL"

**Old Testament:**
EX. 2:11 - ...when Moses was grown, he went out unto his brethren....
[Moses' age at this time was not given. In EX. 7:7, however, Moses was said to be fourscore years old when he spoke to Pharaoh.]
See also under MATT. 4:1-2.

**Perplexing:**
How did Stephen know, or on what did he base his claim, that Moses was 40 years old when he visited the Israelites?

**Language:**
"Moses" is the Greek form of the Egyptian name, "Mose." The Hebrew version is, "Mosche."

7:26 - STEPHEN: "...HE [MOSES] SHEWED HIMSELF UNTO THEM [HEBREWS] AS THEY STROVE, AND WOULD HAVE SET THEM AT ONE AGAIN, SAYING, 'SIRS, YE ARE BRETHREN; WHY DO YE WRONG ONE TO ANOTHER?'"

**Contradiction:**
EX. 2:13 - ...two men of the Hebrews strove together, and he [Moses] said to him that did the wrong, "Wherefore smitest thou thy fellow?"
[Did Moses say, "Sirs, ye are brethren...." or did he ask one why he hit another?]

7:30 - STEPHEN: "WHEN 40 YEARS WERE EXPIRED, THERE APPEARED TO HIM IN THE WILDERNESS OF MOUNT SINAI AN ANGEL OF THE LORD IN A FLAME OF FIRE IN A BUSH."

**Contradiction:**
EX. 3:1-2 - Moses...led the flock to the backside of the desert, and came to the mountain of God, Horeb. The angel of the LORD appeared to him in a flame of fire out of the midst of a bush...the bush burned with fire, and was not consumed.
[Did an angel of the LORD appear to Moses in the wilderness of Mount Sinai, or in the desert by the mountain of God, Mount Horeb?]

**Pagan parallels**: See under MATT. 22:31-32.

**Botany:** See under MATT. 22:31-32.

**Old Testament:** See under MATT. 4:1-2.

7:31-32 - STEPHEN: "...THE VOICE OF THE LORD CAME UNTO HIM, SAYING, 'I AM THE GOD OF THY FATHERS, THE GOD OF ABRAHAM, ISAAC, AND JACOB.'"

**Old Testament:**
EX. 3:6 - He said, "I am the God of thy father [singular], the God of Abraham, Isaac, and Jacob."

**Perplexing:**
Why did God not identify himself simply as God, or God of the universe? Why did He imply that He is only the God of Moses' ancestors? Did the Hebrews believe that other people had different gods?

**History:**
The ancient Hebrews were a polytheistic people before they became monotheistic Jews after the Babylonian Exile in the 6th century B.C.

7:33 - STEPHEN: "SAID THE LORD, 'PUT OFF THY SHOES FROM THY FEET, FOR THE PLACE WHERE THOU STANDEST IS HOLY GROUND.'"

**Old Testament:**
EX. 3:5-6 - He said, "...put off thy shoes from thy feet, for the place whereon thou standest is holy ground. I am the God of thy father, the God of Abraham...."

**Contradiction:**
In EX. 3:5-6, God told Moses to remove his shoes before He identified Himself as the God of Abraham, Isaac, and Jacob.

[Did God say that He was the God of Abraham, Isaac, and Jacob before telling Moses to remove his shoes, as Stephen said, or after telling Moses to remove his shoes, as stated in EX.?]

**Perplexing:** See under 2-3.

**Pagan parallels:**
Ancient Sumerians, Greeks, Romans, and pre-Islamic Arabs believed that shoes, and in some instances all clothes, had to be removed when standing before a god. (Modern Muslims still adhere to the ancient Arab custom by removing their shoes upon entering a mosque.)

7:34 - STEPHEN: "[THE LORD SAID] 'I HAVE SEEN THE AFFLICTION OF MY PEOPLE IN EGYPT, HAVE HEARD THEIR GROANING, AND AM COME DOWN TO DELIVER THEM. NOW I WILL SEND THEE INTO EGYPT.'"

**Old Testament:**
EX. 3:7-8 - The LORD said, "I have seen the affliction of My people in Egypt, have heard their cry by reason of their taskmasters; I know their sorrows. I am come down to deliver them out of the hand of the Egyptians...."
EX. 3:10 - "I will send thee unto Pharaoh...."

**Perplexing:**
Why did God not see the affliction of His people during the 400 years or so of their bondage? Why did He fail to help them? Why did He say that He had to "come down to deliver them?" Why could He not help them directly from heaven? Why could He not help them Himself, without Moses? Why did He not also consider the Egyptians to be His people?

7:35 - STEPHEN: "THIS MOSES WHOM THEY REFUSED, SAYING, 'WHO MADE THEE A RULER AND A JUDGE?' THE SAME DID GOD SEND TO BE A RULER AND A DELIVERER BY THE HAND OF THE ANGEL WHICH APPEARED TO HIM IN THE BUSH."

**Contradiction:**
EX. 2:14 - He [the Hebrew who hit another Hebrew] said, "Who made thee a prince and a judge over us...."
ACTS 7:27 - Stephen: "He that did his neighbor wrong thrust him away, saying, 'Who made thee a ruler and a judge over us?'"
[Did they [the Hebrews] say to Moses, "Who made thee a ruler and a judge?" or did the Hebrew who struck another Hebrew say it?]

7:37 - STEPHEN: "THIS IS THAT MOSES, WHICH SAID UNTO THE CHILDREN OF ISRAEL, 'A PROPHET SHALL THE LORD YOUR GOD RAISE UP UNTO YOU OF YOUR BRETHREN, LIKE UNTO ME; HIM SHALL YE HEAR.'"

**Old Testament:**
DEUT. 18:15 - Moses: "The LORD thy God will raise up unto thee a Prophet from the midst of thee, of thy brethren, like unto me; unto him ye shall hearken."
See also under 3:22-23.

**Perplexing:**
Why did God refer to Himself as "your God" (i.e., "God of the Hebrews"), rather than just "God" or "Lord God?"
See also under 31-32.

**History:** See under 31-32.

7:38 - STEPHEN: "THIS IS HE, THAT WAS IN THE CHURCH IN THE WILDERNESS WITH THE ANGEL WHICH SPAKE TO HIM IN THE MOUNT SINAI, AND WITH OUR FATHERS, WHO RECEIVED THE LIVELY ORACLES TO GIVE UNTO US."

**Contradiction:**
EX. 19:3 - 40:38 - The LORD, not an angel of the LORD, spoke with Moses and the Israelites.
[Did an angel as alleged by Stephen, or the LORD, as stated in EX., speak with Moses and the Israelites?]

7:39-40 - STEPHEN: "WHOM [MOSES] OUR FATHERS WOULD NOT OBEY, BUT THRUST HIM FROM THEM, AND IN THEIR HEARTS TURNED BACK AGAIN INTO EGYPT, SAYING UNTO AARON, 'MAKE US GODS TO GO BEFORE US; AS FOR THIS MOSES, WHICH BROUGHT US OUT OF EGYPT, WE WOT NOT WHAT IS BECOME OF HIM.'"

**Contradictions:**
NUM. 14:2-5 - All the children of Israel murmured against Moses and Aaron, and said, "Would God that we had died in Egypt, or in this wilderness! .... Were it not better for us to return into Egypt?" They said, "...let us return into Egypt." Moses and Aaron fell on their faces before all the assembly of the children of Israel.
[Did the Hebrews thrust out Moses, want to return to Egypt, and say that they did not know where Moses was, as stated by Stephen, or was Moses with them when they said they wanted to return to Egypt, as NUM. reported?]
EX. 32:1 - When the people saw that Moses delayed to come down out of the mount, they gathered together unto Aaron, and said, "Make us gods, which shall go before us; as for this Moses, the man that brought us out of Egypt, we wot not what is become of him."
[Did the Hebrews thrust out Moses, as claimed by Stephen, or had they become tired of waiting for him to return from the mount, as indicated by EX.?]

**Perplexing:** See under 2-3.

7:42-43 - STEPHEN: "...IT IS WRITTEN IN THE BOOK OF THE PROPHETS, 'O YE HOUSE OF ISRAEL, HAVE YE OFFERED TO ME SLAIN BEASTS AND SACRIFICES BY THE SPACE OF 40 YEARS IN THE WILDERNESS? YE TOOK UP THE TABERNACLE OF MOLOCH, AND THE STAR OF YOUR GOD REMPHAN, FIGURES WHICH YE MADE TO WORSHIP; I WILL CARRY YOU WAY BEYOND BABYLON.'"

**Old Testament:**
AMOS 5:25-27 - The LORD: "Have ye offered unto Me sacrifices and offerings in the wilderness 40 years, O house of Israel? But ye have borne the tabernacle of your Moloch and Chiun your images, the star of your god, which ye made to yourselves. Therefore, will I cause you to go into captivity beyond Damascus," saith the Lord....
1 KINGS 11:7 - Then did Solomon build a high place for Chemosh...and for Moloch....

**Contradiction:**
AMOS 5:27 - "I will cause you [the Israelites] to go into captivity beyond Damascus," saith the LORD.... [Did God tell the Israelites that He would carry them way beyond Babylon, as said by Stephen, or that they would be in captivity beyond Damascus, as stated in AMOS?]

**History:**
The ancient Israelites were in captivity in Babylonia for about 50 years during the 6th century B.C. This period is frequently referred to as the Babylonian Exile. They were not carried "way beyond Babylon," as Stephen claimed God had promised. The ancient Israelites prior to and during the Exile and prior to the later development of Judaism were polytheistic as Stephen and the Old Testament indicate.

7:45 - STEPHEN: "OUR FATHERS THAT CAME AFTER BROUGHT IN WITH JESUS INTO THE POSSESSION OF THE GENTILES, WHOM GOD DRAVE OUT...."

**Language:**
"Jesus" was Greek for "Joshua." Therefore, Stephen was referring to the Old Testament Joshua, not to Christ.

7:46-47 - STEPHEN: "[DAVID) FOUND FAVOUR BEFORE GOD, AND DESIRED TO FIND A TABERNACLE FOR THE GOD OF JACOB. BUT SOLOMON BUILT HIM A HOUSE."

**Old Testament:**
PS. 132:2-5 - He [David] sware unto the LORD, and vowed unto the mighty God of Jacob, "...I will not give sleep to mine eyes ... until I find a place for the LORD, an habitation for the mighty God of Jacob."
1 KINGS 6:2-14 - The house which king Solomon built for the LORD.... .... Solomon built the house, and finished it.

7:48-50 - STEPHEN: "HOWBEIT THE MOST HIGH DWELLETH NOT IN TEMPLES MADE WITH HANDS; AS SAITH THE PROPHET, 'HEAVEN IS MY THRONE, AND EARTH IS MY FOOTSTOOL; WHAT HOUSE WILL YE BUILD ME? SAITH THE LORD, OR WHAT IS THE PLACE OF MY REST? HATH NOT MY HAND MADE ALL THESE THINGS?'"

**Old Testament:**
ISA. 66:1-2 - Saith the LORD: "The heaven is My throne, and the earth is My footstool; where is the house that ye build unto Me? Where is the place of My rest? All those things hath Mine hand made...."

**Contradiction:**
1 KINGS 8:12 - Spake Solomon, "The LORD said that He would dwell in the thick darkness. I have built Thee an house to dwell in, a settled place for Thee to abide in forever."
2 CHRON. 7:12 - The LORD appeared to Solomon...and said, "I...have chosen this place to Myself as an house of sacrifice."
2 CHRON. 7:16 - The LORD: "Now have I chosen and sanctified this house, that My name may be there forever; and Mine eyes and Mine heart shall be there perpetually."
[Does God dwell not in temples, as stated by Stephen, or does He dwell in temples (houses) as stated in 1 KINGS and 2 CHRON.?]

7:51 - STEPHEN: "YE STIFFNECKED AND UNCIRCUMCISED IN HEART AND EARS, YE DO ALWAYS RESIST THE HOLY GHOST, AS YOUR FATHERS DID, SO DO YE."

**Perplexing:**
Why did Stephen use the Christian term "Holy Ghost" when addressing Jews? Why did the Jews not inform him that it was not a Jewish concept?
In what way did the fathers of Stephen's listeners resist the Holy Ghost?

7:52-53 - STEPHEN: "WHICH OF THE PROPHETS HAVE NOT YOUR FATHERS PERSECUTED? THEY HAVE SLAIN THEM WHICH SHEWED BEFORE OF THE COMING OF THE JUST ONE, OF WHOM YE HAVE BEEN NOW THE BETRAYERS AND MURDERERS, WHO HAVE RECEIVED THE LAW BY THE DISPOSITION OF ANGELS, AND HAVE NOT KEPT IT."

**Contradiction:**
EX. 20:1 - 23:33, 24:12, 25:1 - 31:18, 34:10-28, 40:1-16, LEV. 1:1 - 8-5, and 11:1 - 27:34 - the LORD spoke directly to Moses and gave him the Law.
Numerous verses in NUM. and DEUT. also have the LORD speaking directly to Moses and giving him the Law.
[Did angels give the Law to Moses, as claimed by Stephen, or was the law given to Moses by the LORD Himself, as reported in the Old Testament?]

**Perplexing:**
Which prophets did Stephen believe were persecuted? When? What did he mean by "persecuted?" Were there any persecuted prophets? If so, who were they? Which prophets showed "before the coming of the Just One" and were killed? Why did the Old Testament not report the killing of prophets? Why did Stephen accuse the Jews of murdering Jesus when he was killed by the Romans for treason for claiming to be a king without Roman authorization? Which parts of the Law did Stephen believe were not kept by the Jews? Why did Stephen give his discourse as though he was addressing people who were ignorant of the Old Testament, rather than knowledgeable Jews who would know that he was deviating from the truth about what was in the Scriptures? Was the writer of ACTS using Stephen to incite hate and possible violence against Jews? Why did Stephen assert that angels, rather than God, as stated in the Old Testament, gave the Law? Was his claim an anachronism? Paul, at a later date said, in GAL. 3:19, that the Law was given by angels. Or, did Paul derive this belief from Stephen? Why did the Jews fail to question Stephen about his assertions, and correct his errors?
Why in his lengthy discourse did Stephen fail to mention any of Jesus' teachings?
See also under MATT. 27:25, 37-38.

**History:** See under MATT. 27:25, 35.

7:55-56 - HE BEING FULL OF THE HOLY GHOST, LOOKED UP STEDFASTLY INTO HEAVEN, AND SAW THE GLORY OF GOD, AND JESUS STANDING ON THE RIGHT HAND OF GOD, AND SAID, "I SEE THE HEAVENS OPENED, AND THE SON OF MAN STANDING ON THE RIGHT HAND OF GOD."

**Perplexing:**
How did Stephen know that it was Jesus who was standing on the right hand of God? How was he able to recognize Jesus and God? What did God look like? How far away were they? How could he see them

clearly? Why did not anyone else see them? Why did Stephen use the term, "Son of man"? Why is he the only one to use the term, since Jesus used it in the gospels? Why is this the only time it is used in the New Testament outside of the gospels?

**Contradiction:**
COL. 1:15 and 1 TIM. 1:17 - God is invisible.
1 TIM. 6:16 - No man has seen, or can see God.
JOHN 6:46 - Jesus: "Not that any man hath seen the Father, save he which is of God...."
[Did Stephen see God, or is God invisible and cannot be seen?]

7:57 - THEN THEY CRIED OUT WITH A LOUD VOICE, STOPPED THEIR EARS, AND RAN UPON HIM WITH ONE ACCORD.

**Perplexing:**
Why did Stephen's listeners wait until now, after he mentioned the Son of man, to scream at him? Why did they not do so earlier when he had distorted and erred about biblical verses and falsely accused them of murder?

7:58 - [THEY] CAST HIM OUT OF THE CITY, AND STONED HIM; THE WITNESSES LAID DOWN THEIR CLOTHES AT A YOUNG MAN'S FEET, WHOSE NAME WAS SAUL.

**Perplexing:**
Who cast him out of the city and stoned him? Was it a mob of people who were incensed at him, or was it the council? He had not said or done anything to warrant punishment under Jewish law, and ACTS did not say that the council ordered him to be attacked. Was the writer of ACTS continuing to try and incite hatred towards Jews? Why did the writer of ACTS depict Stephen as an ignorant, lying, arrogant, religious fanatic, for whom it is difficult to have sympathy?

**Language:**
The Greek word, "neanias," translated as "young man," more accurately means, "adolescent."

7:59 - THEY STONED STEPHEN, CALLING UPON GOD, SAYING, "LORD JESUS RECEIVE MY SPIRIT."

**Perplexing:**
Why did the Holy Ghost, of which Stephen was full (7:55-56), fail to protect him? Why did he fail to perform a miracle to save himself (see 6:8 - he was full of power and did great wonders and miracles)? Why did Jesus and/or God fail to protect him? (In LUKE 10:19, Jesus told his disciples, "...nothing shall by any means hurt you; in LUKE 21:18, Jesus said, "There shall not an hair of your head perish.") Why was an angel not sent to help him escape? Did the Holy Ghost leave him before or after he died?
Was the dispute between the Grecians and the Hebrews (6:1-6) resolved before Stephen's death? If not, was someone appointed to take his place in an effort to settle the dispute? See also under 6:12.

8:1 - .... AT THAT TIME THERE WAS A GREAT PERSECUTION AGAINST THE CHURCH WHICH WAS AT JERUSALEM; THEY WERE ALL SCATTERED ABROAD THROUGHOUT THE REGIONS OF JUDAEA AND SAMARIA, EXCEPT THE APOSTLES.

**Perplexing:**
Who did the persecuting? Why? As the Romans with their military controlled the region, no widespread persecution could have taken place unless they did it or countenanced it. When did "the church" come into existence? Why were the apostles, who were the leaders, not persecuted? Why did the apostles fail to obey Jesus' commands in MATT. 28:19-20 and MARK 16:15 to teach and baptize all nations and to go into all the world and preach the gospel? Why were only the ordinary believers in Jesus forced to flee? Why did the Holy Ghost and God fail to protect the church? Why did the believers fail to pray for protection? Jesus said that anything asked for in his name or in prayer would be received (MATT. 21:22, JOHN 14:13-14, JOHN 16:23, and other verses). Did they perhaps pray, but not have their prayers answered?

8:3 - AS FOR SAUL, HE MADE HAVOC OF THE CHURCH, ENTERING INTO EVERY HOUSE, AND HALING MAN AND WOMEN COMMITTED THEM TO PRISON.

**Perplexing:**
How could Saul, a "young man" (7:58) (or "adolescent, " according to the Greek; see Language under 7:58) make "havoc of the church"? How could he enter every house and commit people to prison? Who gave Saul the authority to engage in such action? Was Saul paid to do so? Why did he not commit the apostles to prison? How did he know who to seize? Why did the Romans allow him to create havoc that might have led to civil unrest? Was ACTS saying that Paul acted alone? If not, who helped him?

**History:**
There is no secular record of Saul (Paul) persecuting Jews who believed in Jesus.

8:4-5 - THEY THAT WERE SCATTERED ABROAD WENT EVERYWHERE PREACHING THE WORD. PHILIP WENT DOWN TO THE CITY OF SAMARIA, AND PREACHED CHRIST UNTO THEM.

**Contradiction:**
ACTS 11: 19 - They which were scattered abroad...travelled...preaching the word to none but unto the Jews only.
[Was the word preached everywhere including to Samaritans, or only to Jews?]

**Perplexing:**
Why did Philip go to and preach in Samaria contravening Jesus' order, in MATT. 10:5, "Go not into the way of the Gentiles, and into any city of the Samaritans enter ye not?" Did Philip forget what Jesus had said? Did the writer of ACTS forget, or was he unaware of what MATT. had written?

8:6-7 - THE PEOPLE WITH ONE ACCORD GAVE HEED UNTO THOSE THINGS WHICH PHILIP SPAKE, HEARING AND SEEING THE MIRACLES WHICH HE DID. UNCLEAN SPIRITS, CRYING WITH LOUD VOICE, CAME OUT OF MANY THAT WERE POSSESSED WITH THEM; MANY TAKEN WITH PALSIES, AND THAT WERE LAME, WERE HEALED.

**History:**
There is no secular record of Philip or any miracles having been worked by him.

**Perplexing:**
Why are there no reports of Philip or his miracles in the literature of that time? What method did Philip use

to perform the miracles? Did he use faith, Jesus' name, touching, or something else? What did the unclean spirits look like? Where did they go?

8:9 - THERE WAS A MAN CALLED SIMON, WHICH BEFORE TIME IN THE SAME CITY USED SORCERY, AND BEWITCHED THE PEOPLE OF SAMARIA, GIVING OUT THAT HIMSELF WAS SOME GREAT ONE.

**Perplexing:**
Why did the writer of ACTS imply that sorcery could bewitch people? Did he believe in sorcery and the ability to bewitch people?

**History:**
It is generally believed that the Simon mentioned was an actual person named Simon Magus. His followers, known as "Simonites, " as well as Christians believed that he could perform miracles. He professed to be "The Word of God," "The Comforter," and "The Image of the Eternal Father"; he was revered as a savior and as a god by his followers.

8:12 - WHEN THEY BELIEVED PHILIP PREACHING THE THINGS CONCERNING THE KINGDOM OF GOD, AND THE NAME OF JESUS CHRIST, THEY WERE BAPTIZED, BOTH MEN AND WOMEN.

**Contradiction:** See under 4-5.

**Perplexing:**
If Simon had performed miracles and had bewitched the populace, how could they have listened to and succumbed to Philip?

8:13 - THEN SIMON HIMSELF BELIEVED; WHEN HE WAS BAPTIZED, HE CONTINUED WITH PHILIP, AND WONDERED, BEHOLDING THE MIRACLES AND SIGNS WHICH WERE DONE.

**Perplexing:**
Why did Simon, who could perform miracles and bewitch people, believe Philip?
See also under 6-7.

**History:** See under 6-7.

8:14-16 - WHEN THE APOSTLES AT JERUSALEM HEARD THAT SAMARIA HAD RECEIVED THE WORD OF GOD, THEY SENT UNTO THEM PETER AND JOHN, WHO WHEN THEY WERE COME DOWN, PRAYED FOR THEM, THAT THEY MIGHT RECEIVE THE HOLY GHOST, (FOR AS YET HE WAS FALLEN UPON NONE OF THEM, ONLY THEY WERE BAPTIZED IN THE NAME OF THE LORD JESUS).

**Contradictions:**
LUKE 1:13-15 - An angel said unto him [Zacharias], "thy wife Elisabeth shall bear thee a son...John. .... ...he shall be filled with the Holy Ghost, from his mother's womb."
LUKE 1:41 - ...Elisabath was filled with the Holy Ghost.

LUKE 1:67 - His father Zacharias was filled with the Holy Ghost....
LUKE 2:25 - ...Simeon...the Holy Ghost was upon him.
[As yet, did the Holy Ghost fall upon only those who were baptized in the name of Jesus, or had It already come upon some individuals who had not been baptized?]
[Was, or was it not necessary for the apostles to pray that people receive the Holy Ghost?]
JOHN 20:22 - ...He [Jesus] breathed on them, and saith, "Receive ye the Holy Ghost."
[Did the apostles receive the Holy Ghost by being breathed on, or did they have to be baptized in the name of Jesus? (There is no mention of the apostles ever having been baptized. See also under 2:3-4.)]
[Was, or was not baptism a prerequisite for receiving the Holy Ghost?]

**Perplexing:**
Why was it necessary for Peter and John to pray for the believers to receive the Holy Ghost? Why could Philip not pray for them to receive the Holy Ghost?
Why did the writer of ACTS say that until then the Holy Ghost had come only upon those who had been baptized in Jesus' name?

8:17 - THEN LAID THEY THEIR HANDS ON THEM, AND THEY RECEIVED THE HOLY GHOST.

**Perplexing:**
If the apostles prayed for the people to receive the Holy Ghost, why was it also necessary for them to lay hands on them? Why was not just hearing and believing enough for them to receive It? (See also under 14-16 - Contradictions.) Why could the apostles not breathe on the people to give them the Holy Ghost as Jesus did to them in JOHN 20:22? On how many Samaritans did Peter and John lay hands? How long did it take? Did the converts speak in tongues as the apostles did in ACTS 2:4? If only two apostles were needed to lay hands on the people, could there have been many believers?

**History:** See under 6:6.

8:18-19 - WHEN SIMON SAW THAT THROUGH LAYING ON OF THE APOSTLES' HANDS THE HOLY GHOST WAS GIVEN, HE OFFERED THEM MONEY, SAYING, "GIVE ME ALSO THIS POWER, THAT ON WHOMSOEVER I LAY HANDS, MAY RECEIVE THE HOLY GHOST."

**Perplexing:**
How did Simon know that the people touched by the apostles received the Holy Ghost? Did It appear as a dove descending on them, as on Jesus in MATT. 3:16, MARK 1:10, and LUKE 3:22, or as the cloven tongues which sat on the apostles in ACTS 2:3? Did Simon, who believed and was baptized (8:13), also receive the Holy Ghost?

8:20 - PETER SAID, "THY MONEY PERISH WITH THEE, BECAUSE THOU HAST THOUGHT THAT THE GIFT OF GOD MAY BE PURCHASED WITH MONEY."

**Perplexing:**
Why do modern Christian clergy willingly and readily accept, and frequently solicit money for prayers and other services rendered in the name of Jesus? Why do they not follow Peter's example and refuse money?

8:21-23 - PETER: "...THY HEART IS NOT RIGHT IN THE SIGHT OF GOD. REPENT THEREFORE OF THIS THY WICKEDNESS, AND PRAY GOD, IF PERHAPS THE THOUGHT OF THINE HEART MAY BE FORGIVEN THEE. I PERCEIVE THAT THOU ART...IN THE BOND OF INIQUITY."

**Perplexing:**
If Simon was a believer, was baptized (8:13), and presumably was prayed for (8:15), touched by an apostles hands, and received the Holy Ghost, how could he be wicked - "in the bond of iniquity?" Did not God or the Holy Ghost know beforehand how he would respond? Why was he not protected from the bond of iniquity? Why could the apostles not protect him. since Jesus said (LUKE 10:19) that he has given them power over all the power of the enemy (Satan)?

8:24 - SIMON SAID, "PRAY TO THE LORD FOR ME, THAT NONE OF THESE THINGS WHICH YE HAVE SPOKEN COME UPON ME."

**Perplexing:**
Why did Simon ask Peter to pray for him, rather than pray himself as instructed by Peter? Did Peter pray for him?

8:25 - THEY...RETURNED TO JERUSALEM, AND PREACHED THE GOSPEL TO MANY VILLAGES OF THE SAMARITANS.

**Contradiction:** See under 4-5.

**Perplexing:**
How much time did they spend traveling around Samaria? How did they travel? Where did they lodge? From where did they obtain the necessary funds? Did Philip return with Peter and John to Jerusalem? See also under 4-5.

8:26-27 - THE ANGEL OF THE LORD SPAKE UNTO PHILIP, "ARISE AND GO...UNTO THE WAY... FROM JERUSALEM UNTO GAZA.... HE WENT, AND BEHELD A MAN OF ETHIOPIA, AN EUNUCH OF GREAT AUTHORITY UNDER CANDACE QUEEN OF THE ETHIOPIANS, WHO...HAD COME TO JERUSALEM TO WORSHIP.

**Language:**
"Candace" was the Roman rendition of a Nubian word meaning "queen, and used as a title for Ethiopian queens. [The term, "Candace queen," may be translated, therefore, as "Queen queen."]

**History:**
The place of worship in Jerusalem was the temple.

**Contradiction:**
LEV. 21:18-23 - The LORD: "Whatever man that hath a blemish.... ...or hath his stones broken.... He shall not go in unto the veil, nor come nigh unto the altar, because he hath a blemish...."
DEUT. 23:1 - He that is wounded in the stones, or hath his privy member cut off, shall not enter into the congregation of the LORD.
[Was the eunuch permitted to enter the temple and worship, or was he kept out because of his physical

blemish? (It is probable that the priests would have recognized a eunuch's physical characteristics, especially if he was castrated when a boy.)]

**Perplexing:**
Was the writer of ACTS aware of the Old Testament verses prohibiting people with physical blemishes from entering the congregation? Was the Ethiopian unaware of the prohibition? Did the priests ignore the prohibition, or not notice him?

8:32-33 - THE PLACE OF THE SCRIPTURE WHICH HE [THE ETHIOPIAN] READ WAS, "HE WAS LED AS A SHEEP TO THE SLAUGHTER; LIKE A LAMB DUMB BEFORE HIS SHEARER, SO OPENED HE NOT HIS MOUTH; IN HIS HUMILIATION HIS JUDGMENT WAS TAKEN AWAY; WHO SHALL DECLARE HIS GENERATION? HIS LIFE IS TAKEN FROM THE EARTH."

**Old Testament:**
ISA. 53:7-8 - "He was oppressed, and afflicted, yet he opened not his mouth; he is brought as a lamb to the slaughter, and as a sheep before her shearers is dumb, so he openeth not his mouth. He was taken from prison and from judgment; who shall declare his generation? He was cut off out of the land of the living; for the transgression of my people was he stricken." [Note that ACTS deleted the phrase, "for the transgression of my people." Isaiah was writing about the transgression of his fellow Israelites.]

**Language:**
The Hebrew reads (according to the Tanach, The Stone Edition, Ed., Rabbi Nosson Scherman, Mesorah Publications, Ltd., 1996):
"He was persecuted and afflicted, but did not open his mouth, like a sheep being led to the slaughter or a ewe that is silent before her shearers, he did not open his mouth. Now that he has been released from captivity and judgment, who could have imagined such a generation? For he had been removed from the land of the living, an affliction upon them that was my people's sin."
[The verses, according to the Tanach, pertain to the end of Israel's exile.]

8:35 - PHILIP...BEGAN AT THE SAME SCRIPTURE AND PREACHED UNTO HIM JESUS.

**Old Testament:**
See under 32-33 - The verses refer to the time of and events during the prophet's life, not to Jesus, hundreds of years in the future.

8:37 - PHILIP SAID, "IF THOU BELIEVEST WITH ALL THINE HEART, THOU MAYEST [BE BAPTIZED]." HE SAID, "I BELIEVE THAT JESUS CHRIST IS THE SON OF GOD."

**History:**
This verse is deleted by many Bibles.
The earliest known appearance of the verse is found in the codex Laudianus 35 which has been dated to the late 6th or early 7th century.

**Perplexing:**
Was the Ethiopian so ignorant of his Jewish faith that he so readily converted to a belief in Jesus as the Son of God?

8:38-39 - ...THEY WENT DOWN INTO THE WATER, BOTH PHILIP AND THE EUNUCH, AND HE BAPTIZED HIM. WHEN THEY WERE COME UP OUT OF THE WATER, THE SPIRIT OF THE LORD CAUGHT AWAY PHILIP, THAT THE EUNUCH SAW HIM NO MORE; HE WENT ON HIS WAY REJOICING.

**Perplexing:**
Why did the Ethiopian, who was Jewish, agree to be baptized - an ancient pagan ritual?
Did the Ethiopian receive the Holy Ghost? Why was the Spirit able to take Philip away from, but not bring him to the Ethiopian? In 8:26, an angel ordered Philip to travel into the Gaza desert, where he met the Ethiopian. Why did the Spirit not move the other apostles from place to place? Why did the Spirit not move Jesus from one place to another? Why did the Spirit prevent Philip from saying, "good-by" to the Ethiopian? Why did the Ethiopian rejoice? Was it because he now believed in Jesus and was baptized, or because he was free of Philip?

**Pagan concept:** See under MATT. 3:5-6.

**History:** See under MATT. 3:5-6.

**Old Testament:** See under MATT. 3:5-6.

9:1-2 - SAUL BREATHING OUT THREATENINGS AND SLAUGHTER AGAINST THE DISCIPLES OF THE LORD, WENT UNTO THE HIGH PRIEST, AND DESIRED LETTERS TO DAMASCUS TO THE SYNAGOGUES, THAT IF HE FOUND ANY OF THIS WAY, MEN OR WOMEN, HE MIGHT BRING THEM BOUND TO JERUSALEM.

**Contradictions:**
ACTS 9:14 - Ananias: "Here he [Saul] hath authority from the chief priests to bind all that call on thy [Jesus'] name."
ACTS 26:12 - Paul: "I went to Damascus with authority and commission from the chief priests."
[Did Paul receive authority to go to Damascus from the high priest, or from the chief priests?]
ACTS 22:5 - Paul: "The high priest doth bear me witness, and all the estate of the elders, from whom also I received letters...to bring them which were there bound unto Jerusalem to be punished."
[Did Paul receive authority from the high priest, or from the high priest and the elders?]
GAL. 1:22 - Paul: "[I] was unknown by face unto the churches of Judaea which were in Christ."
[Was, or was not Paul known in Judaea?]

**History:**
The authority of the high priest and the Sanhedrin (council) did not extend past Judea. Furthermore, the high priest's jurisdiction in theological matters was limited to the Jerusalem temple; he did not have authority over synagogues. Consequently, he could not authorize anyone to make arrests in Damascus, about 200 miles away, outside of Judea, or make arrests in synagogues. In addition, at the time the described events were taking place, Damascus was under Nabatean, not Roman control.
Since the high priest was of the pro-Roman Sadducees who were hostile to the anti-Roman Pharisees (see under MATT. 3:7), it is highly unlikely that he would have even considered allowing Saul, a Pharisee (see ACTS 23:6 and PHILIP. 3:5), and a young man, possibly an adolescent (see under 7:58 - Language), to work for him. Similarly, it is highly unlikely that a Pharisee would have opted to work for a Sadducee.
Early Christians referred to their belief as, "The Way," or "The Way of God."

**Dead Sea Scrolls:**
The term, "the Way, " is used to mean the study of the Torah; and the people of the Qumran community referred to themselves as "followers of the Way."

**Perplexing:**
Why did the writer of ACTS not know about the limitations on the high priest's power? Why was Saul anxious to go to Damascus to arrest people? Why did he not want to remain in Jerusalem and arrest the apostles? Why would the Romans permit Saul to travel to Damascus (in another country) to arrest people and bring them to Jerusalem, thereby, provoking a possible confrontation with the Nabateans?

9:4-5 - HE [SAUL] FELL TO THE EARTH, AND HEARD A VOICE SAYING, "SAUL, SAUL, WHY PERSECUTEST ME?" HE SAID, "WHO ART THOU LORD?" THE LORD SAID, "I AM JESUS WHOM THOU PERSECUTEST; IT IS HARD FOR THEE TO KICK AGAINST THE PRICKS."

**Contradictions:**
ACTS 22:8 - I [Paul] answered, "Who art thou Lord?" He said, "I am Jesus of Nazareth, whom thou persecutest."
[Did Jesus identify himself as "Jesus," or as "Jesus of Nazareth"?]
ACTS 26:14-15 - ...I [Paul] heard a voice saying in the Hebrew tongue, "Saul, Saul, why persecutest me? It is hard for thee to kick at pricks. "I said, "Who art thou Lord?" He said, "I am Jesus whom thou persecutest."
[Did Saul say, "Who art thou Lord," before or after the voice said that it is hard to kick against (at) pricks?]

**Perplexing:**
Why did Saul say, "Lord," before he knew who was speaking to him?
Why had Jesus permitted Saul to persecute his followers? Why did Jesus fail to come to Saul before he began persecuting his followers?

9:6 - HE [SAUL] TREMBLING AND ASTONISHED SAID, "LORD, WHAT WILT THOU HAVE ME DO?" THE LORD SAID UNTO HIM, "ARISE, AND GO INTO THE CITY, AND IT SHALL BE TOLD THEE WHAT THOU MUST DO."

**Contradictions:**
ACTS 26:16-18 - Paul: "[Jesus said] 'Rise, and stand; I have appeared unto thee for this purpose, to make thee a minister and a witness both of these things which thou hast seen, and of those things in which I will appear unto thee...the Gentiles, unto whom I now send thee, to open their eyes, and turn them ... from the power of Satan unto God, that they may receive forgiveness of sins...among them which are sanctified by faith that is in me.'"
[Did Jesus tell Saul to go into the city where he would receive further information, or did he tell Saul what he wanted him to do and tell him to go to the Gentiles?]
[Did Saul ask Jesus what he should do, or did Jesus tell him without first being asked?]
See also under MATT. 9:13.

9:7 - THE MEN WHICH JOURNEYED WITH HIM STOOD SPEECHLESS, HEARING A VOICE, BUT SEEING NO MAN.

**Contradictions:**
ACTS 22:9 - Paul: "They that were with me...heard not the voice of him that spake to me."
[Did the men hear the voice, or not hear the voice?]
ACTS 26:14 - Paul: "When we were all fallen to the earth, I heard a voice...."
[Did the men stand speechless, or did they all fall down with Saul?]

**Perplexing:**
Why did Paul not report this incident on the road to Damascus in his Epistles?

9:10 - THERE WAS A DISCIPLE AT DAMASCUS, NAMED ANANIAS....

**Contradiction:**
ACTS 22:12 - Ananias, a devout man according to the law, having a good report of all the Jews which dwelt there.
[Was Ananias a disciple, or was he a devout man according to the law, with a good report among all there Jews there?]

9:13 - ANANIAS ANSWERED, "LORD, I HAVE HEARD BY MANY OF THIS MAN, HOW MUCH EVIL HE HATH DONE TO THY SAINTS AT JERUSALEM."

**Perplexing:**
Why did Jesus allow Saul to do evil to his "saints" in Jerusalem?

9:14 - ANANIAS: "HERE HE HATH AUTHORITY FROM THE CHIEF PRIESTS TO BIND ALL THAT CALL ON THY NAME."

**Contradictions:**
ACTS 9:1-2 - Saul went unto the high priest, and desired of him letters to Damascus...that...he might bring them bound unto Jerusalem.
[Did Saul receive authority from the chief priests, or from then high priest?]
ACTS 22:5 - Paul: "The high priest...and all the estate of the elders from whom I also received letters...to bring them which were bound unto Jerusalem...."
[Did Saul receive authority from the chief priests, or from the high priest and elders?]
See also under 1-2.

**History:** See under 1-2.

**Perplexing:**
How did Ananias know that Saul had come to Damascus and the reason for his coming? Why did Ananias and Jesus not know that the priests in Jerusalem had no authority to order anyone's arrest in Damascus?

9:15 - THE LORD SAID, "GO THY WAY; HE IS A CHOSEN VESSEL UNTO ME, TO BEAR MY NAME BEFORE THE GENTILES, KINGS, AND THE CHILDREN OF ISRAEL."

**Perplexing:**
Why did Jesus wait until now, after Saul had persecuted and scattered his followers, to make him "a chosen vessel" to work for him? Why did Jesus need Ananias to contact Saul? Why did Jesus not speak to Saul again? Why did the resurrected Jesus not go to the Gentiles?

9:16 - JESUS: "I WILL SHEW HIM HOW GREAT THINGS HE MUST SUFFER FOR MY NAME'S SAKE."

**Perplexing:**
Why did Jesus want Saul or anyone else to suffer for his name's sake?

9:17-18 - ANANIAS...PUTTING HIS HANDS ON HIM SAID, "SAUL...JESUS, THAT APPEARED UNTO THEE IN THE WAY AS THOU CAMEST, HATH SENT ME, THAT THOU MIGHTEST RECEIVE THY SIGHT, AND BE FILLED WITH THE HOLY GHOST."

**Contradictions:**
ACTS 9:4-7 - Saul heard only a voice; no man was seen.
[Did Jesus appear to Saul, or did he just hear Jesus' voice?]
ACTS 22:14 - Paul: "He [Ananias] said, 'The God of our fathers hath chosen thee, that thou shouldest know His will, and see that Just One, and shouldest hear the voice of his mouth.'"
[Did Ananias tell Saul that Jesus sent him that he might see again and be filled with the Holy Ghost, or did he say that God had chosen Saul to see and hear the Just One?]

9:20 - STRAIGHTWAY HE PREACHED CHRIST IN THE SYNAGOGUES, THAT HE IS THE SON OF GOD.

**Perplexing:**
How was Saul able to walk into synagogues and preach anything, especially about something so contrary to Jewish belief as Jesus being the Son of God, without first obtaining permission from the presiding priest? Why did he not preach Jesus' teachings? Was he unaware of Jesus' command in MATT. 28:19-20 - "Go, teach all nations...to observe all things, whatsoever I have commanded you...?"

9:21 - ALL THAT HEARD HIM WERE AMAZED, AND SAID, "IS NOT THIS HE THAT DESTROYED THEM WHICH CALLED ON THIS NAME IN JERUSALEM, AND CAME HITHER...THAT HE MIGHT BRING THEM BOUND UNTO THE CHIEF PRIESTS?"

**Contradictions:** See under 9:14.

**Perplexing:**
How did all the people find out why Saul had come to Damascus?
See also under 9:14.

9:22 - SAUL INCREASED THE MORE IN STRENGTH, AND CONFOUNDED THE JEWS WHICH DWELT AT DAMASCUS, PROVING THAT THIS IS VERY CHRIST.

**Perplexing:**
Since Jesus did not meet the Jewish criteria for being the Messiah (Christ), how could Saul confound any knowledgeable Jews and prove that Jesus is the Christ? Why did the Jews not point out to Saul that, unlike the expected Jewish Messiah, Jesus (1) was Galilean, not Judean; (2) could not have been a human descended paternally from David, if he was the Son of God; (3) did not restore the kingdom of Israel? Were the Jews of Damascus so ignorant of their religion that they could be bamboozled by Saul?

**Contradiction:**
GAL. 1:15-17 - Paul: "When it pleased God...to reveal His Son to me, that I might preach him among the heathen, immediately I conferred not with flesh and blood...but I went to Arabia, and returned to Damascus." [After his conversion, did Saul speak with Ananias and to people in synagogues, or did he not speak to anyone, but go to Arabia?]

9:23 - ...THE JEWS TOOK COUNSEL TO KILL HIM.

**Contradiction:**
2 COR. 11:32 - Paul: "In Damascus the governor under Aretas the king kept the city of the Damascenes with a garrison, desirous to apprehend me."
[Did the Jews want to kill Saul, or did the governor want to apprehend him?]

**History:**
Damascus at this time was ruled by the Nabateans, not by Jews. The Romans had given Damascus to Aretas in A.D. 37, but reclaimed it after his death in A.D. 40. COR., therefore, has placed Saul in Damascus between A.D. 37 - 40. (See notes under 5:36-37; the writer of ACTS placed the apostles in A.D. 46 before Paul began his adventures.)

**Perplexing:**
Why would the Jews want to kill Saul? It was not against Jewish law to claim to be or to claim that someone else was the Messiah or the Son of God. Was ACTS just trying to incite anti-Jewish sentiment? (If the COR. version is accepted, what did Saul do that incited the non-Jewish governor of Damascus to try and apprehend him?)

9:24-25 - THEIR LAYING IN AWAIT WAS KNOWN OF SAUL. THEY WATCHED THE GATES DAY AND NIGHT TO KILL HIM. THE DISCIPLES TOOK HIM BY NIGHT, AND LET HIM DOWN BY THE WALL IN A BASKET.

**Contradiction:**
2 COR. 11:33 - Paul: "Through a window in a basket was I let down by the wall, and escaped his hands."
[Did Saul escape from the Jews, or from the hands of the governor of Damascus? (See under 9:23.)]

**Perplexing:** See under 9:23.

9:26 - WHEN SAUL WAS COME TO JERUSALEM, HE ASSAYED TO JOIN HIMSELF TO THE DISCIPLES, BUT THEY WERE ALL AFRAID OF HIM AND BELIEVED NOT THAT HE WAS A DISCIPLE.

**Contradictions:**
1 GAL. 1:15-17 - Paul: "It pleased God...to reveal His Son in me, that I might preach him among the heathen; immediately I conferred not with flesh and blood; neither went I up to Jerusalem to them which were apostles ... but I went into Arabia, and returned again unto Damascus.
[Did Saul go to Jerusalem from Damascus, or did he go to Arabia and then back to Damascus?]
See also under 9:22.

**Perplexing:**
Why were the apostles still in Jerusalem?
Why were the disciples afraid? Did they not trust God or Jesus to protect them?

9:27 - BARNABAS TOOK HIM...TO THE APOSTLES, DECLARED UNTO THEM HOW HE HAD SEEN THE LORD...HAD SPOKEN TO HIM, AND HOW HE HAD PREACHED BOLDLY AT DAMASCUS IN THE NAME OF JESUS.

**Contradictions:**
GAL. 1:18-2:1 - Paul: "After three years I went to Jerusalem to see Peter.... Other of the apostles saw I none, save James the Lord's brother. .... Afterwards I came into the regions of Syria and Cilicia, and was unknown by face unto the churches of Judaea in Christ.... .... Then fourteen years after I went again to Jerusalem with Barnabas...."
[Did Saul go from Damascus to Jerusalem where Barnabas took him to the apostles, or did he wait three years, then go to Jerusalem to see Peter and James, then wait 14 years before returning to Jerusalem with Barnabas?]
[Did Saul go to Jerusalem and meet with the apostles, or did he meet only with Peter and James?]
See also under 17-18 and 26.

**Perplexing:**
Who was Barnabas? How and where did Saul meet him? Why did Barnabas tell the apostles that Saul had seen the Lord, when according to ACTS 9:4, he just heard a voice, and in 9:7, no man was seen?
See also under 9:26.

9:28 - HE [SAUL] WAS WITH THEM COMING IN AND GOING OUT AT JERUSALEM.

**Contradictions:**
ACTS 22:17-21 - Paul said that he came to Jerusalem, prayed in the temple, and in a trance was told by Jesus to leave Jerusalem; he did not say that he met with the apostles.
[Did Saul meet with the apostles and go in and out of Jerusalem with them, or go to the temple, hear Jesus, and leave Jerusalem?]
1 GAL. 1:17-19 - Paul: "Neither went I to Jerusalem to them which were apostles, but went into Arabia, and returned unto Damascus. Then after three years I went to Jerusalem to see Peter and abode with him 15 days. But other of the apostles saw I none, save James the Lord's brother."
[Did Saul meet with the apostles and go in and out of Jerusalem with them, or did he just meet with Peter and Jesus' brother James?]

9:29 - HE SPOKE BOLDLY IN THE NAME OF JESUS, AND DISPUTED AGAINST THE GRECIANS, BUT THEY WENT ABOUT TO SLAY HIM.

**Perplexing:**
Why would the Grecians (Greek speaking Jews) want to slay him? If all he did was preach about Jesus, he did not violate any Jewish law.
See also under 9:23.

9:30 - WHEN THE BRETHREN KNEW, THEY BROUGHT HIM DOWN TO CAESAREA, AND SENT HIM TO TARSUS.

**Contradiction:**
ACTS 22:24-30 - Paul was seized by Roman troops and set before the chief priests and council.
[Did the brethren take Saul to Caesarea and send him to Tarsus, or was he seized by the Romans and brought before the chief priests and council?]

9:32-35 - PETER CAME...TO LYDDA. THERE HE FOUND A MAN NAMED AENEAS, WHICH HAD KEPT HIS BED EIGHT YEARS, SICK OF PALSY. PETER SAID, "AENEAS, JESUS CHRIST MAKETH THEE WHOLE; ARISE AND MAKE THY BED." HE AROSE IMMEDIATELY. ALL THAT DWELT AT LYDDA AND SARON SAW HIM, AND TURNED TO THE LORD.

**Perplexing:**
Why is there no secular record of this miracle or the mass conversion of all the people in Lydda and Saron? Why did Peter not ask the man whether he had faith before healing him? Why did Peter not have to touch the man to heal him? Why did he not anoint the sick with oil to heal them as was done in MARK 6:13? Why did not Peter heal all the sick people there?
See also under MARK 6:12-13.

**Pagan concept:** See under JOHN 18:5-6.

**History:**
Lydda was the Greek name for the Hebrew, Lod, a town about 22 miles from Jerusalem and ten miles from Joppa.

9:36-42 - THERE WAS AT JOPPA, A DISCIPLE NAMED TABITHA, CALLED DOREAS...FULL OF GOOD WORKS.... SHE WAS SICK, AND DIED.... ...THEY SENT UNTO HIM TWO MEN DESIRING HIM TO COME. PETER WENT. .... PETER...PRAYED, AND TURNING TO THE BODY, SAID, "TABITHA, ARISE." SHE OPENED HER EYES, AND WHEN SHE SAW PETER, SHE SAT UP. HE...LIFTED HER UP, AND...PRESENTED HER ALIVE. IT WAS KNOWN THROUGHOUT ALL JOPPA, AND MANY BELIEVED IN THE LORD.

**Perplexing:**
Why is there no secular record of this amazing resurrection miracle and conversion of people in Joppa? Why were not all the people, rather than just many, induced to believe in the Lord? Why was there no record of Tabitha having been resurrected or of her second death? Did she want to return to life? Why would anyone want to return from the dead, especially to a world filled with evil, if there is a wonderful heaven and a meeting with Jesus awaiting one? Was not bringing someone back from the dead going against the will of God? Why did Peter not use Jesus' name to raise Tabitha? Why cannot other Christians resurrect the dead? In JOHN 14:12, Jesus said, "He that believeth on me, the works that I do shall he do also, and greater works than these shall he do...."
See also under MATT. 9:26.

**Old Testament:** See under MATT. 9:26.

**Pagan parallels**: See under JOHN 11:43-44.

**History:** See under JOHN 11:43-44.

10:1-2 - THERE WAS A MAN IN CAESAREA CALLED CORNELIUS...OF THE ITALIAN BAND, A DEVOUT MAN, THAT FEARED GOD WITH ALL HIS HOUSE...AND PRAYED TO GOD.

**History:**

The terms, "devout man" and "one that feared God," were frequently used to designate people who were not Jewish—they did not accept all of the Mosaic law and were not circumcised—but who worshiped the Jewish God.

Historians tend to doubt that an Italian band (a Roman cohort) was stationed in Caesarea between A.D. 40 - 44 during which time the area was ruled by the Jewish King Agrippa; it is also unlikely that such a band was present at a later date.

10:3-5 - ...AN ANGEL SAYING, "CORNELIUS." .... "NOW SEND MEN TO JOPPA, AND CALL FOR ONE SIMON, WHOSE SURNAME IS PETER."

**Perplexing:**

Why did the angel go to Cornelius? Why did the angel not go directly to Peter and instruct him to go to Cornelius? Why did the angel not take Peter to him?

10:9 - ...PETER WENT UP UPON THE HOUSETOP TO PRAY....

**Perplexing:**

Why did Peter go onto the roof to pray?

10:10-14 - ...HE [PETER] FELL INTO A TRANCE, SAW HEAVEN OPENED, AND A VESSEL DESCENDING UNTO HIM...A GREAT SHEET...WHEREIN WERE ALL MANNER OF...BEASTS, CREEPING THINGS, AND FOWLS.... THERE CAME A VOICE TO HIM, "... KILL, AND EAT." PETER SAID, "NOT SO, LORD; I HAVE NEVER EATEN ANYTHING THAT IS COMMON OR UNCLEAN."

**Perplexing:**

How could Peter have killed the animals? Would he have eaten them raw, if he followed the command? How did Peter know that the voice was that of the Lord?

**Old Testament:**

EZEK. 4:12-14 - God [to Ezekiel: "...thou shalt bake it [bread] with dung that cometh out of man.... Thus shall the children of Israel eat their defiled bread among the Gentiles...." Then said I [Ezekiel], "Lord God...from my youth up till now have I not eaten of that which dieth of itself. ...neither came there abominable flesh into my mouth."

10:17-18 - WHILE PETER DOUBTED WHAT THE VISION SHOULD MEAN, THE MEN SENT FROM CORNELIUS HAD MADE INQUIRY FOR SIMON'S HOUSE, STOOD BEFORE THE GATE, AND ASKED WHETHER SIMON, SURNAMED PETER, LODGED THERE.

**Perplexing:**

Why did the angel fail to give Cornelius specific directions for finding the house, so the men would not have had to inquire for its location?

10:23 - CALLED HE THEM IN, AND LODGED THEM.

**Perplexing:**
How could Peter invite in and lodge people in someone else's house without that owner's permission? Verse 6 said that the house belonged to Simon a tanner. Why did Peter not have the courtesy to speak with Simon first?

10:25 - ...CORNELIUS MET HIM, FELL DOWN AT HIS FEET, AND WORSHIPPED HIM.

**Perplexing:**
Why did Cornelius worship Peter? The angel had not given Cornelius any information about Peter.

10:28 - HE [PETER] SAID, "YE KNOW THAT IT IS UNLAWFUL FOR A JEW TO KEEP COMPANY, OR COME UNTO ONE OF ANOTHER NATION; BUT GOD HATH SHEWED ME THAT I SHOULD NOT CALL ANY MAN COMMON OR UNCLEAN."

**History:**
There was no prohibition against Jews eating with non-Jews who were "God-fearers" (see under 1-2), if forbidden food was not present. Regular social interaction between Jews and non-Jews also took place.

**Perplexing:**
Why did Peter, who said that he was a Jew, believe that it was unlawful for a Jew to associate with non-Jews, when such was not the case?
In 10:15 a voice said to Peter, "What God hath cleansed, call not common." Why did Peter believe that the vision of a sheet with animals of all kinds on it, and the voice he heard in 10:15, pertained to people?

10:30 - CORNELIUS SAID, I WAS FASTING...AND I PRAYED IN MY HOUSE, AND A MAN STOOD BEFORE ME IN BRIGHT CLOTHING."

**Perplexing:**
In 10:3, it was an angel that appeared to Cornelius. Why, throughout the Bible, are angels always described as men? Contrary to Christian tradition, they are not described as having wings; and none are reported to have the appearance of women.

10:34 - PETER SAID, "I PERCEIVE THAT GOD IS NO RESPECTER OF PERSONS."

**Language:**
The term, "no respecter of persons," is interpreted as meaning that God does not show favoritism or partiality towards anyone.

**Contradictions:**
There are numerous contradictory verses about God showing favoritism some of which are:
GEN. 17:1-8 - God selected the Hebrews out of all the earth's peoples to favor with His covenant.
DEUT. 7:6 - Moses: "...the LORD thy God hath chosen thee [the Hebrews] to be a special people unto Himself, above all people. ...."
[Admittedly, this selection and "favor" brought little but disasters and suffering to the Hebrews and their successors the Jews.]

EX. 33:19 - God: " ...I will be gracious to whom I will be gracious, and will shew mercy on whom I will shew mercy."
LEV. 20:10 - God: " ...the adulterer and adulteress shall surely be put to death"; however, in 2 SAM. 11:2-5, David and Bathsheba committed adultery, but in 2 SAM. 12:13, God showed favoritism towards David by forgiving him.
NUM. 12:1-10 - Aaron and Miriam spoke against Moses, but only Miriam was punished; God showed favoritism towards Aaron.
DEUT. 23:2 - God: "A bastard shall not enter into the congregation of the LORD, even to his tenth generation." God, however, showed favoritism towards David who was the tenth generation of the bastard Pharez (GEN. 38:16-29; RUTH 4:18-22), yet the LORD was with David (2 SAM. 7:3) and allowed him into the congregation of the LORD.
JOHN 6:44 - Jesus: "No man can come to me, except the Father which hath sent me draw him." God shows favoritism to some people by drawing them to Jesus.
[Does not, or does God show favoritism?]

10:35 - PETER: "IN EVERY NATION HE THAT FEARETH HIM, AND WORKETH RIGHTEOUSNESS IS ACCEPTED WITH HIM."

**Contradictions:** See under MATT. 10:28 and 19:17-19 (for obtaining eternal life).

**Perplexing:** See under MATT. 10:28.

10:36 - PETER: "THE WORD WHICH GOD SENT UNTO THE CHILDREN OF ISRAEL, PREACHING PEACE BY JESUS CHRIST...."

**Contradiction:**
MATT. 10:34 - Jesus: "Think not that I am come to send peace on earth; I came not to send peace, but a sword."
LUKE 12:49 - Jesus: "I am come to send fire on the earth...."
LUKE 12:51 - Jesus: "Suppose ye that I am come to give peace on earth? I tell you, nay, but rather division."
[Did Jesus come to preach peace as claimed by Peter, or did Jesus say that he did not come to bring peace?]

10:38 - PETER: "GOD ANOINTED JESUS OF NAZARETH WITH THE HOLY GHOST AND WITH POWER, WHO WENT ABOUT DOING GOOD, AND HEALING ALL THAT WERE OPPRESSED OF THE DEVIL, FOR GOD WAS WITH HIM."

**Perplexing:**
If Jesus was God's Son, why was he not born with the Holy Ghost in him? Why did God have to anoint him with the Holy Ghost and power? How did God anoint Jesus? When? If Jesus was one with God, as he said in JOHN 10:30, how could God not be with him? By saying that Jesus of Nazareth was anointed by God and that God was with him, was Peter saying that Jesus was a man of Nazareth who God specially selected to anoint with the Holy Ghost and power?
Why did God allow the devil to oppress people?
See also under 2:22.

**Contradictions:** See under 2:22 and MATT. 1:1.

**Perplexing:** See under 2:22.

**History:** See under 2:22.

10:39 - PETER: "WE ARE WITNESSES OF ALL THINGS WHICH HE DID BOTH IN THE LAND OF THE JEWS, AND IN JERUSALEM, WHOM THEY SLEW AND HANGED ON A TREE."

**Contradictions:** See under 5:30.

**Pagan parallels**: See under 5:30.

**History:** See under 5:30, and MATT. 27:35.

**Perplexing:** See under 5:30, and MATT. 27:37-38.

10:40-41 - PETER: "HIM GOD RAISED UP THE THIRD DAY, AND SHEWED HIM OPENLY; NOT TO ALL THE PEOPLE, BUT UNTO WITNESSES CHOSEN BEFORE OF GOD, TO US, WHO DID EAT AND DRINK WITH HIM AFTER HE ROSE FROM THE DEAD."

**Perplexing:**
If God wanted people to believe in Jesus, why did He not show him openly to everyone? Why was only a small group of "chosen" people allowed to see the resurrected Jesus?
See also under 2:24, 32-33, and MATT. 28:5-7.

**Contradictions:** See under MATT. 16:21.

**History:** See under MATT. 28:5-7, 9-10.

10:42 - PETER: "HE COMMANDED US TO PREACH UNTO THE PEOPLE, AND TO TESTIFY THAT IT IS HE WHICH WAS ORDAINED OF GOD TO BE THE JUDGE OF QUICK AND DEAD."

**Contradictions:** See under JOHN 5:22.

**Perplexing:**
When and how was Jesus ordained? Why was it necessary for God to ordain Jesus, if he was His Son and part of the Trinity?
See under JOHN 5:22.

**Pagan parallel:** See under JOHN 5:22.

10:43 - PETER: "TO HIM GIVE ALL THE PROPHETS WITNESS, THAT THROUGH HIS NAME WHOSOEVER BELIEVETH IN HIM SHALL RECEIVE REMISSION OF SINS."

**Contradictions:**
JER. 31:34 - The LORD: "... I will forgive their iniquity, and I will remember their sin no more."
MIC. 7:18 - Micah: "Who is a God like unto Thee, that pardoneth iniquity, and passeth by the transgression of the remnant of His heritage?...."

[Are sins remitted through Jesus' name by believing in him, or by God?]
JOHN 20:23 - Jesus: "Whose soever sins ye [his disciples] remit, they are remitted unto them; and whose soever sins ye retain, they are retained."
[Are sins remitted through Jesus' name by believing in him, or can the disciples on their own remit sins?]

**Perplexing:**
When did all the prophets give witness to Jesus?

10:44 - WHILE PETER SPOKE THESE WORDS, THE HOLY GHOST FELL ON ALL THEM WHICH HEARD THE WORD.

**Perplexing:**
Why did the Holy Ghost fall on those who heard the word, when in ACTS 8:17, it was necessary for Peter and John to lay hands on people to give them the Holy Ghost? How does the Holy Ghost decide when It will fall onto people? In what form did the Holy Ghost fall onto the people? Why did It come upon these people who had not yet been baptized? It did not come upon Jesus until after his baptism (MATT. 3:16, MARK 1:9-10, and LUKE 3:21-22).

10:48 - HE COMMANDED THEM TO BE BAPTIZED IN THE NAME OF THE LORD....

**Contradiction:**
MATT. 28:19 - Jesus: "Go ye therefore, and teach all nations, baptizing them in the name of the Father, the Son, and the Holy Ghost."
[Were people to be baptized in the name of the Lord, or in the name of the Father, Son, and Holy Ghost?]

**Perplexing:**
Why was it necessary for those who had received the Holy Ghost to be baptized? Why did Peter not baptize them in the name of the Father, Son, and Holy Ghost? Why were they not baptized before receiving the Holy Ghost?

11:3 - [JEWS SAID TO PETER]: "THOU WENTEST IN TO MEN UNCIRCUMCISED, AND DID EAT WITH THEM."

**History:** See under 10:28.

11:15 - PETER: "AS I BEGAN TO SPEAK, THE HOLY GHOST FELL ON THEM, AS ON US AT THE BEGINNING."

**Perplexing:**
Was Peter saying that the Holy Ghost descending on them like tongues of flame, as in 2:3-4, or like when Jesus breathed the Holy Ghost on the disciples in JOHN 20:22?

11:19 - THEY WHICH WERE SCATTERED ABROAD...TRAVELLED...PREACHING THE WORD TO NONE BUT UNTO THE JEWS ONLY.

**Contradiction:**
ACTS 8:4-5 - They that were scattered abroad went everywhere preaching the word. Philip went to the city

of Samaria, and preached Christ unto them.
[Did those who were scattered preach only to Jews, or to everyone?]

11:21 - THE HAND OF THE LORD WAS WITH THEM, AND A GREAT NUMBER BELIEVED, AND TURNED UNTO THE LORD.

**Perplexing:**
If the hand of the Lord was with them, why did not everyone believe and turn to him?

11:26 - .... THE DISCIPLES WERE CALLED CHRISTIANS FIRST IN ANTIOCH.

**Language:**
"Christian," is generally believed to be derived from the Greek "khristianos," ("those who anoint") which was also an ancient Greek word applied to homosexual masseurs who anointed their clients with olive oil in public bathhouses. It is not known whether the name was meant to denigrate the followers of Jesus, or because all or some of them were openly homosexual.

**History:**
Nazarenes was the original name given to those who believed in Jesus.

11:28 - THERE STOOD UP ONE OF THEM [PROPHETS] NAMED AGABUS, AND SIGNIFIED BY THE SPIRIT THAT THERE SHOULD BE GREAT DEARTH THROUGHOUT THE WORLD, WHICH CAME TO PASS IN THE DAYS OF CLAUDIUS CAESAR.

**History:**
A famine occurred in Judea in A.D. 46, but it was not world-wide. There is no record of any world-wide famine ever having occurred. The Judean famine was particularly disastrous, because the following year was a Jewish sabbatical year during which the planting of crops was prohibited. According to ACTS 12:1-2, Herod (Herod Agrippa I) vexed the church and killed John's brother James at the time of the famine; this Herod, however, only reigned until A.D. 44 - two years prior to the cited famine. The reference to the famine occurring during Agrippa's reign, therefore, is an anachronism.

**Perplexing:**
When did Agabus make his prophecy? Why did his prophecy for a famine throughout the world fail? Did the writer of ACTS believe that the Mediterranean region was the entire world? Why was the writer of ACTS ignorant of the fact that the famine did not occur during this Agrippa's reign?

11:29-30 - THE DISCIPLES...DETERMINED TO SEND RELIEF UNTO THE BRETHREN WHICH DWELT IN JUDAEA. ...AND SENT IT TO THE ELDERS BY THE HANDS OF BARNABAS AND SAUL.

**History:**
Helena the queen of Adiabene and her son Izates, the king of Adiabene, arranged to have food sent to Judea from Egypt and Cyprus. Although they were Jewish, the food was sent to all the people of Judea. The reference to elders implies that the Christian community was well established at this time.

12:1-2 - ABOUT THAT TIME HEROD THE KING STRETCHED FORTH HIS HANDS TO VEX CERTAIN OF THE CHURCH. HE KILLED JAMES THE BROTHER OF JOHN WITH THE SWORD.

**History:**
The assertion that Herod killed James is not verified in the secular records of the period. The cited Herod the king was Agrippa I, who was appointed king in A.D. 41 by the Roman Emperor Caligula.
See also under 11:28.

**Perplexing:**
Why did Jesus and/or God permit Herod to kill James? Why did the Holy Ghost or an angel fail to protect him?

12:3-4 - ...HE PROCEEDED FURTHER TO TAKE PETER. (THEN WERE THE DAYS OF UNLEAVENED BREAD.)...HE PUT HIM IN PRISON...INTENDING AFTER EASTER TO BRING HIM TO THE PEOPLE.

**Perplexing:**
Why did Jesus and/or God allow Peter to be put in prison? Why did Herod want to imprison someone who could perform miracles of healing the infirm and raising the dead? Why did the Holy Ghost fail to protect him?
See also under 4:3 and 5:17-18.

**History:**
Easter is an ancient pagan holiday celebrating the resurrection of deities who had died or been killed around the time of the vernal equinox, some of whom spent three full days and nights underground. Some of these gods were, Tanunuz, Baal, Attis, and Mithra. Christians, however, observed the Jewish Passover until the 4th century at which time Emperor Constantine of Rome commanded them to observe the pagan Easter; he prohibited the observance of Passover. It was also this emperor who commanded Christians to cease observing the biblical Sabbath and instead observe Sunday the pagan Roman Sabbath. He ordered the execution of any Christians who continued to observe Passover and/or the Saturday Sabbath. Consequently, the above reference to Easter is an anachronism. (Many other Bible translations correctly use Passover, not Easter.)

12:6-10 - ...PETER WAS SLEEPING BETWEEN TWO SOLDIERS, BOUND WITH CHAINS; KEEPERS BEFORE THE DOOR KEPT THE PRISON. THE ANGEL OF THE LORD CAME...RAISED HIM UP, SAYING, "ARISE UP QUICKLY." HIS CHAINS FELL OFF. THE ANGEL SAID, "GIRD THYSELF...." .... HE SAITH, "FOLLOW ME." HE...FOLLOWED HIM.... .... THEY WENT OUT...THE ANGEL DEPARTED....

**Perplexing:**
Why was an angel needed to lead Peter out of prison? Why did the angel come at night, rather than during the day when he could be seen by the soldiers and others? Why was it necessary for Peter to depart quickly? Why could the angel not carry him away as the Spirit carried Philip away from the Ethiopian in 8:39? Why could the angel not induce Herod to release Peter? Why could Peter not perform a miracle to free himself?
See also under 5:19-20.

**History:**
There is no secular record of Peter's imprisonment and escape.

12:14-15 - WHEN SHE [RHODA] KNEW PETER'S VOICE, SHE...TOLD HOW PETER STOOD BEFORE THE GATE. .... SAID THEY [PEOPLE IN THE HOUSE TO WHICH PETER WENT], "IT IS HIS ANGEL."

**Perplexing:**
Why did the writer of ACTS have the people speak as if there was an angel who looked like Peter? Did they already believe in the Christian concept of guardian angels? Did they have so little confidence in the effectiveness of their prayers that they could not believe that Peter was free? In 12:5, "prayer was made without ceasing of the church unto God for him."

12:17 - .... HE [PETER] SAID, "GO SHEW THESE THINGS UNTO JAMES, AND TO THE BRETHREN." HE DEPARTED, AND WENT INTO ANOTHER PLACE.

**Perplexing:**
Who was the James to whom Peter referred? Was he unaware that James the brother of John had been killed, or was he saying that James was still alive? Was he referring to James the son of Alphaeus (one of the disciples in MATT. 10:3, MARK 3:18, and ACTS 1:13)? Was he referring to James, the brother of Jesus (GAL. 1:19), or possibly to another James? To what place did Peter go? Where? Why?

12:23 - IMMEDIATELY THE ANGEL OF THE LORD SMOTE HIM [HEROD], BECAUSE HE GAVE NOT GOD THE GLORY; HE WAS EATEN OF WORMS, AND GAVE UP THE GHOST [IN CAESAREA (12:19)].

**History:**
Herod Agrippa I died in Caesarea, five days after feeling severe abdominal pain. The cause was not known, but suggestions have been made that he may have been poisoned, had acute appendicitis, or had a perforated or blocked intestinal tract caused by parasitic worms, possibly, *Ascaris lumbricoides*, which can grow up to several inches in length, and may also be vomited up, thereby, giving rise to the assertion that he "was eaten of worms." King Herod the Great was also reported to have died from a disease in which his body allegedly produced worms. Similarly, Sulla the dictator of Rome, was reported to have died from being eaten internally by worms (79 B.C.). After Herod Agrippa's death, Judea was annexed to the Roman province of Syria and governed by Roman procurators.

**Perplexing:**
Why does God want or need glory? Why must an angel kill someone for not giving God glory? Are angels and God exempt from the commandment in EX. 20:13 - "Thou shalt not kill?"

13:2 - ...THE HOLY GHOST SAID, "SEPARATE ME BARNABAS AND SAUL FOR THE WORK WHEREUNTO I HAVE CALLED THEM."

**Perplexing:**
Why did the Holy Ghost need people to work for It? Why could It not do whatever had to be done? Why were Barnabas and Saul needed? In what form was the Holy Ghost when It spoke - was It like a dove, like tongues of fire, or something else?

13:3 - WHEN THEY HAD FASTED AND PRAYED, AND LAID HANDS ON THEM, THEY SENT THEM AWAY.

**Contradiction:**
MATT. 9:14 - Came John's disciples saying, "Why do we and the Pharisees fast oft, but thy disciples fast not?"
[Did the disciples fast, or did they not fast?]

**Perplexing:**
In the gospels, Jesus was not said to have fasted or to have ordered his disciples to fast; and in the Gospel of Thomas, Jesus said, "When you fast, you beget sin for yourself." If Jesus did not command the disciples to fast, and may have opposed fasting, why then did the disciples fast?
See also under'LUKE 2:36-37.

**History:** See under 6:6.

**Pagan concept:** See under MATT. 6:17.

**Judaism:** See under MATT. 6:17.

13:4 - THEY BEING SENT FORTH BY THE HOLY GHOST, DEPARTED UNTO SELEUCIA, AND FROM THENCE THEY SAILED TO CYPRUS.

**Perplexing:**
Why did the Holy Ghost not transport them to their destination as It transported Philip to Azotus in 8:39-40.

13:5 - WHEN THEY WERE AT SALAMIS, THEY PREACHED THE WORD OF GOD IN THE SYNAGOGUES...AND HAD JOHN TO THEIR MINISTER.

**Perplexing:**
How were they able to enter synagogues and preach about Jesus without first obtaining permission from the presiding priests? Did the priests give them such permission?

**History:**
Salamis at that time was the chief city of Cyprus.

13:6 - WHEN THEY HAD GONE THROUGH THE ISLE UNTO PAPHOS, THEY FOUND A SORCERER, A FALSE PROPHET, A JEW, WHOSE NAME WAS BAR-JESUS.

**History:**
Paphos was the site of religious fertility rites related to the goddess Aphrodite.

**Perplexing:**
Was the writer of ACTS trying to incite additional hostility towards Jews by saying that Bar-jesus was a sorcerer and a Jew? Was he trying to equate Jews with sorcery, although Judaism does not condone or involve sorcery?

13:7 - ...THE DEPUTY OF THE COUNTRY, SERGIUS PAULUS, A PRUDENT MAN....

**History:**
There is no historical record of Sergius Paulus.

13:9 - SAUL (WHO ALSO IS CALLED PAUL), FILLED WITH THE HOLY GHOST....

**Perplexing:**
When did Saul become known as Paul? Did he, himself, change his name? When? Why?

**Language:**
In ancient Greek, the word, "saul," meant "wanton" and "loose."
(Therefore, Saul may have deliberately changed his name, before preaching to the Greeks.)

13:10 - [PAUL] SAID [TO ELYMAS (BAR-JESUS) THE SORCORER], "O FULL OF ALL SUBTILTY AND ALL MISCHIEF, THOU CHILD OF THE DEVIL, THOU ENEMY OF ALL RIGHTEOUSNESS, WILT THOU NOT CEASE TO PERVERT THE RIGHT WAYS OF THE LORD?"

**History:**
Paul's words directed against a Jew have been used over the centuries to justify the persecution and murder of Jews as well as other non-Christians. The words of hate and intolerance attributed to Paul, here and elsewhere, have caused him to be viewed as having the ultimate responsibility for religious violence, wars, the Crusades, Inquisition, Holocaust, slaughter of American Indians, and countless other atrocities perpetrated in the name of Jesus; and, consequently, as one of the most evil people who ever lived. There is, however, no historical evidence for the biblical Paul.

**Perplexing:**
Did Paul forget that Jesus was a Jew? What is there about belief in Jesus that incited Paul, and has incited many Christians over the centuries, to intolerance of, and hatred and hostility towards anyone who is not Christian? Did Paul (and centuries of Christians) forget Jesus' words in MATT. 10:16 - "...be ye... harmless as doves," and in MATT. 5:44 - "Love your enemies; bless them that curse you; do good to them that hate you; pray for them which despitefully use you, and persecute you?" Was he unaware of Jesus' words? Did he just opt to ignore and overrule them?
Unlike the Islamic holy book the Koran, which commands Muslims to terrorize and kill all non-Muslims, the Bible does not order Christians or Jews to go on killing rampages.

13:11 - PAUL: "THE HAND OF THE LORD IS UPON THEE, AND THOU SHALT BE BLIND, NOT SEEING THE SUN FOR A SEASON." IMMEDIATELY THERE FELL ON HIM A MIST AND A DARKNESS, AND HE WENT ABOUT SEEKING SOME TO LEAD HIM BY THE HAND.

**Perplexing:**
Why did Paul not pray to convert Bar-jesus? Why did Paul resort to a cruel curse? Why was Paul filled with so much hate towards someone who did not share his religious belief? Was the biblical Paul, if he actually existed, as evil as ACTS depicted him?
See also under 13:10.

13:13 - WHEN PAUL AND HIS COMPANY...CAME TO PERGA IN PAMPHYLLA, JOHN DEPARTING FROM THEM RETURNED TO JERUSALEM.

**Perplexing:**
Why did John leave? Did be become homesick? Did he object to Paul preaching to a Roman? Did he object to Paul's failure to adhere to Jesus' teachings? Did he have a disagreement with Paul?

13:16 - PAUL...SAID [IN A SYNAGOGUE], "MEN OF ISRAEL, AND YE THAT FEAR GOD...."

**History:** See under 10:1-2.

13:17 - PAUL: "THE GOD OF THIS PEOPLE OF ISRAEL CHOSE OUR FATHERS...."

**Perplexing:**
Why did Paul identify God as the God of the people of Israel? Was he saying that other people have different gods? Was he polytheistic?

13:18-22 - PAUL: "ABOUT THE TIME OF 40 YEARS SUFFERED HE THEIR MANNERS IN THE WILDERNESS. WHEN HE HAD DESTROYED SEVEN NATIONS IN CHANAAN, HE DIVIDED THEIR LAND TO THEM BY LOT. AFTER THAT HE GAVE UNTO THEM JUDGES ABOUT THE SPACE OF 450 YEARS, UNTIL SAMUEL THE PROPHET. AFTERWARD... GOD GAVE UNTO THEM SAUL...BY THE SPACE OF 40 YEARS. WHEN HE HAD REMOVED HIM, HE RAISED UP UNTO THEM DAVID TO BE THEIR KING...AND SAID, 'I HAVE FOUND DAVID THE SON OF JESSE, A MAN AFTER MINE OWN HEART....'"

**Contradictions:**
According to Paul the time spent in the wilderness until David became king was 530 years (40+450+40). If Paul had also stated that Samuel ruled for 21 years, the total would be 551 years.
1 KINGS 6:1, however, reported that it was only 480 years from the time the Israelites left Egypt until the fourth year of Solomon's reign. If the 40 years of David's reign and the first four years of Solomon's reign were added to Paul's time frame the total would be 595 (551+40+4).
[Was it at least 530 years from the time the Israelites left Egypt and entered the wilderness until the reign of David, as claimed by Paul, and 595 until Solomon's fourth year, or was it only 480 years until the fourth year of Solomon's reign, as stated in KINGS?]
1 SAM. 13:14, Samuel [to Saul]: "...the LORD hath sought Him a man after His own heart...."
[Did God say that David was a man after His own heart, or did Samuel say it?]

**Perplexing:**
Why did Paul think that it was necessary to recapitulate Jewish history to Jews in a synagogue? Why did he do it incorrectly? Why did the Jews fail to point out his errors? If Paul was a Jew, especially a Pharisee (as he will claim later in ACTS 23:6), how could he err about what was in the Old Testament?
How could God suffer, as Paul asserted, when, as God, He knew what would happen, and was responsible for what happened?

13:23 - PAUL: "OF THIS MAN'S [DAVID'S] SEED HATH GOD ACCORDING TO HIS PROMISE RAISED UNTO ISRAEL A SAVIOUR, JESUS."

**Contradictions:** See under 2:22, 30, and under MATT. 1:1.

**Perplexing:**
If Jesus was descended from David, how could he be the Son of God? Why did the Jews fail to point out to Paul that Jesus did not meet the criteria for being the Messiah - one of which was paternal descent from David through Solomon (2 CHRON. 7:17-18)? (Jews did not recognize a maternal genealogy.) If Paul was a Jew, why did he not know that Jesus did not meet the Jewish criteria for the Messiah?
If Jesus was a savior for Israel, why did he fail to save Israel from the Romans?
See also under MATT. 1:1.

**History:** See under 2:22.

13:28 - PAUL: "...DESIRED THEY [JEWS] PILATE THAT HE [JESUS] SHOULD BE SLAIN."

**History:**
Pilate did not acquiesce to Jewish demands or desires. He was vehemently anti-Jewish.
See also under MATT. 27:17, 22, 24.

**Perplexing:** See under MATT. 27:17, 22, 26.

13:29 - PAUL: "WHEN THEY HAD FULFILLED ALL THAT WAS WRITTEN OF HIM, THEY TOOK HIM DOWN FROM THE TREE, AND LAID HIM IN A SEPULCHRE."

**Contradictions:**
MATT. 27:35, MARK 15:24, LUKE 23:33, and JOHN 19:18 - They [Romans] crucified him.
1 COR. 2:2 - Paul: "...Jesus Christ and him crucified."
2 COR. 13:4 - Paul: "...he was crucified...."
REV. 11:8 - An angel: "...our Lord was crucified."
(Numerous additional verses also said that Jesus was crucified.)
[Was Jesus hung on a tree, or was he crucified? (If being hung on a tree is the same as being crucified, why do the gospels including LUKE use only "crucified?")]
MATT. 27:58-60 - Pilate commanded that Jesus' body be delivered to Joseph [of Arimathaea] who laid it in his own new tomb.
MARK 15:45-46 - Pilate gave Jesus' body to Joseph who laid him in a sepulchre.
[Did the Jews take Jesus' body and place it in a sepulchre, or did Pilate give the body to Joseph who placed it in a sepulchre?
LUKE 23:53 - Joseph took Jesus' body down and laid it in a sepulchre.
JOHN 19:38-42 - Pilate allowed Joseph to take Jesus' body. He and Nicodemus laid Jesus in a sepulchre.
[Did the Jews take Jesus' body down from a tree, or did Joseph take it down from a cross?]
[Did Jews place Jesus' body in a sepulchre, or did Joseph and Nicodemus do it?]
See also under 5:30.

**Pagan parallels**: See under 5:30.

**History:**
The Romans put the bodies of executed prisoners into a common grave.
See also under 5:30.

**Perplexing:**
Why did the Jews fail to question Paul about his claim that they had fulfilled all that was written about Jesus? Why did they not correct his assertion that they took Jesus body down from a tree and put it into a sepulchre?
If the Jews had taken Jesus' body, would they have placed it in a sepulchre?

**Old Testament:**
DEUT. 21:22-23 - The LORD: "If a man have committed a sin worthy of death...and thou hang him on a tree, his body shall not remain all night upon the tree, but thou shalt in any wise bury him that day; (for he that is hanged is accursed of God)...."

13:30 - PAUL: "GOD RAISED HIM FROM THE DEAD."

**Perplexing:** See under 2:24.

13:31 - PAUL: "HE WAS SEEN MANY DAYS OF THEM WHICH CAME UP WITH HIM FROM GALILEE TO JERUSALEM, WHO ARE HIS WITNESSES UNTO THE PEOPLE."

**Contradiction:**
MARK 16:9-19 and LUKE 24:13-51 - Jesus was seen for only one day after his resurrection.
[Was the resurrected Jesus seen for many days, or for one day?]

**Perplexing:**
Why was the resurrected Jesus not seen by anyone other than those who came with him from Galilee to Jerusalem?

**History:**
There is no secular report of Jesus having been seen by anyone after his resurrection, or at any time.

13:33 - PAUL: "GOD...HATH RAISED UP JESUS AGAIN, AS IT IS ALSO WRITTEN IN THE SECOND PSALM, 'THOU ART MY SON, THIS DAY HAVE I BEGOTTEN THEE.'"

**Old Testament:**
PS. 2:6-8 - The LORD: "Yet have I set My king upon MY holy hill of Zion." [The king]: "I will declare the decree: the Lord [LORD, in Jewish Bibles] hath said unto me, 'Thou art My Son; this day have I begotten thee. Ask of Me, and I shall give the heathen for thine inheritance, and the uttermost parts of the earth for thy possession.'" [Paul has taken the Psalm out of context; God is addressing a new Judean king. See below under History.]

**History:**
It was customary for kings in the Middle East including Israelite and Judean kings to be called, "Sons of God," begotten as such on the day of their coronation.
See also under MATT. 3:17.

**Perplexing:**
Why did the Jews fail to inform Paul that the psalm referred to a newly inaugurated king, not to Jesus? Was it possible that Paul wanted to imply that Jesus was God's adopted Son? See ROM. 1:3-4 - Paul said,

"Jesus Christ our Lord was made of the seed of David according to the flesh, and declared to be the Son of God...." If Paul was a Jew, why did he not know that the verse he cited pertained to a newly crowned king, not to Jesus?
See also under 2:24 and under MATT. 3:17.

13:34 - PAUL: "AS CONCERNING THAT HE RAISED HIM UP FROM THE DEAD...HE SAID...'I WILL GIVE YOU THE SURE MERCIES OF DAVID.'"

**Old Testament:**
ISA. 55:3 - The LORD: " I will make an everlasting covenant with you, even the sure mercies of David."

**Perplexing:** See also under 2:24.

13:35 - PAUL: "HE SAITH IN ANOTHER PSALM, 'THOU SHALT NOT SUFFER THINE HOLY ONE TO SEE CORRUPTION.'"

**Old Testament:**
PS. 16:10 - David: "Thou wilt not leave my soul in hell; neither wilt Thou suffer Thine Holy One to see corruption." (Jewish Bibles translate, "Holy One," as "devout one," or "godly one." Thus, David was referring to himself.)
See also under 2:25-28.

**Language**: See under 2:25-28.

**Perplexing:**
Why did the Jews fail to correct Paul's quote of the psalm? Why did Paul, who claimed to be a Jew, a Pharisee, (23:6), not know that the verse referred to David, not to Jesus?
See also under 2:25-28.

13:37 - PAUL: "HE WHOM GOD RAISED AGAIN...."

**Perplexing:** See under 2:24.

13:38 - PAUL: "...THROUGH THIS MAN IS PREACHED UNTO YOU THE FORGIVENESS OF SINS."

**Perplexing:**
Why did Paul continue to refer to Jesus as a "man", not as the "Son of God."
See also under ACTS 2:22.

13:40-41 - PAUL: "BEWARE, THEREFORE, LEST THAT COME UPON YOU, WHICH IS SPOKEN OF IN THE PROPHETS, 'BEHOLD, YE DESPISERS, WONDER, AND PERISH, FOR I WORK A WORK IN YOUR DAYS, WHICH YE SHALL IN NO WISE BELIEVE, THOUGH A MAN DECLARE IT UNTO YOU.'"

**Old Testament:**.
HAB. 1:5-6 - "Behold ye among the heathen, regard, and wonder marvellously, for I will work a work in your days, which ye will not believe, though it be told you. I raise up the Chaldeans, that bitter and hasty

nation, which shall march through the breadth of the land, to possess the dwelling places that are not theirs."

**Perplexing:**
Why did Paul equate a prophecy pertaining to the Chaldeans with Jesus? Why did the Jews fail to correct him? Why was Paul, if he was a Jew, especially, a Pharisee (ACTS 23:6), ignorant of the nature of this Old Testament prophecy?

13:43 - WHEN THE CONGREGATION WAS BROKEN UP, MANY OF THE JEWS AND RELIGIOUS PROSELYTES FOLLOWED PAUL AND BARNABAS, WHO, SPEAKING TO THEM, PERSUADED THEM TO CONTINUE IN THE GRACE OF GOD.

**Perplexing:**
How could Jews knowledgeable of the Old Testament follow Paul who had misquoted and distorted its verses? Was the writer of ACTS being truthful by writing here and elsewhere that Paul spoke in synagogues to Jews?

13:45 - THE JEWS...SPAKE AGAINST THOSE THINGS WHICH WERE SPOKEN BY PAUL, CONTRADICTING AND BLASPHEMING.

**Perplexing:**
Why did it take the Jews so long to contradict Paul? Why did ACTS accuse the Jews of blasphemy when it was Paul who distorted the Old Testament verses?

13:46 - PAUL AND BARNABAS...SAID, "...SEEING YE [THE JEWS] JUDGE YOURSELVES UNWORTHY OF EVERLASTING LIFE, WE TURN TO THE GENTILES."

**Contradiction:** See under MATT. 25:46.

**Perplexing:**
Why did not Paul know that mainstream Judaism does not have the Christian concept of everlasting life? Why did the Jews not point this out to him ?
See also under MATT. 19:16 and 25:46.

**Pagan concept:** See under MATT. 19:16.

13:47 - PAUL AND BARNABAS: "SO HATH THE LORD COMMANDED US, SAYING, 'I HAVE SET THEE TO BE A LIGHT OF THE GENTILES, THAT THOU SHOULDEST BE FOR SALVATION UNTO THE ENDS OF THE EARTH.'"

**Contradictions:**
MATT. 10:5-6 - ...Jesus commanded them [his disciples], "Go not into the way of the Gentiles...but rather to the lost sheep of the house of Israel."
MATT.10:23 - Jesus [to his disciples]: "...Ye shall not have gone over the cities of Israel, till the Son of man be come."
MATT. 15:22-26 - A woman of Canaan asked Jesus to heal her daughter. He responded,"I am not sent but unto the lost sheep of the house of Israel," and "It is not meet to take the children's bread and cast it to

dogs."
[Did the Lord command Paul and Barnabas to bring salvation to the Gentiles, or did he forbid his disciples from going to the Gentiles whom he referred to as "dogs?"] (Note that in the gospels, Jesus preached Old Testament commandments and concepts, whereas in ACTS and the Epistles, Paul preached belief in a resurrected Jesus without references to obeying the commandments.)

13:48 - WHEN THE GENTILES HEARD THIS, THEY WERE GLAD, GLORIFIED THE WORD OF THE LORD, AND AS MANY AS WERE ORDAINED TO ETERNAL LIFE BELIEVED.

**Perplexing:**
How does God decide who to ordain to eternal life? If God has already determined who is to receive eternal life, what difference does it make whether or not one believes? If salvation is predetermined, why is Christianity necessary? What was the point of Jesus coming to earth and preaching? What was the point of Paul traveling around preaching? If eternal life is preordained, is eternal torment also preordained? Is one doomed to eternal torment or eternal life regardless of what kind of life one lives? If God has made the decision about whether or not one will believe in Jesus, does He have the moral right to punish anyone who He has ordained not to believe?
Did those who believed, receive the Holy Ghost? If so, how? Did Paul or Barnabas have to touch them? Were they baptized?
See also under JOHN 6:44.

**Contradictions:** See under MATT 19:17-19 (for obtaining eternal life).

**Dead Sea Scrolls:** See under JOHN 6:44.

14:1 - IN ICONIUM, THEY WENT TOGETHER INTO THE SYNAGOGUE OF THE JEWS, AND SO SPAKE, THAT A GREAT MULTITUDE BOTH OF THE JEWS AND ALSO THE GREEKS BELIEVED.

**Perplexing:**
How were Paul and Barnabas able to walk into a synagogue and speak about Jesus without first obtaining permission from the presiding priest? How could they persuade Jews knowledgeable of the Old Testament to believe that Jesus was the Messiah, or the Son of God, or a man who God chose to raise from the dead? Why did ACTS use the phrase, "synagogue of the Jews?"

**History:**
Iconium was approximately 75 miles southeast of Antioch in Pisidia.
[In 13:14, Paul was reported to have traveled from Perga to Antioch in Pisidia.]

14:3 - LONG TIME ABODE THEY SPEAKING BOLDLY IN THE LORD, WHICH GAVE TESTIMONY UNTO THE WORD OF HIS GRACE, AND GRANTED SIGNS AND WONDERS TO BE DONE BY THEIR HANDS.

**Perplexing:**
What were the signs and wonders that they performed? Why is there no historical record of their accomplishments?

14:5-6 - WHEN THERE WAS AN ASSAULT MADE BOTH OF THE GENTILES, AND THE JEWS WITH THEIR RULERS, TO USE THEM DESPITEFULLY, AND TO STONE THEM, THEY...FLED INTO LYSTRA AND DERBE, CITIES OF LYCAONIA....

**Perplexing:**
Were they ignorant of Jesus' teachings or did they not believe his claims in MATT. 21:22, MARK 11:24, JOHN 14:13-14, 15:7, and 16:23 that anything a believer asked or prayed for would be received? Why, therefore, did they flee rather than pray for the Lord's protection, or everyone's conversion? Or, did they pray, but without success?
Why did the Gentiles attack them?
How did they travel? How long did the traveling take? Where did they rest, stay, and eat? From where did they obtain money for expenses? Did they receive contributions from believers along the way? If so, why did ACTS not say so? Did they beg or, perhaps, steal?

14:8-10 - THERE SAT A MAN, IMPOTENT IN HIS FEET...WHO NEVER HAD WALKED; PAUL... PERCEIVING THAT HE HAD FAITH TO BE HEALED, SAID, "STAND ON THY FEET." HE LEAPED AND WALKED.

**Pagan parallels**: See under MATT. 4:23.

14:12 - THEY [PEOPLE] CALLED BARNABAS, "JUPITER," AND PAUL, "MERCURIUS," BECAUSE HE WAS THE CHIEF SPEAKER.

**Pagan concepts:**
In many pagan myths, gods in the guise of people were said to have come down to the earth. Therefore, the Greeks would not have been surprised to find gods among them. Jupiter (Zeus), king of the gods, was depicted as physically impressive. ACTS may therefore be saying that Barnabas was a big, powerful man. Mercurius (mercury, Hermes) was usually depicted as small, wiry, and verbal (especially adept in lying); he also served as a messenger for the gods. Thus, ACTS may be saying that physically, Paul resembled him. In 2 COR. 10:10, Paul's bodily presence is said to be "weak." As Mercury was Jupiter's son, ACTS may also be saying that Barnabas was older than Paul. Unlike the smooth-tongued Mercury, Paul in 2 COR. 10:10 said that his speech is contemptible, and in 2 COR. 11:6, "Though I may be rude in speech...."

**Perplexing:**
Could the pagan concept of gods coming down to earth and associating with humans have influenced Christians to convert Jesus from an ordinary man favored by God (see under ACTS 2:22) into a divine being or deity who also came down to the earth?

**Language:**
In Hebrew, "Zedek" was the name for Jupiter, a name for Jerusalem, and the name of the god of Salem. In GEN. 14:18-20, Abraham met "the king of Salem," identified as "Melchizedek"; this name may also be translated as "priest of Jupiter," or "priest of the god of Salem."
Some Bible translations use the Greek, Zeus and Hermes, rather than the Roman, Jupiter and Mercurius.

14:13 - THEN THE PRIEST OF JUPITER...BROUGHT OXEN AND GARLANDS UNTO THE GATES, AND WOULD HAVE DONE SACRIFICE WITH THE PEOPLE.

**Language:**
See under 14:12 - the "priest of Jupiter, " in Hebrew would be "Melchizedek."

14:19 - THERE CAME THITHER CERTAIN JEWS FROM ANTIOCH AND ICONIUM, WHO PERSUADED THE PEOPLE, AND, HAVING STONED PAUL, DREW HIM OUT OF THE CITY, SUPPOSING HE HAD BEEN DEAD.

**Perplexing:**
Why was Paul stoned? Why did he fail to pray to the Lord for protection? If he did pray, why was his prayer not answered favorably? Why did an angel or the Holy Ghost fail to come to his aid? Why was Barnabas not stoned? Why did the Greeks, who viewed them as gods, allow Paul to be stoned, especially after he had healed a crippled man (8-10)?
See also under 5-6.

14:20 - ...HE ROSE UP, AND CAME INTO THE CITY; THE NEXT DAY HE DEPARTED WITH BARNABAS TO DERBE.

**History:**
The victim of a stoning was first thrown off a high platform; if not killed by the fall, stones were dropped on him until he died.

**Perplexing:**
If Paul had been stoned so severely that he was believed to be dead, how could he so quickly arise and go traveling about 75 miles from Lystra (14:6) to Derbe? Would he not have been badly bruised and possibly have had some bones broken? How did he travel? How long did the trip take?
See also under 5-6.

14:21 - WHEN THEY HAD PREACHED THE GOSPEL TO THAT CITY ... THEY RETURNED AGAIN TO LYSTRA, ICONIUM, AND ANTIOCH.

**Perplexing:**
How long did they remain in Derbe? Why did Paul return to Iconium and Lystra where he was nearly killed by stoning? Was he seen by any of those who had stoned or seen him stoned? Was he attacked again? If not, why did ACTS fail to say how Paul avoided being stoned a second time?

14:23 - ...THEY...PRAYED WITH FASTING....

**Perplexing:** See under 13:3.

**Pagan concept:** See under MATT. 6:17.

14:24-26 - AFTER THEY HAD PASSED THROUGHOUT PISIDIA...PAMPHYLLA...PERGA... ATTALIA, AND THENCE SAILED TO ANTIOCH....

**Perplexing:**
How was the injured Paul able to travel the approximately 100 miles from Pisidia to Perga and Attalia, then about 350 miles by water to Antioch? How much time had passed since the stoning?
See also notes under 5-6 and 20.

14:28 - THERE THEY ABODE LONG TIME WITH THE DISCIPLES.

**Perplexing:**
What is meant by a "long time?" What did they do while with the disciples? Why was their work with the disciples not considered important enough to report?

15:1 - MEN WHICH CAME DOWN FROM JUDAEA TAUGHT THE BRETHREN, AND SAID, "EXCEPT YE BE CIRCUMCISED AFTER THE MANNER OF MOSES, YE CANNOT BE SAVED."

**Contradiction:**
GEN. 17:10-11 - God: "This is My covenant, which ye shall keep, between Me and thy seed after thee; every man child among you shall be circumcised. Ye shall circumcise the flesh of your foreskin; it shall be a token of the covenant betwixt Me and you."
[Did the practice of circumcision come from Moses, or from God?]

**Perplexing:**
Why was circumcision considered a requirement for being saved? Were the men saying that one had to become a Jew to be saved?

**History:** See under LUKE 1:58-59.

15:2 - WHEN PAUL AND BARNABAS HAD NO SMALL DISSENSION AND DISPUTATION WITH THEM, THEY DETERMINED THAT PAUL, BARNABAS, AND CERTAIN OTHER OF THEM, SHOULD GO TO JERUSALEM UNTO THE APOSTLES AND ELDERS ABOUT THIS QUESTION.

**Perplexing:**
In GEN. 17:10-12, God established the covenant of physical circumcision. In LUKE 2:21, Jesus was circumcised. In LUKE 16:17, Jesus said, "It is easier for heaven and earth to pass, than one tittle of the law to fall." Since the rite of circumcision is part of the law, and Jesus, who was circumcised, said that the law cannot fall, why did Paul and some of the others oppose circumcision? By so doing they were endeavoring to destroy part of the law. Were they ignorant of Jesus' words? Did they not care about the covenant and Jesus' words? Were they too obsessed with converting Gentiles to their sect of Judaism (which evolved into Christianity) to care about what God and Jesus said? Could they be true Christians if they contradicted Jesus by destroying a portion of the law? Therefore, could those who follow them, rather than God and Jesus, really obtain salvation?

15:3-4 - ... THEY PASSED THROUGH PHENICE AND SAMARIA, DECLARING THE CONVERSION OF THE GENTILES.... WHEN THEY WERE COME TO JERUSALEM, THEY WERE RECEIVED OF THE...APOSTLES AND ELDERS....

**Perplexing:**
In MATT. 15:24, Jesus said, "I am not sent but unto the lost sheep of the house of Israel." If Jesus was sent only to the "lost sheep of the house of Israel," why were Paul and other disciples obsessed with converting Gentiles?
See also under 8:1 - Why were the apostles still in Jerusalem?

**History:**
There is no record of Paul or the apostles outside of the Bible.

15:5 - THERE ROSE UP CERTAIN OF THE SECT OF PHARISEES WHICH BELIEVED, SAYING THAT IT WAS NEEDFUL TO CIRCUMCISE THEM, AND TO COMMAND THEM TO KEEP THE LAW OF MOSES.

**Perplexing:**
How could Pharisees, who were well versed in Jewish law and tradition,be believers? They would have known that Jesus did not meet the Jewish requirements for being the Messiah. Why did they not state that circumcision was God's covenant?

15:7 - ...PETER SAID, "...GOD MADE CHOICE AMONG US, THAT THE GENTILES BY MY MOUTH SHOULD HAVE THE WORD OF THE GOSPEL, AND BELIEVE."

**Contradiction:**
ROM. 11:13 - Paul: "I speak to you Gentiles, inasmuch as I am the apostle of the Gentiles...."
ROM. 15:15-16 - Paul: "...because of the grace that is given to me of God, that I should be the minister of Jesus Christ to the Gentiles...."
GAL. 2:7 - Paul: "...the gospel of the uncircumcision was committed unto me, as the gospel of the circumcision was unto Peter."
[Did God make Peter, or Paul the apostle to bring the gospel to the Gentiles?]

**Perplexing:**
Why did God need Peter or any human to give the Gentiles the word of the gospel? Why was God, Himself, incapable of doing it?

15:11 - PETER: "WE BELIEVE THAT THROUGH THE GRACE OF THE LORD JESUS CHRIST WE SHALL BE SAVED, EVEN AS THEY."

**Contradictions:** See under MATT. 19:17-19 (for obtaining eternal life).

**Perplexing:**
Why did Peter not cite any of the requirements Jesus gave for being saved (see under MATT. 19:17-19 - for obtaining eternal life)?
Why after Peter's brief speech, was he not mentioned again in ACTS? What happened to him? Did the writer of ACTS see no further use for him?

15:12 - ALL THE MULTITUDE...GAVE AUDIENCE TO BARNABAS AND PAUL, DECLARING WHAT MIRACLES AND WONDERS GOD HAD WROUGHT AMONG THE GENTILES BY THEM.

**Perplexing:**
What miracles and wonders did they work? Why is there no historical record of these feats?

15:13 - ...JAMES ANSWERED, SAYING, "...HEARKEN UNTO ME."

**Perplexing:**
Who was this James? Was he one of Jesus' brothers?
See also under 12:17.

15:14 - SIMEON HATH DECLARED HOW GOD AT FIRST DID VISIT THE GENTILES, TO TAKE OUT OF THEM A PEOPLE FOR HIS NAME.

**Perplexing:**
Who was this Simeon? Was this a reference to Simon Peter? If so, when did he make the claim attributed to him? When did God visit the Gentiles?

15:15-17 - JAMES: "...THE WORDS OF THE PROPHETS AS IT IS WRITTEN, 'AFTER THIS I WILL RETURN, AND WILL BUILD AGAIN THE TABERNACLE OF DAVID, WHICH IS FALLEN DOWN: I WILL BUILD AGAIN THE RUINS THEREOF, AND I WILL SET IT UP, THAT THE RESIDUE OF MEN MIGHT SEEK AFTER THE LORD, AND ALL THE GENTILES, UPON WHOM MY NAME IS CALLED,' SAITH THE LORD, WHO DOETH ALL THINGS."

**Old Testament:**
AMOS 9:10-12 - The LORD: "All the sinners of my people shall die by the sword, which say, 'The evil shall not overtake nor prevent us.' In that day will I raise up the tabernacle of David that is fallen, and close up the breeches thereof; I will raise up his ruins, and I will build it as in the days of old, that they may possess the remnant of Edom, and of all the heathen, which are called by My name."

**Perplexing:**
Why did James misquote the verse? Why did not anyone correct him?

15:18 - JAMES: "KNOWN UNTO GOD ARE ALL HIS WORKS FROM THE BEGINNING OF THE WORLD."

**Perplexing:**
If God knew everything, why did he not know that Jesus would convince few Jews that he was the Messiah? Why did He not know that the apostles would have to go to the Gentiles, against Jesus' teachings, to gain converts? Why did He not know that His covenant of the circumcision would be broken by Jesus' followers? Why did He fail to know that the Jewish priesthood would end? Did God know that those who believed in Jesus would perpetrate horrendous atrocities, torture, crimes, murders, and wars over the centuries against non-believers and each other? If He did know, is He not then morally responsible for the evils that occurred? Is He not, then, indistinguishable from the devil?

15:19-20 - JAMES: "WHEREFORE MY SENTENCE IS, THAT WE TROUBLE NOT THEM, WHICH FROM AMONG THE GENTILES ARE TURNED TO GOD, BUT THAT WE WRITE UNTO THEM, THAT THEY ABSTAIN FROM POLLUTIONS OF IDOLS, FROM FORNICATION, FROM THINGS STRANGLED, AND FROM BLOOD."

**Perplexing:**
Why did James rather than Peter make the decision? Was James now the leader of apostles? If so, how did he obtain that position? Who gave him the authority to contravene God's covenant of circumcision? Why

did he not say that the Gentiles would have to obey at least the ten commandments of EX. 20, and/or Jesus' teaching? Why was converting Gentiles more important than obeying God's commandments, the covenant, and Jesus' teachings?
See also under 15:2.

**History:**
The rules specified for Gentiles by James were similar to those established by the Pharisees in their "Laws of the Sons of Noah," which were set forth for Gentiles who wanted to attach themselves to Judaism without becoming full Jews. The order to "abstain from pollutions of idols," meant to avoid eating anything used in the worship of idols; "fornication" referred to adultery, incest, sodomy, and bestiality; "things strangled" referred to meat with blood in it; abstaining "from blood" was a prohibition against bloodshed and murder.

15:22 - ...AND SILAS, CHIEF MEN AMONG THE BRETHREN.

**Perplexing:**
Was Silas another name for the Silvanus mentioned in 2 COR. 1:19, 1 THES. 1:1, and 1 PET. 5:12?

15:23-24 - THEY WROTE LETTERS AFTER THIS MANNER, "THE APOSTLES, ELDERS, AND BRETHREN SEND GREETINGS UNTO THE BRETHREN WHICH ARE OF THE GENTILES ....AS WE HAVE HEARD THAT CERTAIN... HAVE TROUBLED YOU WITH WORDS, SUBVERTING YOUR SOULS, SAYING, 'YE MUST BE CIRCUMCISED, AND KEEP THE LAW,' TO WHOM WE GAVE NO SUCH COMMANDMENT."

**Perplexing:**
Why did the apostles and those with them believe that they had the authority to overrule God's covenant of the circumcision in GEN. 17:10-12? Why did they fail to remember and discuss that Jesus was circumcised and did not object to the practice? Did they also forget that Jesus had said, "Till heaven and earth pass, one jot or one tittle shall, in no wise pass from the law, till all be fulfilled" (MATT. 5:18)? And, "It is easier for heaven and earth to pass, than one tittle of the law to fall" (LUKE 16:17)? If Jesus was correct that the law cannot change, why did the apostles believe that they could rescind any of it?

15:29 - THE APOSTLES, ELDERS, AND BRETHREN: "ABSTAIN FROM MEATS OFFERED TO IDOLS, BLOOD, THINGS STRANGLED, AND FROM FORNICATION...."

**Perplexing:**
Do modern followers of Jesus adhere to all of these prohibitions?
See also under 19-20.

**History:** See under 19-20.

15:32-34 - JUDAS [BARSABAS] AND SILAS...TARRIED THERE [IN ANTIOCH] A SPACE.... IT PLEASED SILAS TO ABIDE THERE STILL.

**Perplexing:**
Why did Silas, but not Judas Barsabas opt to remain in Antioch? Barsabas will not be cited again in ACTS. Why? What happened to him?

15:35 - PAUL AND BARNABAS CONTINUED IN ANTIOCH....

**Perplexing:**
In GAL 2:11, Paul reported having a confrontation with Peter in Antioch. Why was this not mentioned in ACTS?

15:37-38 - BARNABAS DETERMINED TO TAKE WITH THEM JOHN, WHOSE SURNAME WAS MARK. BUT PAUL THOUGHT NOT GOOD TO TAKE HIM, WHO DEPARTED FROM THEM FROM PAMPHYLLA, AND WENT NOT WITH THEM TO THE WORK.

**Perplexing:**
Why did Paul here object to taking Mark when in 2 TIM. 4:11 he said, "Take Mark, and bring him with thee, for he is profitable to me for the ministry"?
See also under 13:13.

15:39-40 - THE CONTENTION WAS SO SHARP BETWEEN THEM, THAT THEY DEPARTED ASUNDER ONE FROM THE OTHER; BARNABAS TOOK MARK AND PAUL CHOSE SILAS....

**Contradiction:**
GAL. 2:13 - Paul: "Other Jews dissembled likewise with him [James], inasmuch that Barnabas also was carried away with their dissimulation [about circumcision]."
[Did Paul and Barnabas break up over Mark, or over circumcision?]

**Perplexing:**
Why was the contention between Paul and Barnabas over Mark so great that they had to split up over it? Why was Barnabas adamant about taking Mark with them? Why was Paul so opposed to taking Mark? Why did they not pray to resolve the dispute? Why did the Holy Ghost fail to resolve the matter for them? Barnabas was now the third person to have left Paul (Mark and Barsabas being the other two) . Was ACTS saying that Paul was a difficult person with whom to get along?

16:1 - CAME HE TO DERBE AND LYSTRA; A DISCIPLE WAS THERE, NAMED TIMOTHEUS [TIMOTHY], THE SON OF A JEWESS, AND BELIEVED....

**Perplexing:**
Why did Paul return to a place where he had been stoned? Why was he not recognized and stoned again?

**History:**
The reference to Timothy's mother being Jewish and also believing in Jesus illustrates that the earliest "Christians" still considered themselves to be Jews.

16:3 - PAUL...TOOK AND CIRCUMCISED HIM [TIMOTHEUS] BECAUSE OF THE JEWS WHICH WERE IN THOSE QUARTERS; THEY ALL KNEW HIS FATHER WAS A GREEK.

**Perplexing:**
How old was Timothy? Why was he not already circumcised? If he was a teen-ager or a man, and had not already been circumcised, why did Paul decide at this relatively late date to circumcise him? Did Paul,

himself, do the circumcising? Why did Paul even want him circumcised, when in I COR. 7:19, he said, "Circumcision is nothing," and in GAL. 5:2, "If ye be circumcised, Christ shall profit you nothing." Was not Paul a hypocrite for opposing cicumcision, but then circumcising Timothy? How long did it take Timothy to recover from the procedure and then travel with Paul?

16:4 - AS THEY WENT THROUGH THE CITIES, THEY DELIVERED THEM THE DECREES TO KEEP, THAT WERE ORDAINED OF THE APOSTLES AND ELDERS AT JERUSALEM.

**Perplexing:**
Why did they tell the believers to keep the decrees of the apostles, rather than the teachings of Jesus and/or God's commandments? Why did they consider commands from the apostles and elders to be more important than those from Jesus or the Old Testament God (Jesus' Father)?

16:6 - THEY...WERE FORBIDDEN OF THE HOLY GHOST TO PREACH THE WORD IN ASIA.

**Contradiction:**
MARK 16:20 - They went forth, and preached everywhere....
[Did the Holy Ghost stop them from preaching in Asia, or did they preach everywhere?]

**Perplexing:**
Why did the Holy Ghost contravene Jesus' command in MATT. 28:19 to go and teach all nations...? Why did not the Holy Ghost want them to preach in Asia? When was the ban against preaching in Asia lifted?

**Language:**
Asia at that time was used as a designation for the interior of Asia Minor.

16:7 - ...THEY ASSAYED TO GO INTO BITHYNIA, BUT THE SPIRIT SUFFERED THEM NOT.

**Perplexing:**
Why did the Spirit prevent them from going to Bithynia? From where did Paul obtain funds for travel expenses? Where did they stay? How did they travel on land? How much time was spent traveling?

16:10 - ...WE ENDEAVORED TO GO INTO MACEDONIA, ASSUREDLY GATHERING THAT THE LORD HAD CALLED US TO PREACH THE GOSPEL UNTO THEM.

**Perplexing:**
Who were the "we" and "us?" The writer of ACTS is implying that he was with Paul, but thus far only Silas (14:40) and Timothy (16:1) have been mentioned as accompanying Paul. Was the writer of ACTS accompanying them? If so, why in 16:6, 7, and 8, did he say, "They," implying that he was not with them? (Some theologians contend that the writer was Luke and that he also traveled with Paul. If so, why was he not identified as being with Paul? Why was he not identified by name? When and where did he join the group? Is it possible, however, that the writer had merely inserted himself into the narrative to give the impression that his account was based on firsthand knowledge?)

**History:** See under 1:1.

16:11-13 - ...WE CAME WITH A STRAIGHT COURSE...AND WE WERE IN THAT CITY.... ...WE WENT OUT OF THE CITY...AND SAT DOWN....

**Perplexing:** See under 16:10.

16:14 - A CERTAIN WOMAN NAMED LYDIA...HEARD US....

**History:**
At the time the event is supposed to have taken place, Lydia was not used as a feminine name. It was the name given to the west-central part of Asia Minor.

**Perplexing:**
Why did the writer of ACTS not know that Lydia had not yet become a woman's name?
The "us" implied that the writer, too, spoke to the woman.
See also under 16:10.

16:15 - WHEN SHE WAS BAPTIZED, AND HER HOUSEHOLD, SHE BESOUGHT US, SAYING, "... COME INTO MY HOUSE, AND ABIDE THERE." AND SHE CONSTRAINED US.

**Perplexing:**
Did she receive the Holy Ghost when she was baptized? Why has ACTS failed to mention anything about the Holy Ghost descending on any of the recent converts? How was she able to obtain approval from her household to have strange men stay with them? How large was her house? Was she married? If so, did her husband approve? Why was she not concerned about what her neighbors would think? To whom did the "us" refer? The writer of ACTS again implied that he was present.
See also under 16:10 and 14.

16:16-17 - ...A DAMSEL POSSESSED WITH A SPIRIT OF DIVINATION...FOLLOWED PAUL AND US, SAYING, "THESE MEN ARE THE SERVANTS OF THE MOST HIGH GOD, WHICH SHEW US THE WAY OF SALVATION."

**Perplexing:**
Why does God need servants? See also under 16:10.

**Old Testament:**
GEN. 14:18-20 - Melchizedek ... was the priest of the most high God. ...and said, "Blessed be Abraham of the most high God...and blessed be the most high God...."

**Language:**
In the Old Testament, the Hebrew translated as "most high God" is "El Elyon." This term appears in Phoenician records as the name of a deity.
See also under 14:12.

16:18 - THIS DID SHE MANY DAYS. PAUL, BEING GRIEVED, TURNED AND SAID TO THE SPIRIT, "I COMMAND THEE IN THE NAME OF JESUS CHRIST TO COME OUT OF HER." HE CAME OUT THE SAME HOUR.

**Perplexing:**
Why did the girl follow Paul for many days? Why was Paul grieved at being called a servant of God? Why did he wait many days to order the spirit out of her? Why did he fail to perform a miracle or pray to cause her to stop following him? Why did he want the girl to be free of a spirit that recognized the most high God and the way of salvation? Why did he use Jesus' name to cast out the spirit, something the apostles were not reported in the gospels to have done? Jesus did not tell his followers that it was necessary to use his name to cast out spirits.

**Pagan concept:** See under JOHN 18:5-6.

16:19-20 - WHEN HER MASTERS SAW THAT THE HOPE OF THEIR GAINS WAS GONE, THEY CAUGHT PAUL AND SILAS...AND BROUGHT THEM TO THE MAGISTRATES, SAYING, "THESE MEN, BEING JEWS, DO EXCEEDINGLY TROUBLE THE CITY."

**Perplexing:**
Why were only Paul and Silas seized? Where were Timothy and the writer of ACTS?
Were they still at Lydia's house? If so, why? In 16:40, Paul and Silas will return to Lydia's house and comfort the brethren. In 16:37, Paul will say that he and Silas are Romans. Why did they fail to do so when they were seized? Why did the Holy Ghost or an angel fail to protect them?

**History:**
At this time emerging Christianity was considered to be a Jewish sect.
See also under 16:1.

16:23 - WHEN THEY HAD LAID MANY STRIPES UPON THEM, THEY CAST THEM INTO PRISON....

**Perplexing:** See under 19-20.

16:25 - ...PAUL AND SILAS PRAYED, AND SANG PRAISES UNTO GOD....

**Perplexing:** See under 2:47.

16:26 - SUDDENLY THERE WAS A GREAT EARTHQUAKE...ALL THE DOORS WERE OPENED, AND EVERYONE'S HANDS WERE LOOSED.

**History:**
There is no record of a great earthquake at this time and place.

**Perplexing:** See under MATT. 28:2-4.

16:30-31 - [THE KEEPER OF THE PRISON] BROUGHT THEM OUT, AND SAID, "WHAT MUST I DO TO BE SAVED?" THEY SAID, "BELIEVE ON THE LORD JESUS CHRIST, AND THOU SHALT BE SAVED, AND THY HOUSE."

**Contradictions:** See under MATT. 19:17-19 (for obtaining eternal life).

**Perplexing:**
Why did the prison keeper ask them how he could obtain salvation? ACTS did not say that he was a Jew or Gentile who wanted to become a Christian. If there was an earthquake, why was he more concerned with staying and asking Paul and Silas about salvation than with rushing home to see if his family was safe? Why did Paul not instruct the prison keeper to obey the commandments and Jesus' teachings? Where were the other prison guards?
In MATT. 8:29, MARK 1:24, 3:11, 5:7, LUKE 4:34, 41, and 8:28, devils and unclean spirits expressed their belief in Jesus as the Son of God. Therefore, if belief in Jesus brings salvation, were these devils and unclean spirits saved?

**Old Testament:**
JOEL 2:32 - God: "...whosoever shall call on the name of the LORD shall be delivered...and the remnant whom the LORD shall call."
[It is not clear whether the above and other similar Old Testament verses refer to salvation in the Christian sense, or to salvation from a disaster in the present life of the people being addressed.]

16:32 - THEY SPAKE UNTO HIM THE WORD OF THE LORD, AND TO ALL THAT WERE IN HIS HOUSE.

**Perplexing:**
If there had been an earthquake, why was there no report of damage? Why did ACTS proceed as if nothing untoward had occurred?

16:33 - HE TOOK THEM THE SAME HOUR OF THE NIGHT, WASHED THEIR STRIPES, AND WAS BAPTIZED, HE AND ALL HIS, STRAIGHTWAY.

**Perplexing:**
Where were they baptized? Did they have to travel to where a body of water was located? If so, how were they able to move around at night without arousing suspicion? Did they also receive the Holy Ghost? If so, how? Why was it not reported?

16:35 - WHEN IT WAS DAY, THE MAGISTRATES SENT THE SERJEANTS, SAYING, "LET THOSE MEN GO."

**Perplexing:**
Why did the magistrates decide to free Paul and Silas? Where did the magistrates send the serjeants - to the prison, or to the prison keepers house? Did the keeper take them back to the prison? If it was the keeper's house, how did the magistrates know that Paul and Silas were there?
Why was there still no comment or concern shown about earthquake damage?

16:36-37 - THE KEEPER OF THE PRISON TOLD PAUL, "THE MAGISTRATES HAVE SENT TO LET YOU GO; DEPART, IN PEACE." PAUL SAID UNTO THEM, "THEY HAVE BEATEN US OPENLY UNCONDEMNED, BEING ROMANS. AND HAVE CAST US INTO PRISON; NOW DO THEY THRUST US OUT PRIVILY? NAY, BUT LET THEM COME THEMSELVES AND FETCH US OUT."

**Contradictions:**
ACTS 23:6 - Paul: "...I am a Pharisee, the son of a Pharisee...."
ACTS 26:4-5 - Paul: "My manner of life from my youth, which was among mine own nation at Jerusalem, know all the Jews; ...I lived a Pharisee."
PHIL. 3:5 - Paul: "[I am]...an Hebrew...a Pharisee."
[Was Paul a Roman, or a Pharisee?]
ROM. 11:1 - Paul: "....I also am an Israelite...."
2 COR. 11:22 - Paul: "Are they Hebrews? So am I . Are they Israelites? So am I. ...."
[Was Paul a Roman, or an Israelite?]

**Perplexing:**
Why did Paul assert at this time that he and Silas were Romans? Why did he not do so before being beaten and imprisoned? If Paul was a Roman, would not the apostles have refused to have any dealings with him? If he was Roman, would religious Jews, especially the high priest (9:1-2), have associated with him? Would he have preached belief in Jesus who was a religious Jew? How could he be a Roman and an Israelite? How could he be a Roman and a Pharisee, when the Pharisees were vehemently anti-Roman? Why did Paul not claim to be a Roman in the Epistles?
If Paul and Silas had been guilty of breaking Roman law, would they not be subject to punishment? Were not Roman citizens susceptible to punishment for violating a law?
Out of what, did Paul want to be fetched? Was it out of the prison keeper's home? Was it out of the prison? If the latter, did Paul and Silas return to the prison from the keeper's home? If so, why? Did the writer of ACTS forget that they had escaped from the prison after the earthquake?
See also under 16:35.

16:38-39 - THE SERJEANTS TOLD THESE WORDS UNTO THE MAGISTRATES; THEY FEARED, WHEN THEY HEARD THAT THEY WERE ROMANS. THEY CAME...BROUGHT THEM OUT, AND DESIRED THEM TO DEPART OUT OF THE CITY.

**Perplexing:**
Why did the magistrates believe Paul? Why did they not seek proof that Paul and Silas were Roman? In 15:22, Silas was said to be one of the chief men of the brethren. Would the apostles have trusted and admitted a Roman into their midst?
See also under 36-37.

16:40 - THEY WENT OUT OF THE PRISON, AND ENTERED THE HOUSE OF LYDIA; WHEN THEY HAD SEEN THE BRETHREN, THEY COMFORTED THEM, AND DEPARTED.

**Contradiction:**
ACTS 16:33-34 - [After the earthquake] He [the prison keeper] took them.... When he had brought them into his house...and rejoiced....
[Were Paul and Silas in prison, or in the prison keeper's home?]

**Perplexing:**
When did they return to the prison? Did they return voluntarily, or did the prison keeper take them back? Did the writer of ACTS forget that they had left the prison?
Who were the brethren at Lydia's house? See also under 36-37.

17:1-3 - ...THEY CAME TO THESSALONICA, WHERE THERE WAS A SYNAGOGUE OF THE JEWS; PAUL...WENT IN UNTO THEM, AND THREE SABBATH DAYS REASONED WITH THEM OUT OF THE SCRIPTURES, OPENING AND ALLEGING, "CHRIST MUST HAVE SUFFERED, AND RISEN FROM THE DEAD, AND THIS JESUS, WHOM I PREACH UNTO YOU, IS CHRIST."

**Perplexing:**

How was Paul able to obtain permission to preach in a synagogue, especially on three Sabbaths, when his views were contrary to Jewish belief and based on a misinterpretation of the Scriptures? Why were the Jews so patient with him? Why did they not correct him?

Why did the writer now say, "they," rather than "we," as he had said previously?

See also under 14:1.

**Judaism:**

The Jewish Messiah (Christ) was not expected to die and be resurrected, nor be the Son of God. He was expected to be a king descended paternally from David who would restore the Israelite kingdom.

**History:**

Thessalonica is now known as Salonica, the second largest city in Greece.

17:5 - THE JEWS WHICH BELIEVED NOT...TOOK...CERTAIN LEWD FELLOWS...SET THE CITY ON AN UPROAR, ASSAULTED THE HOUSE OF JASON, AND SOUGHT TO BRING THEM OUT TO THE PEOPLE.

**Perplexing:**

Why did the Jews wait until after hearing Paul preach for three Sabbaths before creating an uproar? Who was Jason? Was Paul staying with him? Why was he not mentioned previously? (In ROM. 16:21, Paul mentioned a Jason who was one of his "kinsmen.")

17:7 - [JEWS]: "...THESE ALL DO CONTRARY TO THE DECREES OF CAESAR, SAYING THAT THERE IS ANOTHER KING, ONE JESUS."

**Perplexing:**

Why did ACTS not mention until now that Paul was preaching that Jesus was a king?

17:10-11 - THE BRETHREN SENT AWAY PAUL AND SILAS BY NIGHT UNTO BEREA, WHO COMING THITHER WENT INTO THE SYNAGOGUE OF THE JEWS. THESE WERE MORE NOBLE THAN THOSE IN THESSALONICA; THEY RECEIVED THE WORD WITH ALL READINESS OF MIND, AND SEARCHED THE SCRIPTURES DAILY, WHETHER THOSE THINGS WERE SO.

**Perplexing:**

Why did Paul and Silas have to sneak away at night? Did they not believe that Jesus would protect them if they prayed to him? Did Timothy and the writer of ACTS also sneak away with Paul? Why did the writer not so state? In 17:15, Timothy will be reported to be with Paul.

How was Paul able to obtain permission to preach his distortion of Scriptures in a synagogue? Were the Jews of Berea so ignorant of their religion that they willingly accepted Paul's assertions?

See also under 14:1 and 1-3.

17:13-15 - THE JEWS OF THESSALONICA...CAME HITHER ALSO, AND STIRRED THE PEOPLE. ...THE BRETHREN SENT AWAY PAUL...BUT SILAS AND TIMOTHEUS ABODE THERE STILL. THEY THAT CONDUCTED PAUL...UNTO ATHENS, RECEIVING A COMMANDMENT UNTO SILAS AND TIMOTHEUS TO COME TO HIM WITH ALL SPEED, THEY DEPARTED.

**Perplexing:**

Why was Timothy's presence just now reported? Why did neither he nor Silas have to flee with Paul? What were they doing while Paul was preaching? How did Paul travel to Athens from Berea which was about 200 miles away? Paul again fled from possible trouble. Why did he not pray to and trust the Lord to protect him?

Why did Jesus, the Holy Ghost, and angels fail to aid Paul?

17:17 - DISPUTED HE IN THE SYNAGOGUE WITH THE JEWS, AND THE DEVOUT PERSONS, AND IN THE MARKET DAILY WITH THEM THAT MET WITH HIM.

**History:**

Athens at this time was open to the free exchange of ideas and beliefs, even those which were not generally accepted. This freedom of speech and tolerance for new or different ideas helped to make the ancient, pagan Athens, of that time, the cultural, philosophical, and scientific leader of Europe. Such freedom was diametrically opposite to Paul's Christianity of intolerance, hate, suppression of differing beliefs, censorship, and violence which dragged Greece and the rest of Europe into the evils of the Dark Ages, Crusades, the Inquisition, the Holocaust, and religious wars; and the wanton destruction of countless tens of millions of human lives worldwide for nearly two millennia, with no end in sight.

See also under 10:1-2.

17:18 - CERTAIN PHILOSOPHERS OF THE EPICUREANS AND THE STOICS ENCOUNTERED HIM. SOME SAID, "HE SEEMETH TO BE A SETTER FORTH OF STRANGE GODS," BECAUSE HE PREACHED UNTO THEM JESUS, AND THE RESURRECTION.

**History:**

Epicureans, followers of Epicurus (341-270 B.C.), believed that happiness was the chief aim of life; that the universe was composed of tiny particles called "atoms"; and that there was no purposeful direction for man or the universe. They supported learning, enlightened discourses, friendship, and moderation in physical pleasures. [One may wonder at how much better and happier the world would be had the Epicurean views prevailed - a world with a minimum of hate, crime, persecution, war, etc.]

The Stoics, followers of Zeno (340-265 B.C.) emphasized the rational over the emotional, a strong sense of duty, and in putting one's self above pleasure and pain by a detachment of mind; they also believed in a supreme deity as well as a number of minor gods.

**Perplexing:**

Why did the philosophers believe that Paul spoke of "strange gods," because he preached about Jesus' resurrection? The resurrection of gods was a relatively common pagan concept.

Why did Paul fail to speak about Jesus' teachings?

17:23 - PAUL: "AS I PASSED BY...I FOUND AN ALTAR WITH THIS INSCRIPTION, 'TO THE UNKNOWN GOD,' WHOM YE IGNORANTLY WORSHIP; HIM DECLARE I UNTO YOU."

**History:**
The altar cited, was not erected to the unknown, but to any important god that the people may not have known about and, consequently, omitted from the local pantheon.

**Perplexing:**
Why did the Athenians not correct Paul's misinterpretation of the altar?

17:24 - PAUL: "GOD...LORD OF HEAVEN AND EARTH, DWELLETH NOT IN TEMPLES MADE WITH HANDS."

**Contradiction:** See under ACTS 7:48-50.

17:28 - PAUL: "IN HIM WE LIVE, MOVE, AND HAVE OUR BEING, AS CERTAIN OF YOUR POETS HAVE SAID, FOR WE ARE ALSO HIS OFFSPRING."

**History:**
The statement, "In him we live....," came from the 6th century B.C. Greek poet Epimenides. "For we are also his offspring," comes from the 3rd century B.C. Stoic poet Aratus.

17:31 - PAUL: "HE HATH APPOINTED A DAY, IN WHICH HE WILL JUDGE THE WORLD IN RIGHTEOUSNESS BY THAT MAN WHOM HE HATH ORDAINED, WHEREOF HE HATH GIVEN ASSURANCE UNTO ALL MEN, IN THAT HE HATH RAISED HIM FROM THE DEAD."

**Contradictions:** See under 2:22, and under JOHN 5:22.

**Perplexing:**
When did God ordain "that man" (Jesus)?
See also under 2:24, 10:42, and JOHN 5:22.

**Old Testament:**
PS. 9:8 - "He [the LORD] shall judge the world in righteousness...."
PS. 96:13 - "...He [the LORD] shall judge the world with righteousness....'
PS. 98:9 - "...with righteousness shall He judge the world."
(Note that in the PS. verses, God does not delegate the power to judge to anyone else.)

18:2 - ... CLAUDIUS HAD COMMANDED ALL JEWS TO DEPART FROM ROME....

**History:**
Claudius was Emperor of Rome during A.D. 41-54. The order was given in A.D. 49 and remained in effect for a few years. It was actually directed at the Christians who were creating disturbances, and who were considered to be Jews.

18:3 - BECAUSE HE [AQUILA] WAS OF THE SAME CRAFT, HE [PAUL] ABODE WITH THEM [AQUILA AND PRISCILLA]...THEY WERE TENTMAKERS.

**Language:**
The Greek word, "skenopoios," translated as "tentmaker," may also mean, "leatherworker" or "weaver."

**Perplexing:**
How did Paul meet Aquila and Priscilla? Why did they allow someone they had just met to move in with them?

18:4 - HE REASONED IN THE SYNAGOGUE EVERY SABBATH, AND PERSUADED THE JEWS AND GREEKS.

**Perplexing:**
How was Paul able to obtain permission to speak and to try and convert people in the synagogue? For how many Sabbaths was Paul permitted to speak in the synagogue?
See also under 14:1 and 17:1-3

18:5 - WHEN SILAS AND TIMOTHEUS WERE COME FROM MACEDONIA, PAUL TESTIFIED TO THE JEWS THAT JESUS WAS CHRIST.

**Perplexing:**
Why did Silas and Timothy go to Macedonia after leaving Athens, rather than to Corinth with Paul (18:1)? Why did the Jews not inform Paul that according to their religious beliefs Jesus did not qualify to be Christ (the Messiah)?
See also under 17:1-3.

18:6 - WHEN THEY OPPOSED THEMSELVES, AND BLASPHEMED, HE SHOOK HIS RAIMENT, AND SAID, "YOUR BLOOD BE UPON YOUR OWN HEADS; I AM CLEAN; FROM HENCEFORTH I WILL GO UNTO THE GENTILES."

**Judaism:**
From a Jewish perspective, Paul misinterpreted Old Testament verses to create his own version of God and endeavored to talk the Jews into accepting as the Messiah (Christ) someone who did not meet their criteria for such.

**Contradictions:** See under MATT. 24:14.

**Perplexing:**
Why did Jesus instruct his disciples to preach only to the Jews and say that he would return before they finished traveling through Israel (MATT. 10:5-6, 23)? Did he not know that most Jews would not accept him? If he and/or God knew that most Jews would reject him as the Messiah, why did Jesus tell the disciples initially to go only to the Jews? Why did he say that he was sent only to the lost sheep of the house of Israel (MATT. 15:24)? Why did he order the disciples to avoid the Gentiles (MATT. 10:5)?
Was Paul's statement, "Your blood be upon your own heads," an effort to incite hate and violence towards Jews?
See also under MATT. 24:14.

18:8 - CRISPUS, THE CHIEF RULER OF THE SYNAGOGUE, BELIEVED ON THE LORD ... MANY OF THE CORINTHIANS HEARING BELIEVED, AND WERE BAPTIZED.

**Contradiction:**
18:17 - The Greeks took Sosthenes, the chief ruler of the synagogue....
[Was Crispus, or Sosthenes the chief ruler of the synagogue?]

**Perplexing:**
After believing and being baptized, did they also receive the Holy Ghost? If so, in what manner?

18:9-10 - THEN SPAKE THE LORD TO PAUL..."I AM WITH THEE, AND NO MAN SHALL SET ON THEE TO HURT THEE, FOR I HAVE MUCH PEOPLE IN THIS CITY."

**Contradiction:**
18:12 - ...Jews made insurrection with one accord against Paul, and brought him to the judgment seat.
[Did the Lord say that no man would set on Paul to hurt him, or did the Lord allow Paul to be seized ?]

**Perplexing:**
Why did God need people to protect Paul? Why could He not do it Himself? Did the Lord lie to Paul when he said that no man would set upon him? Did the Lord not know that Paul would be seized? Where were the Lord's people? Why did they allow Paul to be seized by an angry group of people?

18:12 - WHEN GALLIO WAS THE DEPUTY OF ACHAIA, THE JEWS MADE INSURRECTION WITH ONE ACCORD AGAINST PAUL, AND BROUGHT HIM TO THE JUDGMENT SEAT.

**Contradiction:**
ACTS 18:10 - The Lord said that He was with Paul and no man shall set on him to hurt him; and that he had many people in the city.
[Was Paul seized by an angry group of people, or did the Lord protect him?]

**Perplexing:**
Why did the Lord fail to prevent the Jews from seizing Paul?
Where were Silas and Timothy? Why were they not also seized?
See also under 9-10.

**History:**
Junius Annaeus Gallio became proconsul of the province of Achaia, which included Greece, in A.D. 51. He was born in Spain and his name originally was Marcus Annaeus Novatas; he was the older brother of the Stoic philosopher Lucius Annaeus Seneca. Gallio later committed suicide after a younger brother and nephew killed themselves. There is no documentation that Jews seized Paul and brought him before Gallio.

18:17 - ALL THE GREEKS TOOK SOSTHENES, THE CHIEF RULER OF THE SYNAGOGUE, AND BEAT HIM BEFORE THE JUDGMENT SEAT.

**Contradiction:**
ACTS 18:8 - Crispus, the chief ruler of the synagogue....
[Was Sosthenes, or Crispus the chief ruler of the synagogue?]

**Perplexing:**
Why was Sosthenes attacked by the Greeks? Was it because he was Jewish, or because he was a supporter of Paul (in 1 COR. 1:1, Paul referred to Sosthenes as "our brother")?

18:18 - PAUL...TOOK HIS LEAVE OF THE BRETHREN, AND SAILED INTO SYRIA, WITH HIM PRISCILLA AND AQUILA, HAVING SHORN HIS HEAD IN CENCHREA, FOR HE HAD A VOW.

**Old Testament:**
NUM. 6:2-20 in giving the rules pertaining to a Nazarite vow stated that the head was to be shaved at the completion of the vow at the tabernacle of the people; the hair was then to be burned in the fire under the sacrifice of the peace offerings. The head was also to be shaved, if during the time of the vow, the person caused the sudden death of someone. The entire ritual included bringing offerings of food, drink, and sacrificial animals to the tabernacle. Furthermore, the individual taking the vow was prohibited from drinking wine, grape juice, strong drink, vinegar, and from eating grapes.

**Perplexing:**
Did Paul leave behind Silas, Timothy, and the writer of ACTS? If so, why? What vow did Paul take? When did he take it? When did he complete it? Why was it not previously reported? Why did Paul resort to the ancient Hebrew ritual for a Nazarite vow? Did Paul comply with all of the other requirements for the vow? Had he caused the death of someone? In 21:26, he will make the cryptic remark, "I am pure from the blood of all men."

18:19 - HE CAME TO EPHESUS, AND LEFT THEM THERE; HE ENTERED THE SYNAGOGUE, AND REASONED WITH THE JEWS.

**Perplexing:**
How could Paul enter a synagogue and preach (reason) without first obtaining permission from the presiding priest, especially when his views were contrary to prevailing Jewish belief?
See also under 14:1 and 17:1-3.

18:21 - [HE] BADE THEM FAREWELL, SAYING, "I MUST BY ALL MEANS KEEP THIS FEAST THAT COMETH IN JERUSALEM, BUT I WILL RETURN AGAIN UNTO YOU...." HE SAILED FROM EPHESUS.

**Contradiction:**
In 18:22 - 19:1, Paul left Ephesus and traveled to Caesarea, Antioch, where he spent some time, Galatia, and Phrygia, then returned to Ephesus.
[Did Paul go to Jerusalem, or did he spend time traveling around the region without going to Jerusalem prior to returning to Ephesus?]

**Perplexing:**
Why did Paul not go to Jerusalem? Did he deliberately lie to the people in Ephesus?

18:25 - THIS MAN [APOLLOS] INSTRUCTED IN THE WAY OF THE LORD...SPAKE DILIGENTLY THE THINGS OF THE LORD, KNOWING ONLY THE BAPTISM OF JOHN.

**Perplexing:**
If Apollos only underwent the baptism of John, how did he learn about the way of the Lord? Who instructed him? How could he speak diligently about the Lord if he had not been baptized by a disciple and had not received the Holy Ghost?

**Dead Sea Scrolls:** See under 9:1-2.

18:28 - HE [APOLLOS] MIGHTILY CONVINCED THE JEWS AND THAT PUBLICKLY, SHEWING BY THE SCRIPTURES THAT JESUS WAS CHRIST.

**Perplexing:**
According to 18:24, Apollos was a Jew mighty in the scriptures. If so, how could he use the Scriptures to show that Jesus was Christ, when such a view ran counter to the Scriptures and Jewish belief? Who was Apollos? Why was he allowed to preach belief in Jesus in a synagogue?

**Judaism:** See under 17:1-3.

19:1-3 - ...WHILE APOLLOS WAS AT CORINTH, PAUL...CAME TO EPHESUS, AND FINDING CERTAIN DISCIPLES SAID, "HAVE YE RECEIVED THE HOLY GHOST, SINCE YE BELIEVED?" THEY SAID, "WE HAVE NOT SO MUCH AS HEARD WHETHER THERE BE ANY HOLY GHOST." HE SAID, "UNTO WHAT THEN WERE YE BAPTIZED?" THEY SAID, "UNTO JOHN'S BAPTISM."

**Perplexing:**
Why did Apollos leave Ephesus and go to Corinth before Paul returned to Ephesus? Why did he not wait to meet Paul? Why did Paul return to Ephesus without going to Jerusalem as he said would do (18:21)?

**Contradiction:**
MATT. 3:11 - John: "I indeed baptize you with water...but he that cometh after me...shall baptize you with the Holy Ghost, and with fire."
MARK 1:8 - John: "I indeed have baptized you with water, but he shall baptize you with the Holy Ghost."
LUKE 3:16 - John: "I indeed baptize you with water, but one...cometh...he shall baptize you with the Holy Ghost and with fire."
[Were these disciples ignorant of the Holy Ghost, or had John told them about It?]

19:5 - ...THEY WERE BAPTIZED IN THE NAME OF THE LORD JESUS.

**Perplexing:**
Why were they baptized in the name of Jesus, when in MATT. 28:19, Jesus said, "Go ye...baptizing them in the name of the Father, Son, and Holy Ghost?" Was Paul ignorant of what Jesus had commanded?

19:6 - WHEN PAUL HAD LAID HIS HANDS ON THEM, THE HOLY GHOST CAME ON THEM, AND THEY SPAKE WITH TONGUES, AND PROPHESIED.

**Perplexing:**
Why was it necessary for Paul to lay his hands on them for them to receive the Holy Ghost? Did the Holy Ghost come onto them in the shape of a dove, tongues of fire, or something else? What did they prophesy? See also under 2:6-11, 13-15.

19:8 - HE WENT INTO THE SYNAGOGUE, AND SPAKE BOLDLY FOR THREE MONTHS, DISPUTING AND PERSUADING THE THINGS CONCERNING THE KINGDOM OF GOD.

**Perplexing:**
How was Paul able to obtain permission from the presiding priest to spend three months pontificating in a synagogue on his beliefs and distorting Old Testament verses?
See also under 14:1.

19:9-10 - WHEN DIVERS...SPAKE EVIL OF THAT WAY...HE DEPARTED...DISPUTING DAILY IN THE SCHOOL OF ONE TYRANNUS. THIS CONTINUED TWO YEARS, SO THAT ALL THEY WHICH DWELT IN ASIA HEARD THE WORD OF THE LORD JESUS, BOTH JEWS AND GREEKS.

**History:**
Tyrannus was a rhetorician.

**Perplexing:**
Why did Tyrannus allow Paul to use his facilities? Did Paul have to pay him? If so, from where did Paul obtain the necessary funds? In 16:6, the Holy Ghost prohibited Paul from preaching in Asia. Why then did Paul disobey the Holy Ghost and preach there? Did he forget? Did the Holy Ghost change Its mind? If so, when? Why did ACTS not report it? If Paul just preached in one place, how could all the people of Asia [the word used for central Asia Minor] have heard about Jesus from him?

**History:** See under 9:1-2.

**Dead Sea Scrolls:** Sea under 9:1-2.

19:11-12 - GOD WROUGHT SPECIAL MIRACLES BY THE HANDS OF PAUL, SO THAT FROM HIS BODY WERE BROUGHT UNTO THE SICK HANDKERCHIEFS OR APRONS, AND THE DISEASES DEPARTED FROM THEM, AND THE EVIL SPIRITS WENT OUT OF THEM.

**History:**
There is no secular record of any miracles having been performed by Paul.

**Perplexing:**
In 2 TIM. 4:20, Paul said, "...Trophimus have I left in Miletum sick. If Paul could perform healing miracles, why could he not heal Trophimus? Why did the Holy Ghost fail to inform Paul about the causes, treatment, and prevention of many diseases? By what means were Paul's handkerchiefs and aprons able to heal the sick? Why in 1 TIM. 5:23 did Paul say "...use a little wine for thy stomach's sake and thine often infirmities," rather than say that one should have faith and/or pray?

19:13-16 - CERTAIN VAGABOND JEWS, EXORCISTS, TOOK UPON THEM TO CALL OVER THEM WHICH HAD EVIL SPIRITS, THE NAME OF THE LORD JESUS.... THERE WERE SEVEN SONS OF SCEVA, CHIEF OF THE PRIESTS, WHICH DID SO. THE EVIL SPIRIT SAID, "JESUS I KNOW, AND PAUL I KNOW, BUT WHO ARE YE?" THE MAN IN WHOM THE EVIL SPIRIT WAS LEAPED ON THEM...AND THEY FLED....

**Perplexing:**
Who were these Jewish exorcists? To which branch or sect of Judaism did they belong? How did they exorcise spirits or demons before hearing about using the name of Jesus? Why did ACTS again equate Jews with sorcery (see 13:6)? In MARK 9:38, [Jesus' disciple] John said to Jesus, "We saw one casting out devils in thy name, and he followeth not us...." If at least one other individual could cast out devils using Jesus' name while not being a follower of Jesus, why could not the Jewish exorcists do the same?

19:19 - MANY OF THEM WHICH USED CURIOUS ARTS BROUGHT THEIR BOOKS TOGETHER, AND BURNED THEM BEFORE ALL MEN....

**Perplexing:**
Why was book burning deemed to be necessary? Why did Paul permit it? Why was such religious intolerance acceptable to Christians? Why were Christians fearful of differing beliefs? Jesus did not order book burning or the persecution of those who did not share his beliefs.

**History:**
Because of this biblical acceptance of book burning, it became a Christian practice over the centuries into the present time. The burning of books and other items such as recordings and films that are unacceptable to particular religious sects has also led to the persecution and murder of the authors of such books. The practice of murdering authors of publications deemed unacceptable by religious leaders was later incorporated into Islam as a religious mandate.
See also under 17:17 - the tolerance of the pagans compared to the intolerance of Christians.

19:24-27 - DEMETRIUS, A SILVERSMITH, WHICH MADE SILVER SHRINES FOR DIANA... CALLED TOGETHER WORKMEN OF LIKE OCCUPATION, AND SAID, "BY THIS CRAFT WE HAVE OUR WEALTH. YE SEE AND HEAR, THAT NOT ALONE AT EPHESUS, BUT ALMOST THROUGHOUT ALL ASIA, PAUL HATH TURNED AWAY MUCH PEOPLE, SAYING THAT THEY BE NO GODS, WHICH ARE MADE BY HANDS, SO THAT NOT ONLY OUR CRAFT IS IN DANGER TO BE SET AT NOUGHT, BUT THAT THE TEMPLE OF THE GREAT GODDESS DIANA SHOULD BE DESPISED, AND HER MAGNIFICENCE DESTROYED...."

**History:**
Ephesus was the site of the Temple of Diana (Artemis, in Greek), built in the 5th century B.C.; it was one of the seven wonders of the ancient world. The goddess was worshiped long before the Greeks arrived in Asia Minor and was known as the Great Goddess of Anatolia and the Mother Goddess of Ephesus. Her worship even extended into Egypt. The temple was closed in A.D. 380 by Emperor Theodosius who in an act of religious intolerance also outlawed all religions except Christianity. Temples dedicated to her worship were then converted into churches by Christians.

**Perplexing:**
Why did ACTS say that the Greek Demetrius referred to the goddess by her Roman name Diana, instead of by her Greek name Artemis?
Why do many modern Christians use, pray to, revere, and/or worship such things as man-made icons, crosses, pictures, and stylized fish symbols as did the pagans?

**Pagan parallels:**
Diana (Artemis) was a chaste, virgin goddess with whom Christians later equated Mary.

19:30 - WHEN PAUL WOULD HAVE ENTERED IN UNTO THE PEOPLE, THE DISCIPLES SUFFERED HIM NOT.

**Perplexing:**
Why did the disciples lack enough faith in the Lord to believe that he would protect Paul? Why did they and Paul fail to pray for the Lord's protection? Why did they fail to believe that Paul could perform a miracle to protect himself? Why did Paul fail to perform a miracle to convert the followers of Diana? Did not Paul and the disciples believe Jesus' saying, in such verses as, MATT. 21:22, MARK 9:23, and JOHN 13:14 that believers would receive whatever they asked for?

19:33 - THEY DREW ALEXANDER OUT OF THE MULTITUDE, THE JEWS PUTTING HIM FORWARD. ....

**Perplexing:**
Who was this Alexander? Was he the son of the Simon who carried Jesus' cross (MARK 15:21); the Alexander who was with Annas and Caiaphas (ACTS 4:6); the Alexander that Paul delivered to Satan (1 TIM. 1:20); Alexander the coppersmith (2 TIM. 4:14), or someone else?

**History:** See under 4:6.

19:35 - THE TOWNCLERK SAID, "...THE IMAGE WHICH FELL DOWN FROM JUPITER?"

**History:**
The image is believed to have been a conical stone, possibly a meteorite. It also may have been the odd shaped stone engraved in Greek, "Jupiter the Savior," that is kept in the Church of St. Peter in Rome. The ancient Anatolian goddess Cybele, similarly, had a stone, possibly a meteorite, as a symbol. Muslims also revere a stone (taken from the pagan Arabs) in Mecca as a gift from their deity. Jupiter is the Roman name for the Greek god Zeus.

**Perplexing:**
Why did ACTS say that the Greek town clerk referred to the god by using his Roman name Jupiter, instead of his Greek name Zeus?

19:37 - THE TOWN CLERK: "...THESE MEN, WHICH ARE NEITHER ROBBERS OF CHURCHES, NOR BLASPHEMERS OF YOUR GODDESS."

**Perplexing:**
Why did the town clerk say, "your goddess," rather than "our goddess?" Was he also a disciple?

20:5 - THOSE GOING BEFORE TARRIED FOR US AT TROAS.

**Perplexing:**
When did the writer of ACTS rejoin Paul?
See also under 16:10.

20:6 - WE SAILED AWAY FROM PHILIPPI AFTER THE DAYS OF UNLEAVENED BREAD....

**History:** See under MATT. 26:2.

**Perplexing:** See under 16:10.

20:7-11 - ...WHEN THE DISCIPLES CAME TOGETHER TO BREAK BREAD, PAUL PREACHED UNTO THEM...AND CONTINUED UNTIL MIDNIGHT. .... ...PAUL WAS LONG PREACHING, HE [EUTYCHUS] SUNK DOWN WITH SLEEP, FELL DOWN FROM THE THIRD LOFT, AND WAS TAKEN UP DEAD. PAUL...EMBRACING HIM SAID, "...HIS LIFE IS IN HIM." ...HE [PAUL]...TALKED A LONG WHILE, TILL BREAK OF DAY, SO HE DEPARTED.

**Perplexing:**
Why did Paul deem it necessary to preach to people who were already disciples? Why did he show no compassion for them by keeping them away from their homes listening to him until he had to leave? Why did he not sleep until the break of day?
Did Paul resurrect Eutychus from the dead?

20:12 - THEY BROUGHT THE YOUNG MAN [WHO FELL ASLEEP AND FELL FROM THE LOFT] ALIVE, AND WERE NOT A LITTLE COMFORTED.

**Perplexing:**
Were they comforted because the man was alive, or because Paul had stopped preaching and had departed?

20:13-15 - WE WENT BEFORE TO SHIP, AND SAILED UNTO ASSOS.... WHEN HE MET WITH US, WE TOOK HIM IN.... WE SAILED THENCE...WE ARRIVED AT SAMOS...WE CAME TO MILETUS.

**Perplexing:** See under 16:10.

20:16-18 - PAUL DETERMINED TO SAIL BY EPHESUS...FOR HE HASTED, IF IT WERE POSSIBLE FOR HIM TO BE AT JERUSALEM THE DAY OF PENTECOST. FROM MILETUS HE SENT TO EPHESUS, AND CALLED THE ELDERS OF THE CHURCH. WHEN THEY WERE COME TO HIM....

**Perplexing:**
If Paul was in so much of a hurry to reach Jerusalem that he could not stop at Ephesus, why did he stop at Miletus, and order the elders of the church at Ephesus to travel there to meet with him? How long did it take for his message to reach the elders? How long did it take them to get together and travel to Miletus? Why did he inconvenience them by making them come to him? Would it not have been less time consuming and more convenient for him to have met with them in Ephesus? Was he afraid of returning to Ephesus after the hostility he recently encountered there? If so, why did he not trust the Lord to protect him?
Why did Paul want to be in Jerusalem for Pentecost?

20:23 - PAUL: "THE HOLY GHOST WITNESSETH IN EVERY CITY, SAYING THAT BONDS AND AFFLICTIONS ABIDE ME."

**Perplexing:**
Why did the Holy Ghost permit Paul to be afflicted? Why did the Holy Ghost opt not to protect Paul? If Paul was doing the Lord's work, why would the Lord not reward, rather than punish, him for it?

20:26 - PAUL: "I TAKE YOU TO RECORD THIS DAY, THAT I AM PURE FROM THE BLOOD OF ALL MEN."

**Perplexing:**
Why did Paul make this statement? What did he mean? In 18:18, Paul was reported to have shorn his head because of a vow. See under 18:18 - Old Testament; if while having made a Nazarite vow, the person causes someone's death, he must shave his head. Was Paul saying that he inadvertently killed someone?

20:35 - PAUL: "...REMEMBER THE WORDS OF THE LORD JESUS, HOW HE SAID, 'IT IS MORE BLESSED TO GIVE THAN TO RECEIVE.'"

**Perplexing:**
Why did Paul attribute the above quote to Jesus, when it does not appear as one of Jesus' sayings elsewhere in the Bible? From where did Paul obtain the quote? Why did Paul fail to mention any of those statements attributed to Jesus by the gospels? Was Paul ignorant of Jesus' sayings and teachings? Why do not most Christian clergyman, who have their hands out requesting money, believe that it is more blessed to give than to receive?

20:36 - ...HE KNEELED DOWN, AND PRAYED WITH THEM ALL.

**Perplexing:**
Why did Paul ignore Jesus' command in MATT. 6:6, "When thou prayest, enter into thy closet, and when thou hast shut the door, pray to thy Father which is in secret, and thy Father which seeth in secret shall reward thee openly?" Was Paul ignorant of this command by Jesus? See also under 6:10, and under MATT. 6:5-6, 8.

21:1-3 - ...AFTER WE WERE GOTTEN FROM THEM...WE CAME WITH A STRAIGHT COURSE UNTO COOS...WE WENT ABOARD....WE HAD DISCOVERED...WE LEFT...AND LANDED AT TYRE....

**Perplexing:** See under 16:10.

**History:**
Coos was the birthplace of Hippocrates (450 B.C.) and the site of what was an important medical school in ancient times.

**Old Testament:** See under MATT. 11:20-23.

21:4 - FINDING DISCIPLES WE TARRIED THERE SEVEN DAYS, WHO SAID TO PAUL THROUGH THE SPIRIT, THAT HE SHOULD NOT GO TO JERUSALEM.

**Perplexing:**
Why did the Spirit speak to the disciples rather than directly to Paul?
See also under 16:10.

21:5-6 - WHEN WE HAD ACCOMPLISHED THOSE DAYS, WE DEPARTED AND WENT OUR WAY; THEY ALL BROUGHT US ON THE WAY...WE WERE OUT OF THE CITY; WE KNEELED DOWN AND PRAYED. WHEN WE HAD TAKEN OUR LEAVE, WE TOOK SHIP....

**Perplexing:** See under 16:10 and 20:36.

21:7- WHEN WE HAD FINISHED OUR COURSE FROM TYRE, WE CAME TO PTOLEMAIS....

**Perplexing:** See under 16:10.

**Old Testament:** See under MATT. 11:20-23.

21:8 - THE NEXT DAY WE...DEPARTED, AND CAME UNTO CAESAREA; WE ENTERED THE HOUSE OF PHILIP THE EVANGELIST, ONE OF THE SEVEN....

**Perplexing:**
In 6:1-5, Philip was one of seven men chosen to resolve a dispute between the Hebrews and the Greeks. Was this dispute still in existence? Had it not been settled? If it had been settled, why was Philip still referred to as "one of the seven?"
See also under 16:10.

21:9 - THE SAME MAN HAD FOUR DAUGHTERS, VIRGINS, WHICH DID PROPHESY.

**Perplexing:**
How did the writer of ACTS know that the daughters were virgins? Did he perhaps mean that they were not married? By saying that they "did prophesy, " did the writer mean that they were prophetesses, or that they spoke in tongues?

**Old Testament:** See under 2:16-21.

21:10-11 - WE TARRIED THERE...THERE CAME...A PROPHET, NAMED AGABUS. WHEN HE WAS COME UNTO US, HE TOOK PAUL'S GIRDLE, BOUND HIS OWN HANDS AND FEET, AND SAID, "THUS SAITH THE HOLY GHOST, 'SO SHALL THE JEWS AT JERUSALEM BIND THE MAN THAT OWNETH THIS GIRDLE, AND SHALL DELIVER HIM INTO THE HANDS OF THE GENTILES.'"

**Perplexing:**
Why did the Holy Ghost speak to Agabus, and not directly to Paul?
Why could not or would not the Holy Ghost protect Paul against harm, especially if he was doing the Lord's work?
Was this the same Agabus who prophesied a famine (11:28)?
See also under 11:28, 16:10, and 21:4.

21:12-17 - WHEN WE HEARD THESE THINGS, WE, AND THEY OF THAT PLACE, BESOUGHT HIM NOT TO GO TO JERUSALEM. .... WHEN HE WOULD NOT BE PERSUADED, WE CEASED, SAYING, "THE WILL OF THE LORD BE DONE." WE TOOK UP OUR CARRIAGES .... THERE WENT WITH US...MNASON, AN OLD DISCIPLE, OF CYPRUS WITH WHOM

WE SHOULD LODGE. WHEN WE WERE COME TO JERUSALEM, THE BRETHREN RECEIVED US GLADLY.

**Perplexing:**
How many people traveled with Paul?
Did the brethren include Peter and/or any of the original apostles? If not, why not? What had they been doing while Paul was traveling around preaching? Except for a reference to Philip in 21:8, they have not been cited since ACTS 15. Why were their activities no longer reported?
Why would the Lord want or allow any harm to befall his followers? What was meant by "carriages?" Other Bibles delete the phrase, "we took up our carriages."
See also under 16:10.

21:18 - THE DAY FOLLOWING PAUL WENT WITH US UNTO JAMES; ALL THE ELDERS WERE PRESENT.

**Perplexing:**
Why did they go to James? Had James replaced Peter as the leader of the disciples? If so, when and why? See also under 12:17 and 16:10.

21:21 - [JAMES AND THE ELDERS:] "THEY [JEWS ZEALOUS OF THE LAW] ARE INFORMED OF THEE, THAT THOU TEACHEST ALL THE JEWS AMONG THE GENTILES TO FORSAKE MOSES, SAYING THAT THEY OUGHT NOT TO CIRCUMCISE THEIR CHILDREN, NEITHER TO WALK AFTER THE CUSTOMS."

**Contradiction:** See under 15:1.

**Perplexing:** See under 15:2.

21:23-24 - [JAMES AND THE ELDERS]: "...WE HAVE FOUR MEN WHICH HAVE A VOW ON THEM; THEM TAKE AND PURIFY THYSELF WITH THEM THAT THEY MAY SHAVE THEIR HEADS....

**Perplexing:**
Why was it necessary for Paul to purify himself? Did this refer back to the vow he was said to have taken earlier (18:18)? Why did he have to take the men to the temple?
See also under 18:18.

**Old Testament:** See under 18:18.

21:25-26 - [JAMES AND THE ELDERS]: "AS TOUCHING THE GENTILES WHICH BELIEVE, WE HAVE WRITTEN AND CONCLUDED THAT...THEY KEEP THEMSELVES FROM THINGS OFFERED TO IDOLS, FROM BLOOD, FROM THINGS STRANGLED, AND FROM FORNICATION." PAUL TOOK THE MEN [WHO MADE THE VOW]...INTO THE TEMPLE.....

**Perplexing:** See under 15:19-20.

**History:** See under 15:19-20.

21:27 - ...JEWS WHICH WERE OF ASIA, WHEN THEY SAW HIM [PAUL] IN THE TEMPLE, STIRRED UP ALL THE PEOPLE, AND LAID HANDS ON HIM.

**Perplexing:**
Why did the men with Paul fail to protect or try to protect him? Why did the Holy Ghost fail to protect him? Why did Paul fail to perform a miracle to protect himself, or pray to Jesus for protection? Where was the writer of ACTS who was supposedly with Paul?

21:28-29 - [JEWS FROM ASIA]: "...THIS IS THE MAN, THAT TEACHETH...AGAINST THE PEOPLE, AND THE LAW, AND THIS PLACE, AND FURTHER BROUGHT GREEKS ALSO INTO THE TEMPLE, AND HATH POLLUTED THIS HOLY PLACE." (THEY...SUPPOSED THAT PAUL HAD BROUGHT [AN EPHESIAN] INTO THE TEMPLE.)

**Perplexing:** See under 21:27.

**History:**
Only Jews were permitted to enter the temple, whereas synagogues were open to everyone. [The Church of Latter Day Saints permits only Mormons to enter its temples, but its churches are open to all.]

21:30-32 - ...THE PEOPLE RAN TOGETHER, TOOK PAUL, AND DREW HIM OUT OF THE TEMPLE ....AS THEY WENT ABOUT TO KILL HIM, TIDINGS CAME UNTO THE CHIEF CAPTAIN OF THE BAND, THAT ALL JERUSALEM WAS IN AN UPROAR. WHO IMMEDIATELY TOOK SOLDIERS AND CENTURIONS, AND RAN DOWN UNTO THEM....

**Perplexing:** See under 21:27.

**History:**
Situated just north of the temple was the fort of Antonia; stairs at two locations led down to the court of the temple. Therefore, soldiers could very quickly reach the site where the furor was occurring.

21:38 - [THE CAPTAIN:] "ART THOU THAT EGYPTIAN, WHICH BEFORE THESE DAYS MADEST AN UPROAR, AND LEDDEST OUT INTO THE WILDERNESS 4000 MEN THAT WERE MURDERERS?"

**History:**
An Egyptian Jew claiming to be a prophet brought together about 30,000 men to the Mount of Olives from where he planned to seize Jerusalem. Roman troops attacked and dispersed them, but the Egyptian escaped.

21:39 - PAUL SAID, "I AM A MAN WHICH AM A JEW OF TARSUS, A CITY IN CILICA, A CITIZEN OF NO MEAN CITY.... SUFFER ME TO SPEAK UNTO THE PEOPLE."

**Contradictions:**
ACTS 16:37 and 22:25 - Paul claimed to be Roman.
[Was Paul a Jew from Tarsus, or a Roman?]
In ROM. 11:1 Paul: "I am an Israelite, of the seed of Abraham, of the tribe of Benjamin."
In PHIL. 3:5 - Paul: "[I am]...of the stock of Israel, of the tribe of Benjamin, a Hebrew of the Hebrews, as touching the law a Pharisee."
[Was Paul a Jew from Tarsus, or an Israelite?]

**Perplexing:**
Why did Paul tell the Roman captain that he was a Jew from Tarsus? In 16:37, he claimed to be Roman? In his Epistles, Paul did not claim to be from Tarsus. Why?
See also under 16:36-37.

21:40 - WHEN HE HAD GIVEN HIM LICENSE, PAUL...BECKONED UNTO THE PEOPLE. WHEN THERE WAS A GREAT SILENCE HE SPAKE UNTO THEM IN THE HEBREW TONGUE.

**History:**
At time the event is supposed to have occurred, the people spoke Aramaic and/or Greek.
See also under 2:6-11.

**Perplexing:**
Why did the captain give Paul permission to address the mob? Why did Paul not speak in Greek? Why did the writer of ACTS say that Paul spoke Hebrew? Did the writer not know that Greek and Aramaic were in use?
Why did the people obey Paul and become silent?

22:2 - (WHEN THEY HEARD THAT HE SPAKE IN THE HEBREW TONGUE TO THEM, THEY KEPT THE MORE SILENCE....)

**Perplexing:**
How could the Greek speaking Jews understand Paul? In 21:27, it was the Jews from Asia who first laid hands on him, and they spoke Greek.

22:3 - PAUL: "I AM A JEW, BORN IN TARSUS, A CITY IN CILICIA, YET BROUGHT UP IN THIS CITY AT THE FEET OF GAMALIEL, AND TAUGHT ACCORDING TO THE PERFECT MANNER OF THE LAW OF THE FATHER'S...."

**Contradictions:**
GAL. 1:15-17 - Paul: "When it pleased God, who separated me from my mother 's womb to reveal His Son to me that I might preach him among the heathen, immediately I conferred not with flesh and blood, neither went I up to Jerusalem to them which were apostles before me, but I went into Arabia...."
[Was Paul brought up in Jerusalem, or did he go to Arabia to preach about Jesus before going to Jerusalem?]
GAL. 1:22 - Paul: "[I] was unknown by face unto the churches of Judaea which were in Christ."
[Was Paul brought up in Jerusalem, or was he unknown there?]
See also under 21:39.

**Perplexing:**
Why did Paul not mention Gamaliel in his Epistles? If Paul had been taught by Gamaliel [see under 5:34 - History], why did he frequently misquote and misinterpret Old Testament verses?
See also under 21:39.

22:5 - PAUL: "AS THE HIGH PRIEST DOTH BEAR ME WITNESS, AND ... THE ELDERS, FROM WHOM I RECEIVED LETTERS UNTO THE BRETHREN, AND WENT TO BRING THEM WHICH WERE BOUND UNTO JERUSALEM TO BE PUNISHED."

**History:** See under 9:1-2.

**Perplexing:** See under 9:1-2.

**Contradictions:**
ACTS 9:14 - Ananias: "Here he [Saul] hath authority from the chief priests to bind all that call on thy [Jesus'] name."
ACTS 26:12 - Paul: "I went to Damascus with authority and commission from the chief priests."
[Did Paul receive authorization to go to Damascus from the high priest and elders, or from the chief priests?]
See also under 9:1-2.

22:8 - PAUL: "I ANSWERED, 'WHO ART THOU LORD?' HE SAID, 'I AM JESUS OF NAZARETH, WHOM THOU PERSECUTETH.'"

**Contradictions:**
ACTS 9:4-5 - He...heard a voice saying, "Saul, Saul, why persecuteth thou me?" He [Saul] said, "Who art thou Lord?" The Lord said, "I am Jesus whom thou persecutest; it is hard for thee to kick against the pricks."
[Did Jesus accuse Paul of persecuting him, or ask why Paul persecuted him?]
ACTS 26:14-15 - Paul: "When we were all fallen to the earth, I heard a voice saying, "Saul, Saul, why persecutest thou me? It is hard for thee to kick against the pricks. " I said, "Who art thou, Lord?" He said, "I am Jesus whom thou persecutest."
[Did Jesus refer to himself as Jesus of Nazareth, or just as Jesus and also make the comment about kicking at pricks?]
[Did Paul say, "Who art thou Lord," before, or after a voice spoke about being persecuted?]
[Did the voice say, "I am Jesus of Nazareth," or "I am Jesus?"]
See also under 9:4-5.

**Perplexing:** See under 9:4-5.

22:9 - PAUL: "THEY THAT WERE WITH ME SAW THE LIGHT, AND WERE AFRAID, BUT THEY HEARD NOT THE VOICE OF HIM THAT SPAKE TO ME."

**Contradiction:**
ACTS 9:7 - The men which journeyed with him stood speechless, hearing a voice, but seeing no man.
[Did the men not hear, or did they hear the voice?]

**Language:**
In an effort to eliminate the contradiction, some Bibles erroneously translate the Greek word, "ekousan," meaning, "heard," as "understand," ("did not understand the voice").

22:10 - PAUL: "I SAID, 'WHAT SHALL I DO, LORD?' THE LORD SAID, 'ARISE, AND GO INTO DAMASCUS; THERE IT SHALL BE TOLD THEE ALL THINGS WHICH ARE APPOINTED FOR THEE TO DO.'"

**Contradictions:**
ACTS 26:16-18 - Jesus: "Rise, and stand upon thy feet, for I have appeared for this purpose, to make thee a minister and a witness of these things which thou hast seen, and of those things in which I will appear unto thee, delivering thee from the people, and the Gentiles, unto whom I now send thee, to open their eyes...."
[Did Jesus tell Paul to go to Damascus to learn what he had to do, or did Jesus tell him on the road to Damascus what he was to do?]
[Did Paul ask Jesus what he should do, or did Jesus tell him without being asked?]

**Perplexing:** See under 9:7.

22:12-16 - PAUL: "ANANIAS, A DEVOUT MAN ACCORDING TO THE LAW, HAVING A GOOD REPORT OF ALL THE JEWS WHICH DWELT THERE, CAME.... HE SAID, 'THE GOD OF OUR FATHERS HATH CHOSEN THEE, THAT THOU SHOULDEST KNOW HIS WILL, SEE THE JUST ONE, AND HEAR THE VOICE OF HIS MOUTH. THOU SHALL BE HIS WITNESS UNTO ALL MEN OF WHAT THOU HAST SEEN AND HEARD. .... BE BAPTIZED, AND WASH AWAY THY SINS, CALLING ON THE NAME OF THE LORD.'"

**Contradictions:**
ACTS 9:10 - There was a disciple at Damascus named Ananias....
[Was Ananias a devout man with a good report of all the Jews in Damascus, or was he a disciple of Jesus?]
See also under 9:17.

**Perplexing:** See under 9:19.

**Pagan concept:** See under MATT. 3:5-6.

22:17-18 - PAUL: "...WHEN I WAS COME AGAIN TO JERUSALEM, WHILE I PRAYED IN THE TEMPLE, I WAS IN A TRANCE, AND SAW HIM SAYING UNTO ME, 'MAKE HASTE; GET THEE QUICKLY OUT OF JERUSALEM, FOR THEY WILL NOT RECEIVE THY TESTIMONY CONCERNING ME.'"

**Contradictions:**
GAL. 1:17-20 - Paul: "Neither went I to Jerusalem...but I went to Arabia, and returned to Damascus. After three years I went to Jerusalem to see Peter, and abode with him 15 days. But other of the apostles I saw none save James the Lord's brother. ...I lie not."
[Did Paul leave Damascus and go the temple where Jesus spoke to him, or did he go to Arabia from where he returned to Damascus, before going to Jerusalem three years later to meet with Peter and James, or did he go directly to Jerusalem from Damascus?]
ACTS 9:19-28 - .... Then was Paul certain days with the disciples at Damascus. He preached Christ in the synagogues.... .... ...confounded the Jews at Damascus.... .... When Saul was come to Jerusalem, he assayed to join the disciples, but they...believed not that he was a disciple. Barnabas brought him to the apostles.... He was with them coming in and going out of Jerusalem.
[Did Paul leave Damascus and go to the temple where Jesus spoke to him, or did he remain in Damascus preaching for an unspecified length of time then go to Jerusalem to be with the apostles?]

**Perplexing:**
Why did Jesus fail to know beforehand that the people would not accept Paul's testimony about him? Why

did Jesus tell Paul to flee from Jerusalem, rather than saying that he would protect him there? Why did Jesus not perform a miracle to cause the people to believe in him? Of what value is belief in a deity that cannot or will not assist and protect its adherents?

22:19 - PAUL: "I SAID, 'LORD, THEY KNOW THAT I IMPRISONED AND BEAT IN EVERY SYNAGOGUE THEM THAT BELIEVED ON THEE.'"

**Perplexing:** See under 8:1, 3.

**History:** See under 8:3.

22:21 - PAUL: "HE SAID, 'DEPART; I WILL SEND THEE FAR HENCE UNTO THE GENTILES.'"

**Perplexing:**
Why did Jesus fail to know that he would have to send disciples to the Gentiles, when he told them in MATT. 10:5 not to go to the Gentiles?

22:25 - AS THEY BOUND HIM WITH THONGS, PAUL SAID UNTO THE CENTURION THAT STOOD BY, "IS IT LAWFUL FOR YOU TO SCOURGE A MAN THAT IS A ROMAN, AND UNCONDEMNED?"

**Contradictions:**
ACTS 21:39 and 22:3 - Paul said that he was a Jew, born in Tarsus, a city in Cilicia.
[Was Paul a Roman, or was he a Jew, a citizen of Tarsus?]
See also under 16:36-37.

**Perplexing:**
Did Paul say that he is a Roman, because he had no faith that the Lord would protect him from being scourged? Why did the centurion fail to ask him why, if he was Roman, he had initially claimed to be a Jew from Tarsus? Why did Paul wait until he was seized and bound before declaring himself to be a Roman?
See also under 16:36-37.

**History:**
The Ebionites, early Christians who believed that Jesus was just a man favored by God, accused Paul of having abandoned the Torah to obtain power and influence for himself with the Romans.

22:27-28 - THE CHIEF CAPTAIN: "TELL ME, ART THOU A ROMAN?" HE SAID, "YEA." .... "I WAS BORN FREE."

**Contradictions:** See under 16:36-37.

**Perplexing:**
Why did the captain not ask Paul why he claimed to be a Jewish citizen of Tarsus (21:39), if he actually was a Roman? Why did he not request Paul to provide proof of Roman citizenship?
See also under 16:36-37.

22:29 - STRAIGHTAWAY THEY DEPARTED FROM HIM WHICH SHOULD HAVE EXAMINED HIM; THE CHIEF CAPTAIN WAS AFRAID, AFTER HE KNEW THAT HE WAS A ROMAN, AND BECAUSE HE HAD BOUND HIM.

**Perplexing:**
Why did the captain take Paul's word that he was a Roman without investigating further?
See also under 27-28.

22:30 -...HE [THE CHIEF CAPTAIN]...COMMANDED THE CHIEF PRIESTS AND ALL THEIR COUNCIL TO APPEAR, BROUGHT PAUL DOWN, AND SET HIM BEFORE THEM.

**Perplexing:**
What authority did the captain have to call a meeting of the chief priests and the council? How could it have been convened so quickly? Why did he bring a Roman before a Jewish council (the Sanhedrin) to face possible charges? Why did the priests and Sanhedrin take orders from a Roman captain? Did the council have the authority to interrogate a Roman?

23:1 - PAUL ...SAID, "MEN AND BRETHREN, I HAVE LIVED IN GOOD CONSCIENCE BEFORE GOD UNTIL THIS DAY."

**Perplexing:**
Why was Paul allowed to address the council before it had informed him about why he was there and what charges had been brought against him? Did he want to disrupt the proceedings before they began? Why did Paul not request that James and the elders be present as witnesses for him? Why did Paul fail to inform the council that he was a Roman?

23:2 - THE HIGH PRIEST ANANIAS COMMANDED THEM THAT STOOD BY HIM TO SMITE HIM ON HE MOUTH.

**Perplexing:**
What authority did the Jewish high priest have to order a Roman citizen to be struck? Why did the Roman captain allow a Roman citizen to be struck by Jews? Did the high priest order him to be struck because he was trying to prevent the council from questioning him?

**History:**
Ananias was high priest from c.48-58.
The Sanhedrin dealt with Jewish religious matters; it did not question or try Romans.

23:5 - PAUL: "...IT IS WRITTEN, 'THOU SHALT NOT SPEAK EVIL OF THE RULER OF THY PEOPLE.'"

**Old Testament:**
EX. 22:28 - God: "Thou shalt not revile the gods, nor curse the ruler of thy people."

23:6-7 - WHEN PAUL PERCEIVED THAT ONE PART WERE SADDUCEES, AND THE OTHER PHARISEES, HE CRIED OUT, "MEN AND BRETHREN, I AM A PHARISEE; OF THE HOPE AND RESURRECTION OF THE DEAD I AM CALLED IN QUESTION." WHEN HE HAD SO SAID, THERE AROSE A DISSENSION BETWEEN THE PHARISEES AND SADDUCEES....

**History:** See under 9:1-2, and under MATT. 3:7.

**Contradictions:**
ACTS 21:28-29 - Paul was accused of teaching "against the people and the law," and bringing "Greeks also into the temple." In the ensuing verses he was attacked by the Jews, rescued by the Romans, and then turned over to the council.
[Was Paul brought to the council because he believed in the resurrection of the dead, or because he was accused of speaking contrary to the law and bringing Greeks into the temple?]
ACTS 16:37 and 22:25 - Paul claimed to be a Roman.
[Was Paul a Pharisee, or a Roman?]
See also under 21:39.

**Perplexing:**
Was Paul deliberately lying to stir up dissension to escape being questioned about the accusations that led to his being brought before the council? If he was Roman, how could he honestly affiliate himself with the anti-Roman Pharisees? Did Paul refer to himself as either a Pharisee or a Roman based on what would be most advantageous for him?
In 1 COR. 9:20-21, Paul said, "Unto the Jews I became as a Jew, that I might gain the Jews.... To them [Gentiles] that are without the law [Torah], as without law...that I might gain them that are without law."
Was Paul ignorant of Jesus' sayings about Pharisees? Was he unaware that Jesus had referred to Pharisees (in such verses as MATT. 12:34 and 23:33) as vipers, hypocrites, and evil? Was he unaware that the Pharisees had wanted to kill Jesus (MATT. 12:14 and other verses)? If he was unaware of Jesus' views about Pharisees, why? If he knew about them, why did he boast about being a Pharisee?
Why did Paul's alleged act of desecrating the temple fail to unite the Pharisees and Sadducees regardless of their other disagreements? Why was this not even brought up by the council?
See also under 16:36-37 and 21:39.

23:8 - THE SADDUCEES SAY THAT THERE IS NO RESURRECTION, NEITHER ANGEL, NOR SPIRIT; THE PHARISEES CONFESS BOTH.

**History:** See under MATT. 3:7.

23:9 - ...SCRIBES THAT WERE OF THE PHARISEES' PART AROSE, AND STROVE, SAYING, "WE FIND NO EVIL IN THIS MAN; IF A SPIRIT OR ANGEL HATH SPOKEN TO HIM, LET US NOT FIGHT AGAINST GOD."

**Perplexing:**
Why did the Pharisees ignore the accusations that caused Paul to be brought before the council? Were they unaware that he also had been preaching that Jesus was the Messiah and had been misinterpreting Old Testament verses? Were they unaware that he additionally claimed to be a Roman? Would the Pharisees have said that they find no evil in him, if they had known that he claimed to be a Roman - one of the people they viewed as enemies?

23:11 - THE NIGHT FOLLOWING THE LORD STOOD BY HIM, AND SAID, "...PAUL, AS THOU HAST TESTIFIED OF ME IN JERUSALEM, SO MUST THOU BEAR WITNESS ALSO AT ROME."

**Perplexing:**
Why did the Lord need Paul to bear witness of him? Why could the Lord not make himself known to everyone and, thereby, eliminate all doubts about his existence, resurrection, and divinity?

23:12-15 - ...CERTAIN JEWS...BOUND THEMSELVES...SAYING THAT THEY WOULD NEITHER EAT NOR DRINK TILL THEY KILLED PAUL. THEY WERE MORE THAN FORTY.... THEY CAME TO THE CHIEF PRIESTS AND ELDERS, AND SAID, ".... YE WITH THE COUNCIL SIGNIFY TO THE CHIEF CAPTAIN THAT HE BRING HIM UNTO YOU TOMORROW, AS THOUGH YE WOULD INQUIRE SOMETHING MORE PERFECTLY CONCERNING HIM; WE...ARE READY TO KILL HIM."

**Perplexing:**
Why did these Jews believe that the Roman captain would take orders from the council? Why would the captain even have considered bringing Paul, who claimed to be a Roman, before the council again after the furor that resulted from his last appearance? (In 23:10, the captain and soldiers saved Paul from possible violence by council members.)

23:16 - WHEN PAUL'S SISTER'S SON HEARD OF THEIR LYING IN WAIT, HE WENT INTO THE CASTLE [FORT] AND TOLD PAUL.

**Perplexing:**
How did Paul's nephew learn of the plot? Why did the Roman troops allow him, presumably a Jew, to enter the fort and go directly to Paul? Why did the Holy Ghost or the Lord fail to inform Paul about the plot?

23:23-24 - HE [THE CHIEF CAPTAIN] CALLED TWO CENTURIONS, SAYING, "MAKE READY 200 SOLDIERS TO GO TO CAESAREA, HORSEMEN 70, AND SPEARMEN 200, AT THE THIRD HOUR OF THE NIGHT; PROVIDE BEASTS THAT THEY MAY SET PAUL ON, AND BRING HIM SAFE UNTO FELIX THE GOVERNOR."

**Perplexing:**
Why did the captain opt to bring together 470 men to spirit Paul away at night, rather than just reject the council's request that he appear? Why did he deem such a large number of soldiers necessary to protect Paul? Why was he so anxious to protect Paul, a self-proclaimed Pharisee - a member of a group hostile to Rome? Did he believe that Paul lied when he claimed to be a Pharisee, but told the truth when he claimed to be a Roman? If so, why? Why did Paul not mention the incident in the Epistles?

**History:**
Felix was procurator from A.D. 52 - c.58 with authority over Cilicia and Judea. He had been a former slave but was favored by Emperor Claudius. He had the reputation of being corrupt and a cruel tyrant. There is, however, no record of Paul having appeared before him.

23:25-28 - HE [THE CAPTAIN] WROTE A LETTER - "CLAUDIUS LYSIAS UNTO...FELIX...THIS MAN WAS TAKEN OF THE JEWS AND SHOULD HAVE BEEN KILLED OF THEM; THEN CAME I WITH AN ARMY, AND RESCUED HIM, HAVING UNDERSTOOD THAT HE WAS A ROMAN. WHEN I WOULD HAVE KNOWN THE CAUSE WHEREFORE THEY ACCUSED HIM, I BROUGHT HIM FORTH INTO THEIR COUNCIL."

**Perplexing:**
Did Paul offer any evidence to support his claim to be Roman? If Lysias believed that Paul was a Roman, why did he bring him before the Jewish Council to face questioning about Jewish law? Would Lysias not have been subjected to at least a reprimand for so doing? Why did he fail to write that Paul had asserted that he was a Pharisee before the Council?

23:29 - "I PERCEIVED [PAUL]...TO HAVE NOTHING LAID TO HIS CHARGE WORTHY OF DEATH OR BONDS."

**Perplexing:**
If he believed that Paul was not guilty of anything worthy of death or bonds, why did he continue to hold him captive, rather than releasing him?

23:34-35 - THE GOVERNOR...ASKED OF WHAT PROVINCE HE WAS. WHEN HE UNDERSTOOD THAT HE WAS OF CILICIA, "I WILL HEAR THEE," SAID HE, "WHEN THINE ACCUSERS ARE ALSO COME." HE COMMANDED HIM TO BE KEPT IN HEROD'S JUDGMENT HALL.

**History:** See under 22-24.

**Perplexing:**
Why did a Roman governor hold a Roman imprisoned to await accusations to be made against him by Jews on matters of Jewish law?

24:5 - [TERTULLUS, REPRESENTING THE JEWS, SPOKE TO FELIX]: "WE HAVE FOUND THIS MAN A PESTILENT FELLOW, A MOVER OF SEDITION AMONG ALL THE JEWS THROUGHOUT THE WORLD, AND A RINGLEADER OF THE SECT OF THE NAZARENES."

**History:**
The name "Nazarenes" was the original name applied to the followers of Jesus when they still appeared to be just members of a Jewish sect, during the 40s into the 60s.They followed Jewish customs and beliefs, except for considering Jesus to be the Messiah.

**Perplexing:**
How could Paul be a ringleader of the Nazarenes, if he was a Roman? If Paul was a Jew - a Pharisee - why would Felix involve himself in complaints against him by Jews? If he viewed Paul as a Roman, how could he permit him to be subjected to questioning by Jews? Did Felix take the charge of sedition seriously? If so, why did he not have a Roman trial for him? Where were the apostles, James, Paul's disciples, and the men he had taken into the temple? Why were the original accusations against Paul (in 21:28-29) which involved Jewish law now supplemented with an accusation pertaining to Roman law: sedition?

24:18-19 - PAUL: "CERTAIN JEWS FROM ASIA FOUND ME PURIFIED IN THE TEMPLE, NEITHER WITH MULTITUDE, NOR TUMULT, WHO OUGHT TO HAVE BEEN HERE BEFORE THEE, AND OBJECT, IF THEY HAD OUGHT AGAINST ME."

**Perplexing:**
Why did Paul fail to state that James sent him to the temple with men who had completed a vow? Why

were the Jews from Asia not brought to this trial?
Why did Paul not report his appearance before Felix in his Epistles?

24:22 - WHEN FELIX HEARD THESE THINGS, HAVING MORE PERFECT KNOWLEDGE OF THAT WAY, HE...SAID, "WHEN LYSIAS THE CHIEF CAPTAIN SHALL COME, I WILL KNOW THE UTTERMOST OF YOUR MATTER."

**Perplexing:**
Why was Lysias not present? Why did Felix not demand that he be present from the start of the proceedings? Why two years later, according to 24:27, had he still not come to speak with Felix about Paul? Why did Felix not release Paul if he believed him to be a Roman and the only charges against him were related to Jewish law? Did Felix take seriously the sedition accusation leveled by Tertullus?
See also under 24:5.

**History:** See under 9:1-2 for "The Way."

**Dead Sea Scrolls:** See under 9:1-2.

24:23 - HE COMMANDED A CENTURION TO KEEP PAUL, TO LET HIM HAVE LIBERTY, AND THAT HE SHOULD FORBID NONE OF PAUL'S ACQUAINTANCES TO MINISTER OR COME UNTO HIM.

**Perplexing:** See under 24:5, 22.

24:24 - ...WHEN FELIX CAME WITH HIS WIFE DRUSILLA, A JEWESS, HE SENT FOR PAUL, AND HEARD HIM CONCERNING THE FAITH IN CHRIST.

**History:**
Josephus identified Drusilla as the daughter of the Jewish King Agrippa I. Tacitus identified her as the granddaughter of Cleopatra and Antony; thus, he wrote that by marriage Felix became Antony's grandson. Neither Josephus nor Tacitus mentioned Paul.

24:26 - HE HOPED THAT MONEY SHOULD HAVE BEEN GIVEN HIM OF PAUL, THAT HE MIGHT LOOSE HIM, WHEREFORE HE SENT FOR HIM THE OFTENER, AND COMMUNED WITH HIM.

**History:** See under 23:22-24.

**Perplexing:**
Did Felix believe that Paul had access to or could ottain large sums of money? Did he, therefore, keep Paul captive in expectation of extorting a bribe to release him? Why did James and the other disciples not collect funds with which to secure Paul's release? Did Paul give Felix money (a bribe) to keep him in Caesarea and protect him from hostile Jews?

24:27 - AFTER TWO YEARS PORCIUS FESTUS CAME INTO FELIX' ROOM; FELIX, WILLING TO SHOW THE JEWS A PLEASURE, LEFT PAUL BOUND.

**History:**
Felix had a reputation of being hostile towards Jews, not sympathetic to them. Jews from Caesarea even traveled to Nero in Rome to protest against his actions.
The precise year in which Festus replaced Felix is uncertain. It is believed to have been between A.D. 58 and 61.

**Perplexing:**
Why would Felix who had not been friendly to the Jews and who was being replaced want to placate the Jews? Why did Paul not mention anything in the Epistles about his stay in Caesarea? What happened to the Jews of 23:14 who took a vow not to eat until they killed Paul?
Did they break their vow and eat, or did they starve to death?
See also under 24:22.

25:1 - WHEN FESTUS WAS COME INTO THE PROVINCE, AFTER THREE DAYS HE ASCENDED FROM CAESAREA TO JERUSALEM.

**History:**
In Jerusalem, Festus ordered that a wall in the temple court be torn down. The Jews protested to Nero who decreed that the wall be retained. At this time there was widespread turmoil and violence throughout Judea including Jerusalem. Armed gangs of anti-Roman Zealots were terrorizing communities, burning and plundering villages, and murdering Romans as well as Jews who did not support them. They incited a rebellion against the Roman occupation which eventually led to their destruction and that of the temple and Jerusalem.

**Perplexing:**
Why did the writer of ACTS fail to report the disorder that was then occurring in Judea?

25:4 - FESTUS ANSWERED [JEWS WHO REQUESTED THAT PAUL BE MOVED TO JERUSALEM (25:3)] THAT PAUL SHOULD BE KEPT AT CAESAREA....

**Perplexing:**
Why did Festus want to continue to retain Paul, who had claimed to be a Roman, as a captive in Caesarea? Did Felix not give Festus information about Paul and the charges that had been brought against him by the Jews?
See also under 24:5.

25:7-9 - ...JEWS FROM JERUSALEM LAID MANY GRIEVOUS COMPLAINTS AGAINST PAUL, WHICH THEY COULD NOT PROVE. HE ANSWERED, "NEITHER AGAINST THE LAW OF THE JEWS, AGAINST THE TEMPLE, NOR AGAINST CAESAR, HAVE I OFFENDED ANY THING AT ALL." FESTUS WILLING TO DO THE JEWS A PLEASURE, ANSWERED PAUL, "WILT THOU GO TO JERUSALEM AND BE JUDGED OF THESE THINGS BEFORE ME?"

**Perplexing:**
If the Jews could not prove their allegations against Paul, why was he not released? Why would Festus want to do the Jews a "pleasure?" (See History under 25:1.) If he wanted to please the Jews, why did he not find Paul guilty? Why did he not order Paul to be taken to Jerusalem? (It was Lysias in 23:23-33 who had

Paul taken to Caesarea.) Why did Paul use the phrase, "the law of the Jews," if he really considered himself to be a Pharisee? Would he not have rather said, simply "the law?" Why would Festus be willing to have someone who had also identified himself as a Roman be put on trial in Jerusalem because of unproven accusations made by Jews?
See also under 24:5.

25:10-12 - SAID PAUL, "I STAND AT CAESAR'S JUDGMENT SEAT, WHERE I OUGHT TO BE JUDGED; TO THE JEWS HAVE I DONE NO WRONG.... .... I APPEAL UNTO CAESAR." FESTUS WHEN HE HAD CONFERRED WITH THE COUNCIL, ANSWERED, "...UNTO CAESAR SHALT THOU GO."

**History:**
A Roman citizen had the right to appeal to the emperor. If the charges against Paul were of a Jewish religious nature, however, they would not qualify for a hearing by the emperor. Consequently, the charges against Paul would have had to pertain to Roman law.

**Perplexing:**
By appealing to the emperor, Paul again asserted that he was a Roman. Why did Festus confer with the Jewish council about allowing a Roman citizen to appeal to the emperor? Why did not Festus release Paul as a Roman who could not be put on trial by Jews? What were the charges against Paul that allowed him to request a hearing by the emperor?
See also under 24:5.

25:13 -...KING AGRIPPA AND BERNICE CAME UNTO CAESAREA TO SALUTE FESTUS.

**History:**
The cited Agrippa was Herod Agrippa II. He had been brought up in Rome, and in A.D. 53, was appointed king over parts of Galilee and adjoining territories. He lived with his sister Bernice (Berenice) with whom he was suspected of having an incestuous relationship. She eventually left him to live with the Roman general Titus who later was responsible for the destruction of Jerusalem in A.D. 70.
See also under 25:1.

25:25-27 - "WHEN I [FESTUS] FOUND THAT HE HAD COMMITTED NOTHING WORTHY OF DEATH, AND THAT HE HATH APPEALED TO AUGUSTUS, I HAVE DETERMINED TO SEND HIM. OF WHOM I HAVE NO CERTAIN THING TO WRITE UNTO MY LORD. WHEREFORE I HAVE BROUGHT HIM BEFORE YOU, ESPECIALLY THEE, O KING AGRIPPA, THAT AFTER EXAMINATION, I MIGHT HAVE SOMEWHAT TO WRITE. IT SEEMETH TO ME UNREASONABLE TO SEND A PRISONER, AND NOT WITHAL TO SIGNIFY THE CRIMES LAID AGAINST HIM."

**Perplexing:**
If Festus did not know with what crimes to charge Paul, why did he not release him? What charges was Paul planning to appeal to the emperor?
It is now over two years since he was brought to Caesarea as a captive.

26:4-5 - PAUL: "MY MANNER OF LIFE FROM MY YOUTH, WHICH WAS AT THE FIRST AMONG MINE OWN NATION AT JERUSALEM, KNOW ALL THE JEWS, WHICH KNEW ME FROM THE BEGINNING, IF THEY WOULD TESTIFY, THAT AFTER THE MOST STRAITEST SECT OF OUR RELIGION I LIVED A PHARISEE."

**Contradictions:**
ACTS 21:39 - Paul: "I am a man which am a Jew of Tarsus, in Cilicia, a citizen of no mean city."
[Was Paul's life from the first among Jews in Jerusalem, or was he a citizen of Tarsus?]
See also under 21:39 and 22:3.

**Perplexing:** See under 23:6-7.

**History:** See under MATT. 3:7.

26:6-7 - PAUL: "NOW I STAND AND AM JUDGED FOR THE HOPE OF THE PROMISE MADE OF GOD UNTO OUR FATHERS UNTO WHICH PROMISE OUR 12 TRIBES, INSTANTLY SERVING GOD DAY AND NIGHT, HOPE TO COME. FOR WHICH HOPE'S SAKE I AM ACCUSED OF THE JEWS."

**Contradictions:**
ACTS 21:28 - Jews of Asia accused Paul of teaching "against the people and the law" and bringing "Greeks into the temple."
ACTS 24:5 - Tertullus: "We have found this man a pestilent fellow, a mover of sedition among all the Jews throughout the world, and a ringleader of the sect of the Nazarenes."
[Was Paul accused of supporting a promise he said was made by God, or for teaching against the law, bringing Greeks into temple, and/or for sedition?]

**Perplexing:**
To what promise was Paul referring? Why did Paul not know that the 12 tribes would cease to exist in the future? Why did he fail to address the accusations made by the Jews against him? Why did he say, "I am accused of the Jews," as if he was not a Jew, rather than just, "I am accused," as a Jew would have said?

26:10-11 - PAUL: "...MANY OF THE SAINTS DID I SHUT UP IN PRISON, HAVING RECEIVED AUTHORITY FROM THE CHIEF PRIESTS, AND WHEN THEY WERE PUT TO DEATH, I GAVE MY VOICE AGAINST THEM. I PUNISHED THEM OFT IN EVERY SYNAGOGUE, COMPELLED THEM TO BLASPHEME; BEING EXCEEDINGLY MAD AGAINST THEM, I PERSECUTED THEM EVEN UNTO STRANGE CITIES."

**History:**
The chief priests did not have the authority to order anyone arrested and imprisoned or killed for religious reasons. Only the Sanhedrin had such power.
See also under 8:3 and 9:1-2.

**Contradiction:**
GAL. 1:22 - Paul: "[I] was unknown by face unto the churches of Judaea which were in Christ."
[Did Paul punish people in every synagogue, or was he not known by face to the churches of Judea?]

**Perplexing:**
Why would the chief priests have given Paul authorization to make arrests? Why would a religious Pharisee have taken such a job? Why did the Holy Ghost or the Lord fail to protect those who believed in Jesus? If Paul punished people in every synagogue, how could he have been "unknown by face?"
See also under 8:1, 3, and 9:1-2.

26:12 - PAUL: "I WENT TO DAMASCUS WITH AUTHORITY AND COMMISSION FROM THE CHIEF PRIESTS."

**Contradictions:** See under 9:14.

**History:** See under 9:1-2.

**Perplexing:** See under 8:3 and 9:1-2.

26:14 - PAUL: "WHEN WE WERE ALL FALLEN TO THE EARTH, I HEARD A VOICE SPEAKING UNTO ME, IN HEBREW, 'SAUL, SAUL, WHY PERSECUTEST THOU ME? IT IS HARD FOR THEE TO KICK AGAINST THE PRICKS.'"

**Contradictions:**
ACTS 9:4 - He fell to earth, and heard a voice saying, "Saul, Saul, why persecutest thou me?"
ACTS 9:7 - The men which journeyed with him [Saul] stood speechless, hearing a voice, but seeing no man."
ACTS 22:7 - Paul: "I fell unto the ground, and heard a voice saying, "Saul, Saul, why persecutest thou me?"
[Did Paul and his companions fall to the ground, or did Paul fall to the ground while the men with him remained standing?]
See also under 9:4-5 and 22:8

**Perplexing:**
Why did the voice speak in Hebrew, instead of in Greek or Aramaic?
Why did the gospels not say that Jesus spoke Hebrew?
(Some Bibles use, "Aramaic," rather than "Hebrew.")

**History:** See under 2:6-11.

26:15 - PAUL: "I SAID, 'WHO ART THOU, LORD?' HE SAID, 'I AM JESUS WHOM THOU PERSECUTEST.'"

**Contradictions:**
ACTS 9:5 - He [Paul] said, "Who art thou Lord?" The Lord said, "I am Jesus whom thou persecutest; it is hard for thee to kick against the pricks."
[Did Paul say, "Who art thou, Lord, after (26:14), or before Jesus referred to kicking against the pricks?]
ACTS 22:8 - Paul: "I answered, 'Who art thou Lord?' He said,'I am Jesus of Nazareth, whom thou persecutest.'"
[Did Jesus identify himself as "Jesus," or as "Jesus of Nazareth?"]
See also under 9:4-5 and 22:8.

**Perplexing:** See under 9:4-5.

26:16-18 - JESUS: "RISE, AND STAND; I HAVE APPEARED UNTO THEE TO MAKE THEE A MINISTER AND WITNESS BOTH OF THESE THINGS WHICH THOU HAST SEEN, AND OF THOSE THINGS IN WHICH I WILL APPEAR UNTO THEE; DELIVERING THEE FROM THE PEOPLE, AND THE GENTILES UNTO WHOM NOW I SEND THEE...TO TURN THEM FROM DARKNESS TO LIGHT, AND FROM THE POWER OF SATAN UNTO GOD, THAT THEY MAY RECEIVE FORGIVENESS OF SINS...."

**Contradictions:**
ACTS 9:6 - He [Paul]...said, "Lord, What will thou have me do?" The Lord said, "Arise, and go into the city; it shall be told thee what thou must do."
ACTS 22:10 - "I said, 'What shall I do, Lord?' The Lord said, 'Go into Damascus; there it shall be told thee of all things which are appointed for thee to do.'"
[Did Jesus tell Paul what he was going to have him do, or did he tell him to go to Damascus to learn what he was to do?]
MARK 4:11-12 - He [Jesus] said, "...all these things are done in parables...lest at any time they should be converted, and their sins should be forgiven them."
[Did, or did not Jesus want people's sins to be forgiven?]
See also under MATT. 9:13.

**Perplexing:**
In 9:8-9, Paul could not see for three days after he arose, and in 22:11, he could not see because of the light for an unspecified length of time. Why did Paul not report such a traumatic experience as blindness in the above ACTS 26 verses or in the Epistles? Why is the Lord hostile to Satan? Of what evil has Satan been accused in the Bible?
See also under 9:7, MATT. 13:10-13, and MARK 4:11-12.

**Pagan parallels:**
In Zoroastrianism a god of light, Ahura Mazda (Ormazd), was a good god, whereas the god of darkness, Ahriman (Angra Maintu), was an evil god.
Followers of Orpheus traveled around the Middle East as early as the 6th century B.C. preaching about the forgiveness of sins.
See also under JOHN 6:63.

26:20-21 - PAUL: "[I] SHEWED FIRST UNTO THEM AT DAMASCUS, AT JERUSALEM, THROUGHOUT ALL THE COASTS OF JUDEA, AND THEN TO THE GENTILES, THAT THEY SHOULD REPENT, TURN TO GOD, AND DO WORKS MEET FOR REPENTANCE. FOR THESE CAUSES THE JEWS CAUGHT ME IN THE TEMPLE, AND WENT ABOUT TO KILL ME."

**Contradictions:**
ACTS 9:10-31 - Paul went from Damascus to Jerusalem, then throughout Judea, Galilee, and Samaria.
[Did Paul go from Damascus to Jerusalem, throughout Judea, then to the Gentiles, or did he go from Damascus to Jerusalem throughout Judea, then to Galilee and Samaria?]
GAL. 1:17-22 - Paul: "Neither went I to Jerusalem, but into Arabia, and returned to Damascus. After three years I went to Jerusalem.... .... ...I lie not. Afterwards I came into the regions of Syria and Cilicia, and was

unknown by face unto the churches of Judea which were in Christ."
[Did Paul go from Damascus, Jerusalem, Judea, and then to the Gentiles, or to Arabia, back to Damascus, then to Jerusalem, Syria, and Cilicia, while not being known by face in the churches of Judea?]
[Did Paul go, or not go throughout Judea?]
ACTS 21:27-28 - Jews from Asia accused Paul of teaching against the people and the law and bringing Greeks into the temple.
[Did the Jews want to kill Paul because he told people to repent and do works for repentance, or for teaching against the people and the law and for bringing Greeks into the temple?]
ACTS 24:5 - Paul was accused by Tertullus of being "a pestilent fellow, a mover of sedition among all the Jews throughout the world, and a ringleader of the sect of the Nazarenes."
[Did the Jews want to kill Paul because he told people to repent and do works for repentance, or for being a mover of sedition and leader of the Nazarenes?]
ACTS 23:6 - Paul...cried out, "I am a Pharisee...of the hope and resurrection of the dead I am called in question."
ACTS 24:21 - Paul: ".... Touching the resurrection of the dead I am called in question by you [Jews] this day."
[Did Paul say that Jews wanted to kill him because he told people to repent and do works for repentance, or because he believed in the resurrection of the dead?]
ACTS 26:6-7 - Paul: "I stand and am judged for the hope of the promise made of God unto our fathers ... for which hope's sake I am accused of the Jews."
[Did Paul say that Jews wanted to kill him because he told people to repent and do works for repentance, or because he hoped for a promise made by God?l

**Perplexing:**
Why must anyone repent? Must people repent for not having heard of or believing in Jesus? Is it possible that some individuals may have done nothing for which to repent? What works must be done for repentance? See also under 26:6-7.

26:22-23 - PAUL: "...I CONTINUE...SAYING NONE OTHER THINGS THAN THOSE WHICH THE PROPHETS AND MOSES DID SAY SHOULD COME; THAT CHRIST SHOULD SUFFER, BE THE FIRST THAT SHOULD RISE FROM THE DEAD, AND SHOULD SHEW LIGHT UNTO THE PEOPLE AND TO THE GENTILES."

**Contradiction:**
1 KINGS 17:17-22 - Elijah resurrected a dead boy.
2 KINGS 4:32-35 - Elisha resurrected a dead boy.
MATT. 9:18-25, MARK 5:35-42, and LUKE 8:49-55 - Jesus resurrected a dead girl.
LUKE 7:12-15 - Jesus resurrected a dead man.
JOHN 11:39-44 - Jesus resurrected Lazarus who had been dead four days.
[Was Jesus the first to rise from the dead, as Paul claimed, or were several people raised from the dead before Jesus' resurrection?]

**Perplexing:**
What did the prophets and Moses say about Christ? Where in the Old Testament did they say that Christ should suffer and be the first to rise from the dead, and show light to the people and the Gentiles? If Paul was a Pharisee would he have made these statements about the prophets and Moses? Why did Paul not say that people should follow the teachings of Jesus? Did Paul not know what Jesus had taught? Why did Paul

say that Christ would be the first to rise from the dead? Was he ignorant of the Old Testament resurrection accounts, and of Jesus' resurrection miracles?

26:29 - PAUL SAID, "I WOULD TO GOD...ALL THAT HEAR ME THIS DAY, WERE BOTH ALMOST, AND ALTOGETHER SUCH AS I AM, EXCEPT THESE BONDS."

**Perplexing:**
If Paul wanted God to have all people believe the way he did, why did he not pray to Jesus to make it happen? Was he unaware of such verses as MATT. 21:22; MARK 11:24; JOHN 14:13, 15:7, and 16:23, in which Jesus said that anything prayed or asked for in his name would be given? Did Paul not believe Jesus? Is it possible that Paul did pray for people to convert, but his prayer was not answered?

26:31-32 - WHEN THEY WERE GONE, THEY TALKED BETWEEN THEMSELVES, SAYING, "THIS MAN DOETH NOTHING WORTHY OF DEATH OR BONDS." SAID AGRIPPA UNTO FESTUS, "THIS MAN MIGHT HAVE BEEN SET AT LIBERTY, IF HE HAD NOT APPEALED UNTO CAESAR."

**Perplexing:**
If Paul was not deemed to be guilty of any punishable offense, why was he not released before he appealed to Caesar?
See also under 25:7-9.

27:1 - WHEN IT WAS DETERMINED THAT WE SHOULD SAIL INTO ITALY, THEY DELIVERED PAUL AND OTHER PRISONERS UNTO JULIUS, A CENTURION....

**Perplexing:**
The writer of ACTS said, "we should sail." Was he with Paul while he was a prisoner? Was he also a prisoner? If so, why did he not mention it before? Did he too appeal to Caesar? How many prisoners were there? Did they all appeal to Caesar?
See also under 16:10.

27:2 - ...ONE ARISTARCHUS, A MACEDONIAN OF THESSALONICA BEING WITH US.

**Perplexing:**
Was this the same Aristarchus mentioned in 20:4 as a Thessalonian? Was he also a prisoner? In COL. 4:10, Paul referred to an Aristarchus as "my fellow prisoner." If so, why and when did he become a prisoner, and why was he being sent to Italy with Paul? Did he, too, appeal to Caesar?
See also under 16:10.

27:3 - THE NEXT DAY WE TOUCHED AT SIDON. JULIUS COURTEOUSLY ENTREATED PAUL, AND GAVE HIM LIBERTY TO GO UNTO HIS FRIENDS TO REFRESH HIMSELF.

**Perplexing:**
Was Paul the only one who was treated courteously? Why did a centurion risk his position and possibly his life by allowing a prisoner to leave the ship and visit with friends? Were other prisoners also permitted to leave the ship? When did Paul acquire friends in Sidon?
See also under 16:10.

27:6 - THERE [IN MYRA] THE CENTURION FOUND A SHIP OF ALEXANDRIA SAILING INTO ITALY, AND HE PUT US THEREON.

**Perplexing:**
Why was it necessary for the centurion to put the writer of ACTS on the ship along with the prisoners, if he was not also a prisoner?
See also under 27:1.

27:10 - [PAUL] SAID UNTO THEM, "SIRS, I PERCEIVE THAT THIS VOYAGE WILL BE WITH HURT AND MUCH DAMAGE, NOT ONLY OF THE LADING AND SHIP, BUT ALSO OF OUR LIVES."

**Perplexing:**
Why did Paul fail to pray to the Lord for a safe voyage? Why did Paul not perform a miracle to calm the sea? He had already resurrected a dead man (20:9-12), healed a man who could not walk (14:8-10), performed unspecified wonders (14:3), and special miracles (19:11). Why did the writer of ACTS not report anyone praying?
In JOHN 14:12, Jesus said, "He that believeth on me, the works that I do shall he do also; and greater works than these shall he do....."
In MATT. 8:26 and MARK 4:39, Jesus calmed a rough sea and a strong wind. Therefore, why could Paul not do so?
See also under 26:29.

27:22-24 - "I [PAUL] EXHORT YOU...THERE SHALL BE NO LOSS OF ANY MAN'S LIFE AMONG YOU, BUT OF THE SHIP. THERE STOOD BY ME THIS NIGHT THE ANGEL OF GOD, WHOSE I AM, AND WHOM I SERVE, SAYING, 'FEAR NOT, PAUL, THOU MUST BE BROUGHT BEFORE CAESAR; GOD HAS GIVEN THEE ALL THEM THAT SAIL WITH THEE.'"

**Perplexing:**
Why did the angel fail to bring Paul, those with him, and the ship safely without incident to Italy? Why did the angel allow Paul and his companions to suffer in the storm?
Why does almighty God need Paul or anyone else to serve him? Why does He permit His servants to suffer? Why is He so cruel? Is God sadistic? Does He enjoy causing His servants to suffer? Why did the writer of ACTS fail to report any meeting between Paul and Caesar in the remaining portion of ACTS? Did Paul ever appear before Caesar? There is no record of such a meeting having taken place. Did the angel lie about Paul appearing before Caesar? Did Paul lie about what the angel said? Did an angel really appear to Paul?

27:33-34 - ...PAUL...SAYING, "THIS IS THE 14TH DAY THAT YE HAVE TARRIED AND CONTINUED FASTING, HAVING TAKEN NOTHING. WHEREFORE I PRAY YOU TO TAKE SOME MEAT...."

**Perplexing:**
How were they able to fast for 14 days without becoming too weak to work on the ship? Why did they fast if food was available?

27:35 - ...HE TOOK BREAD, AND GAVE THANKS TO GOD IN PRESENCE OF THEM ALL....

**Perplexing:**
Why did Paul give thanks to God after all the suffering God put him through? Why did he not give thanks to God while the storm was in progress and after the later shipwreck (27:41)?

27:37 - WE WERE IN ALL IN THE SHIP 276 SOULS.

**Perplexing:**
How many of the people on board were prisoners? Other biblical manuscripts, the Vaticanus and the Sahidia, state that there were only about 76 people on the ship.
See also under 16:10 and 27:1.

27:41-44 - ...THEY RAN THE SHIP AGROUND...THE HINDER PART WAS BROKEN WITH THE VIOLENCE OF THE WAVES. THE SOLDIERS' COUNSEL WAS TO KILL THE PRISONERS, LEST ANY SHOULD ESCAPE. THE CENTURION, TO SAVE PAUL, KEPT THEM FROM THEIR PURPOSE, AND COMMANDED THAT THEY WHICH COULD SWIM CAST THEMSELVES INTO THE SEA, AND GET TO LAND; THE REST ON BOARDS, AND PIECES OF THE SHIP.... THEY ESCAPED ALL SAFE TO LAND.

**Perplexing:**
Did any of the prisoners escape from the Romans after they reached land? Why did the centurion want to save Paul? Why did Paul fail to report this incident in his Epistles? In 2 COR. 11:25, he merely said that he had been in three shipwrecks.
Why did the Lord, the Holy Ghost, or an angel fail to prevent the shipwreck?

28:1 - WHEN THEY WERE ESCAPED, THEY KNEW THAT THE ISLAND WAS CALLED MELITA.

**History:**
Melita was a name for Malta, an island bout 500 miles west of Crete. It was the site of an ancient goddess-worshiping people. Some of their temples, which date back to between 5000 - 2500 B.C., are still in existence.

28:2 - THE BARBAROUS PEOPLE SHEWED US NO LITTLE KINDNESS; THEY KINDLED A FIRE, AND RECEIVED EVERY ONE, BECAUSE OF THE RAIN, AND THE COLD.

**Perplexing:**
What language did the inhabitants speak? Since they were somewhat isolated from the rest of the Mediterranean area people, it is likely that they had developed their own language (Maltese, which is spoken today, or something similar), and did not speak Greek, Latin, or Aramaic. How did Paul and the others communicate with them?

28:8-9 - ...THE FATHER OF PUBLIUS LAY SICK OF A FEVER AND OF A BLOODY FLUX, TO WHOM PAUL ENTERED, PRAYED, LAID HIS HANDS ON HIM, AND HEALED HIM. ... OTHERS, WHICH HAD DISEASES IN THE ISLAND, CAME, AND WERE HEALED.

**Perplexing:**

Was the man healed by prayer, or because Paul laid hands on him? How were the others healed? Why did the man and the others not need to have faith to be healed?
See also under 19:11-12.

**History:** See under 19:11-12.

28:10-11 - ...WHEN WE DEPARTED, THEY LADED US WITH SUCH THINGS AS WERE NECESSARY. AFTER THREE MONTHS WE DEPARTED IN A SHIP OF ALEXANDRIA, WHICH HAD WINTERED IN THE ISLE, WHOSE SIGN WAS CASTOR AND POLLUX.

**Perplexing:**

During the three months on the island, from where or how did Paul and those with him get clothes, as they had lost everything in the wreck? Did they have money with which to buy them? If so, how did they obtain it? How were the islanders able to obtain enough supplies for 276 people plus whatever crew and passengers were already on the Alexandrian ship? How large was the vessel that it could take on an additional 276 people? Were these 276 required to pay to board the Alexandrian ship? If so, from where were the funds obtained? Were the supplies used in lieu of money?
See also under 27:1.

**Pagan concept:**

Castor and Pollux (in Greek: Clymenestra and Polydeuces) were considered to be deities associated with St. Elmo's fire and were prayed to for aid at sea. They became the constellation Gemini (the Twins).

28:13-14 - ...WE CAME TO PUTREOLI, WHERE WE FOUND BRETHREN, AND WERE DESIRED TO TARRY WITH THEM SEVEN DAYS, AND SO WE WENT TOWARD ROME.

**Perplexing:**

How was Paul able to find brethren in the city? Did the centurion allow him to wander around at will? Why was a prisoner or prisoners allowed to spend seven days with "brethren?" Why did the centurion permit it?
See also under 27:1.

28:15 - FROM THENCE WHEN THE BRETHREN HEARD OF US, THEY CAME TO MEET US AS FAR AS APPII FORUM, AND THE THREE TAVERNS, WHOM WHEN PAUL SAW, HE THANKED GOD, AND TOOK COURAGE.

**Perplexing:**

If Paul was on his way to Rome, why would brethren make a day's trip from Rome to meet him at the Appii (Appius) Forum, or even travel about ten miles to Three Taverns? How many brethren were there? How did they learn that Paul was coming and where he would be?
See also under 27:1 and 28:13-14.

28:16 - WHEN WE CAME TO ROME, THE CENTURION DELIVERED THE PRISONERS TO THE CAPTAIN OF THE GUARD, BUT PAUL WAS SUFFERED TO DWELL BY HIMSELF WITH A SOLDIER THAT KEPT HIM.

**Perplexing:**
Why was Paul accorded special treatment? Did the centurion or captain of the guard have the authority to allow Paul to dwell by himself? Was the narrator one of the prisoners? If not, why was he with the prisoners? Was the dwelling where Paul resided provided free by the Roman government? Did Paul have to pay rent? If so, from where did obtain the necessary funds?
See also under 27:1.

28:17 - ...AFTER THREE DAYS PAUL CALLED THE CHIEF JEWS TOGETHER, AND WHEN THEY WERE COME TOGETHER....

**Perplexing:**
How did Paul know who the chief Jews were? How was he able to contact them? Why did the Romans permit him do so? Why did they come to meet with him? How many were there? Where did they meet? Why did the Romans allow them to congregate at the residence of a prisoner?

28:18-19 - PAUL: "WHEN THEY [THE ROMANS] HAD EXAMINED ME, WOULD HAVE LET ME GO, BECAUSE THERE WAS NO CAUSE OF DEATH IN ME. WHEN THE JEWS SPAKE AGAINST IT, I WAS CONSTRAINED TO APPEAL UNTO CAESAR, NOT THAT I HAD OUGHT TO ACCUSE MY NATION OF."

**Perplexing:**
The Romans did not take orders from Jews, so they could have let him go. Why did they not do so? What did Paul mean by "my nation?" Did he mean Judea or Rome? How could Paul's nation have been Judea, when he had declared himself to be a Roman (16:37; 22:25-29)? Why did Paul fail to pray to Jesus for his release?
See also under 16:36-37, 25:7-9, and 11-12.

**History:** See under 25:11-12.

28:22 - JEWS: "...AS CONCERNING THIS SECT, WE KNOW THAT EVERYWHERE IT IS SPOKEN AGAINST."

**Perplexing:**
How did Christianity become established in Italy to such an extent that it was spoken against everywhere? Why was it spoken against?

**History:**
Tacitus wrote in *Annals of Imperial Rome* that Christians were "notoriously depraved" and had "anti-social tendencies." They were also suspected of having started the fire that nearly destroyed Rome. Suetonius wrote in *The Twelve Caesars* that Christians professed "a new and mischievous religious belief."

28:23 - ... THERE CAME MANY TO HIS LODGING, TO WHOM HE EXPOUNDED AND TESTIFIED THE KINGDOM OF GOD, PERSUADING THEM CONCERNING JESUS, BOTH OUT OF THE LAW OF MOSES, AND THE PROPHETS, FROM MORNING TILL EVENING.

**Perplexing:**
How many people came to Paul's lodging? Why did the Romans allow him to have many visitors at one

time? Did they all stay from morning to evening? Did Paul provide refreshments for them? If so, from where did he obtain funds to pay for the food and drink?
See also under 28:17.

28:25-28 - ...PAUL HAD SPOKEN, "WELL SPAKE THE HOLY GHOST BY ESAIAS [ISAIAH] THE PROPHET UNTO OUR FATHERS, 'GO UNTO THIS PEOPLE AND SAY, "HEARING YE SHALL HEAR, AND NOT UNDERSTAND; SEEING YE SHALL SEE, AND NOT PERCEIVE; THE HEART OF THIS PEOPLE IS WAXED GROSS; THEIR EARS ARE DULL OF HEARING; THEIR EYES HAVE CLOSED, LEST THEY SHOULD SEE WITH THEIR EYES, AND HEAR WITH THEIR EARS, AND UNDERSTAND WITH THEIR HEART, AND SHOULD BE CONVERTED, AND I SHOULD HEAL THEM."' BE IT KNOWN THEREFORE, THAT THE SALVATION OF GOD IS SENT UNTO THE GENTILES; THEY WILL HEAR IT."

**Old Testament:** See under MATT. 13:14-15.

**Contradictions:**
ISA. 6:8-11 - Isaiah: "I heard the voice of the Lord, saying, 'Whom shall I send; who will go for us?' Said I, 'Hear am I; send me.' He said, 'Go, and tell this people, "hear ye, but understand not; see...."' Said I, 'Lord, how long?' He answered, 'Until the cities be wasted without inhabitant...and the land be utterly desolate.'"
[Did the Holy Ghost tell Isaiah what to say, or did Isaiah respond to the Lord's questions?]
[Did the verses pertain to Jews not accepting salvation through Jesus, or did they pertain to the destruction of cities and their inhabitants?]

**Perplexing:**
Why did the Jews fail to correct Paul's interpretation of the verses?
See also under MATT. 13:14-15.

28:30-31 - PAUL DWELT TWO WHOLE YEARS IN HIS OWN HIRED HOUSE, AND RECEIVED ALL THAT CAME UNTO HIM, PREACHING THE KINGDOM OF GOD AND TEACHING THOSE THINGS WHICH CONCERN THE LORD JESUS CHRIST ... NO MAN FORBIDDING HIM.

**Perplexing:**
What happened to the writer of ACTS and the others who were supposedly with Paul on his trip to Rome? If Paul hired the house for two years, from where did obtain money? Was this the same dwelling to which he was assigned in 28:16? Where did he go after the two years? Why did ACTS end at this point? Why had his case not yet been appealed to Caesar (Nero, at this time)? Why did ACTS fail to report whether or not Paul ever presented his appeal to Nero? Why did ACTS leave the reader in suspense about the remainder of Paul's life and activities?
Why is there no secular record of Paul's escapades, especially the miracles he was said to have performed? According to Christian tradition, Paul along with other Christians were ordered killed by Nero for allegedly starting a fire that nearly destroyed Rome. If so, why did God permit it?
See also under 27:22-24 and 28:16.

## BIBLIOGRAPHY


Aldred, C., *The Egyptians*. Thames and Hudson, 1987.

Allegro, J.M., *The Dead Sea Scrolls and the Christian Myth*. Prometheus Books, 1984.

______ , *The Mystery of the Dead Sea Scrolls Revealed*. Gramercy Publishing Co., 1981.

______, *Physician Heal Thyself*. Prometheus Books, 1985.

______ , *The Sacred Mushroom and the Cross*. Doubleday and Co., 1970.

Angus, S., T*he Mystery Religions*. Dover Publications, Inc., 1975.

*Anon., Aryan Sun-Myths: The Origin of Religions*. Reprinted by Health Research, 1977.

Asimov, I., *Asimov's Guide to the Bible*, Vol. I and 2. Avon Books, 1971.

Barker, G. W., Lane, W.L., and Michaels, J.R., *The New Testament Speaks*. Harper & Row, Publishers, 1969.

Barthel, M., *What the Bible Really Says*. William Morrow and Co., Inc., 1982.

Beltz, W., *God and the Gods*. Penguin Books, 1983.

Bowden, J., *Archaeology and the Bible*. American Atheist Press, 1982.

Bruce, F.F., *History of the Bible in English*. Oxford University Press, 1978.

Budge, E.A.W., *The Egyptian Heaven and Hell*. Open Court, 1989.

Bukyo Dendo Kyokai, *The Teaching of Buddha*. Kosaido Printing Co., Ltd., 1986.

Burrows, M., *Jesus in the First Three Gospels*. Abingdon, 1977.

Callahan, T., *Bible Prophecy*. Millennium Press, 1997.

Campbell, J., *The Masks of God: Occidental Mythology*. Penguin Books, 1988.

______, *The Masks of God: Oriental Mythology*. Penguin Books, 1987.

Carpenter, E., *The Origins of Pagan and Christian Beliefs*. Senate, 1996.

Carter, L., *Lucifer's Handbook*. Academic Associates, 1977.

*Celsus on the True Doctrine*. Translated by Hoffmann, R.J., Oxford University Press, 1987.

Coffman, J.B., *Commentary on the Gospel of Matthew*. Firm Foundation Publishing, 1968.

______, *Commentary on the Gospel of Mark*. 1975.

*The Complete Works of Flavius Josephus*. Translated by Whiston, W., Kregel Publications, 1981.

Condon, R.J., *Our Pagan Christmas*. American Atheists, undated.

Cumont, F., *Oriental Religions in Roman Paganism*. Dover Publications, 1966.

Cutner, H., *Jesus - God, Man or Myth?* Reprinted by Health Research, 1986.

Doane. T.W., *Bible Myths and Their Parallels in other Religions*. Reprinted by Health Research, 1985.

Doresse, L.J., *The Secret Books of the Egyptian Gnostics*. Inner Traditions International, Ltd., 1986.

Drews, A., *The Christ Myth*. Prometheus Books, 1998.

Drohan, F.B., *Jesus Who?* Philosophical Library, 1985.

Ehrlich, E., and Scott, D.H. *Mene, Mene, Tekel*. Harper Collins Publishers, 1990.

Eisenman, R., and Wise, M., *The Dead Sea Scrolls Uncovered. Element*, 1992.

*Encyclopedia of World Mythology*. Galahad Books, 1975.

Finley, M.L., *Christ and the Colonel*. Haldeman-Julius Publications, 1948.

Flanery, E.B., *The Crack in the Bible*. Ashley Books, Inc., 1987.

Floyd, W., *The Mistakes of Jesus*. The Freethought Press Association, 1957.

Foote, G.W., and Ball, W.P., *The Bible Handbook*. Pioneer Press, 1953.

Frye, N., *Words of Power*. Harcourt Brace Jovanovich, Publishers, 1990.

______, *The Great Code: The Bible and Literature*. Harcourt Brace Jovanovich, 1982.

Garbini, G., *History and Ideology in Ancient Israel*. The Crossroad Publishing Co., 1988.

Gillooly, R.J., *All About Adam And Eve: How We Came To Believe In Gods. Demons, Miracles, and Magical Rites*. Prometheus Books, 1998.

Goddard, D., *Was Jesus Influenced by Buddhism*. Reprinted by Health Research, 1971.
Godwin, J., *Mystery Religions in the Ancient World*. Harper & Row, Publishers, 1981.
Goodspeed, E.J., *A Life of Jesus*. Harper & Brothers, Publishers, 1950.
Graham, L.M., *Deceptions and Myths of the Bible*. Bell Publishing Co., 1975.
Grant, M., *An Historical Review of the Gospels*. Charles Scribner's Sons, 1977.
Graves, R., *The White Goddess*. The Noonday Press, 1966.
Guignebert, C., *Jesus*. University Books, 1956.
______, *The Christ*. Carol Publishing Group, 1968.
Hamlyn, P., *Egyptian Mythology*. Drury House, 1966.
Harwood, W.R., *Mythology's Last Gods: Yahweh and Jesus*. Prometheus Books, 1992.
Heinrich, C., *Strange Fruit*. Bloomsbury Publishing, 1995.
Helms, R., *Gospel Fictions*. Prometheus Books, 1989.
Hoffmann, R.J., *Jesus Outside the Gospels*. Prometheus Books, 1984.
Hooke, S.H., *Middle Eastern Mythology*. Penguin Books, 1983.
Ingersoll, R.G., *The Truth about the Holy Bible*. Haldeman-Julius, undated.
______, *What Must We Do To Be Saved?* Haldeman-Julius Publications, undated.
______, *The Foundations of Faith*. Haldeman-Julius, undated.
______, *What Can You Believe in the Bible*? Haldeman-Julius Publications, undated.
Jackson, J.G., *Christianity Before Christ*. American Atheist Press, 1985.
______, *Pagan Origins of the Christ Myth*. The American Atheist Press, undated.
Josipovici, G., *The Book of God*. Yale University Press, 1988.
Kuhn, A.H., *Easter: The Birthday of the Gods*. Reprinted by Health Research, 1987.
Langdon, S.H., *The Mythology of All Races, Vol. 5, Semitic*. Ed., J.A. MacCulloch. Cooper Square Publishers, Inc., 1964.
Lurker, M., *The Gods and Symbols of Ancient Egypt*. Thames and Hudson, 1984.
Maccoby, H., *The Mythmaker: Paul and the Invention of Christianity*. Harper and Row, Publishers, 1987.
______, *Judas Iscariot and the Myth of Jewish Evil*. The Free Press, 1992.
McCabe, J., *The Myth of the Resurrection and other Essays*. Prometheus Books, 1993.
Metzger, B.M., *The Text of the New Testament: Its Transmission, Corruption, and Restoration*. Oxford University Press, 1992.
Neil, W., *Pocket Bible Commentary*. Castle Books, 1997.
Pagels, E. *Adam, Eve, and the Serpent*. Random House, 1988.
*The Origins of Christianity*. Ed., Hoffmann. R.J., Prometheus Books, 1985.
Paine, L., *The Hierarchy of Hell*. Hippocrene Books, Inc., 1972.
Paine, T., *The Age of Reason*. Reprinted by the Thomas Paine Foundation, undated.
______, *The Age of Reason*. Prometheus Books, 1984.
______, *The Age of Reason, Part Three: Examination of the Prophecies*. Ed., Zindler, P., American Atheist Press, 1993.
*Porphyry's Against the Christians: The Literary Remains*. Ed. and translated by Hoffmann, R.J., Prometheus Books, 1994.
Riedel, E., Tracy, T., and Moskowitz, B.D., *The Book of the Bible*. William Morrow and Co., 1979.
Robertson, J.M., *Pagan Christs*. Dorset Press, 1987.
Rocco, S., *Sex Mythology*. Reprinted by American Atheist Press, 1982.
Russell, J.B., *The Devil: Perceptions of Evil from Antiquity to Primitive Christianity*. Cornell University Press, 1988.
Schochet, J.I., *Mashiach: The Principle of Mashiach and the Messianic Era in Jewish Law and Tradition*. S. I. E., 1991.

Schonfield, H.J., *The Jesus Party*. Macmillan Publishing Co., Inc.,1974.
Schürer, E., *The Jewish People in the Time of Jesus*. Ed., Glatzer, N.N., Schocken Books, 1961.
Spong, J.S., *Rescuing the Bible from Fundamentalism*. HarperSanFrancisco, 1992.
______, *Liberating the Gospels*. HarperSanFrancisco, 1996.
Suetonius, *The Twelve Caesars*. Translated by Graves, R., Revised by Grant, M., Penguin Books, 1989.
Tacitus, *The Histories*. Translated by Wellesley, K., Penguin Books, 1988.
______, The Annals of Imperial Rome. Translated by Grant, M., Penguin Books, 1989.
Till, F., Prophecies: *Imaginary and Unfulfilled*. Skepticism, Inc., undated.
______, *The Skeptical Review*, Vol. 3, No. 2. 1992.
Wells, G.A., *Did Jesus Exist?* Pemberton, 1986.
______, *Who Was Jesus?* Open Court, 1989.
______, *Religious Postures*. Open Court, 1988.
Wilken, R.L., *The Myth of Christian Beginnings*. Doubleday and Co., Inc., 1971.